Churchill's Man of Mystery: Desmond Morton and the World of Intelligence
Gill Bennett

The Official History of Privatisation
Vol. I: The Formative Years 1970–1987
Vol. II: Popular Capitalism 1987–1997
David Parker

Secrecy and the Media: The Official History of the D-Notice System
Nicholas Wilkinson

The Official History of the Civil Service: Reforming the Civil Service
Vol. I: The Fulton Years, 1966–1981
Rodney Lowe

The Official History of North Sea Oil and Gas
Vol. I: The Growing Dominance of the State
Vol. II: Moderating the State's Role
Alex Kemp

The Official History of Britain and the European Community
Vol. II: From Rejection to Referendum, 1963–1975
Stephen Wall

The Official History of Britain and the European Community, Volume II

This is the second volume in *The Official History of Britain and the European Community*, and describes the events from 1963 up until the British referendum on the Common Market in 1975.

In 1963, General de Gaulle dashed Prime Minister Harold Macmillan's hopes of taking Britain into the European Community (the Common Market). When Labour Prime Minister Harold Wilson tried again, de Gaulle again said 'no'. Six years later, Prime Minister Edward Heath took Britain into the EEC. But by then the country was split and Harold Wilson, to keep the Labour Party from voting to leave, undertook to renegotiate Britain's membership. When Labour won the 1974 election, that renegotiation culminated in the first nationwide referendum ever held in the United Kingdom.

The British people voted by two to one to stay in the European Community, but British membership has been controversial ever since. This is the story of why three very different Prime Ministers all concluded that, in the British national interest, there was no viable alternative to joining the Common Market. In the words and documents of the time (those of politicians, diplomats and journalists from Britain, France and Germany) it relives the frustrations, successes and humiliations of British politicians as they wrestled with the most important issue of their generation. It shows, with the authority of the Government papers of the day, where and why today's European controversy started and why yesterday's challenges, and the way they were confronted, hold valid lessons for our time.

This book will be of much interest to students of British political history, European Union politics, diplomatic history and international relations in general.

Stephen Wall worked in the British Diplomatic Service. He was Private Secretary to five Foreign Secretaries and to Prime Minister John Major; Britain's Ambassador to the European Union and Tony Blair's adviser on European issues. His book A *Stranger in Europe* was published in 2008.

Whitehall histories: government official history series
ISSN: 1474-8398

The Government Official History series began in 1919 with wartime histories, and the peacetime series was inaugurated in 1966 by Harold Wilson. The aim of the series is to produce major histories in their own right, compiled by historians eminent in the field, who are afforded free access to all relevant material in the official archives. The Histories also provide a trusted secondary source for other historians and researchers while the official records are not in the public domain. The main criteria for selection of topics are that the histories should record important episodes or themes of British history while the official records can still be supplemented by the recollections of key players; and that they should be of general interest, and, preferably, involve the records of more than one government department.

The United Kingdom and the European Community:
Vol. I: The Rise and Fall of a National Strategy, 1945–1963
Alan S. Milward

Secret Flotillas
Vol. I: Clandestine Sea Operations to Brittany, 1940–1944
Vol. II: Clandestine Sea Operations in the Mediterranean, North Africa and the Adriatic, 1940–1944
Sir Brooks Richards

SOE in France
M. R. D. Foot

The Official History of the Falklands Campaign:
Vol. I: The Origins of the Falklands War
Vol. II: War and Diplomacy
Sir Lawrence Freedman

The Official History of Britain and the Channel Tunnel
Terry Gourvish

The Official History of Britain and the European Community

Volume II: From Rejection to
Referendum, 1963–1975

Stephen Wall

 Routledge
Taylor & Francis Group

LONDON AND NEW YORK

First published 2013
by Routledge

2 Park Square, Milton Park, Abingdon, Oxfordshire OX14 4RN
Simultaneously published in the USA and Canada
by Routledge
711 Third Avenue, New York, NY 10017

First issued in paperback 2014

Routledge is an imprint of the Taylor & Francis Group, an informa business

© 2013 Crown copyright

British Library Cataloguing in Publication Data
A catalogue record for this book is available from the British Library

Library of Congress Cataloging-in-Publication Data
A catalog record has been requested for this book

ISBN 978–0–415–53560–1 (hbk)
ISBN 978–1–138–79739–0 (pbk)
ISBN 978–0–203–10327–2 (ebk)
Typeset in Baskerville
by RefineCatch Limited, Bungay, Suffolk

For my son, Matthew

Contents

Acknowledgements

The Cabinet Office series of Official Histories is conducted under the authority of the Prime Minister and I am grateful to the then Prime Minister, Gordon Brown, and the then Cabinet Secretary, Gus O'Donnell for appointing me to write this volume.

I was given all the access I asked for to official documents. I alone am responsible for the statements made and the views expressed

On a day-to-day basis, my access to the National Archives, and all other essential support, including a desk, a cupboard and a computer, were provided by the Knowledge and Information Management Unit of the Cabinet Office under the direction of Roger Smethurst, to whom much thanks. I am especially grateful to Tessa Stirling and Sally Falk, the Head and Deputy Head, respectively, of the Official Histories Team for their professional guidance, painstaking review of my work and for much practical help.

I was helped by a number of those who were players in the story told in this book and who confirmed (or otherwise), and supplemented, my research in particular, Lord Armstrong, Sir Michael Butler, Sir Michael Palliser, Sir Kenneth Stowe, Lord Owen, Lord Hannay, Lord Howe, Lord Hurd and Lord Donoughue.

Some of those cited in the book are people for whom I worked, notably Christopher Soames, Edward Tomkins and Christopher Ewart-Biggs, all of them stars of the British Embassy in Paris. I hope I have done justice to their achievements. Christopher Ewart-Biggs, who was assassinated in Dublin by the IRA in 1976, was one of the most decent people I met in a long career, old-fashioned in appearance, modern in outlook and a wordsmith of mesmeric ability.

Anyone writing a book needs the tolerance of their loved ones. My wife, Catharine, bore with me when I hogged our computer at home and encouraged me when my always poor imitation of Trollopian fluency and efficiency slowed to a feeble trickle. My son, Matthew, to whom the book is dedicated, has been a tower of strength.

Abbreviations

ACP	African, Caribbean and Pacific Group of States
ANF	Atlantic Nuclear Force
BBC	British Broadcasting Corporation
BMC	British Motor Corporation
BMG	British Military Government
BOAC	British Overseas Airways Corporation
BOT	Board of Trade
CAP	Common Agricultural Policy
CBI	Confederation of British Industry
CDU	Christian Democratic Union (Germany)
CERN	European Organisation for Nuclear Research
CFP	Common Fisheries Policy
CO	Cabinet Office
COREPER	Committee of Permanent Representatives of the European Community
CSA	Commonwealth Sugar Agreement
CSU	Christian Social Union of Bavaria
DEA	Department of Economic Affairs
DTI	Department of Trade and Industry
EC	European Community
ECS	Ministerial Committee on European Community Strategy
ECSC	European Coal and Steel Community
EEC	European Economic Community
EFTA	European Free Trade Association
ELDO	European Launcher Development Organisation
EMU	Economic and Monetary Union
EPU	European Payments Union
EQ	Ministerial Committee on European Questions
EQO	Official Committee on European Questions
EU	European Union
FCO	Foreign and Commonwealth Office
FEOGA	European Community Agricultural Guarantee Fund
FO	Foreign Office

FPD	Free Democratic Party (Germany)
FRG	Federal Republic of Germany

All references to Germany in the book are to FRG (West Germany) unless otherwise stated

GATT	General Agreement on Tariffs and Trade
GDP	Gross Domestic Product
GDR	German Democratic Republic (East Germany)
GITA	Go-it-alone
GNP	Gross National Product
GSP	General Scheme of Preferences
HMG	Her Majesty's Government
HMT	Her Majesty's Treasury
IBA	Independent Broadcasting Authority
ITN	Independent Television News
MAFF	Ministry of Agriculture, Fisheries and Food
MLF	Multilateral Nuclear Force
MNF	Multinational Nuclear Force
MUA	Monetary Unit of Account
(N)AFTA	(North) Atlantic Free Trade Area
NATO	North Atlantic Treaty Organisation
NEC	National Executive Committee
NSC	National Security Council
NPT	Treaty on the Non-Proliferation of Nuclear Weapons
OECD	Organisation for Economic Co-operation and Development
OPEC	Organisation of Petroleum Exporting Countries
PLP	Parliamentary Labour Party
PPS	Parliamentary Private Secretary *or* Principal Private Secretary
PS	Parti Socialiste (France)
PUS	Permanent Under-Secretary of State
PUSS	Parliamentary Under-Secretary of State
RAF	Royal Air Force
RDF	Regional Development Fund
SEATO	South-East Asia Treaty Organisation
SHAPE	Supreme Headquarters Allied Powers Europe
SPD	Social Democratic Party (Germany);
TUC	Trades Union Congress
UDR	Union pour la Défense de la République (French Gaullist Party)
USSR	Union of Soviet Socialist Republics (the Soviet Union)
VAT	Value Added Tax
WEU	Western European Union
WTO	World Trade Organisation

Introduction

"Life's but a walking shadow, a poor player that struts and frets his hour upon the stage and then is heard no more."

I thought often about Shakespeare's words as I wrote this book, for most, though happily not all, of the players whose story this is are now dead. And yet, as you read the meticulously comprehensive official records of the period, it is not just their preoccupations, but the people themselves and their personalities that spring back to life off the page. For, day by day, the paper files of the period take you back, not just to a past time, but to the exertions, hopes, fears and exasperations of politicians and civil servants alike.

Here is Harold Wilson's unmistakeable green ink in the margin of a telegram from the British Embassy reporting de Gaulle's selection of Pompidou as his successor in waiting, as his *dauphin*. "I can live with the *dauphin*," Wilson writes. "Send tennis balls?"

Here, a few years later, are now-President Pompidou and Prime Minister Heath, constructing through a mixture of personal chemistry and painstaking diplomacy the beginnings of a historic reconciliation between France and Britain.

As each story unfolds, be it de Gaulle's two vetoes of British accession to the European Community; or the near-collapse of his own Government in May 1968; or the Soviet invasion of Czechoslovakia later in that year, the files recreate, page by page, the build-up of tension, the sense of uncertainty, the questions and doubts about how to act, how to respond, how to advance the British national interest which those whose responsibility it was to advise and to lead faced day in, day out for the duration of their lifetimes in office.

Ambassadors and other civil servants play parts that are intimately woven into this drama. This was a period when those in positions of authority, either as Ministers or officials, had shared the comradeship of wartime service. My late father-in-law, Norman Reddaway, joined the Foreign Office after World War II and became Private Secretary to a young Foreign Office Minister, Christopher Mayhew. Both men had served together (alongside the film star David Niven) in the *Phantom* Regiment. Such stories and such friendships were commonplace and the relationship between politicians and civil servants was, as a result, different from what it is today. Politicians and civil servants did not feel that they were made of different clay. There was, on the whole, greater mutual confidence.

Of course, we have the benefit of hindsight. With that in mind, a leading historian asked me what the basic thesis of my book was going to be. The answer is that there is none. I spent 35 years as a civil servant, seven of them working in 10 Downing Street at three different times. Each Prime Minister, each Cabinet Minister, each Government has its policy and its approach. A whole range of factors goes into the formulation of policy, starting with the view of the Party in power of where the national interest lies, but being constantly affected by the pressures of public and Parliamentary opinion, by events to which a response is required, by the advice Ministers receive, by the personality, beliefs, judgements – and prejudices – of the Ministers themselves, especially the Prime Minister; and by historical memory.

The purpose of an Official History is to use the official records of the day, reinforced by the memories of the participants, to tell the story of why those whose job it was to take decisions on behalf of Britain thought as they did and did what they did. I have thought it best to try to let them tell their own story as far as possible. If, sometimes, the prevailing sense is one of uncertainty then that is no more than a true reflection of what people were feeling at that time.

The Governments of Wilson and Heath, like that of Macmillan before them, came to the painful conclusion that Britain could not maintain influence in the world without joining a grouping of like-minded countries, and that neither the European Free Trade Association (EFTA) nor an Atlantic Free Trade Area was a viable option. Heath was a European of head and heart; Wilson of the head. To me, Wilson's story, as it emerges from the archives, is the more intriguing for being less well known.

Before I started writing, I read Uwe Kitzinger's book, *Diplomacy and Persuasion*, about how Britain joined the Common Market. When I read Kitzinger's comment that "Harold Wilson is almost certainly one of those few men but for whom Britain could not have entered the Community",[1] it gave me pause. Heath, surely, was the European; Wilson the man who put Party before principle. I hope I have accurately portrayed the real story for it is, apart from anything else, a vivid illustration of the huge complex of issues and factors with which all political leaders have to juggle.

My conclusion, after reading the records and talking to people who worked for and with him, was that Wilson, once persuaded of the advantages of membership (and the absence of viable alternatives) held to that view, both in Government and Opposition. If, in Opposition after 1970, he had fallen on his sword for the sake of pursuing the European policy he had espoused in Government, the result would probably have been the end of his leadership and a Labour Party committed to withdrawal from the EEC, or deeply riven, or both. Renegotiation and a referendum were not heroic, but they were the life-raft that kept a workable policy on Europe alive within the Labour Party.

This book also covers the beginnings of a European journey towards two goals, those of European Union and Economic and Monetary Union. If the modern reader wonders what the difference is between the two, so did those who invented the terms some forty years ago. If Europe today is deep in the woods of Economic and Monetary Union, and its problems and implications, the trees we are bumping into are recognisably those planted during the period of this story.

When, in October 1972, the Heads of Government proclaimed their intention of creating a European Union by 1980, not one of them knew, or sought to define, what it meant. It was an expression of hope. Rather clearer thoughts had been expressed about Economic and Monetary Union. But the approach was to be one taken in stages; it was not clear whether the goal was a common currency or a single currency and few had confronted the implications, political or economic. An often deliberate ambiguity, combined with Micawber-like optimism, pervades some of the discussions and decisions.

Some of the clearest thinking was done in Whitehall. Whether even a Heath-led Government would, in the end, have felt able to embrace a single currency is a difficult question to answer. For Heath too it was more aspiration than commitment. But no one in Whitehall who looked into the issue at the time was in any doubt that a single currency would involve a single exchange rate and interest rate and the centralised management of economic and fiscal policy. The need for fiscal transfers from rich to poor was seen as an inescapable component, as were very large transfers of sovereignty from national Governments to a central authority.

The story I have tried to tell is a political and economic one. Some quite technically complex issues, such as Britain's contribution to the budget of the European Community, are covered in detail because they assumed ever larger economic and political importance, going well beyond the period covered in the book. But, by and large, I have not covered the ins and outs of individual pieces of EEC legislation, significant though they may have been. If you are a negotiator, the process is fascinating. If you are not, it can be deadly, especially 40 years on.

I *have* sought to convey, through what was said and written at the time, what British politicians and civil servants believed about the implications of EEC membership for Parliamentary sovereignty and for Britain's ability to continue to decide her own destiny.

I think it fair to say that the implications of European Community law-making were clear to those who studied them. Indeed, much of the Parliamentary opposition to membership was based on the knowledge that European Community legislation, once agreed in Brussels, could not be changed by Parliament without that exercise of Parliamentary sovereignty being tantamount to a deliberate decision to breach the terms of British membership of the Community.

What was much less clear at the time was the extent to which judgements of the European Court of Justice would advance the course of integration. Nor was it at all clear to Ministers that they would find themselves out-voted in the Council of Ministers on significant policy issues. For a start, only a limited number of Treaty articles prescribed majority voting. The big jump in those was to come with Margaret Thatcher's agreement in 1985 to the Single European Act. But, even where majority voting *was* prescribed, it is clear from the records that British Ministers believed that they were safeguarded by the so-called Luxembourg Compromise. In other words, they believed – to a much greater degree than was justified by subsequent events – that if a British Minister, in Brussels, told his colleagues in the Council of Ministers that a very important national interest was at stake, discussion would continue until consensus had been reached. Britain would not be out-voted. In adhering to that view, Ministers were mistaken. But it is what they sincerely believed and they were reinforced in their conviction by the fact that the French Government, the inventors of the Luxembourg Compromise, not only shared their interpretation, but entrenched it by making British acceptance of it one of their conditions for admitting her to EEC membership.

This is a British story, but it is also the story of Europe as a whole, for the reporting and analysis sent to London by Britain's Embassies covered the thinking of European Community Governments, not just on Britain's approach to Europe, but on the progress or otherwise of their own fledgling enterprise. In this wider drama, de Gaulle plays a dominant role. De Gaulle strides outrageously, intolerably and magnificently across the pages of much of this period, holding the whole of Europe to ransom, belittling Britain, bullying Germany and undermining the coherence of the West just as he rebuilt the self-worth of his compatriots. It is questionable whether Monnet's vision of an ever closer union on federal lines would ever have come to fruition as he intended. That it did not is much more down to de Gaulle than to any other single figure.

C S Forester entitled one of his novels *Death to the French*. At this period, perhaps more than any other in the twentieth century, Britain and France alike revisited their old rivalry. Each defined itself in contrast, and often in opposition, to the other. How to deal with the French – meaning how to get round them or defeat them or convert them – was a constant preoccupation of British policy. There were divided views in Whitehall, with a tendency in the Foreign Office to think that the five other members of the European Community could be used to gang up on and overwhelm the French. It did not work. Macmillan, Wilson and Heath all realised that British accession would only be possible if an accommodation could be reached with the French.

Macmillan's hopes effectively died in the autumn fog at Rambouillet in 1962. Wilson skilfully and publicly refused to take 'No' for an answer in 1967, by which time all of Europe was silently praying for the General's demise – politically at least. The significance of Heath's famous two-day meeting with Pompidou in 1971 lay, not just in the undoubted chemistry between the two men, but in the careful preparation, largely bypassing Foreign Ministries, conducted by both sides in readying themselves for the meeting. The one thing most in need of restoration was trust.

Relations with West Germany were both less intense and in a way more unsatisfactory. Macmillan had to contend with Adenauer, who had good reason to dislike the British. The robust Erhard was sadly short-lived and Wilson tried valiantly but unsuccessfully to induce his successor, Kiesinger, to stand up just a little *to* de Gaulle and *for* Britain. It was only with the advent of Willy Brandt that Germany exercised decisive influence on France to allow negotiations for British accession to begin, albeit at a price which Britain is paying to this day.

If there were suspicions in Britain that Germany might be hiding her own private reservations about British accession behind de Gaulle's very public ones, these were more than matched by deep French fears about Germany's place in, and commitment to, a democratic Western Europe. The temptation of a deal with the Soviet Union in the interest of German reunification was thought in Paris to be ever-present in Bonn. As late as 1973, Pompidou was expressing to Heath his fear that Germany could revert to type, a view echoed 15 years later by President Mitterrand to Margaret Thatcher. The true story was one of Germany being consistently willing, within bounds, to spend large sums of her national budget on financing the budget of the EEC. And in the oil crisis of 1973 it was not Germany, but rather France and Britain, who were seen to fail to meet their obligations of Community solidarity.

The disappointments of a decade cannot be laid solely at de Gaulle's door. Macmillan's 'events dear boy, events' permeates every chapter of this history, most pertinently, perhaps, in 1973, the first year of Britain's membership of the European Community, a year which began with a glittering, floodlit gala and ended in three-day week candlelight. The British drama was, of course, not just that of our disappointed European aspirations but also of our national struggle to find economic stability and prosperity. Interestingly, it was not the economics of the EEC which most appealed to Heath and to Wilson, for the balance of economic argument, in study after study, was found to be finely balanced. It was the politics born of the realisation, starting with Macmillan, that Britain was a small country in a world dominated by two super powers, the United States and the Soviet Union. All three Prime Ministers believed that only by membership of the European Community could Britain hope to exercise influence in a world dominated by two nuclear super powers.

The Soviet Union looms as a persistent, if gradually diminishing, threat throughout this history. Soviet nuclear parity with the United States was a real fear and preoccupation. There is no hint of anything other than the assumed continuation of Soviet domination in Eastern and Central Europe, though de Gaulle had a strong sense of the European destiny of those countries and there are glimpses of a similar view on the part of Wilson and Heath as well. The rise of China is foreseen but not felt; that of Japan a new reality. Heath was correct in his view that the predominant place of the United States in the world would be challenged; he was wrong in assuming that it was the enlarged European Community that would be the occasion of it. Writing a history of this kind is a salutary reminder that brilliant analysis, and there was plenty of that, is no guarantee of accurate foresight.

Heath saw, perhaps more clearly than did Wilson, that US interests would move away from Europe towards the Pacific. Both shared the British post-war view that the safety and freedom of the West depended on American military strength and nuclear commitment. They gave no credence to de Gaulle's view of a Europe built in contra-distinction, even opposition, to the United States; nor did any of de Gaulle's partners among the Six. It is that refusal to accept de Gaulle's vision and ambition which accounts in large measure for de Gaulle's monstrously bad treatment of his German opposite numbers during his time in office. He was the author of reconciliation and resentment in almost equal measure.

In 1973, as Nixon's chariot began to plunge to earth because of Watergate, US relations with the European Community went through one of their scratchiest periods. Henry Kissinger's personal, occasionally paranoid, diplomacy and his massively ill-conceived Year of Europe were partly responsible. But the French reacted with Gaullist hostility and Heath's vexation with Kissinger led him to a public outburst of irritation which undoubtedly damaged the UK/US bilateral relationship at the time.

The dogs bark, but the caravan moves on. By the end of 1974, Nixon, Heath and Brandt had all lost power and Pompidou was dead. Yet the genes of national instinct and behaviour pass, in politics as in nature, from generation to generation. Much of this story may seem long ago and emotionally far away. But much of who we, the British, are, and what we do, today, as questioning, and often sceptical members of the European Union, was first written in the official files of forty years ago. The British argument for, against and about Europe that we have today is recognisably the one we were having forty years ago.

Shakespeare's stark statement of the human condition does not embrace one aspect of human life, which his own genius exemplifies to perfection. Men and women do leave footprints in the sands of time. This book is a detailed study of politics and policies, problems and negotiations. But it is above all the story of how serious and dedicated people devoted themselves to trying to find the right answers to one of the great challenges of their generation. I hope it does justice to them and, above all to the memory of Macmillan, Wilson and Heath, the three principal architects of Britain's membership of the European Community.

Had he not fallen ill, this book would have been written by Professor Alan Milward, whose first volume of the Official History of Britain and the European Community is a great work of enduring originality and scholarship. I have been all too aware, as I have sought to follow in his footsteps, that they were larger than I could hope to fill.

1 De Gaulle says "No": 1962–1963

"I think this man has gone crazy – absolutely crazy".

The telephone line between London and Washington was clear on that day, the 19th of January 1963. So there can be no doubt that President Kennedy heard Prime Minister Harold Macmillan correctly. "He is", Macmillan continued, "inventing any means whatever to knock us out and the simple thing is he wants to be the cock on a small dunghill instead of having two cocks on a larger one".[1]

The 'he' in question was of course President Charles de Gaulle of France and on 14 January 1963, in a press conference remarkable for its fluency, authority and patronising disdain, de Gaulle had dashed Britain's hopes of joining the European Economic Community (EEC).

Macmillan's vivid metaphor had not sprung unbidden into his mind. Just five days before de Gaulle's press conference, Britain's Agriculture Minister, Christopher Soames, had reported a conversation with his French counterpart which found its way into Macmillan's diary. "Mon cher", said the Frenchman, "c'est tres simple. Maintenant, avec les Six, il y a cinq poules et un coq. Si vous joignez (avec des autres pays), il y aura peut-etre sept ou huit poules. Mais il y aura *deux* coqs. Alors ce n'est pas aussi agréable"[2].

Much anxious British analysis preceded and followed de Gaulle's press conference. In it, he set out both a rationale for the existence and shape of the European Community as it then was and an argument as to why Britain was not ready to join. The Treaty of Rome, the founding treaty of the EEC, was, de Gaulle argued, a treaty between six continental states of an economically similar nature. They were, moreover, geographically adjacent: "they inter-penetrate; their communications make them extensions of one another". There were no political rivalries or grievances between the Six. Their solidarity was marked by the fact that not one of them was "bound by a private political or military accord". France had had to put her economic house in order to be able to cope. But while the Treaty of Rome had settled a new industrial order, the same was not true of agriculture: "We cannot conceive, and will not conceive, of a Common Market in which French agriculture would not find outlets commensurate with its production". But, de Gaulle went on, no sooner had France got the Common Market's agriculture regime sorted to her satisfaction than up jumped the British with their application to join. And Britain did so only after having, so de Gaulle clearly implied, failed in her attempts to scupper the EEC project in the first place. 'England' was asking to join, but on her own terms. England was "insular . . . maritime. She is linked . . . to the most diverse and often the most distant countries; she pursues essentially industrial and commercial activities and only slight agricultural ones". England, said de Gaulle, as if he were describing someone guilty of unsocial behaviour, "has in all her doings very marked and very original habits and traditions." Could England change in order to accommodate herself to continental Europe? It was doubtful and, in any case, England would bring in other countries in her wake. A Community of 11 and then 13 and then 18 would no longer be the Common Market as constructed by the Six. At these numbers, there would be no cohesion and soon, instead of a community of Europe there would be a colossal Atlantic community under American dependence and direction. That was not what France was about. What France was about was "a properly European construction".

Then, gesturing largely, and at his most magisterial, de Gaulle went on to dismiss the end of Britain's aspirations as a matter of little consequence. Paying tribute, with some, albeit self-serving, sincerity to Britain's role in two world wars, de Gaulle concluded by congratulating his friend, Harold Macmillan, for having had the "great honour" of leading his country "on the first steps down the path which one day, perhaps, will lead it to moor alongside the Continent."[3]

British debate then and later centred on de Gaulle's motives. Was this revenge for perceived humiliations at the hands of the British and Americans in World War II? Was it the deal struck by Macmillan and Kennedy a few weeks earlier in Nassau in which the United States cemented its relationship with Britain by offering her access to the Polaris nuclear missile? Was it hard-headed analysis of French national interests? Was it a hegemonic pipe dream of a Europe rivalling the United States and dominated by France?

Macmillan's own view of de Gaulle, according to his official biographer, Alistair Horne, oscillated between admiration and extreme exasperation.[4] Churchill and de Gaulle were among the greatest men Macmillan had known but the literally large-headed Churchill was constantly thinking forward, as well as backwards whereas de Gaulle, literally, according to Macmillan, pin-headed, could only look backwards.

That was a view Churchill had shared. Under cover of a letter of 1 February 1963, Conservative MP Sir David Robertson sent to Macmillan the record of Churchill's speech to a secret session of the House of Commons in December 1942. Churchill's speech bears the same mixture of respect and resentment about de Gaulle expressed later by Macmillan. This is hardly surprising since, of all British politicians apart from Anthony Eden, Churchill and Macmillan were the ones who, in London and Algiers respectively, had got to know de Gaulle best.

"I consider", Churchill told the House, "that we have been in every respect faithful in the discharge of our obligations to de Gaulle, and we shall continue to the end. I continue to maintain friendly relations and I help him as much as I possibly can. I feel bound to do this because he stood up against the Men of Bordeaux and their base surrender at a time when all resisting willpower had quitted France." But, Churchill continued, that was not the same thing as placing the destiny of France in his hands. That must be for the entire French nation to determine. "Now we are in secret session, the House must not be led to believe that General de Gaulle is an unfaltering friend of Britain. On the contrary, I think he is one of those good Frenchmen who have a traditional antagonism, ingrained in French hearts by centuries of war against the English." Churchill went on to give examples of de Gaulle's dishonesty. In the summer of 1941, travelling through the French colonies of Central and West Africa, de Gaulle had "left a trail of Anglophobia behind him" culminating in an interview in Brazzaville with the Chicago Daily News in which he had suggested that England coveted the African colonies of France and accused the British of in effect "carrying out a wartime deal with Hitler in which Vichy serves as go-between". Vichy, de Gaulle had explained, served Germany by keeping the French people in subjection and England by keeping the French fleet out of German hands.

In July of 1942, Churchill continued, he had facilitated a journey (which he could easily have prevented) by de Gaulle to Syria. De Gaulle had promised him he would behave in a friendly and helpful manner. But in Syria "his whole object seemed to be to foment ill-will between the British military and Free French civil administration and state the French claims to rule Syria at the highest, although it had been agreed that after the war, and as much as possible during the war, the Syrians are to enjoy their independence."[5]

"If Hitler had danced in London we'd have had no trouble with de Gaulle"[6] was one of Macmillan's memorable verdicts. But Macmillan was ambivalent about his nemesis, just as he recognised an ambivalence in de Gaulle. Before meeting de Gaulle at the Chateau de Champs at the beginning of June 1962, Macmillan had had a long talk with Edward Heath who, as Lord Privy Seal in Macmillan's Government, was the man leading the British negotiating team in Brussels. The paradox to Macmillan was that de Gaulle wanted the kind of Europe Britain would be readily able to join. Macmillan noted that the British Ambassador in Paris, Sir Pierson ('Bob') Dixon, (who combined being British Ambassador to France with the role of official head of the UK Delegation to the EEC) and who, Macmillan believed, had "the subtlest mind in Whitehall", thought that de Gaulle had already decided to exclude Britain. But Macmillan himself was not so sure that de Gaulle had made up his mind. He saw him as torn between emotion and reason, the emotion being his hatred of England – and still more the United States – because of the war, because of France's shame, because of Churchill and Roosevelt and because of Britain's access to nuclear weapons. Yet, Macmillan concluded, it was a sort of love–hate relationship – one that must soon resolve itself one way or another.[7]

In terms of atmospherics and substance, the Chateau de Champs meeting on 2 and 3 June 1962 was probably the high point of discussion between Macmillan and de Gaulle about British accession. De Gaulle "did not show the rather brutal attitude which had been attributed to him". He was a charming host "with his natural courtesy and old-world manners". But if Macmillan had been hoping that his discussions would persuade de Gaulle to lean towards Britain for reason's sake, rather than against her because of the sway of emotion, there was scant substantial evidence of a shift. Indeed, de Gaulle trailed many of the arguments he was to use six months later at his press conference. In particular, de Gaulle argued that British accession would change the substantive economic and political character of the Community to France's disadvantage and that Britain was too tied to the Commonwealth and, more especially, to the United States.[8]

Then, as later, the British placed high hopes on the five other EEC members. They were all unequivocal in their wish to see Britain join and the British could not quite bring themselves to believe that, in the end, de Gaulle would gainsay them. Among the Five, Germany was of course the key player. The European Community was, at heart, a vehicle for Franco-German reconciliation; West Germany's economy was already the motor force of the European Community's success, and Germany was the cockpit in which any future nuclear war between the West and the Soviet empire would be triggered. So Macmillan took great pains, following his meeting with de Gaulle, to brief and flatter the German Government.

In a "Dear Friend" letter of 5 June 1962 to Chancellor Adenauer of Germany Macmillan wrote that he believed de Gaulle understood the sincerity of Britain's desire to join, and to play her part in, a larger and more coherent European Community while understanding the British desire to satisfy the legitimate economic expectations of the countries of the Commonwealth. "President de Gaulle and I wished that you had been with us to contribute your point of view to what was a very interesting discussion about the future", Macmillan concluded.[9]

Macmillan's letter crossed with a Despatch to the Foreign Secretary from the British Ambassador in Bonn, Sir Christopher ('Kit') Steel. Until the advent of IT, and greater informality in general, overtook them, Despatches were the common currency of the British Diplomatic Service, not for reporting and commenting on events as they happened (which was done by enciphered telegram) but for deeper reflection on events, trends and policies, the aim being to give Ministers in London as accurate a picture of the local scene as the Ambassador and his staff could muster. They were invariably addressed by the Ambassador to the Foreign Secretary, were usually printed for distribution in Whitehall and to The Queen and often elicited a formal response in the name of the Foreign Secretary himself. In the 1960s, it was rare for one politician to pick up the phone and talk to his opposite number in another country. Telephone communication was not instantaneous or generally secure. Language was often a barrier on both sides. Macmillan, for example, did not speak much German and Adenauer spoke no English. Collective meetings, of the kind which have rendered European Union Ministers more familiar to each other than they are to their own Cabinet colleagues, were in their infancy. Bilateral meetings were infrequent and usually formal.

So it was just such a Despatch from Sir Christopher Steel to Foreign Secretary, Lord Home, that was sent across the road from the Foreign Office to No. 10 Downing Street on 7 June 1962 (probably by messenger but possibly using the pneumatic tube which ran underground between the two offices, mimicking the system in most Department stores of the day). Steel's view was that it was clearly to Britain's advantage that Adenauer must pay attention to the overwhelming weight of opinion in Germany in favour of British entry into the Common Market. But whether that opinion would, in practice, have any positive effect was less certain: "A member of the Chancellor's office told us recently that no one yet had any clear idea as to what, if anything, the Chancellor was prepared to do to overcome French opposition. The Chancellor was more interested in making progress over European political union than in the negotiations in Brussels."[10]

It was probably because of Steel's advice that, on 15 June, Macmillan asked the German Ambassador in London, Herr von Etzdorf, to call on him. The days are long gone since Ambassadors, even those from important countries, have had regular access to the Foreign Secretary, let alone the Prime Minister. Today, if the Prime Minister wants to get across his view to the German Chancellor, he or she either picks up the telephone for a direct conversation or gets one of the No. 10 Private Secretaries to call their opposite number in the German Chancellery. But, largely for the reasons already suggested, Ambassadors were still, in the 1960s, an important vehicle for bilateral diplomatic communication and Macmillan would have known that calling in the German Ambassador in London for a privileged first-hand briefing on his recent talks with de Gaulle would be seen in Bonn as even more significant than if instructions had been sent to the British Ambassador to go in and speak on the Prime Minister's behalf.

The Prime Minister said that he had asked the Ambassador to call because he thought it would be helpful for him to have a little more background on his talks with de Gaulle. Once the Ambassador had been set up to think that he was about to hear something personal and privileged, Macmillan cleverly set out his stall. He did not claim that he had persuaded de Gaulle of the British cause, merely that he thought de Gaulle now better understood the reasons for it. He went on both to set out the world view that he thought would appeal to Adenauer and to dispel some of the misconceptions about the British negotiating stance prevalent in the German Chancellery. Macmillan said that he and de Gaulle had discussed the great changes in the balance of power which had taken place as a result of the two world wars and he thought there had been broad agreement between them that Europe must unite on as wide a basis as possible if it was to recover any of the authority "which it had enjoyed for several thousand years". So, as Macmillan had stressed to de Gaulle, success or failure of the negotiations was not about solving the technical difficulties. Nor was Dr Adenauer right to think that Britain wanted to bring the Commonwealth into the EEC. We had no such intention. But, in having regard to the Commonwealth, the EEC would be having regard to its responsibilities to the outside world. The goal, Macmillan concluded, should be to make Europe strong enough to be a true partner of America.[11]

In making this last point, Macmillan was trying to insert a very subtle wedge between Adenauer and de Gaulle. For de Gaulle's vision of a Europe released from American shackles implied to the German Government a Europe deprived of the protection of American arms, which was politically and militarily unthinkable.

It is unlikely that the Macmillan magic had much impact on Adenauer. Adenauer had good reason to dislike the British. He had been Lord Mayor of Cologne before the war and returned, at American request, to run the city after the fall of Hitler in 1945. Devastation and starvation were the challenges that faced him and the evidence suggests that he put together an effective team to rebuild the city. But the Americans were replaced in June 1945 by the British Military Government. The British tapped his phone line, and he found out about it. If he was authoritarian, so were the British. Nor did local Germans think the British very effective. One well-worn joke was that it would take the Germans three weeks to build a temporary bridge across the Rhine. What if we British helped with all possible resource, asked the BMG. "Ah", in that case "it will take three years."

On 6 October 1945, Adenauer was summarily dismissed and ordered to leave Cologne and refrain from all political activity by the BMG's chief administrative officer for North Rhine, Brigadier John Barraclough. Whatever the reasons, and they seem to have been more political than substantive, it was pretty scurvy treatment of a distinguished official of nearly 70. Although Adenauer often made light of the incident, he reportedly said, not long afterwards, that his three chief dislikes were the Russians, the Prussians and the British.[12]

Macmillan worked quite hard on his relationship with Adenauer. At their first substantive meeting, in Bonn in 1954, Adenauer "delivered a long and fascinating discourse covering . . . the whole history of the German peoples from Roman times until the present day." "During the next nine years" Macmillan continued "I was destined to listen to it on every occasion when we met."[13] Maybe Adenauer was Helmut Kohl's role model when, a generation later, he treated John Major to his own, equally fascinating, equally oft-repeated, discourse on Germany and the post war world.[14]

At all events, by September 1962, Macmillan's Foreign Office Private Secretary, Philip de Zulueta, was warning Macmillan of rumours circulating strongly in Europe (then, as now, nobody talked of Britain as if it were part of Europe) that de Gaulle was determined that we should not join the EEC – at the very least for another two years. This meant, de Zulueta argued, that Britain would have to rely on the other members of the Six to put pressure on France: "We have not yet, I think, reached the stage where General de Gaulle would be prepared to go out openly against us even if the other Five were in favour. The weakness of our position is Dr Adenauer. I do not think that we can change his view but it may be that the Germans will not put up with him for long and we must continue to work hard with our German friends."[15]

The Italian Foreign Minister, Signor Fanfani, took a similar view, advising Edward Heath, who was to call on Adenauer shortly thereafter, to disabuse the German Chancellor of his suspicion that the United Kingdom's object in seeking entry to the European Community was to disrupt it from within. Fanfani judged that Adenauer was unwilling to annoy de Gaulle in any way and was intent on a Franco-German 'Alliance for Peace'. Fanfani also believed that de Gaulle had promised Adenauer that he would be the first President of a European Political Union.[16]

Either Fanfani had an inaccurate view, or de Gaulle was being disingenuous when, on the same day, he told the British Ambassador in Paris, Bob Dixon, that

Britain and others should not worry that France and Germany were embarking on an especially close bilateral understanding. He did not expect that matters would go further than attempts to maintain close and friendly relations with meetings from time to time at the different levels of government. It was true that there were "a lot of theoreticians" such as Monnet in France and a number in Germany and Italy who wanted to work for something like a United States of Europe but this, in his view, was completely unrealistic and would never come about.

When Dixon ventured to suggest that Great Britain belonged to Europe, de Gaulle countered that, as he had told Macmillan at Champs in June, though he did not doubt that we were becoming *more* European, he wondered whether we were yet *sufficiently* European to enter the Common Market with all the rules and regulations we would have to accept.

De Gaulle suggested that the existing friendly relations, and indeed alliance, between France and Britain were satisfactory, that we had broadly the same objectives in foreign policy and that our economic interests were becoming more and more mutually involved i.e., by implication, that that was sufficient. But he recognised that the decision to apply for EC membership was one for Britain to take and that "if we wanted to join the Common Market, accepting the rules of course, he supposed that this was what would happen."

Dixon then chanced his arm by asking for French support in bringing the negotiations for British entry to a satisfactory and early conclusion. Characteristically and significantly, de Gaulle did not respond directly but referred to the fact that, for the French, agriculture was the core of the matter, a cardinal point. France had had the greatest difficulty in getting an agreement among the Six which would protect French agricultural interests. If this could not be maintained the French would have no special interest in remaining members of the Community. The problem for France, de Gaulle said, was quite simple: she must have outlets for the export of her agricultural surpluses.[17]

Commenting on this exchange in a telegram to London, Dixon concluded that "it was plain from what he said that he still hoped that we might decide to withdraw our application, that he would do nothing towards assisting it to be successful but that, in certain circumstances, France might have to reconcile herself to our entry ... The General's attitude does not augur well for our negotiations ... What was striking was that he should have made no effort for the sake of politeness to convey any impression other than that he had no intention of being helpful and that, if we had to come in, he would at least do his best to ensure that France made a financial killing, particularly over agriculture."[18]

Small wonder then that Macmillan commented a week later, in a letter to a friend: "The French enigma remains. But, whatever may be the situation internally, I don't believe they will want to be responsible for keeping us out, with all the terrible consequences that will surely follow to the life and vigour of the old world."[19]

By the time de Gaulle and Macmillan saw each other for their next and, as it turned out, last, meeting, de Gaulle's domestic position had got stronger and Macmillan's weaker. In July 1962, Macmillan sacked one third of his Cabinet.

"Greater love hath no man than this" Jeremy Thorpe famously wrote "than he lay down his friends for his life".[20] Macmillan was 68 and the action was seen to be more an act of desperation than of reconstruction. De Gaulle meanwhile had strengthened his position. On 10 October 1962, de Gaulle dissolved the French National Assembly following the defeat of the Government which had supported his request for a referendum to amend the constitution to allow the President of the Republic to be elected by universal suffrage. With what Macmillan called "splendid disregard" for the vote of the French Assembly, de Gaulle held the referendum anyway and won. Then, contrary to predictions, the Gaullist Party made sweeping gains in the November elections to the National Assembly.[21]

By the beginning of December, it was plain to Macmillan, and to Edward Heath, his negotiator, that the French, strengthened by de Gaulle's recent successes, were both opposing the British in Brussels at every turn and successfully intimidating their other partners. "After his victory both in the referendum and the Parliamentary election, de Gaulle's position is now very strong" Macmillan wrote in his diary. "He is a sort of mixture of Louis XIV and Napoleon – certainly in his own estimation." Yet Macmillan still calculated that the French were afraid of being pilloried as the destroyers of European unity.[22]

Thus the build-up to the meeting between Macmillan and de Gaulle which had been arranged to take place at Rambouillet in mid-December 1962 was not auspicious. Luck, according to most politicians, is a big factor in political fortunes. And Macmillan's ill luck was compounded by a speech made at the US Military Academy at West Point on 5 December by former US Secretary of State, Dean Acheson, the speech in which Acheson famously said that Great Britain had lost an empire and had not yet found a role. Macmillan felt obliged to make a public response, cleverly interpreting Acheson's words as denigration of the resolution and will of the British people and reminding him and others that Acheson had "fallen into an error which has been made by quite a lot of people in the course of the last four hundred years, including Philip of Spain, Louis XIV, Napoleon, the Kaiser and Hitler." The fact that four of these tyrants came from countries on whose goodwill Britain was depending for entry into the EEC and the two French ones were, as we have just seen, de Gaulle's own role models, shows that perhaps even Macmillan felt some of the familiar British ambivalence about continental Europe. But Acheson's speech, which would certainly have come to the attention of de Gaulle, would have done nothing to disabuse him of the notion that Britain, rather than being committed to the EEC as its existing members conceived it, was adrift and looking for a safe port in the storm.

Macmillan's meeting with de Gaulle took place on 15 and 16 December. The first morning was spent in shooting pheasants. In the course of the morning there were four drives and 385 pheasants, of which 77 were allegedly bagged by Macmillan. De Gaulle, who did not shoot, watched the last drive. Macmillan's account implies that Bob Dixon, the British Ambassador in Paris, was one of the guns. If so, he was of the last generation of British diplomats for whom game shooting was a normal accomplishment. When, ten years later, Christopher Soames, as British Ambassador in Paris, peppered his Despatches to the Foreign

Secretary, Sir Alec Douglas-Home (as Lord Home had now become), with shooting metaphors, there was scarcely anyone left at the London end, other than the Foreign Secretary, who understood the language. This generational change was less a reflection of distaste for blood sports than of a class change in the ranks of Foreign Office officials, increasingly recruited from the urban middle class for whom shooting was an unknown pastime.

When formal talks got under way on the Saturday afternoon, the focus was mainly on the world scene. De Gaulle expressed his astonishment at what he called Khrushchev's audacity in putting nuclear missiles on Cuba (the Cuban missile crisis had blown up just two months previously) and speculated that his motive had probably been blackmail, rather than war, doubtless hoping that the Americans would be sufficiently frightened that they would abandon Berlin.

The two men went on to talk about European defence and Macmillan set out the case for the British nuclear deterrent which would be 'independent' in the sense that its ultimate control would remain with a British Government. He told de Gaulle how Britain had been depending on the Americans for the Skybolt missile and that if, as now seemed probable, Skybolt was cancelled, then Britain must have an adequate replacement from the United States – such as the Polaris missile. If that was not available, then Britain would have to develop her own system, submarine or aerial, in spite of the cost.[23] Both that afternoon, and on Sunday morning, de Gaulle and Macmillan met alone apart from the presence of Private Secretaries and an interpreter 'in case of need'. Macmillan spoke good French but his Private Secretary was not confident that de Gaulle had understood everything Macmillan had said given the latter's tendency to speak elliptically.[24]

Discussion of Britain's application to join the EEC, both that afternoon and the following morning, was, in Macmillan's word 'discouraging'. De Gaulle's meaning could not have been clearer. When the two men met alone, de Gaulle suggested that the failure of the Fouchet plan (a plan for a European inter-governmental foreign policy and defence union proposed by de Gaulle in1961) showed what a lack of will there was among other European countries. Even if Britain joined there would be little difference. De Gaulle alluded to the difficulties in the nego-tiations in Brussels. Macmillan expressed himself "astonished and even wounded". He had done a lot to overcome the practical obstacles to British entry only to be told that the whole European idea had failed.

The discussion deteriorated into what Macmillan called "something of a wrangle", before the two men were joined, at noon, by the Foreign Secretary, Lord Home, and the British Ambassador, Bob Dixon. De Gaulle had with him his Prime Minister, Georges Pompidou, his Foreign Minister, Maurice Couve de Murville and the French Ambassador in London, Geoffroy de Courcel. De Gaulle, summing up the earlier discussion, commented that Macmillan had "suggested without actually saying so that ... the European countries did not like the hegemony of France and looked for an equilibrium which British entry into Europe would provide". But de Gaulle did not see any point on which he could base a true European organisation. If the United Kingdom joined, she would be followed by Norway, Denmark, Ireland, Portugal and perhaps even Spain. It was not a desperate situation and, de Gaulle suggested, perhaps something could be worked out gradually. The UK had certainly taken the right road and was working towards a European organisation. The Brussels negotiations were not finished and Mr Macmillan had given the impression that the reasons for this were not, in themselves, very important and could be overcome if the will to do so existed. But, de Gaulle added, the difficulties for France, particularly in the agricultural sector, were real ones.

Thereafter, the discussion became more fraught. Macmillan reproached de Gaulle for his pessimism. The whole future of Europe was at stake, he said. Europe had destroyed itself twice in the 20th century and between the wars the Western allies had lost every available opportunity. For Britain there were two solutions: she could either abandon her traditional role and become a mere client of the United States, or she could help to build up a strong Europe in close alliance with the United States. He wanted the countries of Europe to be both independent and interdependent. If the moment was not seized, it would pass for good. There was no question of any one country having a hegemony in Europe but instead there should be an equilibrium. Britain was ready to work with France, inside the EEC, to create the political base for European construction. He cited both the need for a common monetary system and "the question of defence and of relations with the Soviet Union and the United States.". If the moment were lost it would not be a disaster and life would continue, but it would be "a tragic failure to match the level of events . . . He had taken great political risks for this policy . . . because he believed it to be his duty to the whole history both of his own country and of Europe".

De Gaulle claimed to be much impressed by Macmillan's words. He would only recall, however, that at one point in the war Mr Churchill had said to him that he would always choose Roosevelt rather than de Gaulle and would always choose the larger world rather than Europe. Macmillan responded that, at that point in history, the United States had possessed the overwhelming military power that was essential to Churchill. In any case, when Britain had had the choice, she had stood alone to defend the independence of Europe.

De Gaulle acknowledged that but, returning to basics, he still saw difficulties in Brussels. In the Six, as they existed, France had some weight and could say 'no' even to the Germans. France could stop policies with which she disagreed because in the Six she had a very strong position. Once the United Kingdom and the Scandinavians and the rest had entered the organisation things would be different. In addition, the rest of the world would no doubt demand special arrangements. At that point would the Common Market be strong enough to resist such pressures? The result would be a sort of world free trade area which might be desirable in itself but would not be European.

There was a pause. Then Macmillan said that this was a most serious statement. The view which President de Gaulle had just put forward was, in fact, a fundamental objection to the whole idea of Britain's entry into the Common Market. De Gaulle said this was not the case and Pompidou observed that it was a question of dates. The discussion then ended.

In a discussion after the plenary had ended Couve de Murville told Dixon that the Prime Minister had misunderstood what General de Gaulle had meant. He had not meant, as the Prime Minister had seemed to think, that France did not want the Community to be enlarged or the United Kingdom to join it. Over lunch, the Foreign Secretary, Lord Home, asked Couve de Murville bluntly what the General's remarks had meant if they did not mean that he did not want to see the Community enlarged. Couve de Murville said he was not quite sure what the General did mean. As the meeting dispersed, Pompidou said that the whole point was that France did not want to have to renegotiate the Community's agricultural policy all over again in eight years' time.[25]

A few days later, on 20 December, the French Minister of Information, as was customary, spoke to journalists after the meeting of the Council of Ministers at which de Gaulle had briefed his Ministers on the Rambouillet weekend. Alain Peyrefitte (cousin of the gay writer Roger Peyrefitte whose lifestyle and novels were then considered scandalous but whose fame has outlived that of his political relative) was known to the British Embassy as "a particularly malicious man and well-known to be anti-British". But the Embassy equally believed he would not say or do anything of which de Gaulle did not approve. According to the Embassy's account of Peyrefitte's press briefing, the General had told his Ministers that he had known Macmillan for twenty years and had great personal esteem for him. It was therefore with regret that he had had to refuse Mr Macmillan, who was in difficulties, what he had come to France to ask for. However, major French interests were at stake and he could not do other than refuse. When Mr Macmillan had left he had felt very sorry for him.

The Embassy spared Macmillan the other bit of Peyrefitte's briefing in which de Gaulle had joked that, so upset had Macmillan been that he had felt like consoling him with the words of Edith Piaf's famous song: 'Ne pleurez pas milord'.[26] The Embassy did report that Pompidou (who was either in de Gaulle's confidence or a better interpreter of his master's voice than was Couve de Murville) had been taking the line that the British Government's position was so weak, and the British public's attitude so hostile, that it was difficult for the Six to know how to view the negotiations with Britain. Macmillan wrote in the margins of the Embassy's telegram: "I expect this French line is the one which de Gaulle wants put out".[27] Both then and when de Gaulle again vetoed Britain's application to join the EEC in 1967, the lukewarm nature of British public opinion and the mediocre condition of the British economy made de Gaulle's task easier.

"I'm damned if I'll go there again" Macmillan remarked after his return to London from Rambouillet.[28] But his attention was immediately elsewhere. By 19 December he was in Nassau for one of the most difficult negotiations of his career: what to do about the politically devastating unilateral decision of the US Government to scrap the Skybolt nuclear missile programme. That meeting is significant for this story only because it shows that Macmillan was still capable of a bravura and winning performance, one that remained in the memories of many of his American listeners long after.[29] It was also a reminder, often repeated for subsequent British Prime Ministers, of how dealing with an American President is frequently more congenial than dealing with fellow Europeans. The British Ambassador in Washington, David Ormsby-Gore, a distant relative and a close and trusted confidant of President Kennedy's, wrote to Macmillan after the talks that Kennedy had told him on Air Force One, on the way back from Nassau, that it was the hardest working conference he had ever attended. But a deep impression had been made on him by the fact that, however great the policy differences, that had in no way altered the intimate friendly atmosphere with the flavour of a close family gathering that had become a feature of the talks between the two men. Ormsby-Gore also reported Kennedy's fury at the crass timing by which US Defence Secretary Robert McNamara had authorised what turned out to be a successful firing of the about to be scrapped Skybolt missile. Ormsby-Gore was with Kennedy when he telephoned Gilpatric, the luckless deputy to McNamara (who was away skiing) and described how Gilpatric "received the full blast of the Kennedy fury. It was an awe-inspiring exhibition and was notable for the fact that the President emphasised with the most vivid choice of words the trouble it would cause you in London." The conclusion Kennedy had drawn, said Ormsby-Gore, was that "in a United States Administration where so few of those in responsible positions had ever run for public office, it was absolutely necessary for the President to keep an eye on every conceivable detail day and night if he was to prevent gross errors of judgment." Many British Prime Ministers would have said the same.

With time to reflect over Christmas, Macmillan wrote a personal letter to Edward Heath on Boxing Day 1962 which suggested that he had reservations about his own performance at Rambouillet and that he recognised that the Nassau agreement would have implications for the Brussels negotiations. "I only trust", Macmillan wrote, "that nothing I have done at Rambouillet or Nassau has increased your difficulties. My impression of de Gaulle is that he is friendly to me personally (always remembering the insults which he conceives were put upon him by Churchill during the war), wants friendly relations with Britain, but does not want us now in the Community because he is in a mood of sulks about the future of Europe politically and would prefer to stay where he is with France dominating the Five. At the same time I am not sure that he wants this to be too public. The only thing that seemed to worry him and his advisers were the moments in the discussion where he gave away his hand too obviously and I pounced upon this".[30] Missing from this rather shrewd analysis was one important ingredient. Macmillan, with his strategic view of the sweep of history, almost certainly underestimated the extent to which France's agricultural interests were prominent in de Gaulle's political calculations, as they have been in those of every one of his successors since.

On the same day, Macmillan sent a minute to his Principal Private Secretary, Tim Bligh, suggesting that careful consideration needed to be given as to how the Brussels negotiations were to be broken off should that become necessary. Macmillan accurately foresaw this happening at around the end of January. Macmillan called for work to be done on "what is called the alternative. This needs great care. We must not suddenly return to the Commonwealth like a dog with its tail between its legs. But we must have some imaginative approach on a wide scale. This is a very difficult problem and we must start work on it".[31]

January 1963 began with Macmillan on sharp form. "Everything prophesied by the Treasury has been wrong up to now", he wrote in the margin of a Treasury report on the UK's economic situation. The same could have been said of the predictions of the French Foreign Minister, Maurice Couve de Murville, when Edward Heath had lunch with him at the British Embassy in Paris on 11 January 1963. Heath remarked that the Prime Minister and others present had come away from Rambouillet with the impression that de Gaulle did not want Britain in Europe. Couve replied that this was not true. It was true, however, that de Gaulle was doubtful whether Britain was yet ready to come into Europe. De Gaulle recognised that Britain was in a sense part of the continent of Europe but it would take Britain some time to get used to being European. The General was quite sure that eventually Britain would come into Europe. Couve then said that he did not expect the President, at his scheduled press conference on 14 January to make statements which might have the effect of bringing the Brussels negotiations to a halt.

Heath then asked, in an exchange which is one of the key pieces of evidence in putting together the history of the French veto, whether the French political objections to Britain coming into Europe at the present moment meant that, even if she were able to solve the economic problems of the Brussels negotiations, the French would still oppose our entry. Couve de Murville, according to the official British record, replied with some emphasis that if the economic problems could be solved nothing could prevent Britain acceding to the EEC. Heath then said that this was an important statement of which he took note. So Couve de Murville can have been in no doubt that his words were being treated as a formal statement of the French Government's position.[32] Equally, Michael Butler, First Secretary in the Paris Embassy at the time, is in no doubt that Couve de Murville was being deliberately Delphic. In other words, when Couve spoke of nothing being able to prevent British entry if the economic issues could be solved, he was not saying that they *would* be solved.[33]

That de Gaulle's hostility was not then interpreted in London as outright, terminal, opposition to British entry into the EEC, is borne out by the discussion which had taken place in Cabinet the previous day. Heath led off the discussion and was relatively upbeat. There had, he claimed, been a marked change in the atmosphere in Brussels and the member countries of the Community, admittedly with the exception of France, were again earnestly seeking to reach a settlement on terms acceptable to the United Kingdom. British tactics should therefore be to show determination to agree and to be willing to make concessions, which in turn meant that there had to be an overall package which could be judged on its overall merits, rather than be picked over issue by issue.

Of the outstanding issues in the negotiation, Heath listed tariffs, access for Commonwealth temperate foodstuffs and the UK's own domestic agriculture as the most significant. Tariffs were an issue which was now of residual concern only to the Commonwealth. On Commonwealth foodstuffs, the special position of

New Zealand, for whom Britain was their major export market for dairy products and lamb, had been recognised by all, except the French.

Agriculture was the main outstanding bone of contention and a way forward had been identified by a special committee under the chairmanship of the Vice President of the Commission, Dr Sicco Mansholt. Mansholt had identified five outstanding problems: the extent and timing of changes in agricultural price levels in the UK as a result of British accession; the upper and lower limits of the prices to be fixed by the Community for wheat; the length of the transitional period before the new arrangements applied in full in Britain; the effectiveness of the arrangements for intervention in the event of disruption of a particular commodity market; and the arrangements for horticulture.

Much of the subsequent Cabinet discussion centred on agriculture. Christopher Soames, the Minister of Agriculture, welcomed the fact that Mansholt had forced the French to break cover and deploy their views in detail, but in doing so they had demonstrated the formidable difficulties with which Britain would be confronted if she were required to adapt the practice of the Community, at short notice, to her own fundamentally different system of agricultural price support. The UK market price of wheat, for example, would rise by £11 – 12 a ton, with changes of similar orders of magnitude for other commodities. The United Kingdom therefore needed a long and gradual transition period.

Soames was supported by R. A. ('Rab') Butler, the First Secretary of State and, in effect deputy Prime Minister. Current UK prices, he said, were well below even the lowest price now ruling in the Community. The effect on British public opinion if accession to the Community resulted in a large and immediate increase in the price of wheat would be very serious. Nor could the Government afford to lay itself open to the claim that increased prices in the UK were being used to subsidise agricultural imports into Britain from the Community or third countries.

Duncan Sandys, Commonwealth Secretary and, like Soames, a son in law of Churchill (though in Sandys' case a former son in law since he was divorced) was even more forceful. Britain had been given an assurance by the Community in the summer of 1962 that the Community would pursue a price policy which would offer reasonable opportunities in its markets for exports of temperate agricultural products. At present price levels those opportunities simply would not exist. If the Community did not change its stance then questions of major principle, which were now regarded as having been settled, might need to be reopened.

There is, curiously, no record of any intervention or summing up by Macmillan. The matter was simply referred back to the Common Market Negotiations Committee, which Butler chaired, for further discussion.[34]

Four days later came de Gaulle's press conference. In the light of all the speculation which followed as to de Gaulle's motives, and in the light of the subsequent history of the European Community and of Britain's often controversial role within it, it is worth revisiting what de Gaulle said on the fundamental economics of the EEC as he saw them.

The question de Gaulle was asked at his press conference was about Britain's entry and "the political evolution of Europe". De Gaulle responded by talking about the economics of the issue: "When you talk about economics – and much more so when you practise them – what you say and what you do must conform to the realities, because without that you can get into impasses and, sometimes, you even head for ruin . . . It is the facts that must first be considered. Feelings, however favourable they might be and are, these feelings cannot be invoked against the real facts of the problem. What are these facts?"

De Gaulle then went on to explain how the Treaty of Rome had been concluded between six continental states which were economically speaking of the same nature. Indeed, in industry, agriculture, foreign trade, their commercial clients, their living and working conditions, there were greater resemblances than differences between them. Thus it made sense that what these countries produced, bought, sold and consumed should preferably be bought, sold and consumed within their own group. Moreover, those same countries were keeping pace with each other economically, technically and socially. They were marching in similar fashion and there were no grievances, frontier disputes or rivalries or quests for domination between them. They were bound in solidarity, including through the fact "that no one among them is bound by any private political or military accord".

To reach agreement had been difficult, and to make a reality of it had required the French to put their economic, financial and monetary affairs in order. De Gaulle did not need to remind his audience that this had involved harsh measures amounting to an average wage cut in France of 8% in real terms in 1959. But, de Gaulle continued, while the Treaty of Rome was precise and complete enough as regards industry, the same was in no way true of agriculture. But, for France, this had to be settled. "Indeed" he continued, "it is obvious that agriculture is an essential element in the whole of our national activity. We cannot conceive, and will not conceive, of a Common Market in which French agriculture would not find outlets commensurate with its production".

De Gaulle went on to say that this French imperative had led him to insist on agricultural arrangements satisfactory to France as an absolute condition of the Common Market and its further evolution. How, asked de Gaulle, could any of Britain's agricultural practices, based on imports from the two Americas and its former dominions, as well as on subsidies to its farmers, be anything other than incompatible with the system established by the Six?

De Gaulle went on to cast doubt on whether Britain was sincerely ready to give up Commonwealth preferences, cease to demand special arrangements for her agriculture and wholeheartedly accept the continental system. He was not saying that it would never happen but, in the meantime, if Britain joined then her entry, and that of other countries would "completely change the whole of the actions, the agreements, the balance, the rules which have already been established between the Six . . . Then it will be another Common Market whose construction ought to be envisaged, but one which would be taken to eleven and then thirteen and perhaps eighteen and would no longer resemble, without any doubt, the one that the Six built". Under those circumstances, de Gaulle suggested, the cohesion of its members would not endure for long and "ultimately it would appear as a colossal Atlantic community under American dependence and direction".

Having delivered this body blow to British aspirations de Gaulle proceeded to assert with magnanimous condescension that his consideration and respect for "this great state, this great people" would not be in the slightest degree impaired and, indeed, an association agreement between the Common Market and Great Britain would be perfectly possible "if the Brussels negotiations were shortly not to succeed".

One of the first leaders to respond to the press conference was Kennedy who conveyed a message to Macmillan through Ormsby-Gore in the form of "some crisp and highly critical comments" about de Gaulle. The following day, the 15th, Macmillan replied to Kennedy suggesting that de Gaulle's statement had been more or less what he had expected, that "with all his high-falutin' sentiments what de Gaulle is saying is that he would rather be the only cock on a smaller dunghill" and that British tactics "must be to pay as little attention as we can and to go quietly on with the work in Brussels until the real points at issue can be identified". Macmillan believed that Adenauer had been put in a most humiliating position and that Britain should let anger and pressure develop from the other five members of the Community while trying to get the argument back to the negotiating realities. He undertook to consult Kennedy if this position proved untenable and before any change of British direction. "By a curious paradox", Macmillan concluded "de Gaulle's attitude is cementing that very Anglo-Saxon alliance which he professes to dislike".[35]

Macmillan in 1963, like Harold Wilson nearly five years later, could not quite persuade himself that de Gaulle could sustain his unreasonableness in the face of the united opposition of the Five. But, apart from Adenauer's well known ambivalence about the British, de Gaulle's own track record spoke for itself. De Gaulle himself, in his memoirs, had laid out the approach. He had found, in wartime London, that if he did something to offend the British then he would be treated to the cold shoulder. But if he stood his ground and made no concessionary move in the direction of his hosts, he found, after a while, that they came back to him.[36] Whether or not de Gaulle invented this feature of French diplomacy, it will be familiar to anyone who has had diplomatic dealings with the French and must have been well known to Macmillan with his unique experience of working with de Gaulle in Algeria during the war. But eminently reasonable people find it hard to believe in the intransigence of others. Even though Macmillan had analysed and described de Gaulle's character there was a bit of him which persisted in the hope that the awful consequences, as he saw them, of a divided Europe in an increasingly bi-polar world could be prevented.

And Macmillan was given some comfort by the reaction of the other Member States. They were, the British Delegation in Brussels reported, "hopping mad". They had "the light of battle in their eyes".[37] Macmillan in turn sent written instructions to all Ministers enjoining them to keep their nerve and not be dragged into speculation, still less a battle of words. The pressure and anger should come from the Five and not from Britain in the hope that if, in the end, agreement could be reached on a practical way forward, then what Macmillan called "de Gaulle's philosophical observations" would look a trifle absurd.

Whether or not the French had anticipated so strong an initial reaction from their partners, the intensity of it forced them to wheel out their biggest gun. Couve de Murville told the Five that they could not ignore the General's press conference and his clear statement that Britain was not yet sufficiently European to join the Community. France was opposed to Britain's entry and, unless France's partners rallied to that view, there was a danger of the Community breaking up.[38]

Over the following few days there was a flurry of British official and diplomatic activity in an effort to interpret de Gaulle's press conference and decide how to deal with it. A Foreign Office official, Roger Jackling, told the Cabinet Office Committee on Europe that the French were reportedly preparing a draft Convention of Association between the UK and the Communities. The officials' discussion encompassed all the difficulties and dilemmas faced by the British Government. The Five might not remain united against such a proposal. The French had a right to veto British accession to the Community as a full member so Association could prove to be the only alternative to complete exclusion. Such a scheme might appeal to domestic and Commonwealth opinion if it excluded agriculture. It might be less appealing to British industry if it excluded Britain from the political integration of Europe and there were clear disadvantages in having to accept the common external tariff of the Community while having no effective voice in any subsequent changes to it. In other words, here in a nutshell, was the essence of the British debate about Europe then as since: the attraction of staying on the outside versus the cost of not being on the inside.[39]

Bob Dixon, as both British Ambassador to Paris and official leader of the UK Delegation in Brussels, had the task of interpreting and reporting on events in both places. De Gaulle, he reported, had been in a bad temper before his press conference and an even worse one since. Following the meeting of the Council of Ministers on 16 January his spokesman was instructed to report the President as having told his Ministers that "in today's world there is a sort of universal convention that one should mistrust the realities; that they should not appear but should be carefully hidden away. If someone says that England is an island, everyone is shocked. If one says that NATO is placed under American command it is a scandal". Dixon thought that de Gaulle must be furious. He regarded himself as the embodiment of Europe and his judgement about British accession as absolute. He had made an *ex-cathedra* pronouncement but, instead of accepting the revealed truth, the British carried on negotiating and all the other despicable European politicians contradicted him.[40]

The following day Dixon commented that de Gaulle's press conference on British accession had surpassed in importance "another speech which also modified surgically the ways of thought generally accepted in France on the Right and Left: his televised speech on September 16 1959 about self-determination in Algeria. De Gaulle has been preparing the press conference [of 14 January] for twenty years. One finds in it almost word for word his ideas about Europe, England and the rest in a speech he pronounced in Algiers in 1944, in the speech in Bayeux in 1947 and in a press conference in 1951. De Gaulle is now, after twenty years, able to act on what he had thought necessary for France all his life.

But at the same time he sees that he has only got a few more months, perhaps a few more days, to get his doctrine accepted. A whole system is being organised around him. Britain will not stay out of the Common Market without trying to break up the political organisation of the Six. Mr Kennedy is going ahead with the organisation of the Atlantic world. Dr Adenauer accepts the idea of a multilateral atomic force. In fact, de Gaulle will stake everything next week when Dr Adenauer will be in Paris".[41]

A not dissimilar insight into de Gaulle's long-term thinking was given to Dixon by the French Ambassador in London, Geoffroy de Courcel, a wartime associate of de Gaulle's, when the two men met in Paris in early March. Dixon said it was very hard to know what French policy really amounted to since so many different views were advanced at different times. Courcel responded that the real starting point could be found in the speech made by de Gaulle to the Consultative Assembly in Algiers in March 1944. The General had there enunciated the view that two great powers would emerge as the real victors from the war – the Soviet Union and the United States. Europe would be in ruins and must be built up around recon-ciliation between French and Germans. De Gaulle, said Courcel, had foreseen that Europe must be built up on a strong economic base. The object would be a Europe consisting of sovereign countries but having a European personality capable of holding its own against the vast power of Russia and the United States. It would be a Europe bounded by the Channel, the Atlantic and the Mediterranean. Courcel had gone on particularly to draw Dixon's attention to the mention of the Channel. This, he said, did not mean that the British Isles would be excluded; on the contrary, the General in 1944 had visualised that Britain would be in Europe. But when the war was over it became clear that Britain was becoming strongly drawn towards the United States. It was this latter factor that had influenced de Gaulle during the Brussels negotiations. The Nassau Agreement had finally convinced him that Britain had surrendered her real sovereignty to the United States.

Dixon countered that, if this represented de Gaulle's basic attitude then why had the French not told the British this at the outset? Dixon could agree with much of the approach Courcel had outlined. Where Britain and France seemed to differ was on the relationship of the renovated Europe with the wider world. Britain too wanted to see a Europe built up to a position of equality with the United States and the Soviet Union (and perhaps a position of superiority in economic power) but she wanted to do it on a basis of partnership within the Atlantic Alliance. Was it the case that the French wanted a Europe which would take a different line from that of the Alliance? What had de Gaulle meant when he had told Macmillan that France would be less and less in NATO?

Courcel said that de Gaulle drew a distinction between the Atlantic Alliance, which he supported, and NATO which he thought had been an unsatisfactory organisation. The General recognised that the Atlantic Alliance was a vital neces-sity so long as the Russians remained dangerous. When the cold war ended things might be different, but this might be a generation ahead. Finally, Courcel said, the French had to take into account the possibility of a Labour Government coming into power in Britain and of the fact that the Labour leaders were strongly opposed to British involvement in Europe. If a Conservative Government came back into power after a period of Labour rule, then it might be easier for Britain to come into Europe.[42]

When Cabinet met on 17 January, for the first time since de Gaulle's press conference, Macmillan said it had been right for Britain not to break off the negotiations in response to de Gaulle, particularly in the light of the strong reaction against de Gaulle from the other members of the Community. Now that the French were threatening the very Treaty of Rome it was not certain that the Five would have the strength to resist the political pressure. The attitude of the Federal German Government would be critical.

Some in Cabinet argued that it would be unwise to try to get the US Government to bring influence to bear on the Germans since this might simply make the Germans more susceptible to the French insinuation that Britain's attitude was evidence of an Anglo-American attempt to dominate Europe. Equally, it might be necessary for the British Government to show more readiness to meet the point of view of the Five on issues outstanding in the negotiations in order to secure their continued support.[43]

Despite these doubts about using the Americans to pressurise the Germans, Macmillan, in a message the following day to Heath (in Brussels) hoped that Adenauer might refuse to go to Paris for his scheduled meeting with de Gaulle on 21 January, or at least refuse to make a joint declaration with the French. Macmillan concluded, however, that the most likely scenario was one in which Adenauer made no impression on de Gaulle and agreed to a communiqué which would enable the General to claim that the Franco-German alliance was going ahead in spite of everything. It was essential, Macmillan concluded, to try to stop the last alternative if at all possible: "Of course, if the Americans would tell Adenauer that if he goes with the French alliance this may lead to a reappraisal of their defence commitments, then the Germans would cave in but I fear that the Americans will not do this . . . As you know, I am quite prepared to talk to President Kennedy".[44]

Whether at Macmillan's bidding or that of Ormsby-Gore or quite independently is not clear, but Kennedy told Macmillan on 19 January that he had written to Adenauer. As it happened, the British Ambassador in Bonn, Kit Steel, was that same week in his round of farewell calls prior to retirement. When Steel called on Adenauer on 18 January he found him "really cast down and subdued . . . I nearly felt sorry for him. He looked worse than I have ever seen him". Adenauer told Steel that the negotiations for British entry must not be allowed to be broken off in any circumstances. On the following day, German Foreign Minister Gerhard Schroeder told Steel that the German Chancellor was "faced with a fearful decision. It was almost impossible for him to refuse his signature to a document which enshrined, if in embryo, all his deepest hopes and feelings". Nevertheless, Schroeder promised, the German delegation would go to Paris determined to press the French very hard.

In a speech at lunch in his honour Steel "laid it on the line that in 1954 Lord Hood and I had persuaded Sir Anthony Eden that Germany must come into

NATO. The Americans were helpless and Eden had put this across over Mendes France's furious dead body and at the cost of our undertaking over the four divisions. I appealed to Schroeder to help us in like case." This, Steel believed, had appeared to strike home but he was not optimistic about the negotiations in Paris. He put more store on the impact of the rising tide of anger about French behaviour in the Bundestag.[45]

The omens for any change of heart on the part of de Gaulle, or of effective pressure from Adenauer, remained poor. On 19 January Couve de Murville asked to see Dixon alone and without the knowledge of anyone else in the French Foreign Ministry, suggesting to Dixon that Couve did not want de Gaulle to know that the two were talking. Dixon set out British incomprehension at the turn of events, particularly in the light of what Couve had told Heath just three days before de Gaulle's press conference, namely that if the economic problems could be solved then nothing could prevent British accession. This, Couve muttered, was still his own position. Would some kind of association with the EEC be acceptable to Britain? Dixon said that he did not think a British Government, in the immediate future, would care to embark on another negotiation that might last fourteen months and end up with another French refusal. Couve then said that of course the whole question was really about Europe in its political and defence aspect. Perhaps the French should have discussed the political aspects with the British frankly at an earlier stage. He appreciated that Macmillan had been rather shocked by the General's attitude at Rambouillet. The General, for his part, had been disappointed by the Prime Minister's attitude. Macmillan had not said anything firm about cooperation and building up Europe into an effective entity vis-à-vis the United States. He had noticed that in the vigorous national reaction in Britain to the Polaris arrangement no instinctive desire had been expressed to turn to Europe as an alternative. It was the psychological effect of all this on the General that mattered. After some further inconsequential exchanges Dixon "asked him finally whether there was a prospect of any change in the French attitude at Brussels. He shook his head. He struck me as very uncomfortable about the mess into which the French have got as a result of the famous press conference".[46]

On the following day, the eve of Adenauer's arrival in Paris, the German Ambassador, Blankenhorn, agreed with Dixon that de Gaulle's fundamental objective was to drive the Americans out of Europe and to keep Britain, as a Trojan horse, out of the EEC. Blankenhorn said that he had been warning his Government for some time that de Gaulle's intentions were along these lines. However, Blankenhorn continued "the trouble was that the Chancellor did not much like us and was suspicious of the Americans". Moreover, Adenauer was mesmerised by de Gaulle and Blankenhorn thought that at most the Chancellor might make a rather half-hearted attempt to put the case for a modification of French views. But he would do this mainly for the purpose of being able to say on return to Bonn that he had tried but failed.[47]

Blankenhorn's assessment was confirmed by Steel in Bonn. The strength of German feeling in favour of the French connection, intimately associated in

German minds with de Gaulle himself, was not to be underestimated. German policy was predicated on the Atlantic Alliance but also on European integration and reconciliation with France: "We cannot expect them to throw these overboard merely for the sake of the British. They will almost certainly try to save what they can of these two policies from any wreck, even if it means giving up any idea of bringing the British into Europe in the near future".[48] Moreover, Steel advised a few weeks later, the suspicions of Britain which de Gaulle sowed in Adenauer's mind reinforced a basic mistrust of British motives which was endemic in the UK's relations with Germany. "Many Germans think", Steel advised "that, compared to the French, the British have been petty, mistrustful, critical and often directly hostile. Far from stretching out the hand of friendship they have been cold, reserved and strictly practical. The British Press is the most unfair in the Western world; a permanent current of hostility is apparent from questions in Parliament and the British Government have given little lead to overcome it. After the isolation of the Hitler period, real sincere friendship means a great deal to Germany. In short, a lot of Germans have a sneaking feeling that there is something to de Gaulle's view that the British are not ripe for real collaboration in Europe. (I was told that in a group of young Foreign Service officers about a third felt like this). This sort of feeling is fundamental to the Chancellor's attitude and there is probably nothing we can do to correct it . . . In the longer term we should be able to improve matters by a conscious effort over a period to show ourselves consistently friendly and European in our policies, ready to commit ourselves absolutely to NATO in the European interest and, in return for their support for us, more than ready to accord the Germans a full partnership in all European and Atlantic matters, and in other international affairs as well. It is also very important to be seen by our Allies to be giving a firm lead to British public opinion and the Press, to reply robustly to communist-inspired attacks and insinuations, and generally to demonstrate that we regard the Federal Republic as a trusted Ally, instead of a rather shady business partner to be tolerated but not liked".[49]

Adenauer was in the middle of his Paris visit when the British Cabinet met on 22 January. Heath reported that the strong reaction from the Five to de Gaulle's press conference had compelled the French to retreat sufficiently far to agree that the negotiations in Brussels should be resumed on 28 January. It was, Heath said, possible that Adenauer, in the light of the internal and diplomatic pressures to which he would now be subjected, might persuade de Gaulle to agree to the continuation of the negotiations with French participation. On balance, however, this appeared unlikely, even though a continuation of de Gaulle's present policy might lead to a refusal on the part of the German Government to ratify the Franco-German agreement which was at present under discussion in Paris. Or the Five might suggest that negotiations should continue without the French. But, Heath thought, apart from the fact that this course would merely prolong the present uncertainty, it would be difficult to impart an air of reality to discussions conducted under the shadow of an ultimate French veto. So this course would only be viable if, as a last resort, the Five were prepared to annul the Treaty of Rome and establish a European Community which included Britain and excluded

France. At no point did Heath suggest that this was far fetched. He did, however, advise against pursuing the idea of an Association agreement: it was unlikely that any such suggestion was worth considering on its own merits and it would also revive earlier suspicions that Britain had no interest in promoting greater political unity in Europe rather than merely seeking her own commercial advantage. Moreover, economic association would not enable Britain to take any part in shaping the Community's policies and the Government should be wary of being enticed into so weak a position. In conclusion, Heath doubted whether the determination of the Five would prevail against the uncompromising opposition of de Gaulle. It would then become necessary to consider urgently the action which the Government should take if negotiations finally broke down.

Christopher Soames, the Minister of Agriculture, claimed (with greater optimism than he had evinced in Cabinet on 10 January) that negotiations in Brussels on agricultural issues had been making good progress. There was little doubt that a satisfactory agricultural agreement would have been possible. But Soames advised against trying to continue to negotiate without the French. The French would probably reject any agreement reached and the risk alone would deprive the proceedings of reality and conviction.

The general sense of the Cabinet was that de Gaulle was bent on establishing a French political hegemony in Europe. This would only serve increasingly to isolate France and the pending agreement with Germany might prove to be only a temporary reconciliation. But it would be a mistake to assume that de Gaulle would be greatly affected by pressure from Germany or from any other member of the Five. Equally, there was not much point in continuing to negotiate without France. The national interests of the Five would dissuade them from dissolving the Community and negotiating a new Common Market with Britain and without the French. Public opinion in Britain was prepared to accept some sacrifice of sectional interests as the price of a comprehensive settlement, but not as the price of a limited agreement, still at the mercy of a French veto. Equally, Britain should not turn its back on the goal of EEC membership. The measures which the Government would now be compelled to take should be directed at strengthening the economy, in association with Britain's partners in NATO and EFTA and those policies should depart as little as possible from those the Government had advocated as a potential EEC member. The country had suffered a diplomatic reverse but it also constituted a challenge: an opportunity to redouble the effort to promote greater efficiency throughout the economy.

Cabinet Conclusions are invariably accurate and dispassionate, reflecting the fact that, after vigorous discussion, a collective agreement has to be reached and acted on by all Ministers. The Conclusions of Cabinet on 22 January record Macmillan as saying that "the intervention by President de Gaulle had been due, not to his conviction that the Brussels negotiations had failed but to his realisation that they were within sight of success and that such success would have been incompatible with his ultimate purpose of creating a Franco-German partnership which would dominate Europe to the exclusion of any Anglo-Saxon influence. To this extent the rupture of the negotiations in Brussels could be presented to our advantage. Nevertheless, it was a serious setback to the Government's policies and it might compel us to reconsider our existing commitments in a wider context. It was important therefore that we should not make light of the situation ... or appear to adopt alternative policies on the basis that they would be as advantageous as membership of the European Community. We should now consult our own interests, while refraining from any action which could be represented as an attempt to destroy the Community . . ."[50]

Unusually, however, Macmillan appears to have asked the Cabinet Secretariat for a fuller note of what he said in his summing up and this fuller note, while consistent with the Cabinet record, gives a much darker impression of Macmillan's mood. It had to be admitted, said Macmillan to Cabinet in this version, "that the chance of President de Gaulle retracting from his position sufficiently to make our entry possible was now remote. The Community might in time break up if President de Gaulle continued his present policies, but it would be unlikely to do so on the issue of the United Kingdom's entry. The real struggles were yet to come. President de Gaulle had shown clearly that in order to create the kind of inward looking and autarchic Europe which was his aim it would, in his view, be necessary to remove the American presence from Europe and to break up NATO. This, and not Britain's entry, would be the decisive issue and the other member countries were now beginning to see the extent of the dangers opening before them. There was a kind of logic in the President's approach; he argued that Europe did not need an American presence in their midst because in a major crisis the United States would be bound in her own interest to come to Europe's defence. In the meantime, President de Gaulle might see attractive political possibilities in a deal with Russia leading perhaps to the reunification of Germany ... There was unfortunately little that the Government could do to influence the course of events within the Community in the immediate future; these great issues would probably be settled without us. The Government had consistently presented the UK's entry into Europe as being the right policy for the country. Even the Government's opponents had not argued against the idea of entry, they had only criticised the possible terms of a final agreement ... The failure of the negotiations would be a very serious blow to the Government. There would be severe repercussions on British industry; once the prospect of our entry had been removed even those Commonwealth countries who had been most critical of our conduct of the negotiations would realise the immense advantages which had been lost to them. In a few months' time President de Gaulle's intervention would have faded from people's memory and the failure of the negotiations would be seen as a failure of the Government ... The failure of the negotiations would have political and commercial effects of the gravest kind and it would be a mistake to minimise them. The alternative courses of action which the Government would now have to settle and present to the country should be presented honestly for what they were: defensive measures against the immediate effects of a situation not of our own choosing. It would at the same time be right to re-emphasise the fact that the Government still adhered to the policy for which they had fought for so long: the increasing involvement of the UK in Europe, and the development in an enlarged Community of an outward looking and responsible policy. . . It had been difficult enough to bring public opinion in this country to the point of accepting as a basis for negotiation the idea that we should go into Europe. The failure of the negotiations would make it harder still to preserve that idea as a long-term aim. As a matter of political prudence it might be that we should have to examine again the commitments into which we had entered in 1955 in the Brussels Treaty, which had led to the admission of Germany to NATO. The guarantees which we had then given had been designed to make it possible for France to accept the rearmament of Germany. The political context of these guarantees had been altered out of recognition by subsequent events culminating in the new Franco-German agreement."[51]

This fuller version of Macmillan's summing up is much closer to the mood revealed in the entry he made in his diary on 28 January in what he himself described as a moment of something like despair: "All our policies at home and abroad are in ruins. Our defence plans have been radically changed, from air to sea. European unity is no more; French domination of Europe is the new and alarming feature; our popularity as a Government is rapidly declining. We have lost everything except our courage and determination".[52]

Meanwhile, in Paris, the Franco-German Treaty had been signed and any hope of effective pressure by Adenauer on de Gaulle had been extinguished. The President of the European Commission, Dr Hallstein, together with Jean Monnet, had called on Adenauer at the Bristol Hotel on the Sunday evening of his Paris visit. According to Hallstein, Monnet had made a tactical blunder by attempting to face the German Chancellor squarely with the responsibility of persuading de Gaulle to change his attitude. Adenauer had been furious. He had, he said, come to Paris to finalise the Franco-German agreement, for which he had been working for years and which he regarded as his crowning achievement. The present development in the Common Market negotiations was an entirely new and unforeseen contingency with which he refused to be identified.

Hallstein, on his own, had seen Adenauer again briefly before he left for the Elysée and Adenauer had said he would propose to de Gaulle that the European Commission should be asked to draw up an inventory of the state of the negotiations.[53]

Adenauer did, according to the account which Blankenhorn, the German Ambassador in Paris, gave to Dixon, raise the issue and made the "rather tentative suggestion" that the Commission, besides stock-taking, might go on to suggest solutions to the remaining problems. De Gaulle had neither said 'yes' or 'no' to this idea. De Gaulle, according to Blankenhorn had, however, made it quite clear to Adenauer that he saw no role for Britain in Europe. He had put Britain in a very bad light, conveying the impression that the Rambouillet meeting with Macmillan had convinced him that Britain was not at all suitable as a European partner. He (de Gaulle) had been confirmed in this by the agreement reached by Macmillan and Kennedy in the Bahamas, a point which had impressed Adenauer considerably. De Gaulle had said that he had perhaps given way to his feelings too impulsively at his press conference on 14 January. The Chancellor had recognised this as "a natural reaction of a great man who had been wounded in his feelings". In other words, Blankenhorn concluded, Adenauer had fallen for a line which was clearly designed to exculpate the General from his failure to consult his closest ally in Europe about the line he intended to take on Europe and Britain's entry.

Both the German Foreign Minister, Schroeder, and Defence Minister von Hassel had, in separate interviews with him, spoken their minds to de Gaulle. Von Hassel had "stoutly rejected" de Gaulle's suggestion of Franco-German coopera-tion in arms production and procurement at the expense of existing German arrangements with the Americans arguing that, great as was the importance of Franco-German reconciliation, this could never be at the expense of Germany's relations with the United States and Britain; nor could Germany afford to develop special defence arrangements with France except within the NATO context. Schroeder had spoken in similar terms and had set out the reasons why the German Government considered British entry into the EEC as essential.

Blankenhorn concluded that Adenauer would have gone away from the talks with the impression that de Gaulle was fundamentally opposed to British entry into Europe and Blankenhorn himself was convinced that, whatever report the Commission might produce, at the end of the road the French would object to British entry on political grounds.[54]

President Kennedy, for his part, sought to confront Germany with her respon-sibilities. Ormsby-Gore, whose personal relationship with the US President has been unmatched by any other British Ambassador in Washington before or since, was given a first-hand account by Kennedy of the latter's meeting, earlier in the week of the Franco-German Treaty, with the German Ambassador in Washington, Herr Knappstein. Kennedy had given the Ambassador a rough time. He had started by saying that he naturally welcomed the Treaty as the symbol of the ending of an age-old quarrel. However, the reality was that the quarrel had already been over for years. Kennedy was disturbed that so much attention should be paid to putting to bed a dispute which had been in bed for at least fifteen years, while at the same time the West was confronted with a world-wide threat from the Communist bloc and Western alliances seemed to be falling into disarray. Kennedy had then reminded the Ambassador that in 1958 de Gaulle had proposed the establishment of a tripartite directorate along with the United States and the United Kingdom to the exclusion of the Federal Republic. The US and the UK had turned down this proposal since they felt that it was inconsistent with their obligations to their other NATO allies. Kennedy went on to say that he would, therefore, view with little enthusiasm arrangements between France and Germany designed to impose their collective policies upon the Alli-ance. He followed up with some home truths about the military balance of power in the world and said he assumed that West Germany still saw a need for US conventional and nuclear support in Europe. The President reported that Knapp-stein had been "badly shaken" by all this and the President confided to Ormsby-Gore that he felt he had gone as far as was wise. Indeed, in Ormsby-Gore's own view, he had probably gone a bit further than was wise.

Kennedy showed to Ormsby-Gore a letter from Adenauer, which had infuriated Kennedy by its complacency. In it, Adenauer had reported that de Gaulle had told him that British membership could only be considered when the existing Community had been fully consolidated. Adenauer had responded by saying that a dramatic climax in Brussels should be avoided and, unsurprisingly, de Gaulle had readily agreed. Adenauer had made only the most half-hearted attempts on Britain's behalf and seemed to have no conception of the dangerous implications in the present direction of French policy. Kennedy, correctly as it turned out, thought that the kind of European Commission report that Adenauer had suggested on the organisational and institutional implications of British membership and on what had been achieved so far in negotiation would be no more than a face-saver for France and would constitute delaying tactics which would almost perfectly suit the French. Kennedy told Ormsby-Gore that he was preparing a letter to Adenauer making clear that "the real issue is not the suitability and the timing of British membership, but the future of the NATO alliance. If Germany and the other European countries are prepared to allow de Gaulle to break up this Alliance they should ponder on the consequences of their future relations with the United States and their military and political position vis-à-vis the Soviet Bloc".

Kennedy told Ormsby-Gore that he believed de Gaulle's long-term policy was to put Western Europe in a position to defend itself without the need of American forces stationed on the continent, while at the same time the Russians withdrew from Eastern Europe, agreed to the reunification of Germany and adopted a pacific attitude to the West. That objective in no way shocked him (and with the wisdom of hindsight it shows considerable prescience on his part). But the question in Kennedy's mind was how so favourable a deal, if it were a genuine one, could be extracted from the Russians by a small combination of European states with virtually no nuclear power, when it could not be brought about by the far more powerful combination which included the United States and the United Kingdom. The danger was obvious that, in the absence of any real balance of power, the terms of such a deal would in fact constitute a sell-out to the Russians.

Kennedy held out no hope of the French backing down in Brussels on the question of British accession. But he refused to be too despondent about it and felt that, if the UK and the US stuck together they could survive "the temporary aberrations of a France under Gaullist dictatorship".[55]

De Gaulle's pitch to Adenauer that the European Community needed more time to consolidate before it enlarged was confirmed by an account of the German talks in Paris given by Schroeder to Heath on 28 January. Schroeder had come away from his own conversations with de Gaulle believing that the French wanted to keep Britain out. They wanted three or four years in order to build up their industry and agriculture, develop their atomic weapons and consolidate the Community and its institutions. At the end of that time they would be much stronger and might be prepared to think again.[56]

Couve de Murville had said something similar, from a different perspective, in another private discussion with Dixon (again reflecting a degree of intimacy unknown to modern diplomacy) two days earlier. Couve had said that it was "always a good thing to look ahead, to a time when present personalities were no longer there", a remark which Dixon interpreted as a reference to de Gaulle. In the French view, according to Couve, Britain was likely to be too tied up with the United States for the next decade or so to make it possible for France to work with her inside Europe. Basically, the British were still emotionally, as well as practically, tied up with the United States. Couve recognised that as a result of the "terrible mess in which things now were, France might find herself temporarily isolated, but he believed that in the long run France would emerge in better shape than ourselves". Whether Couve saw the exclusion of Britain from the EEC as something which would contribute to France emerging in better shape he did not reveal.[57]

Kennedy's reference to Gaullist dictatorship was borne out by Dixon's assessment of the French scene. "The situation in Paris" he reported, "is gradually deteriorating. Many of the Gaullist faithful . . . are getting beyond the embryo Fascist stage. The lying propaganda campaign mounted by de Gaulle's machine is extremely disagreeable . . . Our friends in the Quai d'Orsay do not hesitate to say, and not only to us, that the General is in fact a maniac when it comes to power. France is not yet of course a police state but the telephones are widely tapped and in the last few weeks people have begun to grow cautious. The nationalist drum is constantly beaten . . . De Gaulle's foreign policy is based almost entirely on a desire for the grandeur and power of France which he identifies completely with himself and a determination to get his revenge on the British and the Americans for what he regards as the humiliations of the war. When he says that Britain will join Europe one day he is thinking of a moment when Britain herself will have been humiliated and brought to her knees and will be only too glad to come crawling into a French-led Europe. He sees the Franco-German alliance as a step on the road to the expulsion of the Americans from Europe and the reversal of alliances . . . If not defeated, de Gaulle may become really dangerous".[58]

Dixon's telegram reads like something written at a time of huge pressure and fatigue. But Dixon's view is borne out by other accounts. In his book *De Gaulle and the Anglo-Saxons*, published in 1970, which drew on extensive conversations with many of the key players from the period, John Newhouse records the initiation at this time of an anti-American and anti-British propaganda campaign in France of such enduring ferocity that it eventually provoked an official objection from US Ambassador Charles Bohlen.

The campaign was inaugurated by a brief programme on French television (entirely state controlled) called *The Anglo-Saxons* which purported to show the special relations between Britain and the United States since the voyage of the *Mayflower*. In the Paris business daily newspaper, *Les Echos*, the publisher, Emile Servan-Schreiber, said the programme reminded him of the attacks on Britain and the United States made during the war in the Nazi controlled French language press.[59]

The French propaganda campaign was yet more evidence that there was little realistic chance of finding a way to continue the Brussels negotiations. At Macmillan's behest the Treasury prepared a paper on policy in the event of a breakdown. It would be important, the paper argued, not to give the impression of an immediate crisis demanding sudden changes. What had happened was a great disappointment, but it need not be a disaster. Europe had lost an opportunity but Britain's long-term objectives would remain the same. British policy must always be based on the recognition that close association with Europe, as well as with the USA and the Commonwealth, was essential to Britain's political, military and economic purposes. The Government should not close the door now to eventual accession to the Community and, as far as possible, its intermediate policies should be consistent with this. But, the paper argued, Britain also must recognise that it might be some time before the political obstacles to EEC membership were removed and that, in the meantime, as the institutions and policies of the Community developed without Britain, so the technical difficulties of joining would increase. Equally, since one of the main attractions of joining had been the spur this would give to competitiveness, the loss of a large tariff-free market would require national measures to improve productivity, the control of wages and wholehearted cooperation between both sides of industry. Annual growth of 4% was a possibility but this depended on changes of attitude by Government, employers and unions, including willingness to cooperate in ensuring that increases in aggregate money supply kept in step with increases in national productivity.[60]

Since part of the story of the Macmillan years was a persistent failure by Government to pursue these very policies consistently, and of disagreement between Macmillan and his Chancellors at the heart of that failure, it is perhaps not surprising that Macmillan's reaction to the Treasury paper was lukewarm. On 28 January, he wrote to the Chancellor of the Exchequer, Reginald Maudling, who had only glanced at the paper before forwarding it to No. 10: "Perhaps I can summarise it, rather unfairly," Macmillan wrote, "by saying that it offers us the prospect either of going into reverse and adopting a restrictionist policy, or of maintaining our policies as they now are in the hope that in the long run things in Europe will go right for us. What I think we must do, since the wind is temporarily against us, is to tack, since this is the only way of reaching our objective. Therefore, any measures we might adopt which are not in line with what we would have done if we had gone into the EEC should be temporary, not built-in or irreversible." Macmillan went on to list the issues which were immediately on his mind: the Kennedy trade round, Commonwealth relations and EFTA policy. On the latter he posed the question whether British policy should not be "to keep it in being while avoiding anything which would institutionalise it". Finally, Macmillan asked: "Can we use aid to investment as a concealed aid for exports; ought we to restrict imports or float the pound; should there be a quota for British capital invested overseas? Our main objective must remain the same, but we must be careful not to do the long-term cause harm by excessive scrupulosity in this interim period."[61] Macmillan would revert to these themes in Cabinet, in Parliament and in a national broadcast after the Brussels talks had finally foundered.

The end when it came, two weeks after de Gaulle's press conference, was swift and brutal. The EEC and the candidate countries were due to meet in Brussels on 28 January 1963. From there, Heath reported to London that "It begins to look as though none of them [the Five] will have much stomach for the idea of carrying things to the point of breaking up the EEC and making alternative economic arrangements including ourselves . . . It seems to us here that we must dismiss from our minds any possibility of reaching satisfactory economic arrangements with the EEC in the near future".[62]

Cabinet met in special session the following day to consider Heath's reports from Brussels. The situation was changing by the hour but Heath thought it likely that, later in the day, the French Foreign Minister would put an end to the negotiations by refusing to take any further part in the negotiating conference. Heath recommended that, in that event, he should agree a statement with the other five EEC member Governments making it clear that, in their view, agreement could have been reached and that he should pursue with those Governments the idea of promoting some new European initiative, preferably of a political or military nature and linked with NATO, which might strengthen Britain's own position in Europe and serve as a counterpoise to the ambitions of the French Government.[63]

Macmillan's reaction to Heath's advice shows that his mind was focussed on both the domestic handling of the crisis and on its policy implications. The upshot of the Cabinet discussion was a joint telegram from Macmillan and Home to Heath. "You will see" they wrote "that we have been cautious in the wording about setting in hand arrangements for the continued cooperation between ourselves and the Five . . . First, we accept your warning that we should dismiss from our minds any possibility of reaching satisfactory economic arrangements with the EEC in the near future . . . Secondly, as regards defence, we do not want to do anything which would detract from NATO. Discussion in a smaller European group would almost certainly mean pressure on us for increased commitments to the defence of Europe and if the French were absent we might soon expect pressing German demands. It would also, as you suggest, be a mistake to make any move in this direction without prior American agreement . . . Thirdly, as regards the political future of Europe, we must bear in mind that the Five are all in varying degrees in favour of Federalism. While this risk in the long term might have been one thing if we were to enjoy the economic benefits of membership of the Community, it would be quite another if we were to set out on such a course for political reasons alone . . . We have concluded that it would not at this stage be advantageous to commit ourselves to a further early meeting with the Five . . . We should want to have some clear idea of what results might ensue before committing ourselves".[64]

Some fifty years later, this message, from two committed pro European British politicians to a third of similar convictions, still encapsulates everything that has coloured British European policy making ever since. In the face of a brutal assault on European values by de Gaulle, there was an obvious case for a big political gesture by Britain to demonstrate that, where de Gaulle had narrow national interest at heart, the British were ready to embrace and promote a compelling vision of European integration, including in the one area, defence, which would have symbolised the kind of political power that the EEC sought to exemplify. That, instead, Macmillan and Home were so cautious undoubtedly reflects their apprehension about the national mood.

In a minute to Cabinet four months earlier, Conservative Party Chairman, Ian Macleod, had noted that popular support for British membership of the EEC had fallen from a peak of 53% in December 1961 to 40% in the last Gallup Poll survey in August 1962. Opinion was 45/34 in favour among Conservatives and 46/34 against among Labour supporters. Those in favour gave economic reasons for their view, those against political or emotional reasons, such as being 'taken over', 'pushed around', 'surrendering our independence to Frogs and Wogs'. The country's head was in favour but its heart was opposed. Young people and opinion formers were, Macleod concluded, overwhelmingly in favour and that, in his view, gave the key to strategy: "We must I believe present this issue with trumpets as the next great adventure of our country's history".[65]

Now, faced with a contemptuous humiliation at the hands of de Gaulle, leader of a country overtaking Britain economically on the inside lane, and with no obvious alternative to the collapsing central plank of the Government's economic and political strategy, it is small wonder that Macmillan and Home opted for caution, or that Macmillan should write in his diary a few days later: "At home there is a return of the old feeling 'the French always betray you in the end'. There is a great and grievous disappointment (among the younger people especially) at the end of a fine vision".[66]

Meanwhile, in Brussels, attempts to find agreement around the terms and nature of a report by the European Commission on the state of the negotiations were pursued, but in vain. The British Delegation in Brussels were invited to a meeting with the Six on the afternoon of 29 January at which the Belgian chairman announced that the Six had been unable to continue the negotiations. An "extremely dry, matter of fact and short statement" was made by Couve de Murville in which he acknowledged the gravity of the crisis but denied that France was responsible. It was in fact Britain that had not been able to accept the disciplines of the Treaty of Rome, notably its agricultural policy. In any case, new members could not join an uncompleted club.[67] Ministers of the Five spoke emotionally of their deep regret but the Belgian Foreign Minister, Paul-Henri Spaak also stated, significantly, and as the British had calculated, that while the Community spirit had been gravely, perhaps mortally, wounded, the Treaty of Rome itself was not dead. Not for nothing is '*Pacta sunt servanda*' one of the watchwords of the European Union.

Heath made a short and powerful statement ending with the sentence: "We in Britain are not going to turn our backs on the mainland of Europe or the countries of the Community".[68] A statement, on the lines agreed earlier in the day by the Cabinet in London, was also issued by the delegations of Britain and the Five.

So, on the face of it, Britain had been routed. Could de Gaulle's veto have been foreseen or prevented? Was the Nassau agreement on Polaris the last straw as far as de Gaulle was concerned?

Macmillan himself acknowledged, as we have seen, that Dixon had been warning him from before the summer of 1962 that de Gaulle wanted to keep Britain out. There was no illusion on the British side about de Gaulle's wishes in that respect. Where the British were less hard headed was in assessing both the strength of the other five EEC members, in particular Germany, in respect of France and in realising the extent of de Gaulle's intransigence and his willingness to sustain it against all comers. Macmillan and others on the British side found it hard to believe that de Gaulle would precipitate what he, Macmillan, saw as a European catastrophe: one in which the necessary unity of Europe, in partnership with the United States, would be destroyed and replaced by European disarray to the advantage only of the Soviet Union. That was the scenario which Macmillan had laid out at Rambouillet but de Gaulle, while not indifferent to it, was impervious to it, for it played no part in his vision of a world where, perforce, the Americans would be obliged to come to the aid of Europe in the event of Soviet attack but which, otherwise, should develop in radical, French-led, independence.

Did Macmillan make mistakes at Rambouillet? On the whole, the record and eyewitness accounts suggest, rather, a characteristically bravura performance on his part. The question of what was or was not said about Britain's nuclear weapons programme is the one that caused most controversy at the time. It certainly became part of French propaganda after de Gaulle's 14 January press conference that the Nassau agreement proved that Britain was in hock to the United States and uncommitted to Europe. But there is no more than a hint of this in the press conference itself, in de Gaulle's reference to the fact that the Six were "in solidarity through the fact that no one among them is bound by any private political or military accord".

De Gaulle himself never claimed that Nassau lay behind his decision to veto Britain's entry, Macmillan himself confirming that de Gaulle "would not stoop to such meanness".[69] Others did claim that Macmillan had in some way misled de Gaulle and that the misunderstanding had arisen during a walk in the woods when the two men were alone. Macmillan makes no reference to such a walk. Newhouse in *De Gaulle and the Anglo-Saxons* denies that any such walk took place and the accuracy of his account, based on access to some of the participants at Rambouillet, stands up in every other particular when read against the official accounts which were, of course, not available to him.

De Gaulle himself did, however, give somewhat conflicting evidence on the subject. Dixon saw de Gaulle twice between the Bahamas meeting and de Gaulle's press conference and "on neither occasion had he been at all worked up about the [Nassau] agreement. On the contrary, he had told me that he would be very prudent about the whole affair in his press conference".[70]

That version is borne out by a memorandum written by Edward Heath following a call on de Gaulle in 1965, two years after Rambouillet. Heath recorded that "the General confirmed that Mr Macmillan had told him on that occasion that if the US Administration cancelled Skybolt, he would try to obtain Polaris submarines. General de Gaulle had at that point expressed regret that it was not possible for France and Britain to do something together but that he had been in no doubt about Mr Macmillan's intentions".[71]

Yet, at the time, the spokesman of the French Foreign Ministry denied that Skybolt had been discussed at all at Rambouillet and de Gaulle told a group of French Parliamentarians in February 1963 that Macmillan "came to tell me we were right to build a nuclear force. 'We have ours', he told me. 'It will be necessary to reach a point of uniting them in a European cadre independent of America'. There he left me to go to the Bahamas. Naturally, what happened altered the tone of my press conference."[72]

The explanation, insofar as there is one, may lie elsewhere. On 7 February 1963, Louis Joxe, Minister for Administrative Reform in the French Government, told Dixon that French Ministers had been as surprised as anybody by de Gaulle's press conference. At the Council of Ministers the week before, the Ministers concerned had, according to Joxe, been taking the line that a settlement of British entry was in sight and that it was likely to be quite satisfactory from the French point of view. General de Gaulle had not demurred (thus also helping to explain, in Dixon's view, why Couve de Murville had told Heath on 11 January that British accession was likely to go ahead). It was, said Joxe, only about three days before the press conference that he got the impression that de Gaulle had suddenly made up his mind. Joxe had the impression that de Gaulle must have received independent information in the days immediately preceding his press conference, though Joxe had no knowledge of what that information could have been. However, it looked to him as if, quite apart from the Rambouillet and Nassau meetings, something must have occurred which gave de Gaulle the feeling that he was in danger of being cornered or enmeshed, and he had decided to break out.[73]

It may be that for de Gaulle the significance of Nassau was not the offer of Polaris to Britain but in what else was agreed. The first outcome was the, admittedly ambiguous, agreement to a multilateral nuclear force (MLF), a fleet of ships (or submarines) armed with Polaris missiles and jointly owned and operated by NATO members, each with a veto over the use of the nuclear weapons. This idea held no attraction for de Gaulle since it strengthened NATO under American leadership and put Germany within reach of nuclear weapons.

The second outcome was an offer of nuclear cooperation with France. At least some on the American delegation at Nassau feared that the offer of Polaris to the British would "thrust an issue into the hands of de Gaulle and set back the cause of [European] integration".[74] Their fears might have been even greater had Macmillan intimated to Kennedy just how badly the Rambouillet meeting had gone, but he does not appear to have done so. Kennedy, meanwhile, "arrived at Nassau determined not to aid France's nuclear weapons programme" but "left convinced that if nothing else could purchase de Gaulle's cooperation, it would have to be tried".[75]

Both the American Ambassador in Paris, Charles Bohlen, who arrived in Nassau on the last day of the meeting with Macmillan, and returned with Kennedy to Palm Beach at its conclusion, and the British Ambassador in Paris, Bob Dixon, were instructed to call separately on de Gaulle. De Gaulle was to be told that his requirements were understood by the American and British Governments. He was to be offered Polaris. It was to be made clear that, in addition to Polaris itself there could be negotiations on the scope of nuclear assistance, subject to de Gaulle's willingness to put the Polaris missiles at the disposal of NATO, nominally at least.

Bohlen and Dixon both saw de Gaulle, separately, in early January. Dixon gave de Gaulle to understand that whatever France would require in addition to Polaris would be made available. He mentioned the possibility of a *'tridirectorate'* – exactly the proposition that de Gaulle had unsuccessfully made to Britain and the US in 1958.[76]

Commenting afterwards to London, Dixon described the conversation with de Gaulle as typical: "Starting by giving an impression that his mind was open, he gradually revealed what was the heart of the matter for him – determination not to be dependent on an American product or to be dragged into a plan which, to him, is an American plot to ensure their leadership in European defence . . . Nor do I think, after this latest revelation of his sentiments, that help with nuclear matters would dispose him to facilitate our inclusion in the EEC, since he wants a European Community in which we would be acceptable if we were European in the Gaullist sense, not a Community in which we remain tied to the United States".[77]

That de Gaulle did not take the bait is not surprising. A double commitment on his part: to NATO and to British accession, was too high a price to pay. He was by then committed to the development of France's own deterrent and, even at the price of delay, that plan alone fitted with his conception of a Europe led by France. But in the light of the earlier history of discussions between de Gaulle and the Americans in particular, and the evident seriousness with which the American and British démarches to him were made, it would not be surprising if de Gaulle felt cornered or enmeshed as Joxe had surmised.

There is one other passing, but not insignificant, exchange at Rambouillet which may also have stayed in de Gaulle's mind. On the Sunday morning of the talks, de Gaulle referred to the fact that Macmillan "had suggested without actually saying so . . . that the European countries did not like the hegemony of France and looked for an equilibrium which British entry into Europe would provide". In his response, Macmillan said that "there was no question of any country having a hegemony in Europe, but instead there should be an equilibrium"[78]

For Macmillan this was a statement of the obvious but, as Newhouse points out "For de Gaulle, this must have been an extraordinary moment. Macmillan was making his, de Gaulle's real argument. Inside a European Community Britain would of course play her old game of balancing now this one, now that one; that was precisely what de Gaulle could not accept".[79]

Whatever the impact on de Gaulle of comments made by Macmillan at Rambouillet, or of the Nassau agreement, the inescapable conclusion from those talks was that de Gaulle had already made up his mind that he did not want Britain in the EEC. It was nothing Macmillan said that prompted de Gaulle to set out, in comprehensively uncompromising terms, his complete opposition to British entry.

We can only surmise, as Macmillan did, as to the impact on de Gaulle's mentality of perceived grievances from World War II. They undoubtedly coloured his thinking. His vision of a Europe in no way dependent on the United States, politically united under French leadership and with the institutions of the Community under the firm control of national governments, was to prove illusory. But he was surely not wrong to calculate that a European Community with Britain in it would be a very different kind of organisation: larger, more diverse, more outward looking, more economically liberal and more Atlanticist. So it has proved even if de Gaulle's fear of American dominance of the project was not well founded.

The evidence of the records suggests that the one area where the British Government under-estimated the strength of French feeling was over agriculture. For the British, the problems of adaptation to the Community's agricultural policy were almost all negative ones in terms of cost to the UK balance of payments, higher food prices for consumers and damage to relations with the countries of the Commonwealth. That preoccupation, and the focus on finding workable solutions to the problems posed by a common agricultural policy, seems to have led the British Government to underrate the emotional, practical and political importance of the Community agricultural system to the French. At his January press conference, de Gaulle spelled out in terms that, without a Community agricultural policy, designed by France for French farming interests the Community was not an attractive proposition. He surmised – again correctly – that British accession would change it. The fact that, today, the Common Agricultural Policy (CAP) is the stock-in-trade of British political criticism of the European Union and that, equally, the CAP is the banner waved at the Brussels barricades by successive French Presidents, shows how visceral an issue it was and remains.

The British could conceivably have paid greater heed to fundamental French concerns over agriculture, and there is more than a hint of realisation, in the Cabinet discussions just before the end of negotiations, that the British side would need to compromise. But Macmillan and his Ministers faced a sceptical, sometimes hostile, public opinion, resistance within their own Party and an official Labour Opposition whose negative attitude towards British EEC membership was based on the contention that the terms under negotiation, especially as they affected agriculture and the Commonwealth, were unacceptable. So they had very little room for manoeuvre. Ten years later, Edward Heath, as Prime Minister, did seek to tick the French political boxes on agriculture in order to persuade President Pompidou to let Britain in. But by then Pompidou had ensured that the final shape of the Common Agricultural Policy was set before he would even allow negotiations with Britain to begin. And Britain was thus forced to accept a negotiating deal which ensured, not that the issue was finally resolved, but that it continued as a running sore in Britain's relations with her European partners for another decade.

* * *

2 Picking up the pieces: 1963–1964

"The negotiations have broken down. What we've got to decide is what we are going to do next". What indeed? As Macmillan admitted in that national broadcast at the end of January 1963, there was no ready-made plan that was better than the one the Government had been pursuing. But there was, he asserted, "a lot that we can and must do". What that amounted to was a suggestion of consultations with the Commonwealth, with EFTA and with the United States; the pursuit of lower tariffs in the forthcoming Kennedy Round of negotiations in the GATT and, of course, reliance "on our own determination, our own vigour and our own resources. We must be ready to accept change, to modernise, to adapt, to replace obsolete plant and methods which are outdated; to work together, all of us. Is this a gloomy prospect? Not at all. We've been in this kind of situation before. It's always drawn out the best in us. It will again".[1]

Macmillan was putting a brave face on things. The central plank of his foreign and domestic policy had been pulled brutally from under him. He was in his 69th year. While the European drama was playing out at the end of 1962, the Leader of the Opposition, Hugh Gaitskell, had died after a short illness. His successor, Harold Wilson, was twenty-two years younger than Macmillan and would soon take on an almost Kennedy-like aura of vigour, modernity and change.

"I am sure you realise how sorry I am about the great disappointment you have suffered in recent days", Kennedy wrote in a message to Macmillan. "My regret is compounded by my realisation that part of your difficulties resulted from your country's historic association with the United States and your own strong support of this alliance. I count on working closely with you in the coming days."[2]

Macmillan could take some comfort from that, and similar messages of sympathy which poured in, as well as from the widespread anger with France on the European continent. But his immediate tasks were to set a new domestic economic course and work out a European policy based on the British Government's continued wish to join the EEC combined with the knowledge that they could have no idea when that might become possible.

At Cabinet on 31 January 1963, Macmillan confirmed his view that the main objectives of the Government "should be to strengthen relations with the Commonwealth, EFTA and the members of the EEC, other than France, and to work for greater freedom in international trade". None of his colleagues dissented, though the general sentiment in a rather cursory discussion was one of scepticism about how much faith to place in the Commonwealth; appreciation of the protectionist pressures the Government would face and the need to resist them, combined with the faint hope that EEC negotiations might yet resume within a few months.

The following day, Macmillan was in Italy, calling on Pope John XXIII who was described by the British Minister to the Holy See as being "weary" after a strenuous morning, and by Macmillan as "very gay, talked incessantly in French and kept me for thirty five minutes". Macmillan was, however, shocked by the Pope's appearance and surmised, correctly, that he was dying of cancer.[3]

In a long conversation with Italian Prime Minister Fanfani, Macmillan and the Italian speculated about de Gaulle's motives. Fanfani was inclined to think that there was some link in de Gaulle's mind between the proposals for a multilateral NATO force (MLF) and the collapse of the Brussels negotiations. But he still did not really understand why de Gaulle "had changed his mind". The two men had no substantive discussion of what might now be done.[4]

Perhaps conscious of a vacuum, on return to London, Macmillan's Foreign Office Private Secretary, Philip de Zulueta, sent the Prime Minister a minute entitled *A Positive Policy After Brussels*. After analysing de Gaulle's aims (to try to dominate Europe and exclude Britain) de Zulueta advised that "our negative purpose must be to prevent the consolidation, still more the extension, of de Gaulle's Europe. Our positive aim should continue to be to unite a wider Europe and to make her into a powerful and equal partner with the United States in the Atlantic Alliance. Our methods should not be purely 'Atlantic' but should also be 'European' ". By this, de Zulueta explained, he meant using the Western European Union (WEU) as a forum for political action; extending its membership to include Norway and Denmark and perhaps Portugal, Greece, Turkey and even Spain, Sweden and Switzerland. The outdated defence provisions of the WEU Treaty could be renegotiated so that the European element of the proposed Multilateral Force could be commanded by a WEU nominee. On the economic front, he suggested the possibility of a European industrial free trade area through some kind of association between EFTA and the EEC, though he acknowledged that it would almost certainly be vetoed by the French, in which case an alternative might be a series of bilateral agreements with each of the countries of the Six. Unless Britain took the lead in Europe by some positive action, de Zulueta concluded, de Gaulle's bandwagon would be joined by a lot more people.[5]

There is no evidence of a response from Macmillan, though it is perhaps significant that on the same day Macmillan wrote in his diary: "The great question remains 'What is the alternative' to the European Community? If we are honest, we must say that there is none. Had there been the chance of a Commonwealth Free Trade Area, we should have grasped it long ago".[6]

Two days later, on 6 February, Edward Heath chaired a meeting of the official Cabinet Office committee on the EEC negotiations. Heath said it was a time for taking stock and thinking about the future. Whilst initial public reaction had been to suggest a need for major alternatives to the Government's European policies, people were now beginning to feel that a main objective must be to continue to work towards the right solutions for the Europe of the future. He felt there was better mutual understanding between Britain, on the one hand, and the countries of EFTA and the Commonwealth on the other i.e., presumably, a greater understanding that Britain's future lay in Europe.

At the same time, the Foreign Office was giving guidance to its European posts. Guidance Telegrams were the standard means by which overseas posts were kept informed of underlying Whitehall thinking and told what to say on major policy issues. Most European posts at that time would have had same-day access to British newspapers and all were assiduous listeners to the BBC World Service. But they had nothing like the range of information available today through the internet, and useful sources of guidance such as the Hansard record of Parliament only reached them by diplomatic bag a few days after the event. The telephone was not reliable, and certainly not secure.[7]

The Foreign Office saw de Gaulle's veto as part of a conflict between his view of how Europe should develop and that of the rest of the Five and the rest of NATO. De Gaulle posed a fundamental challenge to the Alliance as a whole and it was in NATO that the main effort to thwart him should be made. Strong British doubts were later to emerge about the Multilateral Force but the Foreign Office noted that Britain had already taken the initiative in NATO in leading the discussions on the MLF and "must press on with this, which will have the effect of isolating France". Only Britain could put forward a persuasive view of the part which the European non-nuclear members of the Alliance could play from the start in this NATO nuclear force. If the Americans took the lead that could give credence to de Gaulle's allegations that the Americans were determined on domination in Europe.

NATO was not to be the sole field of action. Use was to be made of the existing Anglo-German and Anglo-Italian economic committees, and active consideration was being given to setting up a similar Anglo-Benelux committee. Equally, however, bilateral action was not enough. Britain had to make her influence felt collectively as well. The Council of Europe was ruled out as being too widely based for concentrated action. Its Parliamentary assembly was useful but the Five were more interested in the European Community's own Assembly, from which Britain was of course excluded. The Foreign Office realistically assessed that "the Five do not seem anxious to underline the split with the French or to take any step looking like a deliberate decision to cooperate with us and exclude the French". This meant that, unless the Five were to break away from the EEC (and with each passing day this was increasingly improbable) the Foreign Office could see no solid economic basis for any other grouping. Nor, with defence questions firmly embedded in NATO, was there much scope for a new political relationship. So, the Foreign Office concluded, WEU looked like the best option. It was not ideal. It was suspect in German eyes because its founding treaty, the Brussels Treaty, contained discriminatory provisions. Countries such as Norway and Denmark were not members. The fact that the French *were* members might inhibit the very developments Britain wanted. But WEU was a ready-made framework for political cooperation and the Brussels Treaty was flexible enough to allow for new initiatives without treaty change. WEU had its own Parliamentary Assembly and, if meetings took place within WEU, it would be easier for the Five to resist French attempts to hold meetings of the Six, excluding Britain.[8]

A structured relationship within WEU was seen as a safer alternative than association between Britain and the Six. For a brief period, a Belgian suggestion of a Customs Union between the UK and the Six was entertained and both Heath and Maudling were in favour but, as Maudling noted, "it would of course be essential to have the French committed from the outset" and the French were not about to concede a large element of what they had just rejected.[9]

The idea of association between Britain and the Six, while not specifically rejected, was viewed by the British with suspicion for the reasons that Heath had given before the formal breakdown of the negotiations: why commit to open-ended negotiations, with no certainty at the end of French agreement and for the sake of an eventual second class relationship in which Britain would be allowed (and required) to implement decisions in which she had had no part?

On 15 February, the Foreign Office told its European posts that any proposal for association would have to represent a firm and effective offer by all its members. Association would still pose the questions of agricultural policy, Commonwealth free entry and the relationship with EFTA. The best that could be said for association was that "it could be of some political value in that it would at least establish a point of contact with the Community".[10]

The American Government were also concerned. In February, Kennedy wrote to Macmillan saying that, while the word 'association' did not in itself hold any terrors for the US, "I ought to add that there are forms of association which would have grave economic disadvantages for us in the United States and that for this reason we hope there can be careful consulting before any major new departure is set on its way".[11] A similar message was delivered by the American Ambassador to Britain, David Bruce, in a conversation with the Foreign Secretary some days later. Bruce told Home that an association between Britain and the EEC "would be an arrangement which the United States would not relish." Then, as later, the Americans were prepared to take what amounted to a protectionist hit from the European Community in the interest of wider European peace and stability and in exchange for Britain being a full member, able to influence policy in an economically liberal direction. They were not prepared to take the hit without the compensating advantages. Home told Bruce that he "doubted if any practical plan would ever be put forward by all of the Six".[12] 'Not ever' is a long time in politics but, although the idea was revived again, particularly after de Gaulle's second veto in 1967, Home's prediction was to prove entirely correct.

The idea did not die immediately. Later in March, when the Italian Foreign Minister called on Macmillan in London, Piccioni sought clarity on the British Government's intentions both about association and about EEC membership. In reply, Macmillan said that the British people had not found it easy to adjust to the idea that their future lay with Europe. But, in the last two years, the great majority had come to that view. The main reason was economic: people could see the benefits of a larger European market. But there were strong political supporters of entry as well, albeit more among the younger generation than among older people. The truth was, said Macmillan, that "the flow of history could not be turned back. British opinion was certainly disappointed by the failure at Brussels, but not disillusioned. This was the end of a chapter, but certainly not of the volume".

As regards association, Macmillan had the feeling that this was not really a serious proposition although, of course, were the Six to make a serious proposal the United Kingdom would consider it. The British Government were not, however, prepared to enter into another long and abortive negotiation in which they could see no prospect of success because the good faith was not there. The British Government "could not overlook the existence of Governments and personalities which might make it futile to put in another application to accede to the Treaty of Rome next week".

The British Government, Macmillan added, would keep up and support the various private and public movements in Britain which were interested in European questions. Those movements would keep the European ideal alive and active. Macmillan made clear that the Government wanted to sustain positive contacts with her friends on the continent, be it through a new organisation or through the WEU and NATO. What was *seen* to be done was just as important as what was actually done. Hence the importance of visits. Hence the fact that Lord Home was going to NATO. That was why the British Government were trying to put more life into the WEU as well as developing their close cooperation with the Five. The British people were, Macmillan concluded, "both practical and proud. They knew that so long as the single veto of France was effective there was no possibility of a new negotiation or a fresh approach succeeding. This was the British people's practical view. Also, being proud people, they did not propose to go on their knees to France".[13]

Macmillan was in effect saying that the central goal of British policy was unchanged but that no amount of displacement activity could disguise the fact that the goal was blocked. Any new activity was therefore going to be a palliative, not a substitute.

None of these ideas dealt with the central problem of how British economic policy was to be conducted in the absence of EEC membership. Small wonder that, when Macmillan met some of his senior colleagues after the 10 p.m. Division in the House of Commons on 4 February (an illustration of the working pressures which politicians have to accept as a matter of routine), he "did not feel that any of them had much stomach for this fight", the fight being the debate on the collapse of the negotiations scheduled for 11 February. So, Macmillan, who had made two big speeches in the House the previous week, given a major television address to the nation and undertaken a three-day visit to Rome, was condemned to do the job himself and spent the whole of 5 February working on his speech.

In his speech, Macmillan reprised the reasons behind de Gaulle's veto. He held out no hope of an early resumption of Britain's accession bid. "This is not a kind of business deal that, if it fails one week, can be taken up the next. It is, for good or ill, a great historic event. It cannot be disregarded but its importance, and perhaps, its permanence, must not be exaggerated. While it would be absurd not to recognise with our heads that Britain's entry is not now capable of early realisation, we should surely strive to keep the vision in our hearts".

He set out Britain's external plan of action: a conference of Commonwealth Trade Ministers; and close cooperation with the Commonwealth, the US, EFTA and, it was to be hoped, the Six, for the Kennedy Round. The EFTA association would be maintained. Britain would work for world commodity agreements. At home, the Government would work for an expanding economy, without inflation, based upon an incomes policy.

Macmillan also went out of his way to heed the advice his Ambassador in Bonn had given him about relations with the Germans. "It is natural" he said "that there should be lingering in our country a certain reserve. The memories of two wars are not lightly wiped out. But the German people are also sensitive over this and, in my view, great harm can be done by ungenerous attitudes, whether in the Press or among any of us. Curiously enough, I have observed that this feeling is often strongest amongst people who have taken the least active part in these great struggles . . . The truth is that just as good Anglo-French relations and a close cooperation between us and the people of France are fervently desired here, we must also recognise that the fruitful development of Anglo-German relations should be one of the props on which the unity of Europe must depend".[14]

Close cooperation with the people of France did not extend to allowing a scheduled visit to Paris by HRH Princess Margaret to go ahead. Macmillan wrote that "we had reason to believe that the General meant to lay on, not a nice cosy luncheon or tea party, but a vast affair – all the Cabinet, half the Diplomatic Corps, cavalry, infantry and all the rest. This seemed to us a bit too much after the way in which he has treated Britain and also too soon, so the Foreign Secretary resisted strongly and so did the Ambassador in Paris. The Foreign Secretary also felt that if HRH went and were to take part in all this it would be regarded as very odd by the other countries of Europe, the friendly Five in particular. However, I need hardly say that this is one of those things in which one is wrong whatever one does. If we had allowed the visit to proceed we would have been criticised; we were equally blamed for insisting on it being stopped".

There was indeed what Macmillan called a great row in the Press, Parliament and the Party and he later felt that it would have been more dignified to let the visit go ahead.[15]

Further evidence of the emotional atmosphere of the time can also be found in the Cabinet's discussion in February of a proposal by the Foreign Secretary to accept the Vatican's suggestion that its diplomatic representation in the UK should be upgraded to the level of Nuncio. Home was in favour on the ground that it "would permit closer cooperation with the Roman Catholic Church in our efforts to contain the expansion of Communist influence". There was some support for Home but an even stronger counter-argument that "it would be wiser not to take any initiative in exciting public controversy on this subject at the present time, particularly having regard to the recent attempt by one section of the popular Press to represent our attempt to enter the EEC as a covert design to bring the UK under RC influence". Macmillan volunteered to arrange for further consideration to be given to the implications of the proposal.[16] When Macmillan reverted to the subject a month later, it was clear that the 'further consideration' of the issue had taken place in his mind alone and that he "was satisfied that action which might be interpreted, even if erroneously, as implying recognition of the temporal authority of the Pope might be regarded as liable to prejudice the favourable development of the current movement towards closer spiritual relations between the Churches". No one questioned this dubious argument and Cabinet, with evident relief, grasped at the pretext to agree that no further action should be taken.[17]

The debate in the House of Commons on the breakdown of the Brussels negotiations was Macmillan's first significant encounter across the Despatch box with Harold Wilson in his role as the new Leader of the Opposition. The two men had previous history. Wilson had been newly thrust into prominence as Shadow Chancellor when Macmillan was still at the Treasury in 1956. Both, according to Macmillan's biographer, D. R. Thorpe, were "essentially outsiders in their own party, even mistrusted figures . . . Both were figures of considerable intellectual capacity, the only Prime Ministers who could be said properly to understand Keynes. Their clashes over the dispatch box as their parties' Treasury spokesmen had all the razzmatazz of a circus act. Both gave as good as they got. Then, public conflict over, they would repair to the smoking room and enjoy a drink and a chat, the performance over . . . Wilson wrote that theirs was 'a happy and stimulating relationship' ".[18]

Macmillan had even expressed admiration for Wilson's handling of the debate in the House of Commons in August 1961 on the Government's decision to open negotiations for accession to the EEC: "The most brilliant speech of the debate was made by Wilson, who opened on the second day. He did not do much by way of discussing the Common Market; he was more intent on attacking the Government. But it was admirably done. Its only fault was that it seemed to come down too much against the European plan, but he retrieved that at the last moment and climbed back upon the official party fence by wishing well to the Government in their endeavours" in what Macmillan called a "reluctant and somewhat disingenuous piece of generosity".[19]

Sixty years later, it is still easy to see why Macmillan rated Wilson's speech so highly. It was informed, serious, reflective and perceptive. It offers more than a few clues to how Wilson would handle Europe in his three terms of office as Prime Minister.

Wilson's opening position in 1961 was that while "we do not oppose the decision of the Government to embark on negotiations to ascertain the conditions on which Britain can join the European Economic Community, we do utterly reserve our position on the decision which must be taken when the Government return to this House from the negotiations". He went on to knock the Government about a bit for negotiating from a position of economic weakness – ironically exactly the predicament he would find himself in 1967, as would Heath in 1971.

From a long-term point of view, he argued, British industry and trade might gain from membership. But, in the short term, British industry was not very responsive to the cold draught of import competition. Between 1958 and 1960, Wilson claimed, imports of manufactured goods from the countries of the Common Market had risen by a monthly average of 49% compared with an increase in our own manufactures of 25%. He foresaw that this might well be the pattern if Britain joined the EEC. The answer lay in "positive, purposive, economic planning". If there was no fundamental change in Britain's internal economic policies then "what we are debating today is whether we shall be a backwater in Europe or a backwater outside Europe, and both are an equally dangerous position to occupy".

Wilson then set out the key criteria by which the negotiations would be judged. The problems of agriculture were not insoluble. It would be the housewife, rather than the farmer, who would feel the draught from the adjustments which would have to be made. The fundamental issue of agriculture was not the effect of EEC membership on the British farmer but on the Commonwealth. Under the last Labour Government, trade with the Commonwealth as a percentage of Britain's total trade had been at an all-time high. The subsequent decline was not due to historical factors, as the Government claimed, but to the Government's destruction of the sterling area as a trading entity, compounded by a lack of enterprise and drive on the part of many British manufacturers. While our exports were falling there had been an overall increase of imports into the Commonwealth countries of the sterling area, but that increase had been scooped by Japan, Germany and the United States.

Wilson then set out in stark terms a problem which remains at the heart of the British argument over Europe to this day. "Anyone reading the economic clauses of the Treaty [of Rome]" he said, "will realise the highly restrictive, even autarkic motivation of the Community. Non-discrimination within the area, yes, but a whole panoply of tariff quotas, import levies and other methods to supplement the tariff provisions . . . All this suggests that there will be a very formidable series of weapons designed to limit the imports into Europe, and into Britain, of the products of many Commonwealth countries. Free trade within the area, yes, but vis-à-vis the outside world – let us be frank about it – this is a highly restrictive, discriminating trading bloc. We should have no illusions about it. It is the sort of bloc which, perhaps, the Conservatives can join and perhaps, with the right safeguards and assurances, the Labour Party could support joining . . ."

Wilson then put a series of direct questions: in seven years' time, if Britain joined, would we expect to see as much Australian and Canadian wheat coming to Britain as today or would it be wholly or substantially replaced by French production? Would there be the same amount of New Zealand meat, or would that be replaced by French production? What about New Zealand butter? There needed to be, Wilson argued, long term, secure arrangements for Commonwealth imports, combined with a promise of association with the EEC for Commonwealth countries.

Wilson concluded this portion of his speech with a moving tribute to New Zealand. Mr Marquand, who was the British Secretary for Overseas Trade immediately after the war, had one day, in Marquand's own words, "sat down with the

New Zealand delegation. I expected a bargaining session as difficult as any other. Instead, the leader of the New Zealand delegation opened the proceedings in words I shall never forget. 'We have not come to ask you "What can you give?" but simply "What do you need?" When you stood alone you preserved our freedom for us. Now tell us what butter, what meat, what grains you need, and – whatever the sacrifice may be for the New Zealand people – we will supply it.'

"I submit to the House" Wilson said "that we cannot consistently with the honour of this country take any action now that would betray friends such as those. All this and Europe too – if you can get it. The President of the Board of Trade last night seemed to think that we can. I hope that he is right, but if there has to be a choice we are not entitled to sell our friends and kinsmen down the river for a problematic and marginal advantage in selling washing machines in Dusseldorf."

Wilson's peroration, like this passage, offers a clear guide to his future policies and evidence of greater consistency than he is often given credit for. "I should like", he said, "to take issue straight away with some . . . sitting below the Gangway opposite, who quite simply regard it as an issue of sovereignty. I respect their arguments but they – and even the word, I think – are really out of harmony with this modern age. The whole history of political progress is a history of gradual abandonment of national sovereignty. We abrogate it when we have a French referee at Twickenham. We abrogated it – some would say that we did not abrogate it enough – when we joined the United Nations. One cannot talk about world government in one breath and then start drooling about the need to preserve national sovereignty in the next . . . The question is not whether sovereignty remains absolute or not, but in what way one is prepared to sacrifice sovereignty, to whom and for what purpose. That is the real issue before us. The question is whether any proposed surrender of sovereignty will advance or retard our progress to the kind of world we all want to see . . . Equally, I do not join those extremists who have been trying to estimate what Britain will become if we do or do not join the Common Market. Stay out, some say, and we shall be powerless and become another Sweden or Portugal. Go in, say the others, and we shall become another Idaho. But I think that these arguments grossly understate the position and role of what Britain is and what Britain could be under the right kind of leadership. The vital issue in the political sense is whether to join the Common Market explicitly or implicitly means a move towards a federal Europe. There is nothing in the Treaty of Rome enjoining federalism, although there is a great deal of supranationalism . . . It is a little myopic of the Prime Minister to refer to it as 'a purely economic negotiation and not a political and foreign policy negotiation'. But, all the same, we warmly welcome his statement of yesterday associating himself with President de Gaulle's approach . . . I hope that the Government will be clear about this. There should be no doubt on this federal issue. There should be no double talk with Europe about it. Our position should be stated so that there is no accusation of bad faith, of dragging our feet, of perfidious Albion if, subsequently Europe seeks to move towards federation and then, and only then, we make clear our opposition to it. Whatever view may be taken concerning these economic negotiations, I hope that we make it clear that we shall not go into a federal system.

I very much welcome the Prime Minister's condemnation of what the right hon. gentleman called 'little Europeans'. We must be outward looking. The Prime Minister is right ... I repeat, we do not oppose the negotiations but on the Government's success in meeting the economic and political anxieties which ... I have expressed – and we wish the Government well in the negotiations – we utterly reserve our position about the package that the Government will bring back ..."[20]

It is clear from that speech that Wilson was not viscerally anti-European, rather the contrary. But then, as later, he had to perform a balancing act between left and right, pro and anti, EC factions within the Labour Party. After Labour's defeat in the 1959 General Election, Wilson had unsuccessfully challenged Hugh Gaitskell for the Labour leadership. Many, on the right of the Party in particular, distrusted him and it was largely for that reason, and because Brown had the support of the Gaitskellites, that he lost out against George Brown in his bid for the deputy leadership in 1962. It was partly because his own position in the Party was precarious and because "if Gaitskell could neutralise the ardent Europeans, who were concentrated in his own wing of the Party, then good luck to him", that Wilson went along with Gaitskell's increasingly anti European stance in the second half of 1962. At the Party Conference that autumn, chaired by Wilson, Gaitskell denounced the European Community and said that the Labour Party should never cooperate with any attempt to join it. Wilson evinced enthusiasm for the speech, though the rallying speeches of Party leaders at Conference are rarely occasions for mature reflection. It cannot have escaped him either, following his defeat by George Brown, that one of the weaknesses in Brown's otherwise strong position within the Labour Party was his "ardent advocacy of the Common Market".[21]

Such was the background to the encounter between Wilson and Macmillan on 11 February 1963. Macmillan recorded that his own speech on 11 February had been "welcomed by the House, and afterwards by the Press, as impressive and suited to a great occasion".[22] Nothing, however, could disguise the fact that Macmillan's task was to explain a débacle. He had defended his goal, but the ball was at Wilson's feet.

Having criticised the terms of entry being negotiated by the Government as woefully inadequate, Wilson could hardly, in responding to Macmillan's speech, paint the breakdown as a tragedy and he shrewdly chose instead to portray it as a débacle. "Even ignoring the long list of unsolved problems ... the fact is that the terms which have been negotiated, the accumulated totality of vital national and Commonwealth interests already surrendered by the Government, already constituted a national humiliation." The nation, Wilson said, would find in Macmillan's speech in the House no positive policies, no inspiration. They would find "nothing but defeatism, a certain amount of peevishness, and a complete policy vacuum".

Wilson was careful not to rule out membership of the Community in the future. "We are not", he said, "slamming the door to proposals to advance European unity – indeed we do not rule out the possibility of further proposals on this ... We certainly do not rule out the possibility of further negotiations in Europe at the right time and under the right auspices". In the meantime, Wilson argued, Britain should take an initiative in the OECD, making clear her willingness to discuss any proposition which covered the whole European area of that organisation. He hinted at some kind of arrangement involving EFTA and the EEC. In addition Britain could show her determination not to turn her back on Europe "and we could show our desire for greater European unity of an acceptable pragmatic kind" by making a formal proposal for regular meetings of Heads of Government of the countries of Western and Northern Europe "not with the idea of imposing federal or common foreign and defence policies on the basis of majority decisions, but to get the widest measure of agreement possible on international questions". "Our future", Wilson concluded "lies now clearly in our own hands, on our sense of purpose, of dynamism, of self-discipline, of sacrifices, if sacrifices there must be, fairly shared. If this failure of the Brussels negotiations has brought this home to us as never before, I thank God for it, because this is the first condition for reasserting our national strength and our national independence . . . The right hon. Gentleman's speech today was one of abdication on behalf of a whole Government. The recovery of Britain's lost dynamic is a task that must and will now pass into other hands".[23]

Harold Wilson himself was riding high in popular esteem. His Party Political Broadcast on 27 February 1963 attracted the largest audience for any British television programme ever. Sixty-four per cent of those polled by Gallup said they liked him, with only 7% expressing dislike. By March, Labour's lead over the Conservatives had risen from 13% before Gaitskell's death to 17%, and was to go up to 20% in June. In the same month, Wilson's approval ratings showed a 19% lead over Macmillan, compared with Gaitskell's 7% in January.[24]

It was perhaps a symptom of the demoralisation of Macmillan and his Government, which was starting to go wider than Europe, that, although the debate was behind it, the Government found little scope to put much more flesh on the bones of future policy than had been outlined to the House of Commons. There is little evidence of detailed thinking about either EFTA or the Commonwealth, doubtless in part because of the realisation, clear from the initial Cabinet debate and from Macmillan's own reflections, that neither offered more than a palliative. The countries of EFTA could not compete economically or politically with the EEC, containing, as it did, three of the largest European economies. British trade with the Commonwealth was already of diminishing importance both to them and to Britain. Commonwealth Governments knew that, given the opportunity, the British Government would re-apply for EEC membership. They themselves would continue to diversify their trade. There was also an increasingly clear understanding at the heart of Government that a new opportunity to negotiate for membership was unlikely to arise before the next General Election in Britain. It is nonetheless noteworthy that, from the end of January 1963 to the General Election in October 1964, there was no further Cabinet discussion of general European strategy. Individual events, such as WEU meetings, were reported. Tactics in the Kennedy Round of GATT negotiations were discussed. There was debate about the Channel Tunnel and about what was then called The Concord.

There was considerable, and anxious, discussion about the Multilateral Force. But, while European issues continued to occupy Macmillan and other individual Ministers, there was no Cabinet discussion since there was, in strategic and policy terms, no new challenge or opportunity to discuss.

At the end of February the Official Committee on EC questions finalised its view on the way ahead in a revised version of a paper drafted by the Treasury. It concluded that it would be necessary to plan on the assumption that Britain would be unable to join the Community for a number of years to come. In consequence:

"(a) We should in our own policies, while not going deliberately out of the way to align ourselves with the Community, avoid action which would positively hinder our eventual accession unless there are, on balance, very strong reasons to the contrary.

(b) We should use our influence with the Community and its individual members primarily with a view to their so far as possible avoiding action which would create new difficulties for our eventual accession. We should positively encourage them to reconsider their policies with a view to harmonious development of world trade and reduction of customs and other barriers.

(c) Departments should bear in mind the factors at (a) above in the formulation of our own policies; and should consider what possibilities there may be, to our own advantage, of our joining in common action with the Community or its members individually.

(d) Departments should consider in the foregoing light what attitude we should take towards individual issues likely to arise within the Community, as these become known.

(e) Machinery should be developed as far as may be practicable to enable close and continuing contact to be maintained with the organs of the Community in Brussels and with its member governments individually and collectively".

The document concluded with a list of the major issues which officials thought might arise within the EEC in the near future:

1. Agricultural policies.
2. Association: requests for association under Article 238 from Spain and Turkey; trade relations with Israel and Iran; future relations between the Community and Algeria.
3. Tariffs: the development of policies, especially in relation to the Kennedy Round. Further decisions concerning the implementation of the Common External Tariff and abolition of internal tariffs.
4. Miscellaneous: External (especially US) investment in Community countries. Freedom of establishment and services. Free movement of workers. Common transport policy."[25]

The work of officials on European economic issues was soon to be swept up into the more general economic steering committee and the specifically European committee disbanded. It is nonetheless surprising that there appears to have been no formal Cabinet endorsement, of this, or any other, agreed strategy for the future. It seems to be a further reflection of the somewhat forlorn feeling of failure and drift which followed the initial adrenalin rush provoked by de Gaulle's behaviour. In any event, from March onwards Macmillan himself was beset by the issues resulting from the Vassall spy case and the Profumo Affair, the latter probably the greatest scandal to afflict any of Britain's post-war Governments to date. Moreover, with a General Election due by the autumn of 1964, and with the Labour Party in the ascendant, there was uncertainty among Britain's potential European partners about the direction of British policy.

De Gaulle, as we have seen, had expressed the view that Labour would come to power in Britain and that after "three or four years of weak and incompetent Labour government" the young Conservatives, by implication Gaullist sympathisers, would sweep into power. Similar thoughts were being aired in Germany. The new British Ambassador in Germany, Sir Frank Roberts, who had been Ambassador in Moscow and was one of the stars of his generation, reported at the end of February that the election of Harold Wilson as Labour leader had caused uneasiness in Germany, and not just because he had suggested that a Labour Government might recognise the Government of East Germany, the DDR. The West Germans, Roberts reported, were facing up to the possibility that Labour could win the next election and were beginning to look, not just at Wilson, but also at some of his front-bench colleagues with "increased interest, but some concern". Defence issues did not worry the Germans. It did not much matter to them whether or not Britain had an independent nuclear deterrent. What mattered to them was the security of NATO and they believed that the Labour Party, like the German SPD, had undergone an evolution towards a common-sense attitude. They were, though, worried that the Party would be pulled by its left wing into too accommodating an attitude towards the Soviet Union and towards a weak policy with regard to East Germany. More particularly, they feared that a Labour Government might turn its back on Europe. The Germans, said Roberts, were better informed about the improbability of a new British Government reversing the commitments entered into by its predecessor. But this reassurance would not hold good in a European situation where (thanks to de Gaulle's veto) commitments had not been made.

The danger, as Roberts saw it, was that fears for the future would begin to affect the present sympathetic attitude of Germany towards the United Kingdom. This was still a tender plant, less robust than German dependence upon the United States or sentimental attachment to France. It was a plant that needed constant care and could wither rapidly without it. There was, said Roberts, already a tendency to feel that, since there could be a Labour victory within the next eighteen months, leading to the abandonment of Britain's attempt to enter Europe, there was little point in collaborating with the present British Government. The result, Roberts predicted, could well be "a progressive dampening of enthusiasm amongst our friends in all parties, and a weakening will to do anything to help us in the difficult post-Brussels situation, and a general lack of interest in cooperation between the United Kingdom and Europe".

The answer, as Roberts saw it, lay in Britain taking the initiative to be more positive. It would not be enough for Britain to say "we are not turning our backs on Europe, but it is now up to you Europeans to find solutions to our difficulties". The British Government needed to come at least half way to meet the Germans, notably by showing themselves keen to make progress on the political front, even if the Government did not think much of the idea of economic association. It did not much matter that ideas for political cooperation – and the Belgians were espousing some at the time – would fall foul of the French. What was important was for Britain to "prove our good European intentions and our determination to explore every possible way out of the present situation".[26]

From Paris, Dixon painted an even starker picture of the evolution of events as it appeared to de Gaulle. By his press conference on 14 January 1963, de Gaulle, Dixon argued, probably believed that he had struck a body blow at British policy which would confuse and weaken the British Government. As a result, they would be incapable of mounting any effective counter-policy, would thus be further weakened and would lose the next General Election to the Labour Party. With the British disposed of de Gaulle, in Dixon's view, probably believed that things would return to 'normal' in Europe. The Germans would follow strong French leadership. The Common Market would go on in some strength while Britain would become still weaker. In de Gaulle's mind, when the Labour Party had won the General Election, they would fail to understand the realities of power, would make no attempt to play a serious role in Europe and would renounce the pursuit of an independent deterrent. Because of the Labour Party's dislike of the Germans, and their desire to appease the Russians, the Labour Government would pursue an anti-German policy which would play into his (de Gaulle's) hands.

Dixon then went a step further in interpreting de Gaulle's mind. NATO would be going badly. The idea of a multilateral nuclear deterrent would be seen to be absurd, and shown up as an attempt to keep all control in American hands, while getting the Europeans to share some of the cost of the American deterrent. Of course, de Gaulle would argue, in the end the British, like other European countries, would not want to be mere American satellites. When the Conservatives eventually returned to power, keen to reverse the plight to which Labour would have reduced Britain they would again take up the cause of EEC membership. But, by that time, French leadership in Europe would be clearly established. France would be the only nuclear power in Europe (Labour having scrapped the deterrent). The young Conservatives would in any case have understood the grandeur of de Gaulle's vision of building Europe independent of the United States. They would perforce become Gaullist. That, concluded Dixon, was what de Gaulle meant when he said that "perhaps one day" Europe would extend to the other side of the Channel.[27]

If de Gaulle really thought that the Conservative Party would espouse the Gaullist vision (and, as we have seen, there is evidence that he did) then, to that extent, he was wide of the mark. But the notion that keeping Britain out of the

European Community so that he could mould it in the French interest, and then allow an economically and politically humbled Britain to join on French terms was then, and later, what he clearly did have in mind. As part of the kind of grand, if perverse, strategy sketched by Dixon, it was to prove deeply flawed. As a calculation of narrow French national interest, it was spot on.

Dixon was also attracted by a similar idea to that put forward by Sir Frank Roberts from Bonn. Somewhat later in the year, Dixon sent a Despatch to the Foreign Secretary, entitled *A Review of the State of French Foreign Policy*. Macmillan saw it, along with comments from Bernard Ledwidge, then Head of Central Department in the Foreign Office. Ledwidge noted an apparent incompatibility between the view expressed by Dixon that Britain should adopt a policy which would isolate France still further and that of Macmillan, conveyed by his Private Secretary to the Foreign Office on 28 June, that "France is necessary to Western policy and it is not in our interest to make her appear more isolationist than she is". The resolution of this apparent conflict, according to Ledwidge, lay in the fact that Dixon distinguished sharply between de Gaulle and France: the latter was indeed necessary to Western policy; the former made any Western policy acceptable to Britain impossible. In Dixon's view, once the General had gone, the French nation would start once more on the journey towards European integration which had been interrupted by the advent of de Gaulle. At that point, said Dixon, Britain would have a good chance of ensuring that a Europe including Britain could establish a natural and fruitful equilibrium with the United States. In Dixon's view, the prospect of bad Anglo-French relations for a year or two was the price which Britain had to pay if she were not to lose all influence over the future course of European events. And the shaping of that European future might also "involve some dilution of the specifically Anglo-American connexion".

This issue: the balance between Britain's commitment to Europe on the one hand, and her political, practical and psychological dependence on the United States on the other, was, and remains, a constant issue of debate at the heart of the British Government. Dixon's perfectly reasonable argument was clearly a bridge too far for Macmillan. In a manuscript note to Home on 23 July, he wrote: "This is a very strange Despatch. Perhaps Ambassador Dixon is going mad too."[28]

That Dixon, far from going mad, was close to the mark in his analysis of de Gaulle's ambition was borne out by a letter to Macmillan from a friend, containing an account of a conversation between the French politician, Maurice Faure, and de Gaulle which had recently taken place. Faure had told his British interlocutor that he had had a talk with de Gaulle lasting thirty-five minutes and had, he believed, created a record by himself succeeding in speaking for ten of them. De Gaulle had said that the whole question of European unity depended entirely on defence. Once defence problems were settled, political and economic questions would fall naturally into place and could easily be reconciled. Europe's defence required its own atom bomb, free from American control. He, de Gaulle, was the only real defender of a united Europe because he alone went to the heart of the problem. He spoke of France shielding her European allies. Europe would eventually find that he was right.

The letter to Macmillan also included a suggestion from René Mayer, former Chairman of the European Coal and Steel Community, that Britain should be invited by the European Commission to sit in Brussels as a Government in a consultative capacity.[29] This was thought to be sufficiently interesting in Whitehall to provoke instructions to the British Delegation in Brussels turning down the proposition. It was thought in London that the absence of any substantive role for Britain would not be acceptable to public opinion. Moreover, "there could scarcely be any prospect of a satisfactory relationship on even this attenuated basis being acceptable to the French since it is abundantly clear that they are determined to block any arrangement which would facilitate the extension of British influence . . . There is no point in courting another French rebuff". If, the instructions concluded, the habit of working together could be developed then the necessary institutional arrangements would follow. Without the will to cooperate, on the other hand, the institutional link, even if it could be set up, would be valueless.[30]

Nonetheless, the idea, or something like it, had legs. In early April the German Foreign Minister, Gerhard Schroeder, floated the idea of regular meetings between the UK Permanent Representative to the European Communities in Brussels and his counterparts in the Six. When he saw the French Foreign Minister, Couve de Murville, in Paris on 8 April, the Foreign Secretary, Lord Home, gave the idea a fair wind. Couve's response was casually offhand. It was true, he acknowledged, that Schroeder had made some such suggestion, though he had qualified it by saying that it must not hold up the work of the Community. The French Government had not really given any serious consideration to the proposal. In any case, he assumed that the British Delegation in Brussels was in contact with the European Commission. Personally, Couve concluded, he would have no objection to some arrangement for contact being worked out. If so, it should be a two-way process.[31]

In a subsequent conversation with Couve de Murville on 9 April, Dixon explained that what was required was more than contact between Britain and the Six. What was needed was an arrangement for regular consultation so as to ensure that the policies of the Community and of HMG did not drift apart. In that case, Couve replied, it would, as he had said to Home, have to be a two-way process, by which he meant that "if the UK was consulted about the work of the Community, the Community should be able to consult HMG about the evolution of economic policies in the UK, for example on tariff questions and agriculture".[32] The Foreign Secretary reported to Cabinet later in the week that "there were indications that the French Government might not oppose arrangements which had been suggested by Dr Schroeder for permanent machinery to enable contact to be maintained between ourselves and the countries of the EEC. This machinery would supplement, and not replace, WEU".[33]

The establishment of regular contact within WEU was indeed the bigger prize as far as Britain was concerned. But the French Government continued to be elusive. By June, Dixon was reporting to London that while the French official line seemed to be changing all the time it was just then particularly deceptive. "For example, they say that they are not opposed to the constitution of the NATO Multilateral Force, though they will not of course participate; that they are in favour of a general reduction of tariffs in the Kennedy Round provided of course that there is a levelling of the American tariff wall; that they are not opposed to WEU Ministerial meetings on various conditions; that they are not opposed to contacts with Britain, only to institutionalising them . . . All these positions in fact conceal strong opposition by General de Gaulle for his own reasons to doing what any of their Allies wish to do".

De Gaulle was shortly to make an official visit to Bonn and Dixon told London that the General was concentrating all his attention on that visit with the aim of making a major effort to align German policies with his own. Dixon identified three subjects to which de Gaulle attached major importance: stiffening the Germans on the Kennedy Round, in particular bringing them into line with French policy on agriculture; the Multilateral Force (which the French wished to sabotage) and, finally, getting the Germans to drop the British, at least for the time being. "At first sight, he seems to be faced with an almost impossible task" Dixon concluded, adding: "It is not I think to be excluded that he will threaten to break up the Common Market if he does not get his way. Whether he could in fact put such a threat into effect is another question".[34]

De Gaulle, according to Britain's Ambassador in Bonn, would have an uphill task in persuading the Germans to align their policies with his, more especially so on the three issues which Dixon had identified. The French had given the Germans the impression that they had no objection to Germany joining the Multilateral Force and any change in that position would come as a real shock to the Germans, facing them with a clear choice between the United States and France on an issue where they must prefer the United States. Nor had Roberts detected any weakening in German support for the United Kingdom – indeed quite the contrary. At the moment of de Gaulle's visit, Roberts concluded, the German Government would still be under the impact of President Kennedy's recent visit. De Gaulle would therefore either have to make some very attractive offer or resort to the threat of breaking up the Common Market. "While this might frighten some Germans," Roberts advised, "I think it would be properly treated as bluff or blackmail by Erhard and others. The French would, in my view, be misjudging the present state of German opinion if they faced the Federal Republic with anything like a direct choice between France on the one hand and the United States and Germany's other allies on the other, since the result would be unlikely to favour France".[35]

Even the usually sour Adenauer seems to have caught the mood, telling his Cabinet colleagues a week later that, while he had had his differences with the British Prime Minister, this had not diminished his respect "for one of the great leaders of the West".

What had prompted this outbreak of bonhomie on Adenauer's part was not, however, a sudden urge to press the British case, but nervousness about Macmillan's domestic position as the Profumo scandal broke about him and deep concern about the growing strength of the Labour Party and of Harold Wilson.[36]

De Gaulle, on the whole an expert judge of the niceties of brinkmanship, did not provoke the kind of *partage de midi* with the Germans that Dixon had described. Without the slightest sense of embarrassment, he even claimed credit for what emerged from the Bonn meeting, telling Dixon on 15 July that "he hoped that we were content with the arrangements for quarterly meetings of the WEU on which he had agreed with the Germans during his visit to Bonn. He said that, as we knew, the Germans had been advocating rather different arrangements [the contact between Permanent Representatives]. However, during the Bonn discussions they had not pressed their point of view very hard and had readily come round to the French point of view. General de Gaulle said that he had insisted with the Germans that something must be done to meet the wishes of the British for contacts with the EEC. They all owed this to the British, to whom great respect was due. It was against this background that 'we, the French' (thumping his chest) had convinced the Germans that they should agree to the WEU arrangement' ".[37]

A series of interlocking issues continued to occupy the British Government as they wrestled with the consequences of exclusion from the European Community. The first was what kind of relationship to have with the Six. And here, no better option was in prospect than that of regular meetings of Foreign Ministers within the WEU Council. The second was the relationship with the other countries of EFTA. But the nature of that relationship was well summed up by the Swedish Minister of Commerce, Gunnar Lange, when Macmillan and Home visited Stockholm later in the summer. "Sweden", Lange said, "had never regarded EFTA as a permanent alternative to the economic organisation of the whole of Europe. Its value was to allow its members to keep closely in contact during the negotiations for a wider economic community and to confer benefits meanwhile. Britain had arranged for consultation with the EEC through WEU. This was not of course a reopening of negotiations. As Heath had said in Strasbourg, we were still virtually in two different camps. EFTA was an outward-looking trading body. For the time being, and very probably for years to come, the EEC would reflect the inward-looking views and foreign policy of the French".[38]

There was nothing in the Swedish statement with which the British Ministers could disagree. EFTA was a useful stop-gap. In economic terms it was well within the British comfort zone for cooperation without loss of sovereignty. But it lacked both economic and political weight compared with the EEC and the British Government had not gone back on the fundamental decision they had taken in 1961: there was no alignment, other than the EEC, which would allow Britain, as its position as a great power declined, to exercise influence in the world commensurate with both its economic significance and its image of itself as an important global actor in political and defence terms.

The third issue was that of Britain's bilateral relationships with France and Germany and the management of the Franco-German relationship so that it did not harm British interests. Much of this centred on defence questions. The key issue remained how far to go in terms of collaboration with the French in nuclear matters and that issue in turn went to the heart of Britain's relationships with Germany and the United States in NATO. Both Britain and France were wary of the Federal Republic of Germany and that wariness was to play a pivotal part in the distinctive ways in which, over the years, France and Britain sought to deal with Germany within the European Community. At the core of the issue was uncertainty about how far representative democracy was firmly rooted in Germany; to what extent Germany, keen to see reunification of its homeland, would allow itself to be tempted by some Russian offer which would in turn weaken the resolve of the Federal German Government to play its full part in the defence of the democratic West. Germany had nuclear ambitions: not to have its own nuclear deterrent, but at least not to be treated as an untrustworthy partner in the nuclear aspects of NATO defence.

De Gaulle was well aware that Germany was, and was likely to remain, the dominant economic power within Europe. He was determined that Germany should be bound into an inextricable political partnership with France in which France, as potentially the only European country with a genuinely independent nuclear deterrent, would be as essential to Germany's security in the future as the United States was now. The creation of a political union in Europe which Germany's leaders keenly sought, both as a badge of their own international reha-bilitation and as a means of buttressing their own national democratic institutions, offered de Gaulle an opportunity. On his part, it involved the reluctant accept-ance of an institutional structure within the EEC which was too supra-national in character for his taste. On their part, as he saw it, it involved their gradual detachment from the dominant US role in European defence.

The Elysée Treaty, signed by de Gaulle and Adenauer with much flourish only days after de Gaulle's January press conference was, so Dixon reported to Lord Home in February 1963 "part of General de Gaulle's grand design to bind Germany firmly to France". The Treaty pledged both Governments to extensive cooperation, especially in defence matters, and to prior consultation on subjects of political importance. Dixon questioned, however, how far de Gaulle was truly committed to the Treaty. De Gaulle had tried to persuade Adenauer to submit the Treaty for approval to the German people in a referendum and had been thinking of doing the same in France. But he was forced to abandon the idea because, as he saw it, Adenauer had neither the strength nor the position to follow his own example by amending the German Constitution so as to provide for direct appeal to the people on important questions of this kind. According to Dixon, de Gaulle saw this failure on Adenauer's part as a major weakness. De Gaulle had told a group of French Parliamentarians on 5 February that the absence of provision for referendums was evidence that the Germans lacked a good Constitution.[39]

De Gaulle may also have been disappointed by the public presentation of the Treaty by Adenauer when he addressed the Bundestag in Bonn on 1 March and claimed that, far from threatening NATO, the Treaty would strengthen it. Nor would it prevent the Federal Government from objecting to French policies – for example over the NATO Multilateral Nuclear Force. De Gaulle would not have been best pleased to hear Adenauer also say that the collapse of the Brussels nego-tiations with Britain had been "wholly unnecessary" and that British entry into the EEC was only a matter of time. And de Gaulle's ego would not have been flattered by Adenauer's advocacy of the Treaty as a Treaty between two peoples, "not just an agreement between two old men".[40]

If reminders of fading glory had stuck in de Gaulle's mind it would account for his remarks, two days before the first of the semi-annual Franco German summit meetings prescribed by the Elysée Treaty in July 1963, at a dinner of French Deputies and Senators. De Gaulle told them: *"Les traités, voyez-vous, sont comme les jeunes filles et comme les roses: ça dure ce que ça dure . . . Hélas, que j'en ai vu mourir de jeunes filles".*[41]

For the Germans, the alliance with France was critical. Germany was not prepared to sacrifice that relationship with her neighbour for the sake of her defence dependence on the British. At no point, apart from his rather Delphic statement in Cabinet immediately after de Gaulle's January press conference, did Macmillan consider using Britain's position as a guarantor of German security as a bargaining chip. The Germans would in any case have been safe in calculating that Britain's own security, her position as one of the four-power guarantors of Berlin, and the importance to Britain of good relations with the United States would all combine to make British blackmail improbable. But the counterpart of that calculation was the obvious truth that France was, by the evidence of two world wars, an easier country to defeat than to depend on militarily, whereas the reverse was true of Britain and, even more so, of the United States. So despite all of de Gaulle's blandishments – and bullying – there is no evidence that the Germans were ever seriously swayed by the overall deal with which de Gaulle both tempted and threatened them. They would not sacrifice their vital national interests to de Gaulle.

For the British, playing the hand in NATO so as to balance their national, NATO and European interests was something of a headache. On 22 February 1963, President Kennedy sent a message to Macmillan in which he said that he and his colleagues had "been doing a lot of hard work here in the last few weeks in an effort to sort out the problems we now have to deal with in the light of General de Gaulle's positions . . . We remain confident that wide arrangements are better than narrow ones, and we have no reason whatever to change our belief that the Atlantic connexion is indispensable on both sides of the Ocean. It seems clear to us that most of Europe shares this conviction with you and us and we are convinced that we have both time and strength with which to sustain this position". Kennedy said he would send the US Ambassador in London, David Bruce, to see Macmillan to "talk with you particularly about the developments in our thinking on the NATO nuclear force and on the particular problem of the Multilateral Force. We continue to think that it is of great importance to maintain a strong and persuasive position on these matters so that the legitimate interests of the non-nuclear members of NATO may be met . . ."[42]

Prompted by the evidence from Kennedy's message that the Americans had almost completed their review of policy, on 27 February 1963 the Foreign Office sent a telegram to the British Embassy in Washington headed *Future Policy towards Europe*. "The broad point we want to get across to the Americans", the Foreign Office argued, "is that in trying to establish close relations with the

Western European countries we are not seeking in any way to undermine NATO. Our purpose, as over the NATO Nuclear Force, is to show the Europeans that there are genuine alternatives to General de Gaulle's idea of Europe and that it is possible in other ways to achieve a more prominent role for Europe within the Atlantic Alliance. By taking the lead and appearing sometimes to act in the name of the Europeans, we believe that we shall be acting in the best interests of the United States and the Alliance and that our policies will fit with the President's grand design of an equal partnership between Europe and North America".[43]

For the British, how far the British independent nuclear deterrent, whose future had been so hard won by Macmillan at Nassau, was to be put at the disposal of NATO was a problematic question. It was also one that went to the heart of the evolution of a European defence policy which would prevent the other European members of NATO from being seduced by de Gaulle's alternative and dangerous vision.

On 25 March 1963, Home told Cabinet it would have to be decided whether or not a new generation of strategic nuclear weapons should be placed at the disposal of NATO and, if so, what system of control and command would be consistent with the British objective of preventing the proliferation of nuclear weapons while maintaining the credibility of the deterrent. It had been agreed by Macmillan and Kennedy at Nassau that there should be a shared NATO nuclear force, which both leaders saw as essential if the proliferation of national nuclear forces was to be prevented. He and Macmillan, Home explained, had interpreted the concept in terms of a multi-national force i.e. a force to which individual nations with a nuclear capability would contribute without surrendering their ultimate sovereignty over the weapons in question. The concept had been endorsed by the NATO Council, apart from the French representative. The Americans, however, had a different perspective. They were convinced that a multi-national force of the kind Home had just described would not suffice to restrain the pressure for independent national nuclear forces. They had therefore evolved the concept of a multilateral NATO nuclear force which would be genuinely international in the sense that all participating countries would subscribe manpower and other resources which could not be withdrawn, even in extreme national emergency. This alternative interpretation had, Home said, attracted a significant degree of support and the Governments of West Germany and Italy appeared to be ready to accept responsibility for the substantial subscriptions for which they would become liable. Home questioned whether the Germans, Italians and others would willingly accept "the inferior status to which their nationals in such a force would be relegated if the US Government were to retain their control over the nuclear weapons with which the force would be armed". There was an additional problem. The US Government would expect Britain to support and contribute to the force by means of warheads, specialised manpower, or even harbour and port facilities. Thus, Britain might be liable for some 5–10% of the total cost of the force which, Defence Secretary Peter Thorneycroft told Cabinet, could amount to £100 million over ten years. Nevertheless, Home concluded, it was for consideration whether Britain should accept this additional liability as "the price of preventing the proliferation of national nuclear forces and of securing for ourselves a place in a force from which we could not afford, politically, to be excluded".

Macmillan summed up that what Britain wanted was a NATO nuclear force consisting of US nuclear forces, British Polaris submarines and a NATO element which might, or might not, consist of the internationally manned force which the US Government were now seeking to create. What was clear was that the Nassau agreement did not oblige Britain to take part in a multilateral force as now envisaged by the US, although it would be wise not to discourage the United States so long as the Nassau Agreement had not actually been signed. "The basic objective of our policy", Macmillan concluded, was "to prevent the Federal Government of Germany and other NATO countries from acquiring their own nuclear forces. It was perhaps doubtful whether either the multi-national concept which we ourselves favoured, or the internationally manned force as proposed by the United States, would be ultimately effective in achieving this aim. The main hope for the future lay in an attempt to conclude an agreement with the Soviet Government for the abandonment of nuclear tests and in the wider international agreements, inhibiting the spread of nuclear weapons, which might be expected to flow from such an agreement. He was maintaining close touch with President Kennedy on these matters".[44]

Thus, on the issue of the Multinational Nuclear Force (MNF), as envisaged by the British and the Multilateral Force (MLF) envisaged by the Americans, the British Government were potentially at loggerheads with the US Government and certainly at odds with both France and Germany who, in turn, were at odds with each other. The Germans were keen on the MLF, while France would have no part of it since de Gaulle was intent on the development of France's own nuclear weapon and intensely suspicious of any Anglo-Saxon initiative. De Gaulle was obliged to tolerate German enthusiasm for the MLF but it was, to him, a symptom of a vexing lack of commitment on the part of Germany to his vision of European integration and independence.

But as the year wore on, the dynamic changed. In July, a Partial Test Ban Treaty was initialled between the nuclear powers: a final international achievement for Macmillan of which he was justifiably proud. The British and Americans were intent on using this treaty as a springboard for further agreements to prevent the proliferation of nuclear weapons. So, by July, Macmillan was able to tell Cabinet, following a visit to Britain by President Kennedy, that "so far as the proposed Multilateral Nuclear Force was concerned . . . it was satisfactory that President Kennedy had been prepared, at least for the time being, to subordinate this project to the need to secure agreement with the Soviet Union, if possible, on a treaty to ban nuclear tests and to prevent the proliferation of nuclear weapons".[45]

The idea, however, did not die and, by September, Macmillan was warning Cabinet that the further work on the MLF, which was now to take place at American instigation, was, in terms of the development of Western strategy, misconceived. The broad parity of nuclear power between NATO and the Soviet Government had greatly diminished the risk of war in Europe itself. The Soviet Government recognised this fact. On the other hand, they were beginning to appreciate the growing danger to their interests from Communist China. On this basis it could, Macmillan argued, be held that the Soviet Government might gradually become willing to work towards a greater degree of understanding with the West and for the maintenance of stability in Europe. The creation of the Multilateral Force at this stage might, therefore, jeopardise the prospects of such an understanding and, by increasing international tension, be liable to disturb the balance of nuclear power at a time when the real interests of the West required a more constructive approach to the Soviet Government and the further development of measures to follow up the initiative of the Test Ban Treaty. "Unfortunately", Macmillan concluded "these views were not shared by the Governments of France and the Federal Republic of Germany who, for different reasons, were anxious to avoid any understanding with the Soviet Government which might either inhibit the development of their own forces [France] or be held to imply an acceptance of the present political and territorial division of Europe [Germany]".[46] Thus, the dilemma for Britain as to whether or not to take part in the MLF remained and the underlying issues also persisted, as a source of potential friction between Britain and France and Britain and Germany.

A few weeks earlier, Home had had a difficult meeting on the subject with German Foreign Minister, Schroeder, leading Macmillan to send Home a handwritten note saying "I have now read the record of your talk with Schroeder on August 14th. It is a very depressing story. The Germans have no sense of guilt or shame". Home had had to tell Schroeder that "the Multilateral Force (MLF) did not have a single supporter in either House of Parliament. To begin with, people considered that NATO was already over-supplied with nuclear weapons. Then there was the question of cost . . . The Force would be beyond the means of most countries. Finally, there was a general belief that the creation of a new weapons system like the MLF would create a new source of tension between East and West for, if the vessels were stationed on the trade routes, the Russians would probably feel bound to react either with submarines or surface weapons; people saw no need to introduce a source of tension at this particular time when it looked as if there were an improvement in East-West relations."[47] But Home's argument had evidently made little impact.

Just as it had in July, the American and British approach of exploratory talks with the Russians designed to build on the Test Ban Treaty held no attraction for de Gaulle. In early September, Dixon reported to London a conversation with the French Foreign Minister in which Dixon had explained to Couve de Murville why the British thought that, on an exploratory basis, we should continue to talk to the Russians. Couve replied that there was certainly a different approach between France and some of her allies. The French view was that the status quo must be maintained. If the Western powers attempted to change it to the disadvantage of the Russians, they ran the risk of war. The Russians, for their part, wanted to exploit it to their own advantage. Their insistence on a non-aggression pact was, so Couve argued, really aimed at the neutralisation of Germany. It was for that reason that the French Government was so strongly opposed to any moves in the direction of non-aggression agreements.

"I did not", Dixon commented, "press this further, knowing that Monsieur Couve had logically no leg to stand on and that the simple fact is that he has no doubt been told by the General that no French representative is to take part in discussions consequential upon an Anglo-American agreement with the Russians (The Tests agreement) in which the French had had (through their own fault) no part".[48]

Macmillan sought from the Foreign Office an analysis of what exactly Couve had meant. "We think", the FO advised in a letter of 18 September, "that Monsieur Couve probably meant that the Soviet proposals were aimed at driving the West Germans towards neutralism, rather than aimed at the neutralisation of Germany. The French thesis is that a non-aggression pact would condone the status quo in Europe and so deepen the division of Germany. This, the French believe, would cause the West Germans to despair of achieving reunification in alliance with the West, and to turn to thoughts of neutralism and independent dealings with Russia. The French argue that this is Khrushchev's aim in pressing for a non-aggression pact".

In a handwritten note on this letter, intended for the Foreign Secretary, Macmillan wrote: "This can only mean, if it means anything, that the French believe that Germany could or should be unified by war. This, a non-aggression pact would prevent if adhered to. It would make no difference to the chances of unification by peaceful methods. This really is the whole point. If it were not for the nuclear weapons I feel sure that such a war would either have happened or be in preparation. M. Couve de Murville likes to believe that he is a logical thinker (like all Frenchmen). But his logic is wrong. Surely the real reason is that de Gaulle will only approve a détente with Russia which he initiated and directs."[49]

If there was any doubt as to whether this was de Gaulle's own view (and there is no evidence that Couve had any discretion in these matters) it was removed by a conversation between Dixon and the President a week later. It was a great mistake, according to de Gaulle, to get involved in discussions of European questions with the Russians. These were bound to centre on the German question, and any agreement about Germany would inevitably perpetuate the division of Germany. Even if the British and Americans maintained that they would not conclude any such agreement, the Federal Government feared that they would. The East German population, who hated the Russians just as much as the West Germans did, would feel the same. De Gaulle felt, therefore, that by getting involved with the Russians at this stage the British and Americans were doing themselves great harm with the Germans and upsetting them. The time to talk to the Russians was when they themselves came along with offers to talk to us.

De Gaulle feared that the result of American and British policies would be to discourage the German Government to a point where they would go neutral. They might in fact neutralise themselves. This would, in de Gaulle's view, be particularly likely if a Socialist Government came into power in Western Germany. If Germany went neutral, then France, de Gaulle predicted, would go neutral too. All this was, no doubt, some way ahead and he, General de Gaulle, would no longer be there. But there might be a Socialist Government in France. "You know what the Socialists are", warned de Gaulle, "with their wild and idealistic notions. A Guy Mollet would be quite capable of working for a neutralist France".

De Gaulle then went on to criticise the underlying political psychology of the Anglo-American approach. The British, he argued, shared in the American nuclear hegemony. He was sure that the combined power of the American and British nuclear force was superior to that of the Soviet Union and was likely to remain superior, since he believed that the Russians had reached their peak in nuclear power. The US and the UK were, de Gaulle said, making a great mistake in assuring the Russians that they would never attack them. He felt sure that no American President would in fact ever take the initiative in launching a nuclear attack. It would take a Napoleon to do that. Or a Charlemagne. Or Hitler. But, even though the Americans might never use their power, why not leave the Russians in doubt? Let them wonder whether the Americans might attack them. Then would be the moment when the Russians themselves would come along, anxious to conclude some useful arrangement with their potential adversaries. By keeping the Russians guessing in this way and leaving them alone in the meantime, we should be greatly adding to the Russians' difficulties with the satellite countries of Eastern Europe. The populations of countries like Romania and Hungary (he did not, of course, he said, mean the present Communist regimes) would become restless, and the resulting unrest would be a factor which the Soviet Union could not ignore.

Dixon, commenting to London on what de Gaulle had said, professed himself unimpressed: "His remarks left me with the impression that, if ever he had had doubts, he had now completely convinced himself of the validity of his own approach to relations between the West and Russia, at the heart of which lay the German question. Despite the virtuosity of the performance, I could not help being reminded of the eccentric philosopher in Aristophanes' play loftily treading on air and thinking about the sun. Though the General is a king as well as a philosopher, and his legs may be firmly planted on the earth in France, his head nowadays is far in the clouds of the international sky".[50]

Yet, less than a week later, the Minister of Defence, Peter Thorneycroft, was telling Cabinet that the French Government had, just the previous day, offered to cooperate with the British Government in the creation of a European nuclear force. The terms of the proposal were, according to Thorneycroft, obscure, but he believed it should be examined closely.

The Cabinet did no more than take note of what Thorneycroft had said, the discussion of the issue revealing some suspicion among other Cabinet members that "the purpose of the offer might be to attempt to delay and confuse discussion of the US proposal for the establishment of a multilateral nuclear force and perhaps to manoeuvre the United Kingdom into a position in which we could once again be represented as faced, in effect, with a choice between Europe and the US".[51]

Macmillan himself had, since de Gaulle's rejection of a post-Nassau deal with Britain and the United States back in January, continued to look for ways in which to re-engage de Gaulle on the question of nuclear collaboration, not least as a route into renewed engagement over Britain's membership of the European Community. On 19 March 1963, Macmillan's Private Secretary, de Zulueta, wrote to his Foreign Office counterpart, Oliver Wright, to ask for advice on what the potential barriers to such cooperation might be, noting Macmillan's view that "in present circumstances we should not wish to make any such arrangement with the French unless the American Administration (or at least the President) were favourable".[52]

Home replied on 27 March, advising that Britain could not share nuclear knowledge with the French without American consent and that, if the Americans wanted to release nuclear information to the French they would equally wish to do it themselves, not through the British.

Macmillan accepted this advice and told Home and Thorneycroft in a minute of 17 April: "I do not see what we should hope to get out of such an approach and I do not think it wise to appear to be running after the French when they have, after all, behaved so badly. My own feeling is that we had better continue quietly to pursue our own policies for the time being without taking too much account of French views".[53]

By mid-July, however, the British and Americans were on the verge of signing a partial nuclear test ban treaty with the Russians and the French Defence Minister, Pierre Messmer, was due to visit London, making the visit that had been postponed, at British instigation, after de Gaulle's January veto. Macmillan's Minister of Aviation, Julian Amery (who was also Macmillan's son-in-law and a fount of ideas which found, in Macmillan, a ready audience) prompted in his father-in-law the thought, based on Amery's own contacts in Paris, that now might be the moment for a renewed attempt to engage the French.

On 15 July, with Messmer due in London three days later, Macmillan minuted Home, Thorneycroft and Amery posing the question whether Thorneycroft should say something to Messmer going beyond the particular collaborative projects which the two Ministers were due to discuss. "This is particularly important", Macmillan wrote, "in view of the Moscow talks and the possibility that we and the Americans may have to speak to the French about the nuclear position if a test ban agreement, and still more a non-dissemination [i.e. non-proliferation] agreement, can be signed with the Russians". Macmillan suggested that it would be helpful if Thorneycroft were to speak to Messmer on lines which he then set out:

"We have had good discussions on certain possibilities of Anglo-French cooperation. There are, of course, certain very important matters in which cooperation is not at the moment possible. In our view, we ought if we can to re-establish the concept of economic, military and political unity in Europe. It is difficult to deal with any of these aspects in isolation; they are all part of one problem. It is difficult, for example, for us to be rivals in trade and for political influence while seeking to be partners in defence matters. This is a problem about which we should be reflecting and in which a test ban might be an element."

The immediate effect of this suggestion was to provoke the threat of resignation on the part of Edward Heath. Heath treated de Zulueta to "a rather difficult interview" on 16 July in which Heath claimed that "the mere suggestion was quite improper and unfair to him. He went so far as to indicate that he found it difficult to serve under such conditions. He said that he must see you . . . The Lord Privy Seal was really very upset both in general and particular".[54]

The nature of Heath's objection became clear from a minute sent by Home to Macmillan on the same day, also opposing Macmillan's idea. "Our political purpose", Home argued, "is to make the General drop his extreme policies and to achieve this with the assistance of our five friends in Europe. We are making quite good progress. The decision has been taken to hold quarterly meetings of the WEU and this was forced on the French by the Germans and others. We know that the Adenauer/de Gaulle meeting went badly for de Gaulle. President Kennedy too has just completed a tour of Europe in which he gained support for the Atlantic concept as opposed to the narrow European outlook of the General. If we were now, by a side door, to throw out hints that we would welcome talks on de Gaulle's chosen ground, we would be accused of bad faith by everyone and be in real danger of getting the worst of all worlds . . . Whatever we do to attract France back into the fold must be done with our allies, and in particular with the assent of the Americans. It would have to be a carefully planned political operation and even then, with the General in his present nationalistic mood, might well not succeed . . . It would certainly involve many exchanges between you and the President. I trust therefore that the Minister of Defence will agree to keep his talks with Messmer to nuts and bolts . . ."[55]

This minute, somewhat impatient in tone by Home's standards, and almost certainly drafted by Heath, reflects a dividing line between the Foreign Office and Number 10 over the years. The Foreign Office tended to want to woo the Five as a means of putting pressure on de Gaulle while No. 10, with perhaps greater realism about the nature of power, and less regard for the sensitivities of smaller European countries, sought a more direct approach to Paris to unlock the door to British EEC entry. This difference of approach was to reach its nadir in the Soames Affair of 1969.

So Macmillan's plan was abandoned, swiftly to be replaced by a new game. On 15 July, Dixon called on de Gaulle. If the past is a foreign country, then Ambassadors certainly did things differently there. Dixon was about to go on summer leave. He asked to call on de Gaulle prior to doing so and de Gaulle readily assented. No present-day Ambassador could hope to achieve such access, let alone on such a flimsy pretext.

The discussion centred on the implications of the nuclear test ban treaty, then under negotiation in Moscow. France, de Gaulle said, would have no objection to the conclusion of such an agreement, though he noted that the Russians seemed anxious to talk to the Americans and to the British, and indeed the Germans, but not to the French. He suspected that the Soviet motive in concluding such an agreement would have less to do with a desire for progress on disarmament than saving resources and gaining some advantage in respect of Berlin. If discussion turned to a non-aggression pact, then that would of course be of interest to France and she would expect to be consulted. De Gaulle added that France herself would be obliged to conduct some nuclear tests, though she was aiming for quality, not quantity. But, in saying that, de Gaulle was of course implying that France would not adhere to the new treaty.

Dixon then turned the discussion to the organisation of NATO, with which he knew de Gaulle was discontented, and to de Gaulle's reaction to US ideas for a Multilateral Force as one solution to that problem. The British Government had noted, Dixon said, that the idea seemed to have been favourably received in Germany. Britain, Dixon implied, was not against it, but by no means committed to it and certainly open to alternatives.

De Gaulle replied that he did not at all deny the "terrible dangers" in the existence of the vast American and Russian nuclear armoury. However, in his view, this would create a balance between American and Russian power and would in effect mean that neither side would be able to attack the other. Both sides had far too much by way of nuclear armaments already, which was probably why the Russians calculated that they could afford an agreement banning tests. When, said de Gaulle, one also took into account the developments both in Russia and America of rockets and satellites, it did not seem to him that there was much danger of war.

De Gaulle then turned to the heart of his argument. The Americans were using their pre-eminence in nuclear power among the Western allies to persuade the latter to rely on them for their security. This, he implied, was an abuse of American power and was why France was determined to have her own independent nuclear force. The Americans had far too much power. Europe must assert herself against it. The Americans used NATO as a platform primarily for their German policy, as well as to keep smaller countries such as Belgium and Holland under their influence on the pretext that only US armed might could protect them. France was, however, prepared to cooperate in NATO to the extent that it was useful in "the battle of Germany".

When Dixon asked if he had any ideas to remedy the situation, de Gaulle said that he had at one time proposed that France, the US and Britain should set up an organisation which would consider the various areas of the world in which military operations might be necessary and take decisions on the political and strategic questions affecting security throughout the world. However, his ideas had not been taken up and he had now renounced them. De Gaulle confirmed that he was referring to his memorandum of September 1958 but that those ideas no longer represented what he felt. So far as the multilateral force was concerned, he had found in Bonn that the Germans favoured this American idea. It would give them no real say in nuclear defence because the arrangements would be under American leadership. "But" said General de Gaulle with a sneer, "the Germans seemed content with that. He had told them that this was their affair".[56]

Commenting to London on his meeting with de Gaulle, Dixon remarked on what he saw as the President's inability to resist the temptation to display his superiority to conventional calculations. To Dixon's mind, the most striking aspect of de Gaulle's discourse was the deep animosity he displayed against the Americans. This was of course the emotional mainspring of his foreign policies but Dixon had never heard it expressed so candidly before. De Gaulle's view was that "the

Americans know, as he does, that there is not much likelihood of a major war breaking out, but that they deliberately exaggerate the danger in order to exercise their political and economic dominance over the weaklings who are foolish enough to be taken in and too feeble to stand up for themselves. In particular, he made no effort to conceal his contempt for the Germans . . . not only in the context of the multilateral force but also in the context of the negotiations about contacts between the UK and the Community".[57]

Against this background, Macmillan was not hopeful of a result when Kennedy proposed to him in the same week that, once the test ban treaty had been initialled, he and Macmillan should send messages to de Gaulle offering nuclear information in exchange for French signature of the treaty. Kennedy himself recognised the difficulty, writing to Macmillan: "I recognise that this is a large dose, but I think it important to make a forthcoming statement to General de Gaulle before the Anglo-Saxons sign a paper in Moscow and before he had his promised press conference at the end of the month."[58]

While Kennedy was primarily concerned to get French buy-in to the new treaty, Macmillan had other concerns. As in January, he was looking for a lever to insert Britain back into the wider European game. Replying to Kennedy's idea of cooperation with the French he posed the question of "what we might hope to obtain in return. For example, what do we want in NATO? What do we want in the European-Atlantic relationship? What do we want as regards European unity both political and economic? Above all, can we use this opportunity to our advantage in at least paving the way towards a new era, in which France would play a full part, both as regards relationships in the Western world and relations between East and West?"[59]

Following the conclusion of the test ban treaty, parallel messages from the two leaders were duly delivered to de Gaulle in Colombey les deux Eglises. De Gaulle's answer came four days later at a press conference on 29 July. He was dismissive of the Americans who "having lost their monopoly of nuclear weapons were now mainly interested in their own survival". It was for this reason among others that France, which was now independent, following a period of total dependence on America immediately after the war, was providing herself with nuclear weapons. He made his strongest attack to date on NATO, saying that the formula of integration was no longer valid for France. There would have to be important modifications in the manner of France's membership of the Alliance. He approved the Moscow test ban agreement but suggested it was of no real importance and made it plain that France had no intention whatever of adhering to it. Nor would he agree under any circumstances to a NATO-Warsaw Pact non-aggression pact. He implied that there was a danger of a new Yalta between the Anglo-Saxons and the Russians. France would have to be very vigilant.

In all this, Britain was lumped in to the odd disparaging remark about the Anglo-Saxons; but Europe did not escape censure either. De Gaulle came close to threatening to break up the EEC if the agricultural policy was not agreed before the end of the year, but he also suggested that, once the agricultural policy was in effect, Europe could go on to political union.

In marked contrast to his 14 January press conference, de Gaulle evinced almost no enthusiasm for Franco-German unity which, he also suggested, hinged on the outcome on the Common Agricultural Policy. The Paris Embassy saw this as confirming what they had been hearing separately: that de Gaulle felt very disillusioned with the Germans.[60]

De Gaulle's formal reply to Macmillan's offer of talks about nuclear cooperation came in a letter of 4 August. There was not a hint in the letter of congratulations on the Test Ban Treaty, which was a major negotiating achievement. De Gaulle was prepared to go no further than writing that "naturally an agreement such as that which has just been reached does not in itself cause any difficulties to the French Government, quite the contrary". As to tests, "the French Government cannot consider abandoning its efforts without achieving the object which it has set itself. You suggest that I enter into conversations with your Government and the Government of the United States in order to examine means of avoiding the need for tests without injuring the French programme. I must say that I find it hard to believe that it would be possible for a State to satisfy itself that armaments indispensable to its defence work properly without being able to verify this for itself. But equally I do not see how France could receive help from other states without accepting conditions limiting her right of using them . . ."[61]

De Gaulle replied in similar terms to Kennedy and went on to set out his objections to the idea of a non-aggression pact with the Soviet Union "and the countries which she holds under her yoke". "Apart from the fact that this kind of assimilation between the two sides could not be accepted by France, the Soviet proposal obviously tends to have the West recognise – that is to say reinforce – the situation that they have created, and which they maintain by force in Central and Eastern Europe, in particular the fiction of the 'German Democratic Republic'. There is, moreover, every reason to believe that the Soviet Government would not fail in this event to renew its demands concerning the status, in other words the fact, of Berlin. The difficulty which would result in Europe, and primarily in Germany, from the acceptance, even partial, of these claims would react too directly on the security and on the policy of France for her not to consider with great wariness anything which might eventually be negotiated in Moscow on this subject . . ."[62]

"From this message", Kennedy wrote to Macmillan, "I think it is safe to say that he not only does not want our help but is unwilling to enter a serious discussion of the problem".

Macmillan and Kennedy were not quite ready to take "no" for an answer, though the British Embassy in Paris were in no doubt that, as the Foreign Office reported to Home and Macmillan on 7 August: "There is no prospect of winning the General over because he is determined to conduct his own nuclear tests . . . Beyond this refusal lies a firm decision not to cooperate with the Americans either about the organisation of the Western Alliance or about organising a détente with the Soviet Union". The Embassy had also advised that the French Government were covering up this negativity "by a propaganda campaign suggesting that no precise proposals were made to France and that the known American requirements are patently unacceptable". The Embassy suggested that the true nature of the offer that Macmillan and Kennedy had made to de Gaulle should be leaked to the Press so that the large sections of French opinion who would not agree with de Gaulle would know the truth. The Foreign Office, however, advised against this course, on the arguable basis that since de Gaulle was in absolute command in France, public opinion was relatively unimportant; and on the very polite grounds that "to leak the text would be a breach of confidence which de Gaulle would resent and exploit". Macmillan and Home accepted this advice.[63]

On the very day that the Foreign Office were evincing such concern for de Gaulle's finer feelings, the French paper, *Telegramme Economique*, published an article which, so they informed the Paris Embassy, had been fed to them by a very high French Government source, probably Prime Minister Pompidou himself.

The article claimed that "people at the very top of the French Government find British participation in the Moscow talks to be distressing for Europe. Britain is not only betraying her past and her future but also giving her approval to a policy of the enslavement of Europe, which is more serious still when seen from France. It may be recalled that General de Gaulle is, despite appearances, favourably disposed towards England and wishes England one day to join Europe fully in order to complete the Franco-German union since, if England, France and Germany created a real union, they could immediately affirm the equality of rights of the future Europe in its relationship with the United States (which would presuppose the possibility of constructing a European nuclear deterrent). Faced with such an entente between France, Germany and England, President Kennedy would be obliged to give in and to allow a real partnership within the Atlantic Alliance. But England, instead of adopting this policy, which would be healthy for herself, for Europe and even for the United States, prefers to remain in the role of a satellite of the US, seeking to join the Common Market, not in order to construct Europe – a Europe equal in rights – but in order to prevent Europe from being born and to maintain its dependence on America. British participation in the Moscow talks reinforces this opinion since they are tending to consecrate the domination of the world by the two great powers and to make it impossible for Europe ever to become politically of age. The reason why the British act in this way is because the Government cannot risk enlightening the electorate about Britain's future without upsetting their ancient ideas and thus losing votes. It is difficult for an Englishman to resign himself to being of the same rank as other Europeans. But it is firmly believed in Paris that the English people will one day react against Britain's present policy and indeed quite soon. Meanwhile, there is no doubt that certain important people in France, including men like M. Pompidou, will work actively in order to bring England nearer to Europe when the opportunity offers. However that may be, it seems to us and to other observers that the British are far too committed to the Moscow affair for one to be able to expect a change of policy from them for a long time".[64]

If this really was de Gaulle's view, and the editor of the paper thought that it was, it is an interesting mixture of the almost paranoid (the notion of European enslavement) and the shrewd (its appreciation of the psychological resistance in Britain to becoming 'European'). It is also a mark of de Gaulle's absolute command, on which the Foreign Office had commented coincidentally on the same day, that a man of Pompidou's intelligence could apparently buy uncritically into de Gaulle's world view and that the newspaper editor, equally, could reproduce it almost as holy writ.

The Ambassador, Bob Dixon, was on leave during this time but clearly felt, on his return, that some stiffening of Home and Macmillan was necessary. He wrote to Home on 9 September setting out his view that de Gaulle was determined not to contribute in any way to détente in Europe between East and West on terms controlled by the Americans. Behind this reaction lay de Gaulle's deep-seated fear that an arrangement of this kind would inevitably lead to a condominium of the world between the two super powers. This, Dixon argued, however irrational, was de Gaulle's constant nightmare. It followed that the more de Gaulle believed that Anglo-American exchanges with the Russians were likely to be successful, the more negative his attitude would become. Dixon feared that the Test Ban Treaty, and its aftermath, might well bring about a really serious clash with the French within the Alliance.

Dixon also expected the French to do their utmost to feed German suspicions about the dangers to them of progress towards a non-aggression pact and to encourage the Germans to maintain the hard line they were taking against any such progression. Opportunities would arise when Schroeder and Adenauer made separate visits to Paris in September, in Adenauer's case on a farewell visit before retirement.

Dixon hoped that Adenauer's departure might offer a better chance of progress, though de Gaulle would try to prevent any such thing. According to Dixon, the German Ambassador in Paris, Blankenhorn, was apprehensive about the damage the French might be able to do with the new German administration.

Dixon was equally clear that de Gaulle would go ahead with his own nuclear missile programme, including testing, and would not at any price make himself dependent on the Americans: "In short, I can see nothing that we or the Americans may offer at present which could buy his signature of the Treaty". Dixon clearly regretted that Macmillan and Home had passed up the opportunity to put de Gaulle on the spot and, in so doing, to detach a section of public opinion in France from him, and came as close as any official would dare to saying that Macmillan had been wrong not to respond to Kennedy's suggestion of a further message to de Gaulle which could be made public and thus make clear where responsibility truly lay.[65]

The idea of a further message from Kennedy to Macmillan was still in play, however, when Home visited the United States at the end of September. The US Secretary of State, Dean Rusk, had been told by German Foreign Minister Schroeder that the Franco-German Treaty, signed with such flourish less than nine months' earlier, was becoming more and more a dead letter. Schroeder's recent talks with Couve de Murville had made no progress on agriculture, on NATO military problems or on East-West relations. Rusk commented that the French had never produced any constructive proposals in any of the fields in which they criticised their allies, and mused that de Gaulle might be unable to hold on to power. Home, more realistically, questioned whether the way existed by which de Gaulle would be forced out.[66] A few days later, at the White House, Kennedy told Home that he was considering one final approach to de Gaulle, with whom he "was almost totally disillusioned".[67]

But, before the autumn leaves had "turned and fallen Kennedy was snatched by an assassin's bullet from the service of his own country and the whole world";[68] and Macmillan himself had been forced by ill health into resignation and retirement. One of Lord Home's first tasks, as Macmillan's successor, was to attend Kennedy's state funeral.

Macmillan was caricatured, especially in the final months of his time as Prime Minister, as a throw-back to the Edwardian age. There was some of that about him, and he enjoyed his family connection through his wife with the Devonshire family, while remaining proud of his Scottish crofting ancestry as well. As MP for Stockton in the 1930s, his one nation Tory-ism was radical, almost Socialist. He was ahead of many in his Party, let alone the country, in seeing what today seems the inevitable direction of events. His 'Winds of Change' speech in South Africa in 1960 is remembered, not just because of the brilliant sound bite, but because it was game changing. Although it was not designed to drive South Africa out of the Commonwealth it did confront her, and the world, with a new and inescapable reality about what Macmillan called the facts of political life.

Macmillan was under no illusion about the world in which he lived and which, by his approach to Europe, he hoped to change. Discussing trade issues with European Commission President, Walter Hallstein, in May 1963, Macmillan said: "Many in the West were now beginning to feel that the Old World was wasting its time and behaving like the Roman Empire in its declining period. By the year 2000 the European populations, even with the United States, would be dwarfed by the enormous masses of Asians and Africans. Someone looking at the Earth from the Moon would regard it as very odd that half the world were trying to reduce their agricultural production while the other half were starving".[69]

Shortly before that, in a private letter to a recent visitor to New Zealand, Macmillan wrote: "I thought New Zealand a delightful place – to retire to. If I were a young man making my life I would prefer Australia. It is full of vigour and an attractive kind of crudity, all the more attractive because so much of our old world civilisation seems so lacking in purpose . . ."[70]

Macmillan's closeness to Kennedy can be seen in similar light. Macmillan recalled, following his last ever meeting with Kennedy at Macmillan's home, Birch Grove, at the end of June 1963, how Kennedy combined "that indescribable look of a boy on holiday with the dignity of a President and Commander-in-Chief".[71] For his part, Macmillan combined the appearance of tradition with, in many respects, the mind of a radical. It was his vision, known in Whitehall as *The Grand Design*, which had set out the challenge on Europe at the end of 1960. And no British Government (as opposed to Parties in Opposition) since then has thought fit to change his fundamental idea, though it remains publicly controversial to this day: the idea that Britain did not simply have vital interests *in* Europe but was an integral part *of* Europe.

On his visit to Rome in January 1963, accompanied by Edward Heath, Macmillan had asked to be taken on a tour of Rome by car. "What is that?" asked Macmillan. "That is the Coliseum, Prime Minister", replied the Ambassador. "I shall never see that again", came Macmillan's reply. And, in Heath's own account, each monument in turn provoked a similar response.[72] Yet Macmillan lived for nearly a quarter of a century after his retirement and was present in Brussels when Heath signed the Treaty of Accession ten years later.

Lord Home (Sir Alec Douglas-Home as he became on renouncing his peerage and winning a seat in the House of Commons) was in office as Prime Minister for just short of a year. As with all Governments condemned by declining popularity to allow the Parliament to run its full five-year course, the national focus was already on the political battle ahead. Some of the Cabinet discussions during the period reflect the atmosphere of phoney war. Cabinet, for example, intervened to save the old street lighting in Westminster, but decided to knock down the Foreign Office, hardly issues of political, as opposed to cultural, significance. Europe was scarcely discussed, save in the context of the Kennedy Round of trade negotiations.

It was by a pure accident of timing that Sir Con O'Neill, the leader of Britain's official Delegation to the European Communities, addressed a Despatch to the Foreign Secretary on 19 October, the day after Macmillan's resignation. The Despatch was addressed to Lord Home but was received by his successor in King Charles Street, Rab Butler.

O'Neill's purpose was to inject some hard-headed rigour into British European policy-making. The most likely opportunity for Britain to negotiate for EEC entry once again would, O'Neill argued, occur if there was a change in French policy. In the meantime, the Government should first of all acknowledge that "our heroic negotiations from October 1961 to January 1963 never had any real chance of success". They could hardly have taken place in less favourable circumstances. Britain's economic position at the time was weak, whereas the Community was still in the flush of economic strength and success. The political cohesion of the Community was strong . . . The British had been obliged, as a condition of negotiating at all, to declare a general acceptance of the Treaty of Rome and of the work done under it. This necessity played into the hands of the French and enabled them, by and large, to organise the Commission and to support them against any attempts the British made to enlarge or modify the terms or spirit of the negotiations. And it was not only the French but other Member States who had "felt in the circumstances of the time some desire to exact from us the full penalty of our long European hesitation, and took pleasure at times in obliging us to swallow the mixture whole".

O'Neill went on to argue that the circumstances of de Gaulle's veto had compelled the British to present the results thus far achieved as more satisfactory than perhaps they were. The Government should now not be inhibited from making valid criticisms of the direction of EEC policy, be it on trade policy, agriculture or relations with the developing world both to embolden some of the existing members who felt critical but were not brave enough to say so, and to demonstrate to the United States that Britain favoured an EEC whose policies were not inimical to their interests.

At the same time, the Government must not allow their friends in Europe to think that Britain had lost her European spirit and motivation. O'Neill was clearly concerned at the potential impact of a speech by Heath on 3 October in which the Lord Privy Seal, anxious to placate sceptics within his own Party, had said: "There have been no discussions with the Community or individually with its Member States about the resumption of negotiations. I see no prospect of negotiations being resumed for some time; certainly not before a General Election in this country . . . and as far as we here in Britain are concerned, in my own view it would be necessary for any future Parliament to give authority for any negotiations of this kind to be resumed".

O'Neill recommended that if Britain wanted to have a stronger negotiating position if accession once again became a realistic prospect, she should be, on the one hand, robust in her policy criticisms of the EEC and, on the other, more ready to express her belief in the need for greater political unity in a future Europe of which Britain would be members, as well as in a more responsible and effective European Parliament.

Finally, O'Neill argued, economic strength at home was the key to all else: "Our comparative economic weakness at the time of our negotiations with the Community was a great misfortune. It combined with other circumstances to make us seem a supplicant. If we are in a position of better economic health, future negotiations with the Community, should they ever recur, could run a smoother course."[73]

Douglas-Home, whose attention was drawn to this Despatch, not by the Foreign Secretary but by another Cabinet member, told his Private Secretary that he would ask Butler to report on it and give his views at a future Cabinet. But there is no evidence that that discussion ever took place.

The attention of the British Government was focussed on the first of the meetings of Foreign Ministers of WEU countries, to which the French had reluctantly agreed, and which took place at the end of October. Butler was able to report to Cabinet that the meeting had been useful, not least because the French Government had finally committed themselves to tariff reductions in the forthcoming Kennedy Round discussions, and all WEU members apart from France had supported the policy of continuing negotiations with the Soviet Union in an attempt to improve East-West relations.[74]

Butler was keen to promote good Anglo-French bilateral relations (a clear demonstration of the validity de Gaulle's wartime negotiating approach of making no concessions and counting on the fact that intransigence on his part would provoke a rapprochement initiated by the injured party). On 23 November, Dixon told de Gaulle that he could assure him that the British Government welcomed the renewed cordiality of Anglo–French relations. De Gaulle replied that he wanted especially good relations with Great Britain. He knew that the breakdown of the Common Market negotiations had been a blow and he was sorry about it. But the more he thought about it the more he was sure that the negotiations could not have been brought to a successful conclusion. There had been too many difficulties still outstanding. However, this did not mean that Britain could not renew the attempt. It was for Britain to bide her time and decide when the moment was ripe. Dixon replied that the question of renewed negotiations for British membership of the EEC was not an issue at the present time.[75]

On that same occasion, de Gaulle also spoke of Kennedy's assassination just three days earlier. De Gaulle described Kennedy as "youthful, vigorous and imaginative" and, in what was for de Gaulle the ultimate compliment "a man who thought like a European".[76]

By the end of 1963, differences between France and Germany over the handling of agriculture in the Kennedy Round led Butler to warn Douglas-Home that, at his January press conference, de Gaulle might say or do something which would lead to the break-up of the European Community. He could, Butler speculated, either walk out himself or make the position of the other five members so difficult that they would have to walk out themselves. Alternatively, de Gaulle might keep the Community in being but get his way enough to leave it in a smouldering crisis.

In the event of the break-up of the Community, Butler argued, Britain should be ready to "take an initiative to reshape Europe nearer our own ideas" which would mean moving "rapidly and decisively to prevent anyone else stepping in with less attractive proposals". Britain's proposals might include an industrial free trade area open to all European countries, with a framework for political cooperation between those countries wishing to take part. The Foreign Office were hard at work on ideas, in consultation with other Whitehall Departments. Douglas-Home expressed himself as being in complete agreement with Butler's approach and ideas, surely an example of wishful thinking, aggravated by the approach of a painful anniversary in the shape of the previous January's press conference.[77]

If France and Germany could not see eye to eye over the conduct of the Kennedy Round, Germany was not going to be easily cowed by de Gaulle. The new German Chancellor, Ludwig Erhard, who had taken over from Adenauer in October 1963, visited London in January 1964.

In a private discussion with Douglas-Home in Downing Street on 15 January, Erhard set out a coherent vision of the balance between economic integration and political direction within the European Community. To Erhard, it was becoming obvious that, if integration within the European Community took place on the economic level only, a situation would arise in which members of the Common Market would be surrendering their national sovereignty in the economic field, not to a political body but to an administrative apparatus (the European Commission). From January 1966, by procedures agreed under the Treaty of Rome, decisions by qualified majority vote would become more usual. Erhard argued that if decisions were taken by majority vote against the interest of one of the Member States, and in the absence of a proper political authority, there would be violent national reactions. So, a political authority was necessary and Britain should be part of that. Erhard was not offering a ready-made solution but wanted to stimulate a debate. Within the Six there was a majority in favour of partnership with Britain, but General de Gaulle was against it. Erhard had explained his position to de Gaulle, namely that he wanted a strong Europe which would carry weight in East-West problems. He did *not* want a third force but a Europe which would be at one end of the Atlantic partnership. If this was on a basis of the Six alone, Erhard had explained to de Gaulle, this would only lead to confusion, and the Franco-German Treaty would become, not a pole of attraction, but a pole of repulsion.

De Gaulle had responded that the first task was to make the Six strong; there would be time for further adherences later on. But Erhard believed the Common Market was already strong, so that de Gaulle's old argument no longer held good.

Erhard told the Prime Minister that, under Adenauer, de Gaulle had been able to expect that Germany would follow France in everything they did. But de Gaulle would have to learn that under a Germany led by Erhard, and with Schroeder as Foreign Minister, all that would change. They were both in favour of Franco-German friendship, but they intended to safeguard the independence of German views and convictions. De Gaulle was sceptical about the value of NATO, wishing to make Europe dependent for its defence on the French *force de frappe*. But that would of course be tantamount to French hegemony in Europe and the Federal Republic, for its part, wanted none of that. If the MLF came into being that would spell the end of French ambitions, which was doubtless why the General was so bitterly against it. But for Erhard, the MLF was tied up with the whole question of European political union and the development of the Atlantic community. For all these reasons, Erhard supported British membership of the EEC.

Douglas-Home's reply was revealingly cautious. Britain, he said, wanted to see EFTA in closer working relationship with the Common Market. But the collapse of the Brussels talks had done great political damage in Britain. Given the feelings on the subject in the House of Commons he had to say, albeit with reluctance, that it would be best if there was some delay before there was a further initiative about the development of European institutions. If Britain once again suffered a rebuff, and there was a fight over her body, that would be very damaging indeed in the run-up to a General Election.

In a subsequent wider discussion, which covered some of the same ground, Erhard said that Germany would never accept the exclusion of Great Britain from the EEC or from a European political community. While Erhard wanted to promote a politically governed European Community, he did not think anything would happen in a hurry. He recognised that, on the substance of the matter, French and British views on the delegation of sovereignty were not far apart.[78]

Similar assurances about German intentions were given a few weeks later when State Secretary Rolf Lahr from the German Foreign Ministry, told Sir Frank Roberts that there was extremely little on which the Five could now agree with de Gaulle, French attitudes, for example, ruling out any progress towards a more representative European Parliament, which was an important part of Erhard's concept for ensuring democratic control of European bureaucracy. Any British Government, after the General Election, which wished to resume discussion on a closer British relationship to continental Europe, would find five out of the six Member States determined to work with the UK. The German position in favour of British membership was firm and clear, which had not been the case in the last months of Dr Adenauer's chancellorship. The Five, individually and collectively, had demonstrated that they were not prepared to accept de Gaulle's concept of a European Community based upon French hegemony, with France using the Community as a platform for purely French policies. If France wished to go her own way, no one could stop her. But she could not speak for the other five or drag them with her. Lahr's conclusion which, said Roberts, struck him as rather optimistic and which he himself admitted might prove so, was that, if Britain and the Five were determined to resume negotiations after the British elections on the basis of full British participation in Europe, then even de Gaulle would be realistic enough to face the facts.[79]

Had Lahr seen the letter sent by Dixon to Harold Caccia, the Permanent Under-Secretary at the Foreign Office on 6 February, he would certainly not have felt so optimistic. Dixon had had a long talk with former French Prime Minister, Paul Reynaud. Reynaud recalled that at the time of the French decision to prevent British entry into the Common Market in January 1963, he had written a letter to General de Gaulle expressing his keen regret at this action and reminding him amongst other things that this was a scurvy trick to play on the British who 'twice saved France'. By return of post he received a letter in General de Gaulle's hand-writing. Or, rather, he received an envelope which proved to contain nothing. It was addressed to M. Reynaud at his house in Paris and underneath de Gaulle had written: "If away, forward to Waterloo, Belgium".[80]

The dilemma for Britain, which lay behind Erhard's reassurances to Douglas-Home was, as Dixon put it in a Despatch to Butler later in the year, that "having first kicked us off while we were boarding the European bus, the General has slowed it down to walking pace. As soon as he is gone, it is likely to pick up speed again. The problem for us is whether, during this transition, we shall be in a position to mount the vehicle. If we can do so, there would be a fair prospect of our being able both to regulate its speed and steer it in the direction we desire – towards Atlantic partnership. In the meantime we must do all we can to maintain the hopes and expectations of the Five that the UK will eventually join the Community and strive to participate in the discussion amongst the Six aiming at political union. But our ability to influence developments amongst the Six is likely to be limited unless a new factor can be introduced to outweigh the pressures for creating a political Europe without Britain. British membership of a Multilateral Force could well provide such a catalyst and, to my mind, should be a very powerful consideration in its favour . . . We might join the United States but could not hope to lead it. We could hope to lead Europe and must try to join it."

In putting this Despatch to the Prime Minister, his Foreign Office Private Secretary, Oliver Wright, minuted: "Sir P. Dixon's Despatch goes right to the heart of our dilemma about Britain's place in the world", to which the Prime Minister responded: "Yes. When the General goes we should try and lead Europe. I don't see how I can do anything until after October."

When the General Election took place, on 15 October, it was Labour who won, albeit by the narrowest of margins and the dilemma of Britain's place in the world was Harold Wilson's to ponder.

It is hard now to remember the sense of anger and humiliation in Britain that followed de Gaulle's veto. Faced with that degree of public disillusionment, it would have been hard for Macmillan or Douglas-Home, at what was by then the fag end of the Parliament, to do more than sustain the aim of accession as a goal of policy for the longer term. Faced with de Gaulle's second veto in 1967, Wilson said straightaway that the British Government would not take 'no' for an answer. But Wilson had won an almost landslide election victory the year before and de Gaulle, who had lost a battle for the soul of the Community at around the same time, was both older and less popular at home than in 1963/64.

Macmillan played the one card he had – nuclear cooperation – with determination, and at times with a greater hope than realism. His domestic position, and the scepticism of public opinion, did not allow him to plant a British flag alongside those of the Five by proclaiming a forward-looking British vision of European political unity. And, as we have seen, the British Government, while clear that they wanted to lead in Europe, had not worked out what they meant by that ambition. In many respects, the country which came closest to sharing British reticence about the institutions of European integration was France but there was no hope of making common cause there. The improvement in bilateral relations sought by Rab Butler as Foreign Secretary was largely defined by common projects such as the Channel Tunnel and Concorde, which the British could ill afford but dare not cancel, partly because they knew that, in de Gaulle's propaganda, they were symbols of Britain's commitment to Europe.

On the issue of Europe, Macmillan had been out ahead of many in his own Party. The Conservative Party, following their election defeat, would soon have a new leader, Edward Heath, of equal European commitment. But what of Britain's new Prime Minister, her youngest thus far in the twentieth century?

When, in 1966, Harold Wilson interviewed for the job of his Foreign Office Private Secretary Michael Palliser, son in law of one of the EEC's founding statesmen, Paul-Henri Spaak, Palliser thought it only fair to warn his prospective boss that he was a convinced and enthusiastic pro-European. "In that case", Wilson replied, "you and I will have no trouble getting on".[81] In October 1964, few would have thought such a reply by the new Prime Minister probable.

* * * *

3 The Labour Government: a toe in the water: 1964–1966

In the summer of 1964 Sir Con O'Neill sent a Despatch from the UK Delegation to the European Communities. The Despatch was addressed to the Conservative Foreign Secretary, Rab Butler, but O'Neill declared his purpose as being to assemble and assess the facts and arguments which the *next* British Government would need in order to determine its policy on Europe. And it was clear from the tenor of the Despatch that, like most of his compatriots, it was not a Conservative, but a Labour, Government that O'Neill had primarily in mind.

A year of direct dealing with the European Community had removed such illusions as O'Neill had held on arrival and he cleverly positioned himself tactically as the slightly sceptical and unbiased observer who could, from that standpoint, capture the attention of a strategically sceptical incoming Labour Government.

"At one extreme", argued O'Neill, it [the EC] can be regarded as the most hopeful experiment in international relations embarked on for generations. . .For those who see it so, it is an enterprise we should be proud to join if we can for both idealistic and interested reasons, paying almost any price entry might involve. At the other extreme it can be regarded as constituting potentially, and already to some extent in fact, the kind of European structure against which we have repeatedly throughout our history gone to war. For those who take this view, the Community has almost succeeded, by stealth, in achieving what Napoleon and Hitler failed to achieve by force: a Europe united, without Britain and therefore against her".

The problem, according to O'Neill, was that there was some truth in both extremes and in all possible views in between. And he thought that, in assessing the true nature of the European Community, the British tended to underestimate the extent to which the EC had always been concerned with politics and power. The Commission President, the German Walter Hallstein, had always declared that he was in politics, not business: "He may well believe that power grows out of regulations on the reference price of Tilsit cheese or the price of grain a hen needs to lay one egg. I think it does".

"Almost all our troubles in the last 300 years (except for the last 20) have come from France and Germany," wrote O'Neill. "What could have suited our aims, conscious or subconscious, better than the situation in 1945 when both were powerless and a new, strong, friendly English-speaking Power, on whom we were prepared to rely and with whom we had and believed we could maintain a specially intimate relationship, was ready to assume their protection and ours?"

It was, O'Neill argued, scarcely surprising that many Europeans doubted the wholeheartedness of the British commitment to an independent Europe and, while for Britain the question of her relationship with the Community was crucial, for the 'Europeans', on the whole, it was not. The tide of indignation following Britain's exclusion by de Gaulle had ebbed away almost out of sight. The British problem was on the whole forgotten or, if raised, used as a stick to beat another partner rather than to help the United Kingdom.

Interest would revive after the General Election. But there would be intense relief in some quarters, and not just in France, if Britain's attitude then allowed the Community to forget about her once again. Nowhere was this attitude more firmly held than within the European Commission. For them, life was complicated enough at Six. They did not want a Seventh to come along and ruin it.

O'Neill went on to advise that, although the pace of development of the Community might slow down, it would be most unwise for a British Government to base its policy on any assumption other than that, over the next five or ten years, the Community would remain in being and probably both prosper and continue to act as a powerful magnet. Experience, including Britain's own, had shown that the Community could not be changed from the outside. A large, if unavowable, part of the British objective in negotiating for membership in 1961 was precisely that of changing the character of the Community. Britain's entry would have changed it. That was why she had been kept out.

O'Neill was convinced that, on balance, Britain would gain economically by entering the EEC but he based his argument on the belief that, if Britain did not join, "our decline towards isolation and comparative insignificance, which it seems to me has already begun, is likely to continue, and cannot be arrested". There would be three great centres of effective power for the rest of the century: the United States, the Soviet Union and Western Europe. All states outside those groupings would become increasingly peripheral and irrelevant. Perhaps, O'Neill teased, Britain should accept this. Nations had no right to eternal influence and Britain herself had been pretty peripheral in European and world affairs in all but the last 250 years. She could decline again but, in that event, the decline would probably be rapid.

O'Neill rehearsed the arguments for and against association, as opposed to full membership, but thought the former unattainable and the latter not within realistic reach for the next three or four years. This would coincide with the end of the Community's own transition period. Majority voting would begin in 1966 and the Common Market would be achieved in 1970. The Kennedy Round of trade negotiations would have been completed. The CAP would have proved either workable or unworkable. In three years' time de Gaulle might be dead – or at least gone.

The United Kingdom had, argued O'Neill, no early results to gain by continuing to be positive about her European ambitions. But a negative signal from Britain would change the present situation profoundly: it would close doors, cancel commitments, relieve consciences, comfort enemies and bitterly discourage friends. 'Yes', or even 'Yes, but' was infinitely preferable to 'No'. Equally, the British Government should not try to hold back the political development of the Community because Britain was not inside it. He doubted if the results of any such development within the EC would have a very supra-national character, so Britain would lose little by the Six going ahead and a lot by trying to restrain them.[1]

Thoughts of Europe had not been high on the agendas of either the Conservative or Labour Parties in the General Election campaign. "Entry into the EEC is not open to us in existing circumstances", said the Conservative Manifesto, "and no question of fresh negotiations can arise at present. We shall work, with our EFTA partners, through the Council of Europe, and through the Western European Union, for the closest possible relations with the Six consistent with our Commonwealth ties". In other words, given the French veto and the unpopularity of the idea of membership, a Conservative Government would keep its European ambitions, at least publicly, on the back burner.

The advantage for the Labour Party was that there were thirteen years of "Tory misrule" to attack and their manifesto took a Cooks' tour of Conservative failures starting in 1951, passing through Suez, and ending with the Common Market. While Labour, under Attlee, had begun transforming a white colonial empire into a multi-racial Commonwealth, the Tories had broken faith both with the countries seeking independence and with the old colonial settlers. This failure of faith and enthusiasm had reached its lowest point "when Harold Macmillan and Alec Douglas-Home both declared there was no future for Britain outside the Common Market and expressed themselves ready to accept terms of entry to the Common Market that would have excluded our Commonwealth partners, broken our special trade links with them, and forced us to treat them as third class nations. Though we shall seek to achieve closer links with our European neighbours, the Labour Party is convinced that the first responsibility of a British Government is still to the Commonwealth".

While Europe was not high on the to-do list of the new Government, European issues quickly wrote themselves onto the agenda. The French Government, never ones to neglect an opportunity to sour the atmosphere, set the ball rolling within a fortnight of the General Election when Foreign Minister Couve de Murville told the National Assembly that "assessments made of the aptitude or will of Great Britain truly to participate in European construction have evolved in a more and more pessimistic direction".[2]

Britain alone was not Couve's target. French newspapers had been reporting that France might leave both NATO and the EEC and the French media, largely in the pocket of the Government, would not have so reported unless officially steered to do so. The British Embassy described Couve's speech as one of his toughest to date although two days later they were reporting that "the tone of French Government statements is mounting. We understand this is because General de Gaulle had expressed dissatisfaction at the Council of Ministers yesterday with the muted tone of the Foreign Minister's remarks in the National Assembly".[3]

The new Foreign Secretary, Patrick Gordon-Walker, reported these developments to Cabinet on 5 November 1964, recommending that Britain's most effective counteraction would lie in seeking to strengthen EFTA, particularly since morale in the Association was low.[4]

This was something of an understatement. One of the first acts of the Labour Government had been to impose a surcharge on imports which, in the case of EFTA, was contrary to the rules of the organisation and done with no prior consultation. With an EFTA Ministerial meeting due later that day, Jim Callaghan, the Chancellor of the Exchequer, reported to Cabinet that the Ministerial Sub-Committee on External Economic Policy had considered a number of proposals designed to calm things down, including a possible commitment to relax the surcharges by the middle of 1965. This had, however, been ruled out since the Government could not afford to commit themselves so far ahead. There was, predictably, much more British enthusiasm for a Danish proposal to set up within EFTA a Standing Committee to review economic developments.

With lofty disregard for the illegality of their own action, and the anger and dismay of Britain's partners, Callaghan advised that "our partners should be reminded that, although they would suffer temporary embarrassment as a result of import surcharges, they had derived great benefit by way of increased trade with this country since the Stockholm Convention was signed and that it was in their interests to await the opportunity for a further expansion of trade which would arise as soon as the surcharges were removed".[5]

When Cabinet met the following week, the reality of EFTA anger had become apparent. Gordon-Walker said that the EFTA meeting, which he and the President of the Board of Trade, Douglas Jay, had attended "had provided convincing evidence of the shock which our unilateral decision to introduce import surcharges had inflicted on both official opinion and public sentiment in the other member countries of the Association". The Foreign Secretary had only narrowly avoided Britain's EFTA partners formally invoking Article 31 of the EFTA treaty which would have enabled them to take retaliatory action against Britain. This action which, he feared, could have led to the disintegration of EFTA, would have been gravely damaging to Britain's interest, not just in respect of EFTA but the EEC as well. To head off a crisis, the Foreign Secretary had been obliged to undertake to begin to reduce or abolish the import surcharges in a matter of months which meant that some action would have to be at least imminent by the time of the next meeting which Gordon-Walker, with much difficulty, had managed to have postponed until February 1965. Failing action on Britain's part by then, "the Association might well be finally disrupted". Jay endorsed this assessment and Wilson summed up that the Cabinet would have to keep the situation under close review.[6]

This experience, so early in the life of the new Government whose members, apart from Wilson himself, had little previous Ministerial experience, was chastening. Wilson's Foreign Office Private Secretary, Oliver Wright, believed it influenced Wilson's gradual subsequent move towards EEC membership.[7]

In its Election Manifesto, the Labour Party had avoided committing itself to unilateral nuclear disarmament, but it had undertaken to "submit the whole area of weapons supply to a searching re-examination" and to propose the renegotiation of the Nassau Agreement. "We are against the development of national nuclear deterrents and oppose the current American proposal for a new mixed-manned nuclear surface fleet (MLF). We ... will put forward constructive proposals for integrating all NATO's nuclear weapons under effective political control so that all the partners in the alliance have a proper share in their deployment and control".

By 26 November, a group of Ministers under Wilson's chairmanship had completed their initial review and Wilson reported to Cabinet on that day that the UK could no longer sustain its three major defence roles: a commitment to the defence of Europe under NATO; the role of a nuclear power, which the Government had inherited from the previous Administration; and the maintenance of a world-wide military presence based on her overseas commitments. Wilson wanted to retain a significant British role in the Mediterranean and east of Suez, not least as a means of maintaining the Commonwealth connection. As regards Britain's nuclear weapons, he noted that construction of some of the Polaris submarines was now so far advanced as to make it unrealistic to cancel the orders, but his group of Ministers had agreed to propose an Atlantic Nuclear Force (ANF) to which Britain would commit, irrevocably, her V-bomber force assigned to Europe, and her Polaris submarines. The control of such an ANF would raise difficult problems but it must work in close cooperation with the command system of NATO and both the US and UK governments should possess a veto, not only on its use, but also on any change in the method of control. It seemed unlikely that the French Government would participate in the project at the outset; but the way should be left open to them to join later.

Gordon-Walker observed that one of the main political objectives of the plan was to prevent a nuclear alliance between the United States and West Germany. This reflected a preoccupation in the Labour Party that there should be no German finger on the nuclear trigger as well as a broader fear, shared by the United States, that if Britain were not fully integrated into Europe and if France were increasingly detached, a potentially risky German-American alliance would be the only remaining option.

Cabinet endorsed the proposal for an ANF as a basis for opening negotiations in Washington. There was some concern that the commitment of British forces to an ANF would mean that the French Government would enjoy independent control over their own *force de frappe*, while Britain would have surrendered such independent control in relation to our own deterrent. Others, however, thought that, by the time it became operational, the *force de frappe* was unlikely to be credible as a deterrent.[8]

Wilson worked hard to sell the idea. When the Belgian Deputy Prime Minister and Foreign Minister, Paul-Henri Spaak, visited London early in December, he warned the Prime Minister that the UK's willingness to renounce any entitlement to withdraw nuclear forces from the Alliance, even in the event of a supreme national emergency, was a concept that France could never accept; and that the only result of going ahead on that basis would be to force France into isolation.

That would, in turn, confront Germany with the stark issue of choosing between Paris and Washington, a choice with an unpredictable outcome. He urged Wilson not to renounce the "supreme national interest" clause of the Nassau Agreement. Just as de Gaulle had used the original Nassau Agreement to stop Britain joining the Common Market, so all the signs indicated that he was prepared to do the same thing to Germany with the Multilateral Force.[9]

The Foreign Secretary told Cabinet the following day that Spaak had left him and Wilson "in no doubt about the extent to which, in his opinion, the other European members of the Alliance were becoming subservient to the personal dominance of General de Gaulle".[10] The Foreign Secretary did not point out, however, that Spaak's own attitude had been a clear illustration of just that tendency.

A week later, Wilson was at pains to explain the new policy to German Foreign Minister, Gerhard Schroeder and to explain away his own public remarks on the subject which had been, he claimed, incorrectly reported. He (Wilson) was not irrevocably opposed to a mixed-manned surface fleet. What he irrevocably opposed was any diminution of the US veto on the Western deterrent. Schroeder said that any talk of 'a German finger on the trigger' touched an exposed nerve in Germany. Germany had renounced the production of nuclear weapons but public opinion did not like to see Germany portrayed as an inferior within the Alliance. Wilson replied that he proposed no fingers on the trigger at all. What Britain was proposing amounted to a credible deterrent with all participating countries being equal in status. *The Times* the previous day had described this policy as the biggest act of self-abnegation in British history.[11]

On the same day, Wilson was able to report to Cabinet that, during his own visit to Washington, just concluded, he had found that the American Government were no longer as unanimously in favour of a mixed manned surface fleet as they had been and that it might be possible for decisions on this whole issue to be postponed until the late autumn of 1965.[12]

A week later, the Foreign Secretary reported to Cabinet that he had had a discussion with Couve de Murville in which he had made "considerable efforts" to improve relations with the French Government and to promote a more sympathetic understanding on their part of the objectives behind the ANF project. But he had clearly got nowhere. Couve had admitted that the French Government had no solution of their own to the problem of containing German nuclear aspirations within the Alliance. He had, instead, indicated that, unless NATO could be reorganised in a way that was more in line with French views, the French Government would be compelled to dissociate themselves progressively from the work of the Organisation.[13]

In the meantime, the German Government was proving, from a British standpoint, less stalwart than Erhard had indicated in his talk with Douglas-Home only a few months earlier. In January 1965, Roberts reported from Bonn that Adenauer's influence was more in the ascendant than at any time since he had retired as Chancellor over a year earlier. Roberts noted that German moods were notoriously mercurial and much of the current talk within the CDU/CSU appeared to the outside observer so irrational as to make both diagnosis and recommendations for a cure difficult. But the net effect was a recurrence of old German suspicions about the UK, and particularly about the new Labour Government, loss of faith in the US Government and a tendency to turn to de Gaulle and France as rocks of stability in a sea of troubles.[14]

A week later, Erhard paid an official visit to Paris, where he and de Gaulle declared themselves ready to deepen Franco-German cooperation. They also announced that the time had come for a fresh examination, with the other members of the European Community, of the problems of political cooperation i.e. foreign policy coordination. In other words, the very discussion which the British Government wanted to be part of was to take place without them and with no reference to their interests and possible contribution.

On 23 January, Erhard told Roberts proudly that one of his main objectives in going to Paris had been to persuade de Gaulle to agree to further moves towards European Political Union. The initiative would be confined to the Six although he, Erhard, continued to favour a wider Europe. When Roberts reminded Erhard of Britain's repeated desire to take part in such talks from the outset, Erhard expressed doubt as to whether the UK, under its present Government, was really interested in membership of the Common Market. Roberts retorted that the reason for that was that the door to entry remained barred and Britain could not risk a second rebuff. Accession was, in any case, not the issue. Talks on political unity were a different matter and the British Government believed it should be involved in them from the start. If the Six felt that they had to start without the United Kingdom then at least proper arrangements should be made for consultation, and not merely for keeping the British Government informed.

Erhard justified his approach on the ground that, ever since the War, European unity had become an important goal for the Germans as an alternative to German nationalism, and a failure to make progress could be dangerous. He added, unconvincingly, that since de Gaulle was already thinking in terms of bringing even the Communist East European countries into his concept of Europe, he could hardly keep Britain and the Scandinavian countries out for much longer.

Roberts eventually got Erhard to say that he still wanted to use the WEU and bilateral channels for consultation with Britain. But Roberts commented to London that Erhard would have to be kept up to the mark. Fortunately, he added, Foreign Minister Schroeder had been present at the conversation.[15]

Before the month was out, the death and funeral of Winston Churchill gave Wilson the opportunity for his first meeting with de Gaulle. De Gaulle began the conversation with a characteristically self-serving version of British EEC aspirations: "On the one hand Britain said that they wished to join the Common Market; on the other hand it became evident that, not only for domestic political reasons but also because of Commonwealth ties, membership of the Common Market simply was not possible for Britain. Then the negotiations had broken down. France had gained the impression that the United Kingdom tended to bear a grudge against France for stating what was obvious".

Wilson, in his reply, implicitly accepted de Gaulle's version of events. The policy of the Labour Government was different from that of the Conservatives. At the time of the negotiations, the Labour Party in Opposition had stressed many of the things which de Gaulle had stressed, particularly the problem of the Commonwealth. He himself could not see how the links with the Commonwealth could be reconciled with the spirit of the Common Market. The Labour Party had also strongly opposed the supra-national element in the Treaty of Rome and were certainly not prepared to abandon to a supra-national authority control over foreign policy and defence. The Labour Party's view was much closer to the President's own concept of *l'Europe des Patries*. He found the President's view entirely realistic. Britain was dependent for 40% of her trade in foodstuffs on Commonwealth countries. It was an illusion to imagine that the irreconcilable could be glossed over. That did not mean it was not possible to develop close and harmonious relations between Britain and France but it was likely that these relations would have to be in fields other than the economic.

De Gaulle replied that Wilson had been wrong to talk about integration for that was not exactly what the Common Market was aiming for. There was no supreme authority which took decisions. Each of the six Governments was master in its own house. There was, it was true, a Commission in Brussels, staffed by experts of all sorts. They were clever, and even useful, men; but they were certainly not a Government. There was also a political side to the Common Market. He did not imagine that any British Government could consent to a supra-national authority. France would never accept such an authority and therefore he approved of the British Government's position.

In reply, Wilson said that the Fouchet Plan (a French plan for the inter-governmental development of political cooperation in Europe) might have gone a bit far but it was on the right lines. He had heard it described as '*l'Europe à l'Anglaise*'; that was to say it typified the English concept of functional cooperation, not supra-national authority. Wilson thought that Britain and France had a common interest in defence matters but they also had to recognise that Britain and France had a different conception of the American connection. And there, since this was a working funeral and each of the two leaders had others to see, this first conversation ended.[16]

That Wilson was not just being tactically ingratiating in what he said to de Gaulle is borne out by his conversation later on the same day with the Danish Prime Minister, Jens Otto Krag. Wilson told Krag that there was no prospect of a new negotiation for British adherence to the EEC. So long as adherence to the Community would deny Britain the right to buy cheap food from the Commonwealth, there was no basis for a negotiation. On top of this underlying fact was the uncompromising attitude of de Gaulle himself. Perhaps, in the long run, a closer relationship with the Six would develop in the context of a defence arrangement, but the British Government were not seeking a European solution but an Atlantic solution. Britain expected to have, moreover, a continuing and probably increasing role east of Suez and her trade links with the Commonwealth continued.[17]

On the following day, Wilson met Erhard. The tenor of the conversation suggests that neither man was thinking then of British membership of the EEC. Erhard remarked that, valuable though the Community of the Six was, it was not, in itself Europe. He hoped it would be possible for the United Kingdom to "come closer" to the Community and create a larger Europe. Erhard had the impression, from his meeting with de Gaulle earlier in the month, that de Gaulle seemed less intent on isolation and more open to German ideas.

Wilson agreed that the question was how to develop closer relations between Britain and the EEC. On the economic side, progress in the Kennedy Round was one way. Membership of the Common Market was not in the realm of practical politics at present. This did not mean that the Government were neutral on the issue. On the contrary, the Labour Party regarded the formation of the Community as one of the historic landmarks of our time and Franco-German reconciliation as a great step forward. On the political side, the British Government wanted to be closely associated with any development for political union. On the economic side, they wanted to take all steps to increase trade between Britain and the EEC. In defence matters, they wished for an even closer Atlantic partnership, particularly now that NATO seemed to be coming under strain.[18]

Thus, the European policy of the new Government was, while not ruling out EEC membership in time, to take no active steps to promote it; to see the political development as something distinct from the Treaty of Rome and essentially inter-governmental, and therefore to seek participation in it; and to use British membership of EFTA as the principal vehicle for promoting economic cooperation in Europe.

The first indication of new thinking came in a minute from Michael Stewart to Wilson in February 1965. Patrick Gordon-Walker, the Foreign Secretary, had lost his seat of Smethwick in controversial circumstances at the General Election. He was nonetheless appointed as Foreign Secretary on the basis that he would immediately stand for re-election. The sitting MP in the safe Labour seat of Leyton was persuaded to stand down so that a by-election could be held. Not surprisingly, there was a local backlash by the electorate, who felt they were being used as pawns in a bigger political game. Gordon-Walker was again defeated and resigned from the Government in January 1965. Michael Stewart, until then Secretary of State for Education, was appointed to succeed him.

Stewart had held a meeting at the Foreign Office with British Ambassadors from EFTA countries as well as the Heads of British Delegations to EFTA, the EEC, OECD, NATO and the Council of Europe. The meeting, Stewart told Wilson, had discussed European policy on the basis of a Foreign Office paper "which pointed to our increasing and dangerous isolation from Europe." The meeting had agreed that "in present circumstances we must hold onto those organisations which we had, with EFTA as our principal instrument of economic policy in Europe, the OECD as the economic arm of the Atlantic Alliance and NATO (with, if possible, an Atlantic Nuclear Force within it) as the military arm".

Although the conclusions of the meeting had been cautious, the paper that had been discussed, and which Stewart sent to Wilson, pulled no punches. Current developments in different fields were sharply increasing Britain's isolation from Europe. The European Community had passed the point of no return. It was bound to become more cohesive, dominating and assertive. Conversations about

Political Union would be taking place among the Six and Britain would not be allowed to take part. In those conversations, defence issues would be discussed, in the absence of both Britain and the United States. EFTA (quite apart from the problems caused by Britain's 15% imports surcharge) could not develop beyond what it was: an industrial free trade area. French obstruction in NATO and WEU prevented Britain from using either organisation for effective consultation or integration. All these factors, coupled with the political weakness inevitably resulting from her present balance of payments difficulties, "are resulting in what may be described as a creeping isolation of Britain from Europe".[19]

A few days later Wilson was asked in the House of Commons about Britain's future relationship with the EEC. He replied that the circumstances which had led to the breakdown of the Brussels negotiations had not changed but that "if a favourable opportunity were to arise for negotiating entry into the EEC, we would be prepared to negotiate if, and only if, the necessary conditions relating to essential Britain and Commonwealth interests could be fulfilled. At the same time we are most anxious to do anything in our power to avoid the further economic division of Europe and to do all we can to build a bridge between EFTA and the EEC. . ." When one of Wilson's Private Secretaries submitted the Hansard entry to the Prime Minister, reminding him that, when the reply had first been drafted Wilson had indicated that the Hansard extract should be drawn to the attention of all Government Ministers, Wilson wrote, in the green ink which he favoured, "It wasn't very good, so I'd say no".[20]

With time to reflect on his discussion with de Gaulle, Wilson was not under any illusion about French attitudes. In mid-February, he told the US Ambassador in London, David Bruce, that while de Gaulle was putting on a show of great friendliness towards Britain, on all major issues, such as nuclear matters and the organisation of NATO, the British Government were in total disagreement with the French. It was nonetheless his wish to get bilateral relations with France onto a normal working basis and to make progress on a narrow, functional basis.[21]

This was not made easy when, within days, one of the French representatives at an EEC meeting in Brussels spoke out against Britain's export rebate policy and tried (unsuccessfully) to persuade other EEC members to take the matter up in GATT. On seeing the report of the meeting, Wilson wrote in some exasperation: "Getting a bit tired of this. If EEC are going to raise export rebates in GATT, how long, O Lord, how long before some publicly spirited citizen is going to raise EEC agricultural policy, which is totally opposed to the spirit, and almost certainly the letter, of GATT".[22]

Wilson was to pay official visits to Bonn and Paris in March and April. In late February, Cabinet decided to reduce the imports surcharge, which had caused so much ill feeling in EFTA, from 15% to 10% from 27 April, but not to promise future reductions.[23] But if the Government had done the minimum necessary to repair relations with its EFTA partners, its wider European prospects remained unpromising. At the beginning of March, Roberts warned that, while the German Government still wanted a wider Europe with Britain as part of it, the objective of getting political cooperation started was important enough to the Germans to warrant going ahead without us.[24]

The Foreign Office shared this view, advising in their brief for the visit that "as it now seems likely that political talks among the Six will begin without us, it might be better not to say specifically that we want to take part in talks from the beginning. But we should leave the Germans in no doubt that we think it unrealistic to discuss defence problems among the Six without American and British participation, and unwise to discuss European political cooperation without Britain".[25]

Roberts also advised that in Germany political union was widely seen as emanating, and not separate, from European economic unity. This integration of two aspects of European unity, which the British had tended to see as separate, was a cause of concern to the Foreign Secretary.

Michael Stewart was not an instinctive European as George Brown was but nor would he have been a pushover for the pro-European ideas of Foreign Office officials. For a start, Labour had returned to power after thirteen years of Conservative Government suspicious that the Civil Service was imbued with Conservative ideology, so the natural tendency of incoming Ministers was to aim off for anything that looked like Tory business as usual. In addition, Stewart, though mild-mannered and unforceful, had been a leading player in the Fabian Society, the think tank of the Labour in Party in all but name. So it is reasonable to suppose that the minute he sent to the Prime Minister on 3 March, just days before the two of them were due to visit Bonn, was the result of genuine reflection on his part.

"I am concerned", Stewart wrote, "that the EEC is becoming a power unit of the kind that EFTA can never become. Our present attitude and policies are not enough to prevent General de Gaulle achieving his objective of making this unit into a closed shop. If this happens, we face the following risks: the United States will be forced to make deals with the Six, bypassing Britain, as they now look like doing over the Kennedy Round. The Commonwealth will fix up their own arrangements with the Six, as Nigeria is now trying to do, in which case the EEC will inherit our place in a large part of Africa. This is a process which could spread to other areas. The continuance of an integrated Atlantic policy in defence will become increasingly difficult".

Stewart argued that there could be no question of renewing Britain's application to join the Common Market as things stood. But one day the Government might wish to do so and it was in its interests to keep the option open. Stewart was worried that the Government were not doing enough to encourage Britain's friends among the Six. This could be done, he argued, largely through the presentation of the Government's policies as a coherent and positive whole; and by giving them as European a slant as possible, short of suggesting that membership of the EEC was a real practical issue. It served little purpose, he contended, to reiterate our inability to join the Common Market now. We should, instead, make it clear that, provided our essential (but unspecified) interests were safeguarded, we should ultimately want to join a wider European market. The Government should also make clear that membership of the Commonwealth, and Britain's relationship with the United States, were not incompatible with membership of "the right sort of Europe".

Stewart concluded by attaching to his memo some fairly anodyne ideas for closer cooperation, adding that "our ultimate vision of Europe should of course include the East European countries too. But we should not over-emphasise this when it antagonises those Atlanticist Europeans on whose support we rely to defeat General de Gaulle's purposes".[26]

Wilson commented, again in green ink, that he agreed with a lot of what Stewart had written but his worry related to what 'the right sort of Europe' was. "Unless it is genuinely outward looking and not autarkic", he wrote, "it must be inimical to Atlantic, and more particularly Commonwealth, links. The real test is agricultural policy, which in its present form is autarkic and would deal a death blow to Commonwealth trade".

Wilson's comment was scribbled on the back of another document which he read alongside Stewart's minute: a memorandum from the Ministry of Agriculture on the effect that membership of the EEC would have on British agriculture, now that the arrangements for the EEC's Common Agricultural Policy (CAP) were coming into force. The Cabinet Secretary had submitted this note to the Prime Minister under cover of a flesh-creeping memo of his own: "So violent would be the change in prices of food in this country if we joined that complete reshaping of agricultural production would take place, with cereals and butter receiving much the greatest boost. In a market as sensitive as that of cereals the slightest disturbance to world demand might bring about large and possibly catastrophic changes to prices. Thus there is a danger that Commonwealth producers would suffer double loss . . . Calculations made in the Treasury at the time of the negotiations suggested that the addition to the import bill for foodstuffs might have been of the order of £60 – £100 million a year".[27]

Stewart, the bit between his teeth, responded to both Wilson's and Burke Trend's comments in a further minute when he and Wilson had returned from Bonn. He acknowledged that the continuing sharp increase in European agricultural production was a major problem – one of technological advance as well as of price. The high Community grain prices would, however, inevitably create surpluses and the EEC's agricultural policy would sooner or later have to be drastically revised on the basis of much lower prices. But that was a problem which existed independently of Britain's relations with Europe and one whose solution depended on devising some equitable means of dealing with agricultural surpluses on an international basis. So it would be wrong to suppose that the present agricultural policy of the Community was immutable. Nor were Britain's Commonwealth interests either homogeneous or static.

Stewart then turned to what he meant by "the right sort of Europe". "I have in mind", he said "factors going rather beyond the trade field. My main worry is that the Community may, if we are excluded from it, develop in course of time into a 'Gaullist' bloc, set upon achieving its self-appointed and self-centred policies, and hostile to our whole concept of European development in an Atlantic framework. The real test therefore of 'the right sort of Europe' is whether it is a Europe which is prepared to accept Britain as a full and equal member and to make proper provision for the other members of EFTA".[28]

Stewart would have been reinforced in his concern by the fact that the visit he and Wilson had made to Bonn and Berlin from 6 – 9 February had been only, as Wilson told Cabinet "reasonably successful", a view borne out by German Press comment as reported by the Embassy in Bonn, where most newspapers agreed that Anglo-German relations were now warmer and that a number of misunderstandings and points of friction had been removed but that equally there was no evidence of any real progress on the questions of nuclear defence or Britain's relationship to Europe".[29] Roberts' own comment to London was that "no progress in developing closer links with Europe was to be expected and none was made" but he did observe that the Prime Minister's reminder to Chancellor Erhard of Britain's desire to take part in political talks with the Six, and Stewart's own remarks to the same effect at a subsequent WEU meeting in Rome, had at least led to renewed German declarations of intent to keep Britain informed of the discussions among the Six, even if they did not go so far as to promise to try to have Britain included.[30]

Wilson and Stewart had sought to make a favourable impression on the German Government and on German public opinion by visiting Berlin en route to Bonn and in this they had succeeded. In his talks with Wilson, Erhard was fairly forthcoming about his desire to achieve functional unity within Europe, including Britain. Wilson's response was less than the Foreign Secretary might have hoped for after his earlier plea for a change in presentation, at least. Wilson's response to Erhard's overture was to say that he must make clear that Britain could not agree to supra-national solutions in defence or politics, though Britain could take part in the forthcoming political talks. In other words, Britain wanted to take part but on a clearly delimited basis. Surely, Erhard retorted, the Prime Minister could at least go as far as General de Gaulle over supra-nationality. The Prime Minister agreed that, as he had told de Gaulle, the latter's Europe was an English Europe without the English. The new British Government had gone much further than the General had ever done in its willingness to abandon nuclear sovereignty within NATO. But he admitted, this was a commitment within and to NATO, and not to a European grouping. When Erhard commented that Britain's willingness to surrender sovereignty clearly did not apply to the economic field, Wilson replied that he had to look at each case on its merits. The Treaty of Rome had not been the real difficulty for the Labour Party but, rather, their insistence that trade with the Commonwealth must not be hampered. That problem had not been solved and had now become more difficult because of the new EEC arrangements for agriculture. Britain imported wheat at £20 a ton, whereas the EEC price was now £36. To accept the Common Market price would kill Britain's Commonwealth trade, increase the cost of living and add to Britain's balance of payments burdens.

Despite the slightly scratchy tone of this conversation, agreement was reached during the talks, and in the communiqué, on the importance of strengthening the links between EFTA and the EEC, and Wilson, in his report to Cabinet, noted that "the Federal authorities had been not unsympathetic to our suggestion that, despite the absence of any prospect that the UK could accede to the EEC in the near future, discussions should now be undertaken about the means by which closer functional links between the Community and EFTA might be created. It would be desirable therefore to give further consideration to the basis on which we might recommend to our associates in EFTA that such discussions should be set in train". Cabinet agreed that such "a fresh initiative in establishing closer functional cooperation with the EEC" was indeed desirable. And Michael Stewart reported that WEU members, "with the exception of the representative of the French Government, who had adopted an uncooperative attitude throughout", also supported such an initiative.[31]

Within a week, however, Stewart was pointing out to the Prime Minister the limitations of any approach by EFTA to the EEC. Association with the EEC under the Treaty of Rome "would probably require acceptance of most of the obligations of membership without a corresponding degree of control. We should appear as second class citizens and the effect could even be to frustrate, rather than promote, the achievement of the type of European policies we want". Stewart thought that, short of formal association, there might theoretically be a closer relationship between EFTA and the EEC. But the obvious development – complete removal of the tariff barrier – would raise the problems of the 1958 negotiations for a free trade area and it was scarcely conceivable that these could now be overcome on a basis which would be beneficial to British interests.[32]

Stewart was saying that the most desirable form of relationship between the two organisations was one all too similar to the ill-fated Maudling plan, often criticised by de Gaulle as a wrecking tactic by the British. Stewart was too tactful to remind Wilson that in his meeting with de Gaulle in London less than two months earlier, Wilson had told de Gaulle that "he had criticised the Maudling initiative at the time on the grounds that it was based on a total misunderstanding of what the European powers were trying to achieve; it had failed to appreciate that Europe was uniting economically for non-economic motives."[33]

Stewart's advice reflected the views of the new British Ambassador in Paris, Sir Patrick Reilly. Wilson was due to visit Paris at the beginning of April and Reilly advised that it would be unwise for the Prime Minister to refer to the possibility of some association for Britain with the EEC. If the Prime Minister were to raise the possibility now, the French would, Reilly feared, seize on it as evidence that the British had finally abandoned hopes of full membership and were no longer pressing to participate in any political development among the Six.[34]

Reilly offered even bleaker advice a fortnight later as he analysed the prospects for the visit. "The principal French objective", he wrote, "is to show to the world in general, and to the French people in particular, that Britain's exclusion is now accepted by the British as a permanent feature of the landscape . . . The General will therefore gain significant advantage from the mere fact that a British Prime Minister has visited France again after the unhappy encounter which Mr Macmillan had with him at Rambouillet . . . Provided that this visit can be said to have passed off in a friendly manner, French propaganda will be able to present it as effectively putting an end to the period of coolness in Franco-British relations . . . Nothing does the General's image more good than to be able to show that his toughness pays and that he actually gets what he wants for France without losing her friends in the process . . . There is a third objective in the General's dealings with the British which I fear is never very far from his mind. This is to use any opportunity which offers to drive wedges between ourselves and our two principal allies – the United States and Germany. Moreover, the French are no longer among those close friends to whom we can speak with confidence that what is said will not be exploited in repetition to others for whom it is not intended".[35]

A meeting between Reilly and de Gaulle a week later found the President "friendly and relaxed" though his "little speech about his respect and liking for the British people" (an aspect of de Gaulle's view of the world which permeates his memoirs) could not be taken as having any policy significance. Rather, de Gaulle was benignly patronising. The British people were, he said, "at a difficult point in their history and undecided which way to turn. It was neither their fault nor anyone else's, but until they had made their choice there was nothing to be done." This was classic de Gaulle: Britain's exclusion from the EEC was not due to his opposition but to the fact that the British had not yet decided to accept to be Europeans on his terms.

Reilly's advice to London had implied that the very act of the Prime Minister going to France would be interpreted as a success for French policy but since de Gaulle was a Head of State protocol dictated that, if there was to be any meeting at all, Wilson would have to go to Paris. It had, in any event, been the policy of the Conservative Government, who had every reason to feel resentful towards de Gaulle, to heal the breach and Wilson could hardly neglect Britain's closest neighbour, collaborator in various bilateral projects and, above all, the key to whatever relationship Britain was to have with her potential continental partners.

The meeting between the two was friendly. Macmillan had commented, after de Gaulle's visit to his home at Birch Grove in 1961 that, while de Gaulle "has extraordinary dignity and charm, 'unbends' delightfully, is nice to servants and children and so forth, he does not apparently listen to argument".[36] It was that same de Gaulle who was on display on 3 April 1965. He treated Wilson to an expansive view of Europe. When, in 1958, he had "taken over the direction of French affairs he had found a treaty for the organisation of the Common Market. Some aspects of the Treaty had been satisfactory, particularly those which encouraged freer trade between the Six countries. Other aspects were not satisfactory, such as the tendency to assume that decisions in the economic and political field might in time be taken, with the support of Governments it was true, but by organisations of experts who were not Governments themselves: by the so-called executive at Brussels. Moreover, there was provision for a legislature, consisting of elected members from the various countries, who were supposed to control the executive by a sort of Parliament. This was nothing but fiction. Decisions affecting the lives of people could only be taken by responsible Governments. De Gaulle rejected any sort of supra-national institutions. There existed an Economic Community . . . They had tackled the terrible problem of agriculture. What they had in fact done was to construct a free trade area between themselves and to arrange for the Six to eat what they themselves produced. But there was no progress, and there could be no question of any progress, towards an abdication from national responsibilities. In the political field he had made modest proposals for the Six to cooperate in political matters. For a start, there might be regular meetings between Governments. The trouble was that the good people of Bonn and Rome and of Brussels and The Hague did not want any discussions on a confederal basis. If there were to be discussions on that basis, they invoked Britain; but Britain was not there. The fact was that all these so-called Europeans could not bring themselves to propose and apply a European policy. In political matters they were bound by American decisions. It was the Americans who defended them. Whenever the Americans wanted to do something in Europe, these Europeans were forced to yield and be happy. This was a wrong and thoroughly bad policy".

As regards Eastern Europe, de Gaulle continued, "which meant in reality the Soviet Union, both the internal life of Russia and Russian relations with the outside world were evolving in a more liberal direction. The West too had changed. The difference in system between East and West was now diminishing. Of course, there was the biggest problem of all, the German problem. In the East they did not accept that Germany could ever be reunited. The West subscribed to the idea of German unity. There was in fact a fundamental difference between East and West on this question. One day, the question of Germany, its unity, its frontiers, its armaments would have to be solved within a European context. He did not exclude the United States from these arrangements; but the solution of the German problem could not be an exclusive American-Soviet arrangement. We had already paid a high price for Yalta."

Talk of Russia gave Wilson an opening, for this was a subject on which he knew a great deal having, as he told de Gaulle, visited Russia twelve times since the War. Wilson thought the essence of the present relationship between the Soviet Union and the West was one of fluidity. There were new men with new ideas and the feelings on both sides were less tense. Since the Cuban confrontation, no country would lightly embark on limited war. Paradoxically, there was greater relaxation under the shadow of nuclear terror. Each time he had visited the Soviet Union he noticed a growing pragmatic approach to certain problems. An exception was the problem of Germany. Britain started in her dealings with the Soviet Union from a position four-square within the Western Alliance. The German problem was central to Russian thinking. Throughout their history the Russians had been obsessed by Germany. Russia had lost twenty million dead in two World Wars. France had as much reason to be concerned by the German problem but France's reaction had been to cooperate with Germany and to sign the Franco-German Treaty. The Russians, however, were still fearful. They feared the possibility of a national German nuclear capability; they feared the possibility of a Franco-German nuclear collaboration; they feared the ANF and the MLF. It was impossible to exaggerate Russian feelings on this score. Britain would be firm in Berlin but Khrushchev had made it very clear that the present division of Germany suited Russia very well. The reunification of Germany would be a long process. Nevertheless, he looked forward to the time when it would be necessary to have neither NATO nor the Warsaw Pact.

Wilson then turned to the Common Market, whose establishment the new British Government welcomed. The issue now was whether, and on what terms, the United Kingdom could join the Common Market. The terms which had previously been under negotiation would virtually have meant, Wilson contended, the disappearance of primary commodities from the Commonwealth. Britain would, however, always be prepared to talk about joining on terms which would reconcile her national and Commonwealth interests. Taking a realistic view, it could not be said that that situation obtained today. Britain would like to take a pragmatic view and see what could be done to prevent divisions between the Six and the Seven. As for European political union, Britain would like to take part in political talks. She did not imagine that in the foreseeable future supra-national relationships would develop within the Six. Nor would Britain herself view with any sympathy supra-national institutions which meant that British foreign or defence policy was determined by majority voting. Like France, for reasons of history and geography and national character, Britain had a window on the world and her interests in world affairs went wider than the continent of Europe. Britain would be alarmed by developments in Europe leading to a majority voting system and the British Government were concerned by these developments whether Britain was inside or out.

Characteristically, de Gaulle did not respond directly to the issue of British membership of the EEC, or even to that of relations between the EEC and EFTA. He merely remarked that "there need be no fundamental conflict of interest between Britain and France. It was for this reason that he agreed that Britain and France should get together in practical matters rather than dwelling on past historical heritages or on such organisations as NATO which were becoming fictions".[37]

In his memoir of his first Government, Wilson makes no comment on the substance of his talks with de Gaulle, though in his letter of thanks to de Gaulle he commented that he had been "much encouraged, since my return to London, to find virtually unanimous public support, in Parliament and in the country, for this resumption of normal, friendly, neighbourly relations with France".[38]

Wilson's aim in this first substantive meeting with de Gaulle was limited: to establish a relationship. He would naturally have been wary. Despite his criticisms of Macmillan, Wilson had a shrewd appreciation of Macmillan's strengths and would have known that Macmillan's failure with de Gaulle was sign enough of how formidable an opponent de Gaulle could be. More importantly, Wilson's own thinking was starting to evolve. There is a slight, but not insignificant, shift between what Wilson said to de Gaulle in January and what he said to him in April. In January, Wilson had said that he did not see how Britain's links with the Commonwealth could be reconciled with the spirit of the Common Market. In April, he said that Britain would always be ready to talk about how that reconciliation might be achieved, even though that situation did not apply at that moment. De Gaulle cannot fail to have picked up on Wilson's statement that "the issue now was whether, and on what terms, the United Kingdom could join the Common Market".

Wilson's policy was twofold: to seek to establish a relationship between EFTA and the EEC and to continue to express keen interest in taking part in talks about political union. On 27 April, Wilson told Cabinet that during an informal meeting of leaders of Socialist Parties at Chequers the previous weekend he had made it clear that there was no question of Britain seeking to join the EEC at the present time, if only because there appeared to be no prospect of obtaining satisfaction on the various conditions Britain had always attached to her accession. On the other hand, he had emphasised the increasing need to establish closer links between EFTA and the Community. There had been general agreement that the possibilities should be explored at the next EFTA Ministerial level, which might be held at Head of Government level. A meeting of this kind, Wilson advised, should help both to avert the growing threat to the cohesion of EFTA itself and to strengthen the connections between the EEC and EFTA, even though little progress could be expected in this respect until after the forthcoming elections in Germany. Cabinet endorsed the approach and agreed to consider at a future meeting what the substance of British proposals to strengthen EEC/ EFTA links might be.[39]

On the following day, Wilson was in Rome for talks with Italian Prime Minister Aldo Moro. According to the record of the meeting, taken by a young First Secretary in the British Embassy in Rome named Douglas Hurd, Moro was clear about Italian ambitions for the gradual development of a supra-national authority in Europe, while recognising that it was not possible in the immediate future. Wilson said that there was equally no immediate prospect of Britain making another application for membership: the necessary unanimity among the Six was not present. But Wilson did set out what for him was a new exposition of the issue. He alluded to the fact that, during the Macmillan negotiations, the position of the Labour Party had been set out by its then leader, Hugh Gaitskell in the form of five conditions. These five conditions had been: safeguards for the trade and other interests of the Commonwealth; safeguards for EFTA; safeguards for British agriculture; freedom to pursue Britain's own foreign policy; and the right for Britain to plan her own economy. Now, Wilson told Moro, times and conditions had changed. Some problems now seemed less difficult than they had a few years ago. It was not the Treaty of Rome as such which posed major problems for Britain. The insuperable difficulty at present was the agricultural policy of the Six which was based on the idea of autarky (clearly a favourite Wilson term in this context) and of resisting agricultural imports from outside countries. If Britain joined the EEC she would have to accept its price levels and this would greatly increase her food bill.

Against this background, Britain was aiming at bilateral agreements of a functional kind with her European neighbours, the major issue being that of relations between the EEC and EFTA. A relatively modest proposal might be for an exchange of Ambassadors between the two groupings. A more ambitious idea was that of lowering tariffs between them.

In response, Moro was sympathetic, while also pointing out that the CAP might be adapted as a result of the Kennedy Round.[40]

That achieving closer EEC/EFTA relations would be an uphill task was soon illustrated by a meeting early in May of Jean Monnet's Action Committee for the United States of Europe. Monnet, as the inspiration behind the European Community, and its principal designer, had long been a champion of British membership and, for that and other reasons, had fallen out with de Gaulle. Given Monnet's far reaching ambitions for the Community it was hardly surprising that his Action Committee should, at their meeting, call for a new treaty which would apply the institutional system of the Common Market to the conduct of foreign policy and defence. The Foreign Office view of this, set out in guidance to its European missions, was a classic expression of opposition wrapped up in politeness: "Our view remains that, while a European point of view may emerge on defence, it does not follow that this should be given separate institutional expression . . . The defence of Europe can only be assured through an integrated Atlantic defence system." In one form or another, that view was to remain a constant of British policy from then on.

But what irked the Foreign Office was that the Action Committee "still tend to treat the Six as Europe. We should have liked to see them acknowledge the need for the EEC to adopt policies which will facilitate the creation of a wider European unity and, in the meantime, reduce the effect of the existing division of Europe. EFTA countries are mentioned (as a unit not as individuals) only once and in the same breath as Japan and countries with which the EEC should examine 'questions affecting these countries' interests'. The Declaration makes no mention of the need, to which we attach great importance, to secure closer relations between the EEC and EFTA".[41]

Despite the inward focus of the EEC, Wilson was sufficiently encouraged by his talks with Erhard and Moro to put flesh on the bones of his ideas for closer EEC/EFTA cooperation. On 10 May, he approved for circulation to Cabinet a memorandum in his name on links between the two organisations. Although approved by Wilson the document was clearly not written by him since there was quite a wide gap between the document and what Wilson said, on the same day, to Danish Foreign Minister, Per Haekkerup, at a meeting in Downing Street. Wilson put forward an ascending order of priorities for cooperation: an exchange of Ambassadors between the two communities; a joint consultative committee at Ministerial level; active cooperation in the Kennedy Round perhaps leading to a reduction of tariffs on commodities of specific interest to European trade along with a most favoured nation clause for the rest of the world. He also suggested a variant of the Muenchmeyer Plan. Muenchmeyer was a German industrialist who had proposed that the EEC might, as a single economic unit, join EFTA, or some wider grouping, while maintaining its own integrated union among its own members. This appealed to Wilson, not least because it was close to an idea he had put forward from the Opposition front bench in 1962, namely for a free trade area consisting of eight members: seven EFTA countries, together with the Six, who would join as a single unit.[42] In speaking to Haekkerup, Wilson acknowledged that it would not be reasonable to expect the EEC simply to join EFTA but he thought it might be possible for both EFTA and the EEC to join a larger organisation.

Wilson's final idea was that of 'Five Years After', namely the idea that five years after both EFTA and the EEC had reduced their own tariffs to nil, they should reduce tariffs between them to nil also.

These ideas did not take account of the reality, which was that the EEC was an organisation on the rise, while EFTA was starting to look somewhat ramshackle, not least as a result of the action taken by the British Government on tariffs. The memorandum for Cabinet, in Wilson's name but drafted within the Cabinet Office, showed greater realism. The paper recognised from its outset that the attraction of the Common Market was weakening Britain's own spheres of influence. Thus Austria, Nigeria and East Africa were already in negotiation with the EEC for association with it and others would be tempted to follow. "We must", the memorandum argued, "maintain the aim and hope of establishing closer political and economic unity in Europe in some form in which the United Kingdom can play a full and integral part. We cannot . . . expect the Six to abandon the Community arrangements. Thus the ultimate solution seems only feasible in terms [of] the inclusion of the UK and other EFTA countries in a Community based on the Treaty of Rome but developing and adopting policies acceptable to us . . . Because of the General's veto on us . . . the problem is one of keeping up hope and direction at a time when it is not possible to take major initiatives to merge the two groups."

The paper concluded: "In the light of these considerations I feel that our objectives at the Vienna Meeting should be to restore the cohesion of EFTA, so far as we can do so without detriment to our longer-term prospect for entry into the EEC. . ." In other words, in the paper in his name, as opposed to the ideas Wilson was himself articulating, EFTA and the EEC did not appear as organisations of equal standing. Rather, managing EFTA was a necessary step on the road to eventual membership of the EEC by Britain and such other EFTA countries who, as individual nations, chose to join her.[43]

Wilson's paper and more detailed papers from the Foreign Secretary were discussed in Cabinet on 13 May. Wilson spoke of preventing a loss of confidence or cohesion within EFTA and of bringing EFTA and the EEC closer together. Stewart went further. There could be no question, he admitted, of renewing the application to join the Common Market in present circumstances. But the Government might wish to do so at some point in the future and it was in their interest to keep the options open. They should make it clear that, "provided that our essential interests were safeguarded, we should ultimately wish to join a wider European market, together with any other members of EFTA who wished to accompany us". Few listening can have been in any doubt that the "wider European market" in question was the Common Market and not some new hybrid composed of EFTA and the EEC together.

At the same meeting, Cabinet also agreed in principle to move to adopting the metric system, another clear signal that Britain was moving towards the Continent and away from the Commonwealth.[44]

Immediately after Cabinet, Foreign Office missions in EFTA countries were instructed to deliver a message from the Prime Minister which raised the possibility that EFTA should propose the establishment of a standing joint consultative committee of EEC and EFTA Ministers, supported by a subordinate committee of senior officials. The terms of reference might be questions of general economic and commercial policy.[45]

Within days, the Swedish and Danish Ambassadors in London were calling on Wilson, on instructions from their Governments, to warn him that they believed the Six would oppose the idea and that if it were put forward, it would receive an instant rebuff, which would be bad for EFTA and bad for Europe. Wilson replied that EFTA leaders could not go to the planned meeting in Vienna and come back leaving the world with the impression that nothing had happened. If one did nothing for fear of a rebuff, then one would be condemned to do nothing all the time. However, ever realistic, Wilson suggested that it might, after all, be better to remit the idea to the Permanent Council of EFTA in Geneva so that they could report back on it to the next Ministerial Meeting.[46]

Wilson was moving cautiously, partly because his own thinking had not advanced as far as that of George Brown and Michael Stewart, and partly because it fell to him to manage the evolution of thought within the Cabinet and the Labour Party more widely. He was not therefore best pleased to read an article in *The Guardian*, on the eve of the Vienna EFTA summit, by the paper's Political Editor, Peter Jenkins. The Prime Minister's Principal Private Secretary, Derek Mitchell, noted that George Brown was certainly the culprit who had briefed Jenkins and that Wilson wanted to raise the issue of confidentiality at the next meeting of Cabinet. But Mitchell also noted that the article gave a full run-down of the Prime Minister's policy for the Vienna Meeting.

Under the heading *Labour takes another look at Europe* Jenkins wrote that the Prime Minister's visit to Vienna "may mark the opening of a new phase in Britain's relations with Europe. The attitude of Mr Wilson and some senior Cabinet Ministers towards the EEC has undergone a gradual but considerable change since the Government took office. The Government's policy has taken this new direction without any revival in the Cabinet of the old arguments which came near to splitting the Labour Party in 1962. The Prime Minister is not yet counted a convert. (One pro-European Minister put it like this: 'Wilson is dipping his toe into the water to see how cold it is. . .'). But the Foreign Secretary, Mr Michael Stewart, once classed as an 'anti', is now claimed as a 'pro'. All the Ministers at the Foreign Office are now said to have discarded for all practical purposes the five conditions placed by Hugh Gaitskell on Britain's membership of the Common Market . . . Obviously, [Wilson] will be reluctant to reopen the Common Market question in his party or in the country while there is no imminence about British membership. But there is no doubt about the direction in which the Government's thinking is now moving".[47]

At about the same time, a record reached Downing Street of conversations in Brussels between leading European Commissioners and Cecil King, owner of the Mirror Group of newspapers. King was almost as influential in his day as Murdoch in later decades. King had reportedly commented that if Wilson did not get himself a sensible European policy in the near future, King's newspapers would cease to support him, and that meant that he would not win the next election.[48] The Prime Minister's Private Secretary, Oliver Wright, marked the record to Wilson but then thought better of it.

EFTA Heads of Government met in Vienna on 25 May and "decided that the Council should be charged with the task of recommending what procedural arrangements might best facilitate contacts between EFTA and the EEC and what substantive issues of policy might be the subjects of discussion between them." Wilson claimed the meeting as a success which, in a limited way, it was. But Swedish and Danish caution had prevailed. And similar caution was maintained in the instruction sent to British Embassies in the EEC at the Prime Minister's behest. Their "ostensible object should be only to convey the information contained in the communiqué, since it does not constitute an immediate, nor foreshadow an early, approach to the Community". But Embassies were also instructed to "learn any views which Representative or Community Governments or the Commission may care to express". The reaction of the Italian Government, among the more friendly towards Britain's European aspirations, was illustrative. The Italian Director General of Economic Affairs told the Embassy that the progress made in economic integration within the EEC was now so far advanced that EFTA and the EEC were two entirely disparate entities. Any invitation from EFTA to the EEC would have to pay due regard to the supra-national character of the Community. This was a polite way of saying that the EEC had turned into a butterfly, while EFTA was still only a caterpillar.[49]

One document which Oliver Wright did show to Wilson was a telegram from the British Embassy in Paris reporting that de Gaulle had been touring the French provinces, attended by various of his Ministers. De Gaulle had shown an unprecedented mark of favour to his Prime Minister, Georges Pompidou, by allowing him to share a platform with the General. This had caused the French Press to suggest that Pompidou was now the accepted dauphin. Wilson commented in green ink: "No objection to the dauphin. Send tennis balls?"[50]

The gradual shift in the Prime Minister's thinking, picked up by Peter Jenkins, was clearly not lost on Douglas Jay, President of the Board of Trade and a man who would prove to be, over the years, one of the most strenuous opponents of British EEC membership. In mid-June, Jay produced, unbidden, a memorandum for the Prime Minister on the balance of advantage to UK trade of membership of the EEC. Jay's conclusion was "that, economically, the application of the EEC's agricultural and levy system to the UK would be heavily disadvantageous to us on balance in the long run as well as the short. There is no clear evidence that other factors would outweigh this. Adherence to the EEC on terms which left us free to purchase our food and materials as now would of course be a totally different proposition".

Jay's approach was a clever one. He was not claiming to be opposed to EEC membership but he must have known that the conditions which he described as acceptable – no change in the pattern of British imports – would render membership unnegotiable. Jay made clear in a covering note to Wilson that he was not pressing for the paper to be discussed "as the issue is not actual at the moment". So, it was just a warning shot across Wilson's bow. Unsurprisingly, Wilson, for different reasons, wanted to avoid a fight and wrote on Jay's paper: "I should keep in cold storage".[51]

Work continued on follow-up to the Vienna EFTA summit. Commenting to the Prime Minister on a Foreign Office submission to the Foreign Secretary, Cabinet Secretary Sir Burke Trend endorsed the Foreign Office's flexible approach whereby EFTA would suggest to the European Community joint discussions "not so much of cut and dried proposals, as of fields and ideas in which closer collaboration might be fruitful and how we might jointly work towards such collaboration". Trend thought "this approach is the best way of avoiding the twin dangers of causing dissension in EFTA (which would be leaked) over proposals which, because they are firm and specific, ipso facto sharpen the differences between EFTA countries; and of presenting the hostile and critical elements in the Community with firm propositions to reject or to criticise".

Wilson endorsed the approach but still hankered after something more specific. "The key", he commented, "is tariffs. We should not hang back on Muenchmeyer and should be prepared to suggest an agreement to reduce tariffs between the two blocs, at a rate of e.g. 20% of the difference in each year 1967–1972".[52]

At the beginning of July, Michael Stewart was able to tell Cabinet that at the WEU meeting he had just attended the other members had responded favourably to the EFTA initiative, albeit asking for more detailed information at the next quarterly meeting. So, the British Government's decision to proceed cautiously was matched by equal caution on the other side.[53]

Cautious or otherwise, cooperation between the two organisations was abruptly aborted by the biggest crisis in the life of the European Community to that date, and probably in its entire history. On 30 June 1965, following a meeting of the Council of Ministers of the EEC in Brussels, the French Minister of Information told the Press: "There is no question for the moment of France participating in fresh meetings concerned with the Common Market at Brussels. Everything is now at a standstill. No further meeting is foreseen".[54] A few days later, the British Embassy in Paris confirmed, from official French sources, that the French Government was withdrawing its Permanent Representative in Brussels. The members of the French delegation had orders to take no further part in the work of the Community.[55]

The Head of the UK Delegation to the EEC, Sir James Marjoribanks, explained the background in a Despatch the following day entitled "The Crisis within the EEC over Agricultural Finance". "In March 1965", he wrote, "the European Economic Commission produced, on instructions proposals for the future financing of the Community's agricultural policy, including provision for direct income to the Community, and increased budgetary control by the European Parliament. France demanded that only the first of the three elements in the Commission proposal should be accepted i.e. they were prepared to meet in principle the obligation to provide for expenditure in the final stage while postponing indefinitely the question of direct income for the Community. By 25 June, it appeared likely that France would accept a vague declaration of intent on further progress in completing the Community in other fields as well, but on that day she refused to consider a Luxembourg counter-proposal which appeared reasonable to other Member States. At the meeting of the Council on 28th, France refused to consider as a further alternative an interim agreement only. On 29 June, France offered largely meaningless concessions to Italy . . . and the meeting was broken off. . .M. Couve de Murville gave the impression of not genuinely seeking agreement. The French case that a solution must be reached by 30 June was both logically and legally weak. It would now be hard for the Commission to give in to it. The crisis is now more serious than that of January 1963 [provoked by the French veto of the British application] since it relates to the basic principles of the Community. The French action in breaking off negotiations must make a compromise solution harder to reach".[56]

From Paris, the British Ambassador did not think the French would compromise. He believed that de Gaulle was characteristically maintaining at least two options. If the Five gave in, then France would achieve a satisfactory Common Agricultural Policy and supra-nationalism would have been avoided for the time being, and possibly for good. If the Five did not give in, then an arrested Common Market might still prove a valuable substitute. De Gaulle would have demonstrated to the French people that the development of the Common Market had threatened to compromise the independence on which the economic progress and restoration of the international standing of France had been based since 1958.

Reilly saw no reason to expect de Gaulle to give way. He thought de Gaulle would insist on some major concession on supra-nationalism. He would seek to reduce the powers and prestige of the Commission and to induce the Five to adapt the machinery of the Commission so as to favour instead dealings between national representatives and governments. De Gaulle was reportedly particularly incensed with Hallstein, the Commission President, and a reliable contact in the Elysée had told the Embassy that the French Government would not resume normal relations unless there were changes in the Commission.[57]

At the heart of the dispute was indeed an argument about the nature of the European Community. De Gaulle had been out of power when the Treaty of Rome was negotiated. On his return to office in 1958, he had been obliged to accept an organisation whose supra-national characteristics, enshrined in the Treaty of Rome, he could not change but heartily and openly disliked. For de Gaulle, the price of acceptance of the EEC as he had inherited it was always going to be securing an agricultural deal uniquely favourable to France and, if possible, diluting the powers of the Commission and stalling the automatic progression to greater use of majority voting foreseen in the original Treaty provisions. As Michael Stewart explained it to Cabinet on 8 July, the French Government had been concerned to press financial proposals in connection with agriculture which would have been of maximum advantage to themselves. The other five Governments had sought to extract, in return, concessions which would have emphasised and enhanced the supra-national character of the Community. The repercussions in a wider context, for example in relation to the Kennedy Round of tariff negotiations could not, in Stewart's judgement, be anything but unfavourable and, for that reason, the British Government should refrain from appearing to derive any satisfaction from the situation. On the other hand, Stewart concluded, it was not impossible that circumstances would now develop in such a way that the question of UK participation in the Community might be reopened; and the Government should be prepared for this possibility.[58]

It was not surprising, therefore, that the Paris Embassy should have pricked their ears up when the French Information Minister, Alain Peyrefitte, ever the General's faithful spokesman, and not known as an Anglophile, made a speech at the Calais Fair on 12 July in which he said that "two great nations, France and Britain, are fated . . . to develop that which unites them more than that which separates them, to draw progressively closer to each other, and together to build a future based on exchanges, cooperation and friendship".

Similar sentiments were expressed on the same day by the French Undersecretary for Scientific Research, M. Bourges, prompting *Le Monde* to comment: "In all this tumult [the EEC crisis] at the bedside of Europe, remarks which, in other circumstances might appear conventional, acquire a new significance. Observers have therefore noted with more than usual care the allusion made in Calais on Sunday by M. Peyrefitte to the ever closer interconnection of French and British interests".[59]

There appears to have been little more to this flurry than a desire to signal to France's partners that there were other fish than them in the sea. There was certainly no sign that, as far as her partners were concerned, France was ready to compromise. According to Reilly, de Gaulle's price for France's return to the conference table would almost certainly include an agreement to reduce the powers and pretensions of the Commission and to confine it to a technical role. Nothing short of a fundamental shift in the nature of the Community itself was likely to satisfy him. Nor was there any pressure of public opinion on the French Government to come to terms. A new public opinion poll indicated that the majority of the people did not understand the problem at issue, but were confident that de Gaulle would get the best bargain for France.[60]

There were, however, already signs that this crisis would not be like others, in which French intransigence would provoke capitulation by her partners. The German Foreign Minister, Schroeder, told Sir Frank Roberts that the period of unrequited German concessions in the EEC, financial or otherwise, was now over and was unlikely to return. Apart from the fact that eyes had finally been opened in Germany as regards French policy and tactics, German budgetary stringencies were likely to increase and it would not in future be possible for any German Government to, as it were, throw its bread upon the European waters.[61] At the same time, Marjoribanks from Brussels was telling London that, although the Commission had revised their proposals on agricultural finance so that they were now very close to what the French had been seeking, the main purpose of the Commission's revision had been to make it as difficult as possible for France to consider the new proposals. And, Marjoribanks added, "There are some new and important factors which may help to strengthen the Five and keep them together. Perhaps the strongest factor is the feeling that the present institutional pattern is necessary to protect the interest of the smaller countries in general and, in particular, to avoid the danger that the Community may degenerate into a Franco-German partnership, with Italy and the Benelux countries obliged to accept what Paris and Bonn dictate." Marjoribanks pointed out that the Community's institutions were consciously designed to provide a safeguard against these very dangers, dangers which the Franco-German Treaty of January 1963, and the subsequent conduct of each major negotiation within the Community had only served to underline. "The fear runs deep", Marjoribanks concluded, "that if the institutions of the Community are revised in a sense acceptable to de Gaulle the position of Italy and Benelux will be dangerously exposed".[62]

De Gaulle was insisting that a financial regulation agreed within the EEC in 1962 required the Community to provide by 30 June 1965 for the further financing of the CAP. But he did not accept that there was a corresponding obligation to provide for further supra-national content in the Community. The Five disputed this but, whatever the rights and wrongs, the main issue was, according to a paper put forward to Ministers by the Department of Economic Affairs (DEA) in August, following inter-departmental consultation in Whitehall, that de Gaulle "has always made clear his dislike of the supra-national element within the Community and of the role of the Commission and has had in mind the desirability of demonstrating that any attempt by the Commission to play the full initiatory role envisaged for them by the Treaty of Rome, and any attempt to apply the full rigour of majority voting provided in the Treaty, is entirely unacceptable to him".

The French Government had withdrawn from all meetings of Common Market bodies apart from those concerned with day to day matters and, although the Five did meet at the end of July, they did so only to discuss and not to decide. With some understatement, the DEA paper predicted that "a period of paralysis is likely to ensue"; serious attempts at reconciliation were unlikely to precede the German elections in mid-September; and the French were insisting that any efforts to patch things up should be made by the Governments of the Five, and certainly not by the Commission.

The paper advised that resumption of the Community's activities in some degree was more likely than disintegration. But it could not be ruled out that, if de Gaulle failed to achieve a clear limitation on the supra-national content of the Community and an outcome on agricultural financing which continued to give France a high proportion of Community support, he might prefer to withdraw from the Community altogether. Even if that did not happen, it seemed unlikely that, for so long as the General was in power, the Community would be able to develop as its founders had intended and as other EEC Governments wished to see.

The paper also advised that work on the EFTA initiative (largely a British construct at all times) should continue even though some in the EEC had advised that the crisis there would be fatal to it. Whatever else was done, the paper concluded firmly, "any suggestion that we might wish to play a part in the settlement of the present [EEC] difficulties would be regarded by all the Six as unhelpful. Our Delegation in Brussels has reported that those who wish to see the Community stand up to de Gaulle devoutly hope that our attitude will be one of sympathetic inactivity".[63]

This advice was repeated in a Foreign Office brief prepared for the Prime Minister a month later. "It seems clear", said its authors, "that General de Gaulle is seeking, not merely a settlement of the agricultural dispute on his terms, but the abandonment of the supra-national features of the Community . . . The worst solution for us would be a submission of the Five to French domination". "Yes", Wilson wrote, "but here, as in all other documents, we ought to avoid appearing to take sides in the EEC dispute. Nor should we say anything about supra-nationality which, in any case, we oppose".[64]

When Cabinet reviewed Britain's foreign policy later in September, the future of NATO was a greater preoccupation than that of the EEC, though the two were clearly linked. Michael Stewart listed 'France' as the first of NATO's problems because of de Gaulle's statement that by 1969 there should be no foreign troops under foreign command on French soil. Britain, said Stewart, had no wish to quarrel with France; but the Government took the view, which the US now shared, that in the last resort NATO could exist without France.

"In the EEC", Stewart continued, "the Five had always given way hitherto to French intransigence; but they were now standing firm against the latest French demands. It was in our interest that they should continue to do so. Although French views on the undesirability of supra-national organisations might seem close to our own, a Community which was wholly subservient to France would inevitably become progressively more inward-looking and less satisfactory as a partner in our politico-military policies in Europe".

In the ensuing discussion, some argued that in terms of economic and technological potential the UK was no longer able to compete independently with the other countries of Europe and that the diminishing commercial value of Britain's Commonwealth connections meant that these were no longer sufficient compensation for Britain's exclusion from the market represented by the EEC.

Others argued that EFTA gave Britain a market of more than 100 million people and that, even without being members of the EEC, British trade with the members of it, had more than doubled since the Community's foundation.

The Prime Minister summed up the discussion, saying that it was generally accepted by Cabinet that this was not an opportune moment at which to seek to reopen negotiations for UK membership of the EEC. Nor should Britain intervene in the current dispute within the Community. The Government might in due course reassess their attitude to the Community and re-examine, in the light of developments in recent years, the conditions which the Labour Party had hitherto attached to UK accession. But, Wilson added, it should be recognised from the outset that the principles of a planned economy, to which the Government were committed, would not easily be reconciled with the economic doctrines of the EEC; and the approach to membership of the Community should therefore be directed, not merely to whether it would be to Britain's advantage to join it, but also to the question whether the Government could succeed in insisting on whatever terms and conditions they felt that they must stipulate.[65]

The EFTA Ministerial Council was due to meet in Copenhagen at the end of October and George Brown advised Wilson that British Ministers, meeting in the External Economic Policy Committee, were all agreed that the question of EEC/ EFTA relations should not be allowed to die merely because of the present difficulties within the EEC. On the other hand, while the Danes (encouraged by the Germans) wanted to press on, the Swiss were averse to making any approach to the EEC until the latter were in a position to respond.[66]

In practice, both the EEC and EFTA were marking time. German State Secretary Lahr told Roberts on 21 October that there was now a trial of strength and of patience and it was essential to show the French that their partners had even better nerves than they did. To Roberts' contention that it was easier for a one-man Government in Paris than for five independent and democratic ones, Lahr responded that, having had the experience of one-man rule in Germany, he preferred the alternative. In any case, most of the General's opponents were fortunately younger than he was and would outlast him, even if they had to wait five years.[67]

A month later, the German Foreign Minister told the Foreign Secretary that there should be no difficulty about settling the French concern about excessive use of majority voting under the arrangements due to come in to force on 1 January 1966. Everyone was clear that no majority voting decision would be imposed on a country if it affected its vital interests. The bottom line was that none of the other five Governments of the EC, let alone their Parliaments, would accept any amendment to the Treaty of Rome to accommodate French wishes.

As regards the European Commission, Schroeder said that the French wanted to turn it from being an initiator of Community policy into a mere executant of the decisions of the Council of Ministers. The French wanted some sort of declaration by the EEC Governments in favour of replacing the Commission with a different kind of body. But to attempt to put a new head on the machine in this way would have a disastrous effect on the Community.

In short, in Schroeder's view, if the Community was allowed to develop as it was, it should not be difficult to arrive at a settlement. But if attempts were made to change it there would be great difficulties. He could not predict what France's attitude would be to cooperation between the EEC and EFTA (confirming by implication that nothing could be done for the time being) but he hoped discussions between the two groupings could begin at the start of 1966. He mentioned the importance of Britain doing more to emphasise its interest in a positive European development. The closer Britain could come, the better. He was, he said, thinking more in psychological terms than of statements of Government policy. Stewart replied that Schroeder would be aware of the difficulties which had stood in the way of British entry into the EEC. The British aim was a wider European market embracing both the EEC and EFTA, in which others could also participate.[68]

In late November, de Gaulle's spokesman, Information Minister Alain Peyrefitte, reported another of de Gaulle's utterances on Britain's European prospects. Edward

Heath, who had succeeded Alec Douglas-Home as Leader of the Opposition, had given a speech in Paris on 22 November in which he said that recent changes in Conservative policy, for example in favour of moving to a levy system for agriculture, were both justified in their own right and designed to make it easier for Britain to join the EEC. Britain, he said, ought to take the first favourable opportunity to become a member. Heath also called on de Gaulle and the President had taken then opportunity to tell his Cabinet that the issue of British membership seemed to be "ripening in a positive sense" and that, if this evolution should take more precise form, it would be considered by France with sympathy.

The Foreign Office viewed this hint of a shift in French policy with suspicion. It instructed its missions to make clear that this statement derived from no official contacts between HMG and the French Government and that the British Government interpreted it as being mainly designed to influence the French internal situation, as well as the position within the Community.[69]

But, according to the British Embassy in Paris, this was not how matters were seen in France. There, it was very exceptional for Peyrefitte's briefings to include the verbatim text of what de Gaulle had said in the Council of Ministers and the Embassy thought that the initial reaction of the British Government, which had been reported in the French Press, would be regarded as very negative. The Ambassador sought authority to make positive-sounding enquiry of the French as to what they had in mind. But this appears to have come to nothing.[70]

There is a whiff of premonition of the Soames Affair three years later in the evident lack of effective consultation of the Paris Embassy on the part of the Foreign Office before they responded to the apparent French overture. On the other hand, on this occasion, the Foreign Office were almost certainly nearer the mark than the Embassy. The significance of the fact of Peyrefitte's briefing does not invalidate the Foreign Office's conclusion that this was more about sending a signal to France's partners than to Britain, the message being that France did have alternatives to the Five.

It was also scarcely surprising that de Gaulle's friendly remarks about Britain should be made following the visit of the Conservative Opposition leader. De Gaulle had spoken before about his hopes for the Conservative Government which he expected to follow a Labour interlude. De Gaulle's remarks would have been seen by British Labour Ministers as wilfully damaging to them, which was no doubt part of his intention.

In December, the first Presidential election by universal suffrage of the Fifth Republic, indeed the first such election by universal suffrage since 1848, took place in France. In the first round on 5 December, de Gaulle won 44.6% of the popular vote, the Socialist candidate, Francois Mitterrand 31.7% and the centrist Jean Lecanuet 15.5%.

Stewart told Cabinet on 9 December that de Gaulle was likely to gain over 60% of the vote in the second round on 19 December and that this might go some way to restoring the prestige which he had forfeited by failing to win an overall majority in the first round. The immediate outcome, he feared, would be to increase British difficulties in her relations with France, and therefore with the EEC, since de

Gaulle might react to the personal rebuff he had received at the hands of the electorate by pursuing all the more strongly his individualistic policies. In the longer run, the demonstration that there was a genuine political Opposition in France, might help Britain because it would make it harder for the French Government to pursue a wholly unilateral course.[71]

In the event, de Gaulle won the second ballot by 55.1% of the vote against Mitterrand's 44.8%, a respectable showing for both men and one which confirmed Michael Stewart in the view he had expressed in Cabinet. But, regardless of the French elections, Stewart's own position about Britain's European future had hardened in favour of a declaration of intent by Britain: "a declaration of our readiness to negotiate the entry of the UK into the EEC as soon as the Member States of the EEC are ready to enter into such a negotiation", as he put it in a minute to Wilson, and an accompanying paper, on 10 December.

Stewart argued that "as long as it remains possible for France to dismiss Britain from active consideration . . . and for the Five to profess that they do not know where we stand about membership or otherwise of the Common Market, I believe that French influence in Western Europe will continue to grow and British influence to diminish". He argued that the Government should announce, preferably in January 1966, that they were in principle willing to accept the Treaty of Rome and join the EEC; that they had re-examined the Five Conditions attached by the Labour Party to British membership in 1962 and found them capable of being met; that there was, from the British side, no obstacle to early British entry into the Community and that they were convinced that British entry into the EEC would be in the best interests of both Britain and the rest of Europe.

As regards the Five Tests, Stewart believed that the second (freedom to pursue one's own foreign policy); fourth (the right to plan the economy) and fifth (safeguards for the British economy) should present few difficulties. The most serious problems would be presented by the first condition, relating to Commonwealth trade. Here, said Stewart, real difficulties undoubtedly remained, though he did not believe them to be insuperable and certainly not so much of a problem that they should stand in the way of a British declaration, which should be made before the Community crisis had been resolved. "Two of the principal reasons for the proposal I am making", Stewart continued, "are, first, my conviction that a settlement of the crisis on broadly French terms would be extremely dangerous for British interests; and, second, my belief that the action I propose would make such a settlement less likely . . . Economically, French predominance would make the Community even harder for us and the rest of the world to live with than it has been up to now. Protectionist tendencies would be strengthened in every sphere . . . And the veto, prolonged into the indefinite future, would ensure that no progress was made in the economic field except on French terms. The political consequences of a settlement in favour of France could be even graver . . . The risk would be real that some of France's partners, having bowed to her will, would be tempted to adopt her methods. The example of French nationalism might finally prove contagious in Germany, and Germany might begin to see her future in a closer partnership with France in the defence sphere, as in others. Of such a partnership Germany might hope, in due course, to become the leader. Were these consequences, or some of them, to ensue it would be difficult for us, even in conjunction with the Americans, to exercise a decisive contrary influence . . . The sum of these arguments is that a settlement in favour of France would be bad, and even dangerous, for our interests".

Today, Stewart's argument thus far sounds faintly paranoid. But, as seen then from the British side of the Channel, French national self-interest was being pursued by de Gaulle regardless of the impact on his erstwhile allies. He was seen as unprincipled and ruthless. Britain, like France and Russia, had a real fear of the resurgence of the kind of German nationalism that had led to the two world wars. The two things in possible combination spelled the kind of continental encroachment that was seen by Britain as dangerous to her survival. Stewart's argument would have seemed far-fetched to very few of his compatriots.

Stewart was not, however, oblivious to the likely counter argument, which he addressed in his paper, namely that, whatever happened in the Community, Britain would be the gainer. If the French won, then supra-nationalism would be checked, the independence of Member States would be safeguarded and the resulting Community would be an easier one for Britain to join without sacrifice of national habits and principles. If, on the other hand, the Community was destined to collapse why intervene to prevent it?

Stewart's answer was twofold: firstly, that a failed European Community would make Europe a much more dangerous continent. Germany, in particular, had made a large investment of faith in the Community's ideals and their bankruptcy could lay her open to dangerous temptations; and, secondly, that Europe, including Britain, really did need the kind of real economic integration which the Community was attempting to achieve. The Labour Party, Stewart contended, had never objected to the Treaty of Rome as such, or to the Community system, or to its principal features, notably the Commission and the system of majority voting, both of which the French were now attacking. Indeed, Stewart argued that majority voting might on the whole suit British interests better than the retention of a veto by each Member State. It was, after all, the French veto which had led the Community to adopt most of the principles and practices which it would be hardest for Britain to accept, and which could prevent their modification if the Community survived.

Stewart concluded: "I have made no attempt in this paper to re-examine the economic case . . . On the whole I incline to feel that, on economic grounds, the case for joining is the stronger case, though I am conscious of the force of some of the contrary arguments. The economic case is arguable, but in my view the political case for our joining is compelling".

Wilson was not convinced. He wrote on the paper (and his view was passed back to the Foreign Office) "This should not be circulated until I have had a chance of a long talk with the Foreign Secretary, on his return from Latin America. There is a lot I find hard to swallow. Why should we find acceptance of French conditions dangerous since they reject supra-nationality, play down the Commission and oppose majority voting? These ought to help us – and also minimise the danger of an exclusively 'European' foreign policy and an ultimately European deterrent. On agriculture and the Commonwealth, there seems to be no analysis of the cost to our balance of payments. All the figures I have seen would seem to be ruinous to our already vulnerable balance of payments. It is still a recipe for high prices and therefore high wages and industrial costs. On 'planning' I am sure that, had we been in the EEC last year, we would have had to accept full deflation as Italy was forced by the EEC to do".[72]

In January 1966, after the Christmas break, the Foreign Office returned to the charge, sending the Prime Minister a further paper which sought to address some of his earlier criticisms. Wilson sent the paper, and its predecessor, to his Special Adviser, Thomas ('Tommy') Balogh, who commented that they lost the woods for the trees: "The most important point about the Treaty of Rome – entirely neglected in these documents – is that it is based on the belief that the free opera-tion of the Market mechanism should be the dominant principle underlying economic policy. The idea of a Government deliberately using a whole series of instruments in order to steer the economy in particular directions and improve its performance is not one that is enshrined in the Treaty. Yet it is the idea which underlies the economic policy of the present Government".[73] There is no evidence of a response from Wilson to this minute, or indeed to any of Balogh's other minutes of advice on EEC issues.

Although Stewart's paper had initially received short shrift from the Prime Minister, the drip of water on stone clearly had its effect. On 18 January George Brown sent a note to the PM, following a private talk between the two of them, proposing that he should instruct Eric Roll (Permanent Undersecretary in George Brown's Department, the DEA) to organise "some very quiet work that would make it easier, as and when we would wish to consider these matters among ourselves, to have official advice available without too much delay".[74]

Three days later, the Foreign Secretary sent a minute to Wilson, following a talk between the two of them on the same subject. Stewart recorded that they had agreed that his paper would not be circulated to other Ministers but would go to a limited number of officials as the basis of a "further examination of the implica-tions for us of a move into Europe", which was to include a study of the economic consequences, with particular reference to the effect on the balance of payments.

"While you were not prepared to proceed at this juncture with a declaration of intent, you suggested instead that some very prominent figure in British political life should undertake a tour of the capitals of the Six. The object of the tour would be first an overt demonstration of our continuing interest in Europe, and secondly to obtain an up to date reappraisal of the attitude of each of the six Governments to our making a renewed attempt to negotiate entry. You felt that this would achieve a good deal of what we hoped to get out of a declaration of intent, while avoiding the political repercussions to be expected from so precise a commitment to a new policy".[75]

Stewart said he would think about who might undertake the tour Wilson had in mind but, unwisely, and in a minute which bore all the hallmarks of official advice, he returned to the charge less than a week later, suggesting that the task of a tour would be much better undertaken by officials. Stewart also tried again to nudge the Prime Minister along by suggesting that whoever made the tour should be authorised to express willingness to accept the Treaty of Rome. Wilson minuted that he was getting at odds with Stewart and Brown.[76]

Before this matter could be taken any further, the Six ended their dispute. The British EEC Delegation reported to London on 30 January that, early that morning, the Six had agreed on four texts covering relations between the Council and the Commission: recognition of disagreement on majority voting (the normal work of the Community to be resumed despite this); agreement that unanimity should in any case apply to the main outstanding agricultural decisions; and a general indication of subjects to be dealt with when normal work resumed.

Marjoribanks was in no doubt that this was a defeat for France. "The Five clearly found it difficult to believe until near the end", he wrote, "that, after so many years, the French were at last in retreat . . . The measure of France's diplomatic defeat is the difference between her earlier conditions for her return to Brussels and the few minor concessions now made to her . . . In the statements made by de Gaulle and Couve de Murville on 9 September and 20 October, in the remarks made to Ambassadors of the Five in Paris and the uncompromising terms put forward by Couve on 17 and 18 January, French conditions for return were, at the least, agreement on no majority voting, a new Commission with a more subservient role and agreement on agricultural finance. France has now agreed to return on the basis of a unilateral declaration on majority voting from which her partners dissent, and minor points, nearly all presentational, affecting the Commission.

On the debit side, French action since 30 June 1965 has built up opposition and suspicion among the Five; further threats of a walk-out will lack conviction; France no longer has a date for completion of agricultural finance arrangements; and has built up an atmosphere where all her objectives, including the choice of new Commissioners, will be harder to achieve . . . France's bluff has been called and the balance of power in the European Communities will not be the same again. As Schroeder, whose performance during the meetings was by all accounts masterly, said privately afterwards, France can never again make her partners believe that she will walk out of the Community".[77]

At Cabinet on 3 February 1966 Stewart gave a more nuanced assessment. The outcome, he said, had not been wholly satisfactory to either party; but it might be thought that the Five had, on balance, derived greater profit from the encounter. The French Government could claim that they would still retain a virtual veto on the issue of majority voting in the Community but . . . it had always been implicit in the working of the Community that the principle of unanimity could not, in practice, coerce any member Government to accept a decision which they judged to be contrary to their major national interests . . . The results . . . did not suggest that there was likely to be any opportunity in the immediate future for an initiative by Britain to enter into closer relations with the EEC.[78]

Stewart's interpretation of the so-called Luxembourg Compromise was at odds with the interpretation put on it by the British Delegation in Brussels. The

Luxembourg Compromise, as British officials later recognised and advised, was an agreement to disagree. It did indeed accept that *"where, in the case of decisions which may be taken by majority vote on a proposal of the Commission, very important interests of one or more partners are at stake, the Members of the Council will endeavour, within a reasonable time, to reach solutions which can be adopted by all Members of the Council while respecting their mutual interests and those of the Community."* But the French had felt it necessary to add: *"With regard to the preceding paragraph, the French delegation considers that where very important interests are at stake the discussion must be continued until unanimous agreement is reached"*. But the 'Compromise' went on to state that *"the six delegations note that there is a divergence of views on what should be done in the event of a failure to reach complete agreement"*.

Thus, the Luxembourg Compromise was never, as the British Government often termed it, a veto. It was a political agreement with no legal status and it was to prove a broken instrument in British hands when, eighteen years after the Luxembourg meeting, the British Government invoked it for the only time in our membership and were nonetheless voted down by other member Governments, including the French. None of that, of course, could Stewart foresee but neither he nor his officials seem to have worked out the other consequence of the gradual increase in majority voting. It was a commonplace of British views that no country would be outvoted on its important national interests, and the record shows that the number of occasions on which Britain has been outvoted remains relatively small. But the effect of majority voting over the years was to put political pressure on any Member State that found itself in a minority of one or two (i.e. insufficient to form a minority to block) to rally to the majority in the end game rather than be seen to have been defeated in a vote. Thus, many more Member States are outnumbered than are formally outvoted, and a formal consensus often disguises the underlying extent of political disagreement.

On the same day as Cabinet, Stewart wrote to Wilson to advise that, with the EEC back in functioning order, its members would be extremely busy for the time being mending their own fences and would in all probability be too busy to be thinking about the British. This meant, in his view, that in the new situation the idea of a 'prominent person' to tour EEC capitals would be less useful than when Wilson had originally suggested it. Indeed, it would look rather odd if the British were to pursue the idea. "It might even look as if we had missed the bus and were sending someone to find out where it had gone".[79]

However, on the other side of the European argument, Douglas Jay, the President of the Board of Trade, clearly saw that Stewart had been trying to shift policy in a more pro-European direction. Jay wrote to Wilson on 3 February to tell him that he had told Stewart privately that he did not agree with some of his recent statements about the European Community. "I believe", he wrote "that any talk of the UK 'seeking membership' of, or negotiating separately with, the EEC does harm, because it alarms EFTA and weakens our bargaining position. Any unilateral negotiation would lead straight, as in 1962, to our being forced to accept the common external tariff and agricultural levies, with great damage to our balance of payments – or to another breakdown". Wilson subsequently noted on the minute that he had had a talk with Jay and "told him the form".[80]

Others were also stirring. On 10 February, Balogh alerted Wilson to the fact that "the Informal Committee organised by Roll has now given rise to an equally informal Organising Committee which is commissioning papers. Its membership is Sir Con O'Neill of the Foreign Office, Mr Frank Figgures of the Treasury and someone from the DEA. You will remember that Sir Con O'Neill made a violently anti-French speech implying advocacy of our entry. Mr Frank Figgures is one of the greatest protagonists of supra-national institutions. Unless measures are taken to get a balance in the composition of both the Organising Committee and the papers, I fear all this will get out of hand and we shall be confronted with *faits accomplis*". In putting this note to Wilson, Derek Mitchell, the Principal Private Secretary (through whom all such papers would have had to pass on their way upwards), wrote "They are unlikely to open negotiations without Ministerial authority". And Wilson appears to have paid little heed to Balogh's note.[81]

At around the same time, the Minister of Housing, Richard Crossman, who was a consistent opponent of British EEC entry, wrote to Stewart to suggest that de Gaulle's attitude to supra-nationality surely suited British interests rather well and that the peace of Europe would be safeguarded if Britain were to concert with France and Russia to keep Germany in a condition of permanent inferiority. Not surprisingly, Stewart did not accept this view, arguing that French objectives were at odds with British interests, that European security depended upon the creation of trust and a spirit of cooperation between a partnership of equals and that a successful basis for a rapprochement between East and West could not lie, as de Gaulle seemed to think, in the assertion of one nationalistic European presence against the interests of a European neighbour, Germany, and against the United States. Stewart concluded, in words that have been echoed by every Foreign Secretary of every British Government since, "I believe France to be a natural partner . . . and that in any case it is neither practicable nor desirable to make a stark choice between France and Germany in our European policy. In the long run, sound relations between ourselves, France and Germany will be the best basis on which to build economic and political stability in Europe".[82]

In late February, de Gaulle gave a press conference in which he said that the Luxembourg settlement made possible a return to the reasonable procedures of earlier years. He spoke about the possibility of an initiative among the Six to re-launch political unity and about cooperation with neighbours such as Britain, Spain and Scandinavia and did not rule out "adherence or association" in due course provided that the resulting Europe was powerful and independent vis-à-vis the United States.[83]

Three weeks later, de Gaulle asserted that independence, as far as France was concerned, by withdrawing France from the integrated military structure of NATO. In a handwritten letter to Wilson of 9 March de Gaulle claimed that Great Britain, "constant ally, proven with glory, of France and a great European state", would understand France's reasoning.[84]

Wilson was indeed not wholly unsympathetic. Stewart warned Cabinet that the effects of the French decision would be grave and costly and that, without showing hostility to France, it would be necessary to demonstrate clearly British determination to maintain the North Atlantic Alliance. But a few days later, Wilson sent Stewart a minute in which he wondered whether some at least of de Gaulle's "assessments of the way things are moving in the world may be more up to date and in tune with the times than our own . . . He is in my view on firm ground when he concludes that the likelihood of war in Europe has greatly receded over the past few years; and that, if this is so, the Western powers ought now seriously to be looking for ways of promoting a détente with the East. What have we armed for, if not to parley?"[85]

Wilson may have been hoping that de Gaulle's signal at his press conference about Britain and Europe could be built on. His response to de Gaulle's letter was unusually warm given that de Gaulle had just pulled the French rug from beneath the feet of his allies: "I much appreciate the generous remarks which you make about Great Britain in your letter. You who know this country so well will fully understand that it is the overwhelming desire of the British people, animated as they are by a spirit of respect and affection for France and her achievements, to have the closest possible relations with their French neighbours".[86]

However, the signals were more positive than the reality. The German Foreign Minister told Stewart in mid-March that he had recently asked de Gaulle what his attitude was and, while the tone was more positive, de Gaulle had made it clear that the question of British accession would not arise for two or three years. Schroeder concluded that the basic French position had not really altered and that the British would be deluding themselves if they thought that the French position had changed in any essential particular since January 1963.[87]

At about the same time, the Diplomatic Adviser at the Elysée confirmed to the Paris Embassy that there had indeed been no change in the French attitude. The Adviser attributed to inexperience the positive remarks made by de Broglie, the French representative at a recent WEU meeting.

The evidence suggests that, despite their being no substantive shift in French attitudes to British membership, Wilson's own attitude was hardening in favour of another attempt. Wilson had just called a General Election, half way through his term, hoping to capitalise on a lead in the polls to increase his wafer thin majority in the House of Commons. He made a significant intervention on Europe during the campaign, in a speech in Bristol on 18 March 1966. The previous day, he had received confirmation from the Foreign Office, in response to an enquiry made at his behest, that de Gaulle had indeed said in 1963 *"Les Anglais, je les aurai nus"*. The comment had been made to the Swiss Ambassador in Paris with, according to the Foreign Office, the intention that the remarks be reported and circulated. It was also characteristic of de Gaulle that he would not allow any official version of the remarks to appear so that he could deny them if he so chose.[88]

In his speech of 18 March, Wilson chose, against the evidence, to put the most favourable interpretation possible on recent French comments. "The Government regard recent statements in France . . . as removing one major impediment to Britain joining the EEC if suitable terms and conditions can be agreed. We welcome the French statements . . . Although there is deep imprecision in what French leaders are saying, the present French attitude is markedly different from the situation three years ago ... The French refusal at that time was due to the inept handling of Anglo-French relations and the duplicity shown by the Tory leaders concerned. In the meetings with President de Gaulle at Rambouillet they failed to deal straight with him. It was the Nassau Agreement that slammed the door of the Common Market in Britain's face. Since the Labour Government came into office we have worked to improve relations with the French Government ... It is this relationship which has helped to produce a change of attitude ... The Government's position is that we are ready to join if suitable safeguards for Britain's interests, and our Commonwealth interests, can be safeguarded. . .So far, all we have been told – this week – is that we can look forward to joining 'one day'. We have been told we must enter 'without reservations', 'naked'. There is a lot more probing, a lot more exchanges, before anyone can start rushing fences ... We believe that given the right conditions, it would be possible to join the EEC as an economic Community ... The Common Market is no cure-all for Britain's economic problems. There are strong industrial arguments for being in Europe ... Unless we modernise, streamline our industries, base our attitudes on a full day's work for a full day's pay ... then the Common Market choice is simply a choice between being a backwater inside Europe and a backwater outside Europe. If the conditions are right, and we are able to enter the wider Community from a situation of industrial strength, we shall be facing a challenging adventure . . ."[89]

In many respects, Wilson's speech in 1966 is close to the one he had made in the House when Macmillan first applied to join the EEC five years earlier. Politicians live by words and the speeches they make are nearly always careful and deliberate. Wilson's speech was a campaign speech, designed to close off any conceivable Tory advantage from appearing pro-European by comparison with Labour and, speciously, to claim that a sea change had occurred as a result of the change of Government from Conservative to Labour in 1964. He used the opportunity to get de Gaulle's 'naked Britain' remark out in the open and, in so doing, performed the politician's trick of reinterpreting it. In de Gaulle's version, there is little doubt that what he meant was that he wanted Britain to come crawling to him on its knees. In Wilson's version 'naked' was simply another way of saying 'without reservations'. But Wilson was also advancing the position of his Party on the subject of Europe; doing so in circumstances where his colleagues in the Labour Party could hardly gainsay him without damaging Labour's electoral prospects; and putting himself in a position where, if re-elected, he could claim that his speech formed part of the Party's electoral platform. And win he did, transforming a majority of 4 in 1964 to one of 96 in 1966.

Within two weeks of the General Election, Eric Roll had submitted to the Prime Minister the outcome of the work of officials under his chairmanship. The officials' paper was procedurally cautious, taking the view that Britain's own economic health must be restored before she joined the EEC, and equally thorough in its analysis of the pros and cons across each of the main areas of EEC activity. Its assumptions were equally realistic: "We have assumed that the Six will continue to make progress towards the creation of an economic community, though more slowly and with more difficulty than appeared likely before the crisis of 1965/66. In particular, we have assumed that the CAP will be completed as originally planned . . . and that the Financial Regulation will be agreed on the basis that import levies have to be handed over to the Community . . . Looking further ahead, the Community will acquire a more political character as it progresses to economic union . . . If we were to join we should be accompanied by other members of EFTA, and the Irish Republic would also be admitted at the same time. We have assumed that before joining the Community our own economic position and our balance of payments will have been restored to reasonable health . . . We have also assumed that preliminary soundings might be initiated before measures to restore our economy had taken full effect."

"The reasons for joining the Community can equally well be expressed as the disadvantages of exclusion or the advantages of being inside", the paper continued. "The practical issue relates to participation in – as opposed to exclusion from – a larger aggregation of economic, political and military power and potential than Britain possesses. While the countries composing the EEC are capable of constituting a political and military influence of the first order, this power would derive in large measure from economic achievements and prospects based on a Customs Union which its members are resolved to build up further into an economic union . . . A detailed examination of the economic implications of joining indicate a considerable number of consequences which we would prefer to avoid e.g. the Common Agricultural Policy. Nevertheless, they belong to disciplines which apply to the others no less than they would to ourselves . . . Whatever the balance might be, it needs to be set against the British position if we stay out . . . The central case for membership is for becoming part of a larger market and a larger economy . . . It is the assured access to what is virtually a single market [of 280 million] that is of great significance . . . The size of Britain's population and of her economy is already proving, and will increasingly prove, to be too small to maintain an expanding economy and standard of life at home as well as to sustain the role which all parties desire us to continue to play in world affairs . . . In contrast, there have emerged in the rest of the world three major economic and industrial complexes (the US, the USSR and the EEC) . . . The UK will move into a position of increasing disadvantage as the years go by. Failing marked success in world tariff negotiations, which seems unlikely, only integration of the UK in a larger grouping seems likely to change the prospects of falling into a position of progressive competitive inferiority. From this point of view, only the EEC offers us the prospect of integration in conditions of partnership rather than subordination."

The document went on to make the case for membership on political grounds; in brief that the EEC could be expected to grow in strength and influence while Britain, outside it, would diminish. Moreover, with Britain inside, responsibility for the operation of the Community would remain even more firmly in the hands of individual Governments. If Britain stayed out, by contrast, Germany would come to dominate, leading either to the EEC, not Britain, being the principal partner of the United States, or to a dangerous increase in nationalism, perhaps in the form of an exclusive Franco-German partnership.[90]

Wilson did not comment on the substance of the paper but he referred it to a newly established Cabinet Committee on Europe, which he would chair and which would have among its members the First Secretary of State (Brown), the Chancellor of the Exchequer (Callaghan), the Foreign Secretary (Stewart), the Defence Secretary (Healey), the Commonwealth Secretary (Bottomley), the President of the Board of Trade (Jay), the Minister of Agriculture (Peart) and the Chancellor of the Duchy of Lancaster (Thomson). Thus three of the members (Brown, Stewart and Thomson) were pro Europeans; three (Jay, Bottomley and Peart) were sceptics and three (Wilson, Callaghan and Healey) could be said to be swing voters. The terms of reference of the Committee were: "To keep under comprehensive review the political, economic and military relations between the UK and Europe".[91]

To this new Committee, on 6 May, George Brown and George Thomson submitted a paper which argued that the Government needed to decide what it was going to say about its policy on EEC membership. But that was merely the lead-in to what was in practice a paper about the strategy and tactics of an application. The first question, the paper argued, was whether French intentions with regard to NATO need be an obstacle to probing and testing with the French the possibilities of EEC membership. The paper did not answer its own question but speculated that de Gaulle might hope, by appearing to treat Britain in a relatively friendly way over the EEC, to foster the impression in the minds of other NATO allies (especially Germany) that Britain was not above doing a deal with France behind their backs.

Overall, Brown and Thomson thought that France was probably still hostile to Britain's entry and that recent signs to the contrary were probably attributable to NATO considerations. The rest of the EEC members were well disposed but, given the recent EEC crisis and the current NATO one, even they thought that membership could not happen before late 1967 or 1968. The state of the British economy was also a factor. Complete recovery need not be a pre-condition of entry, particularly if the Government had established its authority in other ways, which the paper did not specify. But the economic state of health of Britain would be of prime relevance to the negotiation and it was important that we should be on the "economic up-grade".

The paper devoted a lot of attention to what it called the tactical alternatives: "Whether we ought to concentrate on the French or on the Five. The argument for concentrating on the French is that they hold the key. The argument against is that to do so would strengthen the French position when our object is to weaken it. The French would be tempted to force the price up to a level which we could not afford to pay". A key question, the paper argued, was whether Britain could count on the Five, who were even more fed up with the French than usual because of French action in NATO, to force the issue and "to get us in, in spite of the French". There was, it said, a view in Germany that Britain could count on this. Whatever the truth of the matter, nothing need or should prevent the British Government from probing EEC intentions, and this should be done by taking advantage of bilateral meetings already arranged.[92]

On the basis of the paper, Wilson wrote himself a green-ink memo:

"1. Do we want *Europe des Patries* or *Europe de la Commission?*
2. Do we envisage long-term collective political (and Military?) commitments. If not, should we say so?
3. Study of Treaty of Rome, including constitutional aspects. How give effect to Regulations?
4. Capital Movements.
5. Agriculture in relation to Commonwealth imports: cost of enlargement; cost to import bill.
6. Probing – especially President de Gaulle.
7. NATO vs. EEC (a) tactical; (b) long term objectives. Are they exclusive?
8. The EFTA – EEC dialogue".[93]

Wilson's minute is a characteristically shrewd summary of the essential key issues for Britain, both substantive and tactical. The fact that the EFTA-EEC dialogue was ranked last, when it had been the cornerstone of the Government's policy only a few months earlier, illustrates the extent to which the Prime Minister's own thinking had evolved. The active pursuit of EEC/EFTA rapprochement appears, in practice, to have been quietly dropped.

On the same day, the Cabinet Secretary advised the Prime Minister that the time had come to give more detailed consideration to the practical implications of EEC membership in both political and economic terms. The time had therefore also come, he recommended, to replace the informal group led by Eric Roll by formal – and neutral – interdepartmental machinery, consisting of a steering committee and such subordinate 'subject matter' committees as might be necessary. In other words, Trend too was suggesting a shift in gear to reflect a shift in policy.[94]

Wilson, nonetheless, remained cautious. In a meeting on 6 May with George Thomson who, as Chancellor of the Duchy of Lancaster, had been given special responsibility for European matters, Wilson said that "it was arguable that in the past we had appeared to be dragging our feet about possible membership of the EEC. Now it might be said that we were tending to go a little too far in the opposite direction". Thomson assured the Prime Minister that, in his contacts with European Ministers, he had been at pains to make it clear that the Government did not think that progress on the EEC front by Britain could be made very rapidly. He and Wilson agreed that particularly careful study needed to be given to the internal problems of adjustment that would arise for Britain if she joined the EEC and of the legal problems involved.[95]

Wilson's own position had shifted but he would proceed at a deliberate pace, partly because he himself needed to be convinced that the political wish to move towards the EEC was underpinned by sound analysis and argument and partly because he had to carry his Cabinet and Party, where views were divided, along with him.

As Wilson and Thomson were meeting, George Brown was making a major speech on Britain and the EEC to a conference of the Socialist International in

Stockholm. His central message was that Britain was part of Europe and that her aim was a common European market embracing the EEC, Britain and any other European countries that wished to participate. In words that prefigured those used over two decades later by Margaret Thatcher at Bruges, Brown described as the greatest tragedy of all the gulf now dividing Eastern and Western Europe: "We should remember that the countries of Eastern Europe include some whose contribution to the development of our history and culture have been very great in the past and could be great again in the future. My purpose in referring to them is to remind us, in considering the problems of Western Europe, that the continent of Europe does not end at the Iron Curtain".

Brown went on to set out the British domestic considerations. "There is in Britain today a growing awareness at all levels of society that our own future is closely linked with that of our continental neighbours. In reality there have been two domestic debates. The first has been concerned with whether Britain should join the EEC at all; the second with the question whether, when the time comes, we could negotiate the terms that would provide for our vital interests. The first debate has never been wholly on Party lines and is now over. There can be few people in Britain who do not recognise that the future of Britain, a major European country, lies with the rest of Europe. The second is very much on Party lines and was in fact at the centre of the election arguments". It was of the greatest importance therefore, Brown continued, that there should be the clearest understanding abroad of the newly elected Government's position. "I want to make it quite clear", he continued "that Britain stands ready to enter the EEC provided that our essential interests are safeguarded . . . The question then is not whether we should join the EEC but when and on what terms . . . We do not question the institutions of the Treaty. But surely in an expanded Community it would be reasonable to foresee adjustments . . . However . . . we would not be asking for special treatment or the freedom to avoid commitment to the basic rules of membership".

Brown then took his audience through Labour's Five Conditions. They were not, and never had been, five reasons why Britain should not join. But there were some real issues. Britain could not, for example, join the EEC without there being profound effects on the pattern of her imports from New Zealand, Canada and Australia. Foodstuffs represented 80% of all of New Zealand's exports to Britain, 58% of Australia's and around a quarter of Canada's. Nor was Britain's own agriculture insignificant. True, agriculture accounted for less than 4% of Britain's working population but it remained a major industry. Britain's agricultural productivity had been increasing by about 6% annually and Britain's agricultural production was nearly three times that of Denmark and two and a half times that of the Netherlands. Community agricultural prices could not be ignored, especially for cereals where membership would impose the greatest price increase. That in turn would be reflected across the livestock sector in the shape of higher-priced animal feed with consequent negative effects on the profitability of products such as pig meat, poultry, eggs and milk. And it would be consumers who would have to pay. These problems were not insuperable. But they required hard and patient study if they were to be resolved.

Brown quoted Wilson's phrase –"We are in Europe, but our influence and power are not, and must not be, confined to Europe" – to argue that there was no incompatibility between the EEC and Britain provided that the Community was willing to look beyond its own frontiers. He assured his audience that Britain should only enter the Community with a healthy economy and a strong balance of payments. Britain had applied once before and been unsuccessful. On any future occasion the British Government would want to be sure that all parties to the negotiations were equally determined to bring them to a successful conclusion. He could not say when or in what circumstances British membership was again likely to become the subject of negotiations but, with each year that EFTA and the EEC travelled along different roads the problems of bringing them together grew no easier. "We want an expanded EEC", Brown concluded. "We want to be a member of it and we want to find the basis on which this would be possible. And the Labour Government in Britain, deeply conscious of its responsibilities to Europe, and of Europe's responsibilities to the world, is determined to play its full part in bringing about the European unity which is so fundamental to both".[96]

Brown kept up the pressure on Wilson, writing to him on 16 May that, in order to make progress towards membership of the EEC it would be necessary for the Government to state at an early stage that it accepted the Treaty of Rome. Brown noted that he had already gone some way in that direction in his Stockholm speech, and the Foreign Secretary had, he said, spoken in similar terms. The principal obstacles which Britain would need to overcome arose from EEC Regulations and other arrangements, rather than from the Treaty of Rome as such, so it would be possible to declare acceptance of the Treaty of Rome without prejudicing any important British interests.

Wilson remained cautious. On 19 May, on advice from the Cabinet Secretary, he minuted to Brown agreeing with him that officials should examine the extent to which it was the Treaty of Rome, or the measures adopted under it, which might prejudice British interests if the Government publicly endorsed the Treaty. He concluded: "I am bound to say that, until we have a considered recommendation of this sort before us, I should continue to be reluctant to invite the political controversy which would undoubtedly be aroused if we gave any public indication that we were prepared formally to accept the Treaty".[97]

Meanwhile, Balogh was telling Wilson, following a conversation with Eric Roll, that the latter was advising George Brown that France could be made to accept Britain i.e. that de Gaulle could be outflanked. "I fear this is completely misguided and such a view might well put us into a position of repeating our mistakes of 1963". Michael Palliser, who had recently taken up the post of Foreign Office Private Secretary to Wilson, endorsed Balogh's advice.[98]

The German Foreign Minister might have given some comfort to Roll's view when he told the British Ambassador in Bonn, Frank Roberts, that he "remained convinced that France under de Gaulle did not want UK membership of the EEC." France must therefore be put under effective pressure, Schroeder said. He thought the best way of achieving this would be for the practical problems relating to British entry to be very carefully studied. Once that had been done to the satisfaction of the Five and the UK, France should be confronted with the result and then brought to take a definitive position. Europe could not go on with half-truths and half promises. Germany's favourable balance of trade depended on EFTA more than on the EEC. Moreover, the EEC, like NATO, could in the last resort exist without France, but hardly without Germany. Even de Gaulle could hardly persuade the French that they should go it alone, not only without NATO but without the EEC. France's partners, said Schroeder, therefore had good cards in their hands.[99]

On the same day, Erhard spoke to the Ambassador in similar terms. Like Schroeder he had noted and welcomed the recent British public expressions of interest in the EEC. Membership for Britain remained his goal but he feared the French attitude remained the one expressed recently i.e. that Britain must simply sign on the dotted line. This, said Erhard, was clearly out of the question and some way round this difficulty must be found.[100]

Germany, like Britain, was juggling with two issues: how to respond to the French and others on British membership of the Community; and how to handle the French withdrawal from the military structure of NATO. The British, supported by the Americans after a hesitant start, were leaders of a robust line which included the belief that it would not be politically or practically sensible to keep the political headquarters of NATO in Paris when the French were requiring the withdrawal of SHAPE, the military planning arm of the Organisation. The German Chancellor faced a dispute within his own Party on the handling of NATO and Wilson told Cabinet, following a visit to London by Erhard on 23 May, that it was not surprising that Erhard wanted to get the NATO and other related issues out of the way before turning his attention to the question of British EEC membership. Wilson also told Cabinet that it was perhaps significant that Erhard had been inclined to discount the indication that the French Government might now be more favourably disposed to British entry.[101]

At the same Cabinet meeting, the Foreign Secretary reported that British Ministers had suggested to Erhard that a statement by the Six supporting the principle of UK entry into the Community would be helpful. What Stewart did not report to Cabinet was Erhard's response to this suggestion which was that he would like to examine it with colleagues of the Five but that any initiative which he took within the Five could not be kept secret and would be regarded as an attack on de Gaulle.[102]

Later that same day, Wilson sent to President Johnson a message about Erhard's visit in which he recorded that "we also had a useful short exchange about our own future relations with the EEC. The Chancellor made it clear that he did not think there was any real likelihood of an effective negotiation for British entry at present, even supposing that this could be done with due regard for our essential interests. But we were able to make clear our continued willingness to enter into such a negotiation if the opportunity presented itself, and I was encouraged by the evident anxiety of the Chancellor to see us and other EFTA countries in an expanded Common Market on satisfactory terms. I felt that we were thinking along very similar lines".[103]

The state of thinking within the British Government and more broadly was well summarised at the end of May in an article by Andre Fontaine in *Le Monde*, following a visit Fontaine had made to London. Fontaine noted that, after their serious disappointment in 1963, the British feared that they would again be thwarted if they advanced too quickly, with many in the Foreign Office believing that de Gaulle had no intention of letting Britain enter Europe. Moreover, according to Fontaine, the British did not want to go against American wishes because they feared that separation from the Americans would weaken Western pressure in negotiations with the Russians. Most importantly, Fontaine noted, "it is difficult for many British people to accept the idea that France and Britain can really be regarded as equals when Britain held the fate of the world in her hands for an entire year . . . Many Labour voters are from a modest background. . . They are naturally inclined to retain old prejudices about European vices and parochial illusions". But Fontaine thought that this trait would, paradoxically, make the Europeanization of Britain, under Wilson, easier. For, while a Conservative Prime Minister could count on the hostility of Labour, were Wilson to take the plunge he could count on the support of the Conservative Party "without having much to fear from his own party since he has several years of assured power ahead of him. This makes us hope that when the right moment comes this able and wise man will be able to make the gesture on which the whole future of Europe depends".[104]

So, the British Government was faced with a number of puzzling issues. Should they, in effect, wait upon the demise of de Gaulle, or try to push forward in the hope that de Gaulle could be outflanked by Britain and the Five, or at least, put in a position where even he was not strong enough to resist the combined pressure? What kind of state did the British economy need to be in both before we joined and before we applied to join? Were acceptable conditions of membership attainable?

On the first question, Wilson was more inclined than the Foreign Office to believe that de Gaulle could not be outflanked, though he might be pressured. But at the end of the day, there was no escaping that de Gaulle would have to assent if Britain was to gain entry to the EEC. This view was confirmed by a weekend discussion at the end of May between Wilson's new Foreign Office Private Secretary, Michael Palliser, and Palliser's Belgian in-laws, including his father-in-law, the Belgian statesman, Paul-Henri Spaak. All agreed that Britain could not get in without the assent of de Gaulle and that such assent was probably not attainable on terms acceptable to Britain. It followed that a negotiation for British entry was probably some way off. Views in the Spaak family differed as to the degree of change in French attitudes that would follow the departure of de Gaulle. Spaak himself, like Palliser, believed that change would be very rapid indeed. Others did not.[105]

A letter a few days later from Reilly in Paris to George Thomson did not take a different view although it did lodge the seductive thought that the politics of British entry might be tackled positively by a personal approach from the Prime Minister to de Gaulle. That, however, would only work if de Gaulle could be persuaded that Britain was able to accept the essential economic terms of entry.[106]

Reilly returned to the charge in a Despatch later in June with advice which was perceptive but ambivalent reflecting, not only the innate instinct of all advisers to hedge their bets, but also the very real difficulty of knowing what was in de Gaulle's mind. So supreme was the President and so disposed to keep his own counsel, that there were few wholly reliable external guides to his intentions. So, for example, Maurice Schumann had told Thomson in mid-June that thinking Frenchmen realised that the united Germany which it was de Gaulle's declared policy to achieve would have too much weight in an EEC that did not include Britain. Hence the growing support in France in general for British entry. Reilly drew from this the conclusion that the French Government, and probably the General himself, therefore considered British entry inevitable sooner or later. If, Reilly concluded, de Gaulle could bring himself to take the risk of letting Britain into the EEC, in the nature of things forces would start to work which would bring her both politically and economically in the direction in which de Gaulle wished to see Britain move. However, his political objections to British entry could only have been strengthened by the results of his action over NATO.[107]

As to the question of the necessary degree of economic health that must precede membership, the collective view of British officials, with input from Balogh, was that Britain could enter the Common Market only from a position of economic strength, with a strong balance of payments in prospect. If Britain entered in a weak position, competition from the Six would cause too many British industries to decline. If Britain entered from a position of weakness, the chances of her gaining from membership would be small. The group doubted whether these necessary conditions for successful membership would be fulfilled during the next four or five years.[108]

George Brown remained the principal advocate of outflanking de Gaulle. His advice to the Prime Minister was to leave the economic arguments to one side and to outflank the General politically. "If", he wrote, "we could create a situation in which we, with the Germans, were seen to be leading in the construction of a truly European approach to security, defence and foreign policy arrangements and one which, unlike de Gaulle's, is explicitly based on partnership with the United States, it would, I think, be very difficult for de Gaulle to prevent the Five, and no doubt large sections of French opinion too, from rallying to such a position".

Wilson minuted: "First Secretary and I had a preliminary talk about this. My view is that in present circumstances the United States would not lift a finger to help in this exercise, that it is George Ball, not LBJ, who is interested in Europe, LBJ only in Vietnam, that our attitude on South East Asia and SEATO is driving them into hostility and that, even if this could be overcome, we should get a deal with the United States and Germany only on the basis of conceding the German case on nuclear sharing".[109]

More domestic reasons for Wilson's caution remained. At the end of June, George Thomson gave a speech at a WEU Ministerial meeting in which he declared that the political will to join the EEC was present in Britain and implied that the will to a new British application to join was present if only the Six were equally committed. The speech provoked a minute from Balogh to Wilson warning that the Government was being committed to policies without due consideration.[110]

The Minister of Housing also weighed in with a minute to the Foreign Secretary: "Some of us have been alarmed for many weeks", Crossman wrote, "by the impression, which seems to have been deliberately created in a number of speeches, that there was some change in our attitude to the Common Market and also the emergence of new objective conditions favouring our adherence to the Community. Each time this alarm was expressed we have been reassured that there is no change of attitude and that, anyway, any recent changes in the objective conditions have not diminished but actually increased the obstacles in the way of British adherence. I hope you can reassure me that . . . the attitude adopted will be that to which we agreed in Cabinet . . ."[111]

The following day, the President of the Board of Trade, Douglas Jay, wrote in support of Crossman, obliging Stewart to defend the position. In his response, Stewart claimed that Thomson's speech was a repetition of that given by George Brown two months earlier, that policy was as defined in the Queen's Speech and by the Prime Minister in Parliament and that Thomson's speech, like Brown's, had been cleared with the Departments directly concerned. "As you will know", Stewart concluded "the Europe Committee has commissioned a series of studies covering the implications of British membership of the Common Market. I assure you I have no wish to prejudge the decisions which will have to be taken in the light of these studies . . . In my opinion, nothing that has been said, when read in proper context, can be held to have done so. I realise that there are differences of approach between some of us but I think we would be well-advised to postpone the debate between us on these large issues until the material I have referred to had been made available and sifted by the Europe Committee".[112]

While these shots across the bow were being exchanged, and while, much more seriously, the Government was beset by a run on the pound grave enough to raise the question of a devaluation, Wilson, Brown, Callaghan, Stewart and Thomson were receiving in London a French delegation led by the Prime Minister, Georges Pompidou and including the Foreign Minister, Maurice Couve de Murville. If the visit led Pompidou, as Heath claimed, to return to Paris disgusted and convinced that Wilson did not mean business over joining the Community,[113] then some of the blame must rest with Heath who refused to defer a debate of his choosing on Vietnam, thereby forcing Wilson to curtail the talks with Pompidou and, since he had to wind up the debate in the Commons which ended with a 10 p.m. Division, to arrive hopelessly late for a dinner in his honour at the French Embassy.

Wilson himself acknowledged that Pompidou was "somewhat annoyed, and understandably so" and that Press reports showed that the incident rankled.[114] More serious, however, was the lack of any meeting of minds.

Pompidou started the meeting on 7 July with a lengthy account of de Gaulle's view of the Common Market, including the claim that the General had told Pompidou that one of his preoccupations over the EEC was that it risked causing difficulties between its members and others, especially the United Kingdom. The element of self-fulfilling prophecy in this observation appears to have escaped

Pompidou. Pompidou went on to describe in familiar terms the difficulties of adaptation to the rules of the Common Market which France had experienced, her own severe internal economic measures in 1958/59 including devaluation and a tough wages policy, and the critical nature of agriculture for France's national interests. The problem for France, and for Britain, Pompidou concluded, was to know if Britain had really decided to engage on the path to the Common Market. If so, there would be no lack of good will on the part of France.

In response, Wilson said that the Government had the political will to join and wished to do so, provided Britain's essential interests could be met.

This prompted Couve de Murville to raise a number of difficulties, notably Britain's economic state and British objections to the CAP. Wilson expressed confidence that the UK was back on the road to economic strength. He did not minimise the problems of agriculture. But the British approach was pragmatic. The Government did not judge the advantages of the Common Market in terms of whether it would lead in the long run to political unity. There were many who did, but the Government judged the enterprise primarily on the practical plane. He understood that was the general position of the French Government and wondered whether there would now be advantage in more detailed bilateral discussions with the French Government and others.

Pompidou said there was no doubt that, in the minds of the authors of the Treaty of Rome, the political had been more important than the economic but, as things had turned out, it was the economic aspect that had opened up the greater possibilities of progress. Of course, in the long run, political federation might be possible as new joint policies emerged in the social, fiscal, transport and other fields, so there would develop a greater political unity. Pompidou noted that officials of the two countries were already in touch and he agreed that those talks should continue and be intensified. The French, Couve added, were at Britain's disposal for any talks which were necessary.[115]

When the same British Ministers met Pompidou and Couve de Murville the following day at the French Embassy, under persistent questioning from Wilson as to whether the British could once again find themselves up against the kind of veto Macmillan had incurred for not being sufficiently European, the French Ministers offered limited reassurance. Pompidou set out the need for Europe, and the countries of Europe, to have the friendliest of relations with the United States while also preserving their own distinctive identity. The Common Market was a regional organisation. Britain was in the region; the United States was not. It was difficult for a country to be situated in a certain region but to pursue different economic policies from other countries in that region. Europe might develop gradually into a Confederation – or even a Federation.

Couve then retraced the history of the talks at Champs and Rambouillet and the agreement at Nassau which, he asserted, had led France to conclude that Britain had decided, contrary to what the French had earlier been led to believe, on Anglo-American, rather than Anglo-French, nuclear cooperation.

Wilson and Brown reverted to the issue of basic French attitudes. They asked whether, if Britain entered a negotiation to join the EEC, the French would still at some point adduce an argument against her entry on the grounds that Britain was too outward looking towards the Commonwealth and the United States. Couve said they would not. The Prime Minister pressed the point. The basic issue was whether Britain would, at the end of further negotiation, be told that, because of her foreign policy, she was back in a Rambouillet/Nassau situation. Both Pompidou and Couve said that this would not be the case.

Couve then said, as he had the previous day, that there were three possible options open to Britain: accept the CAP as it stood; reach agreement with France and the Six on something different; or make an agreement excluding agriculture. Both Brown and Wilson ruled out the third option as amounting to Association only. The PM said the third option was unacceptable. He was not prepared to be "only a country member of the club".[116]

At the end of the two days, an agreed communiqué was issued in which: "Mr Wilson reaffirmed the readiness of Britain to join the EEC provided her essential interests could be met. M Pompidou recalled that nothing prevented the entry of Britain into the Common Market provided that she accepted the Treaty of Rome and the arrangements subsequently agreed. It was agreed that the two Governments would remain in contact with each other, as with the Governments of Member States of the EEC other than France, for further discussion of these questions".

Alan Campbell, Head of the Foreign Office's Western Department, noted afterwards that the British side had queried whether the French really wanted to refer to "the arrangements subsequently agreed" given that Pompidou himself had not done so. But the French insisted on it. The reference to continuing contacts was put in by the British.[117] "The arrangements subsequently agreed" was, of course, a reference to the Common Agricultural Policy, in particular, as well as to the *acquis* in general. Thus, in French minds, the parameters of any negotiation were to be confined to the first of the three options described by Couve the previous day i.e. Britain would have to accept the agricultural arrangements as they stood.

Tom Balogh noted in a minute to Wilson that, while George Brown's Department were interpreting the outcome of the talks as a sufficient basis for opening bilateral discussions, the Foreign Office interpretation was entirely negative. Balogh said that, on the basis of the records, he shared the Foreign Office interpretation, even though he suspected the FO of reaching that conclusion because they still had it in mind to try to force Britain's way into the EEC via the Five – an attitude which, Balogh reiterated, he thought unrealistic.[118]

The overall view of the visit by British Ministers was realistically gloomy. In a Despatch of 14 July, Patrick Reilly noted that the discussion confirmed what the Embassy had been reporting: "There is undoubtedly much popular support now in France for British entry into the EEC. A second French veto would therefore be unpopular in France. . .The French Government would not welcome British entry now [but] they want to avoid another veto if they possibly can. Their line therefore is that there is no obstacle to Britain's entry provided that she can accept the Treaty of Rome and the *arrangements made thereafter*. I have little doubt that this formula, which occurred in M. Couve's BBC interview recorded on 4 July, and which the French delegation were instructed to get into the communiqué, although neither Pompidou nor Couve had actually used it, was laid down by the General himself. It represents a hardening of the position recently taken in French Ministerial statements...When on 8 July the PM and his colleagues again and again pressed the French Ministers to say frankly whether there was still a political objection to British entry the latter repeatedly evaded the issue".[119]

There was not much comfort from de Gaulle's own view of the talks. At an Elysée Bastille Day reception, de Gaulle told Reilly that he thought the frank discussions had been useful. It all depended on Britain. According to Reilly, "I tried to suggest that this was not entirely the case, but I cannot say that he took much notice".[120]

At Cabinet on the same day, the Foreign Secretary reported that the discussions with Pompidou and Couve had "as was expected, little concrete result. We had at least mitigated the French suspicion that our firm policy in NATO was motivated by hostility to the French Government and there had been further agreement in respect of the construction of the Channel Tunnel...We had also attempted to persuade the French representatives of the desirability of reviewing the programme for the construction of the Concord in view of the rapid increase of its cost, but it appeared that the French Government remained determined to continue with the project".[121]

If agriculture remained one of the main obstacles to British entry to the EEC, as seen from both sides of the Channel, the detailed arrangements agreed within the Community later in July did not make accommodation any easier. The French Council of Ministers discussed a report on the agreement from the Minister of Agriculture, Edgar Faure, on 27 July and the French Defence Minister, Pierre Messmer, who happened to be seeing his opposite number, Denis Healey immediately afterwards, told Healey that one consequence of the agreement would be to make it more difficult for European countries outside the Six to obtain either full membership or association. The EEC would be able to show less flexibility in negotiating with third parties now that the agricultural framework had been fixed. Joining the Six would in future be a question of whether one could accept the rules of the organisation.[122]

It was perhaps because of the new agricultural framework that the Secretary of State for Commonwealth Relations, Arthur Bottomley, suggested to Wilson that it might be worth looking again at the option of making an agreement with the EEC which excluded agriculture. Such an agreement would, he believed, dispose of most (if not all) of Britain's difficulties from the point of view of the Commonwealth, and might well be the most satisfactory course for British agriculture as well.

Wilson's reply was significant. He agreed, he told Bottomley, that there could be some economic attractions in Couve's third possibility. "But, I remain firmly of the view that it would not be politically acceptable, nor give us any kind of effective role within the EEC, which must be our objective, if we are to join in due course and on satisfactory terms".[123]

A sub-text to the British debate was the US attitude. Throughout the early summer, the US Secretary of State, George Ball was, both privately and publicly, pressing the view that Britain should join the EEC without delay. Early in July, Ball told the British Ambassador, Sir Patrick Dean, and the Cabinet Secretary, Burke Trend, who was on a visit to Washington, that the President was deeply interested in the matter and that it was his strongly held view that Britain's economic survival could only be assured if she joined the EEC. Ball considered that Britain's position was much weaker as a suppliant than it would be once she were inside the organisation. He even hinted that the continued support of the United States for sterling and for the modernisation of the British economy depended on Britain joining the Six.

Ball repeated these comments in a talk at Chatham House in London later in the month, speaking publicly but unattributably. A Foreign Office minute of the occasion had him arguing that Britain should apply to join the EEC without specifying conditions in advance. Moreover, if Britain would give up her independent nuclear deterrent this would help her to join the EEC and help to solve the German problem which he defined as being one of equality with Britain. The health of the British economy was more important than the British role east of Suez.[124]

Wilson was never anything but sceptical of the pertinence of Ball's view, commenting that President Johnson was not personally interested in the EEC and that one word to him to the effect that France's condition for British entry would be the renunciation of the link with the United States would end the matter.[125]

When, at the end of July, Wilson visited Washington, Palliser's opposite number, the National Security Adviser, Walt Rostow, told him that the President did not intend to go into detail with the Prime Minister about Europe. Johnson, said Rostow, wanted the British Government to know how much he hoped that we should continue to maintain the momentum for eventual British membership of the EEC. This was not a plug for the rather more extreme ideas of George Ball. The President did not mind Ball saying what he did but recognised that Ball's view was unrealistic. On the other hand, the President did not believe that it was enough for Britain just to wait for de Gaulle to disappear: the more we prepared European opinion for eventual British accession, by a continuing demonstration of our political will to join the Community, the greater pressure we should generate within the Six to work for British membership. The President wanted the Prime Minister to know that this remained an objective of US policy.[126]

Against that background, Wilson wisely took the initiative to raise the subject with President Johnson, and in terms which were designed to present British policy in the most favourable light from the American perspective. There were those in Britain, Wilson said, and perhaps even a majority of the British Press, who would prefer Britain to give up her worldwide role and to concentrate instead on getting into the EEC, even if that meant accepting terms dictated by the French Government. In principle, accession to the Community might be to British advantage and it was a step which the Government wanted to take – but only on terms which took proper account of British and Commonwealth interests. The British

Government were not prepared to accept the French terms, which would imply both the end of Britain's present relationship with the United States and the surrender of her worldwide role. The Prime Minister was not prepared to endorse the concept of a merely inward-looking European role for Britain, with no Atlantic or Pacific part to play. It would be better to wait until the ordinary laws of mortality removed the French obstacle to Britain entering the European Community on acceptable terms.[127]

The evidence of this and other official records suggests that, at this juncture, Wilson had reached a decision about the overall strategy: to join if terms could be negotiated. He had implicitly rejected the view of Balogh and others that the very nature of the Community would be inimical to the policies of a Labour Government. But he had not made up his mind about tactics and timing. The Foreign Office view, and certainly the view of George Brown at the DEA, tended towards at the very least clear signals of intent. Brown was also tempted by the idea of using the Five to outflank de Gaulle. Wilson was always sceptical of that approach. He knew that British accession could not happen without French assent, but he was far from clear in his own mind as to how far de Gaulle could be pressured into a situation where the unpopularity of a veto, both with France's other partners and with her own public opinion, would make it too difficult for de Gaulle to say no.

The evidence of what Wilson said to Johnson at the end of July 1966 suggests that, at that point, Wilson believed that only the departure of de Gaulle would open the way for British membership of the EEC. But there were also good reasons for not waiting. If Britain waited until de Gaulle had gone, could she then count on the same level of support from the other EEC members, or would their enthusiasm have faded for lack of British interest? The longer Britain delayed the greater the degree of economic integration that would have happened without her. The recent EEC agricultural settlement had already added an extra hurdle. With delay, there would be others. In addition, it was becoming evident that discussions of political unity, in effect of the beginnings of an EEC foreign policy, would not be delayed much longer. This was the Government's biggest fear: that Britain would be faced with a Community dominated by France and Germany, and that Germany might, by force of economic power and because of American fears of a Germany drifting towards neutrality, replace Britain as the closest partner of the United States.

In addition, significant bureaucratic momentum had been created by the work by officials on the pros and cons of membership which Wilson had commissioned. By the end of July, a raft of papers had been produced. The Prime Minister had asked about potential conflicts between Britain's NATO obligations and EEC membership, given de Gaulle's attitude towards Britain's relationship with the United States. He had also asked whether Britain should favour a Europe based on the nation state, or one organised on supra-national lines (*Europe de la Commission*, as he termed it).

The official answer to the first question was a lengthy 'no', on the premise that, while de Gaulle, and indeed his successors, might wish it so, there was no way a

British Government could agree to the kind of defence arrangements de Gaulle had in mind. On the whole, officials thought that French policy in this field was likely to survive de Gaulle because it was based on traditional and national considerations which were likely to have enduring force. But they identified two countervailing tendencies. France, post-de Gaulle, might become more 'European', so that French opinion might change or, at least, a successor French Government might be more susceptible to pressure from the Five. Secondly, French fears of German domination of the Community could alter their attitude towards British accession. "On balance", officials concluded " it seems safer to assume a continuation of present policy; but it is equally safe to assume that a French successor regime will be less effective than the present one in putting its policies into effect against strong opposition from outside". This judgement was to prove, in the event, quite close to the mark.

On the question of nation states v supra-nationality, officials concluded that there was both a short-term and a long-term question. Given French attitudes, in particular, it was likely, so officials thought, to be some time before the question of supra-nationality, in any context other than the limited economic one of the present Community, became actual. "Whether at some later, and probably remote, date, the future of Europe lies in the creation of a genuine United States of Europe, embracing economic, political and defence activity, or whether the nations of Europe will continue to wish to preserve a large measure of national independence and sovereignty, is a question which can only mature gradually over a period".

Officials went on to examine each component of the problem, starting with majority voting. Britain would, at least technically, be committing herself to a range of provisions involving the potential for majority voting. Those obligations "could subsequently be translated into specific obligations by means of a decision, regulation or directive adopted by the Council of Ministers without Britain's consent and which would operate directly in this country with the force of law. . .This is a commitment of a kind different from the obligations Britain has accepted under other treaties". On the other hand, the range of fields with which the Community was concerned was strictly limited by the Treaty of Rome to economic and commercial policies and related subjects such as certain fields of social legislation. Nor did the Treaty of Rome envisage that unanimous voting would be given up in respect of major questions such as the scope of the Community. Nor, in the previous eight years, had there been any question of the EEC attempting to impose decisions by majority vote against the major interests of any Government. Even before the recent crisis in the Community it had never been seriously thought that if any Member State declared that its own vital interests were at stake, the others would seek to outvote it. Officials thought the Luxembourg settlement of the crisis rendered the risk of being outvoted in such circumstances "even more remote".

Interestingly, in the light of subsequent and continuing political controversy in Britain over the issue of majority voting, officials took the view that, while in every country there was a healthy dislike of being outvoted, majority voting was necessary to ensure progress rather than stagnation. Enlargement would anyway make it probable that, at the very least, Britain could usually hope to form a blocking minority on legislation which she did not like.

The official advice to Ministers was similarly sanguine about the role of the European Commission which was "not to be compared with that of a Government. It resembles most nearly an official executive, possessing considerable discretion to propose and advise on policy together with certain regulatory and delegated functions. . .Final power in the EEC is firmly vested in the Council of Ministers, which approves or rejects the Commission's proposals".

Officials were, however, not blind to the powers of the Commission. They noted that it had the sole right of initiative; that its proposals could only be amended by the Council acting unanimously and that from these provisions flowed great power which could be abused; perhaps, some thought, already had been abused. But the Commission was a safeguard as well as a threat and, unless it had enjoyed a limited independence and power of initiative, there would have been less economic progress and more political friction. It was hard to see, officials concluded, how progress could be made in an enlarged EEC unless the Commission (which would of course include two British members) was allowed to play the part foreseen for it under the Treaty of Rome.

Officials accurately described the role of the European Parliament as advisory and supervisory. It had, they said, no real powers vis-à-vis the Council of Ministers but it did serve as a limited check on the powers of the Commission. Officials did foresee that any radical growth in the powers of the European Parliament would be at the expense of national Parliaments but concluded that this made it unlikely that either national Governments or Parliaments would welcome any fundamental change in the powers of the EP "at least in the foreseeable future".

In this last piece of advice, officials were understandably lacking in foresight. The members of the EP at that stage were appointed, not elected, and, although the Treaty of Rome envisaged direct election in due course, it prescribed neither the method nor timescale, or even the inevitability of that development. But of the three main institutions of decision making in the European Community (Commission, Council and Parliament) it is the last that has most dramatically increased its powers over the years and at the expense of the other two.

Officials concluded that "any conceivable form of European Common Market will have elements of nationalism as well as of supra-nationalism. . .However, the scale has always been heavily tilted in favour of national control. . .But, in the long run it would not be in our interest to see progress hampered by the possibility of a French (or other) veto on any question of significance; nor is it likely to be necessary for the protection of our own interests that we should possess a formal power of veto, since in an enlarged Community our prospects of finding friends to form a blocking minority should always be good. Nor would an effective Commission, within the limits laid down by the Treaty, be likely to operate to our disadvantage".[128]

The economic analysis provided by officials contained even more informed and intelligent surmise than the political. In August, as the work progressed, Balogh minuted to Wilson that there had been "a very sharp cleavage between the unanimous view of the economic advisers (and, I may add, a large part of the Treasury) which took an unfavourable view of the implications [of membership] and the rest of the membership of the official body which, I fear, refused to contemplate the implications in a realistic manner".[129] A month later, Balogh was warning the Prime Minister (who appears to have paid scant heed to Balogh's advice, a fact borne out by the observation of one of his Private Secretaries at the time) that officials had tried "to fudge the problem of our joining the EEC because of the obvious impossibility of squaring the circle i.e. protecting both the Commonwealth interests and getting into Europe on terms acceptable to the Five, let alone the Six. The brief seems to me a changeless repetition of the posture of the Conservative Government which you so effectively and devastatingly criticised and I wonder whether it is a posture which is really compatible with our policy".[130]

The report of officials, which underwent a number of revisions, was presented on 9 September 1966. It started with the point that the central question was whether Britain would gain or lose economically by joining the EEC. The short-term impact on Britain's balance of payments was likely to be adverse, particularly if she joined at a time when sterling was still weak or only convalescent and the reserves were low. The long term effect on the balance of payments would depend on whether British industry could remain competitive at the time of entry and was able to take advantage of its new opportunities. If it were, then the balance of trade could move in Britain's favour; if not, it would get worse, especially because of the costs of moving towards full adoption of the Common Agricultural Policy.

The paper faithfully recorded the view of the Economic Advisers (including Balogh) that "if we entered while in a weak position there is a danger that competition from the Six would cause too many of our industries to decline, and give insufficient opportunity for expansion of industries in which we have a competitive advantage. We should be forced to pursue deflationary policies to safeguard the balance of payments because our freedom to adopt other policies to this end would be severely limited; and this would lead to stagnation of output, low investment and a slow growth of productivity. All this would in turn weaken our competitive position still further. The vicious circle which has beset this country since 1947 would remorselessly turn further around. Entry from strength would thus appear to be a necessary – though not a sufficient – condition for a favourable outcome. . .More precisely, they [the Economic Advisers] maintain that before joining the Common Market we must foresee a satisfactory balance of payments at a reasonably high level of employment and with demand expanding in line with the productive potential of the economy. . .Whatever the long term consequences, the initial effect of membership on our balance of payments would be adverse, probably by several hundred million pounds a year, because of a worsening in the trade balance and on agricultural account and because of the need to liberalise our capital exports".

Having recorded the view of the Economic Advisers, the official paper eschewed a balance sheet of advantages and disadvantages and concentrated instead on identifying the salient issues and the implications of membership. For British industry, the short term effect of the reduction in tariffs arising from entry would be to accelerate existing trends in British trade towards an increasing surplus in machinery and transport equipment and an increasing deficit in consumer goods. Overall, Britain might expect to gain rather more than she would lose, but the net improvement would be small.

As regards agriculture and agricultural trade with the Commonwealth, the report noted that "our farmers would lose the security and long-term assurances of the guaranteed price system in exchange for a system which aims to secure producers' returns by managing the market (through a combination of variable frontier levies, tariffs and support buying) for the major commodities". Whatever the overall result for farm revenue and profit, cereals growers would prosper and cereal production would rise above the highest levels envisaged under the National Plan. But cereals accounted for only about 12% of total farm sales, whereas the livestock sector (beef, mutton and lamb, pigmeat, milk and milk products, poultry and eggs) accounted for about 70%. The effects of high cereals prices (reflected in the increased costs of animal feeding stuffs) would reduce the profitability of pigs, poultry and eggs, though beef and sheep producers might benefit because they were least affected by high cereal prices. The profitability of milk (accounting for nearly a quarter of present farm income) would also be reduced unless the industry were left to adapt to cheaper summer production – so accepting the possibility of a liquid milk shortage in winter.

Much of Britain's horticultural production would also suffer severe damage because it would lose the protection of high tariffs against the highly competitive advantages of European growers. On the other hand, it was thought that, because the Community was a net importer of fish, the British fishing industry should stand to gain from entry to the markets of the Six or at least from the reduced pressure on the UK market if Norway and Denmark also joined the EEC. The paper could not, and did not, foresee that Britain's future partners would fix a Common Fisheries Policy on the eve of British accession deliberately so as to maximise their relative advantage at British expense, thus creating a commercial advantage for themselves and provoking a source of political friction which has persisted to the present day.

As regards Commonwealth trade, the official paper noted that Britain spent some £2,000 million annually on imported foodstuffs. The Government would need to negotiate special arrangements for some Commonwealth imports, particularly for New Zealand butter, cheese and lamb where the problem had at least been recognised by the Community. Overall, officials thought that the total Community expenditure on agricultural guarantees could involve a gross cost to the British balance of payments of between £200 and £300 million, resulting from the loss to the Exchequer of the levies and duties which would, with membership, accrue to the EEC instead. Of course, Britain would get something back in terms of payments to UK farmers from the Agricultural Fund but this might be as little as £25 million. Thus, it was realistic to expect a net cost to the British balance of payments of between £175 and £250 million.

There would be a further cost to the consumer because it was the consumer (as opposed to the taxpayer) who would have to pay, not only for the full cost of producer support at the higher Community prices, but also for the cost of bringing the prices of foodstuffs imported from outside the EEC up to the higher levels necessary to protect the internal Community market. The increase in food prices might be of the order of 10–14%, adding between 2.5% to 3.5% to the cost of living by the end of the five-year transitional period.

The officials' paper also devoted attention to the issue of taxation. Article 99 of the Treaty of Rome specifically envisaged the harmonisation of the legislation of Member States concerning 'turnover taxes, excise duties and other forms of indirect taxation'. It was by no means certain, at the time officials were writing, that it would be a precondition of membership that Britain moved to a system of VAT, though it was thought to be possible and in reality turned out to be essential. Officials also viewed with relative equanimity the prospective harmonisation of systems of indirect taxation though they predicted that harmonisation of rates was unlikely to arise until the UK had become a member. "Though there is implicit in the Treaty an undercurrent in the direction of the abolition of fiscal frontiers, a formal decision to adopt uniform rates of tax would have to be unanimous under Article 99", officials advised. Equally, while the Treaty of Rome did not refer specifically to direct taxation, the Commission had done some fact-finding work on the taxation of companies and officials thought that eventually the Community might move towards the harmonisation of direct taxes even though the possibility was very remote. In the event, European tax issues were to become one of the more vexatious issues for Britain as a member of the EEC.[131]

The final piece of work for Ministers was that of a Legal Affairs sub-committee of the Official Committee on Europe which drew on, and updated, the studies prepared for the Conservative Government in 1962. Membership of the Communities, Government lawyers advised, "involves a transfer of legislative and judicial powers in certain fields to the Community institutions and an acceptance of a corresponding limitation of the exercise of national sovereignty. . .Adherence to the Treaties would involve the passing of an Act of Parliament applying as law in the United Kingdom so much of their provisions and of the instruments made under them as had direct internal effect as law in Member States; and also providing that future instruments similarly took effect as law here. Such an Act would be an exercise of Parliamentary sovereignty, and Community law, existing and future, would derive its force as law in this country from the Act. The Community law so applied would override our national law so far as it was inconsistent with it. After the Act was passed it would be necessary for Parliament to refrain from enacting legislation inconsistent with Community law and thus to avoid breaches of our Treaty obligations". The report went on to set out in detail the implications for law and Parliamentary sovereignty of British membership.[132]

Its views were reinforced by a minute to Wilson of 29 July from one of his Special Advisers, Stuart Holland. Holland thought that officials generally had underestimated the likely impact of majority voting, given too much weight to the Luxembourg Compromise and failed to emphasise the scale of the Commission's powers, particularly by failing to make plain that "there are but a handful of provisions by which the Council may legislate without the initiative of a proposal from the Commission. . .The Commission's legal power to issue binding judgements on its own authority has implications for our legislative freedom. Such powers cover not only all State aids to industries or regions. . .but also public enterprise and enterprises. . .In general the Report [does not] express the extent to which the scale of provisions for majority voting in the Treaty will limit our own legislative freedom. They spell out the difficulty or ease of administering existing Community legislation rather than the degree to which it restricts us in legislating for ourselves".[133]Wilson asked for Holland's minute to be circulated to other Ministers but, for reasons not apparent from the documents, this was not done.

It might be thought that the continued hostility of de Gaulle, the state of the British economy and the potential costs of membership would all have contributed to the issue of British membership of the EEC being put on the back burner. Had Harold Wilson himself been hostile to the project, he could have persuaded George Brown and Michael Stewart, the prime movers for early action within the Cabinet, that early action was ruled out by the state of the British economy. But that was not his position. "A great deal of work had gone on since the General Election on the question of closer relations with Europe", Wilson wrote in his memoirs. "I felt that, instead of taking this further through Cabinet committees and formal Cabinet meetings, it was the kind of decision which would gain from a full-day meeting at Chequers. Many Ministers felt strongly on this issue; it was better to have a 'second reading' debate with no vote. . .I re-read the papers which had been prepared. . . and considered what I should aim for at the end of the discussion. The case for applying to join the EEC had been strengthened in my mind. But on what terms? What would the European reaction be?"[134]

All of that was true. But Wilson's biographer, Pimlott, offers another explanation: "The massive deflation caused by the run on the pound had disposed of much of Labour's economic and social crusade, at least for the time being. Ministers, and especially premiers, like to have a collective goal: the prospect of European membership, hitherto kept in reserve, offered itself as an obvious candidate. After the July crisis, in Roy Jenkins's words, Wilson 'required constant bounce to get back'. The Common Market option, in this context, looked like a trampoline".[135]

Thus was the stage set for what was possibly the most crucial meeting of the Labour Government in its progress towards adopting a policy of seeking membership of the EEC.

* * * *

4 Once more unto the breach: 1966–1967

The special Cabinet to discuss Europe met at Chequers on Saturday, 22 October 1966. On the previous day, 144 people, including 116 children, over half the pupils at the Pantglas Primary School in the Welsh village of Aberfan, were killed when a coal tip collapsed, overwhelming them in an avalanche of slurry.

Wilson was in Skelmersdale when news of the disaster reached him. He flew directly from there to Aberfan and, many weary and distressing hours later, reached Chequers at 2.30 in the morning on Saturday.

It is one of the features of political life at the top level that Prime Ministers can allow themselves little time for emotional reflection. Personal feelings have to be processed in haste and translated into action. Wilson's feelings about Aberfan were, however, reflected in a memo he dictated in the days immediately after the tragedy and in the recollection in his memoirs that, when he awoke at Chequers on the Saturday morning "beside the sudden waking realisation of those hours I could see my suit hanging and my filthy shoes, both covered with Aberfan slurry. Somehow it was weeks before I could bear to have them cleaned and much longer before I could wear them".[1]

But the business of the day had to be executed. Before Cabinet began, Wilson put to George Brown the idea that the two of them might make an exploratory visit to EEC capitals. "There was a momentary suspicion", Wilson wrote later, "that he would prefer to go alone in the first instance, but this quickly disappeared. As a convinced pro-European I think he suddenly sensed that it was important that I should go too, not only because it would emphasise to our hosts our sense of purpose, but also because I should be able to put directly to European Heads of Government the doubts which were still troubling me and get them answered".[2]

Brown certainly expressed to Wilson's Private Secretary, Michael Palliser, his puzzlement and unease at Wilson's intention. Palliser advised him to seize the chance to get the Prime Minister fully engaged in the European project.[3]

In August, Brown and Stewart had swapped roles in a Cabinet reshuffle, with Brown becoming Foreign Secretary and Stewart First Secretary. Getting the Foreign Office had been the price demanded by Brown for staying in the Government. Stewart, a great loyalist, was rewarded by being advanced to number three in the Cabinet pecking order.[4] The two were still in tandem over Europe and it was their paper that went to the Chequers Cabinet. Both men clearly felt that they had to answer some of the negative assessments in the analytical papers prepared by officials. They tackled the issue head on:

"The official paper on the economic implications indicates inter alia the disadvantages of entry into the Community, including the adverse balance of payments effects", they wrote. "On the other hand, and not dealt with there, are the balance of payments and other implications of our staying out of the Community. It seems to us that we should pay a considerable price if we did not join". They set out the reasons for their view. The best of British industry was convinced that its interests lay in the Community and the effect of not seeking to join would be damaging psychologically and lead to demands for greater (and by implication costly) protection. If Britain did not join she could nonetheless expect Austria and Denmark to seek to do so, thereby truncating EFTA, whose remaining members would probably also seek entry. In those circumstances, other Commonwealth countries would be likely to follow the example of Nigeria and seek association arrangements with the Community which would switch trade preferences from being in Britain's favour to being against. Kenya, Uganda and Tanzania were already discussing just such an option.

For Brown and Stewart the political consequences of failure to join the Community would be even more decisive. The very announcement that Britain had abandoned the probe which it had begun after the General Election would damage Britain's ability to exercise influence over European and Atlantic issues. Britain would, in practice, be handing over much of her influence to Germany. Nor was a prosperous 'little Britain' readily achievable: "The implications of our carrying on outside are, even on an optimistic view, of a slow recovery to a separate and modest status against increasing competition and discrimination, in which we are without the offset of belonging to a larger market with its opportunities for industrial growth and without the protection that membership of this large market would give us against competition from the world at large."

America, the paper argued, would be forced, with Britain out of the EEC, to pay more and more attention to the expanded Community as the effective power centre of Europe. Britain would be bypassed within the Alliance and become a declining influence without having the economic strength to assert herself as America's indispensible ally in the Far East. While China and 'Community Europe' joined the United States and the Soviet Union as super powers, Britain would have allowed itself to decline to an offshore island of a Europe which would be the weakest of the four great powers. With Britain inside the Community, on the other hand, Europe would be a major factor in the developing world power pattern and Britain a major influence.

Brown and Stewart said that if there were prospects of engineering an alternative grouping (based on the Commonwealth, EFTA or the old Commonwealth and the USA) they had been unable to discover them. The choice was between joining the EEC or carrying on as we were.

"These considerations suggest", the two men concluded, "that, with due regard for putting our economy in good shape, we should aim at achieving our objective of negotiating satisfactory terms for membership of the European Community sooner rather than later; and that in judging the terms we should regard as satisfactory, we should bear in mind that it may pay us to forego some of the objectives we would like to secure if this would advance the date when we could join . . . The immediate point we wish to put before our colleagues is our belief that, disagreeable as some of the short term implications of joining the EEC may be, the implications of carrying on broadly as we are now are, in our view, worse. Over the longer term, there can be no question of which is the right choice to make". The paper concluded with a recommendation that the Government should declare its readiness to accept the Treaty of Rome, as a starting point for negotiations on the changes Britain would need to the arrangements made under the Treaty and for negotiating suitable transition periods.[5]

Balogh had given Wilson his comments on the Brown/Stewart approach in a minute of 20 October. Balogh argued that the most crucial condition of having political influence within the Common Market was survival as a first class industrial power. If we became a derelict industrial slum that would destroy our political influence and, with it, a very large part of the arguments of Brown and Stewart. Balogh had earlier argued that membership of the European Community would be incompatible with the kind of control economy which the Labour Party favoured and that the beneficial boost of membership to Britain's export capacity would be outweighed by the overwhelming nature of the competition from more efficient European industries, as well as the unavoidable cost to Britain's balance of payments of the EEC's expensive and protectionist system of agricultural support. In addition, he now argued, Britain could not join without renouncing the special relationship with the United States and accepting the French approach to trans-Atlantic relations. Instead, Balogh recommended consideration of the alternatives to EEC membership, namely the Atlantic Alliance, by which he meant effectively the 51st state approach; or the Little England approach which, he argued, had never been considered at all but which would decisively reduce Britain's commitments in international affairs, free up the resources to double productive investment and rationalise British industry, continue British aid to the ex-British countries and establish close collaboration with Sweden and Norway if the Danes went into the EEC.[6]

If Balogh thought that Wilson, or indeed any British Prime Minister, was likely to be attracted by the Little England approach, it was a mistaken judgement. The phrase alone might have told him that. Wilson paid no heed to the advice.

The Cabinet Secretary, Sir Burke Trend, nonetheless put the same idea, as at least needing consideration, in his brief for the Prime Minister. But Trend was politically savvy enough to call it 'going it alone' and he entertained the idea only to dismiss it and to move on to what he saw as the more realistic options, which were either Association with the United States in a North Atlantic Group, or the EEC. Trend thought the first option unrealistic. The Americans wanted Britain to integrate into Europe. There was no sign that they were prepared to see Britain integrate with them. Even if they were, would the notion be politically acceptable in Britain? Would we wish to find ourselves in a state of economic dependence comparable with that of Canada?

So, the alternative was membership of the EEC. What would this mean for Britain's future policies and prospects? Trend thought that the official papers on the politico-military implications were more reassuring than the economic, which drew attention to the risk that Britain's balance of payments might suffer to the tune of £300–400 million a year. Even on the politico-military front Trend wondered whether, as EEC members, Britain would remain free to maintain policies such as an independent nuclear deterrent and an East of Suez presence if her new partners were able to argue that these policies involved a political or economic price which rendered the UK incapable of pulling her full weight in the Community. He also thought it arguable whether Britain would gain in terms of her relations with the Soviet Union and her capacity to promote better East-West relations if she shifted from the Anglo Saxon to a European (i.e. German-biased) posture. Finally, Trend argued, it was arguable whether, if Britain joined the Community, she could hope to retain the indefinable but not insignificant advantages, in terms of international prestige and influence, which she derived from being the senior partner in the Commonwealth.

Trend thought that the report prepared by Government legal advisers on the legal and constitutional implications of membership suffered from the same deficiency as the economic study in that it did not bring out the progressive limitations on Britain's constitutional and political freedom of action which membership would entail. On the one hand, Trend argued, Britain's effective sovereignty was already circumscribed by a wide range of treaties and conventions; her political independence by the extent to which she relied on military partnership with others; her economic independence by her need to avoid retaliatory action by others; and her financial independence by her position as banker for the sterling area. Experience so far suggested that there need be little immediate practical embarrassment from accession. In so far as there might be, as members Britain could anticipate and minimise the risks. But, Trend continued, "as against these considerations, Ministers will wish to consider how far, in accepting the obligations of membership, we should in fact be surrendering both political and legislative control over our own social and economic policies – and surrendering it not merely to an association of fellow sovereign states with whom we could argue on equal terms, but also to an independent supra-national Commission whose motives would not always be apparent".

The final issue, Trend advised, was whether to accept the advice of Brown and Stewart that the Government should declare its acceptance in principle of the Treaty of Rome. Would such a step lay Britain open – indeed invite – a negotiation for which she was not yet ready (certainly economically but perhaps also politically) and one in which the power to seek derogations from the Treaty of Rome (as distinct from purely transitional provisions) would have been conceded from the outset?[7]

As Cabinet Ministers made their way to Chequers that Saturday morning, most of them, ensconced in their Ministerial Rovers, would have read that week's *Economist* fresh from the newsstands. Under the heading *Pushing the Door to Europe* the paper considered that "so far there have been two major reasons for waiting. One was the antipathy to Europe of the Labour Party. Provided the Prime Minister himself is not antipathetic, and this has always been in doubt, that reason is now quite unimportant. This autumn's docile Labour Party conference has shown that, in all aspects of policy, Mr Wilson has a free hand whatever action he means to take. The other obstacle has been, and is, the French veto . . . Nevertheless, since the French boycott of the Brussels institutions last year something has changed among the Six. It is no longer certain that General de Gaulle, who has wielded the axe so often already, can feel confident about the consequences of wielding it yet again. As matters stand between the Six, a British challenge to France to rebuff its attempt to join the European Community would be a sound diplomatic investment . . . And waiting entails risks. It builds up the familiar image of Britain as a reluctant dragon. Political attitudes in Europe are changing rapidly. It is not likely, but still conceivable, that a period of European doldrums might finally find Germany and others indifferent to British entry into the Community . . . Britain has nothing to lose, and an insurance policy to gain, by making its presence felt in Europe as soon as it plausibly can . . . A rebuff to a British attempt to enter the Common Market would be far from all loss for [Wilson], for the attempt would show that he is not just a tactics-wise, strategy-foolish, opportunist. A success would be a major gain . . . The Government is divided between Departments which see the political issue, but have to keep their noses out of technical affairs, and others which know the nuts and bolts, but have no political view an practise an instinctive nationalism as a substitute for one . . . Can the Ministers at Chequers this weekend . . . start to make the Sphinx in Paris answer questions instead of asking them?".[8]

It was not, however, that aspect of *The Economist*'s coverage which interested Wilson but rather a piece about the importance of technology in the modern world. The scope for European collaboration in technological development and, indeed, the difficulty of mustering the necessary resource without such collaboration, was one of the factors that attracted Wilson to EEC membership. He had copies of the article put round the table for all the participants to read.[9]

Wilson divided up the Cabinet discussion into two sessions. In the morning, with officials present, the Cabinet explored the factual analysis contained in the official papers prepared over the preceding weeks. As the afternoon session opened without officials, other than the Cabinet Office secretariat, Wilson made clear that there was no question of Ministers taking decisions at the meeting. It was, rather, an opportunity for a wide ranging discussion of the major issues.

The first of those issues, according to George Brown, was whether discussions with the Governments of other European countries should be continued and what further clarification of the Government's own position should be given. So far, it had not been possible to discover whether de Gaulle would again veto British entry. It seemed probable that he would wish to do so, but the other five Member States would be strongly opposed to a veto, and it was beyond even the General's power to take France out of the Community. The Five wanted Britain in. So too did the United States. The idea of some kind of association with the US was not an alternative to accession to the EEC. The Dutch and Germans, in particular, were asking how they could help. To answer them required additional authority from Cabinet since there had until now been no cover for exposing anything of the British negotiating position. If the Government were to discover whether British needs could be accommodated in a negotiation then they would have to be ready to say, not that they had decided to join the Communities, which would depend on what could be negotiated, but whether they accepted the Treaty of Rome which was the basis for any negotiation. If negotiations were opened then they could start in 1968, with a view to entry in 1969. Brown recommended that timeframe, as compared with joining in the mid-1970s, which some had favoured in the morning discussion. The Government should, in short, begin an active phase of investigation.

There were, not surprisingly, assorted views in the subsequent discussion. Attention focussed on the formidable difficulties which accession would pose for the British economy, especially in respect of the freedom of capital movement, the CAP, Britain's ability to maintain economic controls and her trade with the Commonwealth. Entry would also restrict Britain's political sovereignty. Some thought the overwhelming priority should be for Britain to regain her own economic strength before anything else. This might take between two and five years, with a further two years beyond that to demonstrate that she could maintain that strength without a further crisis. The United Kingdom's resources, they argued, only permitted her to play a secondary role in the world and entry into the EEC would in no way enlarge that role.

Others thought that, on the contrary, the Cabinet would not be holding their present meeting were it not for the fact that Britain could not hold her own on her own. If the Government did not initiate further and more far-reaching discussions the Five would be disillusioned and opinion within the EEC might harden against British entry at a future date. In the meantime British influence with the United States would diminish and Germany, in ever closer association with the United States, would become the dominant Western European power.

There were differing views about the likelihood of another French veto. No one thought the French would do other than place obstacles in Britain's path, even after the departure of de Gaulle. But some thought a combination of the greater strength of the Five, and electoral factors within France, might make it difficult for de Gaulle to veto once again. Others believed that de Gaulle would veto and be able to sustain that veto against the opposition of the Five. He had made it clear that he wanted Britain 'naked' – stripped of any special position she might have as the centre of the Commonwealth and Sterling Area, and of any special relationship with the United States. However, the general view of both 'tendencies' within the Cabinet was that the possibility of a French veto should not in itself be decisive in determining whether the Government should pursue further the terms on which membership might be possible.

Cabinet agreed that the Government should first of all satisfy itself that there was no superior, or at least satisfactory, alternative to EEC membership.

One suggestion was that if the Government cut defence expenditure, Britain could recover her economic position and that EFTA, with a home market of 100 million people, should be an adequate basis for the development of industrial groups large enough to maintain a competitive global position, as well as trading links with Canada, Australia and New Zealand. On this view, the idea that EFTA might not survive indefinitely was given little credence. If Britain indicated that she had decided not to pursue EEC membership then it was likely that only Austria would leave the Association.

Other Cabinet members thought this unrealistic, that other members of EFTA would leave and that the Association would probably break up. Nor could Britain count on continuing trade with the Commonwealth given the increasingly close association of Canada with the US and the determination of Australia to seek wider markets.

Some were attracted by the idea of an Atlantic/Commonwealth Association, especially if the Kennedy Round were to fail and if the French continued to disrupt the Western Alliance. But others thought this unlikely to be practicable and that, even if it were, such a relationship with the United States would place Britain in a position of unacceptable economic and political subservience. In any event, the US strongly favoured British membership of the EEC as a further guar-antee of the western Alliance and, for that reason alone, would be unlikely to contemplate a different relationship.

There was understandably quite a debate about whether the Government should indicate their acceptance in principle of the Treaty of Rome. The general view of Cabinet was that it would be imprudent to make a clear-cut declaration of British acceptance of the Treaty at this stage. To do so would weaken Britain's bargaining position and might have serious and damaging implications for the British economy by implying that the Government intended at an early stage to abandon the economic controls that were vital for the recovery. It was, however, the general view that the Government should be able to indicate that if satisfac-tory transitional arrangements and adjustments in the Community's existing arrangements could be obtained in negotiation, then the provisions of the Treaty of Rome would not in themselves, in the last resort, constitute an impassable barrier to British membership.

The Prime Minister summed up thus far. The discussions had brought out that the risks and difficulties involved in joining the EEC were formidable and the balance of advantage difficult to strike. On the economic side, the Government did not know what terms they could get on issues which involved hundreds of millions of pounds of expenditure, notably in regard to capital movements and the effect of the Community's agricultural policy on Britain's imports, exports and payments.

On the political side, Wilson argued, a similar problematic range of difficulties arose. The balance of advantage would depend hugely on the terms: good, bad or indifferent; and upon whether the British economy was strong when we joined. That might not be achievable for between two and four years. However, we could not carry on without clarifying our position. On that score Brown was right. Nor did the probing that had been done so far provide an adequate basis of fact on which to make a judgement. Nor had there been sufficient study of the possible alternative associations with, for example, the Commonwealth or the United States.

Wilson went on to give his personal estimate of where matters now stood on the five conditions for entry formulated by the Labour Party in 1962. First, EFTA was no longer a stumbling block: the EEC's negotiations with Austria showed that the fact of Austria's neutrality was no longer an issue. Second, it now seemed unlikely that British agriculture, taken as a whole, would do badly in the Community. The problem would be that production would be unbalanced. For example, cereal growing would be unduly favoured and dairying would be penalised, and Britain would have to seek some accommodation on this. Third, experience and enquiry now suggested that Britain's external financial and economic obligations already limited her freedom to play the economy as much as, or more than, membership of the Communities seemed likely to do in practice. Fourth, the example of General de Gaulle did not suggest that Community membership would trammel the independence of British foreign policy – which seemed likely to depend more on her economic strength or weakness than on the Treaty of Rome. Fifth, the major problem of safeguarding Commonwealth interests now came down to that posed by the Community's agricultural policy.

Wilson suggested that the next steps might be:

To give first priority to rebuilding Britain's economic strength, considering all necessary measures including the possible limitation of her defence commitments;

To study in greater depth the possible alternatives to membership of the Communities. These included the idea of a North Atlantic Association. It would be a great weakness if, in negotiating with the Communities, the Government had no alternative course open to them;

To find out what terms the Government could get for entry. This would have to be done by informal probing of the six member countries individually. In the case of France this could only be done by an approach to General de Gaulle himself.

Wilson then launched his idea that he and the Foreign Secretary should travel to see the Heads of Government of the Six "for frank discussions, stating what our major difficulties were, and seeking to ascertain how far they would be met, and whether there would be any conditions in regard to e.g. our relations with the US. If asked whether we could accept the Treaty of Rome, the reply might be that, provided we received satisfaction on the points on which we still saw difficulty, adherence to the Treaty would not in itself be a sticking point. It would of course be necessary for the Cabinet to consider this matter before a decision was taken".

In subsequent discussion, "doubts were expressed on the prudence of such a course at the present time". Wilson summed up that an exploratory mission would, of course, be without commitment and that, in any case, a formal decision would have to be taken by Cabinet. In any event, there was no question of negotiating with the Six for some time. Officials would look in detail at how far some form of North Atlantic Association might offer an alternative to membership of the EEC as well as what options would be open to Britain if that, or EEC membership, did not prove practicable.[10]

Cabinet was to meet again, formally, on the subject of Europe on 1 November and the Cabinet Secretary advised the Prime Minister that he could sum up the Saturday meeting at the outset of Cabinet by saying that the Chequers meeting "had concluded that, on balance, it would probably be worthwhile to make a fresh attempt to discover whether we could now obtain, by fresh negotiation, acceptable terms for our entry into the Community". Wilson thought this went too far, commenting in the margin of Trend's memo: "Can't quite say that. No conclusions. Only mine".

The Foreign Secretary, meanwhile, felt that the cautious version in the minutes as to what could be said in reply to the question whether the Government accepted the Treaty of Rome was an inaccurate representation of the meeting at Chequers. He was, Palliser warned Wilson, "very worked up . . . and feels that the minutes are a considerable withdrawal from what you actually said".[11]

Brown felt in retrospect that it had taken "tremendous pressure" to persuade Wilson to be positive towards the EEC. Douglas Jay, by contrast, as an opponent of EEC entry, believed that, while Wilson tried to give the impression to the anti-Marketeers that he was still a sceptic, in reality he had sold out to the supporters of British entry.[12]

Wilson, in his own memoirs, was careful on this as on other issues to describe what he did and said, rather than what he thought. It is clear from the analysis of Labour's five tests that he gave to his colleagues on 22 October that his own thinking had moved in a positive direction. For the convinced pro-Marketeers the political case for joining was overwhelming, just as for the anti-Marketeers the sovereignty and related arguments against joining were as powerful as the economic ones. For Wilson that never seems to have been the case. He was a sceptic with a small 's'. For him, the terms of entry were the principal determinant of whether it would be in Britain's interest to join. The attractions of exercising political influence as part of the EEC were evident. The legal and policy constraints involved in accepting the Treaty of Rome were not in themselves an insuperable obstacle to joining. But, for Wilson, the impact on the British balance of payments and on the economies of the countries of the Commonwealth, as well as on Britain's relations with those countries, were real and significant factors in his thinking. The issue of membership was, and remains, so polarised that it has become almost an article of faith to believe or not to believe. It is hardly to Wilson's discredit that he wanted to make up his mind on the basis of the evidence, rather than on instinct.

There were also of course divided views within Cabinet with Douglas Jay suggesting that, at the time of the Chequers meeting, there were ten in favour of membership, eight against and three undecided.[13] Against that background, and given Wilson's own views on the substance, it would have been surprising if he had led boldly from the front. Opinion was still too finely balanced for him to risk a defeat in Cabinet and he had a much better chance of capturing undecided opinion by playing a long game. So, even if he himself had been as decisively in favour as Brown or Stewart, it would have been out of character, as well as tactically rash, to pin his colours firmly to the mast. Moreover, whatever decision was eventually to be taken by Cabinet, it would fall to him as Leader to carry the party, where opinions were also divided.

Two days after the Chequers meeting, the *Daily Telegraph* carried a Gallup poll showing a remarkable degree of cross-party support for accession in the country as a whole. 68% of those questioned were in favour of membership (72% for the Conservatives, 70% for the Liberals and 69% for Labour – differences which were well within the margin of statistical error). Among European business and other professional leaders Gallup found an extraordinary degree of support for British membership: 91% across the EU, ranging from 98% in Germany to 84% in France.[14]

Only de Gaulle did not seem to catch the mellow autumn mood. In a press conference on 28 October he lauded the action taken by "the French authorities" i.e. himself, in 1963 in preventing British membership, and in 1965 "when we had to interrupt the Brussels negotiations". He went on to make comments about the German Government which, even forty five years later, are striking for their directness. "So far as Germany is concerned" de Gaulle said, " despite the terrible losses which the wars launched by the First and Third Reich inflicted on us, we offered her a frank reconciliation, and I have myself visited her cities, factories and countryside to proclaim this to her people, in the name of eternal France. Almost four years ago, we even went so far as to conclude with the Federal Republic, at her request, a treaty which could have provided the basis for a special cooperation between the two countries in the political, economic, cultural and defence fields. It is not our fault if the preferential links between Bonn and Washington, contracted without France and constantly tightened, have deprived the Franco-German agreement of inspiration and substance. It is quite possible that, as a result of this, our German neighbours have lost several opportunities for common action by the two nations, because while they were applying, not our bilateral treaty but the unilateral preamble which changed all the sense of the Treaty and which they themselves had added [the German Parliament had insisted on referring to the importance of transatlantic relations and of an inclusive EEC as a condition of ratification], events moved in another direction, notably in the East, and even perhaps in Washington, altering the situation which existed at the outset. However, we have not gone back either on the burying of our grievances or on the practice of cordial relations with Federal Germany, and while we maintain complete control over our forces there, as elsewhere, we agree to keep for the time being on her territory an important military force which obviously contributes to her security, which we will withdraw as soon as she wishes us to do so, and for which, in contrast with her other allies, we ask for no financial contribution. In fact, so far as Germany is concerned, how could we have been more deserving or more accommodating?"[15]

De Gaulle's message to Germany was to achieve over time its desired effect. It was designed to intimidate, and it did.

Cabinet met again on 1 and 3 November, this time formally in London, to take up the discussion of EEC membership. About two thirds of the full Cabinet had been present on 22 October (those Ministers with a clear Departmental interest), so the 1 November meeting was the first full discussion by the full Cabinet. Wilson summarised what had seemed to his colleagues at the earlier meeting to be the principal issues: freedom of capital movements; agricultural policy; the effects of membership on Britain's competitive ability, though these last had not been thought to be serious since Britain would gain from the abolition of tariffs, and gain still more from the large market which would result and from economies of scale; control of our own economy, especially as regards industrial development; the constitutional, legal and political consequences of membership, though here it seemed that practice was different from theory and that "on that basis, Ministers had been advised that it would be unnecessary to seek to have the Treaty of Rome amended before we joined the EEC". Finally, Wilson said, the Chequers discussion seemed to have established that there need be little fear that EEC membership would interfere with the conduct of an independent foreign policy. It had not been possible to reach a conclusion about de Gaulle's intentions or conclusions.

Wilson described the recommendation made by Brown and Stewart that there should be further exploratory discussions with the members of the EEC, on the basis of a public declaration of the Government's willingness to accept the Treaty of Rome, provided that the means could be found of meeting Britain's own difficulties.

Thus far, Wilson's summary of the Chequers discussion had been neutral but he went on to put some of his own cards on the table for the first time: "As regards the balance of advantage of membership of the Community, in his view the arguments based on the advantages of scale to be derived from membership of a much larger market were of greater weight than those related to the 'cold douche' of competition to be expected in those circumstances." He then cleverly used the 'advantages of scale' argument to introduce, and dismiss, the possibility of a North Atlantic Free Trade Area. "It was unfortunate", he said, "that the arguments of scale had not been considered five years ago in relation to possible economic arrangements on a North Atlantic basis, though there must be considerable doubts whether the US would be willing to forsake her protectionist policy sufficiently to make such arrangements possible." So Wilson made it appear as if, somehow, the idea of an Atlantic Free Trade Area might have been viable if only the Tories had pursued it but they had neglected to do so and now the idea was one whose time was irrevocably past.

Wilson was similarly adroit in telling Cabinet that he agreed with Brown and Stewart that further soundings of EEC Governments should be made; in rejecting the idea that there should be a prior declaration of willingness to accept the Treaty of Rome (a declaration without conditions would be dangerous; a declaration with conditions would simply repeat the position of the Conservative Government) and in concluding that the only way through the impasse would be for him and Brown to make a tour of EEC capitals to ascertain what the conditions and timing of UK entry to the Community might be. He proposed that, if asked about acceptance of the Treaty of Rome, the British response should be that, given satisfaction on the major points of capital movements and the CAP, the Government would be prepared to sign the Treaty of Rome.

Of course, since the CAP embraced the British budget contribution and its associated impact on the balance of payments, and the entire future of Britain's relations with the rest of the Commonwealth, Wilson's formula was close to being simply a shorthand version of the Conservative list of conditions. More significant than its departure from the Conservative approach, however, was its divergence from the Labour Party approach hitherto enshrined in the five conditions.

Finally, Wilson acknowledged that some colleagues had expressed doubts about the proposed visits to EEC capitals. But, he asserted, such visits would reduce to a minimum the possibilities of misrepresentation at home and abroad of the Government's position. What he did not say was that such visits would also, of course, ensure that the soundings attracted the maximum media attention and that, if Wilson and Brown came back with a favourable report, it would be very hard for anti-Marketeers to gainsay it without damage to the standing of the Government as a whole.

Brown took up the argument: either Cabinet agreed to the joint visits by himself and the Prime Minister or, if Cabinet felt that such a tour might appear too dramatic, then the Government should make a declaration in respect of the Treaty of Rome, followed by lower level investigations. Thus, Ministers were being told that the only way to avoid the controversial Declaration was to accept the high-level tour.

Needless to say, since other Cabinet members were not political slouches, they did not automatically accept the Morton's fork on which Wilson and Brown were seeking to impale them. Some Ministers argued that neither a declaration nor a programme of visits was wise at this stage. Such a course could lead Britain into premature negotiations, risk a rebuff from the French and be hugely damaging to the prestige of the Prime Minister and Foreign Secretary.

Wilson sought to recapture the initiative by suggesting that the discussion should concentrate on a few issues, taking account of the different points of view. There was, he said, substantial agreement that the Government could not maintain the present position; and that they needed to find out the conditions of membership they hoped to secure before they could decide whether or not to seek entry. That information could only be obtained at a higher level, and on a different basis, from previous discussion. Entry from weakness would be disastrous, but to take no further action while Britain regained her strength might damage the recovery. The purpose of the proposed visits would not be to seek entry, but to ascertain the likely conditions of entry. If the conditions turned out to be unacceptable – or if he and Brown were rebuffed – that would constitute the strongest defence of the Government's subsequent position.

Wilson then wrapped up his basic proposal in an accompanying flurry of diplomatic activity. There should be a conference of EFTA Heads of Government in London in December, followed by an announcement reaffirming Britain's willingness to enter the EEC on appropriate terms and announcing the proposed visits. He would then attend the January meeting of the Council of Europe in Strasbourg and make a full statement of the Government's attitude to Europe. Cabinet would consider and approve the terms of what he should say. Then the visits, which would not just be about EEC membership, but about urging a forthcoming attitude to the Kennedy Round. The studies of alternatives to EEC membership should be urgently pursued. Consultation of the Commonwealth should be organised.

By turning the issue into a series of procedural proposals, Wilson was able to sum up that the Cabinet were on balance in agreement with the broad lines of the programme of action which he had put forward. But he did not push his luck. He promised Cabinet a further paper from the Foreign Secretary setting out in detail the programme of action and the statement of intent.[16]

That paper was duly considered by Cabinet on 9 November, when there was rather more resistance to the Wilson/Brown scheme than they might have anticipated, probably because its opponents realised that, if they approved it, they were in effect firing the starting gun for a process that would lead to a new negotiation for membership. But the extent of opposition was not such as to prevent Wilson from summing up that on balance the Cabinet agreed to the intensified exploration that he and the Foreign Secretary had proposed, subject to the qualification that it would be necessary to negotiate certain permanent adaptations to the arrangements under the Treaty of Rome, as well as suitable transitional provisions. He would seek the approval of Cabinet for a statement which he would make to Parliament. At the end of the exploratory discussions "the Cabinet would then have to decide whether the terms which we might reasonably hope to obtain in formal negotiation were adequate to justify our joining the Community . . . Meanwhile, the Cabinet had taken no decision on whether or not we should in due course apply to join the EEC or on whether we should start negotiations to that end". The Foreign Secretary added that further thought would need to be given to the timetable for the visits to capitals of the Six. The visit to Paris should be neither the first nor the last.[17]

Wilson made his announcement to Parliament the following day, with support from the Conservative and Liberal benches (albeit of the 'joy over the sinner that repenteth' variety) and criticism of a 'perilous adventure' only from the veteran Labour Member, Emmanuel Shinwell.

Francois Mitterrand, the leader of the French Socialist Party, was in London on the same day and, together with Guy Mollet, called on Wilson. According to Michael Palliser's account of the conversation, Mitterrand did not reveal whether he himself would be a candidate in the next Presidential Election though he believed the Gaullists would be hard to beat in the next Assembly elections. He and Mollet both thought Pompidou would be de Gaulle's *dauphin*. But Mitterrand disagreed when Mollet spoke rather contemptuously of Pompidou's political ability. Mitterrand thought that Pompidou had acquired considerable political flair and was by far the ablest and most effective of the current Gaullist leaders. Indeed, he clearly regarded Pompidou as a dangerous proposition in any future election.

Both Mollet and Mitterrand had been in the Gallery of the House of Commons to hear Wilson's statement on the European Community. Mollet was slightly grudging in his recognition that Wilson's statement represented an advance in the British Government's position but Mitterrand, "characteristically, rather inscrutable throughout" seemed more enthusiastic about what the Prime Minister had said. It was, according to Mitterrand, a regrettable fact that the French public on the whole supported de Gaulle's anti-Americanism. The same was not true in respect of de Gaulle's anti-British feeling. There was also widespread support in France for the Common Market, and de Gaulle's boycott in 1965 had undoubtedly lost him votes in the Presidential Election. If de Gaulle now persisted in an anti-British attitude in response to the Prime Minister's initiative, this would not be popular with the French people as a whole.

The meeting concluded with a brief exchange about Herr Kiesinger (the news of whose election by the German CDU as successor to Chancellor Erhard had just arrived). Mollet said that he knew Kiesinger quite well, respected his ability and regarded him as a good European. Of course, Mollet added, he had been a Nazi, but "find me the German who hasn't".[18] What none of the participants in the meeting could foresee was that Erhard's resignation (his FDP partners had broken the coalition because of a budget disagreement) and his replacement by Kurt Kiesinger at the head of a grand coalition, would lead to a rapprochement between Germany and France, which would have consequences for Britain's European prospects.

Wilson and Brown were thinking actively about the next steps. They agreed that the Cabinet Office, rather than the Foreign Office, should provide neutral chairmanship of the inter-departmental coordination that was now needed. Wilson had agreed with Trend that there should be meetings at Deputy Secretary level, or thereabouts, chaired by Bill Nield of the Cabinet Office, with Permanent Secretaries meeting under Trend's chairmanship as necessary. Brown agreed, adding in manuscript to his formal minute of acquiescence: "And don't let anyone say I'm not trying to help".[19]

Brown also agreed to the proposal put to him by Wilson in a private note that an Advisory Committee for Industry should be established to help the Government through the "varying phases of Common Market negotiations". "In view of the feelings of DEA that they are now being by-passed in the whole Common Market operations . . . it would provide a means of integrating DEA and the First Secretary [Michael Stewart] in the whole operation."[20] Wilson and Brown were, on this evidence, already thinking ahead to formal negotiations for entry and Wilson was clearly anxious, not just to gruntle Stewart, but to have him actively engaged as a pro-European ally.

Wilson also wrote to President Johnson to bring him up to speed on the Government's shift of policy. "As you know", he wrote on 11 November, "I have never been one of the little band of so-called 'Europeans'. I believe that the way our predecessors set about things five years ago was the wrong way; the failure of their attempt was inevitable and no Government under my leadership is going to get into a similar situation. Moreover, it always seemed to me doubtful . . . whether the Six, left to themselves, were likely to develop into a Community dedicated to a concept of ever widening and freer world trade; or whether the trend would not be towards a tight little inward-looking group of countries concerned essentially with their own affairs . . . This tendency represents a real danger for all of us . . . On the other hand, I believe that the situation in Europe has changed pretty fundamentally since 1962 and is continuing to change; that the prospects of building a new and wider Community including, as well as ourselves, a number, if not all, of our EFTA partners, are now much more promising than they were; and that if we can build such a Community, it will greatly strengthen not only Britain and Europe, but the West as a whole. Obviously, this concept of an outward looking European Community, designed to play the constructive role in world affairs that each of us is now finding too difficult, is bound to raise once more the fundamental issue of our own relationship with the United States which stuck in de Gaulle's gullet last time. The prophets of gloom say that this remains as total an obstacle to our present approach as it proved for our predecessors. We shall see. My own belief is that the General had not changed one iota in his general view of the world or of our own relationship with yourselves. But . . . Europe and the world are changing around him and so is the situation in France itself . . . Clearly, our talks in Paris will be by far the most difficult and delicate of any we shall have. But if I despaired of them, I would not have said what I said yesterday . . . There shall be no change in the fundamental relationship between our two countries and in our own basic loyalty to, and belief in, the Atlantic concept . . . We are going into this in the firm belief . . . that the sort of European concept I have outlined above is the right one and that our efforts to achieve it shall succeed . . . in what I personally regard as an historic initiative".[21]

That message was scarcely one that Wilson would have felt able, comfortably, to show to his more sceptical Cabinet colleagues. Its tone was barely reconcilable with the cautious summing up Wilson had given to Cabinet two days earlier. It is clear that Wilson intended his fact-finding mission to EEC capitals to produce answers that would allow a bid for EEC membership to be launched. That too was how Johnson read Wilson's message. He replied on 15 November that he was "immensely heartened by your courageous announcement about joining the EEC".[22]

Wilson would have been less than human if he had not hoped that he might succeed with de Gaulle where Macmillan had failed. His comment to Johnson that "no Government under my leadership is going to get into a similar situation" to that experienced by the Conservatives, reads as somewhat vainglorious. Yet, it is evident from what Wilson went on to say about de Gaulle's position that he was under no illusion about de Gaulle's hostility. The 'mistake' Wilson was determined not to repeat was that of giving de Gaulle grounds for turning Britain down. So, Britain would not get into a negotiation where there was a huge list of problems to be resolved, thus giving the French the excuse for claiming that they were incapable of resolution. Nor would there be ambiguity about defence and possible nuclear collaboration. The hope on the British side was that, by avoiding a repetition of what they saw as past mistakes, by exploiting the good will of the Five and their relatively greater strength vis-à-vis France following de Gaulle's failed blackmail of 1965 and because of the favourable shift in French public opinion, they could make it too difficult for de Gaulle to do what he undoubtedly would want to do, i.e. to veto a British application yet again.

Britain's Ambassador in Paris, Patrick Reilly, thought that de Gaulle had probably hoped that the cold remarks he had made about Britain and the EEC at his press conference on 28 October would serve to discourage HMG from making an early move. The French Press, according to the Embassy, had certainly been briefed, and had dutifully commented, that the Prime Minister's remark in the House on 10 November that there was nothing about defence in the Treaty of Rome and that such matters were dealt with in NATO indicated strict limits to Britain's European conversion. Reilly advised that Britain could expect no helping hand from the General. On the contrary, the French were likely to do all they could to spread among the Five doubts and suspicions about HMG's real intentions (e.g. that she was out to sabotage the hard-won CAP) as well as fears that British entry would bring with it financial liabilities for the Six. The French Press, with unsurprising egocentricity, were suggesting that Paris should be the first capital to be visited by Wilson and Brown. With equally unsurprising tactical thoughts in mind, Reilly advised that Paris should be visited last.[23]

From Bonn, Sir Frank Roberts reported on the welcome generally accorded to the Prime Minister's announcement. On the other hand, Roberts was already warning that the new German Government would put some degree of improvement in Franco-German relations high on its list of priorities and that this in turn would mean even greater reluctance than the previous Government would have shown to face a showdown with de Gaulle over British entry. The successor to Erhard, Dr Kiesinger, had added to his welcome for the prospect of British accession the comment that this would require the agreement of all the Six and that the Six included France, with whom Germany must strengthen her friendship. Thus was delivered the first intimation of the "all assistance short of help" which was to characterise Kiesinger's approach to British membership.[24]

Crucial as Germany's attitude would be, the key issue was how to overcome French objections. The Chancellor of the Exchequer took some informal soundings among fellow Europeans in the margins of an OECD meeting in late November. There was general agreement both among the EFTA countries and the Five, Callaghan found, that Britain could not be expected to risk another veto and a feeling that such a veto would probably mean the final division of Europe, which was not to be tolerated. On the other hand, Callaghan continued, "we cannot rely on the Five standing up to the French, and further, it would be unwise to try to line them up. In a talk I had with a group of French journalists they all emphasised that one of Heath's mistakes was that he appeared to be lining up with the Five and in the end he was left alone with them". Callaghan had found the French journalists strongly of the view that everything would hinge on a direct confrontation between Wilson and de Gaulle. In the end, the remaining members of the Six would not, in the view of the journalists, with which Callaghan agreed, count for very much. A fairly common view among the French journalists had been that the Common Market was not a large matter to de Gaulle; the important issue was the political independence of Europe from the United States. Callaghan had also drawn the conclusion that, despite all the gossip in the *couloirs*, no-one, including French officials, had any idea what French policy was. They were waiting for word from on high. De Gaulle, Callaghan was certain, would take a personal decision, albeit after discussion with his colleagues and after listening to Wilson and Brown. Foreign policy and defence would play a large part in determining the General's attitude.[25]

There were other discouraging signals to validate Callaghan's shrewd appraisal. Pompidou told French journalists at about the same time that, while Britain was undoubtedly close geographically to Europe, it was doubtful whether she was close in other respects. It was not up to France, or to the Six, but Britain, which had to show that it would accept the rules of the Common Market, including its inconveniences which encompassed, as far as Britain was concerned "the efforts we [the Six] have made to resist international competition".[26]

Christopher Soames, former Conservative Cabinet Minister who had lost his seat in the 1966 General Election, called on the French Foreign Minister on 24 November. He was told by Couve de Murville how badly de Gaulle's last substantive meeting with the British [Rambouillet] had gone and Couve did not give Soames "the impression that he hoped the next meeting will go well. Neither, on the other hand, did he say anything to lead me to believe that the reverse was true . . . My general impression, for what it is worth, is that, though the French Government does not welcome the British Government's initiative, he feels that it is possible that it may have to succeed. All is to play for but the stakes will be high".[27]

One of the few Frenchmen to acknowledge the importance of Wilson's initiative was Jean Monnet, who was doing what he could to counter the briefing being given to French journalists by Couve and others which dismissed it as of little importance and as showing no new evidence of any real desire to enter the EEC. Monnet thought it important for Wilson to say, in Paris and in the clearest terms, that Britain wanted to join, accepting both the Treaty of Rome and the CAP. The simplest possible approach, leaving all special arrangements to be sorted after accession, would make it impossible for de Gaulle to say no. Things had moved on since the 1963 veto. The young were bored with the old quarrels and wanted Europe with Britain in it.

Reilly asked Monnet whether he thought that an offer by Britain of cooperation in some political or defence field of interest to the French might help secure agreement to British accession. Monnet completely rejected the idea. It was impossible to catch the General with any gimmick. Heath was quite wrong in his belief that de Gaulle's acquiescence could be bought by some agreement in the nuclear field. De Gaulle did not want such an agreement. He had an obsession about not being dependent in any way on anyone. He detested the EEC, but he could not get rid of it. He would detest British entry but, if the British played their cards right, he could not prevent it . . . In any case, the General was coming to the end of the road. What more could he do but leave the Alliance? On the whole, Monnet thought it likely that he would do so, but would this matter? Everyone regarded France as virtually out of the Alliance already. The best course for Britain, Monnet insisted, was to seize the initiative with a simple, straightforward declaration, sticking firmly to the economic issues alone and asking before entry for nothing more than an adequate transitional period.[28]

Reilly believed Monnet was broadly right in believing that there was a strong current of opinion in France in favour of British entry to the EEC. But he equally thought it essential not to exaggerate the influence of French public opinion on de Gaulle, not least because the General was expert at manipulating it. Even if the British Government was able to make the kind of dramatic proposal which Monnet had advocated (and Reilly correctly assumed that it was not), Reilly doubted if it could be exploited to British advantage in the French election campaign. The French elections should not therefore be a key factor in planning British tactics.[29]

Armed with the unanimous support of EFTA countries following the meeting of EFTA Heads of Government in London on 5 December, Wilson and Brown prepared for their odyssey. Wilson was looking for some hook to engage de Gaulle, or at the very least for ways of minimising his opposition. One such hook was conceivably the old Fouchet Plan, to which de Gaulle had referred in his October press conference, saying that it could be taken up again as soon as France's EEC partners showed that they were pursuing truly 'European' policies. "Could we make a move forward by accepting Fouchet?" Wilson asked. "It seemed quite reasonable at the time. Or at any rate make encouraging noises?"

The attraction of the Fouchet plan, from the British perspective, was that it had proposed what the Foreign Office, in advice to Wilson, called "a fairly loose form of political cooperation". For exactly the same reason, the plan was unattractive to the Five, especially the Belgians and Dutch who wanted a more institutionalised political structure with, built into it, a series of checks and balances to protect the smaller members of the Community from the dominance of France and Germany. The plan had lain dormant since 1962 when two versions, one representing French views and the other those of the Five, had been on the table. So, as the Foreign Office pointed out, the problem for Britain was that, if we declared support for the Fouchet Plan (French version) we should alienate the Five.[30]

Wilson agreed with Palliser's advice that thought was needed before the tour of European capitals about British ideas on future political cooperation and about how these should be presented. Palliser thought it essential that the Prime Minister and Foreign Secretary should say exactly the same things on the subject to the French on the one hand and the Five on the other. British thinking might well prove more palatable to the French than to the Five but the French could be counted on to ensure that whatever was said to them by the British would be retailed, in terms somewhat to our disadvantage, to the Five. So it would be essential to take a consistent line throughout. "Yes", said Wilson, "but our whole strategy should be based on the fact that the Five, at the end of the day, will probably not oppose our entry e.g. on these grounds, and the French might – indeed probably would. Can we be more definite?"[31]

The grand tour was not due to start until late January 1967 but there were two significant preliminary visits to France in mid-January – by the Chancellor of the Exchequer, Jim Callaghan, and the Foreign Secretary, George Brown, whose visits overlapped.

Callaghan was in Paris on Treasury business but his French opposite number, Michel Debré, raised with Callaghan the subject of British accession, speaking, he said, to express his own thoughts rather than those of the French Government. There were, said Debré, two big problems. The first was that if Britain entered the Common Market, the Common Market itself would not be the same with Britain inside it. Eight years had passed since the creation of the EEC. Change would seem all the greater because habits and rules had been created. The Community could not remain the same with Britain inside it, but to say that was not the same as to have reservations about Britain's admission. It was not just a question of what would be the economic and political tendencies of the new Community. A Community had been created which was in some ways wider and in some ways more narrow than the Treaty of Rome had envisaged. What would be its future political and economic policies? How would it work? These questions had to be faced if 'reservations' were to be avoided. After de Gaulle's return to power he had had to decide whether to apply the Treaty of Rome, signed the previous year, or not. Politically, he had been in favour of it. He had been forced to accept its economic features, involving the determination of the proper value of the Franc in relation to the DM and the other currencies of the member countries. Britain's entry now, when the internal tariffs were disappearing, capital movements were being freed and consideration was being given to harmonising taxes and capital movements, would raise similar questions, in particular the consequences of membership for the value of the pound.

"Debré would like us in if the General would let him", wrote Wilson in the margin of this account. For Debré was indeed implying that British accession was possible if Britain was prepared to make the same radical changes required by membership that France had had to make. But he was also saying that, whereas de Gaulle had faced these decisions only one year into the life of the Community, now, eight years on, the process of adaptation would be that much harder for Britain. Implicit in Debré's comments was the thought, as well, that France had painfully shaped the Community to suit her interests and the very act of letting Britain in would put those achievements at risk.[32]

On the same day, George Brown was speaking to Couve de Murville, the French Foreign Minister. The record shows Brown saying a lot and Couve only a little. But what Couve said was significant. When Brown asked whether French attitudes mirrored the British Government's serious desire to enter the EEC, Couve replied that the French Government were indeed taking the matter very seriously. They considered it a very big problem, one that would continue to exist for as long as it remained unresolved. In January 1963, the French had known that what had happened was not the end of the story and that the problem would be posed again sooner or later, though they did not know that this would happen "less than four years later". It was impossible to say what would happen. Couve referred to the need to understand Britain's problems. Brown replied that it was also necessary to discuss solutions. The British Government had been continually told that they must say clearly that they wished to enter the EEC. They had now said this. He had, however, never heard M. Couve de Murville say that the French Government also wished this to happen.

Brown did not wait for Couve to reply before going on to spell out the serious consequences of another failure i.e. that Britain "would see other ways of arranging her affairs". This allowed Couve to say no more than that he fully understood this.[33]

On 16 December, Brown called on de Gaulle. Brown opened by assuring de Gaulle of Britain's sincerity in applying for EEC membership. It was not a political ploy. He himself had long been in favour of entry and British public opinion generally had come to the same view.

De Gaulle replied that he understood why there were many reasons for Britain to wish to join the EEC. But Britain had not joined in to make the EEC in the first place. Under what conditions did the British Government wish to enter now? He had discussed all this at great length with Macmillan. Macmillan and Heath had also said that they wanted to enter but they had never indicated that they could accept the conditions that would make it possible for them to join the kind of EEC that already existed. Macmillan, de Gaulle implied, had wanted to join a different EEC than the one created by the Treaty of Rome. So the French Government's answer to the question whether they wanted Britain to enter the EEC would depend on the conditions for British entry. British entry was not an easy matter. Britain was a maritime country, with advantages and disadvantages. Britain had her Commonwealth. She had the sterling zone. These were facts. How could Britain accept rules which were Continental rules for Continental countries, which had nothing corresponding to the Commonwealth, to the sterling area or to Britain's maritime economy? The French did not know, and did not see how it could be possible for Britain to come in.

Brown responded that, of course, there were particular difficulties for Britain but politicians existed to find solutions to such problems. France had had to make big changes. If France could do so, why not Britain?

De Gaulle changed tack. He would like to draw Brown's attention to the political aspect of the EEC and he would speak frankly about it. He had not made the Treaty of Rome. The men who did had done so with a political aim. This was to make Europe after their fashion, which was not his own. Many things had changed since then. The urge towards supra-nationalism had diminished. Nevertheless, there was a political aim which remained, which was a reality, and which had enabled the Six to overcome the difficulties which they had faced in order to make the EEC. What was this essential European element? It was something that was not American. If it was American, it would not be European. This essential fact could not be disregarded. Where did Britain stand on this? It was not a detail or a matter of ways and means: it was one of aims and spirit. Not all the Six were as convinced or as bold as France over this essential European element; but to some extent all had this European spirit. Where were the British? What were their intentions?

De Gaulle continued that he was old and had lived a long time and through many difficult moments. In these, he had always seen that Britain was bound to the United States and neither could nor would break her links with the United States. He understood that Britain had a special position in all this and that her position with regard to the United States was different to that of France. There was the language. There was the sea.

Brown dealt with this view of the world as best he could. British and French views on supra-nationality were close. On the United States there were indeed differences which had to be faced frankly. Speaking, Brown said, with much respect to an older and wiser man, he did not believe that the problem, of links with the United States was such a great obstacle as the General seemed to think.

De Gaulle replied that the French had always considered a European Europe very important. Now they thought it more important than ever. All of Eastern Europe was changing both internally and vis-à-vis the West. The Cold War had been left behind and great possibilities were opening up. It was difficult to reconcile this extension of Europe eastwards with the maintenance of special relations with the United States. This did not imply any hostility to the United States. But the US was so vast and powerful that the French believed that if they did not exist independently, on their own feet, one day they would be annexed. Those were the reasons why he considered that the American issue was fundamental.

Brown sought to reply. To move from a situation in which one bloc confronted another was an important goal and Britain and France together could be the heart, if not the head, of such a shift.

De Gaulle professed himself much interested in what Brown had said, though he slightly spoiled the effect by adding that of course he had known in advance more or less what Brown would say to him, and vice versa. He would sum up. The EEC existed. Therefore for its members there were no problems; but for the British there were. The British wished to come in. Thus they had set the problem for themselves. The French needed to know in what circumstances the British would come in. This was a question which was as important as it was unresolved. There was the present and there was the future. The British had changed much. They might change more. The future was open.

Brown replied, as he had to Couve two days earlier, that if Britain's bid failed there would be heavy pressure on Britain to seek some other way of organising her affairs. Thus, in a European sense this was their common problem – a problem for France as well as for Britain. Europe had been well run only when France and Britain had stood together.

De Gaulle concluded that he, and all of France, had the greatest regard for Britain. The two countries had a long common history. At times, France had suffered from it. At times she had profited from it, and he himself in particular. He had the highest regard for British worth and qualities. Whether now France and Britain would achieve something together, or whether they should simply remain as before, good friends and neighbours, who could say? Both countries had lived long without the EEC and they would continue to do so even if Britain did not enter the EEC. On that Delphic note, the meeting ended.[34]

In the light of subsequent events, it is easy to see fatal warnings in many of de Gaulle's statements during his meeting with Brown. There were two barrels to de Gaulle's gun. The first was the rules of the EEC and the basic conditions of entry. De Gaulle made it clear, by implication, that whatever the British Government might say about their willingness and ability to accept and abide by the rules he, de Gaulle, did not believe it. But just in case they did and could, then there was a further, innate and indelible, feature of British policy that appeared to make it impossible for Britain to join: her relationship with the United States. Brown was compelled to deploy the same kind of arguments that Macmillan had used at Rambouillet. And, at the end, de Gaulle allowed a chink of light just big enough to allow Brown to go away thinking that the game was not up. Perhaps the hardest aspect of de Gaulle's stance for anyone else to grasp was its very immutability. Insofar as de Gaulle had not ruled out British entry, he had only entertained the possibility on the premise that the EEC stood, and would stand, solid and unchanging. All the moves would have to come from Britain and all the moves would have to be of a fundamental nature.

If Harold Wilson and George Brown had, among their Christmas reading, Sir Patrick Reilly's Despatch from Paris of 22 December on France and the EEC, they would have found little in it for their comfort and no absolute markers to enable them to make up their minds about de Gaulle's intentions. "France's likely attitude to the political problems facing Europe", the Ambassador wrote, "must be seen in the context of General de Gaulle's whole policy. His aim is still to create a new Concert of Western and Eastern Europe. He believes that increasing détente in Europe will encourage the Five in favour of a more independent policy. A successful Franco-Soviet rapprochement will set the pattern, France will lead in the EEC in discussions aimed at freeing Europe of the United States ... The French speak of the French and Soviet economies becoming complementary. The idea is hard to reconcile with the further development of the EEC, which de Gaulle may see only as a temporary system. General de Gaulle's attitude to British membership of the EEC is derived from his vision of the future of Europe. In his attitude to Britain he will not compromise his long-term objectives but will court the minimum of risk. To sum up, General de Gaulle is probably satisfied with the present situation in the EEC. Supra-nationalism is checked for the time being. The French can be expected to play an active part in economic and technical discussions at Brussels which might help the Six to withstand American competition. The General will remain ready to consider political cooperation on Gaullist terms. As regards the UK, he is aware that the Five are in favour of our entry. But he will want to prevent our entry unless he can feel satisfied that, once in the Community, we will have to follow the French lead."[35]

"For de Gaulle politics is what the whole thing is about", wrote Michael Palliser, in a minute to Wilson early in January 1967, both analysing de Gaulle's motives and trying to chart a way through de Gaulle's defences. Economics, Palliser thought, were simply the handmaiden of politics and any economic arguments that de Gaulle might adduce (e.g. about sterling or the CAP) would be adduced for political reasons. De Gaulle had no doubt that he was the greatest Frenchman since Napoleon and, said Palliser, to be fair he probably was. But de Gaulle wanted to go down in *history* as the greatest Frenchman since Napoleon and Palliser thought that Wilson could confront de Gaulle fairly bluntly with his place in history: surely he would not wish to be known to future generations as the Frenchman who irrevocably split the old continent and condemned the countries in it to a permanently declining world status, as compared with the current (US and USSR) and the future (China and Japan) giants of the world.

Palliser knew that his line of argument was not flawless. De Gaulle's economic arguments against British accession were indeed highly political but they were not simply the product of de Gaulle's desire for a Europe cooked to a French recipe. France under de Gaulle had had to make a huge effort of economic adaptation to be able to compete within the framework of the EEC and the CAP, especially hard won, was fundamental to the French Government's perception of France's economic interests. Equally, had de Gaulle perceived his place in history as dependent on the ultimate creation of a Europe with Britain as a key player then the kind of appeal which Palliser envisaged Wilson making might have been irresistible. But the problem for Palliser, and ultimately for Wilson, was that de Gaulle's conception of a united Europe was one that marginalised Britain insofar as Britain was a close ally of the United States. So there was no conceivable premise on which the British Government – any British Government – could both safeguard its essential national security interests (which had the Atlantic Alliance at their core) and placate de Gaulle. And whereas de Gaulle, however hard he tried, could not compel his EEC partners, Germany in particular, to accept his vision (which they all viewed as more or less misguided), he *could* singlehandedly safeguard his vision from the principal threat to it: that of Britain acceding to the EEC. And he probably had a more accurate sense than did the British of the impact this would have on his partners in the Five. The cards might be stacked against him in terms of the overall attitude of the Five, the evolution of French public opinion and his own advancing years and diminishing popularity. But if he calculated that he could still play his ace – in the form of a veto on British entry – he could do so in the knowledge that Britain's threats to look to her interests elsewhere than at the heart of Europe were empty ones and in the knowledge also that Britain was a country in economic decline whose accession would cause problems in the short term for all the EEC's existing members. He could also count increasingly on the acquiescence of the new German Government.

The attitude of the Germans was a cause of concern in London. Monnet had told the British Ambassador in Paris that, while the Social Democrats, and especially Brandt, could be helpful, little reliance could be put on Chancellor Kiesinger and the Christian Democrats.[36] But, at a meeting of European Socialists in Rome early in January 1967, George Brown found even Brandt to be negative and unhelpful. Brandt had displayed no enthusiasm for British membership and had clearly implied that he regarded the Franco-German alliance as of overriding importance. He had given Brown the clear impression that he was not disposed to help Britain if this seemed likely to lead him into difficulties with the French. Brandt had subsequently claimed to Brown that the latter had misunderstood him but Brown did not consider that he had misunderstood at all, particularly as Brandt's unhelpful attitude had contrasted with the constructive approach of all the other Foreign Ministers.[37]

The British Ambassador in Bonn, Frank Roberts, confirmed Brown's impression. "I am not over confident", he advised, "even of the SPD voice within the Government and was not surprised to see that Brandt did not give you a very reassuring impression in Rome. Brandt's own intentions, and indeed German intentions generally, are I am sure of the best, but he and the Chancellor in particular are anxious to come back from Paris with at least the appearance of a successful meeting . . . Their main objective this weekend, apart from improving the climate of Franco-German relations, is to find out how far they can go together with France in improving relations with the East. There is therefore a real danger that what they say on British membership of the EEC may be so perfunctory as to leave General de Gaulle with the impression that the new German Government feel less strongly on this subject than its predecessor." Bang on cue, *Die Welt* carried a headline: "De Gaulle intends with the help of Bonn to prevent British entry into the EEC".[38]

The reluctance of the German Government to engage in more than token fashion on behalf of British accession continued to be a preoccupation for the Prime Minister. On Palliser's minute about tactics and strategy towards de Gaulle Wilson had written some notes for his own guidance: "Politics – not economics. France and Britain politically stable. If we give a pledge we can deliver. Unlike Germany (also Belgium, Lux, Netherlands and Italy). In a sense more stable than US, who are more subject to Congressional pressures. The General and I can sign a treaty and carry it. LBJ can't be certain. [He couldn't pull out of Vietnam if he wanted to]. Another bond – can help to unite and develop Africa. Technology widening from aircraft. Though using US for late 60s generation for our main aircraft (forced there by improvidence of our predecessors) we shall be indissolubly tied to joint French aircraft interdependence in 1970s. Nuclear- Nassau. We opposed, as he did. Killed MLF on coming into office. Opposed to any collective pooling involving hardware solution."[39]

Wilson told the American Ambassador in London, David Bruce, on 10 January 1967 that he regarded the operation on which he was embarking as essentially a political one, particularly so in dealing with de Gaulle who was not only perhaps the key figure but also a consummate politician. We had to recognise that our basic problem was that in order to get into the Common Market we had to find a way of winning over the General.

The Prime Minister said that he was concerned about the stance of the Germans, as reflected in Willy Brandt's rather unhelpful attitude. We must expect the Germans broadly to toe the French line and could certainly not regard them as an ally. The Germans were clearly thinking more of how to develop the Franco-German alliance. If de Gaulle accepted British entry then the Germans would certainly also support it. But the British Government could not count on them to exert any pressure on him.

Bruce agreed. One of the main problems with Brandt was that he talked too much and too freely. His long period as Mayor of Berlin, a large part of which was essentially public relations to project the importance of Berlin onto the world scene, had enhanced a temperamental tendency to excess of speech. He would "be well advised to keep his mouth shut rather more frequently in future, more particularly since he combined this tendency with a certain naivety of political thought".[40]

Later that same day, when the *New York Times* arrived in Downing Street it was seen to carry a report from the paper's Bonn correspondent under the headline 'Bonn won't push British EEC issue in talks at Paris'.

There was a crumb of comfort in the Annual Review for 1967 from the British Delegation to the EEC in Brussels. There was, the Delegation reported, a growing feeling in Brussels that the momentum the Community now lacked could only come to an end through British membership. But Sir James Marjoribanks also reported that the Community was continuing to live under the shadow of de Gaulle. It had survived the crisis of 1965–1966 but every step taken in Brussels was taken in the knowledge of the existence in Paris of a Head of State who could not be pushed far with impunity. There was a clear desire to avoid provoking him unnecessarily.[41]

A Foreign Office compendium of French quotes on British accession made even more depressing reading. Most telling, not least because it was current, was de Gaulle's New Year message for 1967 which spoke of France continuing to work for "a reconciliation of the European continent". This, France would achieve "by practising friendly and fruitful relations with Soviet Russia. She will do it by renewing her former close ties with Poland, Yugoslavia, Czechoslovakia, Romania, Bulgaria, Hungary and Albania. She will do it by cultivating her contact with each of her neighbours in a friendly manner and by working to construct an economic, and perhaps one day a political, grouping of the six Western powers. All that will be carried out in order to help our continent to gather together all her nations from one end to the other to form a European Europe". Clearly, there was nowhere for Britain in this grand design.[42]

With less than a week to go before the first of the exploratory visits to EEC capitals (Rome) Wilson and Brown did receive some comfort from the Germans. Roberts called on Brandt and spoke to him candidly of British anxieties about German attitudes. Brandt said he understood that Brown had been disappointed with his attitude at the Rome meeting of Socialist leaders. But all he had meant to say was that the idea raised by Nenni, the Italian Socialist leader, that the Five might substitute Britain for France as their partner was not possible. That did not mean that Germany preferred France to Britain. For Germany, relations with London were as important as those with Paris. It was a vital German interest to widen the EEC and for this Britain was the key. The Germans would speak clearly to de Gaulle in Paris. He hoped that Britain, for her part, would be able to clarify and simplify her position and to base her main requirements for entry on transitional arrangements. An approach of this kind would ensure the full support of the Five and would, Brandt hoped, enable "us all" to confront de Gaulle with a position where it would be extremely difficult, if not impossible for him to repeat the veto of 1963.

Roberts commented to London that he had found Brandt's whole attitude "thoroughly sensible and responsible" and that Brandt had conveyed considerable reassurance.[43]

Four days later, Roberts was sent for by Kiesinger to be given a personal account by the Chancellor of the Franco-German talks which had just taken place in Paris. Kiesinger had, he said, stated German views on NATO and on the EEC quite clearly and de Gaulle had accepted that their views differed. De Gaulle had spoken with respect and even admiration of Britain but had questioned whether, because of her many overseas connections and responsibilities Britain was a suitable member of the EEC and whether British entry would not change the whole nature of the Community. At one stage in the discussions de Gaulle had made relatively little of the differences between France and Germany compared with what could unite them. But there was, de Gaulle had suggested, one exception, British entry, which could be very serious. The Germans, de Gaulle had said, were much more inclined than the French "to take chances and hope for the best".[44]

On 16 January, Wilson and Brown left for Rome, the first stop on their tour of EEC capitals, for talks with Prime Minister Moro and Foreign Minister Fanfani. As Brown recorded in a personal telegram to Britain's EEC ambassadors, "The PM and I feel that the visit to Rome got us off to a very good start. If the Italian Ministers had any doubts before we met them as to the sincerity of our intentions, and the strength of our determination to enter the Community if we can get the right terms, they can have none now. They themselves said as much. They welcomed especially the clear confirmation they received that the Treaty of Rome is not in itself an impediment to our entry provided that we can receive satisfaction in appropriate ways on the points which cause us difficulties. We made clear that we were determined to play our full part in the search for greater political unity in Europe once we had joined the Community. We also expressed our strong hope that the members of the Community would not embark on some new search for political unity without us, and use it as an excuse for delaying consideration of the problem of our entry". The Italian welcome for Britain's intention to enter the Community was, Brown concluded, strong, sincere and repeatedly expressed. Moro had summed up by saying that while some of the problems associated with accession were more difficult than others, none was insuperable.[45]

When Wilson made a statement on the visit to the House of Commons, Opposition Leader Edward Heath challenged him as to whether he had or had not told the Italians that Britain accepted the Common Agricultural Policy. Wilson's response was characteristic. It admitted nothing that would alert his Party's sceptics, threw up a considerable amount of obscuring dust but also sought to secure for himself the maximum negotiating space: "We stressed the very great difficulties of the levy system with particular reference to the fact that it would mean a big change to the pattern within Europe because, unlike the Six, we are a major food importer and it would mean a very big transfer across the exchanges . . . The suggestion that we accept in full, without any question of amendment, adaptation, transitional provisions or anything else, the CAP, was inaccurate."[46]

One week after the Rome visit, Wilson and Brown were in Paris. Wilson had told Cabinet a few days earlier that "it seemed clear that General de Gaulle would again seek support for a rejection of our approach to Europe on the basis that the British were not sufficiently European, despite the extent to which he himself had pursued policies which other European nations would not regard as being in the general European interest".[47]

"The discussions took place in a frank and cordial atmosphere throughout", the Foreign Office reported. "Although they produced no concrete results the result was certainly not such as to discourage us from our purpose. We believe that the French Government cannot but have been convinced of our sincerity and determination in seeking British entry to the Community".

At the last of the two days of meetings, de Gaulle had given his impressions of the talks. A considerable change had taken place in Britain's thinking over the last few years and Britain was now prepared to moor herself alongside the Continent and to loosen somewhat the special relationship she claimed with the United States. The EEC had been formed, albeit with great difficulty, from six homogeneous continental nations. Now Britain, with all her extra-European connections, wanted to join them, and this at once raised the question whether the EEC's fundamental character would not be destroyed if she were to do so. Were there then no alternatives to full British membership given that membership seemed difficult, if not impossible? This question could not of course be answered without further reflection and the French Government had come to no conclusion, but he asked the British Government to consider two alternatives: something 'new and different' or association with the Community in some form.

The Prime Minister had responded briefly: only membership of the Community would provide a sufficient basis for the wider political unity inside Europe and between Europe and the outside world which must be the aim. An offshore relationship would not suffice.[48]

One of the more challenging tasks facing any Ambassador is to report his or her impressions of a visit by the great ones from London. The Ambassador's telegram will be seen right across Whitehall. It dare not risk inconsistency with the possibly more upbeat account that the visitors may themselves have given to their Cabinet colleagues. It must not gild the lily, but nor can spades be called spades, let alone bloody shovels. Britain's Ambassador in Paris, Patrick Reilly, had plenty of experience in the diplomatic art of reporting a Ministerial Visit.

"I have no doubt", Reilly reported, "that the Prime Minister and yourself made a very considerable personal impression on General de Gaulle. There could be no doubting the impact on him of the sincerity, force and what he called the solidity of your approach . . . He was also clearly much impressed by what you said on the general theme of an independent Europe, and I would hope that less will now be heard of the political objections to British entry. On the other hand, Couve's brief remarks at the last meeting were, I think, a warning that we have not heard the last of them . . . On the main issues affecting our entry, however, the French gave nothing away . . . The General himself referred to the economic obstacles to British entry as being such as to make it very difficult, if not impossible. He went on to suggest that HMG should consider two alternative solutions . . . It is difficult to believe that either of these is seriously meant . . . No one has yet explained how an Association Agreement admitting Britain to the industrial Common Market, but allowing her to maintain the present system of agricultural support, could conceivably be acceptable to France. It would be equally objectionable to French agriculture and industry.

As for the General's first suggestion . . . the General really meant starting again from scratch and negotiating something which could take the place of the EEC, in which Britain and others could participate . . . I think it may represent something which the General would in his heart of hearts like to see; but he must know that at the present time the suggestion has no relation to practical realities . . ."[49]

In a message to Willy Brandt, Brown was upbeat, concluding that he remained convinced that, provided a solid front was shown by Britain and the Five, he would acquiesce in the end.[50]

Palliser, more analytical and judicious than Brown, showed the latter's message (which had not been cleared with Wilson and to which Palliser himself had only got access through the Foreign Office grapevine) to the Prime Minister, taking issue with some points: the General was far from having 'accepted' that the British attitude had changed. He was much too suspicious for that. He was, rather, as the PM himself had put it, now scratching his head and trying to figure out how far Wilson was to be trusted. Nor had the General, as Brown claimed, moved to a second line of defence, that of alternative suggestions. He was, rather, indulging in a diversionary manoeuvre on the British flank; his own main battle line was intact.[51]

Wilson's own report to Cabinet on his visit to Paris was not notably upbeat. The visit did not appear to have changed de Gaulle's view that he would prefer Britain not to join the EEC at present. However, de Gaulle had recognised a clear difference between the attitude of the British Government now, compared with that of the then Government in 1961–63.

Wilson and Brown described de Gaulle's notion of establishing 'something new and different'. Their suspicions of de Gaulle's motives were shared by other Cabinet members, not least because, if Britain were seen to favour such an approach, she would damage her position in relation to the Five and, with it, the possibility of their being willing to use their influence with the French.[52]

Reports from elsewhere in Europe of the French reaction to the visit of Wilson and Brown were somewhat more upbeat. *Agence France Presse* (AFP) described the meeting as 'encouraging'. The French Ambassador in Rome told his British colleague that, whereas the Italian Government's response to Wilson had been 'yes, but' that of the French was 'Well, why not?'. According to the Frenchman, Wilson's statement to de Gaulle that, after the delivery of the Polaris submarines the UK would no longer be dependent on the United States in the matter of nuclear defence, had had an important effect.[53]

The Embassy in Paris were less bullish. The information available to them suggested that the French were making much of their reservations about the sterling issue. The French conceded that the British position had changed in the past few years but official guidance to French embassies on Wilson's visit emphasised that British entry would alter the whole character of the EEC.[54]

Back in London, Sir Con O'Neill was professing himself "to some extent elated" by the fact that the General, who had talked about Britain 'one day' mooring alongside the Continent, when he had vetoed the application in 1963, was, four years later, willing to say that Britain was now prepared to do just that. "I feel", O'Neill wrote in a letter to Palliser, "that this echo of an almost classical phrase was of real significance; indeed to my mind it was the most significant thing that happened during the Paris visit". "This is a very good point", Wilson noted.[55]

As in the past, it took the Danes to pour some realistically cold water on British hopes. Palliser's predecessor in Downing Street, Oliver Wright, had become Britain's Ambassador in Copenhagen. Danish Ministers and officials had visited Paris in the wake of Wilson's visit. According to the account they gave to Wright, all their French interlocutors had spoken to a tight and identical brief. The nature of the French reaction to the British visit had been neither a welcome nor a flat refusal, but discouragement shrouded in ambiguity. Several defensive positions had been erected, all of which Britain would have to get through to enter the Community. These defences were of two sorts: concrete issues and political issues. The concrete issues were agriculture, sterling, amendments to the Treaty of Rome, and so forth. The French had indicated that none of these need represent an insuperable difficulty if Britain were really determined. However, according to the Danes, even if Britain succeeded in demolishing these lines of the French defence they would then come up against the second, political, line of defence. This was that the entry of Britain into the Community would change the entire nature of the enterprise. If, on the other hand, Britain were to appear ready to follow de Gaulle's suggestion of looking for something new, then of course she would find the Five ranged in opposition against her which, in turn, would relieve de Gaulle of the need to press his own objections. So, the French were raising fears in the minds of the Five that they might be willing to contemplate something new in order to accommodate British entry and, at the same time, raising doubts in the minds of the Five as to whether, if Britain joined the EEC as it now existed, that would fundamentally change the nature of something which all the original Six held dear. A consequence of the General's tactics was that, because the Five wished above all not to prejudice the nature of the Community as it now was, the British would receive little more than touch-line support from them. The match was really between Britain and France. Only the Dutch might be more than passive spectators and they did not carry much weight.[56]

Further realism was injected by a conversation a few days later between Wright and the Danish Minister of Trade and European Integration, Tyge Dahlgaard. Dahlgaard said that he had two main impressions of French attitudes following the visit of Wilson and Brown. The first was that the French would rather 'see us hanged' than as members of the Common Market but, secondly, that they did not wish themselves to be the executioners this time. Dahlgaard said that the French did not think the British could count on much support from the Five. For Italy, the present agricultural policy worked well and Britain would not get much support from that quarter, at least on agriculture. The present German Government was trying to repair its relations with France and would not wish to offend de Gaulle. The Benelux countries did not count for very much, except perhaps for the Netherlands.

Dahlgaard thought that this candid French assessment might well be right. He concluded, therefore, that, although the French would be less inclined to veto a second time, the Five would not give Britain as much support as they had last time, nor be as shaken this time if the General did once again cast his veto. The best that could be said was that the British Government had the French seriously worried.[57]

Even the German Chancellor, Kiesinger, was realistically downbeat, telling Roberts in early February that, while he had made German support for British membership quite clear, as being both in the German national interest and that of European unity, de Gaulle's reaction had left him with the firm impression that the General remained opposed to British entry.

Kiesinger went on to test Britain's attitude to the political development of the European Community. For him (Kiesinger) the main purpose of the EEC remained political, despite its considerable and surprising economic success. The basic thinking behind de Gaulle's conceptions, disappointing though they were in many ways, was the political unity of Europe. What Kiesinger wanted to know, therefore, was whether the United Kingdom saw the European Community in this light or whether she regarded it mainly as an economic institution.

Roberts replied that the British Government were quite as much, if not more, interested in the political as in the economic side of the Community and were determined to play their full part in promoting greater political unity inside Europe. Having seen the Community at work in recent years, many of Britain's early worries, e.g. over sovereignty, had been removed. As regards British public opinion, the big majority which had now developed in favour of full participation in Europe was motivated mainly by political considerations and not only by the thought that British membership would be better economically for Britain and for Europe.[58]

British fears, or lack of them, over sovereignty did not necessarily translate into unqualified support for the political development of the Community. On the former, Wilson had been as robust as he had been consistent when challenged at a Brussels press conference on 1 February by Peter Snow of ITN as to whether he was prepared to accept that "joining the Community means some surrender of sovereignty by Britain to the European Commission, and specifically are you prepared to accept the principle of majority voting?".

Wilson replied: "When you use the phrase 'surrender of sovereignty' I want to make it quite plain that this emotive phrase is – has never been – one that has frightened me. In debates on the Common Market four years ago, I said then that a progressive surrender of sovereignty is a mark of an advancing civilisation, that we did it when we joined the International Postal Union a century ago. I said then that we did it when we had a French referee at a rugby match at Twickenham. And certainly we did it when we agreed without protest to a Swiss referee from

Zurich, I think, at the World Cup final – that the final result to whatever loss of sovereignty was involved did not mean any loss of the match. So I'm not worried about the phrase 'sovereignty'. So far as the Commission is concerned, and majority voting, we have made it plain that whatever we put our name to we shall carry out fully, and we shall carry out all our obligations on entering the Community on exactly the same basis as the founder members and our partners in this venture".[59]

On the issue of Political Cooperation, the Government were more cautious. When Wilson and Brown were in Brussels early in February, the Belgian Prime Minister and Foreign Minister had outlined a new initiative in the field of European Political Cooperation. They suggested that the Six, and any members of NATO who were potential applicants for EEC membership, should agree that, in a few specified fields, they would not take external action without first consulting each other. This procedure might first apply to European technology (an area which Wilson had forcefully promoted as central to the EEC's purpose in a speech the previous November), economic détente with the East and the formation of a solid European front at international conferences.

In a telegram to Brussels on 14 February, the Foreign Secretary said that he realised that the Belgian suggestion was designed to be helpful to the British. It was tempting to support it, in the hope that the French would refuse to "be tied down in this way". But, since the French could not be relied on to kill the idea and therefore to protect Britain from having to implement it, the British Government could not take the risk of supporting it. In other words, it was too bold for British liking. The British Ambassador in Brussels was accordingly instructed to tell the Belgians that Britain supported the objective of close consultation, harmonisation of external policies and, wherever possible, coordination of the actions of Member Governments. But progress could only be made when Britain was a member of the EEC.[60]

Wilson and Brown were about to embark on the second most critical of their visits to EEC capitals: to Bonn. Immediately before their departure on 14 February, Wilson told Cabinet that "although it was clear that the Germans would welcome our joining the Community, it seemed doubtful whether they would be prepared to press their support against the French . . . They would probably attach greater importance to the maintenance of the recently re-established cordiality of their relationship with the French Government, though they might later become somewhat disillusioned by French actions".[61]

The visit itself was, in the words of the Foreign Office telegram reporting its outcome, friendly and constructive throughout. Wilson had told Kiesinger that Britain was prepared to accept the Community as it was (subject to arrangements to meet Britain's difficulties) and, once she had become a full member, to join with other members in the development of the Community towards economic unity and the harmonisation of policies necessary for that purpose. As a result, Kiesinger had said at the end of the two days that what he had heard from the British had confirmed the German Government in their conviction that they should continue to support British entry.

Kiesinger had sought some assurance as to the British attitude towards majority voting. It was not, he said, a question of dogma on the part of Germany but of efficiency in the operation of an enlarged Community. The British had responded that they would be willing to conform to whatever decision on majority voting was acceptable to the Community as a whole. The British did not think that the accession of a number of EFTA partners would produce block EFTA voting within the Community. Voting patterns would change with different issues. As to the Treaty of Rome, the only adaptations which the British saw as necessary were those affecting formal voting rights and allocations of contributions etc. Similarly the British attitude to the regulations established under the Treaty was that she could accept them, provided that the special difficulties raised for Britain could be overcome.[62]

The Foreign Office's optimistic view was borne out by what was said to the Bonn Press corps by the German Government spokesman, speaking on the record and attributing his remarks personally to the Federal Chancellor. "The talks", said the spokesman, "were impressive, good and useful. The German mind has been strengthened in its conviction that we should help to bring Britain into the Common Market. We hope that the talks on this and the efforts for British entry can be brought to a positive result".[63]

This upbeat tone was reflected in German Press coverage of the visit. The British Press, by contrast, and perhaps because they had been expecting the Germans to pull British chestnuts out of the fire, was pessimistic, and this tone was in turn reflected in some of the continental Press, including in France.[64]

Summing up the visit, the Ambassador in Bonn felt that the British Government could, at this stage, expect from the Germans in Paris persuasion but not pressure. This had come as a disappointment to friendly German officials but not to the Embassy who had not expected to achieve more. Roberts hoped that calmer reflection would lead the German Government to realise that the British, as well as the French, could affect German interests for good or ill, for example in the whole field of East-West relations, and that that was an additional reason for getting Britain into the EEC. In short, Roberts believed, while Kiesinger did not yet see his way to confronting the General firmly, he had been brought to realise that he must do more than merely keep the door open for Britain, which had been his original intention.[65]

On the day after Wilson's visit, Kiesinger was asked on German television whether it was correct to conclude from the visit that, while German support for British entry had not changed, Germany would not press the British case in Paris in order not to endanger the friendly relations between Bonn and Paris which had only recently been renewed. "We do indeed want to see Great Britain enter the EEC", Kissinger replied. But he went on to add: "We have no pressure to exert on France. We would have no means to exert such pressure. Nor would we wish to do so in view of our friendly relationship with that country. Therefore, we must represent our view patiently and with the necessary tact. But we shall fulfil honourably the promise we have given to our British visitors . . ."[66]

An article by the *Financial Times* Political Editor, Ronald Butt, on 18 February was commended two days later by Wilson in discussion with the Swedish Prime Minister. Wilson, who had almost certainly briefed the paper himself, commented that the article gave "an impression of the way in which the next stage might have to be handled". Butt had written: "There is apparent a rather greater optimism about the prospects than might be found in the capitals of the Six. Mr Wilson, it is clear, is determined to conduct his European campaign as a flexible, running political operation – adapting his tactics to changes in the situation as they occur. One of his main strategic objectives is to avoid getting into a position which gives President de Gaulle the chance to exercise his veto on one of the basic problems. The British tactics are to hammer away at each of the basic problems until reasonable French objections are removed in the belief that, if President de Gaulle is reduced to saying that the French simply do not want us, this will be an untenable position. To say this is not to suggest that the Prime Minister is pessimistic about the impression he has made on President de Gaulle. He obviously believes he has convinced President de Gaulle of Britain's earnest wish to join and also that Britain's position vis-à-vis the French is very different from that during Mr Macmillan's negotiations. Mr Macmillan had offended the French President on the nuclear defence issue and the Anglo-American connection. If London reads the situation aright the defence issue is no longer of major importance, nor is Britain's relationship with the United States. Equally, the older notions of a supra-national political community have gone out of fashion, and the more nationalistic Gaullist view of the EEC is more compatible with the British approach. Mr Wilson has been able to invite President de Gaulle to look around at the other Common Market countries and join him in the conclusion that Britain and France are the only really stable Governments in Europe at the moment . . . Mr Wilson has no illusions about President de Gaulle's falling on his neck and inviting him to come inside. To President de Gaulle, the EEC is a nicely running concern, very much to the advantage of the French, and with the French President in the top seat. President de Gaulle never wanted to vacate that seat to install Mr Macmillan. But he might accept that in the changed conditions of 1967 it would suit him to share his position with Britain in a vastly enlarged market. Despite the reports of a certain coolness in Bonn, the PM appears to be confident that he has wholehearted support . . .

Surveying the rising tide of discontent in the Labour Party over the Common Market, one might well feel that we have been here before. Was not Mr Macmillan obliged by the weight of critical opinion in his own party to stand more stiffly by his terms than he otherwise might – thus inviting the ultimate veto? Mr Wilson is now faced with criticism in his Cabinet from Mr Douglas Jay, President of the Board of Trade, and in a substantial section of his Party. The Prime Minister, plainly disturbed by Mr Jay's critical intervention this week, has sent for his exact words. If the British Cabinet decides to go ahead with an application this summer, Mr Jay might well resign. Another possible resigner is Mrs Castle, who remains suspicious. But even she is likely to be driven to this step only if she happens to be angry about something else at the time. For the rest, Mr Peart is now not apparently reckoned as an intransigent . . . To sum up, the Cabinet will probably want to make a clean 'yes-no' decision this summer. It could go either way . . . If it is 'yes' the Opposition backbench Labour Party is not expected to constitute an obstacle. There should, it is thought, be nothing more than a number of abstentions if a vote were taken on an application to join.'[57]

If this article reflected briefing by Wilson himself or by someone close to him and reflecting his views, it was perhaps less clever vis-à-vis the Six than Wilson thought. Many on the Continent would have had direct access to the *Financial Times*. Embassies in London would have read it, seen its significance and reported it in detail. Neither its treatment of de Gaulle, nor its reported comments by Wilson on the Five *to* de Gaulle, were calculated to win Wilson any friends. It was Wilson in his most Artful Dodger guise.

Rather more clever was the manner in which Douglas Jay's opposition to EEC membership was exposed. When Jay read the article, his only possible conclusion can have been that if he played the resignation card, it had already been discounted by Wilson. Similarly, if Barbara Castle went, it would be from pique, not principle.

One element missing from Butt's analysis, and presumably from the briefing that inspired it, was any mention of the prospects for the British economy and their relevance to the attitude of EEC members to British accession. When the Chancellor of the Exchequer, Jim Callaghan, met the Commission Vice President, M. Marjolin, in Brussels in February this aspect was, however, at the centre of the discussion. Marjolin reminded Callaghan that unanimous agreement was required for new members to join the EEC. All Six would be involved in the conduct of negotiations. Back in 1962, an issue such as tariff reduction within the EEC had been in its infancy and for Britain to align her tariffs with those of the Six would not have been problematic. But now the reduction of the tariffs of the Six would reach 85% in July 1967 and 100% a year later. For Britain to match those reductions without an excessive jolt to her industry would require a transitional period of up to three years, which would have to be negotiated. Economic and financial problems would also certainly arise. As a matter of history, each member of the Community was increasingly giving its complete guarantee to the others, so that if any Community country found itself in economic difficulty the others would be under an obligation to make their help available. This development was, in turn, changing the extent to which the traditional instruments of economic policy could be used by individual member countries. They were no longer free, for instance, to use at their own discretion quantitative restrictions on trade, or Exchange Control. Devaluation, too, was becoming increasingly difficult, partly because of the CAP itself and partly because the main agricultural prices, for instance, for cereals, meat and dairy produce, were fixed in terms of a unit of account. closely related to gold. For Britain to convince the doubters among the Six (and Marjolin suggested that there was more than one) the British Government would have to convince them that over the next three or four years Britain would make enough economic progress to solve her economic problems as they arose. In particular, she would need to show that she was going to have a balance of payments surplus in 1967 and to maintain it over the years, not only to repay borrowing from the IMF but also to build up her reserves. Insofar as Britain's problem was to meet crises of confidence in sterling, this problem would be largely solved if she were earning a balance of payments surplus on current account year by year. Marjolin's contacts with the representatives of the Central Banks of France, Germany, Italy, Belgium and the Netherlands suggested to him that they regarded sterling as a vulnerable currency. This belief was founded on the experience of the past decade in which sterling had suffered recurring difficulties; but it would be changed by a substantial period of, say, five years, in which Britain was seen to be achieving economic expansion without a balance of payments deficit. Since, however, Britain could not wait for such a period before attempting to secure entry into the Common Market, it was necessary for her spokesmen in the negotiations to carry conviction that the policies being pursued by the British Government would secure the desired result of balance of payments surplus and expansion.

Revealingly, Callaghan's response to Marjolin's analysis was not to challenge it, let alone to suggest that Marjolin's criteria could be met, but to offer two different reasons as to why British entry was necessary. The first was that there would be much less likelihood of damage to the Community from difficulties in Britain if Britain were in the Common Market than if she were outside it. The second argument made by Callaghan was that, if Britain, having made up her mind that "if the path into Europe were open, it should be trodden", were rebuffed, then this would mean that "we would have to make extensive changes in our arrangements". If the EEC, in turn, showed itself to be too timid to absorb a country whose obligations were of a different kind from those of the existing members, then the EEC might, as a result, become not only an inward-looking organisation, but also one that would be left on one side in the main development of history. Whether Callaghan's Lear-like threat of some unspecified but significant action by Britain if her application failed; or the notion that it was the success of the EEC, just as much as that of Britain, was at stake, carried much conviction with his audience must at the least be questionable.[68]

Officials in London were well aware of the difficulties. On the day Callaghan was meeting Marjolin, Bill Nield, the Cabinet Office Deputy Secretary responsible for European coordination, minuted to Palliser that "unless General de Gaulle's attitude undergoes a radical change, our chances of securing entry in the foreseeable future depend upon our eliminating or reducing his opportunity to obstruct or veto negotiations; that these must therefore be short, limited to major issues, and with the heads of agreement worked out so far as possible in advance with the Five or Six, *and timed to coincide with the clear recovery of our economic strength*" [author italics].

Wilson and Brown accepted that Britain would not be able to compete as an EEC Member State unless she had recovered economically but Wilson was upbeat about the prospects; George Brown even more so. On 24 February, Brown told Walt Rostow, President Johnson's Special Adviser on International Affairs, that European matters were still going better than he would have expected. The newness of the German Government was a complication, as was their natural desire to maintain warm relations with France. De Gaulle had played skilfully on this desire and the Germans were proceeding cautiously. He and the Prime Minister had, however, achieved a major success in their rounds of discussions by eliminating suspicions that the United Kingdom wanted to have long technical negotiations before going into the Common Market. He saw no evidence that there would be a veto from France and some evidence that de Gaulle could not, in any case, declare a veto for internal political reasons.[69]

The Prime Minister and Foreign Secretary held the final substantive discussion of their visits to capitals in The Hague at the end of February. The discussion was revealing because it contained further evidence that, while Wilson was suspicious of supra-national federalism in what he would have seen as its most extreme form, he did not have significant reservations about the extension of majority voting – an issue which would bedevil later British Governments. The Dutch Prime Minister, Professor Zijlstra, and his Ministerial colleagues explained the importance they attached to majority voting and their own belief that it would become progressively more opera-tive as the Community developed. They also explained the strength of feeling in the Dutch Parliament on the need for Parliamentary control within the Community.

Wilson agreed on the importance of majority voting as an issue. It would not be appropriate for the British Government to express a view so long as we remained outside the Community. But the Government accepted the provisions of the Treaty of Rome no less than other members of the Community. Brown said that there need be no fear of rigid patterns of alliances or of voting within an enlarged Community. There would be shifting patterns according to various interests on various topics.

As regards the European Parliament, Wilson said that Britain had a strong interest in good financial management within the Community and in the political development of the Community. Wilson also responded positively to Dutch talk of the importance of progress towards political union, suggesting that, important though the economic aspects of Britain's present initiative were, the political moti-vation was perhaps even greater. The British Government were concerned to ensure the political strength, independence and unity of Europe so that Europe should have a more powerful voice in world affairs. Somewhat Delphic though these utterances were, and obviously geared to their audience, there was nothing in them to suggest that institutional issues were a central preoccupation for the Government as it approached the possibility of negotiation for entry.[70]

With their tour behind them, Wilson and Brown reported to Cabinet on 9 March 1967. Wilson, with characteristic tactical sense, confined his comments to procedure. It was now necessary to consider the procedure which would, he said, afford the Cabinet the fullest opportunity to consider what steps should be taken next. The issue of whether to apply for membership of the EEC was so momen-tous that the Cabinet must clearly have ample time to consider and discuss it. Both undue haste and procrastination were to be avoided. He and the Foreign Secre-tary would circulate a full factual account of their talks with the Governments of the Six in a paper which would also set out the points of difficulty which had been raised by the Six themselves, in particular their anxieties about the change in the character of the EEC which would result if the UK and other EFTA partners were to accede to it; and also their anxieties about the position of sterling in the UK economy. Before Easter, the Cabinet should devote at least a full morning to the discussion of this paper, with further discussion after Easter if necessary. In the light of these Cabinet discussions, he and the Foreign Secretary would circulate a further paper making recommendations on whether negotiations for entry should be started and, if so, when and how. A considered decision could thus be reached without undue haste or undue delay.[71]

The attitude of the French Government, meaning, in practice, the attitude of de Gaulle (for there is no evidence of French views being formed by collective Ministerial discussion in Paris) was to be the dominant political consideration overshadowing Cabinet's discussion of British prospects. In the French legislative elections in March the Gaullists won 284 seats (a loss of 49 seats) the Socialists 116 (91 before) and Giscard d'Estaing's Independent Republicans (who formed part of the overall Gaullist majority) 44 (35). The Communists also made significant gains, going from 41 to 73 seats.

"The results" commented the Embassy in Paris "have come as a surprise. Even the opposition leaders and public opinion polls had allowed the Government a clear majority. The most striking aspect has been the discipline of the left electorate in voting for a single candidate of the left in each constituency . . . In the last resort, the Gaullist reverse may have been due to economic and social factors, and a desire for change coupled with a feeling of protest after almost nine years of authoritarian Government. But bad political tactics undoubtedly contributed. By crying victory after the first round, Gaullist propagandists helped rally the left . . . The respectability [de Gaulle] has in the last years conferred on the Communist Party took the conviction out of his and his Ministers' evocation of the red peril at the last moment . . . The polarisation of French politics is more marked than before".[72]

If there was any expectation on the British side that humiliation in the elections would lead to humility in the Elysée there was no sign of it when Sir Patrick Reilly called on the President on 20 March.

Reilly told de Gaulle that Wilson and Brown had in general been encouraged by their tour. The points of difficulty had been identified and clarified and, while the British Government did not wish to minimise them, the number of problems appeared to have been reduced.

De Gaulle replied that it would be a mistake to rush things (*brusquer les choses*). The economic situation was not very good anywhere in Europe, save perhaps in Italy, or in the United States. In France, things were not going better. There was no real expansion anywhere. This was not the moment for anything.

Reilly asked whether the General could say how long he had in mind for this delay. De Gaulle said that he could not. It all depended on Britain. The problems were both practical and political. The practical problem was not one so much of principles but of dimension: the problem of absorbing into the Community a country of the size of Great Britain. The political problem was that of how Britain could fit into the creation of something which was truly European in the light of her special ties with the United States. The attitude to the United States was the real criterion, the true touchstone. Reilly said he had hoped that the Prime Minister and Foreign Secretary had convinced the President of their deep interest in Europe. De Gaulle replied that he was in no doubt of British wishes, but he was still by no means sure of British requirements. In addition to Britain's relations with the United States there was, for instance, British interest in the non-proliferation treaty. Would these British needs allow her to be truly

European? The Germans of course had comparable needs too, but they were different from the British ones.

Commenting to London on his exchange with de Gaulle, Reilly said he had found de Gaulle relaxed and friendly as usual. The General's staff claimed that he was in excellent health and form generally. But, while Reilly did not doubt that de Gaulle could still draw on great reserves of strength and energy, he had, throughout the interview, been more conscious of the President's age than ever before. In particular, his language seemed less clearly phrased than usual.

On the substance of the conversation, Reilly judged that everything de Gaulle had said about British entry into the EEC had confirmed the view that he was deeply reluctant to accept it at the present time. It was also clear that he did not want to see an early British application. His remark about not moving too quickly had been as quick and spontaneous as his subsequent explanation of it by reference to the economic climate had been unconvincing. "He remains, I fear", Reilly advised "entirely untouched by any spark of feeling or glimpse of vision of what British entry might mean for Europe. He admits that British opinion about Europe has changed since the last negotiations, but he considers that the facts compel Britain to remain tied to the United States to an extent which makes her still a dubious candidate for the EEC. He seemed more than ever obsessed with the Americans, about whom he grumbled again and again in language which at times I found difficult to follow. At the same time, his mind seemed full of the need to construct some kind of 'Europe' of which, however, one could sense no conception more positive than that which he gave to the Prime Minister and yourself, namely that it should not be American".[73]

A further straw in the wind was the line which, according to the Paris Embassy, was being actively purveyed in the French Press and by French officials, to the effect that the Five (with the possible exception of the Dutch) were becoming more and more convinced of the difficulties involved in British accession to the Community and increasingly sceptical of Britain's chances. The Embassy had picked up from various sources word that the Germans were making no secret of their reservations about the practicability of early British entry. Kiesinger's interview in *Der Spiegel*, with its emphasis on the primacy of Germany's relations with France, was seen in France as significant and important. The Diplomatic Correspondent of *Le Monde*, André Fontaine, had told a member of the Embassy that officials from member countries of the Five were speaking much more bluntly and critically among themselves about British chances than they were to the British.[74]

On 21 March, Cabinet had the first of a series of discussions of what was termed The Approach to Europe. The Prime Minister and Foreign Secretary set out the major issues which they had sought to focus on, and to narrow down, during the tour of EEC capitals: the CAP and the difficulties arising from the current system of levies (a particular problem as Wilson saw it and one which could not be tackled solely through the length of any transitional period); the issue of capital movements, particularly the freedom of portfolio investment required under the Treaty of Rome; and the residuum of major Commonwealth problems, especially those related to New Zealand agricultural exports and to the future of the Commonwealth Sugar Agreement. There had, Wilson said, been a lot of discussion of the sterling area and the British balance of payments, against a background of fear that, since the economic troubles of any member of the Community must inevitably affect the rest, any further sterling crisis requiring, for example, deflationary measures in the UK, would seriously damage the interests of the Six. The worries of the Six had, however, been greatly mitigated, Wilson claimed, by his willingness to state explicitly that Britain would not, in such circumstances, seek to use the provisions of article 108 of the Treaty of Rome to seek assistance from other Member States. Problems arising from the role of sterling as a reserve and trading currency would be dealt with by the British in the appropriate international fora.

In the ensuing discussion, the Foreign Secretary, according to the Cabinet record supplemented by the Cabinet Secretary's notes of the meeting, put a favourable interpretation on recent events. The Five were less scared of de Gaulle than doubtful about the sincerity of Britain's European vocation and on that score they were now more convinced. Brown claimed that de Gaulle in discussion with the British Ambassador in Paris the previous day had said that the problem was not one of principle but of dimension. The Five were looking for new leadership politically, not unnaturally did not see the French Government as being the people to provide it, and would accordingly welcome British accession. It was important for Britain to be inside the Community by 1969 when a number of important issues were due either to be decided for the first time or negotiated, as was the case for the financing of the CAP.

The Defence Secretary, Denis Healey, pointed out with characteristic sharpness that there was no evidence from any of the records of discussion with the Five that any of them, with the possible exception of the Dutch, would be ready to stand up to de Gaulle; and the Dutch carried less weight with the French than any of the other countries of the Five. Moreover, the Dutch were the strongest supporters of the supra-national aspects of the EEC and were the keenest on high agricultural prices, so the most they would concede on agriculture was something on the transitional period.

Wilson disputed this. The Germans would press the French, albeit only in private. Healey said that was not what the record of discussion showed. But, Wilson retorted, that reflected what had been said in semi public session. In private, the Germans had been more positive. However, he agreed that it was an open question whether they would push this to the point of endangering the coalition or their new honeymoon with France.

If we applied to join, were we likely to fail? Callaghan asked. Or were we likely to succeed provided that, for example, we made clear that we accepted the Treaty of Rome? Wilson thought that, in the last resort, the Five would not stand up to de Gaulle. But, if de Gaulle vetoed Britain once again, the EEC would never be the same again. On balance, he did not think de Gaulle would veto but the odds would be only marginally in our favour. And much would depend upon how many conditions we made.

To the suggestion that the Government should concentrate on out-manoeuvring de Gaulle, Wilson gave a cautious 'maybe'. First of all, the Cabinet had to be clear about its decision on entry i.e. on the essential safeguards we needed for our own and the Commonwealth's essential interests.[75]

When Cabinet met again on 6 April, Jim Callaghan warned that if Britain entered the EEC without making provision for the continuation of exchange controls, there would be unacceptable consequences for the British balance of payments. Britain would need a transitional period which lasted until such time as the strength of Britain's balance of payments had been increased and established.

The Lord President, Richard Crossman, a leading sceptic about EEC entry, argued that the removal of foreign exchange controls would lead to industry moving both from Britain to the rest of the EEC and to those parts of the UK which were closest to the Continent, notably the South East of England, especially after the completion of the Channel Tunnel. He thought the motor industry might well move to the Continent.

Crossman was supported by Douglas Jay, President of the Board of Trade and Cabinet's leading opponent of EEC accession. At present, he argued, many US concerns took the view that, so long as there were two *blocs* in Europe, EFTA and the EEC, it was advantageous to maintain a factory or factories in each *bloc*. But if the *blocs* were merged, and there was only one market, then EFTA countries might prove to be the second choice only, after the EEC.

Wilson disputed this. The three principal US companies (Ford, General Motors and Chrysler) were already well rooted in the UK. Ford had said they would have transferred their activities in Dagenham to the EEC but for their expectation that the UK would join the Community. Chrysler's investment in Rootes had been similarly protected by specific pledges. General Motors were expanding in Lancashire and the British Motor Corporation (BMC) would remain a British firm. Roy Jenkins, the Home Secretary, added that it was only with EEC entry that BMC would consider creating new assembly plants on the Continent.

The discussion was striking for the extent to which Wilson, while not minimising the risks, nonetheless argued the overall case for EEC entry: Regional Policy would benefit on balance. Mine closures, mentioned by Cledwyn Hughes, the Welsh Secretary, would happen regardless of whether Britain entered the EEC. If Britain did not join it was, given the size and wealth of the Community market, even more likely that there would be a slow transfer of investment and economic activity from the UK to the rest of Europe in order to avoid the tariff barrier. Hard as it was to quantify, there would be a dynamic effect from accession. Account should be taken of what Europe would produce (instead of importing from the United States) when it was producing for a still larger market following enlargement.[76]

Before Cabinet met again on Europe, on 13 April, the Cabinet Secretary submitted to Wilson the results of the studies commissioned by Cabinet on alternatives to EEC membership i.e. an Atlantic Free Trade Area (AFTA) or what was known as 'Abstention' i.e. going it alone and not belonging to any new grouping of countries.

The report found that there was no possibility of an AFTA coming into being in the existing world economic order and, for that reason, an AFTA was not negotiable. Decisions about future economic strategy had to be taken in the context of what was possible and AFTA was not an option open to the UK. It was conceivable that an AFTA might become a possibility in the event of a breakdown in economic relations between the US and the EEC, for example if there were a total failure of the Kennedy Round as a result of the European Community's policies and attitudes. But such a crisis would inevitably involve a parallel change in US defence policy and would thus be extremely dangerous to Britain in every respect. There would be a deep cleavage between Britain's present major allies and she could not expect membership of an AFTA, in which she would be very much a junior partner to the United States, to compensate for the risks to British interests, and perhaps to Britain's security, which, in an increasingly unstable world, it would be difficult to countervail.

As regards Abstention, the Report argued that the UK could continue to earn a reasonably good living if she continued in the existing situation. But it would be no soft option. She should have to be ready to accept the social disruptions inherent in the radical reorganisation of her pattern of production necessary to enable her to prosper. It would not be easier for Britain to do this on her own than it would be inside an enlarged EEC: in form Britain might have more freedom; but it would be a freedom to submit to disagreeable necessities.

Burke Trend felt that the Report did not assign sufficient importance to the risks and difficulties for the UK in the long run arising from the formation and consolidation of other trading blocs. Even if tariff levels were on average reduced, the consolidation of other trading blocs would create discrimination against UK products. The only way for Britain to compete effectively would be through rapid economic adjustment with big social, industrial and political consequences. Of course, the report acknowledged that Britain would face big pressures to adjust inside the EEC, "but it would certainly be more difficult for us to react purposively to them if we were on our own than in the more dynamic economic conditions which we would expect if we were within the EEC".

Trend was more at ease with the political analysis in the report. A conscious and definite long-term policy not to seek accession to the EEC would inevitably adversely affect Britain's relations with the Six. Over the years, such influence as Britain now had with the United States would diminish. Britain's ability to prevent a split between Western Europe and North America and her ability to promote desirable developments, such as better relations between the Soviet Union and the West, would be further reduced. Britain's own security would be harder to guarantee.

Trend agreed with the Report's overall conclusion which, in effect, ruled out Abstention as a long term policy: "For ourselves, it seems more probable that if we were again rebuffed by the EEC, or if we decided not to apply to join, we should continue to pursue our present trading policies, including as far as possible in the face of their steady erosion, of the privileges which we enjoy in Commonwealth markets; in short that we should not make any overt and declared change of policy but should continue much as we are in the hope (in which we should be encouraged by the United States) that at a later stage a more favourable opportunity might occur".[77]

On 13 April, Cabinet discussed sterling, immigration and the legal and constitutional implications of EEC membership. In the light of the preoccupations of later British Governments over matters of sovereignty, it is interesting that relatively little discussion of that issue took place.

The Lord Chancellor, Lord Gardiner, introduced the topic, saying that entry to the EEC would inevitably involve a substantial diminution of sovereignty, but this was true of every international treaty which Britain ratified and which subsequently restricted her freedom of national action. So the issue, therefore, was one of degree, not of principle.

This rather sanguine view was questioned although, since the Cabinet Secretary's own notes of the meeting are very cursory on this topic, it is not clear who made the key point, namely that there *was* a difference of principle in the extent of the restriction on sovereignty imposed by entry into the EEC, on the one hand, and the signing of other international treaties, on the other. The latter clearly specified the extent to which subsequent freedom of national action was restricted by signature of the treaty in question, and this restriction could not therefore be increased thereafter except by an amending treaty. If Britain were to become a member of the EEC, however, there would be a progressive limitation of her national sovereignty through the legislation which the Community was empowered to pass and the Government would, therefore, not know at the time of entry how extensive the restrictions on British sovereignty would subsequently prove to be.

The Minister of Transport, Barbara Castle, thought that this aspect of EEC membership might be particularly acute in respect of transport policy where Community policy threatened to be based on a system of rigid controls and restrictive quotas, whereas the Government's own policy was moving to a much more flexible system, based on qualitative, rather than quantitative, regulation.

Wilson thought the Government could probably veto any measures contrary to their interests but Callaghan pointed out that the EEC was progressively moving to majority voting. How could we ensure that, at least during the initial period of membership, substantial minority interests would not be overridden?

The discussion concluded, inconclusively, with the Lord Chancellor commenting (according to the Cabinet Secretary's notes; the point does not appear in the formal conclusions) that the Government must recognise that EEC membership would represent a derogation from Britain's power to conduct independent foreign and trade policies.[78]

After Cabinet was over, Wilson Brown and Callaghan held a meeting with German Foreign Minister, Willy Brandt. The main purpose on the British side seems to have been to make Brandt's flesh creep given that all the evidence reaching the British Government suggested that, while the German Government wanted to see Britain join the EEC, they saw it as no part of their role to do more than make their position clear to de Gaulle. Indeed, Kiesinger had been explicit that, in his view, pressure was pointless as well as undesirable.

Both Wilson and Callaghan spelled out to Brandt that, if Britain were again turned down, she would not "wait patiently for a few years until de Gaulle's death and then reapply . . . The pride of a great nation could not be expected to stand this kind of treatment twice . . . If Britain were rejected she would be bound to look elsewhere . . . The result would be the inevitable creation of two rival groups, both intrinsically inward-looking – the 'little Europe' Common Market, and a group of countries (of which Britain would certainly be one) formed around the United States, which would tend increasingly to withdraw from a policy of cooperation with the countries of continental Europe." This, Wilson threatened, would present an appalling dilemma to the German Government, in particular, since in a number of fields they would be torn between their Common Market loyalties and their wider relationships, particularly with the US. Wilson was at pains to point out that this was the last thing he wanted to happen. But the Common Market countries should be under no illusion that something on these lines would be the consequence of a second rejection of a British attempt to join the EEC.

How far Wilson and Callaghan believed their own line must be questionable in the light of the advice they had received that the alternatives to EEC membership certainly did not include an intimate and new relationship with the United States. How far Brandt believed it is unclear. He confined himself to explaining the reason for Germany's favourable view of France. In particular, he explained that, for Germany, influence with the Soviet Union was critical and most Germans felt that France, which had a close relationship with the Soviet Union, would better advance the German case (which included reunification) than would Britain. Brandt also believed that the Soviet Union would also see France as a useful interlocutor on German matters, not least because to some extent France could help, within Europe to 'contain' Germany.[79]

On 18 April, Cabinet discussed the implications for Britain of the Common Agricultural Policy (CAP) of the EEC. The Minister of Agriculture, Fred Peart, argued that the costs of the CAP, and its distorting effects on the pattern of British agriculture, meant that it would be against British interests to join the Community unless, in other fields, compelling reasons to join were established. Even so, serious damage to Britain's agricultural industry, and heavy burdens for the balance of payments, would be involved.

But Peart was not, at heart, making a case on agricultural grounds for not seeking to join, for he went on to propose the "minimum easements" which he considered it necessary for Britain to obtain to make the CAP acceptable. These were a long (10 years) transitional period; special arrangements in respect of certain major commodities, such as milk; relief from the burden which the CAP would impose on Britain's balance of payments, whether in the form of smaller levy contributions, finance for adjustment and production grants from central EEC agricultural funds, or some other means.

Wilson agreed with these proposed measures. Nor, he said, should the Government accept suggestions from the Six that Britain should await the outcome of the review of their agricultural financing arrangements in 1969–1970, unless it were clear that in that review Britain would be in a position effectively to defend her interests i.e., by implication, by having secured membership by that date.

The Cabinet Secretary made no notes of this part of the discussion so it is not possible to work out which member of Cabinet made the prescient observation, borne out by subsequent events, that "it would be unrealistic to think that the French would agree that we should enter the Community without prior agreement on the arrangements for financing the CAP after 1970". But, in the main, Cabinet accepted the advice of Peart and the Prime Minister on palliative measures and Cabinet also seems to have accepted the argument that the CAP, being still in its infancy, was bound to be susceptible to change, especially so if new members, of the agricultural importance of the UK and Denmark, were admitted. Thus did Cabinet agree that the condition of British entry should be that the Government obtain adjustments to the CAP, especially with a view to lightening the burden of the policy on Britain's balance of payments.[80]

Two days later, on 20 April, Cabinet met again, this time to discuss AFTA and GITA – the idea of a North Atlantic Free Trade Area or a policy of Abstention or 'Go it Alone'.

The discussion reveals Wilson at his cleverest. By focussing the debate on what would happen if a British bid to join the EEC was rejected, Wilson reinforced the assumption that a bid to join was inevitable. That was why, half way through the discussion, Wilson turned to the Cabinet Secretary and said: "We are home and dry".

The Prime Minister pressed his advantage by summing up the discussion thus far. While the papers before the Cabinet, and some part of the discussion "might have underrated the influence which the United Kingdom could maintain if we were to become a member of a wider grouping, regard must also be had to the important and perhaps decisive role which we might play as a member of the EEC. In the event of our becoming a member we should be in a very strong position to influence the policies of the Community as a whole. If we were to be rebuffed, there was general agreement that the Government should make it clear that we could nevertheless maintain political influence and a strong economy and should seek to create a national spirit which would enable us to do so with success. We should not therefore in that event adopt the policy of waiting upon events and upon a favourable opportunity to join the EEC at a later date. Equally, however, we should not turn our backs on Europe. We should, while not planning to join Europe at some later date, therefore not rule out that possibility. We should also bear in mind the risk that without our membership the EEC might, in both political and economic terms, become too inward looking, with consequent damage both to themselves and to the rest of the world. We should also bear in mind that a decision on the part of the Government not to seek membership at present would encourage such inward looking policies. It was arguable whether, if we were to join the Community, we should automatically acquire the economic dynamism which had characterised the European economy in recent years: it could indeed be argued that that period of dynamic growth was now coming to a conclusion. But there was good reason to think that if we were to join, this act would of itself create a new economic dynamism, the more especially if some of our partners in EFTA were to join the EEC at the same time."

There was then an exchange, reflected rather banally in the Cabinet Conclusions, but vividly noted by the Cabinet Secretary. If de Gaulle vetoed Britain,

Wilson argued, the United States might then turn and fight France for the soul – and pocket – of Germany. Not only the US, but the Soviet Union too, wanted to see Britain in the EEC since both countries feared a German revival, especially if France were to relapse into political anarchy when de Gaulle disappeared. The vulnerability of Western Europe if the Vietnam War ended and the US balance of payments moved from deficit to surplus should not be overlooked. If at that time Britain were pursuing a robust policy of her own, the EEC might need and welcome Britain. But that was not an argument for pursuing GITA now – or even for applying to the EEC in the hope of rejection.

This last comment prompted Denis Healey to intervene to say that it would be very dangerous to play for a rebuff by de Gaulle. A collapse of confidence in the UK was a more likely consequence than a revival of the Dunkirk spirit. But, Wilson responded, it would be even worse to approach the jump and then refuse. That, said Healey, was an argument for not approaching the jump in the first place. "But we are at the jump now" Wilson said. "No", replied Healey, "I cannot accept an argument based on the need to maintain momentum. I argued that at Chequers last autumn. An unwise decision then is not a reason to take another unwise decision now".

Wilson again: "But we were at the jump last autumn. And your arguments about the disastrous results of a second rebuff apply equally to a refusal to take the jump which has faced us ever since we formed this Cabinet."

Douglas Jay intervened: "But the decision then was explicitly without commitment. I cannot accept that momentum since then requires us to take the wrong decision now".

Wilson: "I agree. But it does require us to take a decision".[81]

George Brown, the Foreign Secretary, was not at Cabinet. He was on an official visit in Washington. That evening he received a personal telegram from the Prime Minister: "This is a cheer-up note you may be in need of after a hard week. But please treat it as Top Secret. It is vital nothing of this be said to the Americans, still more to the Press, or we may create a powerful counter-reaction. The fact is that, this morning, Cabinet on GITA and AFTA was a real turn up for the book. The fence sitters moved over. With the exception of Jay and Healey, the prevailing mood of those who were previously anti or floating was that, to quote, Barbara [Castle], we should 'have a bash' and, if excluded, do not whine but create a robust British dynamic. Dick [Crossman] and surprisingly Dick Marsh, and less surprisingly Tony Greenwood, took the same line. Scotland and Wales also moved perceptibly. We could now have at best a 19-2 settlement. More likely, 4 or 5 against, though I fear the consequences of the balance of payments paper in causing a counter swing. Our joint paper can now be more decisive . . ."[82]

In the light of Cabinet, and of Wilson's clear wish to see an early decision on an application for membership, the Cabinet Secretary prepared for the Prime Minister and Foreign Secretary a paper for circulation to Cabinet setting out the pros and cons of four courses of action: a negative decision; postponement of a decision in order to seek further information; a decision in principle to apply but to engage in a further period of probing before actually applying; a decision to apply now for negotiations for early membership. Not surprisingly, the paper opted for the final course: apply now on the basis that the sooner Britain joined the sooner she could influence the development of the Community; it was what Britain's friends in the Community wanted; it was the only way of finding out what terms were available; it would give the French less room for hostile manoeuvre and was, in any case, the only way of determining whether the French would actually stop Britain from joining; even if an application failed, the Government would have demonstrated their sincerity and determination and have the best available basis for moving to some alternative arrangement.

To this draft Wilson added the following: "At the meeting of Cabinet on 20th April, the view was widely expressed that the dynamic required to make a go-it-alone policy workable could best – some argued could only – be achieved in the climate of a rejection of Britain's application by the Community. It was further argued that while AFTA was not an immediate possibility, encouraging developments in an AFTA, or partial AFTA, direction might follow a hostile EEC decision, particularly if the United States as a result moved into a more aggressive posture vis-à-vis France."

Wilson's tactics were clear – to lead even the reluctant members of Cabinet to the view that the only realistic route to a future for Britain outside the EEC was, in any event, via an application to join. The logic might be flawed, but the tactics were not.

For similar reasons, Wilson deleted from the Cabinet Office draft the words "We believe our decision, whatever it is, and the Parliament in which it is taken, will be an historic one", with the marginal comment: "Might put waverers off".[83]

That the Cabinet's decision was imminent was evident from the enquiry which the Foreign Secretary made of Britain's EEC Embassies late in April as to what the reaction would be if Britain were to decide to apply, or not to apply, for membership. The predictable response from almost all capitals was that an application would be welcomed and delay viewed with dismay. The exceptions were Brussels, where the British Delegation to the EEC noted that all the Commissioners, except for the President, Hallstein, were in favour of an early bid. And Paris.

Reilly had already told Foreign Office Minister Fred Mulley, in a letter of 20 April, that de Gaulle remained deeply reluctant to accept British entry at the present time and that his Ambassador in London, Geoffroy de Courcel, was demonstrating by his activities there that he must be under instruction to do everything possible to discourage and delay a British application. The official line in Paris was extremely negative. Pompidou had made a statement in the National Assembly in which he referred repeatedly to the Six while making no suggestion that the Community might before long be enlarged.[84] Now Reilly advised that, while a number of French Ministers were positively in favour of early British entry, including Messmer, Joxe, Pisani and even Debré, Couve de Murville would remain unhelpful, Pompidou noticeably discouraging and all of them entirely subject to the personal reaction of de Gaulle which would determine that of the French Government as a whole. Reilly thought that de Gaulle had probably not yet made up his mind.[85]

Wilson had one more opportunity to find out at first hand. Adenauer was dead and the world gathered in Bonn for his funeral. De Gaulle knelt and Lyndon Johnson wept, the German Press noted. At the British Ambassador's Residence on the Rhine at Bad Godesberg, the Union Jack was lowered, a bagpiper played 'Flowers of the Forest' and the Last Post was sounded. 400 million television viewers reportedly watched Adenauer's last journey. But, as with all such funerals, the leaders were there to work as well as mourn. On 25 April, Wilson had separate meetings with de Gaulle and Kiesinger.

Wilson tried a new tack with de Gaulle. There was, he told de Gaulle, a whole range of world problems where the British and French Governments could work together so as to maximise, not just their combined influence in the world, but that of Europe as a whole. He proposed that the two of them should, before long, have a private exchange about these wider world problems.

De Gaulle was not easily to be hooked. He listed a raft of objections: people would speculate that they were talking about Britain and the EEC. (Wilson said they could deny it.) May was not a convenient month since he had to give a press conference. Towards the end of May there would be a meeting of the Six. But he eventually conceded that, after that, they could meet.

Wilson hoped that nothing would be said at de Gaulle's mid-May press conference which would create difficulties for the British approach to the EEC. It was most undesirable that anything should be done to create undue rigidity or inflexibility in relation to the issue. De Gaulle replied that he certainly intended to say nothing which could give offence to the British Government, the British people, whom France regarded as their friends, or to the Prime Minister himself. He hoped that nothing he said would be regarded in Britain as ill-disposed. Wilson said he hoped so too and repeated "most earnestly" the view that Britain and France should seek to achieve a far greater degree of understanding and cooperation, not only in Europe, but in world affairs generally. Historically, whenever Britain or France had been able to work together they had in the end jointly achieved great things. Whenever they were divided their divisions were exploited by others to their disadvantage. De Gaulle said that he agreed with this general approach, though he himself could not of course expect to be there much longer to see the realisation of these ideas.[86]

Wilson also had a substantive meeting with Kiesinger as part of what Wilson called 'repeating his EEC tour in miniature'. Kiesinger had just met Johnson, for the first time. Wilson described the President as a straight shooter. He shot, but he was always straight in the way that he did it.

When Kiesinger asked about the British approach to Europe, Wilson said that some members of the Cabinet were still not very enthusiastic. He had deliberately allowed the fullest information and time for discussion, but he was now stepping up the pace. His own evaluation was that Britain would have to pay a heavy economic price if she joined the EEC. In the long term – though this was essentially an act of faith – he believed that British membership would be economically advantageous. Just as the original formation of the Community had given an élan to the Six, so Britain would benefit from something similar. But if the decision rested solely on economic arguments it would be exceptionally difficult to justify. But, looking back on his tour and the conclusions he drew from it, the political arguments for joining had become stronger in his mind. During the coming week, he would bring the argument in Cabinet to an end and reach a decision. If that decision was that Britain should apply to join then the Government should limit the points for negotiation to three or four major issues, leaving the numerous other points of detail for settlement once entry had been achieved. If the British application failed for one reason or another, there was no question of Britain hanging about for two or three years pending a fresh application. The Government were not saying that they had to 'get in or die'. But if they failed to do so now, it was difficult to envisage any situation in which a third application might be possible. Britain would be bound to seek some other grouping. Nonetheless, any feasible alternative would be a second best to membership of the EEC.

Kiesinger probed the reasons behind Wilson's political conversion to the EEC. It was, he thought, especially important because of the suspicion in Europe that Britain did not realise the political importance of European unity or seek the achievement of a political Europe. He himself had, since 1950, sought British membership of the Communities for precisely those political reasons.

Wilson said that a Europe that was economically strong and much more cohesive politically could engage on more effective terms with the Soviet Union. At present, Europe tended to be too apologetic, insufficiently strong and "not willing enough to dictate terms".

Equally, the technological arguments for European unity were extremely strong. Unless Europe kept its edge then it would sink back into a state where the United States and the Soviet Union would be making the next generation's products and Europe would be left making those of the last generation. Britain, for example, was about to achieve a fresh breakthrough in the field of nuclear energy that would again carry her far ahead of the United States. Much could be done jointly between Britain and Germany in the civilian development of nuclear energy. Similarly, in computers, great prospects were open but Britain needed a market as great as that of the US in order to succeed.

Turning to the difficulties of membership, Wilson said he was certainly not suggesting that Britain should join the EEC for the pleasure of accepting the CAP. But, as a realist, he recognised that the CAP would not be changed. The Government were, however, very concerned at the whole levy system and something must be done to meet the British case in that respect. He was sure that adequate solutions could be found to the three or four major problems.

Wilson reiterated that if the British application, which would be a major turning point, were to fail, or if negotiations were to be deferred for another two years, nothing would be the same again. Britain would have to seek an alternative solution, worse for Britain and worse for Europe.

Kiesinger said that he could not conceive that a British application would be rejected a second time. Wilson said that he did not intend to follow the only existing precedent. He would keep the direction of the British application in his own hands and those of George Brown. Their intention was to treat this as an essentially political exercise and not as an exercise in greengrocery. The negotiations must not become bogged down in a morass of detail. They could not afford to waste time. History did not wait.

Kiesinger said that he had had only a short exchange with de Gaulle (presumably on the occasion of the funeral). But he believed the General's attitude was different, even though he could not precisely define the change.[87]

Wilson received similar assurance from another mourner in Bonn, Jean Monnet. Monnet said that no-one knew what de Gaulle wanted, perhaps not even the man himself. But it would be much more difficult for him to veto Britain this time than it had been in 1963, both because of the political evolution in France and because of the disorder into which such an act would throw the whole Community.

Wilson spoke of de Gaulle's dislike of the kind of change in the nature of the EEC which British accession would represent. Monnet replied that he agreed on the need for change so long as it was in a progressive, and not a retrograde, direction. De Gaulle had steadfastly objected to progress towards the political integration of Europe, which was one of the basic principles underlining the Treaty of Rome. Any further weakening of this concept would be retrograde because without not only economic, but political, integration the kind of Europe that its members were talking about would have no hope of emerging. If it was that kind of change, i.e. retrograde change that Wilson had in mind, then it was only fair to warn him that it would not be welcomed in Europe, except by a very limited circle.

Wilson replied that if Britain joined the Community she would carry out all her obligations under the Treaty. What seemed important to him was the practical development towards economic and political cooperation and unity. He accepted that there had to be very close unity if Europe was to be able effectively to have any influence in world affairs.[88]

The straight-shooting President Johnson was also on Wilson's 'to see' list and the two men met in Bonn on 25 April. The meeting began in robust fashion with Johnson accusing the British Government of going crazy in wanting to pull out of South East Asia when its main allies were fighting Communism in Vietnam. Wilson promised to consult his allies. "They're the best damned allies you've got", Johnson retorted.

Johnson calmed down when Wilson set out the rationale for his European policy. Since the War, one of the main thrusts of western policy had been to ensure that Germany was able to develop a democratic form of Government within the kind of Western framework that would prevent any reversion to earlier and more dangerous tendencies there. Now, as the whole pattern of relationships in Europe, between Europe and America, and between East and West was changing, it was becoming harder to contain Germany within this kind of system, as current trends in German policy tended to demonstrate. The present German Coalition was, Wilson thought, somewhat unnatural. Brandt was a less firm and imaginative leader than Erler (Fritz Erler, German Social Democrat) would have been and the latter's early death was a tragic loss. Brandt's main concern seemed to be, having achieved the Grand Coalition, to remain in office. Brandt had reached a kind of understanding with Kiesinger based on the latter's support for Brandt's détente policy in return for Brandt's support for the Chancellor's pro-French policy. From Kiesinger's viewpoint, this was fine since he did not think Brandt would get very far in the detente. Wilson thought that Johnson might find Kiesinger a less easy person to come to terms with than his predecessor. This was in part because Germany was going through a phase of deliberate dissociation and disengagement from the United States and of closer association with France.

Wilson recalled an earlier conversation in which the President had told him that somewhere in Germany there was a boy in short pants who might one day lead the German nation into fresh and disastrous adventures. In his view, the youth was now in long pants. He and George Brown had both been unfavourably impressed during their previous visit to Bonn by Strauss, an extremely powerful personality, with some dangerous political ideas. At present, Kiesinger seemed quite skilfully to be holding the balance between Brandt and Strauss and, of course, the second Franco-German honeymoon might well, like its predecessor, never be consummated. But General de Gaulle, as he had admitted to Wilson that morning, was not immortal. After his disappearance, France might well go through a period of political weakness and uncertainty. If Britain were not by then linked with the other European countries within the tight association provided by the Community, the latter would be dominated by a very powerful Germany, about whose political dispositions confident prediction was impossible but anxiety seemed only too justified. The consequences of this would be extremely dangerous, not only for France, but for the whole of Europe and thus for the United States. In Germany's present mood, the United States could not expect, from 3,000 miles away, to control developments in Germany. This was why the Prime Minister saw such political importance in British membership of the European Community; and why this was also in the interest of France and of the United States. From outside the Community Britain could exert little control over events; inside, her position could be most influential and she could help also to lead the Community towards more constructive policies in relation both to East-West issues and to the outside world in general.

Michael Palliser, the author of the record, reported that the President made little comment but did not dissent from what Wilson had said. Wilson himself subsequently commented to Palliser that, despite the President's tough friendliness, he did not find the overall exchange encouraging. The President had struck him as being in an extremely tense and emotional condition and to be obsessed with his Vietnam problem. There was, Palliser noted, a decidedly hawkish flavour to some of Johnson's remarks and the Prime Minister foresaw a difficult period ahead in Britain's relations with him.[89]

Wilson had had better luck with Kiesinger. A close associate of Kiesinger's reported something of a turnaround in Kiesinger's attitude to British membership following his meeting with the Prime Minister. But Roberts, the British Ambassador, added a corrective. When he had reported to State Secretary Schutz how well the conversation between Wilson and Kiesinger had gone, Schutz commented: "The trouble with Kiesinger is that conversations with him always tend to be satisfactory".[90]

On the eve of the British Cabinet's final and decisive two-day discussion of Britain and the EEC at Chequers, the prospects for a British bid did not look encouraging. Roberts reported from Bonn that Brandt had played a blinder on Britain's behalf in discussion with Couve de Murville, to the point where Couve had been uncomfortable, forced onto the defensive and very chilly, and where Brandt's own future relations with Couve had probably suffered significantly. Brandt had got Couve to agree that any British application would at least be taken into consideration by the Six before the summer break. But on substance, Couve had been very negative. He had argued that, since there was nothing political in the Common Market, Britain's strong political interest in joining was irrelevant. It was, according to Couve, difficult enough to find any common political interest among the Six so the addition of Britain would only make matters more difficult. Couve had repeated de Gaulle's argument that British accession would change the whole nature of the Community, thus clearly revealing to Brandt that the unavowed French objection to full British membership of the EEC was that it would frustrate the basic French concept of a Western Europe under French hegemony.[91]

Cabinet met over two days at Chequers on 29 and 30 April 1967. After an initial session with officials present, Cabinet met in its normal format i.e. with only the Cabinet Secretary and officials of the Secretariat in the room with Ministers. The first item of business was a report by officials and economic advisers on the effect of entry into the EEC on the UK balance of payments.

Jim Callaghan, as Chancellor, introduced the paper. The truth was, he said, that it was impossible to quantify accurately the total effect of membership on the balance of payments. It was clear that the immediate effect would be disadvantageous and serious. But he agreed with the conclusion of officials that the effect would be manageable and that therefore, if other arguments pointed in favour of joining, the balance of payments issue need not stand in the way. If Britain were to join she should need to make an additional economic effort in order to meet the impact over a period of five to six years, but even these early adverse impacts would be offset by the impetus which joining could be expected to give to industrial investment and economic growth. If there were an adverse impact of, say, £600 million over six years that would be offset by the élan generated by membership which was probably worth £300 million.

Michael Stewart (First Secretary of State) thought that Britain could expect to see an increase in her growth rate from 3% to 3.3% as a result of entry. Britain's economic difficulties had proved to be greater than anticipated, regardless of whether Britain was in or out. But the dangers of staying out were greater than those of going in. The Government should therefore try to get in – and do so while the policies of the EEC were still fairly flexible and pragmatic. Moreover, the disadvantages of staying out would grow rather than diminish with time, and so would the realisation of that fact and the regret that would accompany it of an opportunity missed. These factors outweighed the negative immediate impact of joining.

Douglas Jay (President of the Board of Trade) accepted that an exact quantification of cost was impossible. But orders of magnitude could be indicated. A basic consideration was that it appeared Britain must accept the substance of the Common Agricultural Policy (CAP). He estimated the adverse impact of joining at somewhere between £400 million and £900 million. Meanwhile the long-term advantages were not clear or certain enough to offset this loss, mainly because the increase in British exports to the EEC would be more than offset by the loss of exports to the rest of the world as a result of the loss of Commonwealth preference, higher export costs as a consequence of the CAP and increased imports both from the EEC and the rest of the world. These factors weakened the argument for membership based on economies of scale since those benefits would not materialise if Britain's exports did not increase in net terms.

Tony Crosland (Secretary of State for Education) argued that these factors were only critical if the decision to join turned solely on the short term impact of membership on the balance of payments and not at all on political factors. The paper by the experts adopted the worst-case assumption on every point.

Barbara Castle (Minister of Transport) countered that it was important to quantify as far as possible. Otherwise the Government would be relying solely on the mystique of the élan of joining. Was the Government going to insist on adequate safeguards for British interests or not? The Party would not swallow an unconditional application. What was the real value of this so-called élan? It seemed to mean the hope of more investment but not a guarantee of more exports. The experts' report emphasised the handicap to British exports but seemed to rule out the remedy for this i.e. devaluation which the Government could anyway have adopted, therefore getting the benefit of élan without the distortion of the EEC's agricultural policy and so on.

Roy Jenkins (Home Secretary) thought more precise quantification was impossible. Even on the assumptions in the paper (which were anyway too pessimistic) the adverse effects could be offset if Britain benefitted from an extra one third of one per cent of growth between 1970–1975. Moreover, although the transitional period would not begin until 1970, the élan would begin from now i.e. giving Britain two years of extra growth.

Fred Peart (Minister of Agriculture) argued that the figures in the official memorandum were the only ones available. Was an adverse impact of £600 million manageable, especially as it would be aggravated by the introduction of VAT? Callaghan responded that VAT could not be introduced unless there was unanimous agreement to it within the EEC. There was a long way to go before fiscal harmonisation would be achieved within the Community.

Richard Crossman (Lord President of the Council) said that the balance of payments was only coming right as a result of deflation i.e. stopping growth. To cope with EEC membership the Government would have to make that still worse – even worse than had been indicated in the Budget speech without reference to the EEC. There were two things that could help: a major cut in overseas defence expenditure – and therefore in Britain's overseas commitments; or devaluation even though one must obviously not admit that. The Government could not assume that the interval between an application to join the EEC and actual entry would generate élan unless the period was short and something was said or done to offset the fears he had expressed.

The Prime Minister intervened. The Cabinet must beware of leaks about devaluation. It had to be kept open as one option though in present circumstances it would not be right. Others would follow if Britain devalued and the tour of capitals had shown that the Six, particularly France, would resent it. Therefore it should be retained as an option but the fact of doing so should be kept secret. Devaluation was not a one-way option; it could have economic consequences no less unpleasant than those of deflation.

Callaghan said that so long as he was Chancellor he would not devalue. It was not an option that was open to him personally – he had given too many pledges to holders of sterling for him to be able to remain as Chancellor in those circumstances. But outside pressures could force a devaluation, not least if it were thought that Cabinet were inclining towards it. The difficulty would be to choose a rate which would be credible i.e. it must be large enough, but not so large as to provoke retaliation. Assuming the right rate was chosen, imports would not rise *pro tanto* since the sterling area would follow the UK. The same was true for a reduction in export prices since exporters would look to make extra profits. On balance, there would be substantial damage to the balance of payments but it would be much more than offset by a cut in imports and by the stimulus to exports. He could not really quantify how much the net gain would be but, on the basis of the French experience, the first year might turn out level in balance of payments terms but the diversion of resources might need to be about twice as great as the damage to the balance of payments. Part of this diversion would come from the deflationary impact of price rises, the rest from an increase in taxes greater than the diversion of resources – perhaps 25% greater. This was on the assumption that unemployment would be no higher than the Government envisaged at present – say 1.8%. £600 million of resources might have to be diverted and taxation increased by about £400 million in the first year – in addition to the Government's present measures.

If, Callaghan continued, there were retaliatory devaluations by others the effect would be aggravated by loss of confidence among sterling holders and a general flight from reserve currencies and a contraction of international liquidity. A floating rate would provide no remedy: it would merely provoke an assumption that the Government intended to let the rate go on going down and would generate confusion in international trade and payments. It was arguable that Britain should devalue on entering the EEC. But that risked precipitating trouble the Government would not be able to control and his own past pledges would make it impossible for him to remain as Chancellor of the Exchequer.

Barbara Castle wanted to know why, when the French devalued, their action had not provoked similar problems? Because, in part, Wilson replied, the Franc was not a reserve currency; and partly because devaluation had been followed by price increases and compulsory wage stabilisation, estimated to have produced wage reductions of 8% in real terms. This had only been possible because of the personal authority of de Gaulle and the weakness of the French Parliament. Would it really be feasible in Britain to reintroduce and reinforce Part IV of the Prices and Incomes Act allowing prices to rise but without wage rises?

Asked by Crosland how much the balance of payments would improve by the third year, Callaghan said it was impossible to quantify, except to say that it would be better than in the first year – if the Government had survived the first year politically. Jay observed that it would be wrong to assume that the impact of the CAP could be offset by devaluation. Indeed, if devaluation were beneficial why not have the benefit without having the CAP at all?

Crossman said that if entry to the EEC might force the UK to devalue then a decision on devaluation and its timing was a relevant issue. It was not something that could be stopped because of a threat by the Chancellor to resign. But if Britain did not devalue then the Government must also accept a considerable increase in deflation. Was that what Ministers wanted?

Wilson replied that devaluation was not an alternative to deflation. Devaluation would require deflation as well until an export-led boom was in train. That would take time and the interim effects of deflation, in terms of tougher wages policies and increased unemployment, could be electorally unfortunate.

George Brown said that entry to the EEC would not require Britain to devalue, though it might be the right moment to devalue if that were the right thing to do on other grounds. The study on the balance of payments effects was misleading because it assumed Britain would join without setting any conditions and because it ignored the pragmatic way in which the Community worked. 1969–1970 would be the first year of effective membership and after that there would be lengthy transitional periods. So the full effect would not be felt until 1975. In the meantime, the critical year would be 1969 when Britain, as a member, would have a voice in decisions on the CAP and the harmonisation of economic policies. Moreover, the savings on defence and foreign policy which were likely to emerge from the forthcoming Defence Review should produce substantial savings in foreign exchange by 1975. The Government should also have discharged the remaining debts to the IMF by 1970. Further, only free access to the larger market of the EEC would give British industry the necessary stimulus for investment and growth, the effects of which would be an increasing force in Britain's favour in the years 1970–1975. If so, there was no need to consider whether entry would require devaluation – even if devaluation was the right thing to do for other reasons.

The Prime Minister said that it had been right to consider the issue of devaluation in the context of the approach to Europe. There were, however, extremely powerful objections, as outlined by the Chancellor of the Exchequer and in discussion, to devaluation as a way out of Britain's present and prospective difficulties. Nobody was bound by the discussion that had just taken place. But it was of the highest importance that no hint should be given that the question of devaluation had been under discussion. It was not to be disclosed by those present to anybody else, including to junior Ministers. If there were any leak, even if the evidence of authorship was not conclusive, the leak would lead to the person concerned being discharged from the Cabinet.

Reverting to the issue of the balance of payments, Michael Stewart said that the real issue was the adequacy of the measures the Government were taking to improve British industrial efficiency. But Jay thought that the report which had been prepared for Cabinet did not make unduly pessimistic assumptions. The estimates about the costs of the CAP were realistic. In any event, one could not take lightly the threat of an extra burden of £600 million on the balance of payments. The Government did not take the issue lightly when they were trying to achieve much smaller sums on overseas military expenditure or on overseas investment. Could we rely on élan to see us through? If that meant an investment boom, Britain had not had one of those recently precisely because of her existing balance of payments difficulties. If an élan meant an export boom deriving from the larger market then it was to be noted that 80% of British exports went elsewhere than to the EEC. No good case had been made for accepting the burden implied by accession.

Barbara Castle reverted to the issue of VAT. Could Britain veto in 1969 a decision to introduce VAT in 1970? Callaghan said that the principle of such a tax was one thing, its detailed application another and that would have to be agreed unanimously. It was not necessary to accept the picture as set out in the document, even if the principle of VAT was accepted. Moreover, many other changes in the tax system would have to be made at the same time.

Discussion turned to EFTA and the Foreign Secretary reported on the Ministerial meeting of the organisation that had taken place on 28 April. Britain's EFTA partners had been less concerned with Britain joining than with their own prospects if she did so. The Portuguese had been very gloomy but all the rest had supported a British application with varying degrees of enthusiasm, and of optimism about the chances of success. They were ready to waive the London Declaration (which had effectively given a veto to Britain's EFTA partners in respect of her entry into the EEC unless all other EFTA members also entered or agreed to the terms of Britain's entry) provided Britain was prepared to give an undertaking not to re-erect tariff barriers. This would, Brown said, have been unrealistic and would have given the French a new ground of objection to British membership. In the end the London Declaration had been replaced by a new statement that it would be the purpose of EFTA Governments, should it be necessary, in order to give a reasonable opportunity to other partners in the organisation to conclude negotiations, to arrange for sufficient transitional periods so as to avoid disruption in European trade patterns.

Brown thought that EFTA would hold together during British negotiations for accession to the EEC and there was no real risk of a precipitate break-up. But he thought that Denmark and Norway would quickly follow Britain in seeking EEC membership, and Sweden and Switzerland would probably follow with applications for Association soon after. Denmark would apply to join even if Britain did not and several other EFTA countries would probably apply, under pressure from their business interests, even if Britain did not. They all favoured a direct, simple application by the UK – implying that they too would leave the detail of the conditions of membership for negotiation after entry.

Douglas Jay argued that it was important to keep EFTA in being as a fall-back if Britain's own accession bid failed. And it was important to try to avoid any re-erection of trade barriers against Britain's EFTA partners.

After a brief discussion of the attitudes to British membership of other EEC members and of the United States, Wilson brought the Sunday morning discussion to an end, proposing for the afternoon a general debate following an opening statement by the Foreign Secretary. At the end of the session he would sum up the sense of the Cabinet's discussions as a whole, but no decision whether or not to make an application to enter the EEC should be made until the Cabinet met in Downing Street.

When the meeting resumed in the afternoon, the Foreign Secretary advised that the attitude of the French Government was crucial to the progress of any application. The French would prefer that the British Government not apply at all, thus saving them from expressing a view on British membership. It was for that reason that they had suggested the alternatives of associate membership or of 'something new and different'. But associate membership would impose on Britain most of the obligations of membership with few of the rights, while 'something new' was in reality no more than a delaying tactic on the part of President de Gaulle.

There were five broad courses before the Government. First, the Government could decide not to apply for membership. If they decided not to join the EEC it was most unlikely that they would succeed in joining any alternative economic grouping. In such circumstances they could expect little support from the United States for the formation of an Atlantic Free Trade Area (AFTA), even though the American view might be different if Britain applied to join the EEC and were then rebuffed. If Britain failed to seek membership of the EEC and remained outside any economic grouping, it was likely that public opinion would be critical and that private investment would fail to revive.

The second course of action was to postpone a decision while further information was sought on the terms which might be available, but it was unlikely that much more would be learned from further discussions and the French would use the opportunity to cast doubt on Britain's sincerity and determination. Conversely, those EEC countries which most keenly supported British entry would be discouraged and the momentum generated by the tour would be dissipated.

The third possibility was to decide in principle that Britain would apply for membership but to engage in a further period of investigation before putting in an application. This course would provide little more information, and a declaration of intent without an early application might well be taken as discouraging by Britain's friends in the Community who were urging the Government to press ahead quickly.

The fourth possibility, which was not described in the memo which he and the Prime Minister had prepared for Cabinet, was to follow the example of the previous Administration and to apply for entry on a conditional basis 'to see if the conditions we required could be met'. The Six, however, might well respond by refusing to start negotiations at all on the ground that such an approach did not constitute a genuine application; or negotiations might start, only to break down later in prolonged arguments over detail. The responsibility for the failure would then be placed on the UK, and the Government would be accused of having learned nothing from their predecessors' mistakes.

The fifth course was to apply now for negotiations for early membership of the Community. If this course were followed it would be better to make a new application than to ask for a resumption of the negotiations which had broken down in 1963. The timetable argued that the Government should make an early application with a view to membership in 1969 or 1970. In 1969, the Community would have to negotiate new arrangements both for agricultural finance and for their associated states. The Government should so time entry as to be able to influence the revision of these arrangements in Britain's own interests from within the Community. From the point of view of the strength and stability of the domestic economy, Britain would not be ready to enter the Community until 1969; but if entry were deferred much beyond that time many of the dynamic effects on the British economy would be lost, US investment would turn away from Britain towards Europe and industrial confidence within Britain would decline. By 1969–70 the Government should be in a position to relax the stern policies they had undertaken in order to restore a healthy economy, and that would be the appropriate time at which to undertake new obligations arising from membership of the Community.

If it were decided to apply now, the application should be made before the meeting of the Heads of Government of the Six in late May. If this were not done the French would be able to postpone the start of serious negotiations for the greater part of a year; and if negotiations did not begin until 1968 Britain would not achieve membership until after the renegotiation of Community arrangements in 1969. It was therefore important that the Government should apply at a very early stage.

The case for joining the Community, Brown concluded, could be made on both economic and political grounds. Although the EEC was at present dominated by France, this dominance rested solely on the personality of President de Gaulle whose eventual departure from the scene would end French dominance of the Community and create a vacuum that could only be filled, if the EEC remained as at present constituted, by Western Germany. There were already signs that the United States was paying increasing regard to Western Germany among her European allies and it seemed probable that, if Britain failed to pursue the opportunities for leadership in Europe, Western Germany's influence on the US would more and more replace her own. Both for economic and political reasons, therefore, the Prime Minister and he had recommended in their paper that the UK should make a clear application now to negotiate for early membership of the Community.

Denis Healey was first into the fray. In his view, the case for joining had not been made. Accession would aggravate Britain's short term problems by creating a strain on the balance of payments ten times greater (at an estimated maximum of £900 million) than overseas defence expenditure. The only advantages of membership were the larger market and that of élan. But the report on the balance of payments demonstrated that there would be a loss of exports because of the loss of existing preferences.

If the economic case was so weak, what then was the political case? That there would be a European foreign policy which Britain could better influence from within than without? But there was no European foreign policy; and the US penchant for Germany was actually less now than it had been. Britain could therefore influence European countries as effectively from without as from within.

What about the élan? There was no guarantee how long it would last. It would depend on the creation of a larger market and, even if that happened in the end, the short term impact of membership would be a fall in Britain's standard of living. As for changes within the EEC, well those could be vetoed by others just as much as by Britain.

All that said, Healey believed that an expectation had been created which was eroding EFTA and the Commonwealth. A decision not to join was therefore no longer politically practicable. So the decision now was about when Britain should join and what concessions the Government should seek to offset the short-term disadvantages; and how to anticipate the impression that, if Britain did not succeed in getting in, she was finished. De Gaulle did not want us in. He would therefore spin things out for as long as he could and his will might well prevail. So long as de Gaulle was there, Healey warned, it would be impossible to negotiate accept-able terms for rapid entry. And no one knew whether the UK economy would anyway be strong enough to carry rapid entry. He therefore believed that the third option (decide in principle in favour but not actually apply immediately) was the best course. If the Government opted for the fourth course (the Macmillan precedent) they would have to spell out their conditions publicly, which was tantamount to putting them in an application. Applying in the hope of being rebuffed would be a practical nonsense and politically unwise. The negotiations would destroy the basis of alternative courses and the Government would be bound to maintain the posture of waiting until de Gaulle went and the 'Marseillaise' was replaced by 'Inward, Christian Soldiers'.

Roy Jenkins believed that the political arguments were more important than the economic. But even taking the latter, it was easy to exaggerate the adverse impact of membership, which would be medium term rather than short term. The political case did not depend on there being a European foreign policy. The US/ German line-up was not a mere dream. The argument about Britain's overseas defence expenditure was a false antithesis. The case for cutting overseas defence expenditure was that it was out of scale with Britain's world position, and that position was being further weakened by the country's non-membership of any cohesive grouping. To achieve membership of such a grouping, it was worth accepting some temporary disadvantages. There was no reason for delay. The Gaullists would not change with the departure of de Gaulle himself. What the

French wanted Britain to do was to delay because they knew that the position against the UK would harden as time passed and the Five became discouraged. Britain's application should not be cluttered with too many conditions: otherwise it would fail, the Government would be thought to have failed by their own fault, would lose friends as a result and have nothing visible to fall back on. Therefore he favoured an early application to join.

Richard Marsh (Minister of Power) thought the political reasons for entry were very strong. But the issue was whether Britain could afford to join, in terms of the short term impact entry would have. Here, the burden of proof lay with those who advocated entry. The issue of élan was one of mystique. It could not be proved; nor could the alleged merits of the large market. Sweden was very successful without such a market. Equally not proven were the merits of competition: the British motor car industry had not benefitted all that much from competition. His conclusion therefore was that the Government should decide not to apply and should thereby put an end to the uncertainty. The alternative was a French veto with a final result which would be even worse.

The Minister of Technology (Anthony Wedgwood Benn) said that the task of revitalising British industry would be basically the same whether Britain was in or out. The difference lay in the short term impact of entry, and in the greater risk of devaluation. He noted the growing threat of US industrial domination. Set against that were the growing prospects of European technological collaboration, which must be influencing France as well as Britain. There was an increasing realisation of the need for large scale operations in technology and of Britain's own inability to plan her own economy as efficiently by herself as had been expected. The Government also had to take into account Britain's inability to play the same role in the Commonwealth as she used to, as well as her waning influence with the United States. So, for him, all these arguments suggested that, despite the short term disadvantages, the Government should go ahead in order to give Britain a clear new role.

Lord Gardiner (the Lord Chancellor) said that postponing a decision was not a realistic option. Deciding in principle only would play into French hands and be a further disincentive to British industry. It was not Britain's role to try to link up with the United States – or to try to do the same with the Soviet Union. Since Britain could not stand alone she should link up with Europe, which she could lead. De Gaulle knew that the Soviet Union was no longer a threat to Europe and that the real danger lay further in the East. Britain could contribute to European political stability and should therefore go in, leaving as much detailed negotiation until after entry as possible.

Ray Gunter (Minister of Labour) agreed on the last point. One could not really quantify until one began to negotiate. The Government should therefore apply to join now and without any more prior conditions than were absolutely necessary. As to German revanchism, he did not think this a mere bogy.

Herbert Bowden (Commonwealth Secretary) said that the economic arguments were inevitably inconclusive. However, Commonwealth trade, though diversified, was real and it would suffer if Britain applied to join. Nevertheless, he supported entry provided British interests were safeguarded. But if the achievement of those safeguards was left until after Britain had joined the Government might fail to get them and yet be unable to withdraw. So the best course was to take the decision in principle and establish a minimum of conditions. It would be easier to withdraw from that course than from the course of making an application to join and seeking early negotiations.

Fred Peart (Minister of Agriculture) said that the adverse impact of the CAP was not in dispute. British agriculture would suffer from a more competitive system. The levy system would increase prices – contrary to what the Government had promised in all their speeches, manifestos etc. Britain's traditional food policy would be destroyed and the country would move to a system which was not as good as its own and which would damage many Commonwealth interests – not just those of New Zealand but the sugar producers as well. The Government were being hustled by an artificial momentum, accelerated by a campaign in the Press. Some sections of public opinion would regard an application for membership as a betrayal of what the Government had stood for and fought the election on. Therefore, if the Government were going to apply, there would have to be conditions. He questioned the political argument that something could be made of 'Europe' as an entity distinct from the United States and the Soviet Union – even in terms of technological collaboration. In conclusion, it would have been wiser not to embark on this exercise. But, if the Government could not resile outright, then they must not go in unconditionally.

Patrick Gordon Walker (Minister without Portfolio) believed that now was the most favourable moment to go into the EEC. The present check to supra-nationalism allowed Britain to get in in time to shape the movement towards political unity when it started again. The need to control German revanchism was another strong argument. The wider market was essential for proper technological development and to arrest the brain drain. He favoured an application for early entry. It was of the essence to avoid a French veto and to get a clear, quick outcome. So the Government should apply, in the hope of success but also as the best insurance against failure. The application itself should be unconditional (and therefore new, not a reactivation of the old one) and the conditions should be set out in a separate announcement and in the Parliamentary debates. The conditions stated before negotiations began should be the minimum: New Zealand, Commonwealth sugar, periods of adaptation; and the Government should make it clear that they would be as free as others to interpret matters according to their own needs. The fall-back position should be clearly stated in the debates. Finally, he wondered whether the impact of membership on British agriculture need be so bad. Cereals would do well and those areas which would be hard hit would be those which were also eligible for help from the pool.

Cledwyn Hughes (Secretary of State for Wales) stressed the need to protect Britain's vulnerable areas, which included Welsh agriculture. Any withdrawal of production grants would be catastrophic. Therefore, if Britain went in to the EEC she must do so in time to take part in the renegotiation of the CAP in 1969. Per contra, he did not think the Government should overrate the interests of the

Commonwealth: they had not paid much attention to British interests. UK accession would generate élan and therefore growth – in the EEC as a whole as well as in the UK. It was not certain that de Gaulle would veto a second time. But if he disappeared, and Britain were not in the EEC, Europe would suffer politically. He therefore favoured making an application for early negotiations.

Barbara Castle (Minister of Transport) believed that the economic arguments and the political arguments could not be separated – unless the political argument meant only foreign policy. If Britain went in it would be out of the failure of the Government's economic policies and the adoption of Tory policies which gave priority to the parity of the pound and to the Anglo-American link. The Government should have devalued in October 1964. They had not done so and been shown to have no effective alternative to Tory policies. If Britain entered the Community before the economy was competitive, the impact on the balance of payments would be worse than if she did not go in; and if Britain entered, the Government's emphasis on competitiveness would have to be even more desperate and stern. If we increased our growth rate by half a per cent – to over 3.5% – that would mean that by 1975 we should just have recouped the cost of entering now; to say nothing of the difficulties of achieving it. The Government could probably not survive the next General Election given the intensification of the prices and incomes policy which they would have to enforce and the gloomy prospect which they would be offering the country. At the same time, they would have destroyed the last economic link with the Commonwealth and adopted an immigration policy which would have given Europe priority over the Commonwealth. What would they get in return? Freedom from US policy? Freedom to say what they really thought about Vietnam? Her preference would be to decide not to apply. But if the Government were now committed too far then she opted for a conditional application, if only to show that they were not applying out of sheer despair.

Tony Crosland (Secretary of State for Education) said that the economic arguments were not conclusive, though he believed that they were, on balance, favourable in the long term. In any event, all that was involved was a shift, over five years, of half or one per cent of prospective growth. The political arguments, on the other hand, were decisive. Firstly, the EEC already existed as a very powerful, but inward looking, political force which Britain could reinforce and transform. Secondly, every country needed a role and, having lost an empire, mere leadership of the modern world was not adequate. Nor was an independent world role any longer practicable. Europe was a real role. Thirdly, failure to apply would leave Britain friendless and without influence in Europe, and it was not possible to recreate the old spirit in EFTA and the Commonwealth. There was no merit in postponing the decision, and the Government should not miss out on being inside the Community by 1969. Britain's Ambassadors in the countries of the Six and her colleagues in EFTA were advising that the Government should apply now. The application should be clear and simple but the Government's conditions should be stated in debates etc.

Anthony Greenwood (Minister of Housing and Local Government) said that objections to the EEC as part of the apparatus of the Cold War were weaker than they had been. Indeed the contrary might be true. But doubts remained. There were no grounds for thinking that de Gaulle would not block Britain again. Therefore he favoured a decision to go in principle only. The economic arguments, especially the balance of payments study, pointed strongly to going no further. And the Government's ability to plan the economy would be handicapped. Commonwealth links might be weaker than in the past but there was still scope for making a reality of the new Commonwealth and racial discrimination would be as distasteful as the sugar regime would be damaging to producing countries.

Lord Longford (Lord Privy Seal) wholly supported the Foreign Secretary. The Government must safeguard New Zealand and sugar producers. But otherwise the economic arguments, though inconclusive, were in favour of entry. On political grounds, the objective must remain world government. The reinforcement of Europe was not incompatible with Socialism in Britain.

Richard Crossman (Lord President) said that the Government were now committed to entry. The issue was not whether to apply but when and how. They must face up to the possibility of devaluation if they went in, as well as the prospect of several years of misery thereafter. A decision in principle only was unrealistic and would play into French hands. A quick decision was needed and the Government should indicate that when they applied. It was only after Britain had been excluded that Go-it-alone or "insular Socialism" could have any chance. He therefore favoured an application for early negotiations.

William Ross (Secretary of State for Scotland) said that if it was essential to go into Europe from a position of strength, then Britain had not got that strength. If Britain must give leadership to Europe, the Government had better make sure of their own political leadership and their control in the UK. If Britain's prospects after going in were as suggested then there would no longer be a Labour Government. The structural changes in Scottish agriculture required by EEC membership would affect more than 80% of it. It was not affordable to go in on that basis, unconditionally. If Britain were to go in, and he would prefer not to go in at all, then the Government must state their conditions.

Douglas Jay said that British agriculture would be hurt and the Commonwealth damaged. So would Britain's regional policies, and so on. That was what all the argument until now had shown. In exchange all that was being offered was the 'larger market' and 'élan'. The Cabinet were all in agreement that the balance of payments must be put right. So what was being proposed was to add a new burden to the balance of payments and to weaken Britain's defences of it. As a result, Britain would exchange her dependence on North America for dependence on Europe, particularly Germany. The best course would be to join the EEC without the CAP and if that was not acceptable the Government should simply wait until it was. Moreover, the prospects of success if Britain did apply were not good. He therefore favoured a statement of principle in favour of joining together with a clear statement of conditions.

Michael Stewart said that further probing would not produce more knowledge. And how would it be done? Another probe would either lead into negotiations or give an impression of complete indecision. It would be indistinguishable from a rejected application which all were agreed would be very damaging and even more unsatisfactory than deciding against applying at all. Even the option of a decision to apply and to seek early negotiations was not unconditional. It was a prelude to the actual negotiations in which the Government would get as much as they could. The choice was between deciding not to apply and deciding to apply and it rested on a combination of political and economic arguments. We were at a turning point in history when new political groupings were beginning to emerge, and we could not afford to stand aside. Things did not stand still. The EEC itself would develop and the argument about the benefits of a larger market would prevail. The Six would become more formidable as competitors against the United Kingdom and we should find ourselves excluded. Britain's influence in the world would decline as a result. As to the strain on the balance of payments, the report showed that it should be manageable unless the country was hopelessly effete. And the strains on the balance of payments if Britain went in must be compared with the strains to which it would be subject if she stayed out. Entry to the EEC would make no more difficult – but if it stimulated investment would actually make easier – democratic control over the conditions of life, distribution of wealth and so on. Political developments if Britain stayed out were unpredictable. If French domination persisted, the ensuing increasing estrangement from the United States would be very dangerous for Britain. If Germany came to dominate the Community there would arise a US/German link from which Britain would be excluded. And if Britain were excluded she would be unable to influence world developments and would become politically impotent whereas, as a member, she should be able to ensure that Europe and the US remained on close terms, especially since the US was the only other power which defended the principles of political liberty to which Britain subscribed. A Europe adrift from the United States could go wrong on this point. Therefore he opted for an application to apply for early negotiations.

Jim Callaghan said that the Government should apply simply, but with conditions stated separately in debate. The option of applying in principle and probing further was not feasible. The Government could succeed, or be rejected, or have to break off negotiations but if they were driven to that last course they must be free to develop an alternative strategy before the next General Election in, say, 1971. Only the option of applying for early negotiations allowed Britain either to get in quickly or to break off in good time. An application might lead to a weakening of the pound, which the country could withstand since the balance of payments was now in surplus. But that surplus must be maintained over the next few years if Britain applied for membership and the Government would have to go for long transitional periods.

Sir Elwyn Jones (Attorney General) said that the Government now knew that derogations were possible within the EEC 'when arrangements have shown themselves to be inadequate'. It should therefore be possible to negotiate easements provide that the Government acted while arrangements within the EEC were still fluid. Politically, OECD and other organisations had shown how it was possible to 'surrender sovereignty' without damage. A further example was the agreement that UK citizens could address petitions to the European Court of Human Rights under the Convention. Indeed, experience showed that Britain's main problem would be to avoid dominating, rather than being dominated by, these European activities.

As between a decision only in principle to apply and an application for early negotiations, the wording of article 237 of the Treaty of Rome pointed to the latter as the safe course.

John Silkin (Chief Whip) thought that a decision to apply for membership might provoke 40–50 expressions of dissent within the Parliamentary Labour Party. A decision not to apply might provoke twice as many. The probe had created momentum but it was itself created by an existing momentum. As between the option of an agreement in principle to go in and an actual application, the latter would not prevent the Government from withdrawing their application if their conditions were not met. And he drew great reassurance from the flexibility of the EEC in practice, not least as regards developing countries. On her own, Britain might not be able to do much in that field.

The Prime Minister said that he would not seek to sum up the discussion. In considering some of the points which had been made Ministers should recognise that, so far as Britain's foreign policy was concerned, they were not considering the possibility of a Europe organised on federal lines. What was involved was the degree of influence Britain might be able to exert on major decisions of foreign policy in the future. Major difficulties, and perhaps a period of disorder, might occur in France after the death of President de Gaulle and disquieting tendencies were discernible in Germany. If Britain were inside the EEC she should be able to exert her influence in the formative stages of policy, whereas outside it she should not be able to do so and might be forced into closer association with US policy in the Far East. Similarly, if Britain were a member of the EEC she could influence developments of Community policy on world liquidity. So far as the economic aspects were concerned, he had said in public speeches that the case for British entry was not proven, but this statement related explicitly only to the basis of quantifiable information available at present; this did not take account of changes that the Government might secure in the course of negotiations. Relations with the Commonwealth in recent years in economic matters had been disappointing. There had been little attempt on the part of the other Commonwealth countries to look other than to their narrow national interests. There had been a complete failure to take concerted Commonwealth action, even in respect to Government purchases. New Zealand and Australia preferred to purchase American aircraft of types not superior to Britain's own. Canada had done nothing to redress Britain's adverse trade balance with her and, although she was giving economic aid, she was doing less in proportion to her GNP than Britain was. In the Far East, the policies of Australia and New Zealand were increasingly divergent from those of Britain, with a very strong emphasis on their narrow area of interest in South-East Asia.

As to future procedure, the Cabinet had already agreed that their formal decision whether or not to apply for membership should be taken at their next meeting in Downing Street. In the light of the discussion, he would prepare a short draft statement to Parliament which the Cabinet could consider on Tuesday, 2 May and which, if the Cabinet agreed, he would make shortly thereafter. Consideration of this statement would give the Cabinet the opportunity to decide to what extent and in what sense any application should deal with the question of safeguards for our essential interests. It might be convenient to hold a debate in Parliament over three days in the following week. Before the debate a White Paper should be published giving an account of recent visits leading up to the Cabinet's decision.[92]

Cabinet had taken no formal decision. That it would do so was enough of a foregone conclusion to enable the Foreign Office on 1 May to forewarn its European posts of an announcement in the House of Commons the following day and to instruct them straightaway to pass a message from the Foreign Secretary to his European opposite numbers to the same effect. Wilson sent a personal message to de Gaulle recognising that Britain's decision raised "issues which are difficult for you, as they are for us". The decision had been weighed with the utmost care and taken in the confidence that it was the right one for Britain and for the future of Europe. "I know too", Wilson concluded, "that you too will consider it with the utmost care and in a spirit of friendship and goodwill".

De Gaulle replied by return. "Whatever may happen", he wrote "I appreciate the full importance of this decision. As you say, for the United Kingdom to adhere to the Treaties of Paris and of Rome raises for yourselves and for us and for all the countries concerned very tough problems. We have already had the opportunity of discussing them and you know that France is under no illusion about the difficulties. Rest assured that, so far as France is concerned, she will act in the spirit of friendship which characterises the relationship between our two countries and which, more than ever, corresponds to the needs of our time".[93]

When Cabinet met on the morning of 2 May Wilson presented the draft of his statement to the House announcing the Government's decision to apply under article 237 of the Treaty of Rome for membership of the EEC. A number of amendments were agreed. Wilson then put the question: "Who dissents from the decision?" Richard Marsh, the Minister of Power, and Barbara Castle, Minister of Transport, both said that they dissented.[94]

That afternoon, Wilson addressed the House, to warm congratulations from both the Conservative and Liberal front benches and little dissent elsewhere. This was, he told MPs, "a historic decision which could well determine the future of Britain, of Europe and, indeed of the world, for decades to come".[95]

* * * *

5 We shall not take "No" for an answer: 1967

Letters from the Private Secretary at the Foreign Office to his opposite number in Number 10 were the customary means of official communication between the two Departments. "Yours (with, on this occasion, some emotion)" was, however, an unusual sign-off. Yet that was how Murray MacLehose, George Brown's Private Secretary, signed off the letter he sent to Palliser on 4 May 1967 enclosing draft letters for the Prime Minister to send, formally lodging the British application for membership of the European Communities. "I too submit this to you with some emotion", Palliser wrote in putting the drafts to Wilson.[1]

There was not much time for emotion. At Cabinet on 4 May, Wilson had to warn his colleagues against leaks, of which there had been plenty purporting to tell who had voted how on the subject of Europe within Cabinet. He reminded them of the principle of collective responsibility and, a few days later, secured their agreement that the proposal which had been put forward within the Parliamentary Labour Party for a free vote on the Government's motion in favour of entry should be turned down.[2]

The initial signals from Paris were not encouraging. At two meetings of the French Council of Ministers de Gaulle asked each of his Ministers to declare his opinion. Of senior Ministers, Couve de Murville stood out as the least favourable and Debré as one of the most favourable. Ministers were told not to give too negative an impression in public but de Gaulle himself reportedly took a hard position and his arguments tilted against British entry. He had recognised that important changes had taken place in Britain since 1963 but he was not yet convinced that the time had come for British entry.[3] The Italian Ambassador in Paris told Reilly the following day that the French were giving to their EEC partners the impression that they would press strongly for Britain to be offered Association, but not membership itself.[4]

On 10 May 1967, the House of Commons voted by 487 votes to 26 in favour of Britain applying for EEC membership. It was the highest majority recorded in the House on any issue for a century. On the following day, the EEC Council of Ministers in Brussels agreed to consider the British application at their next meeting in June, despite what was reportedly a non-committal, and indeed sarcastic, attitude on the part of the French Foreign Minister.[5]

When they met at Adenauer's funeral, de Gaulle had promised Wilson that he would say nothing at his May press conference that would cause offence. That promise was doubtless fulfilled in his mind when, in his press conference on 16 May de Gaulle prefaced his substantive comments on Britain by saying that "there could not be, and, moreover, has never been, any question of a veto. It is only a question of knowing whether a successful conclusion is possible in the framework and within the conditions of the Common Market as it is, without introducing destructive difficulties . . ."

The Common Market, the President went on to say, constituted a sort of miracle and to introduce now massive new elements would bring it into question. He set out at length his familiar argument about the homogeneity of geography, economics and politics among the Six, compared with Britain "which is not continental, which because of the Commonwealth and because she is an island is still engaged in the far-distant seas, which is linked to the United States by all sorts of special agreements, has not identified herself with a Community of fixed dimensions and strict rules".

De Gaulle came close to describing the British application as a confidence trick. Britain, he noted, declared herself ready to subscribe to the Treaty of Rome. Yet she wanted exceptional and prolonged delays in applying the Treaty. It was obvious that Britain could not accept the CAP and if Britain entered the Community "that system would consequently break up, which would completely upset the balance of the Common Market and take away from France one of the principal reasons which she has for being a member of it".

If Britain joined, then so would other EFTA countries and, de Gaulle argued, "the organisation of the Six would be replaced by an inspiration, by dimensions and by decisions which would be completely different . . . As for France, the conditions in which she would then find herself as regards her industry, agriculture, commerce, currency and finally her policies, would for certain have no relation with those she now accepts within the Common Market. With what then would we finish, unless perhaps the creation of a kind of West European free trade area, while waiting for the establishment of an Atlantic zone which would deprive our continent of all real personality?"

Of course, de Gaulle continued, the Treaty of Rome was a dynamic treaty and it would be possible to offer Britain some sort of free trade area or an Association Agreement. Or, finally, why not wait "until this great people, so magnificently endowed with capabilities and courage, should themselves have accomplished, first of all, and by themselves, the profound economic and political transformation which is required so that its union with the continental Six could be effected . . . If one day, this were to come about, with what joy would France greet this historic conversion".[6]

It is small wonder that the British Press treated de Gaulle's comments as a second veto. The British Government were less sure. Reporting from Paris, Patrick Reilly noted how de Gaulle had been on impressive form, achieving the astonishing intellectual feat of making two separate statements of more than half an hour each, virtually word perfect and with only one or two slips of memory. While de Gaulle had, Reilly noted, said little that was in itself new about Britain, he had been more negative than Reilly had expected. And in a subsequent telegram Reilly noted what was the most disconcerting aspect of de Gaulle's press conference from the British perspective, namely that "apart from the brief and rather grudging recognition at the start and at the end of some movement in Britain, he gave no sign that any impression had been made on him by all that has been said by British Ministers to himself personally in private or in public either on the economic issues or on the whole political background. He exploited, exaggerated and even distorted the difficulties which we have admitted ... The whole statement is so negative that one must ask oneself whether the General's object has not been, while disclaiming any veto, to follow HMG's application with a counter-attack so powerful as to prevent a negotiation from ever starting at all". The only consolation, if it was one, was that de Gaulle had been even harsher in his treatment of French domestic politics. He put the Opposition outside the pale of the Fifth Republic and condemned Giscard d'Estaing and the Independent Republicans within the Government majority for activity contrary to "political morality and the public interest".[7]

Jean Monnet's reaction was to take comfort from the fact that de Gaulle had not in fact said 'no', and he advised that it was vital that the British Government should not treat him as having done so.[8] The Dutch Government reacted with robust indignation and the Dutch media called de Gaulle "preposterous and unbending"; showing the "enclosed qualities of an old time, an old man, an old regime"; and concealing his true motive – his desire for France to be the leader of continental Europe.[9]

German reactions were more nuanced. The German Press reaction was described by the British Embassy as "not unsatisfactory". There was no evidence of indignation, but equally no sign of acquiescence in what de Gaulle had said. Most of the German Press headlines suggested that the door had not been shut.

The German Government spokesman, speaking after a meeting of the German Cabinet, had reaffirmed its open door policy on British membership. Schiller, the Economics Minister, who was present at the Press briefing had "said rather more openly than was perhaps necessary that Germany wanted to keep her hands free to play a mediatory role between the UK and France". However, the Embassy thought, behind the scenes the German Government were expressing their views rather more firmly, despite a tendency in the Foreign Ministry to argue that it might have been better for the British Government to have accepted their earlier advice to delay putting the question until the autumn. Overall, Frank Roberts' conclusion was that the most dangerous feature of the General's statement might be his suggestion that the time was ripe for the Six to complete their own integration without outside complications. This was bound to be seductive, though Roberts concluded with the optimistic assertion that there were also signs that the Germans had, since 1963, learned to be more wary about de Gaulle.[10]

In London, Parliament was in recess so the Government were not obliged to make an immediate statement, and the tactics which quite quickly emerged were not to respond in public to de Gaulle's provocation but, instead, to reaffirm the Government's intention to seek negotiations for membership for which an application had been lodged as required under the Treaty of Rome. In this the

Labour Government's response was not, in immediate terms, very different from that of the Macmillan Government in the face of de Gaulle's similar press conference of January 1963, i.e. not to accept that a press conference was a veto, which could only come as a result of action by the French Government at the Council of Ministers in Brussels.

In a speech to the CBI on 17 May, Wilson said that the interest of everyone in Europe, including Britain, required that speedy progress should be made. "We must all of us know before many months are up exactly where we stand". In reporting this, Ronald Butt of the *Financial Times*, who had been a previous recipient of the Prime Minister's authorised views, commented that there was certainly no question of allowing the negotiations to drag on for two or three years: if Mr Wilson became convinced that this was the prospect he would probably break off the negotiations himself. Palliser showed the piece to Wilson, advising him that the British side would have to be patient. Of course de Gaulle would want to drag things out indefinitely but, equally, if the British were thought to be adopting a 'take it or leave it' attitude that would play straight into the General's hands and allow him to say that it was we who had vetoed ourselves. Wilson saw the note but made no comment on it.[11]

By contrast, Wilson was much more taken by Palliser's analysis of de Gaulle's position as revealed in his press conference. Palliser, in a lengthy minute to Wilson, described the General's resistance to British entry as being in reality resistance to the arrival on the scene of a powerful and vigorous partner. His generally negative attitude throughout the press conference reflected his growing disappointment and disillusionment with his own country. De Gaulle had always held his fellow countrymen in contempt and his general message was still that only he could save them from themselves. At the same time, de Gaulle must be conscious that the sands were running out. The elections and the generally increased ferment of political and social opposition in France were a reminder to de Gaulle of the essential unreliability of the French people and that even his iron grip was increasingly being challenged. It would be exceptionally difficult to overcome the General's resistance to Britain, and great resistance must be expected. But Palliser thought the task was not impossible provided the Prime Minister could shake de Gaulle's convictions about the continuing non-European character of Britain's associations and objectives. But this in turn would require the Prime Minister's own constant attention. "My main doubt now", Palliser concluded "is whether the old man does not feel his back so much against the wall as to force him to lash out in any case. During his career he has tended to be at his most intransigent when he felt himself to be weakest. It could still mean that, when it comes to the crunch, he will still be unwilling to take the gamble and let us in".

Wilson wrote back: "I have had an illuminating first reading and certainly accept the main thesis – not necessarily the pessimistic conclusion".[12]

But Palliser was close to the mark. Con O'Neill at the Foreign Office was shown by a member of the US Embassy staff in London a report of conversations in Paris between US Ambassador Bohlen and Alphand, Secretary General at the Foreign Ministry, and Debré. Alphand had been quite categoric that what de Gaulle had said at his press conference should be taken as in fact a rejection of the British application. Debré had taken a different, but equally unwelcome, line, namely that de Gaulle's central idea was that the Six should negotiate with the British on the basis of offering the UK Association for a five-year probationary period. If, at the end of that period, the British had become sufficiently European, then they might be allowed to take their place in the EEC.

George Brown sent Wilson a copy of O'Neill's minute with the comment: "All this is a war of nerves – to see whether your nerve is as strong as the General's. My money is confidently on yours! But equally, of course, defeatist stuff in the pro-Market papers plays his game. My advice is 'bash on regardless' and I give it because it is just what he does not want you to do". Wilson commented: "I agree".[13]

But when Lord Gladwyn, former Ambassador in Paris, sent Palliser a note on 22 May suggesting Association as a fall-back, provided the British Government was always consulted on major decisions and had observer status in the Commission, Wilson agreed with Palliser that this might, just possibly, constitute an eventual fall-back position.[14]

Wilson was due to go to Washington in early June and to Paris in the middle of the month. On a reconnaissance visit to Washington, Palliser found a "disturbing new current of uncertainty" about Britain, partly because of doubts about British prospects of getting into the EEC and partly because of the state of the British economy. The President was being briefed to probe about British economic prospects since it was clear that the Americans had made a pessimistic assessment of British growth prospects, of likely levels of unemployment and of the chances of Britain escaping the stop-go economics of recent years. If it seemed that Britain had a good chance of getting into the EEC soon, then American confidence would flow back. But there was no such optimism and, as a result, the Americans were sceptical about the British Government's chances of restoring the British economy.[15]

While Wilson, in Washington on 2 June, was having some success in persuading President Johnson of the viability of Britain's European vocation, British missions in Europe were also picking up signals which might have given them some hope that de Gaulle had gone too far when the Six had met in Rome at the end of May. Rey, the Commission President, thought that de Gaulle had overreached himself and created a widespread feeling among the Five that they could not put up with that sort of treatment much longer. The result of de Gaulle's tactics, according to Rey, had been to make the British application an issue of principle on which no extraneous political arguments would be allowed to intrude.[16]

M. Harmel, the Belgian Foreign Minister, told the British Ambassador in Brussels that the recent Rome summit had been a most disagreeable experience. De Gaulle's behaviour had reminded him of a 12th century ruler haranguing his vassals. The sad fact was that the General, who knew what he wanted and was of course a brilliant orator, had dominated the proceedings. Moro had been an ineffective chairman. Kiesinger had been very feeble. The Dutch Prime Minister had been courageous but clumsy and had been severely mauled by de Gaulle who had reprimanded him for his anti-French attitude and made it clear that in his view 'European' Europe did not stretch as far as The Hague, and probably not as far as Brussels.[17]

In Whitehall, work was being pursued on two tracks: preparations for the Prime Minister's meeting with de Gaulle in Paris on 19 June, and preparations for the conduct of negotiations on entry to the EEC.

The Foreign Secretary, "in consultation with the Prime Minister", had been put in general charge of the negotiations and of coordinating the work of the Ministers and Departments concerned and he – and other Ministers as required – were to take part in the actual discussions when they started. Lord Chalfont, Minister of State at the Foreign Office and a former Defence Correspondent for *The Times* was to have responsibility for the day-to-day conduct of the negotiations, supported by an official delegation headed by Sir Con O'Neill.[18]

When the Cabinet Ministerial Committee on the Approach to Europe, chaired by Brown, had its first meeting on 5 June, it also had its first spat. Douglas Jay, President of the Board of Trade, proposed that Britain's negotiating objectives should be to secure arrangements allowing Britain, after accession, to continue to import cereals, meat and dairy products free of levy or duty. Brown judged that Jay's proposal was inconsistent with the conclusions on the CAP previously reached by Cabinet. Jay disagreed. Cabinet, he said, had agreed that it would be necessary for Britain to seek adjustments to the CAP, going beyond a simple transitional period. Nor had the statement made by the Prime Minister in the House of Commons on 2 May ruled out such an attempt. Jay recognised that, at the end of the day, it might not be possible to secure the objective he had proposed, but that was not an argument for failing to make the attempt.

Brown told Jay that, if he wanted to pursue his proposal, he would have to circulate a paper to the Committee. Wilson, on seeing the Committee's minutes, wrote that, in his view, what Jay was proposing was not compatible with the conclusions of Cabinet and that, if he wanted to pursue his idea he should prepare a Cabinet paper for submission to him in the first instance. Wilson would then decide whether the paper should in fact go to Cabinet or not.

Wilson must have correctly judged his man because, on 13 June, Jay wrote to him saying that, while he maintained his view, he saw no need to circulate a paper. Jay's bluff had been called. Wilson made sure he had the last word, writing to Jay on 27 June: "I do not regard this [i.e. Jay's] view as consistent with the decisions reached by the Cabinet and particularly with the terms of the statement of Government policy of 2 May, as agreed by the Cabinet. I do not therefore consider that this matter should be raised further, or that it would be appropriate for you to circulate a paper on the subject, now or at a later stage". Jay had been warned that he must toe the Cabinet line or face the consequences.[19]

As regards Wilson's meeting with de Gaulle, the French Embassy in London had warned No. 10 that, while there need not be a formal agenda, the British "should remember that the General was now an old man and set in his ways; and he disliked surprises". Wilson's response to Palliser was that "I would wish to talk frankly to him about the so-called Anglo-American relationship, and our

Commonwealth relationship. In the main, however, to see how far our ideas coincided on all the main problems – especially West-Soviet relations. I would not rule out any subject he wanted to raise. I agree IMF (if he wanted to raise that – I don't) should not be handled on a technical basis, but with a broad brush as symptomatic of our approach to great world problems. Politics not economics – both in Europe and more widely. In fact *haute politique* and pretty *haute* at that".[20] Wilson subsequently told the Cabinet Secretary that he also felt he must be in a position to deal with two aspects of British policy on which de Gaulle held misconceptions. These could be summarised in two questions: 'Are we – or are we likely to be – good Europeans?' 'Are we likely to be good members of the EEC?'[21]

From Paris, Patrick Reilly advised that Britain's main asset in France was what he called a basic current in favour of British entry, though this translated, according to the most recent opinion poll, into 13% in favour of British entry and 47% more in favour than not. Reilly believed that de Gaulle's anxiety at his May press conference to paint himself as a good European was evidence that Europe was the one subject on which de Gaulle really took some notice of French public opinion. Reilly did not make the obvious point: that to portray the EEC as a great success made it easier for de Gaulle to argue that it would be disastrous to allow the British in to ruin it, but he did draw the conclusion that public opinion in France was never likely to be so strong as to oblige de Gaulle to give way. The General himself probably accepted that full British membership could not be avoided indefinitely, but he did not want it to happen and would try to prevent it while avoiding, if he could, a clear French veto. His immediate aim would be to delay the opening of negotiations.[22]

Jean Monnet, whose assessments of de Gaulle's likely actions were as persuasive as they were inaccurate, went even further, advising Reilly that, while de Gaulle would delay things as much as he possibly could, in the last resort he could neither prevent negotiations starting, nor break them off, as last time, once they had started. He was sure the General could not afford another veto, which would be very unpopular in France. There was, Monnet thought, another consideration, which might seem far-fetched, but which he believed to have some influence on the General's mind. De Gaulle, Monnet argued, was always conscious of himself as a figure in history and was mindful of how he would look to future generations when he had passed from the scene. He must realise that, if he went on opposing British entry as long as he remained in power, and then, when he went, Britain came in quickly, as she surely would, then he himself would look foolish; and he would not wish to do that, even when he was dead.[23]

Monnet and de Gaulle disliked each other. Monnet had been only briefly part of de Gaulle's circle during World War II, finding de Gaulle's autocratic methods difficult to live with. De Gaulle gave Monnet little credit for the vision which gave birth to the European Community and dismissed him as an unrealistic idealist. Monnet was almost certainly right in surmising that de Gaulle had at least one eye on his place in history. But he was wrong in assuming that, in thinking about his historical reputation, de Gaulle was subject to doubts about the rightness of his judgements. That had never been his way. The aspect of de Gaulle's policy-making that looks to a later generation most eccentric is his obsession with the United States and the need for Europe to define its independence in terms of separateness from the US. But that was precisely the cornerstone of de Gaulle's world view and he was therefore extremely unlikely to think that his place in history would be less secure for his having kept Britain out of the EEC and thereby preserved the European independence which he saw as essential to its survival. On a narrow view of the French national interest, it is equally unlikely that de Gaulle would have thought it damaging to his reputation to have preserved the CAP and other aspects of French national advantage within the EEC from the inevitable erosion which they would suffer upon British accession. If that was his calculation, then he was right.

The most potent arguments against de Gaulle's world view were those advanced by Macmillan and, subsequently, by Wilson, namely that only a united Europe could exercise real economic and political influence in the world and that the preservation of the peace on which all else rested could only be guaranteed by 'the West' i.e. Europe, North America and, in effect, the Old Commonwealth, acting in concert. On those issues, neither protagonist has turned out to be completely right or completely wrong. De Gaulle was correct (though not alone) in seeing that the threat of nuclear conflict with the Soviet Union had diminished dramatically after the Cuba Missile Crisis. But he was wrong in his estimation of what would happen in the short-term in Eastern and Central Europe, and the Soviet invasion of Czechoslovakia in August 1968 did, as we shall see, drive a coach and horses through his foreign policy. Equally, however, the European Community never established itself as the power on the world stage that Macmillan, Wilson and Heath believed it would. All three of those leaders were right in calculating that, without entering the EEC, Britain's influence would diminish. But Britain's entry into the EEC did not lead to a qualitative shift in European world influence – for a whole variety of reasons, prominent among them being the resilience of the nation state and of the national interest and the consequent difficulty of defining and implementing game-changing policies at European level.

If the British Government in mid 1967 did not correctly judge that de Gaulle's very negative press conference was tantamount to another French veto on British accession, it was in part because of the signals they were getting from Monnet and others. Wilson had, in any case, hit on a public formula which he used in the media and in Parliament from the time of the press conference onwards, namely that Britain would not take 'no' for an answer. He described the underlying thinking at a meeting with the New Zealand Prime Minister on 12 June. Wilson told Marshall that the French attitude was difficult to assess. The French were filibustering but probably did not wish to veto British entry. He had made it clear in Parliament and on television that Britain did not propose to take 'no' for an answer and he wished by the end of this year to have some idea of Britain's prospects. He intended to maintain the sense of urgency. The British Government had received much encouragement from the Five and it would be difficult for France to maintain a continuing veto on negotiations or even too blatant delaying tactics. De Gaulle's main objections were to the Anglo-Saxon character of British policies and to any major change in the structure of the EEC which would reduce France's preponderance.[24]

However close de Gaulle's press conference had come to being, in effect, a veto on Britain's EEC application, it certainly did not constitute a veto in formal terms and was not taken as such by any of the other EEC members. Wilson's "we shall not take 'no' for an answer" was therefore a way of maintaining momentum and trying, pre-emptively, to devalue any French veto if it came. It also had the effect of determining future British policy. Cabinet had concluded that it would not be feasible to pursue alternatives to EEC membership, such as 'go it alone' or NAFTA without first trying the route of an EEC application. Wilson's mantra became the de facto policy of the Government: the alternative to a successful application to join the EEC was not 'go it alone' or NAFTA but to keep banging on the door until Britain was successful. Of course, if de Gaulle had not already read the hollowness between the lines of earlier threats by Brown and Wilson that a rejection of Britain would force her to turn away from Europe to alternative partnerships, he would now have done so. For Wilson's 'not taking no for an answer' was a clear signal that in practice a 'vetoed' Britain would wait for better days. It is doubtful whether that factor entered significantly into de Gaulle's calculations and, as events were to unfold, Wilson's formula was undoubtedly the right one vis-à-vis British public opinion, the Five and probably even de Gaulle himself. It carried within it the implication that de Gaulle would not be there forever and that the British application would, if need be, endure until after he had gone.

While the Government could not be faulted for political determination in its EEC policy, the question of whether a different approach could have been taken was raised privately by Selwyn Lloyd, former Chancellor of the Exchequer and Foreign Secretary under Macmillan, who told a British official privately in June that, strong supporter of British accession though he was, he could not understand the timing of the British application. The only reason he could adduce for it was the assumption that the Government had received private assurances from across the Channel which they were not at liberty to refer to in public. A much better course, in Selwyn Lloyd's view, would have been for the Government to start immediately making the necessary adaptations to bring British systems into line with those of the Six e.g. by beginning now to move over from the deficiency payments arrangements to the levy system for agriculture. This process of adaptation would necessarily take some years. When it was well on the road to completion, e.g. about 1970, Britain could then lodge her application, having demonstrated to the Six that she was in earnest, and making it much harder for the French to veto. The Opposition would have been open to such a bipartisan approach and, Lloyd implied, would still be so.[25]

Under Edward Heath's leadership, the Opposition did start to adapt their own policies on just the lines Lloyd had suggested. But Lloyd's proposal would have been difficult politically and practically for the Wilson Government. Agriculture had been one of the sticking points in the Cabinet discussion of whether to apply for membership. A number of Cabinet members reluctantly acquiesced in a bid in the expectation that it would fail and that Britain could fall back on existing policies. It would have been very difficult to secure support in Cabinet or in the Parliamentary Labour Party for a radical shift in British domestic policy on the off-chance that the French would let Britain in. Moreover, Brown had made a compelling case for an early application i.e. so that Britain could be on the inside when the crucial decisions were taken in the Community in 1969 about the definitive shape and financing of the CAP. The correctness of Brown's judgement was borne out when, after de Gaulle's second veto, decisions on agriculture and its financing were taken by the Six, in the absence of Britain, in a form massively to Britain's economic and political disadvantage.

Now, on the eve of Wilson's visit to Paris, came further evidence of de Gaulle's attitude. Former German Chancellor Erhard told the British Ambassador in Bonn on 16 June that he was convinced that de Gaulle remained fundamentally opposed to British membership, since this would conflict with his aim of establishing French hegemony in Europe. Erhard recalled that, at a meeting between himself and de Gaulle in 1964, the latter had said that if France and Germany agreed on a common policy they had no need to worry about the other countries of Europe; these would be on their knees. De Gaulle, Erhard thought, might now hesitate to use a veto but he would certainly seek to impose conditions and find pretexts for delay which would in practice make British entry unattainable for a long time. For his part, Kiesinger would not wish to have a row with de Gaulle and indeed maintained that the best way to help Britain was to preserve Franco-German friendship in the hope that de Gaulle could gradually be induced to accept Britain's entry as being in the interests of France. Erhard was sceptical about the wisdom or effectiveness of such tactics.[26]

Wilson and de Gaulle had lengthy discussions at the Grand Trianon palace at Versailles on 19 June. Wilson, and this was almost certainly a mistake on his part, reverted to his earlier approach of threatening de Gaulle with a "quite powerful and indeed aggressive" NAFTA-like arrangement if Britain was not able to enter the EEC. Wilson added that this was not, of course, what Britain wanted. Britain had consciously and deliberately made her choice in favour of Europe. He submitted, "with much respect, regard and affection", that President de Gaulle now had to make his choice. De Gaulle responded that Britain would always be pulled towards the United States. As regards the growing tension between the United States and the Soviet Union, the French Government did not yet see clearly where the UK's sympathies lay. Even if Britain would not make up her mind now, she would be compelled, sooner or later, to choose between staying with the United States – and therefore siding with them in their quarrels – or leaving them. The French Government guessed that Britain had not yet decided. The French Government, however, had decided. In both the Middle East and the Far East they had disengaged. US disputes were not their disputes; and if these led the US into wars, those too would not be France's wars. France had done this, not from any hostility towards the US but because she realised that, now that the US were the greatest power in the world, they would behave as France and Britain had behaved when they had occupied that position i.e. they would consider only themselves and their own interests. For a country like France this inevitably posed the basic question, whether to go down the same route as the US or not.

Wilson responded that de Gaulle's analysis failed to take account of the extent to which British policy enabled her to exert influence on the US. Moreover, it was an over-simplification to draw a distinction between France and Britain simply in terms of their being willing or unwilling to be involved in a war. If ever a thermo-nuclear war broke out, every country in the world would suffer. British views and influence were of real value at a time when President Johnson was under constant pressure to escalate the conflict.

Wilson went on to argue that the lesson of what France had achieved in disengaging from world affairs, and the progress made by Britain in reducing her overseas commitments, was that they must work together to create a united Europe so powerful that the two super powers would have to take account of it. Wilson went on to play the 'anti-Nassau' card. By contrast with Macmillan at Rambouillet he could present the President at the Grand Trianon, not with a Nassau agreement, but with a Nassau in reverse, in the sense that he had told President Johnson that Britain was not proposing to acquire a further generation of US missiles i.e. Poseidon. Britain would work out her own military and political destiny; and an important part of that would be in partnership with France, for example in the construction of military aircraft.

Wilson went on to make a powerful case for industrial, technological and civil nuclear collaboration between France and Britain and de Gaulle responded that nothing stood in the way of such collaboration. But he clearly saw it as a bilateral matter. As far as British membership of the Community was concerned, he reverted to his earlier question. Was it possible for Britain at present – and was Britain willing – to follow any policy that was really distinct from that of the US, whether in Asia, the Middle East or in Europe? It seemed to him that Britain was now some way down that road; she was acquiring independence in missiles, in aircraft and in atomic energy; and it appeared that she saw herself as having a distinctive role and wished to maintain and develop it. There was certainly scope to do a great deal in common – in missiles, atomic energy and aviation – and France would readily do this; indeed the two countries had done a certain amount already. But the whole situation would be very different if France were genuinely convinced that Britain really was disengaging from the US in all major matters such as defence policy and in areas such as Asia, the Middle East and Europe.

Wilson replied that on all matters of foreign policy, Britain was able to take her own decisions. If her views happened to coincide with those of the US Govern-ment, that was the result of a deliberate British decision. To be a good European surely it was not necessary to be anti-American. He was being asked how far Britain really was dependent on the US. Industrially, she was still dependent to a greater extent than he would wish and he had told President Johnson that Britain intended to fight for her industrial independence. But time was not on our side. It might be said that we could afford to wait another five years. But this would give a decisive lead to the US, while Britain and France went on with a parish pump type of industry, tempered perhaps by a little bilateral cooperation. If he and the

President met again in ten years' time, perhaps at another moment of world crisis, would they expect then to be more, or less, dependent industrially on the US – and possibly also on the Soviet Union? Surely they should use the next ten years to establish an independent and united Europe. Both France and Britain should be pressing ahead on industrial research and development both jointly and on a wider European basis. But Britain could only do this if she were confident that she would be within a wider European market. Time was not on the side of Britain, of France or of Europe as a whole. But if we moved quickly we could use the time available constructively. We were at a turning point. He understood the message President de Gaulle had been seeking to convey at his recent press conference, which he had read with great care. He had replied promptly that Britain was not prepared to take 'no' for an answer. Admittedly, the President would say that he had not said 'no', but only that more time was required to examine Britain's application. But more time was not in fact available. On 2 May the British Government had announced their application for membership of the EEC. The application was clear, unconditional and unequivocal. If Britain had not done that, then President de Gaulle could fairly have said, as he had in January, that there was no proposition before him.

Wilson repeated the threat that the British Government had not taken their decision because they regarded it as the only course available to them. Some future arrangement, such as an Atlantic Free Trade Area might be a loose arrangement but it could become quite powerful and indeed aggressive. In political terms – and he wished to speak very frankly – there could be, as we had sometimes seen before, a struggle between the United States and France for the soul of Germany. If Britain were not a member of the Communities, she would have to decide her attitude. Britain's first choice was to be integrated, with France politically, and economically with Europe. If this failed, however, Britain would have this other choice, though he did not wish to be forced to make it. Moreover, in such circumstances Europe would be subject to constant pressures, divisions and temptations and would never come to represent a force in the world.

De Gaulle said he had listened, not only with interest, but with real gravity, to the Prime Minister's remarks. The Prime Minister had depicted an Atlantic grouping which would constitute an even greater and more complete domination by the US in technology, industry, finance and politics than ever before. He had implied that, if Britain could not join the Communities, this grouping would be the consequence. This certainly did not appeal to France. Indeed they had accepted with resignation a policy of European integration or, to be more exact, of organised cooperation in Europe, precisely in order to escape from such domination. But they could not be completely certain that, if Britain joined the Communities, such an Atlantic Community would not one day emerge. Even if Britain were in the Communities, she might seek this, unless she changed substantially. But even if the Prime Minister himself, and his Government, did not seek such a development, the fact remained that British entry would introduce to the Communities an element broadly favourable to the 'Atlantic' concept. Moreover, certain members of the Six were also favourable to it, though perhaps less so than Britain. Holland was strongly in favour; Belgium too to some extent, and Germany would be very tempted, while the "poor Italians", being directly dependent upon the US, could not hope to prevent it. If during and after the War, and even more recently, Britain had seemed to be separate from the US – and this did not mean opposed to the US, but separate and determined to make her own way – then France would have been less circumspect; and he too, who had observed Britain over the last 27 years, would not be as cautions towards her as he was. But he always observed, in war and peace, and whether or not Britain really wanted this, that she was linked to the United States. Thus, if Britain joined the EEC in her present condition she would introduce an element that inclined towards an Atlantic type of Community. This was why he was cautious. In this attitude there was no hostility to Britain and it did not result from any failure to recognise British capabilities; but simply because he saw Britain as she had been so far. Lately, however, it had been possible to detect certain changes; and the Prime Minister had spoken on such matters as missiles and aircraft as the President liked to hear him speak. The same was true for nuclear energy. This was indeed welcome. Nevertheless, the question remained: where did Britain stand? If Britain joined the Communities, in two or three years time what would her attitude be in discussions within Europe in regard to the United States; and in such matters as agriculture, food production, currency questions, capital movements – all fundamental to the EEC – what would Britain's attitude be? At the Rome meeting, France and her partners had all been favourable in principle to British entry; but in practice the Five agreed with France that they should carefully examine the likely effect on the EEC of British membership in respect of the issues he had just referred to. This examination would naturally take some time. They had taken note without comment of the British application and they had to see where it would lead the Six. But this depended essentially on the British. Would Britain bring to this European enterprise something that would really be European; or would her entry, on the contrary, lead simply to an Atlantic Community that was all too easy to envisage, or possibly some Free Trade Area arrangements even looser than the Kennedy Round? He himself had had no part in the establishment of the EEC; it might well have been preferable to set up something wider. But this was what had been established – a Community with certain rules and obligations. He hoped that the Prime Minister would put himself in his place and understand why he asked these questions. It was conceivable that one day the Atlantic concept would submerge them. But in that case there would be no Europe – or at least no European Europe, and no specifically European character or personality. They did not wish this to happen. But they might be unable to prevent it.

Wilson said that de Gaulle overstated the dangers of a possible Atlantic Community. Only de Gaulle could in fact create such a Community in the light of the attitude he took to the British application. He himself shared some of the President's apprehensions. Any such Community would not be only an Atlantic grouping. The United States was a Pacific, as well as an Atlantic, power and some of its major partners, such as Australia and New Zealand, were now to be found in the Pacific. He would not welcome such a development. Nor did he wish to see a death struggle for the soul of Europe. The British Government had made their decision. The President had said that he had no hostility to Britain, but that he was hesitant and needed to be convinced of Britain's attitude. But this could not take an indefinite period. The British Government would like discussions with the Community to begin. This was an urgent matter and Europe could not wait; nor could France or Britain. Of course this involved risk for both countries. But the greatest risk of all was that of delay while the rest of the world drifted towards a disaster which could possibly be averted by a strong Europe acting independently and without fear or favour as regards anyone.[27]

With the wisdom of hindsight it is easy to see how Wilson's tactic of trying to frighten de Gaulle into accepting Britain's EEC application because of the danger that, if spurned, she might become even more Atlanticist than de Gaulle already feared, was destined to backfire. The record suggests that it had exactly the effect of reinforcing de Gaulle's prejudices. Wilson would perhaps have been on firmer ground had he stuck to his positive agenda of increasing British independence of the United States and of collaboration with European partners, especially France. That line seems to have gone some way towards persuading de Gaulle that Britain had changed, and was still changing, in the direction which de Gaulle sought. However, if de Gaulle's fundamental premise – that Europe could only be built in contradistinction to the United States – was fatally flawed, his assessment that Britain remained firmly tied to the United States, and was likely to go on looking first and foremost in that direction, rather than towards the rest of Europe, was close to the mark. De Gaulle would have been even further reinforced in his view had he known that Wilson had outlined to President Johnson on 2 June the fact that he might have to make to de Gaulle a number of tactical statements or gestures "that might seem a bit non-American, or even anti-American", for the purpose of proving Britain's Europeanism. He might, Wilson told Johnson, need a Nassau in reverse. "The President", according to the record "took this well and grinned". Thus, Britain's shift of public focus from the United States to Europe, had been cleared with the United States Government in advance.[28]

Wilson told Cabinet on 22 June that his conclusion from his talks with de Gaulle was that the Government should continue to press their application for membership of the Community. It might be that by the autumn they would have further indications of the attitude of the Six and that would be the time to review where matters stood.[29]

The day before, Wilson had given a more impressionistic account in a personal message to George Brown, who was in New York. "De Gaulle's gloomy, apocalyptic mood characterised much of our discussion", Wilson wrote. "He is visibly ageing, not only physically, but also in the sense of being unwilling to contemplate any new thinking. But I think he is still realistic enough to recognise that his own foreign policy, based on his past experiences, prejudices and humiliations, has left France with woefully little world influence. I suspect that his talk with Kosygin last Friday was traumatic. He claimed that the Russians still attached importance to their links with France, but he dismissed Pompidou's forthcoming visit there as purely a courtesy trip. He spoke with some bitterness about Johnson's failure ever to consult or talk to France; but he admitted that France made no effort herself at such consultation and was now separated from the United States – as he now seemed to recognise she was also from the Soviet Union. The general theme that ran through the whole discussion was that, as he put it at one point, the US, which was now the greatest power in the world, behaved (as France and Britain had done in their heyday) exclusively in her own interests. The only way for a medium sized power like France (or in his view Britain) to conduct their affairs in such a situation was to disengage and 'to make it clear that America's quarrels are not our quarrels and their wars will not be our wars'. All this was of course related primarily to Vietnam and the Far Eastern situation and to the danger of world war arising from it. This, he said, was the main reason for France's withdrawal from NATO, so that she could keep her hands free. Britain's involvement with the US made it inevitable that we should be dragged into their wars. It also affected us damagingly in such areas as the Middle East where we were now suffering because we were regarded by the Arabs as indistinguishable from the pro-Jewish Americans. I rubbed it into him that, in the thermo-nuclear age, it was unrealistic to think that France could keep out of wars in this way and that, far from being disengaged, he and we should try to be jointly engaged in a positive exertion of influence designed to avoid the eyeball to eyeball situations.

"This led on naturally to our European discussion. We had a useful run over the ground on technological and industrial cooperation and on the lesson that political influence is related to economic strength. Here again his constant theme was our involvement with the Americans and the danger that if we came in all the weaker brethren in the Six ('the poor Italians', 'the poor Belgians', the Germans exposed to constant temptation and the Dutch, already on our side anyway) would follow our lead and the whole thing would become an American dominated Atlantic arrangement. It was to prevent this that France was in the Community.

Painted in this way, the picture looks pretty sombre for our prospects. And so, on the basis of what he actually said, I suppose it is. But in practice I and those with me believe this to have been a useful visit. In the broader context I think he was genuinely attracted at the possibility of Britain and France playing a more effective role together in world issues – and particularly over the Middle East; while in the European context he showed unmistakeable interest in what I told him about our willingness to cooperate (if we got in) in the advanced technologies and particularly the civil nuclear field. The fact that we were not buying Poseidon was also a bull point. He accepted that in these major economic and industrial areas we were now becoming increasingly independent of the Americans.

To sum up (and even if this sounds a shade far-fetched) I found myself watching this lonely old man play an almost regal 'mine host' at Trianon, slightly saddened by the obvious sense of failure and, to use his own word, impotence that I believe he now feels. His concept of France's role as he described it is oddly reminiscent of the days of the Maginot line. There is nothing he can do but sit behind his *Force de Frappe* and watch the world move towards Armageddon. Against this background I feel paradoxically encouraged. He does not want us in and he will use all the delaying tactics he can (though incidentally the word Association was not once mentioned, nor anything like it). But if we keep firmly beating at the door and do not falter in our purpose or our resolve I am not sure that he any longer has the strength finally to keep us out – a dangerous prophecy, as prophecy always is with the General. But I thought you should have my personal impression for what it is worth".[30]

The tenor of Wilson's comments to Brown was repeated in the instructions the Foreign Office sent to its European posts. The principal impression which had emerged, British Embassies were told, was the somewhat resigned and fatalistic, not to say despondent, attitude of the French President towards current affairs and developments and the General's extreme hostility to any Atlantic influence within Europe.

In giving an account to Governments of the Five, Embassies were instructed to refer to the fact that "in reporting on the visit to the House of Commons the PM made clear that he would not claim that General de Gaulle was more enthusiastic about British entry than he had been at any other time. But, although there may appear to have been no advance by General de Gaulle, there is certainly in consequence no retreat by us". Embassies were also instructed to warn their host Governments against a study of the issues surrounding British accession being used as a mechanism to delay the opening of discussions with Britain.[31]

A few days later, on 26 June, Home Secretary Roy Jenkins had separate conversations in the British Embassy in Paris with Mitterrand and Giscard d'Estaing. Mitterrand told Jenkins he was sure that Gaullism could not survive de Gaulle and that he himself could beat Pompidou in a Presidential election. Wherever he [Mitterrand] went, he obtained astonishingly large and enthusiastic audiences. Mitterrand was on the whole pessimistic about the prospects for British entry into the EEC. He thought it unlikely that de Gaulle would relax his opposition.

Giscard d'Estaing identified two currents of opinion in France about Britain's EEC application. One, which was much influenced by fears of the consequences of the final establishment of the Common Market in July 1967, was hostile to anything which would increase foreign competition, and therefore to British entry. On the other hand, another current of opinion felt that British entry was necessary for Europe sooner or later. While Giscard showed himself to be generally favourable to British accession, it was, the Embassy reported, clear that he thought it reasonable that, during any transitional period, Britain should have a status falling short of full membership. Giscard also rather firmly linked the accession of Spain with that of Britain. He thought the addition of a Latin nation to the Community was desirable in order to prevent the EEC from acquiring too Nordic a character.

Giscard did not say much about the political situation in France other than to speak rather scathingly of Mitterrand as a man of no principles. He had begun on the extreme right and had moved to the left, not from conviction, but from calculation of his best chance of achieving power. But Giscard did not believe Mitterrand would ever be President of France.[32]

The next stage in Britain's application should, in the normal course of events, have been for the Government to make an opening statement in the EEC Council of Ministers. But the French Government, in the Council, had opposed this. The Foreign Ministers of Belgium and Germany had ingeniously proposed that the British should, instead, make their statement in the Council of the WEU (in effect the Six plus Britain). This was not a proceeding that France could veto.

The Foreign Secretary accordingly brought to Cabinet on 3 July the draft of what he proposed to say at the WEU the following day. There was a general feeling in Cabinet that the statement implied that the Government had gone further than hitherto towards accepting that political considerations were overriding, that those considerations were wholly in favour of our joining the European Communities and that the Government were prepared to accept in negotiation almost any economic price in order to succeed. However, it was also the general view that, since the main aim of the speech was to get the negotiations started, it was necessary to highlight those things which would particularly appeal to the Six. On this basis, George Brown's draft was accepted.[33]

Brown's speech at the WEU was one that, of the senior members of the Government, probably only he could and would have made in such portentous terms. His language certainly fitted the occasion. This was, he said, a decisive moment in Britain's history. It would shape the country's future for generations to come. Unless Europe, with Britain as a member, was equipped to meet the challenge of the modern world she would drift further and further to the margin of events. For Britain, the balance of economic advantage was a fine one. Some of the most decisive considerations for Britain had been political. Political power, and the ability to assert a European influence on events, could only grow out of economic strength. If that unity could be achieved, then Europe would maintain a commanding position in the international competitive markets of the world. But the aim was not simply material prosperity. It should lead to a greater political purpose for Western Europe, in short as a power for peace.

Brown went on to deal with fears that British accession would lead to some radical alteration in the nature of the EEC. There would of course be changes. But they would be changes of dimension, not of the fundamentals, which would remain unaffected. Britain accepted all three EEC Treaties, subject only to the adjustments needed to provide for the accession of a new member. Britain recognised that the Community was a dynamic organisation which had evolved and would continue to do so. If the EEC was to be true to the spirit of the Treaties which established it, its institutions would develop and its activities would extend to wider fields beyond those covered by the existing provisions of the Treaties. Britain would play her full part in that process. Indeed, it was the realisation of Europe's potential which had, above all, aroused her desire to join the Communities. As a member, Britain would accept whatever responsibilities the evolving Community might decide to assume and would join as eagerly as other members in creating opportunities for the expression of European unity.

Brown noted that the existing arrangements for financing the CAP would put an inequitable burden on the United Kingdom. He looked forward to taking part as a full member in the negotiation of the financial arrangements for the Community post-1969.

Brown concluded: "Today, the European spirit flows strongly in the movement towards a greater unity. With Britain as a member of the Community, Europe will be enabled to play a greater role in terms of power and influence, and to contribute in far greater measure not only to the development of her own potential but to that of the world as a whole . . . History, I am sure, will judge us all harshly if we fail in this endeavour".[34]

That evening, the Duty Clerk at Number 10 sent a note up to Harold Wilson: "The Foreign Secretary's Private Secretary has just telephoned from The Hague to let us know that the Foreign Secretary's speech went over 'very well indeed'. The response from the Five was all that could have been expected and they clearly realised the importance of the statement and greatly welcomed it. The French, as expected, were non-committal".[35]

George Brown's speech was probably the most forthcoming statement of British European policy ever made by a Foreign Secretary. Certainly, no such speech has been made by a British Minister for at least the past thirty-five years. Particularly remarkable, and especially so in the light of the reluctance of subsequent British Governments, was the clear signal Brown gave that if the existing European Treaties were not adequate to the dynamic mission of the EEC then Britain was ready to participate in changing them.

The speech also bears witness to the fact that the British Government consistently under-estimated the extent to which hard-headed attachment to the CAP was a significant factor in de Gaulle's hostility to British membership. De Gaulle would certainly have read Brown's speech. The notion that Britain would be inside the EEC by 1969 and therefore able to reshape the CAP, and its financing, in her own interest and, ipso facto, against that of France, would certainly have hardened de Gaulle's determination to keep Britain out.

It is tempting to wonder how de Gaulle viewed the importance of the CAP as against the great sweep of history, together with his own place within it. But de Gaulle the statesman was also de Gaulle the Party politician seeking, and depending on, popular votes. He could not afford to alienate his core voters. It is anyway clear that de Gaulle saw the CAP as part of the price which France had successfully extracted from her EEC partners in exchange for her acceptance of other, institutional, elements which were not seen as in France's national interest. It is doubtful if de Gaulle saw his championing of the CAP as anything other than a significant part of his legacy which, for most French people, it indeed was and is. An apt comparison might be with Margaret Thatcher's later championing of the British financial rebate: viewed by Britain's partners with distaste but, generally in Britain as one of her triumphs and as an achievement in the British interest that her successors, regardless of Party, consent to undermine only at their political peril.

This view of France's national interest was confirmed when the French Finance Minister, Michel Debré, came to London in July. Debré, so Palliser told Wilson, was a sincere anglophile. That went back to the War and to the fact (often forgotten) that Debré was Jewish. Like many other French Jews (Mendès-France being another) Debré was profoundly suspicious of, and hostile to, Germans. He had opposed French entry into the EEC at the outset largely because Britain was not to be in and France was to be left in uncomfortable juxtaposition with Germany. But Debré was also passionately loyal to de Gaulle. The General had forced Debré (as Prime Minister of France) to accept Algerian independence (to which he had been implacably opposed for years) and to accept Franco-German friendship. As long as de Gaulle was there, Palliser argued, Debré would do whatever de Gaulle told him. Debré was equally passionately anti-American, largely from the feeling that it was as a consequence of American policy that France was driven out of Indo-China and had to abandon Algeria. He was, said Palliser, in political terms, a kind of left-wing blend of Julian Amery and Enoch Powell – complex, of passionate convictions and beliefs and with a kind of fiery integrity. Debré, while he would always be personally well disposed towards the British, would not (so long as de Gaulle was there) stray an inch from the path which de Gaulle had laid down. That in turn made him less flexible and correspondingly less easy to do business with than the much smoother Pompidou – Debré's principal rival for the post-de Gaulle era.[36]

When Debré met Wilson and Callaghan in Downing Street, Wilson again set out the possibility of Britain seeking a wider free trade area with the United States, Canada and other Commonwealth countries and the other members of EFTA if she was denied membership of the EEC.

Debré replied that this was indeed a very serious matter and one of great interest to the whole of Europe. For her part, France, in joining the Common Market, had made a determined effort to break away from her traditional protectionism. The Common Market was possibly only a stage in the process but the French interest required that the stage should be a relatively long one. Moreover, France had only been able to abandon this traditional protectionist concept under three conditions: the existence of a substantial external tariff protecting her industries; a European agricultural policy under which French agriculture would continue to be protected; and the restriction of capital movements to a specific geographical area. This situation would have to be maintained for a long time so that France's agricultural problems could be resolved and French industry satisfactorily adapted and modernised. Debré added that, speaking personally, he was more English than the English as regards any supra-national system. But the French could not afford to give up the advantages they enjoyed under the present system of the Common Market and take a leap into the unknown of a far wider Free Trade Area.[37]

That was Debré, the Anglophile, speaking. De Gaulle himself, a week earlier, had been a good deal blunter in speaking to Britain's Ambassador in Paris. Reilly said to the President that he had been much struck by what de Gaulle had said in his most recent press conference when he had spoken of building a Europe that would be able to balance any power in the world. Reilly hoped that the Prime Minister had convinced de Gaulle that this was what Britain too wished to join in doing in entering the EEC.

De Gaulle said that he knew that this was what the British said, and he believed that the British meant it. But they were not capable of actually doing it. There were all the problems of agriculture, capital movements, New Zealand and so on. Britain could not change her longstanding habits, the sources of her food etc. She was, in any event, irrevocably tied to the United States.

Reilly (who, interestingly, is never on record as taking Wilson's line that Britain would look for some new free trade area if denied EEC membership) responded that Britain hoped to show in negotiations that the difficulties mentioned by de Gaulle were much less great than he believed. But he did remonstrate with de Gaulle at the fact that Couve de Murville, so far from accepting that Britain was necessary to a Europe which could balance any power in the world, had said that the entry of Britain and its EFTA partners would be a grave danger to Europe, reviving the Cold War and creating a new iron curtain. De Gaulle replied that this was exactly what the Russians had said to Pompidou and Couve in Moscow the previous week.

Reilly, quite bravely, responded that he hoped the President would forgive him for saying that, having served in Moscow (where Reilly had been Ambassador), when he had first read what Couve had said it had struck him as typically Soviet language. De Gaulle said that the Russians, who had never liked the Community, were generally horrified at the prospect of Europe dissolving into some vast Atlantic organisation. It was only the true Europe of the Six which could form the element of balance.

Did this mean, Reilly asked, that Europe must be confined to the Six for ever? Not for ever, de Gaulle replied, but until Britain had changed enough for member-ship, and in all respects (which Reilly interpreted as meaning both as regards Britain's economic practices and her political allegiance).

Reilly drew de Gaulle's attention to Brown's WEU statement. De Gaulle confirmed that he had read it. Reilly argued that it surely showed that the British Government had reduced the terms for which they were asking to narrow limits. "Terms, yes", de Gaulle replied "But you have not dealt with the facts". He repeated 'the facts;' three times, shaking his head and making a sweeping gesture of dismissal that the British could not do what they said they would. Britain, de Gaulle continued, was asking for transitional periods and all kinds of derogations; and there was sterling, about which the British Foreign Secretary had said nothing. Britain was simply ignoring the problem.

Reilly said that the British Government did not believe that the sterling problem which the French Government identified really existed. But the British were quite ready to discuss it anyway, as the Prime Minister had himself told de Gaulle, not excluding, even, discussion of the possibility of a European currency one day. At this, Reilly reported, de Gaulle looked slightly non-plussed, having evidently forgotten that part of his conversation with the Prime Minister. Reilly concluded that it seemed very difficult to convince de Gaulle that the British would do what they said they would. De Gaulle replied that it was indeed so. Reilly recalled that de Gaulle had told the Prime Minister that there was no question of a French veto. Of course there would be no French veto, de Gaulle replied. But it would all take a very long time.

Finally, de Gaulle spoke about his forthcoming visit to Canada to which he was clearly much looking forward.[38]

On the following day, de Gaulle was in Bonn for a meeting with Chancellor Kiesinger. The French Government took the unusual step of issuing the text of what de Gaulle had said in the plenary discussions. De Gaulle had set out his view on the necessary relations between Europe and the United States. A Franco-German coincidence of view was necessary in order to avoid American hegemony. There needed to be cooperation with Eastern Europe so as to ensure that there was something else in world policy other than a system of two blocs. This preservation of national personality, of "our Europe of the Six" and of a policy of détente with the East also implied French support for German reunification, based not solely on philosophical arguments but also on its desirability from the point of view of French interest.

Having, in effect, told the German Government that the price of French support for German reunification was German acquiescence in de Gaulle's world view, the General turned to Britain. "If one day", he said, "and we can hope for this, Great Britain becomes what we are ourselves, that is to say really European in her way of life, in the procurement of her food supplies, in her monetary system, in her practice of capital movements, in her world situation, in her links with the Commonwealth and in her relations with the United States – in short if Great Britain becomes really European, there is no reason why she should not be in our Community. But if she joins before this evolution has taken place then this Community which we have established with such difficulty between the Six will no longer exist. It will be completely changed. Of course we could change everything but in that case this is what should be proposed. One cannot do what we have done amongst ourselves and at the same time bring in countries with different conceptions. Perhaps the evolution of Great Britain will continue; we certainly hope so. But this is the development which must be brought about before everything is destroyed".[39]

That the British Government did not at this point conclude that the game was up was down to a number of factors. From Paris, Reilly was reporting that semi-public criticism of de Gaulle in France had reached unprecedented levels. There was a feeling around that de Gaulle would not last very much longer. His anti-Israeli Middle East policy was partly to account. A British journalist had told Reilly that his newspaper was constantly asking him the question: 'Is the General gaga'? According to Reilly, this was far from the truth: "To anyone who saw his last press conference, or who had an account of his discussions with the Prime Minister or had the sort of talk I had with him on 11 July it can only seem grotesque to describe him as gaga or senile. His intellectual powers are still remarkable. His staying power is extraordinary, his grip on the governmental machine complete. Yet, he is unquestioningly ageing, and with age all his dominating characteristics and prejudices are becoming still more accentuated. Thus his judgement is clouded by his compulsive anti-Americanism and his obsession with independence and with French dominance in Europe. He seems genuinely to believe that the Russians now coo like a sucking dove; and facts that do not suit him, like the real nature of the British application to the EEC, are simply pushed away as non-facts. We must therefore expect all his present policies to be maintained and indeed accentuated".

Reilly went on to predict, with considerable prescience, that there would be a clash which would lead to de Gaulle's departure before the end of his mandate at the end of 1972, and probably a good deal earlier, but not before 1969. Reilly thought that de Gaulle would try to avoid a clear veto because of its domestic unpopularity. He clearly also set some store by the fact that the Embassy were continually being told by official sources that a veto was impossible.

Neither Reilly nor anyone else seems to have dissected this assurance. Since de Gaulle's definition of a veto was clearly whatever he chose to make it (he consistently, for example, denied that he had vetoed Britain's application in 1963) it was rash to put more weight on those assurances than on the fact that de Gaulle had found numerous ways over several weeks of making clear, in public and in private, that he was not prepared to have the British in the EEC for the foreseeable future. Reilly, like others in the British establishment, believed that de Gaulle would try to find ways, short of a formal veto, of blocking the opening of negotiations indefinitely. The British Government, in his view, should therefore play a long game.[40]

Palliser, following a two day visit to Brussels, reported a similar view among Eurocrats: France would not be able to prevent a negotiation because de Gaulle would not wish to veto one. Although Palliser himself tended to this view he had been struck, as he reported to Wilson, by an authoritative account of a conversation at the end of June between Maurer, the Romanian Premier, and de Gaulle in which de Gaulle had said two things in categorical terms. The first was that he had no intention of accepting British membership of the EEC. The second was that he intended to withdraw from the Atlantic Alliance in or by 1969. The Private Secretary to Harmel, the Belgian Foreign Minister, had reported his master's view as being that de Gaulle would have to block negotiations with Britain simply because George Brown's statement to the WEU had made it so crystal clear that a negotiation was bound to succeed.

Paul-Henri Spaak's son told Palliser that the French were saying to the Germans that one of the main reasons why they were opposed to British entry was that it would prevent Franco-German domination of the Community. At the same time, they were saying to their other partners that if Britain were allowed in this would be bound to lead to Anglo-German domination of the Community. Palliser was struck by the fact that, however much other members of the Community resented French patronising and de Gaulle's autocratic methods, they all implicitly accepted Paris as the de facto capital of Europe. To that extent, they slightly justified the contempt in which de Gaulle held them, and they certainly justified to him his belief that the only way to keep Paris as the real capital of Europe was to keep Britain out and thereby to prevent London from superseding Paris, as eventually he believed it would.

The general view of those to whom Palliser spoke was that if de Gaulle decided to take France out of NATO in the next year or two he could probably get away with it as regards French public opinion. But they equally thought that de Gaulle was probably no longer strong enough to take France out of the EEC and that, if he tried to do so, it might result in his downfall. That, Palliser concluded, immeasurably strengthened the hand of the Five, did they but realise it, in dealing with de Gaulle in the context of British membership.[41]

Authoritative German accounts of Kiesinger's meeting with de Gaulle in Bonn bore out the consistent picture of total opposition to British membership of the EEC on the part of de Gaulle. Kiesinger had given an account of the meeting to the US Ambassador in Bonn, George McGhee. Kiesinger claimed to have taken the bull by the horns and to have told de Gaulle that he neither understood nor sympathised with de Gaulle's anti-American policies. De Gaulle had repeated his well-known view of the need to prevent American domination of Europe. When Kiesinger had asked him why he felt it necessary to attack the United States in public, de Gaulle had replied that it was necessary for him to do so for internal French political reasons. There were certain Frenchmen, such as Monnet, who were willing to give up French national identity by accepting American domination and he felt it necessary to neutralise their influence.

Kiesinger had told the US Ambassador that de Gaulle's attitude to British entry to the EEC had been adamant. De Gaulle had claimed not to have reached a final judgement and said that, if Britain could prove herself qualified for full membership then that could be considered. But de Gaulle had gone on to list a series of conditions, including that Britain must 'change its nourishment' i.e. stop taking its main food supplies from outside Europe. He had also cited the problems of Aden and Singapore as obstacles to British membership.

Kiesinger had told de Gaulle that European public opinion was so strongly in favour of British membership that this could not be prevented. De Gaulle had replied that no one could force France to accept Britain into the EEC. In giving this account to the US Ambassador, Kiesinger had commented that he himself thought that it might not be possible to attain the kind of European political unity which Germany sought in the EEC if Britain became a member.

In putting this report to Wilson, Palliser commented: "I wish I had a little more trust in Kiesinger". "Yes", wrote Wilson.[42]

Kiesinger also gave an account of his meeting with de Gaulle directly to the British Ambassador in Bonn. This version did not differ substantially to that given to the American Ambassador save that, not surprisingly, Kiesinger portrayed his support for British accession in more heroic terms. But the impression of de Gaulle's adamant opposition to British accession was the same. Indeed, Kiesinger had found de Gaulle much harder than he had been at their previous meeting six months earlier. Summing up the visit, Kiesinger told Roberts that there remained total disagreement between Paris and Bonn on two basic issues: British membership of the EEC; and NATO and relations with the United States and with the Soviet Union.

Despite these basic disagreements, which would not easily be removed, Kiesinger thought it important still to maintain an improved climate in Franco-German relations and to preserve the Franco-German reconciliation which had been one of the main achievements of the post-war years. He also thought that Germany had something to gain and nothing to lose from French support for her policies aimed at detente with Eastern Europe. De Gaulle, Kiesinger believed, realised how deeply divided France and Germany were on important questions and that this lay behind the story de Gaulle had told at the official dinner in his honour of the two men who had gone looking for treasure but had found nothing beyond the fact that they had become friends in the process.

Kiesinger struck Roberts as being tired and depressed. So he might be, Roberts thought, given his domestic troubles over the budget, foreign relations and defence which had combined to bring rudely to an end the six months' honeymoon period of the Grand Coalition and which had, for the first time, checked the impressive rise in the Chancellor's own popularity.[43]

These accounts of de Gaulle's visit offer an interesting insight into de Gaulle's capacity to read the wind and to judge how close he could sail to it. His dinner-time story was a clever way of signalling that the policy differences between the French and German Governments were not significant compared with the friendship that had gown up between the two countries, and that the differences were not enough to undermine that friendship. For all of Western Europe, confidence that there was a fundamentally sound Franco-German relationship was ultimately more important to their sense of security than was British accession. The Governments of the Five all knew that, in the last analysis, they could count on Britain, and the umbilical link between Britain and the United States that de Gaulle insisted on severing was a further guarantee of that dependability. Paradoxically, a Britain which had distanced itself from the United States in order to be an acceptable EEC member in French eyes would, by that very fact, have been a less desirable partner for the rest of the membership.

Sailing close to the wind was certainly what de Gaulle did when, on 24 July, he gave his famous rallying cry of "Vive le Québec libre" on the steps of the City Hall in Montreal. After two emergency meetings, the Canadian Government issued a statement saying that "Certain statements by the President tend to encourage a small minority of our population whose aim is to destroy Canada and, as such, they are unacceptable to the Canadian people and its Government". De Gaulle promptly cut short his visit. The British Government, anxious not to get on bad terms with France, made no official comment.

However, on his return to France, de Gaulle gave a full account of his actions to the French Council of Ministers and ordered that they be issued in the form of a public statement. More almost than any other of de Gaulle's public utterances at that time, his comments give an insight into his state of mind and his image of himself. "General de Gaulle noted", said the Elysée press release, "the immense French fervour which manifested itself everywhere he went. He observed among the French Canadians the unanimous conviction that after the century of oppression which in their case followed the English conquest, the second century ensuing under the system laid down by the British North America Act of 1867 had not assured them, in their own country, liberty, equality and fraternity. Taking account of this indescribable wave of emotion and resolution, General de Gaulle indicated unequivocally to the French Canadians and to their Government that France intended to help them to gain the emancipating objectives which they themselves had fixed upon. The President of the Republic returned to Paris without passing through Ottawa as he had at first agreed to do. In fact, a declaration published by the Federal Canadian Government describing as unacceptable the wish that Quebec should be free, such as General de Gaulle had expressed, evidently rendered this visit impossible. It goes without saying, concluded the President of the Republic, that France had no aim to direct or even less to exercise sovereignty over all or any of present day Canada. Given, however, that France founded Canada, given that she alone through two and a half centuries administered and peopled Canada and gave it importance, given that she takes note there of the existence and the ardent personality of a French community comprising six and a half million inhabitants, four and a half million in Quebec, France could certainly not either disinterest herself in the present and future destiny of a populace sprung from her own people and admirably faithful to their original motherland, or consider Canada as a country foreign in the sense that any others would be".[44]

All of this was characteristic de Gaulle: outrageous, intolerable, disingenuous, distorted, embittered, ungrateful and graceless – even dotty, but dotty on a grand and magnificent scale. His statement was that of a man both in full control and out of control. Bravura stuff that it was, it started more widespread speculation in France than had ever been heard before about whether the General was starting to 'lose it'.

Whatever the truth of that conjecture, de Gaulle's action in Canada and his representation of it to the French people showed his continued dominance and his capacity for disregarding the norms of acceptable behaviour. Thus when Palliser submitted to Wilson, with a question mark against it, a minute from Lord Chalfont which maintained that de Gaulle was not strong enough either in the Six or in France to impose a veto of the brutal sort which had ended the previous negotiations, Wilson wrote: "I agree with your question mark. We are past the point of forecasting his actions on the basis of rational analysis".[45]

On 10 August, in a televised address to the French people, de Gaulle indirectly addressed the criticisms of him: "So it is that the apostles of decline are stupefied and indignant at the fact that France, without in the least giving up the friendship she bears for the Anglo-Saxon nations, but nevertheless making a break from absurd and outward conformism and effacement, should take up a really French position towards the Vietnam war, or towards the Middle East conflict or towards the construction of a European Europe, or towards the overturning of the Community of the Six which would be consequent upon the admission of England and four or five other states, or towards relations with the East or towards the international monetary question . . ."[46]

British cinema audiences four decades later cheered at the moment in the film *Love Actually* when Hugh Grant, playing the British Prime Minister, denounced the American conduct of the special relationship as an insult to the nation of Elizabeth I, Churchill, Margaret Thatcher – and Harry Potter. There must, to a French audience, have been something almost equally absurd, disturbing but patriotically arousing in de Gaulle's words in 1967. They were theatre, and potentially costly theatre, in terms of France's real interests but they struck a chord in a nation that wanted to feel as if it could relive old glories.

The day after de Gaulle's broadcast, Frank Roberts in Bonn compared notes about it with Willy Brandt. They agreed that de Gaulle had said nothing new about the British bid for membership. Brandt went on to tell Roberts the following story. After de Gaulle, during his visit to Bonn in July, had made his statement in plenary about how the British had to become more European, and that this involved feeding themselves with food produced from European soil, Brandt had laughingly said to the General that he would have had some sympathy for his approach if he had taken the line that English cuisine must be brought up to the French level. De Gaulle, not a man for jokes, especially other people's, replied that he had said nothing in Bonn that he had not said directly to Harold Wilson shortly before in Paris. De Gaulle went on to comment that the Prime Minister had not said much in reply but that he, de Gaulle, had guessed what he was thinking, which was that things would be very different after he, the General, had departed. De Gaulle had added "C'est possible mais pas sur". According to Brandt, this was the first time he had heard de Gaulle talk so philosophically about the situation after his own departure.[47]

In Roberts' judgement, the Grand Coalition in Bonn was beginning to pay a price for its policy towards France. In a Despatch addressed to the Foreign Secretary in mid August, Roberts argued that, while the CDU/CSU and SPD had vied with each other in injecting an excessive amount of warmth into the Franco-German relationship, it had long since been clear to Germans outside the coalition that, despite fine phrases and toasts of Gallic grandeur to a united Germany, de Gaulle himself had contrived to keep the real temperature of Franco-German relations near to freezing point, above all by his handling of the Middle East crisis and by his behaviour in Canada which had been openly, universally and mercilessly criticised in Germany. De Gaulle's behaviour in those instances had, above all, strengthened the suspicion that he could not be relied upon as an ally and that his rabid anti-Americanism was now driving him into the arms of Germany's chief enemy, the Soviet Union. The coalition in Bonn were, the Embassy believed, running the risk of making themselves look slightly ridiculous by continuing to act as an unrequited but loyal lover. The corollary to the French policy of Kiesinger and Brandt had been the risk of a deterioration in German-American relations, as well as the more obvious failure or inability to give effective support to the British application for EEC membership. For the overwhelming majority of Germans, amicable Franco-German relations were highly desirable, but the maintenance of the alliance with the United States and of NATO were vital to German national interests. It followed that the German Government's almost subservient attitude to de Gaulle was beginning to cause annoyance and criticism.[48]

Speculation about de Gaulle's motives and intentions buzzed around the capitals of Europe after the *rentrée*. But the first authoritative account of French intentions came in mid-September 1967. Crispin Tickell, First Secretary in the Embassy in Paris, was told by Peter Strafford of the *Times* bureau in Paris that, on 18 September, his bureau chief, Charles Hargrove, had told him that the Head of the Press section at the French Foreign Ministry had informed him, for his own personal information, that the French Government had decided to veto the opening of negotiations for British entry into the Common Market. This veto would be imposed when the subject was discussed at the meeting of the Foreign Affairs Council of the EEC on 23 October. Hargrove, a man whose distinction as a correspondent was more than matched by his own self-regard, had instructed Strafford not to pass this information to the Embassy but Strafford had felt under a responsibility to do so.

In a letter to London, covering Tickell's note, Reilly wrote: "As you know, I have for a considerable time thought it possible that the General might decide to act in this way in order to put a complete stop to our candidature before it could get any further . . . It would be in character with his recent behaviour for him to say a quick 'no' now."[49]

In advice to the Foreign Secretary (who was in New York), Foreign Office officials advised that the Government should await further evidence of French intentions before taking the Hargrove story as Gospel and that it should certainly not be taken up with the French. But, the Government should take seriously the increasing evidence that it might be subjected to an outright veto in the near future rather than to delaying tactics.

Wilson commented: "We should be ready for possibility. [Should we] make another immediate application and keep the ball before every meeting?"[50]

The Foreign Secretary was in New York for the UN General Assembly and had a meeting with the French Foreign Minister on 24 September. Brown asked Couve de Murville to tell him frankly what the French attitude was. Couve replied that Britain was bound to enter the EEC. His precise words were "It is bound to happen". Brown asked Couve when he thought the negotiations could begin. Was it possible to get them going before the end of October? Couve said he was doubtful whether the negotiations could begin so soon but, in his opinion, they would certainly begin before the end of the year.[51]

Was Couve out of the loop or telling an untruth? His first answer was ambiguous and could have meant that British membership was inevitable one day. His reply to Brown's supplementary question suggests that he was either lying or out of the loop. Yet it is hard to believe that the Foreign Ministry's official spokesman would have known more of the intentions of the French Government than his own Minister.

Whatever Couve's real position, his comments seem to have persuaded Brown that they could be taken at face value. On 28 September, Brown told Cabinet that "he had had an interesting talk with the French Foreign Minister, who had been unusually friendly. In reply to direct questions he had appeared to accept that we were bound to join the EEC, and to agree that negotiations might begin by the end of the year."[52]

On 30 September, the European Commission produced their formal Opinion on the British application. "With one major exception, the passage on economic and financial questions, the Commission's opinion is basically helpful to our candidature", commented the UK Delegation in Brussels. The broad conclusion, namely that the next step must be negotiations, was precisely what the British had hoped for. The section on agriculture and the treatment of subjects such as New Zealand and Commonwealth sugar, while offering no great encouragement to Britain, were largely factual and left the field wide open for solutions to be found. The section on monetary policy was, in the view of the Delegation, tendentious writing. It was out of tune with the confident sketches of solutions in other fields. The conclusions were very unfavourable to Britain and to the future prospects of the British economy and the passages on sterling were drafted with the sort of vagueness which would prove grist to the French mill. According to Marjoribanks, the British Representative to the EEC, the influence of French Commissioner Raymond Barre had obviously been applied to this section. That in turn had been the price that the rest of the Commission had been obliged to pay for acquiescence in the Opinion as a whole on the part of the two French Commission members.

The section on economic and financial questions was entirely devoted to the problems of the United Kingdom, on the basis that Denmark, Norway and Ireland posed no problems. There was a brief description of the conflict since World War II between the policies encouraging the growth of the British economy and the limitations imposed on those policies by the weak balance of payments. The continued cycle of stop and go had demonstrated that the problems of the British economy were not only short-term ones, but structural. Although the economy was now in a better state than it had been in 1963/64, the fundamental situation had not changed. Industrial investment had stagnated during 1966 and would show a sharp drop in 1967. In this way the seeds of further crises already existed. The wage freeze and the rise in unemployment were making the pursuit of an appropriate economic policy politically difficult. There was a need for reflation but this had dangerous implications for the balance of payments. The marked improvement in the balance of payments achieved towards the end of 1966 had recently been reversed. At the same time, there had been a reversal in the flow of short-term funds. In general, the balance of payments situation was deteriorating again. The problem presented by the need to repay debts to the IMF was worse now than it was at the beginning of the year. Even the projected 3% growth rate risked overstraining the balance of payments.

The Opinion then turned to the question of the sterling balances. It suggested that the possibility of violent fluctuations in the future could not be excluded. Although the basic trend was one of slow shrinkage of the relative importance of the sterling balances in world monetary reserves, there could be large net with-drawals. These in their turn could upset the UK economy and, if the UK were then a member of the EEC, could upset the economies of the Community.

Having cast this pall of gloom, the Opinion went on to deal with the likely effect on the UK economy of joining the EEC. There would be advantages. Tariff-free access to the European market would more than compensate for the loss of Commonwealth markets, which were, in any case, not growing so rapidly. There would be a real incentive for major industrial modernisation. But there would also be increases in prices and in industrial costs and there would be a net adverse burden on the British balance of payments arising out of the application of the CAP and the raising of tariff barriers against Commonwealth countries. A further factor would arise from the freezing of capital movements and the opening of the British market to the competition of manufactured goods from the Community. Steps would need to be taken during the transitional period to enable the British economy to meet these additional problems. It would be up to the British Government to take those steps but all members of the EEC would be interested parties in the matter and ought to be consulted. The offer made by the British Government not to make use of the provisions of Article 108 of the Treaty to seek support for sterling in its international role was not considered sufficient protection for the Community. Much wider measures would be needed after consultation between all the parties concerned. It was difficult to see how sterling could continue to play its existing separate role when the UK had joined the Community. Nor could sterling in its present form become a European reserve currency. A major adaptation of the British economy would seem to be necessary.[53]

"In general", said the Foreign Office in a guidance telegram to its posts a few days later, "the views expressed in the section of the Commission's Opinion which deals with economic and financial questions are pessimistic and in contradiction of the views which we hold about our own economy, but they are not susceptible either of proof or disproof. Our general line will therefore be that of stressing our belief in the prospects for continued improvement in the UK economy but making clear our preparedness to discuss economic and financial problems with the Community".[54]

Whistling in the dark, where the British economy was concerned, was an essential core skill for any British diplomat throughout the period. But that aspect of the Opinion could not be wished away or glossed over. For the British Government, the political advantages of membership had outweighed the economic uncertainties in their calculations. For the Five, in making their calculations, equal but opposite considerations would have to apply. They could not ignore the significant weaknesses of the British economy and the risk of those weaknesses being imported, like a millstone, into the still buoyant EEC. The Commission Opinion on the British economy was stark but, in the light of subsequent developments, realistic. Its adverse nature would make de Gaulle's task easier.

The man himself summoned Reilly for a 35-minute meeting on 5 October. The General referred to "these interminable discussions" about the EEC and British entry. Speaking rather formally, according to Reilly's account, de Gaulle then said he wished Reilly to understand that, contrary to what seemed to be the impression in the UK, there was not, either on his part personally, or on that of France, any objection of principle to the entry of Britain into the EEC. On the contrary, once Britain was ready to come in, she would be welcome. It all depended on the British. It was for them to make the decisions which would make it possible for them to join. But in Britain's present situation, she could not do so. Britain was not ready and, if she came in as she was, she would bring about the break-up of the Community. Perhaps that was what she wanted. Alternatively, British entry would require the transformation of the Community into something entirely different. It would be quite understandable if that was indeed the British object.

Reilly asked whether, by his reference to Britain's 'present situation' de Gaulle meant the economic situation. De Gaulle replied that he did and went on to refer to all the issues associated with the CAP. He then said that the Six would now be discussing among themselves the Opinion of the Commission. He did not know what the upshot would be. He had to ask himself whether it was better to negotiate now, when Britain was not ready to come in, or to wait until Britain was ready and then start to negotiate. He repeated that France had no basic objection to British entry but there was a doubt and reticence about engaging in negotiations which could have no immediate point, since Britain could not come in now, and which might end in failure, like the Heath negotiations.

De Gaulle spoke in this vein, with some repetition, for about a quarter of an hour. Reilly asked for permission to reply. Firstly, he could not believe, after his conversations with the Prime Minister and Foreign Secretary, that de Gaulle really thought that HMG's object was the disruption of the Community. The General acknowledged that he had perhaps exaggerated on that point. Reilly said that HMG had no desire to seek major changes in the EEC. For instance, the Government accepted the CAP. This, perhaps predictably, prompted de Gaulle to say that no doubt the British Government sincerely believed that they could accept the essential principles of the Community, but the truth was that they could not.

Reilly spoke of the British economic situation. There was, he suggested every reason to think that during the two years or more before British entry the British economy would greatly improve, so that the difficulties de Gaulle foresaw would disappear or be greatly reduced.

De Gaulle accepted that a recovery in the British economy, whose problems HMG were facing with a courage which he admired, would make the problem of the agricultural levies easier. Nevertheless, it would remain. Things might be different if Britain could accept some form of Association, which might of course have to last quite a long time. But he knew that HMG would not contemplate this. He was sorry. Surely to accept it would be better than to embark on fruitless negotiations for full membership. Reilly said that de Gaulle knew HMG's objections to Association. It would do nothing to meet the political aim of candidature. De Gaulle said that would only be true if the Association were to be permanent. Reilly replied that Britain would, in an Association, be bound by economic decisions in which she would have no say. De Gaulle said that this would depend on the terms of the Association. But he realised that it was no good pursuing this subject.

Reilly ventured that the only way to get out of what looked like becoming a dialogue of the deaf was to accept the Commission's recommendation and get down to negotiations round a table. It would be very sad and hard to understand if Britain were told that this was not now possible. There followed a long silence while the General seemed to consider his reply. In the end, he made none.

The conversation then turned to other matters but, at the end of it, de Gaulle brought it back to the EEC. He repeated in the same formal manner that there was no objection of principle on France's part to Britain's entry. If only Britain could change sufficiently and take the necessary decisions – the economic decisions which would make her entry possible for her, and the political decisions, by which he meant of course decisions to put an end to Britain's excessive dependence on the United States. On this last point (to which de Gaulle had not previously referred during the interview), de Gaulle admitted that Britain was moving a little. He then came back to the economic problems, which were very great: the balance of payments, the stability of the pound, the international role of sterling. He implied, without saying so explicitly, that it all added up to an insurmountable series of obstacles.

Reilly said that he could only repeat that the British Government were convinced that the problems were not as great as de Gaulle feared and that they could prove this in negotiations, A refusal to let Britain do so would not be understood by the British Government and people and, Reilly felt bound to add, that it would be a very serious step.[55]

It was, Reilly told London, the General who had summoned him, which was very unusual. He must therefore have had some purpose directly related to the British candidature. His general attitude had been, if anything, more negative than ever. What he had said was consistent with his not having decided to oppose any negotiations at the present time, but it also showed clearly that he was seriously considering doing so. Reilly had given him two opportunities to say that he would agree to negotiations. De Gaulle had conspicuously refrained from taking them. On the other hand, he had implied that the French would acquiesce in a possibly prolonged discussion among the Six, so that an immediate 'no' on 23 October looked unlikely in Reilly's opinion.

Reilly's overall conclusion was that the main aim of the interview had been to enable de Gaulle to say once again, if he decided to prevent negotiations, that there was nothing new in whatever French statement was then made, and that the British Government had received a full and fair warning. Yet Reilly also had the feeling that there was more to it than that. The way in which de Gaulle had started with an assurance of no hostility of principle, and the way he had come back to the same thought at the end, was striking. He seemed to Reilly to be saying: "If only you would drop all this nonsense about coming into the EEC now, how happy we would be to collaborate with you in all sorts of ways".[56]

Unlike Reilly, Palliser found the general tone of the conversation "distinctly encouraging". De Gaulle, so Palliser advised the Prime Minister, was for once on the defensive and obviously uncertain how best to play his hand. All of this was unlike his usual behaviour and Palliser believed it showed that the Government's patient persistence had for once shaken de Gaulle's stubborn obstructionism. The conversation showed de Gaulle as reluctant to take the extreme step of a veto. Pressures were bearing in on de Gaulle: internally with farmers' riots, local elections and a general feeling of national malaise; and externally, where the rebellious Eurocrats had not been brought to heel and where de Gaulle risked a further major crisis within the Six. To have got de Gaulle to make such an evident demonstration of his own uncertainty was a signal success for the Prime Minister's policy of not taking no for an answer. The Government should therefore, firmly but courteously, maintain that policy. The Government must not give de Gaulle any excuse for blaming Britain or for driving wedges. It was not over-optimistic to believe that Britain could be negotiating in one form or another by the end of the year, or early in the next. Palliser wisely concluded this upbeat analysis with a caution: "We cannot of course avoid an irrational response by the General in the shape of a veto. Indeed we must, I am afraid, in common prudence, expect one".[57]

"The General" said the Foreign Office, in a Guidance telegram more than usually Delphic, "gave no indication that he is ready to agree to negotiations; but, equally, he stopped short of saying that he is determined to prevent them".[58]

Behind the scenes, the Cabinet Committee on the Approach to Europe was looking at action to be taken in the event of a veto. On 6 October, the Foreign Office put a note to the Committee which posited four broad courses of action which were open to HMG in the event of a French veto:

1.   To attempt to build a North Atlantic Free Trade Area;
2.   To pursue a neutralist policy;
3.   To abandon the effort to join the Communities for the time being, making it plain that this abandonment was temporary only, but taking no specific action. This would, in effect, be the same course as that pursued by the Conservative Government in 1963;
4.   To reaffirm the Government's determination to join the Community and to counter-attack against the French veto.

Course 1, the Foreign Office argued, had been carefully studied already and its prospects of achievement were as hopeless now as they had been then.

Course 2 would destroy Britain's chances of leadership in Europe. It would destroy NATO and the basis for Britain's security. It would hand the leadership of Europe to France, and later to Germany. It would lose Britain influence and support in the United States. It would do more than any other course of action to produce a sharp and general run on sterling.

There seemed little, in the FO's judgement, to commend Course 3 as opposed to Course 4. Britain would not win respect in Europe or elsewhere by lying down to a French veto; and from the domestic point of view there were obvious disadvantages in appearing to do so. Public opinion in Britain would expect action. However, by adopting course 4 (reaffirmation of Britain's determination to join and a counter-attack against the French veto) the Government should be able to profit from the general reaction against France throughout Europe so as to secure certain objectives of value to the United Kingdom.

The FO paper went on to argue that de Gaulle's position was weaker in 1967 than in 1963 – in Europe, in France and actuarially (i.e. he was older). If Britain stood firm and counter attacked quickly she might still turn French action to some account.

From this rousing mixture of Kings Lear and Henry V the Foreign Office derived the following somewhat more prosaic conclusions. Britain could not expect the Five to re-sign the Treaty of Rome, with Britain, in an attempt to expel

France. Nor could Britain negotiate with the Five given that any terms of entry so agreed would still be subject to a possible French veto.

On the other hand, Britain could and should review her policies towards France in all fields, using the present moment "to settle outstanding questions in the sense of our own national interest to the total disregard of French interest".

Once again, however, following this rhetorical call to arms, the Foreign Office concluded rather tamely that "there is probably not much scope for action of this kind". Such possibilities as there were included "butter [presumably boycotting the French brands], Concorde and the exclusion of France from the aluminium smelter project."

More broadly, came the general objective of "Paralysing the Community's development". If it was still the British objective to join, then it was also in the British interest that the policies of the Six should develop as little as possible prior to Britain's accession. The more decisions that were taken by the Six without Britain, the harder it would be for Britain to assume the resulting obligations. The British objective could be attained by encouraging the Five to maintain the British application on the agenda of all EEC Council meetings for, while France could veto negotiations, she could not unilaterally reject the British application. Britain should encourage individual Member States to block progress on particular items where their own and the British interest coincided, e.g. Germany on the Financial Regulation and the Netherlands on energy policy. More positively, there might be opportunities for cooperation with European partners on technology and defence. The key thing was speed. Once a French veto was clear, not even a few days should be lost. The ideal would be a quickly summoned Summit of the Five plus Britain (and any other vetoed candidates). Germany held the revolving Presidency of the Council and would be the natural host. But, the Foreign Office argued, firm leadership would be essential and, for that reason alone, Germany was probably ruled out. Of the remaining possibilities, only three (Italy, Belgium or the UK itself) were realistic hosts. Of those, the unreliability of Fanfani meant that Belgium was the best bet. Failing that, Britain should herself call the meeting.[59]

The Foreign Office's minute amply illustrates the relative helplessness of the British position. The terrors they hoped to summon up, in the face of a French veto, were terrors for children. And the notion that Britain could summon a Summit which the Five would attend in the absence, and in the face of the anger, of France was fanciful. That illusion should have been dispelled in any event by the message reaching London from Bonn at about the same time. Remarks made to the Ambassador by officials in the Chancellor's office there suggested to Roberts that the Germans were already under strong French pressure to watch their step lest German support for Britain might provoke General de Gaulle too far.[60]

The susceptibility of the Germans to such pressure was a further illustration of the fact that, for Germany, relations with Britain did not weigh nearly as heavily in the balance as those with France. De Gaulle's unpredictability and unreliability, as witnessed by his behaviour in Canada, made people outside France respect him less but fear him more. His threats might not just be idle ones.

Wilson and his Ministers still believed, however, that the game was not up and, in separate meetings on 10 October, Wilson and Callaghan briefed a group of visiting French journalists. Callaghan, revealingly in the light of the anti-Common Market stance he was to espouse in Opposition after 1970, declared his belief "that Europe would have to march on the path of economic integration, and this would take Europe towards the establishment of a European currency".[61]

Wilson was asked outright why he had changed his mind about joining the Common Market and replied that he had not done so. It was he who had drafted the Labour Party statement at Brighton in 1962 which had welcomed the progress towards European unity represented by the EEC. During the 1966 General Election campaign, he had referred to the Common Market as 'an exciting adventure'.

Wilson said that there was room for argument about the economic motives for membership, though he felt they were strong. But the political motives were even stronger, not only for Britain, but for the whole of Europe. He then advanced the political case though much more in terms of the advancement of European technology than in either institutional or foreign policy terms.

Asked about federalism, Wilson replied that if it meant one Government with its own defence forces, its own foreign policy, one Head of Government and one Defence Minister, etc., then, even though many sincere people within the Six might still be looking forward to such a situation, he was bound to say that the impetus for it seemed to have fallen away recently. It was certainly not on the horizon – or just over the horizon. Britain would go as fast as the rest were ready to go. As regards a common defence policy, there too he did not see a common line within the EEC. Britain would continue to work through NATO and WEU. But he had the feeling that, when Britain was inside the EEC, and meeting regularly with her other partners to discuss other matters, it would be easier to talk about defence too.

Wilson was asked how he had come to realise that membership of the EEC was necessary for Britain and gave an answer whose slightly surprising character almost certainly bears witness to it being his true view. It was, he replied, firstly because of aircraft. The R & D of modern aeroplanes was excessively costly when a country did it on her own. By joining in a cooperative project, say with France, Britain could halve her research and development costs and double the market. But one could not push that analogy too far: two countries could cooperate in a military project and could by themselves guarantee the market for the product e.g. a military aircraft. But this was not the case in the field of civil technology such as computers. Supposing the French and British industries cooperated to make a new computer, the existence of an 18% tariff between them would make it an unsaleable proposition. They had to have a tariff-free Common Market.

Wilson had clearly decided to steer clear of awkward questions about the Commission Opinion on the British bid. He had, he said, no official copy of the report in English. Britain's dealings with the Community were only through the Foreign Office and he did not know whether "George Brown had received a post card from them". He had heard arguments used in Paris that the European train with its six coaches would become less powerful, and might even lose its sense of direction if it had more coaches. His reply was that if Europe got more coaches it would also get at least two engines. Britain's entry would increase the size of markets and technological resources, and hence the power of each industry and of each scientist would increase. He did not accept that the train would go off the rails. All had the same idea about the direction in which they should go. Nor would British accession lead to an increase in American domination: "One of our main purposes is to become less dependent on American industry as a by-product of developing European industry". We needed a larger base to hit back.[62]

George Brown gave to Cabinet on 11 October an account of recent developments and an analysis of the Commission's Opinion. He told Cabinet that he was putting contingency planning in place to cover various eventualities, including the exercise of a French veto, although that was perhaps unlikely at the EEC meeting on 24/25 October.

There was no discussion in Cabinet of the likelihood of a veto but anticipation of one was clear from the concern expressed in discussion about the wisdom of saying publicly that Britain would maintain her application however long the resistance to it, and of publicly writing down Britain's relationship with the United States in a way that could be interpreted as being positively anti-American.

Wilson defended the position. The statement that 'we would not take 'no' for an answer' had been used repeatedly and was a correct description of the British position over the past year or more. It was important to maintain that attitude in relation to the French Government. As regarded the United States, recent statements, while over-emphasised by the Press, were also consistent and were not a source of friction between the British and US Governments.

Wilson also downplayed the concern of some of his Cabinet colleagues that the Commission Opinion on the British economy would compel Britain to concert its economic policies with the Community. That section of the Opinion was almost certainly a French draft and was probably the price that the Commission as a whole had had to pay for securing the crucial recommendation that there should be early negotiations.[63]

The French Government were meanwhile showing signs of resentment at being paid in their own coin. The information effort being mounted by the British Government and by the British Embassy in Paris in support of the Government's EEC application (and of which the visit to London by French journalists was part) was being characterised by the French Press, heavily influenced by the French Government, as "*l'offensive anglaise*" and "the British cavalry charge". Even well-disposed French observers had, according to Reilly, commented that Britain's activities might appear to the French as arrogant, displeasing and un-British. Couve de Murville was said to have described them as "undiplomatic".

The French authorities, Reilly believed, were worried by what the British were doing and they might well try to disarm the British by feigning to be offended. Nevertheless, there was a real danger that French opinion would become much less receptive to British arguments if the French Government could persuade them that the British were trying to carry the French position by storm. It was a nice calculation. The sense of urgency on the British side must be maintained in order to make it the more difficult for the French to run our initiative into the sands; but Britain should avoid giving the impression of trying to stampede the French. We should not present the issue as a confrontation between Britain and the General and still less as a single combat between the General and the Prime Minister.

Whatever happened during the next weeks or months it would be right, Reilly was convinced, to avoid any personal attacks on de Gaulle, or even light-hearted remarks about him. Experience showed that they were always counter-productive. The French in these affairs allowed themselves little humour (and in any case British humour could be misunderstood) and they were taking this matter desperately seriously – at any rate when it suited them to do so.

In putting this letter to the Prime Minister, Palliser commented: "I have long believed that, when we try to take a tough line with the French we tend to do it in the wrong way. It is no good getting obviously shrill and bad-tempered (e.g. the Princess Margaret cancellation) since this plays straight into their hands and delights them. Equally, however, we have tended in the past, when we were not being shrill and bad-tempered, to be too yielding and gentle. I think that we can perhaps be a shade more persistent and determined. It is a very old French ploy to pretend that it is we who are being 'arrogant, displeasing and un-British' or indeed 'undiplomatic'. The French themselves indulge these qualities without any scruples and would firmly resist any attempt to prevent them doing so".

Wilson commented: "I agree with your note. The line should be sustained kicking the ball into his 25, without malice, but firmly on the basis that we intend to get over the line"[64]

Before the Six next met in Luxembourg, Wilson was due to meet the German Chancellor in London. On 18 October, Kiesinger and his wife spent the evening with the British Ambassador in Bonn and his wife at a small dinner "almost entirely taken up with a very full, frank and friendly discussion of the EEC problem and of Germany's role". Roberts found no difficulty in persuading Kiesinger of the firmness of Britain's European conviction and of her determination to achieve membership. Kiesinger said he had had his doubts earlier in the year but was now convinced. Kiesinger regarded de Gaulle's opposition as purely political and based on simple reluctance to share European leadership with Britain. As regards Germany, Kiesinger assured Roberts repeatedly that he personally, and the overwhelming majority in Germany, wanted to see the UK as a full member of the EEC as soon as possible and that the German Government would do their best to achieve this. It had been his dearest wish in the early post-war years to see Britain take over European leadership.

As to how to handle de Gaulle, there Kiesinger's position was, Roberts found, absolutely firm but much less satisfactory. Kiesinger said several times that he had studied de Gaulle carefully and knew him well, perhaps better than anyone else in Europe. He was firmly convinced that what he called the Dutch method of handling de Gaulle was wrong and would lead everyone to disaster. Of course de Gaulle wanted to delay matters as long as possible and hoped for some mistake on the part of the British or of the Five which would help him. But even de Gaulle accepted that history and the force of events were on the British side. De Gaulle had never tried to refute Kiesinger's argument that there was an overwhelming majority inside Europe, and even a majority inside France, in favour of British membership. But de Gaulle was a proud, unbending figure who, if too openly thwarted or put under what he regarded as intolerable pressure, was capable of a dangerous reaction. If, however, he was handled with the right mixture of firmness and understanding he could be brought round. Kiesinger was convinced that de Gaulle could be brought round on British accession (as he had been on world financial reform), but only if a bridge were built over which he could retreat.

Roberts warned Kiesinger that, while the British Government understood and sympathised with the difficult position in which Germany found itself, those in Britain who did not know what Kiesinger had done in private with de Gaulle were inclined to believe that the public statements made by himself and his Ministers showed excessive solicitude for French susceptibilities. Kiesinger responded that the importance his Government attached to restoring a better climate in Franco-German relations by no means meant that there was political agreement between the two Governments. On most issues, French and German views were diametrically opposed and he had never tried to conceal this in his dealings with de Gaulle. But he continued to consider European unity impossible without Franco-German reconciliation. Roberts agreed but added that continued Anglo-French friendship was equally important, and not least for Germany.

Roberts told London that he was impressed by Kiesinger's obvious sincerity and his clear conviction that success could be achieved. There was not much, if any, chance of persuading Kiesinger to change his tactics in favour of a more forceful line e.g. of five-power solidarity and pressure within the EEC. Kiesinger had spoken to Roberts of his own disappointed romantic love affair with England in the immediate post-war years. He accepted Roberts' suggestion that the two countries were now well placed for a marriage of reason and went on to quote Disraeli's example in that a political marriage of reason had become a romantic relationship of a different kind.[65]

The following day, Brandt told Roberts that, while he believed, having just returned from speaking to Couve de Murville in Paris, that the French would prefer delaying tactics to an early veto, the latter could not be excluded. Brandt complained about British criticism of Germany. Each country, he added with a smile, seemed to be behaving out of character. The British had become hectic, the French illogical, the Germans eager for compromise and the Italians firm and intransigent.[66]

Palliser commended Roberts' advice to Wilson. Kiesinger would resent it if the PM tried to twist his arm and might become more, rather than less susceptible to French pressures. It remained to be seen whether Kiesinger was a statesman as many had thought or, as seemed more probable, simply a skilful politician. Palliser was struck by Roberts' reference to Kiesinger's disappointed romantic love affair with England in the immediate post-war years. Kiesinger was not unique in that respect. Many Germans had had the same disillusionment largely because, "being

Germans, they emerged from the War extraordinarily insensitive to the hostility generated against their country in Britain and failing to realise that, while they expected bygones to be bygones, memories in this country were rather less flexible". But, Palliser argued, 22 years after the end of the war, if the Prime Minister could bring himself to play on this aspect of Kiesinger's character, he could have a considerable political and psychological impact on him. Kiesinger had had a difficult and rather unhappy early life. He was a more complex character than some had so far believed. To win him over was a fascinating challenge.[67]

Wilson's meeting with Kiesinger on 23 October covered much the same ground that Roberts had covered a few days earlier. Kiesinger did, however, add one interesting piece of analysis of de Gaulle's motives. In March 1950, Adenauer had proposed a Franco-German union. That idea had been cold-shouldered by the Quai d'Orsay but had received an enthusiastic reception by de Gaulle in retirement at Colombey as a means, as he saw it, for the two European countries to break free from American influence and exert their own influence in and outside Europe. A few weeks later, the then French Prime Minister, M. Bidault, in what had been described as Europe's funeral oration, had advocated total Atlantic Union. But then, on 9 May 1950, Schumann had announced his plan for the European Coal and Steel Community, with the full support of Adenauer and de Gasperi but, once again, to the surprise of the Quai d'Orsay.

According to Kiesinger, when de Gaulle returned to power he took up the threads exactly where he had left them on his first retirement. To understand de Gaulle one had to understand how far back his basic policies drew their origin. Kiesinger himself, while a staunch supporter of the Atlantic Alliance, had never believed in an Atlantic Union as a realistic proposition. De Gaulle, on the contrary, feared that it would happen and believed that many who advocated European unity did so because they regarded it as a first step towards Atlantic unity.

Wilson agreed with this analysis. De Gaulle believed basically that Britain and Germany sought this kind of Atlantic unity. De Gaulle's fear was not only that, if Britain joined the game being played by the Six, she would try to change the rules, but, fundamentally, that, if Britain joined, "we should all of us find ourselves in the end playing baseball".[68]

That the very same evening, Wilson gave instructions that contingency planning should be done for a possible French veto, including the possibility of cutting British troop levels in Germany, does not suggest that the two men had got beyond the level of normal courtesies in their relationship.[69] Subsequent German Press reporting of their relations was even more revelatory.

The following report appeared in *The Observer* of 29 October 1967:

"Hans-Ulrich Kempski, star correspondent of the *Sud Deutsche Zeitung*, who was present at a conversation between Mr Wilson and the Chancellor in what Herr Kempski described as 'the boudoir' on the first floor of 10 Downing Street, wrote this description of the incident:

'It was 20 past 11 at night, as Wilson entered. He let himself fall into an armchair and silently listened to the Chancellor's reflections. He looked detached. Then suddenly he sat up and fixed the Chancellor with a look so threatening that he seemed about to spring at him. It happened as the Chancellor, asked by an English journalist whether he really believed that de Gaulle was in favour of German reunification, hesitated for an instant before answering 'Yes, I am sure of it'. It was now that Wilson began to speak in sentences whose fast-hitting brutality would have been shattering for Kiesinger if Wilson had not expressed them with rosy good humour, full of cheerful self-satisfaction, as if it were all a good joke. What he said boiled down to this: Britain had the best of relationships with the United States, but no less good a relationship with the Soviet Union. So the Germans should reflect for just a moment about who could most effectively represent their vital interests; and they should reflect, too, on the question whether, in a crisis, Moscow would pay more attention to France than to the combined voices of Britain and America. Kiesinger was still gripping his glass tightly, still pressing his feet in their patent leather slippers deep into the carpet, as James Harold Wilson sprang up and said: 'Our hot line to Moscow starts working at one minute after midnight'. He looked at the Chancellor with a hypnotic smile and, after another glance at his watch, pronounced: 'We have 26 minutes left to get our reports off to Moscow".[70]

Der Spiegel of 30 October contained two articles on Kiesinger's visit to London and the Downing Street reception to which journalists had been invited. Palliser submitted them to Wilson over a week later with the understated comment "Not too helpful".

On the Downing Street evening, the reporter had written: "The Chancellor gave a lengthy and elaborately dressed-up 'no' to Press questions as to whether a German initiative might move de Gaulle away from his obstructive position. Harold Wilson took possession of a baby-blue armchair on Kiesinger's right and, after listening for a time with an impassive face, he was overcome by the tense nerviness of a man who hears a gnat humming somewhere near but does now know where to hit. While Kiesinger continued to hold forth in a stately manner, Wilson dug his thumbnails between his front teeth and pulled all kinds of faces behind the fan made by his fingers. Or he drew so hard on his pipe that a silver hair which had been dramatically ornamenting the shoulders of his smoking jacket was dislodged and floated to the ground. Only when Kiesinger, with a glass of gradually warming whisky in one hand, and a long dead cigar in the other, followed up his plea of powerlessness in the face of de Gaulle with the admission that he really believed that the General, who was on such good terms with Moscow, was working for the reunification of Germany – only then did Wilson intervene. He rose with the emphasis of a host who is resolved to prevent anyone at his party from letting his hair down. The Chancellor had already been more than generous with his time, Harold Wilson pronounced metallically, and added with a laugh, but unrelenting: besides, thanks to their outstanding relationship both with Washington and Moscow, the British Government was in the habit of exchanging the latest news with both capitals over the hot line and the line to Moscow would come on shortly, at exactly one minute past midnight. It was therefore time to break up the party. Kiesinger stifled any doubt he may have had at the questionable taste of this pleasantry with a weary, forced laugh. Then he rose obediently and went submissively out."

On the visit as a whole, the article concluded that "London was not really a good place for Dr Kiesinger. If anything, the Chancellor's natural inclinations were towards France rather than towards Britain, and it was difficult to see how the visit could have been a success. Kiesinger lacked conviction; he did not see how he could impress upon the French the advantages of British entry, nor how he could convince the British that he was unable to make any headway with the French. He only became enthusiastic in Westminster Hall, where he was impressed by a sense of history. In general, the impression left by the visit was one of sadness and of a certain resentment on Kiesinger's part. Perhaps he felt that there was some justice in the fact that Britain was in difficulties. Had he not advised the British ten years ago that they should direct their efforts towards Europe and should it now be his fault that they had not done it at the right time?"

Wilson, clearly vexed, wrote in manuscript "Should Trevor [Lloyd Hughes, his Press Secretary] (a) not clout this man (b) point out that we were not in the habit of using the hotline as it was not connected till that midnight? This wording suggests it comes on every midnight. We're not having these German types here again".

Palliser responded to the FO, who had sent the German Press extracts, reporting the Prime Minister's comments but noting that no action was called for given that the correspondents in question had, at the Prime Minister's suggestion, been excluded from future briefings with him.[71]

While Kiesinger was enjoying a visit of mixed blessings in London, the EEC's Foreign Ministers, at their Council meeting in Luxembourg, were coming to no conclusion on the question of British entry. The meeting, according to the British Delegation, was unmistakeably five versus one. The arguments advanced by the French Foreign Minister had been no more realistic than before but, on this occasion, he had taken up a more extreme position than he need by giving a clear 'yes' in response to the question 'would enlargement of the Community affect its fundamental objectives?' He had also suggested that the abolition of the reserve function of sterling was a precondition for British entry. The British Delegation concluded that "after this meeting, the point of near crisis or near veto seems much closer than hitherto appeared."[72]

Further consideration of the British application had been deferred to the next meeting of the Council of Ministers on 20 November and, so Brown told Cabinet on 26 October, it was his intention to emphasise to Parliament that afternoon that the British Government "did not regard the objections to our application which had been raised by the French Foreign Minister at the Luxembourg meeting as amounting in effect to a veto on our application".

Wilson told his Cabinet colleagues that if there were a veto Britain would have to consider how to protect her interests and he had accordingly instructed officials to examine how best in those circumstances to maintain our application. Wilson also instructed his colleagues, in so far as it was necessary to say anything publicly about the French comments on Britain's economic and financial situation, to follow closely the speech which the Chancellor, Jim Callaghan, had just made at the Lord Mayor's Banquet.[73]

Callaghan had told the Lord Mayor's guests, and the nation, that "in the context of our application to join the Common Market the sterling balance question has been greatly exaggerated". Nevertheless, Callaghan went on to say, if his view was not shared by some of Britain's friends in Europe, the British Government were prepared to take part in constructive discussions provided, of course, that such discussions were not intended to delay negotiations on entry to the EEC. He was ready to "seize the opportunity which is now open to us to approach these problems in a constructive and European spirit".

The question of a European common currency was, Callaghan said, another matter and "it would be a much longer one, since it could come about only if members of the Community, including ourselves, had achieved a much greater degree of economic integration than at present. But our application to join the EEC does present an opportunity for bringing our thinking and, we hope, in due course our policies, much closer together".[74]

The state of the British economy was both a source of concern for Britain's prospective EEC partners and fertile ground for French propaganda. Reilly, who was cautious in his judgements, but punctilious and precise, wisely advised the Foreign Office not to base policy on assumptions about de Gaulle's vulnerability. It was indeed possible, as one shrewd French observer had said, that a veto on British accession might be the "fourth nail in his coffin" after his recourse to Government by ordnance, his controversially pro-Arab Middle East policy and his remarks in Quebec. Yet, according to Reilly, none of this seemed to affect de Gaulle's grip on affairs. There had been a new crop of rumours about the General's health. But when Reilly had seen him on 5 October he noticed nothing special to confirm those rumours. He had been, as usual, left with the impression of a man who was undoubtedly ageing. *The Times* correspondent had told the Embassy that Pompidou had grumbled to a French journalist about the growing difficulty of getting de Gaulle to concentrate on important matters in hand. Yet, in Reilly's view, the only safe assumptions were that de Gaulle might go on for years and that he would prove more and more obstinate. Reilly's own meeting with de Gaulle on 5 October had confirmed that his personal opposition – and indeed aversion – to British entry within the foreseeable future was as strong as ever. So much so that there had been a moment when Reilly had thought it possible that, influenced by his behaviour at Quebec, de Gaulle might have gone for a quick 'no' that very week, and there had been Press reports that he was considering doing just that. If the Five were to force him to choose openly at the present moment, he would say 'no'. But the French had managed to persuade the Germans not to bring things to the crunch.

Reilly thought that the basic current of French opinion was still flowing in Britain's favour, if anything more strongly than before. It was influenced by considerations which were political, psychological and even sentimental, rather than economic. Indeed, except in areas and among people directly concerned with exports to the UK, it was rare to find anyone in France who considered that

British entry would have real economic advantage for France. Many special interests were reserved or even hostile. The discontented small farmers were too disenchanted with the EEC itself to be interested in British entry. Financial circles were sceptical about the British economy and about sterling.

Thus, Reilly advised, there was abundant material on which the unscrupulous French Government propaganda machine could feed. It was now clear that the main weight of the French Government's attack would be put on sterling and the British economy and it had to be admitted that "at this moment the wicket favours the French bowling on this subject". It might not, therefore, be difficult for the French Government to convince their public that, in opposing negotiations at the present time on those economic grounds, they were not in reality applying a new veto.

Reilly added, with great prescience, and he appears to have been the first person to see and say it, that "we would now be wise to assume that the General's objective is to ensure, not only that we do not enter the Communities, but also that we are not able to influence their decisions though our participation in negotiations for entry until at least 1970, by which time the French could hope to have the agricultural regulation permanently settled, and much else besides". For that reason, if de Gaulle were forced by the Five to pronounce himself clearly for or against negotiations, he would be prepared in the last resort to impose what would amount to a veto at a moment of his own choosing and he would be fairly confident of being able to ride out any resulting storm. Maurice Schumann had told Reilly only a few days earlier that de Gaulle had said at the Council of Ministers that he had had many crises with the British and that they had all ended by settling themselves.[75]

The British Government had a small crisis of their own to tackle. On 26 October, Lord Chalfont, the Minister of State at the Foreign Office responsible for European matters, gave an unattributable Press briefing at the conclusion of an EFTA meeting in Lausanne. During the briefing Chalfont got into discussion with the correspondents on what would happen if Britain's application to join the EEC were to fail. His replies led to British Press stories, inevitably picked up and replayed in the Continental Press, to the effect that, in the event of a French veto, the Labour Government would withdraw the army of the Rhine from Germany and would rethink the situation in West Berlin. All decisions would be concerted with the United States.

The Foreign Office denied that there was any basis for the stories. But, for several days, Wilson and Brown considered whether Lord Chalfont had a future in the Government. On 28 October, in the second of two telephone conversations with Brown, Wilson said that "if this morning's Press was the end of the affair it would probably be best to do nothing since any action in these circumstances would be taken as a panic measure and the Press might again take up the totally unjustifiable story that there was a split on this matter between himself and Brown. On the other hand, if things did not die down and a hunting party started chasing Lord Chalfont's scalp, it would be preferable to take early action". Brown said that, if Chalfont was not asked to resign, "it would be necessary to cut him down to size a bit" and to make the seriousness of his action quite plain to him. The Prime Minister said that if Lord Chalfont remained a Minister in the FO there was no need for an immediate decision about his future responsibilities. It was not likely that negotiations would start with the EEC for six months or so and the position could be considered again then. What was particularly damaging about the reports was . . . their effect on European opinion. This would need watching very carefully.

In another telephone conversation the next day Brown said that his present view was that Chalfont should remain a Minister. "All Ministers made boobs from time to time and Lord Chalfont had not made many previously. He would see Lord Chalfont the following day and give him a lecture. The Prime Minister said that he might be asked to submit all his future speeches to the Foreign Secretary".

On 29 October, the German Ambassador in London telephoned the Permanent Under-Secretary at the Foreign Office "in some consternation" to seek reassurance on what Chalfont had said. Gore-Booth told him that the Foreign Office statement that the reports of British policy were baseless was the true Gospel.

Wilson himself felt obliged to send messages of reassurance to both President Johnson and Chancellor Kiesinger. To Johnson, Wilson said that he was "particularly sorry to see the scandalous accusation that you and I had been in some kind of consultation beforehand about all this". To Kiesinger Wilson wrote "I feel I owe it to you to confirm that there is not a word of truth in the fantastic stories about British attitudes and policies that have been flying about Europe this weekend . . . As I told you, we are not taking no for an answer and are not thinking about alternatives, still less about fundamental changes in British policy."

Palliser, clearly the drafter of these messages, cleared them with the Foreign Secretary during the course of another meeting, presumably Cabinet. Brown commented: "Quite good. But it does all put some inhibitions on any rethinking we might do later. That's the real nuisance. So we must get it to die as soon as possible."

On the following day, Wilson had to defend Chalfont in the House of Commons. Wilson told the House that Chalfont had offered his resignation, that he (Chalfont) had deplored the nature of some of the reports which had appeared and that he (Wilson) had told Chalfont that he could best serve his country by remaining at his post. Wilson also confirmed that there was absolutely no change in British policy.

Kiesinger replied to Wilson on 7 November that he had never believed the Press reports and had no doubt about the unchanged British position towards Germany and Europe.[76]

The French Government, as an unnamed senior French official told his friend Palliser they would, exploited the 'Chalfont affair' to the maximum. Even *Le Monde* had taken the bait in giving much more credence to the affair than it deserved and in giving the impression that Britain had lost its *sang froid*.

Palliser's friend thought that Callaghan's Mansion House speech had helped staunch worries about the role of sterling but that a bigger problem was the British balance of payments. The British, he argued, saw this as a national problem which they had undertaken to settle. Nevertheless, the Europeans (including the Commission) were not convinced and believed that all the additional burdens which would result, at least unofficially, from Britain's entry into the Common Market, would accentuate the elements of imbalance which could produce very great difficulties for the whole of the enlarged Community.

A similar issue arose, in this Frenchman's view, over agricultural levies. Obviously, it would be unfair if Britain had to pay into the Agricultural Fund between £175 and £200 million straightaway. Some kind of refund might be possible, reducing the burden to around £140 million, though not less than that. But Britain would have to accept the principles of the agricultural regulation.[77]

As if on cue, Couve de Murville told the French National Assembly a few days later that acceptance by the British of the Treaty of Rome did not dispose of the problem. What exceptions would have to be envisaged? "Especially in France", he argued, "the questions which immediately come to mind are those concerning the CAP and, in the first place, the financial regulation because it constitutes the framework. Everyone knows that it will have to be completed before 1 January 1970 in order for this to become the definitive regulation. As things are at present, we can envisage that there will be no insurmountable difficulties. But what would it be like if Britain participated in the discussion? In any case, we cannot imagine that, prior to a negotiation, the Six would not adopt the definitive regulation involving, as the Commission says, the transfer to the Agricultural Fund of at least 90% of the levy proceeds, even if subsequently other arrangements might form the subject of discussion." There could have been no clearer signal that France would not allow negotiations with Britain to begin.[78]

The Prime Minister's Guildhall speech on 13 November did not address these controversial matters. Instead, Wilson reverted to the theme of his Guildhall speech of a year earlier and of his speech in Strasbourg back in January, namely the need for an effective and organised technological component within the enlarged Community.[79] This was a subject Wilson cared about deeply and, in addition, the tactic was clearly to demonstrate the added value that Britain could bring to the Community. But the significance of Couve's remarks in the French National Assembly was not lost on Wilson. In a meeting with the Belgian Prime Minister and Foreign Minister the day after the Guildhall speech, Wilson drew their attention to the fact that Couve had appeared to suggest that it was necessary for the Six, and the Six alone, to reach final decisions on certain economic questions, especially agriculture, before the British entry. This kind of approach, Wilson warned, tended to intensify the impression in Britain that "we were being forced to cool our heels outside the closed door. The longer the present situation continued, the more support grew in Britain for alternative courses." Harmel warned against defeatism and against any Atlantic alternative, which would simply confirm de Gaulle in his opposition to Britain and in his view that the time was not ripe for British entry. De Gaulle's line could not, however, be held forever.

Palliser, the record taker, added a rider in sending his record to the Foreign Office. Where Harmel was reported to have said that De Gaulle's line could not be held forever, he had in fact said, but did not want it so recorded, that "the fact is that General de Gaulle is not immortal".[80] From the British perspective, this offered only limited comfort because it implied, on the part of the Five, a willingness to await the whim of fate and not a readiness to try to force the pace.

On 15 November, acting on instructions, Reilly made one further effort to influence the French Foreign Minister. The Foreign Secretary, Reilly told Couve, had personally asked him to say that, in the light of what Couve had said to him in New York, namely that he expected negotiations to begin before the end of the year, he (Brown) would be very disappointed, and would find it very difficult to understand, if the position of the French Government made it impossible for negotiations to be opened by the end of the year or soon after.

Couve, in Reilly's account, interposed that what he had said to Brown was that he would know where Britain stood by the end of the year. Reilly responded that this was not what Brown remembered Couve saying and that Brown was certain that there was no possibility of his having misunderstood. Couve would remember that Brown had taken note with satisfaction of President de Gaulle's statement to him (the Ambassador), a statement repeated by Couve more than once since, that France had no objection of principle to British entry.

Reilly then said that speaking personally and, with Couve's permission, very frankly, one thing that had greatly struck him in all the recent arguments and declarations of the French position was that one could look in vain in them for any admission of the undeniable fact that the entry of the United Kingdom would have real advantages for France and for the whole of Europe, not least in the political, technological and agricultural fields. British entry would provide good prospects for new markets for French agricultural products. It would result in a reduction of French financial contributions to the common funds of the Community. In the technological field, the possibilities were enormous as spelled out by the Prime Minister just recently. The Prime Minister's Guildhall speech answered exactly the preoccupation which the General had expressed in a memorable phrase at his last press conference when he had spoken of the threat represented by the Americans' 'conquering wave'. The more, said Reilly, he thought about the present situation, the more puzzled he was by the contradiction between the aspiration expressed by the President that 'Europe should one day constitute an element which could weigh equally with any country in the world', and what seemed in practice to be the policy and practice of the French Government, namely that of course Britain must come into the Common Market one day, but that this date should be delayed as long as it possibly could. If one member of the Community refused to accept a request for the opening of negotiations for entry into it, could one hope that the mutual confidence and cooperation now existing between that member and the candidate could be maintained? Any attitude which amounted to a refusal of negotiations, whether by an open veto or by the laying down of prior conditions or by the indefinite dragging out of discussions among the Six, could not be understood by the British public and could not fail to make a most unfortunate impression in Britain.

Couve made a written note of all this, which was rare for him. He had, he said, been struck and touched by Reilly's language. He could assure Reilly that in the French Government's consideration of this whole problem, one of their principal anxieties was that in this affair essential Franco-British relations were at stake. He added that in its public statements the French Government did not give sufficient weight to the advantages which British entry into the EEC would bring. The main advantage would come from the enlargement of the market in general. He would make a careful note of what Reilly had said. He did not expect much to happen at the Council meeting on 20 November. The meeting in December would be more important. He confirmed that de Gaulle would give a press conference on 27 November at which he would speak abut the British candidature. Couve added, jokingly, that he had been too discreet to say anything about an Association agreement between Britain and the EEC since he knew only too well the views of HMG, and of the Foreign Secretary in particular, on that subject.

With the distance of the decades, the interview looks like something of a wasted opportunity on Reilly's part, or perhaps that of George Brown, to probe whether Couve's statement to the National Assembly did not in reality mean that the French had decided to keep Britain out until 1970 at least. Reilly noted, in commenting to London, that Couve had responded to what he clearly understood to be an important and carefully worded communication, made on instructions, with the punctilious professional courtesy which was characteristic of him. Reilly was surprised not to have been exposed to a tough argument and concluded that Couve no doubt thought that no useful purpose would be served by an argument and perhaps that, in present circumstances, the French Government's position was too strong to need restatement. Yet, Reilly added, it was not the first time "that with a phrase and a quick look, half shy, half frank, he has given me a glimpse of another Couve who does not like what he is doing". But, in Reilly's judgement, Couve would continue to apply de Gaulle's policy with his usual hard cool skill. The General would make the essential pronouncement at his press conference and Couve would be its executant at the December meeting of the Council in Brussels. Reilly thought that the General would not agree to the opening of negotiations or to full membership but that Couve's reference to Association tended to confirm the general impression that de Gaulle would make an offer to negotiate some kind of Association. Reilly doubted, however, whether de Gaulle would give the idea of Association any content.[81]

On 18 November 1967, in the face of a severe run on the pound in international currency markets, the British Government devalued the pound from a parity of $2.80 to $2.40. As they did so, Wilson sent a message to each Head of Government of the Six, telling them that "the decision about the changed sterling rate does not affect our resolve to pursue our declared European policy and that it is our intention to prosecute an application to join the Community with energy". To EFTA Heads of Government Wilson said: "Our application to become a member of the European Communities stands unchanged and we shall continue to press it vigorously. We believe that the decision we have taken in regard to the pound sterling, by strengthening our economy, will enable us to make an even more positive contribution to the common European effort".[82]

Jim Callaghan, true to what he had told Cabinet months earlier, resigned as Chancellor of the Exchequer after devaluation was announced. He and the Home Secretary, Roy Jenkins, swopped roles and Jenkins became the new Chancellor.

Wilson clearly thought that the new situation created some opportunities. He sent a minute to Jenkins on 23 November inviting him to begin asking what devaluation implied in terms of reshaping the Government's basic economic policies and its forward economic strategy. Putting in hand a study would give reassurance to the rest of the Cabinet and to the inter-departmental machinery in Whitehall. The study would, Wilson thought, have to cover a very wide field, embracing not only the Government's policies for agriculture, fuel, transport etc., but also the whole range of the Government's measures to assist industrial output, to promote productivity and to save imports. It would also have to look overseas and to consider the implications of devaluation for Britain's external commercial policy and her application for EEC membership.[83]

On the following day, Wilson sent a minute to George Brown, expressing his "deep thanks to you for the very steadfast line you have taken throughout the whole period". Wilson went on to suggest that Brown was doubtless already working out how sterling devaluation could be turned to account in relation to Britain's EEC application. "Clearly", Wilson wrote "it ought to help. Certainly it undermines part of Couve's stated position. But I doubt whether it will in any way affect the General's long-term strategy. But no doubt you will be thinking how we can use this new situation. I suppose it will not be possible to get any clear news until after the General's press conference. . . .[84]

In his reply to Wilson's message about the devaluation, President Johnson tended to see the policy change in rather apocalyptic terms: "I have read several times your courageous message. If it is a comfort to you, I can tell you that my faith is deep that the British people have the will and the means both to pay their way and to continue to play the part they must in the world. This faith is in my blood and in my life's experience with Britain. Our prayers are with you and with the men and women of your land, for it is somehow just wrong for Britain to be off balance in this way. I was much heartened by the response around the world in the wake of the devaluation of the pound. There are strong currents of international understanding and good will, and there ought to be for those like you and me who lived through the unnecessary tragedy of the Great Depression after 1929, and who also lived through the other great tragedy when Britain saved us all".[85]

The British Government's decision was both necessary and prudent in economic terms and Wilson had positive reactions from the Governments of the Netherlands, Luxembourg, Belgium and Germany, all looking forward to positive discussions between Britain and the Six. The immediate fallout when the Council of Ministers met in Brussels on 20 November was, however, mixed. An account given to the British Embassy in Bonn by State Secretary Lahr confirmed that the British devaluation had proved the essential backdrop to the whole discussion at the Council. There had been a general feeling among all delegations that the Commission Opinion was now no longer wholly actual and the suggestion was made that it be supplemented by a new chapter which would be based on talks with the UK. This was clearly an opportunity for the British, and the French accordingly opposed it. There was then a procedural wrangle which lasted for hours and led to an eventual compromise under which the President of the Commission was charged with the task of giving an oral report on the implications of the devaluation to the next meeting of the Council in December. Lahr said that, in the discussion of devaluation Brandt had taken the line that the British decision opened up great opportunities, that it was indeed up to the British to exploit these opportunities, but that it also behoved the Six to do all in their power to help. Lahr added that the attitude of the French Foreign Minister had been thoroughly negative throughout and, although Couve had found himself up against a united front of the Five both on substance and on procedure, it was now absolutely clear that the economic arguments advanced by the French against British accession were only pretexts and that, even if Britain were to perform the impossible feat of abandoning the reserve role of sterling tomorrow, France would still find other reasons for opposing British entry.[86]

This downbeat conclusion was more than echoed in a report from the UK Delegation in Brussels: "This was not a good meeting from our point of view. No progress was made towards the opening of negotiations. There was no substantive discussion of the problems raised by the French and Couve's clear statement . . . his superiority in tactics and his greater familiarity with the subject matter enabled him to disarm the opposition. The circumstances of the meeting were unpropitious: there was a strong feeling of disorientation after the events of the weekend and we could in any case not have hoped for much progress".[87]

Then, on 27 November, categorically and contemptuously, de Gaulle dismissed Britain's application. The tone, as Palliser noted in a minute to Wilson, was "heavily ironical, not to say sarcastic in places, and in general substance confirms that he has not moved an inch from his general approach. Two points are new. First, the very clear rejection of any negotiations for our entry; secondly the willingness to discuss an 'arrangement', whether one calls it association or something else, which would favour commercial exchanges between the continental countries on the one hand and the British, Scandinavians and Irish on the other. But the latter carries with it no implication of an arrangement that would lead to ultimate British membership of EEC and we shall have to do all we can to discourage the Five from clutching at such a totally unsubstantial straw".[88]

From Paris, Reilly reported de Gaulle as having been "in good form". His tone had been one of lofty tranquillity but in substance it had been, of his sixteen press conferences as President, the most outrageous yet. In the realm of foreign policy he had repeated all the themes which had provoked the most criticism in recent months and had pushed his demands for Quebec even further than before. That part of his speech was the one which, according to Reilly, "displayed the greatest contempt for normal standards of international behaviour" but he had shown almost equal disdain for the opinions of France's five partners. Several of de

Gaulle's references to Britain had been "tinged with hostility and malice." He had said that the recent devaluation might explain the extraordinary haste which Britain had been displaying to open negotiations. He as good as said that Britain was only trying to join the Common Market because her earlier efforts to break it up or dominate it had been frustrated and because she now found that the EEC was leaving Britain behind while the Commonwealth broke up. He referred to a possible change in the British national personality, evidently a reference to the recent by-election successes of the Scottish and Welsh Nationalist parties. He had raised both his arm and his voice when referring to its working conditions as one of Britain's problems. "From our point of view", Reilly commented "the only redeeming feature in the General's performance was that it was so exaggerated and divorced from reality that it did not seem to carry much conviction to his audience of a thousand or so journalists. There was very little applause at the end".[89]

That evening, the Foreign Office issued a statement which read: "Under Article 237 of the Treaty of Rome any European state may apply for membership of the EEC. The reply is to be given by the existing members of the Community as a whole. We have made such an application in full accord with the terms of Article 237 and we expect a reply from the Community. The Council of Ministers are due to meet on December 18/19".[90]

On the following morning, Wilson and Brown met to discuss the situation. Wilson said that, in answering questions that afternoon in the House he would stick firmly to the line taken the previous evening by the Foreign Office, with which he entirely agreed.

Brown said that he had discussed the situation with his senior officials and that there was some difference of view. Some of his advisers thought he should play the hand long and slowly. But he was convinced that the only dignified and sensible course was to work for a firm decision one way or the other at the next meeting of the Council on 18/19 December. If there was to be a firm French veto, then we should seek to have it imposed at that meeting; equally this would compel the Five to face up to the resultant situation. They might, Brown believed, then decide to freeze all further programmes within the Community; and this would be intrinsically desirable from Britain's point of view. The Prime Minister fully agreed. He had two comments. He took it that the line proposed in relation to the December 18/19 meeting was not meant to imply that, if a French veto were confirmed, the Government should then seek to change course in the sense of withdrawing their application or looking for NAFTA-type solutions. Brown agreed. Secondly, Wilson said, although the Government's aim should certainly be to achieve a fully cohesive attitude by the Five, this was not strictly speaking necessary. Kiesinger might prove a somewhat weak link in the chain though there would be an opportunity of bringing pressure to bear on Brandt. But Luns was robust. The argument used against his tactics hitherto by some of the Five, that they were counter-productive and encouraged France to take a firmer line, no longer held much force. Surely the Government's purpose should now be to stiffen Luns (and any others possible) to take the line within the Community that France's attitude was a monstrous abuse of the unanimity rule and that, in consequence, he (or they) gave notice that they intended in future to block any progress within the Six on matters of interest to France, especially, for example, the agricultural renegotiation over the next eighteen months. As the Foreign Secretary had said, there was an advantage in seeking to freeze the situation within the Six.

Brown thought it would be useful to discuss before long with the Americans both the kind of tactics that should be deployed in Britain's European approach and also what other steps could be taken to make life more difficult for de Gaulle. We should have to make it absolutely clear that this was not an attempt to discuss with the Americans either a NAFTA or any other alternatives to our application to join the EEC. The Prime Minister agreed. He said he was completely opposed to the pursuit of alternatives. In this connection he thought it was also essential to nail any proposal for so-called Association with the EEC. Wilson and Brown agreed that Brown would circulate a paper to Cabinet.[91]

The initial reaction of Brown and Wilson is revealing. They were clear that the British application remained on the table and that nothing short of full membership would do. They were equally clear that if the French were going to turn de Gaulle's 'no' into a formal veto, it was better for that to happen than to be strung along beyond December. Wilson was resolute in his opposition to looking for alternatives to membership such as NAFTA. Where both men were unrealistically optimistic was in their expectation that the Five would have both the interest and the will to sustain effective action against French interests. In assessing Luns' willingness to act they do not appear, for example, to have calculated where the Netherlands' own agricultural interests might lie. They were realistic in their estimation of German effectiveness.

Wilson was true to his word when he answered questions in the House later in the day. He refused to accept that de Gaulle's rebuff was a humiliation for Britain: "I do not agree", he told Labour MP Renee Short. "We have slammed down our application on the table. There it is and there it remains". He was clear in confirming that while he had in the past said that there were possible alternatives to EEC membership in the future, "they are not there now". He affirmed the Government's intention of maintaining "our closest relationship with the Five and indeed the best possible relationship with France as well. There must be no peevish reaction, or any action which would imperil our otherwise good relations with France. I have never had anything but courtesy from General de Gaulle in all my dealings with him. I do not think that the present situation will be helped by any insults, direct or indirect, across the Channel. However, I feel that where there have been misstatements of fact, or any distortions based on a rather out of date approach to some of the problems of the modern world, these should be answered so that in the great debate which will continue in Europe some of these misconceptions can be dealt with once and for all".[92]

Peter Shore, Secretary of State for Economic Affairs, a leading sceptic but liked by Wilson whose Parliamentary Private Secretary he had been, did not agree. He wrote to Wilson that evening: "While I appreciate your wish not to react petulantly to de Gaulle and to await the December meeting of the Council of

Ministers, I do feel strongly that, with soft answers, we are in danger of losing a unique opportunity of rallying opinion, of asserting self-reliance, and of identifying ourselves with the national cause. People in Britain, as you have so often observed, are tired of being pushed around. The General's veto compounds the feeling of national humiliation which followed last week's devaluation. You put the very point in your broadcast last Sunday when you concluded: 'It's Britain first now'. Surely this is the moment, in a measured and serious way, to be 'Gaullist' in the British sense and to rally the nation (including the CBI and the TUC) in the task of making ourselves strong and independent."[93]

Wilson saw the minute but made no comment on it and did not reply. He had the capacity, a great gift in any politician, not to allow himself to be riled. As he had also made clear in his discussion with Brown, the strategy remained to gain entry to the EEC and, while that could encompass pressure by the Five on the French, it also had to involve ultimate acceptance by the French of the British candidature, so it would not be in Britain's interest to burn any bridges.

On the eve of the Cabinet's discussion of the next steps, Thomas Balogh, who had seen the Foreign Secretary's memorandum for Cabinet, put it to Wilson that it suffered from the alternative hypotheses that (a) France can be forced to give way or (b) it is in our interest to create havoc in the relations of the five Community members with the sixth. In Balogh's view, (a) was not tenable and (b) carried the grave danger that, not only the Gaullists, but the French themselves, would regard the British as mischief makers. That in turn would strongly diminish Britain's chances of eventually getting into the Common Market after de Gaulle. Balogh said that he had always thought the Foreign Office tactic of trying to alienate France and then overcome her resistance either with American or with the Five's help was mistaken.

In putting Balogh's memo to Wilson, Palliser commented that he agreed with (a) but much less with (b). Wilson made no comment but he did agree with another minute from Balogh warning against the temptation to accept an inferior status through Association.[94]

The Foreign Secretary presented his memorandum at Cabinet on 30 November 1967. He was not, he said, examining the position which would arise if the French imposed a veto at the December meeting of the Council of Ministers but, rather, the situation as it was following de Gaulle's press conference. His proposal was that the Five should be urged to insist at the December meeting on fixing a date in January for the opening of negotiations, and so force the issue with the French either at the December meeting or at a further meeting in January. It would be a mistake to take it for granted that the French were in fact prepared formally to veto the opening of negotiations with Britain and it was important, for two reasons, to resolve the uncertainty. The first was to hold firm the position of the Five who, with the exception of the Germans, who were less firm because of the difference of views between Kiesinger and Brandt, had reacted staunchly to de Gaulle's statement. If, said Brown, we were in any way to let the Five feel that we were prepared to tolerate much further delay in answering our application, the waverers among them would be encouraged to seek alternatives to early negotiations for full membership and notably to explore the possibilities of associate membership. It was therefore essential to convince the Five that the Government stood firmly by their application and sought immediate negotiations on it, and would wish the Five, at the meeting of the EEC Council in December, to press this issue to a decision.

The second reason for maintaining strong support for our application was the political situation at home. In response to statements as hostile and malicious as those made about Britain by de Gaulle it was essential for the credibility and standing of the Government to insist on their right under the Treaty of Rome to early negotiations for full membership. The longer the uncertainty, the greater the damage to the Government and, if the delay persisted for some months, the support of Britain's friends abroad and of public opinion at home would be lost.

Brown added that his view was not shared by Tony Crosland (who was absent from Cabinet). Crosland felt that the Government should say to the Five that, while they hoped they would be able to settle Britain's application at their December meeting, the British side would not press them to do so if they felt this was unwise; and that, in general, the Government should not press the Five to courses involving extreme conflict with the French and possible disruption of the Community.

Denis Healey agreed with Brown, but thought his proposed course of action was not without risk, the biggest danger being that de Gaulle might agree to start some sort of negotiations which might then drag on interminably or end eventually in a veto: the Government must not lay themselves open to a third humiliation of that kind. It was imperative therefore to tell the Five, not only that Britain wished negotiations to start early in the new year but that any such negotiations must offer the prospect of a satisfactory conclusion in a reasonable space of time.

In the meantime, Healey continued, we should prepare ourselves for a situation in which there were no negotiations. He doubted whether there were viable international groupings which Britain could join instead of the EEC, though the possibilities of a NAFTA might perhaps merit further consideration. However, there were three contingency studies which were now urgently required: an examination of the extent to which the United Kingdom would be free over the next three years to change her policies – political, economic and military – to her own advantage, where hitherto the Government had been inhibited by the need to avoid disturbing France and the other members of the Community; an examination of areas such as technology where, despite exclusion from the Community, the Government might still want to act in ways which would maintain and develop good relations with the Five or with the Community as a whole; and an examination of wider relationships between Western European states, including, among others, the possibility of a collective relationship between EFTA and the EEC such as had been considered at an earlier stage.

In general discussion, the Cabinet supported the Foreign Secretary's proposal that the Government must seek an end to the uncertainty. It was suggested that it might be better to accept that de Gaulle had already cast a veto rather than wait for the formal procedures of the Treaty of Rome to be played out. There were dangers in continuing with what appeared to the British public to be a humiliating process. But the more general view was that the Five would regard that as a capitulation and a betrayal and as recognition that de Gaulle had the right to speak for the Community as a whole.

Wilson concluded that the Cabinet had agreed to the Foreign Secretary's proposals. The French President had blatantly abused the unanimity rule with the purpose of causing the Community to act in breach of their obligations under Article 237 of the Treaty of Rome to negotiate with any European state applying to join. The Dutch and other Governments might now reasonably take the stand that, as the French Government had abused the unanimity rule to make Article 237 inoperative, they proposed to do the same, for example in relation to the renegotiation of the agricultural finance provisions which were due in 1969 and which also required unanimous agreement, unless the British were by then admitted. While the French President would not change his opinions, it was not inconceivable that he might be brought to realise that his obstruction of the will of the rest of the Community would not pay. The United Kingdom must meanwhile turn its attention wholeheartedly to strengthening its own position by its own efforts and look to its national interests. Officials should now undertake the studies suggested by Healey covering, inter alia, agricultural policies; defence, including NATO, WEU and the offset arrangements for the British Army of the Rhine, as well as defence procurement; and UK relations with EFTA and EFTA relations with the EEC.[95]

It is not clear on what basis Wilson suggested that the Dutch might turn the tables on de Gaulle in the manner he described to Cabinet, unless he had private information to that effect. The Dutch were certainly robust but discussion among the Five soon turned to the possibility of what the Luxembourg Foreign Minister called, in a meeting with Brown the day after Cabinet, a third alternative to the 'all or nothing' approach of the British and the 'nothing' approach of de Gaulle.

Brown did not like this one bit. He was not sure, he said, if it was fully appreciated on the Continent that Britain had found it difficult to decide whether the balance of economic advantage was in favour of joining the Community. If the argument had rested on the economic merits of membership it was doubtful whether those in favour would have carried the day. What had changed the situation was the growing realisation in the Labour Party and in the country of the political arguments for the integration of Europe, of the political necessity for Europe to take on a shape, character and size with an equal voice and equal influence on events. From this it would be clear that Association was of no interest to Britain at all. An Association, in which Britain was precluded from taking part in voting on the construction of the new Europe, would mean that there would be no new Europe at all. The experts could study whether Britain might derive economic advantage from such an arrangement. But this would not be going to the heart of the problem. Even if there were a guarantee of full membership at the end of it, Britain would have contracted out of what she wanted to do. Britain had now wholeheartedly, in letter and in spirit, accepted the Treaty of Rome. There was no way round this. The Six must decide on whether to apply Article 237 of the

Treaty. If he was now expected to try and commend a form of association, that was frankly out of the question.[96]

The idea did not die, however. In early December, the Belgian Government floated the idea of making progress through a series of steps which would lead to full membership. Pierre Harmel, the Belgian Foreign Minister, told the British Ambassador in Brussels on 4 December that if the Five sought to open negotiations with Britain in order to draw up a final Treaty of Accession straightaway, France would certainly refuse. Instead, what he thought feasible was the immediate opening of negotiations with Britain, leading to an agreement on full membership, but it should be *a* negotiation rather than *the* negotiation. Harmel did not think that pressing for a straight 'yes' or 'no' from France would be the right course and would not command a united front among the Five. Etienne Davignon, then a senior Belgian official, had earlier told Barclay, the Ambassador, that 'pulling down the temple' was not necessarily what the Five – even the Dutch – would be willing to do.

Brown remained adamant, telling Harmel, via Barclay, that "his proposals contain too many loopholes and are open to too many interpretations. The point as I see it is that we are now approaching the moment when we must expect a decision from the Community as to whether we can start negotiating together the terms of an instrument of accession of Britain to the EEC".[97]

The Belgian plan would not have given Britain a voice in the Community's institutions until final agreement had, the Belgians hoped, been reached. Con O'Neill, the senior Foreign Office official dealing with Europe told the Belgian Ambassador in London that his Government's proposal would involve "at best a period of twilight in which many important decisions would be taken by the Six without Britain having a voice, and at the end of which Britain would have to accept these decisions and would be subject to a unanimous vote of approval before she could enter the Community as a full member".[98]

Commission President Jean Rey, also a Belgian, was due to visit London on 4 December and Palliser, apart from advising Wilson to be polite and positive about the EEC institutions (something which evidently did not come naturally to him) since Rey was fundamentally on Britain's side, also thought that a bit of water should be put in the Foreign Office wine of opposition to any kind of Association. Palliser was sure Rey would want to discuss Association or other compromises and equally confident that the Prime Minister would want to take a firm line as advised in the Foreign Office brief for the meeting. But, Palliser advised, the Prime Minister would not wish finally to shut off any reasonable options, not least because this was a useful opportunity to get a first hand impression of the kind of ideas which were going around in Brussels and the other capitals of the Six. Realistically, it had to be recognised that the British Government would probably only manage to get the Five and the Commission to take a robust line with the French if, in the last analysis, they did not close the door completely to some kind of 'reasonable compromise'.

A day later, Palliser showed to Wilson a minute from Chalfont to Brown in which Chalfont argued that, while Cabinet had agreed that the Government should play hard for an early decision on the single question of whether or not negotiations for accession were to be opened, the point had also been made in the meeting that there might be dangers in that course if it appeared that the Five would be very reluctant to follow it. The morale of the Five, according to Chalfont, was not good. The Germans were clearly out for some compromise between what they regarded as the two extremes of the French position on the one hand and the British on the other. Even Luns had mentioned an idea which bore all the hallmarks of the Harmel proposal.

Chalfont also thought that, partly because of constant Press reports about compromises, there were persistent doubts in the Community as to just how tough the British Government would be in the end. There was a feeling around that Britain would probably accept something on the lines of the Harmel plan at the end of the day, but that British Ministers could not yet say so for tactical reasons. Some people, Chalfont continued, would indeed argue that something on the lines of Harmel's proposal would be better than nothing. It would enable close relations with the Community to be maintained; it might enable Britain to ensure that the development of the Community in the long period before Britain attained full membership remained consistent with her interests; and, when de Gaulle died, it might enable Britain to achieve membership more quickly.

Chalfont then set out all the arguments against the Harmel solution, concluding that it should be possible to get the Five back in line but that the Government would have to consider how to proceed if that effort failed.[99]

Palliser showed Chalfont's paper to the Prime Minister, commenting: "I am sure we must go on taking a firm line with Rey and the Five; but equally they will not want to face up to a showdown with the French unless it is clear that, not only negotiations for full membership, but any form of what they would regard as a 'reasonable compromise' is totally excluded by the General". "Noted – very good", commented Wilson.[100]

When Commission President Jean Rey came to London he did so preaching, not so much compromise, as patience. Britain, Rey told the Foreign Secretary, was clearly waiting with patience for a decision by the Community on her application. Britain was not looking for a half-way position and nor were the Commission. They hoped, rather, that the Council would "in due time" take a decision in favour of starting negotiations.

Brown baulked at this. He personally found patience a hard virtue to preach. It sometimes brought people to accept a situation which they ought not to accept. The British Government had brought Britain to a position in which she was willing to make one of the biggest choices in her history. But it would be increasingly difficult to keep up the momentum. At present the Government had on their side Parliament, Industry and the Trade Unions. But the political climate was changeable. He was worried by Rey's use of the phrase "in due time". Was it not already high time? It was true that Rey had added "the sooner the better". How soon could this be?

Rey replied that all Brown had said was true. But in political life things did not happen merely because it was necessary and important that they should happen.

What was needed was "patience in London and perseverance in Brussels". Brown repeated the danger that public opinion might go off the boil.

Later in the day, at a meeting with the Prime Minister, at which Brown was also present, Rey repeated that the Association for which the Treaty of Rome provided would not be appropriate for Britain. He had been concerned with the negotiation of all the existing or pending Association agreements and there was nothing in any of them which led him to think that this formula would provide a quicker or better solution for Britain.

Wilson reaffirmed his own view that de Gaulle's extremely vague references to arrangements other than membership had given no clear indication of what he had in mind, and to negotiate such arrangements could well take far longer than to negotiate membership under the Treaty of Rome where all concerned knew the rules and what it was they were negotiating. If there was to be some vague Association arrangement, the Six might take a very long time even to agree what they meant by it. It was not clear, for example, whether what de Gaulle had in mind would include agriculture. There was total uncertainty about anything except full membership. British public opinion would never accept 'candidate' membership as when, for example, a junior Russian politician aspired to the Politburo and his eventual membership was subject to his good behaviour. More-over, whatever Britain might have done during this period of candidacy, a single member of the Six could still veto her eventual entry to the Community. Thus she might remain a very long time in a twilight state without any guarantee that there would not be a further veto at the end of the road.

Rey, who had at no point sought to make the contrary case, said that the Commission had always believed that Britain could not be expected to make the necessary economic effort required for effective participation in the Community unless she received firm assurances for the future. He thought that even the French Government themselves were probably rather unhappy at the situation which had been created for them. Couve de Murville had hitherto taken a much more nuanced line than that expounded in de Gaulle's press conference. In these circumstances he thought it probable that the Five would press at the 18 December meeting for a decision about negotiations. If this was not secured then a situation comparable to the 1963 crisis would arise. He did not think that the Community itself would be in danger. But he equally did not think that the Five would resign themselves to the situation as they had in 1963. He did worry about a possible shift in Britain away from support for membership, and Wilson and Brown effectively told him that he was right to worry. If there was a further serious delay, Wilson warned him, he was not too optimistic about the Government's ability to hold public opinion to support for the Government's policy. Brown agreed.

Rey said that the Commission remained unanimously of the view expressed in their report that negotiations for British membership should begin. He wished to underline (which he could more readily do since M. Barre was not present) that this view was fully supported by Barre. He had been disturbed by suggestions in the British Press that Barre had drafted the chapter of the Commission's Opinion dealing with the British economy and that he therefore in some respects bore responsibility for it. The whole report had been very fully discussed within the Commission and represented the agreed view of the Commissioners. Wilson advised him not to pay too much attention to Press reports, neatly side-stepping the fact that British Government sources were almost certainly at the root of the reports in the first place.[101]

Needless to say, the Foreign Office lost no time in sending instructions to its European Embassies: "We do not want to appear to give anything approaching a full account of these discussions [with Rey], which originated in an informal and courtesy visit, to the Governments of the Six. But it would be helpful if you could inform the Government to which you are accredited discreetly, but at a fairly senior level, that the view that full membership was the only appropriate solution for the UK, and that Association was inappropriate, was firmly put forward by the Commission".[102]

Not surprisingly, the search, on the Continent at least, for a compromise continued. Two days after Rey's visit to London, Con O'Neill travelled to Bonn for talks with State Secretary Lahr, his German opposite number. Lahr told O'Neill that the German line would proceed from the proposition that Britain could not be offered less than full membership of the Community; but the time at which Britain achieved that full membership might have to be the subject of compromise. Britain's full and unrestricted membership of the Community at the earliest opportunity must be the aim. But the French could not possibly be brought to discuss any play involving this as the immediate outcome of negotiations. Britain's presence in the Council, and her right to speak there, would have to be guaranteed from the very start. But Britain's full participation in the Council's decisions would not be negotiable with the French. Could the British Government therefore consider one of the following: either that Britain should have consultative rights in the Council of Ministers, under which all would be obliged to take her views into consideration before they moved to a decision or, alternatively, that Britain should have a vote in the Council from the start, but less than the full vote to which she would eventually be entitled?

O'Neill declined to entertain these ideas, assuring Lahr that if he rejected his proposals it was not because he thought them premature, but because he thought them unacceptable. He (O'Neill) was speaking from a position of principle, not from a tactical position.

At one point Lahr threw out the suggestion, which he described as a personal one but which he had tried out on Brandt who had also found it attractive. This was that, if the worst came to the worst and Britain could not enter the existing Community, a new Community of ten members (i.e. including the French) should be founded with exactly the same scope as the existing one. The existing Community would continue and the new Community would rapidly catch up with it. Lahr seemed to think that an idea of this kind might be hard for the French to oppose. O'Neill did not share Lahr's optimism.[103]

The ideas put forward by the Germans were well-intentioned (if, in the case of a new Community of Ten running in parallel with the Community of Six, lacking close touch with reality). But they were also self-interested. With Brandt leaning towards Britain and Kiesinger determined to appease the French, the Grand Coalition's only hope of an outcome which kept the conflicting pressures in balance was that of a compromise, which would also have the benefit of limiting Kiesinger's exposure to further criticism in the German Press. Unsurprisingly, therefore, the Embassy in Bonn were picking up signals of equidistant German Government discontent with both Britain and France: "a growing tendency to argue that what is described as our present all-or-nothing [approach] is almost as intransigent as the French line and, although more understandable in some ways, more unreasonable in so far as the French are at least in the Community and have the power to keep us out, while we are not yet in and can only get in if the Five find some method of overcoming or circumventing French resistance. There is the immediate danger that the very recent and welcome tendency of the Germans to act as one of the Five, rather than to stick to their earlier preference for the concept of one plus four, could be reversed, in which case it will be impossible for the Five to agree upon a common line on 18 December, and Couve will once again be able to run rings around them. There is also the longer-term danger that, if only and perhaps even unconsciously as an alibi for themselves, the Germans will be tempted to share the blame for failure between us and the French. This would of course be in complete contrast to the position after the breakdown in 1963 and would make our subsequent relations much more difficult".[104]

Roberts, the Ambassador, was skilful. At no point did he risk the wrath of George Brown by suggesting a change of British tack. But the reference to the risk of being in a worse position than in 1963 was a clever one. Wilson, in particular, set great store by the superiority of his tactics and strategy in 1967, by comparison with the mistakes made by Macmillan in 1963. The notion that, in this respect at least, he might be wrong-footed by comparison with Macmillan is not one he would have enjoyed. It is not therefore surprising that, when Palliser suggested to Wilson that he might have a word with Brown before the latter gave dinner to Brandt at Dorneywood on 8 December, Wilson wrote back: "I am prepared to accept observer status *while* negotiations are going on. But they [the French] won't."

As a skilful media manipulator himself, Wilson would also have realised that an editorial in the *Frankfurter Allgemeine Zeitung* of 7 December, reported by the Embassy to London by telegram, would not have appeared there by accident. The paper claimed that it would have been obvious at an earlier stage that Britain could not enter the EEC in a single step had Wilson not over-estimated Britain's political weight. Before de Gaulle's press conference everyone had shied away from advising Britain to steer towards an Association agreement with the EEC, or something on similar lines. Since de Gaulle's press conference, many had been urging Britain to start from the facts of the situation, even if they were annoying facts, and to find an interim solution. Was muddling through, a frequent characteristic of British foreign policy, suddenly not to count any more? The Federal Government, the paper went on, had shown reserve hitherto and indeed was in a more difficult position than France's other EEC partners (although annoyance with de Gaulle did not constitute a policy for the Dutch, Belgians and Italians either). The paper stressed, with apparent approval, the desire of the Bonn Government to avoid a collision within the EEC. The great uncertainty, it concluded, was whether Britain would finally accept an interim solution. Since Britain had no political alternative to EEC membership, the paper hoped that Britain would eventually decide to adopt a more flexible line.[105]

At Dorneywood on 8 December, the Foreign Secretary told Brandt that the British position was clear. The British Government were not interested in anything short of full membership of the EEC and wanted the Six, at their meeting on 18/19 December, to decide on their answer to the British application.

According to a telegram to Bonn and other European posts from the Foreign Office that evening, Brandt said that he would support the British attitude and (as chair of the Council meeting) would go for a straight vote on the issue of whether or not to negotiate. He also agreed that, if the vote went against Britain, he and Brown would discuss next steps together.[106]

What the French Foreign Minister would do on 18 December was the principal topic of discussion, not only in London and the capitals of the Five, but in Paris as well. Two poles of thought were, according to the Paris Embassy, discernible. The first was that Couve de Murville would show himself trenchant and unyielding and would demand that discussion of the British application should be terminated. This thesis rested on the assumptions that complete inflexibility would be consistent with the General's ever harder attitude to this and other foreign policy issues; that the ensuing crisis among the Six would have erupted and subsided before the nettle of France's membership of NATO had to be grasped; that a temporary freeze in the Community would not harm France; and that if the present indiscipline among the Five (i.e. resistance to French wishes) were tolerated much longer it could quickly spread to other fields (defence and monetary, notably) with serious consequences for Gaullist strategy. A good source in Debré's cabinet had told the Embassy that Couve would indeed be totally negative in Brussels and that, in the long run, this might be better for Britain than protracted procedural red herrings in the form of proposals for Association. Britain's European faith would thus not be extinguished but simply put into the deep freeze for a period. The same source was convinced that de Gaulle's attitude towards Britain's candidature would in any case not survive the General's departure by more than a few weeks.

The other pole of thought, according to the Embassy, was that Couve would not seek to stop all further discussion but would allow the Council to spend time talking itself into recognition of the validity of de Gaulle's conclusions. A pointer in this direction had been Couve's statement in the National Assembly on 7 December when he had said that France's attitude towards the British application had not changed but that there had to be a discussion in depth, and agreement between the Six, before a decision could be taken.

There was, Reilly reported, a substantial body of French opinion which continued to hope that, however justified Britain's claim to full membership, the British Government would accept present realities (a local euphemism for the period of de Gaulle's survival) and agree to accept something less than full membership during an interim period. That view was widely held by French people of many shades of opinion, who argued that to insist on what Britain knew to be unattainable in present circumstances cast doubt on the sincerity of her attachment to Europe.

In the light of these conflicting impressions, Reilly played safe in his own predictions by doubting whether de Gaulle himself had yet made up his mind. What was clear was that the French were confident that, in the last resort, Kiesinger could be relied on not to be very firm in support of Britain. The Embassy's contacts with their German colleagues in Paris showed that the French were threatening that failure on the part of the Germans to support them would lead to the break-up of the Community and that these threats were succeeding in making German flesh creep. The German Embassy in Paris took the view that de Gaulle was prepared to go at least as far as he had in 1965 in paralysing the Community, this time in order to keep Britain out. Reilly concluded that his own Embassy's best information suggested that, whether or not the Five presented a solid front on 18 December, "there is a shade of odds in favour of the General choosing a very tough line".[107]

Evidence of the success of French policy, which anyway played to Kiesinger's instinctive sympathies and judgement, came in a meeting a few days later between the German Chancellor and members of the SPD in the Bundestag. At that meeting, Kiesinger warned against a policy of banging the table and doubted if it was wise of the British to demand all or nothing. He understood it but it would not produce the desired result.

This line did not go down well with SPD Parliamentarians who cross-questioned Kiesinger toughly and forced him to admit that his policy of bridge-building and of trying to reason with de Gaulle had so far shown no sign of success.

The Bonn Embassy reported a strong and general feeling in the German Parliament that de Gaulle had gone too far and that a tougher line on the part of the German Government was overdue. But this did not mean that Kiesinger was in any way shaken in his belief that his kid-glove approach was the right one. Kiesinger had told the SPD members that he would not allow the issue of British membership to put Franco-German relations to the test. Helmut Schmidt who, as a leading SPD coalition member, was at the meeting, had added that Germany could not pursue its present Eastern policies without France.[108]

On the same day, the Foreign Ministers of the Five met alone at breakfast in Brussels and, after it was over, Brandt, at their request, met with George Brown, who was in Brussels (probably for a NATO meeting) to tell him of their conclusions. All had agreed that a decision should be reached the following week on the basis of the Commission's report recommending the opening of negotiations with Britain. The other four had asked Brandt to tell Couve de Murville that the five Governments were afraid that a unilateral 'no' by France would cause serious damage to the Community. Brandt would give that message at lunch later the same day.

Brandt added that there was no agreement among the Five about how to interpret Article 237 of the EEC Treaty. Was a unanimous decision needed to open negotiations or not (the issue being that a decision to admit a new member required unanimity but a decision to open negotiations might be considered a procedural one requiring only a simple majority)? But they had all agreed that this was not a relevant question. The issue was not a legal one. There would be no point in taking it for decision in the European Court of Justice, which would only waste infinite time. The Five had therefore decided that if France refused the opening of negotiations they would reserve their position. This meant that they would then discuss among themselves and with others (i.e. the British) what to do. Among the possibilities they would consider would be whether to open negotiations, or talks, between the five Governments and the British.

Brandt asked Brown whether there was a danger that the British Government, in the face of a French refusal to open negotiations, would withdraw its application. Brown assured him that this was extremely unlikely. Ministers would have to consider the matter. But Brandt could assume that the British application would remain on the table. Brown reminded Brandt of Wilson's statements that the British application was in and would remain in, and of his determination not to take 'no' for an answer. Britain's purpose would remain to get into the Community. The main danger from the British perspective was that if the British were kept hanging around inconclusively, support at home would be eroded.[109]

On the following day, Brown called on Couve de Murville, who was also in Brussels. He asked Couve what his attitude would be at the Council meeting the following week. Couve said his attitude was well known. France was not prepared to agree to the opening of negotiations because the United Kingdom was not yet ready for membership. When Brown asked whether this meant that Couve would cast a veto, the latter replied that it meant 'nothing of the kind'. France would merely express the view he had just stated. When Britain was ready, negotiations could begin and these need not be long. A few months should suffice for settling a small number of matters relating to membership of the institutions etc. which would arise. He could not understand the talk about long negotiations.

Later in the conversation Brown asked Couve if he would pass a message to General de Gaulle. Couve said he would be delighted to do so. Brown then asked him to inform the President that if the French, on 19 December, were to veto the opening of negotiations with the United Kingdom for membership of the Community, this would do tremendous damage to Anglo-French relations.[110]

Quite what Brown hoped to achieve by this threat is hard to discern. Had he studied de Gaulle's form he would have known that the President had lived from 1940 onwards with expressions of grave British displeasure and had learned that the best tactic in dealing with them was to ignore them. Moreover, it was only two weeks since the Prime Minister had told the House of Commons that he was intent on maintaining good bilateral relations with France so the threat implied in Brown's warning to Couve of 'tremendous damage' to Anglo-French relations was not one that would have disturbed Couve de Murville, let alone de Gaulle.

Brown had fared better in his dealings with Brandt. On return to Bonn from Brussels Brandt went straight to the Bundestag where he gave German Parliamentarians an account which, in the words of Frank Roberts who heard it, was "firm and clear and excellent from our point of view". Brandt said that the German Government fully agreed with the British position that a decision on Britain's application for full membership should not be delayed. That would be his objective on 18/19 December and he would be prepared to sit right through the night and into the next day to get it. Brandt spoke throughout in terms of the Five and made it clear that they were united in support of Britain's application and of the immediate opening of negotiations and that the only opposition came from France. But, Brandt argued, even a French refusal to agree to open negotiations now would not end the matter and if, as Brandt hoped, the British and the other three applications remained on the table, the Five would individually or collectively find means of considering the situation and, he hoped, find appropriate solutions in discussion with Britain and the others. Brandt concluded that German national and European interests demanded British membership, and the consequences of a refusal to negotiate could be incalculable within the Community and for Europe generally. The further development of the Community would be bound up with British entry. Brandt ended with a strong appeal to France to reconsider her position before the meeting.[111]

This was, as Brown put it in a personal message to Brandt, "splendid stuff".[112] But the British Government still feared that Kiesinger would remain weak and instructed the Embassy in Bonn to repeat to any waverers that British opposition to any arrangement falling short of full membership was not a tactical position but one of compelling reasons of principle.[113]

On the eve of the Brussels meeting, State Secretary Lahr gave to Roberts an account of the meeting Brandt and Couve had had in Brussels and which Lahr had attended. Couve had deployed an 'offensive of smiles' and had argued that de Gaulle's position at his press conference had been misunderstood. It had been clear that Couve was embarrassed by the situation into which his President had put him. He had sought to persuade Brandt that France, far from being opposed to British membership, wanted it, but that negotiations should only begin when prospects of success were better i.e. when the British themselves had got their economy and finances into better order. Couve, without being at all precise, had then talked about a possible compromise which seemed to be based upon industrial arrangements between the Six and the applicants, but with some agricultural content as well. Couve had shown that he realised that this would be unacceptable in itself and that anything which stopped at Association, under whatever name, would not do. He had therefore indicated for the first time that he had in mind an arrangement which would be based upon full British membership as part of the package even it this were delayed for some time. Lahr said that, while this was unsatisfactory, it at least marked a shift in the French attitude. Lahr assured Roberts that the Germans did not intend to get drawn in Brussels into discussion of compromise proposals. But Roberts commented to London that he was in no doubt that indications from the Dutch were correct and that the German Government would want in the New Year to consider ways in which to break the deadlock. The Germans saw their role as being to save the Communities while also ensuring British entry and Roberts had picked up signals that Brandt would consider an absolutely inflexible attitude on Britain's part in the New Year as unrealistic.

Roberts' judgement was borne out by a statement from the German Government spokesman on 18 December saying that the German Cabinet had confirmed its support for British entry. The Federal Government was not, however, of the view that the meeting in Brussels meant the end of the examination of the problem of British entry. After a pause, probably in the New Year, a new phase of negotiations might begin. The Federal Government saw nothing as a final cut-off.[114]

"This morning's information from Brussels" wrote William Nield from the Cabinet Office in a minute to the Prime Minister on 20 December "shows that the Five have stood up well to the French and declared themselves in favour of early negotiation, with the French saying that our economic recovery must be completed first. The Five met after the Ministerial Council and Brandt subsequently said that they must use the Christmas period to think about the problem facing them, and that he hoped Britain 'would give us a chance in the coming weeks to see how to bring the matter up with a better chance of success'. All pending meetings of the Six, including those of the Finance and Agriculture Ministers, have been cancelled, and it is clear that the French action, though expected, is causing great bitterness. There is likely to be an even stronger reaction from political and public opinion on the Continent which is of course not under the same restraint as the Five Governments vis-à-vis France. If we now avoid hasty decisions and play our cards right with the Five, the development of the Community may be paralysed for a time, and therefore made so difficult, that the French may be faced with a choice between a non-cooperative Community of Six, or the enlargement of the Community. The Five have stood up to the French much more strongly than we thought possible, and it would be wrong now for us to let them down, and improvident for us not to encourage them to maintain their resistance to France".[115]

From Brussels a statement had been issued by the Council of Ministers which recorded that five Member States had agreed with the recommendation of the Commission that negotiations should be opened with the applicants for membership. One Member State had said that the process of recovery of the British economy must be brought to its conclusion before the British application could be recognised. "There has not been, at the present stage, agreement in the Council on the continuation of the procedure".[116]

The Foreign Office issued a statement which had been cleared with the Prime Minister: "It is a matter of grave concern that the Government of France has been unable to accept the unanimous view of its partners that negotiations for Britain's accession to the European Communities should start at once, This can only delay the inevitable progress towards a united Europe including Britain, which is in the interest of Europe as a whole. There is no question of withdrawing Britain's application. Her Majesty's Government believe that, given the support of the five Governments and the overwhelming majority of opinion throughout Western Europe, European unity is bound to be achieved. HMG will be consulting about the implications of the present situation with other European Governments who share Britain's views on the future of Europe."[117]

For the second time, De Gaulle had vetoed Britain's application for membership of the EEC with consequences for Britain's relations with her future partners which were to outlive him, Macmillan and Wilson and to resonate in British politics for the next half century.

* * * *

6 To woo or to win: Britain, France and Germany: 1967–1969

Neither Harold Wilson nor George Brown, in their respective memoirs of the period, offers any analysis of whether the British Government might have prevailed against de Gaulle with a different strategy or tactics.

The Cabinet minutes make no mention of it but it is clear from a subsequent exchange between William Nield and Michael Palliser that there had, at the Cabinet immediately following de Gaulle's November press conference, been a tendency among Ministers to blame officials for failing to give the Government an accurate assessment of de Gaulle's intentions.

George Brown liked to play the blame game. He was suspicious of officials and, with a memory of the British Embassy in Paris having failed to spot de Gaulle's imminent return to power in 1958, drew the conclusion, to which he adhered when he became Foreign Secretary, that "the Embassy was in all kinds of ways totally out of touch with what was really going on". He brought Patrick Reilly's tenure as Ambassador to a premature end, blaming him and the Embassy in part for the "arid frigidity which seemed to him to have settled down over all official relations between Britain and France".[1]

The reality was somewhat different. Ministers, not officials, determined the timing of Britain's application. Nield, in a minute to Palliser of 14 December commented that, had he been asked, he would have advised against starting for another six months to a year, not least to allow for careful preparation. But a strong recommendation not to carry on with the approach to Europe would, Nield argued, have been clean contrary to the express instructions of Ministers. On the narrow point of the likelihood of a veto, Nield had, he said, never advised or envisaged that the risk of a veto could be ignored, but had rather taken the line that the French position was an obstacle to be eroded. He did not believe that anybody, Ministers or officials, was under the delusion that there was a clear possibility, indeed perhaps probability, of a veto.

Palliser took a similar view and the record bears him and Nield out. That de Gaulle was consistently negative from the first meeting between him and Wilson onwards is clear. No one on the British side doubted that de Gaulle wanted to keep Britain out of the EEC and, if Wilson ever thought he could succeed where Macmillan had failed, the evidence suggests that he did not hold that view for long. Rather, the British hoped that the strength of feeling among the Five, the support for British membership in France itself and de Gaulle's relative decline in domestic popularity would all make it hard for him to veto, as opposed to using obstruction short of a veto. Wilson worked hard at convincing de Gaulle that Britain had changed since 1963 and that the British Government wanted a Europe that would be a strong economic and commercial competitor of the United States. He made a little headway. But de Gaulle, while acknowledging that Britain had changed, never accepted that she had changed enough. And, in his veto press conference in November 1967, he reverted to arguments dredged up from a long litany of ancient grievances.

Once the British Government had concluded that it was in the British national interest to re-apply for membership, and once it was clear that Parliamentary and public support was almost uniquely favourable, it would have been counter-intuitive to mark time. The tour of capitals which Wilson and Brown undertook confirmed the strong support of the Five for Britain's application and a general view that de Gaulle would not, as in 1963, have the strength within the EEC to say 'no'. In addition there were good arguments, more than borne out by subsequent developments in Britain's absence, for Britain to be inside the EEC when crucial decisions came to be taken in 1969/70 on the long-term financing of the Community and, in particular, of the CAP.

From quite an early stage the Danes, fellow applicants, were realistically downbeat about British prospects and spot on in their assessment that it would actually be easier for de Gaulle to say 'no' a second time because the rest of the EEC would know, as they had not known on the first occasion, that a French veto would not put the whole future of the EEC in jeopardy. There is no evidence that the British disputed that judgement, though it is equally clear that it was balanced by more optimistic voices on the continent.

The British Government did not over-estimate the influence on France of the German Government. They tried hard to convince the German Chancellor, Kiesinger, of the sincerity of their European vocation and, by and large, seem to have succeeded. But they were never in any doubt that Kiesinger was intent on seducing France, not strong-arming her and they were therefore under no illusion about the prospects of success. For his part, the British Ambassador in Bonn, Frank Roberts, was at pains to portray Kiesinger in as favourable light as reality allowed but he too never strayed from believing in the sincerity of Kiesinger's intentions into advising that goodwill towards Britain would translate into effective action on her behalf.

From the records, the British Embassy in Paris comes across as well informed and sound in its judgements. Sir Patrick Reilly had good access to the President and Foreign Minister. Reilly did not predict with certainty a veto on de Gaulle's part but he certainly advised consistently of de Gaulle's determination to keep Britain out of the EEC and was in no doubt of de Gaulle's preparedness to cast a veto if he had to.

Reilly's relations with George Brown were unhappy ones, as much because of Brown's personal bad behaviour towards Reilly's wife as for any professional reason. But mutual respect and trust are an important adjunct to the successful prosecution of policy, a point made cogently by Nield in his minute of 14 December 1967 to Palliser when he wrote: "The element I most deplore in the criticism to which you have referred is the underlying implication that in some way the responsibility of Ministers and of their officials for the adoption of a policy and for its success can be clearly separated so that if there is a failure the officials can be separately blamed and thereafter discounted. This seems to me a total negation of the concept of collective responsibility of Ministers and of the concept of loyalty of officials to Ministers, both of which are indispensable to good Government in this country."[2]

The strategy of the British Government was not, then, determined with their eyes closed. Perhaps the cleverest part of it was Wilson's decision to make clear, months before de Gaulle's veto, that Britain would not take 'no' for an answer. That drew some of the sting in advance from de Gaulle's opposition, perhaps contributed to his own admission that Britain would be ready to join one day, and certainly encouraged the Governments of the Five to seek ways of strengthening their ties with Britain in expectation of de Gaulle's eventual departure from the scene.

Willy Brandt, as Chair of the EEC Council of Ministers and as the representative of the one Government powerful enough to deal with the French on equal terms, had been given the role of reflecting on the next steps following de Gaulle's veto and of coming forward with suggestions, in consultation with others of the Five and with Britain, in the New Year.

But Brown was not for hanging around. On 19 December, he sent to Wilson and to other Cabinet colleagues a minute on European policy after the veto. In it, he acknowledged that it would not be realistic to think in terms of full membership as long as de Gaulle was in control. Nor would British requirements be met by Association in any form. More effective would be some arrangement for common action with the Five and it was for that that Brown sought the approval of Wilson and the Cabinet. His proposed means was through an early high-level meeting with the Five, called either by the British or, since they had shown themselves interested, by the Italians.[3]

The only Minister who responded in writing was Anthony Wedgwood Benn, Minister of Technology, who had "considerable misgivings" about organising an early high level meeting with the Five and who urged that "before committing ourselves to this course, I should like to be much more certain about the support it would enjoy in Europe and particularly the support which the idea would have from the Germans. Unless they are wholeheartedly behind the idea, the project could miscarry. I would therefore suggest that careful soundings should be taken of the Five individually . . ."[4]

Officials, meanwhile, had completed the study commissioned by Cabinet on 30 November on the consequences of the UK's exclusion from the EEC. Their conclusions were unsurprising: an Atlantic Free Trade Area was no more a negotiable option in December than it had been six months previously.

Whatever Britain might say and do, other Commonwealth countries would expect that if a favourable opportunity arose in the future for the UK to enter the EEC then Britain would take it. They would act accordingly.

Other EFTA members would, similarly, continue to believe that Britain would make a fresh bid to join the EEC as soon as the opportunity arose and, in so doing, leave the rest of EFTA to make whatever arrangements they could in the circumstances.

"The conclusion we draw", officials wrote, "is the same as that drawn from the previous examination in April, namely that there is no new trade bloc or grouping which we could hope to establish in the foreseeable future as an alternative to joining the EEC . . . We still need to form a part of the enlarged Community in relation to our political objectives in a united Europe and in relation to our industrial and commercial needs for a wider domestic market . . . Concentration now on the policies needed to put the economy right will not reduce our future prospects of joining the Community. The present objections on the part of France to our membership will be greatly reduced if we are then economically strong".[5]

At Cabinet on 20 December, Brown secured ready support for his policy and its three main aims for the immediate future: to maintain the longer term objective of full membership of the Communities; to ensure as far as possible that the Communities were prevented from developing in ways which would make it more difficult for Britain to join later; and to preserve, to the greatest extent compatible with the first two aims, Britain's freedom of action in the economic field pending the achievement of full membership. Cabinet agreed that Brown should make a statement on the policy they had just agreed to Parliament that afternoon, which he duly did.[6]

Brown was determined not to let the grass grow. On 20 December, the Foreign Office sent guidance to its European posts: "We must move quickly if we are to make the most of the current irritation with France. And there will be obvious advantage in taking the first steps before Kiesinger meets de Gaulle in mid-January . . . One possible approach could be the conclusion of a multilateral agreement to consult and to undertake joint action wherever possible . . . The aim might be to establish a form of political union between the Five, Britain and the other applicants for membership. What we achieved together could be taken into the Community when French policy makes possible its enlargement to include Britain . . ."[7]

This outburst of euphoric unreality does not appear to have been dampened by a cold shower of Nordic realism provided by the Norwegian Foreign Minister, John Lyng, when he told the British Ambassador in Oslo the following day that he doubted whether the Five would agree to act as a group. He had had talks in Brussels the previous week with Luns, Harmel and Rey and had got the distinct impression that individual members of the Five would be glad to develop bilateral contacts with the applicants, but no more.[8]

A similarly realistic assessment was given in Copenhagen by Norgaard, the Minister of Market Affairs, when he told the Ambassador, Oliver Wright, that, while there could be no harm in an initiative of the sort the British were proposing and that Denmark would take part in any meeting with the Five that was eventually set up, he was not confident that much useful action could come out of it. If there was any real alternative to the enlarged European market which had been once again denied to the applicants, "we should all have thought of it before".[9]

The British Ambassador in Bonn called on Brandt after Christmas for "a relaxed conversation over a glass of sherry" at Brandt's home. Roberts' purpose was to explain to Brandt that the British Foreign Secretary was flying to Rome the following day to propose a meeting between the Five and the applicants.

Brandt's reaction was far from relaxed. He hoped there would have been bilateral discussions, including direct talks between himself and Brown, as Brown himself had at one point suggested, before the German Government found itself confronted from Rome or elsewhere with the rather more far-reaching and urgent suggestions the Ambassador had outlined to him. It had also been agreed between the Five that they would meet together to consider the situation in the New Year and that meant, in his view, separate consultations by the German Government with the other EEC members, with the French and with the British and the other applicants. Quite frankly, Brandt said, he had not been thinking in terms of such rapid or demonstrative developments as the British were now proposing. He doubted whether there was enough solid material to justify early high level discussion. He would prefer to determine the topics where progress might be made rather than have a meeting which, without obvious practical results, could do more harm than good. Brandt felt that it was the duty of the Five, or perhaps of Germany ("which has so often been criticised and perhaps sometimes deservedly") to smoke out the French and try to get from them some clear proposals which might be acceptable to the British.

When Roberts expressed strong reservations about getting involved with anything of that kind with the French, Brandt pointed out that the Brussels meeting, though most disappointing, had not been entirely negative and there were certain points on which one could seize. For example, it had been agreed that there was no objection of principle to British entry, that the question remained on the agenda to be taken up at any time and that there was a connection between British entry and British economic stability. He was not thinking in terms of compromise solutions, which he thought a bad concept, nor of anything to replace full membership, but rather of a procedure which would lead to full British membership. Whereas the French veto had been clearly expressed in 1963 this was not, at least formally, the case now. France had been clearly isolated in Brussels and the French Foreign Minister put firmly on the defensive. There were many people in France, even some close to de Gaulle himself, who were most unhappy about the present position. Surely it was wiser to work upon these possibilities than by some demonstrative act of solidarity, with little solid content.

In reporting the conversation to London, Roberts noted that Brandt was "undoubtedly a little peeved" that Brown had taken Rome and The Hague into his confidence before him. It was important, Roberts urged, to keep Brandt closely in the picture from now on, more especially as the Italians were unlikely to take any step without consultation, and probably agreement, with Bonn.[10]

When Brown and Fanfani met in Rome, the Italian wisely suggested that, rather than organise a special meeting of the Five with Britain and the other applicants, the best opportunity for a meeting would be the scheduled WEU meeting on 29 January. Brown accepted this on two conditions: that the meeting should be seen to be taking place (which was anyway unavoidable) and that it must be prepared in advance so that it would be known and accepted that it would lead to more formal meetings and to some continuing machinery to service them.[11]

When Roberts in Bonn reported this outcome to the Foreign Ministry, it was clear that the two Governments were still at cross purposes. Brandt, Roberts was told, had hoped to have a little more time in which to work out, first among the Five and then in consultation with Britain, a possible approach to the French. Brandt thought that he had agreed the general approach with Brown and had therefore been taken aback by the speed at which the different approach discussed by Brown and Fanfani in Rome had developed. The Germans discouraged any notion of British Ministerial visit to try to sort things out. Bilateral discussions at senior level would be preferable.

Roberts concluded from his exchange that it was quite clear that, even if Brandt could be convinced that the British approach was the right one, which was by no means certain, he would have great difficulty in so persuading Kiesinger, who was setting great store by his forthcoming meeting with de Gaulle. The British Government should not try to lay too heavy a load on Brandt and should now hold back, leaving it to the Belgians, supported by the Italians and the Dutch, to propose, and press for, the January meeting.[12]

On the following day, Roberts was summoned to the Foreign Ministry by State Secretary Lahr. Lahr had been instructed to make it clear that Brandt had been upset by the British approach to the Italians. After the Brussels meeting, the Five had asked Brandt, since Germany was in the chair, to consider how best the question of British accession should be pursued after the holidays. Brandt had undertaken this responsibility and had informed the British that he was so doing. He had therefore assumed that the British agreed. The next thing he had heard was a report from the German Embassy in Rome who, in turn, had been told by the Italians of an official British approach to them asking them to take the initiative of calling an early meeting between Britain and the Five. In these circumstances, Lahr said, Brandt felt himself relieved from any responsibility he might have undertaken in Brussels and would leave it to the Italians of Belgians to take over. Nor was it his intention to attend the WEU Ministerial meeting in Brussels.

Lahr then said that the Germans did not regard the maintenance of the British application, as affirmed at the December meeting in Brussels, as a simple declaration of intent with no practical validity until de Gaulle had disappeared, but as imposing on the Five, and in particular on the Germans, the duty to press the French to explain their position and, if possible, to obtain from them some solution which might be acceptable to Britain. Lahr asked Roberts to remind Lord Chalfont of a conversation he and Lahr had had in London in October when Chalfont, fresh from Rome, had reported Fanfani as saying that if the consultations among the Six on British membership were not completed at the 22 October meeting of the Council he would walk out. Fanfani had not done so. The Germans, Lahr added, saw their task as to give the British, not lip service, but effective help, and to offer reliable advice rather than simply telling us what we wanted to hear. Lahr fully understood British feelings about de Gaulle, which he shared. He had

had sixteen bitter years of negotiating with the French. They could, however, be worn down by equal obstinacy and stubbornness. Nothing would please the French more than for the battle for British entry now to be abandoned and for the EEC field to be left to them for so long as de Gaulle remained in the saddle.[13]

Given the extent of Anglo-German friction, arrangements were made for Lord Chalfont to go to Bonn on 8 January for talks with Lahr. Chalfont, who was a shrewd observer and, unlike Brown, an unemotional one reflected afterwards that the Germans, who probably regarded the British as obsessed with the French, seemed themselves to be obsessed with the French too, albeit in a different way. Chalfont had been struck by the fact that Lahr had scarcely referred to the Italians, Belgians, Dutch or Luxembourgers. Only the German and French positions and requirements seemed to be in his mind. Lahr had tried quite hard to get Chalfont to endorse the proposed German approach to the French which the Germans were determined to make, but had had to be content with Chalfont's statement that, although the British were extremely sceptical of such an approach, they could not stop the Germans from making it.[14]

Privately, Chalfont was less convinced that the British Government should pursue their own approach regardless. In a minute to the Foreign Secretary of 11 January, Chalfont warned that "the Germans would [not] engage in consultation with us on the pattern which you discussed in Rome, except in the unlikely event that the French took part themselves or (equally unlikely) that they raised no objection to the Germans doing so. We have therefore to decide whether the continuation of our hard line with the Germans, and our intensive effort to promote consultation on a 5 + 1 or 5+ 4 basis is likely to be successful. My own view is that to continue to pursue it single-mindedly would mean that, in the event, we should be faced with the prospect of consultations with four members of the Common Market at best, and probably with the Benelux countries alone. We shall also have exacerbated our relations with the Federal Republic which, if Brandt's reaction to the Rome visit is a reliable guide, are under some strain already . . . My own personal feeling is that, having pushed this matter to the brink with the Germans, we should now cut our losses to some extent and adopt a more flexible policy."[15]

Palliser, who had a black market copy of Chalfont's minute, showed it to Wilson with the comment that it was "a good but gloomy account". Wilson commented that he would "prefer to see the Germans draw a blank – then let all of us, including them, review the situation".[16]

Wilson had already made his substantive views clear at a meeting a few days earlier with US Under-Secretary Nicholas Katzenbach, who was touring Europe to explain the recent foreign exchange measures taken by the US President. Katzenbach told Wilson that the Germans had pressed him strongly to urge the British Government to take half the loaf. The Germans appeared to have certain ideas in mind, definitely involving trade concessions of some kind.

Wilson's response was that this was pure escapism on the part of the Germans. They had a coalition, all members of which wanted British membership. But half wanted it passionately whereas the other half were perhaps more concerned to preserve what Wilson called the fiction of the Franco-German alliance. To attempt a solution on the lines suggested by the Germans would be folly for Britain. If we were involved in negotiations for entry to the Community, we at least knew and understood the rules under which this would happen. But no one had the least idea what was meant by Association, least of all de Gaulle himself. It would take the Six far longer, first to agree on what they themselves meant by Association, and then to seek to negotiate with Britain, than for Britain to negotiate full membership. However, if the arrangement was simply an industrial free trade area, there was no way this should be more acceptable to France now than at the time in 1958 when de Gaulle had vetoed Maudling's proposals to the same end. Indeed, the French would seem to have everything to lose by it. There was already profound alarm in France at the likely consequences of free trade within the Six and French industry had already been afraid of British competition, even before devaluation. They were much more so now. Thus France was bound to seek vast concessions from Britain in the agricultural field and no doubt would also raise all the other problems they had used in the context of negotiations for membership, such as sterling, capital movements etc. In short, Britain would be in precisely the same situation in terms of difficulties and points for negotiation as if she were seeking full membership; but without any rules on which to base the negotiation. This was out of the question.

Palliser, who was present, recorded that Katzenbach was clearly impressed by the Prime Minister's firm rebuttal of the German ideas and added that Arthur Hartman (State Department Director and former head of the economic section of the US Embassy in London) had commented to him that he thought it extremely salutary that the Prime Minister should have used such robust language.[17]

In putting Chalfont's minute to Wilson, Palliser had warned him that Brown's approach to following up the Brussels meeting of the Council had "got a bit off the rails". On 17 January, on the eve of Cabinet and of a visit by the Foreign Secretary to Bonn, Palliser spoke to Chalfont who, along with Foreign Office officials, thought that further pressure on the Germans would simply give Brandt and Kiesinger an excuse to get off the hook and drive them more closely into French hands. The Foreign Secretary had taken a different position, believing that, if the Germans were to be kept in line over the longer term, the British Government must remain totally intransigent with them, dissuade them from accepting any French suggestions and, in general, force them to make a choice.

If this attitude of total intransigence were in fact to be taken by Brown in Bonn then, Palliser argued in his minute to Wilson, there was a real danger of very serious consequences for the Government's European policy. "I have always believed", Palliser wrote, "and I think you have shared this belief, that the real danger for ourselves and for the French of current French intransigence about letting us into the Common Market lay in the possibility that, when in due course the French obstacle is removed, we should find that it had been replaced by a German obstacle. At all events – and whatever one may feel about the Germans and the way they conduct their affairs – there will be no solidarity of the Five without at least German acquiescence. If we play our hand tactically in such a way as to give the Germans an excuse to snuggle up again to the French, we shall find ourselves out on a limb alone, with perhaps Joe Luns half way along the branch with us. This is not a basis for policy".

Palliser's view of German attitudes was mirrored by that of Lord Chalfont who told the Foreign Secretary on 17 January that "my assessment of the German position is coloured by my experience of Germany over recent years which has led me to believe that they are not sincere in their expressed wish to get us into the Common Market. I believe that the position can be summed up in the aphorism that 'as soon as de Gaulle disappears in Paris, he will re-emerge in Bonn'. In other words, I suggest that overt German support for our application has been a tactic that they have felt they can safely employ knowing that the effective opposition would be provided by the French. I believe that we can come to one clear conclusion. It is that Germany will not, at least as long as the present political structure there exists, take the slightest risk of damaging their relations with France in order to further our interests".[18]

That Germany would put her relations with France before those with Britain was one thing. It did not, of course, therefore mean that Germany was fundamentally and secretly against British membership altogether, even if Kiesinger was temperamentally and politically lukewarm. What can be said, however, is that, once Brandt was firmly at the helm as German Chancellor, his intervention on Britain's behalf was positive, determined and decisive.

Palliser, in his note to Wilson, went on to say that a later conversation with Brown's Private Secretary, Donald Maitland, suggested that Chalfont's arguments might have made some impression on Brown. Brown had apparently admitted privately that he had been wrong to go to Rome (although, characteristically, he blamed Foreign Office officials for advising him to do so), that the tactical handling of the situation had not been too skilful and that the main purpose of his visit to Bonn should be to smooth Brandt's ruffled feathers, while making it clear that the Government had no intention of being fobbed off with half a loaf and that the Government's desire for full membership had not changed in one degree.[19]

None of these self-doubts were evident from the Foreign Secretary's presentation to Cabinet on 18 January. Brown presented his hasty and unprepared visit to Rome as simply a response to an invitation from the Italian Foreign Minister. Brandt's irritation at Brown having gone back on an understanding to allow Brandt to take the lead in consultations was given no weight, other than as an unreasonable taking of umbrage and as "a change of the attitude of the Federal German Government and especially that of Herr Brandt who had supported us strongly at Brussels on 18/19 December but seemed since then to have moved to a position much nearer that of the Federal Chancellor".

Wilson summed up an inconclusive discussion, saying that it was clear that de Gaulle would seek to persuade Kiesinger to endorse the French attitude to British membership of the EEC. It was essential that the German Government should be left in no doubt that, after the meeting between Kiesinger and de Gaulle, we could not tolerate further delay arising out of a prolongation of the Franco-German discussions of Britain's position in relation to the EEC. There was, Wilson said, general agreement in Cabinet that it would be right to consider a comprehensive review of Britain's external policy. But he warned Cabinet "to beware of promoting discussions among the European countries of a degree or a kind which might prove divisive and therefore counter-productive". Thus, quietly, a little water was added to Brown's wine.[20]

In the event, Brown's meeting with Brandt did help clear up the misunderstandings and resentments. There remained a clear difference of perception. Brown told Brandt that he had no doubt that the French had vetoed British accession. But he would do nothing to discourage the Germans from carrying on with their own approach to the French. He would be very happy if the Germans discovered that a veto did not exist. Brown also suggested that nothing could happen in any meeting between the Five and Britain which would prevent the Germans from going on with the exploration which they had in mind. The two could proceed *pari passu*. Indeed, it would be better still if the meetings were to include the French.[21]

The French meanwhile had not been inactive. On 11 January Prime Minister Pompidou made a 45 minute appearance on French television. His performance, according to the British Embassy, was impressive. By contrast with his first efforts back in 1965 he was confident and decisive. His remarks about Britain were, however, disobliging. "Lovely word", wrote Wilson in the margin of the Embassy telegram. "I like disobliging".

Pompidou was asked in his interview whether it would not be preferable for a strong French Government to embark on negotiations with Britain rather than to leave this to a Government which might not have the same prestige. Pompidou replied that France's policies were based on the principle of cooperation with the whole world. No one had cooperated more inside the Community, so as to make the Community go forward, than France. No one had done more to establish links between East and West. No one had cooperated more, due account being taken of her means, than France had with the Third World. And France already cooperated with Britain. As for Britain's entry into the Common Market, it was as clear as the sky was blue that Britain was not ready to take on the disciplines of the Community. He noted that, in the recent economic measures, President Johnson had made a distinction between underdeveloped countries, the developed countries with which the US was closely linked, and others. The 'others' were in essence the European Community. Great Britain was among those closely linked with the United States. This was the first time that the Americans had said openly that Great Britain was closely linked to them. For this reason, it was permissible to say that Britain was not all that much in Europe. The problem of negotiation was not to know whether there were people who were weaker or stronger than others round a table. It was possible that the Government of France tomorrow would be less strong than the present Government. But the problem of Great Britain's entry was to know when she would be in a position to enter the Common Market, when she would renew herself, and – so as to enter Europe – turn her back on all that attracted herself elsewhere. The date of the negotiation therefore depended on Britain and not on the strength or weakness of the French Government.[22]

While Pompidou was stressing the present impossibility of Britain qualifying for membership of the EEC, the French Government generally were making much of the fifth anniversary of the Franco-German Treaty of Cooperation. Couve de Murville took prime time on French television on 22 January (less a mark of the intellectual curiosity of the French audience than of French Government control of the TV channels) to praise the part the Treaty had played, not just in the permanent reconciliation of Germany and France, but also in the construction of Europe, of which Franco-German cooperation was now an essential element. The settlement of the German problem, Couve said in remarks that were both a promise and an implied threat to the German Government, would only become possible on the basis of close Franco-German collaboration and in an atmosphere of détente and agreement.

Brandt, in the same programme, struck a friendly but somewhat cooler note, admitting that not all the hopes which had been placed on the Treaty had been fully realised. "I do not believe", he said, "that the present situation is favourable to efforts aimed at creating concrete political cooperation. This will doubtless only change when it is known what will happen about the enlargement of the Communities".

There was, the British Embassy reported, a strong element of official orchestration in this publicity build-up. Kiesinger's successive assurances that he would brook no tough line towards the French were being highlighted and on French television Kiesinger had been singled out for praise for his 'European' attitudes, in contrast to Erhard and Schroeder.[23]

For its part, the Foreign Office was worried that the impression was being spread on the continent that Britain's 'all or nothing' policy was just as much an obstacle to progress as the position of France itself. Kiesinger had been reported as telling a meeting of his Parliamentary Party that the British policy was just as wrong as the French one. Several speakers in a debate in the European Parliament on 23 January had taken the same line.

The Foreign Office therefore sent a Guidance telegram to its European posts on 25 January explaining that the 'All' that Britain was accused of demanding was no more than the British request for EEC membership in what had always been described as an open Community, and indeed a Community whose open character was specified in the Treaty of Rome. None of the members of the Community (other than France) had reproached Britain in any way for seeking membership, or said that the British were asking too much. On the contrary, all of them, and the European Commission, had urged Britain to apply for membership and had subsequently supported and welcomed the British Government's decision to do so. It was only since the French veto that Britain had begun to be told that she was asking for too much. The British Government had decided to ask for membership after a review which had included other possibilities, such as some form of Association. Its rejection of those possibilities and its concentration on membership had been wholeheartedly approved in five member countries of the Community, who had endorsed the view that the political requirements of an integrated Europe could only be met by enlargement of the Community.

It therefore appeared, the Foreign Office argued, that 'Nothing' in this context meant that Britain was to blame for not accepting an objective (membership) which, before the French veto, everybody had told Britain she should discard. The British Government's view remained that membership was the right objective. In present circumstance, given the attitude of France, it could not be attained. That did not mean that Britain should lower her sights. Membership remained the objective and there were solid and practical reasons for the British objection to interim or compromise solutions, which presumably constituted the 'something' which others now thought Britain should accept. These reasons rested, among other things, on doubts as to whether any such interim compromises would, if put to the test, actually be available. Moreover, the British attitude was not one of 'all or nothing'. There were many things which European countries could usefully do together.[24]

The impact of these powerful arguments on some of Britain's would-be partners (and the arguments in Guidance telegrams were meant to be deployed by Britain's Embassies) might have been somewhat diluted had they known that the British Government's policy had the strong support of the US Government. But the US Government *had* made its view clear to the Germans and had done so for reasons of self-interest. Discrimination against US interests, such as was involved in European Community protection, was, the Americans had said, tolerable to the US Government if it was caused by moves which could be represented as a genuine move in the direction of greater unity in Europe, but partial measures, whether in the economic or technological fields, could not be justified on those grounds and would be liable to provoke resistance on the part of Congress or of the US interests affected.[25]

The British Government found itself in an unenviable situation. France had clearly vetoed her application for EEC membership. Yet the Germans were disinclined to accept 'no' as meaning 'no' and were intent on looking for some alternative arrangement which would salve their bad conscience vis-à-vis the British, keep them in good standing with the French and yet, in British eyes, do nothing substantive to advance the British case and a lot to undermine it through ambiguity and prevarication.

A brief respite was provided by the presentation, on the day of George Brown's visit to Bonn but too late for him to discuss them with Brandt, of Benelux proposals for political and technological consultations between, on the one hand, the Six, or the Five, or even some of the Five and, on the other, the United Kingdom and other European States.

Brown told Cabinet on 25 January that the proposals represented a compromise between the position of the Dutch Government, which had been advocating a freeze on all future development within the EEC, and their other partners in the Benelux grouping. Britain was being offered the opportunity of continuing European consultations and collaboration, without being required at this stage to accept any obligations or commitments.

Never loath to look a gift horse in the mouth, Cabinet moithered over the proposal at some length but Wilson summed up in Brown's favour and authorised Brown to welcome and accept the Benelux proposals on behalf of the Government at the WEU meeting scheduled for 30 January.[26]

The outcome on 30 January was, as Brown told Cabinet two days later, "a good deal better than we might have feared and indeed than we could reasonably have hoped". Brandt had come under strong criticism from both Fanfani and Luns for Germany's determination to explore the ground with the French. Brandt, while unable to accept the Benelux ideas in advance of the meeting between Kiesinger and de Gaulle, had welcomed "the basic principles on which the Benelux proposals were based". All others (apart, predictably, from the French who nonetheless did not reject them out of hand) welcomed the proposals and it had been agreed that the Belgian, Dutch or Italian Governments would call a meeting at official level of all concerned to prepare the ground for a Ministerial gathering.[27]

All eyes were, however, on the Franco-German summit scheduled for 16 February. In a conversation between Wilson and the Canadian Prime Minister, Lester Pearson, on 10 February, Pearson wondered whether de Gaulle would even allow Brandt to accompany Kiesinger to Paris. Wilson agreed. De Gaulle was playing a dangerous game with the Germans trying, it seemed, to drive a wedge between Kiesinger and Brandt. If he succeeded, he might well precipitate the downfall of the German coalition Government, with unpredictable consequences. Was that what he wanted? Pearson interjected that de Gaulle had certainly been trying to break up Canada and added, jocularly, that on the fall of the Belgian Government (which had just occurred) he had considered whether he should send an appropriate message to the Flemish separatists.

Wilson went on to say that de Gaulle might find that he had overplayed his hand, just as he had recently overplayed it economically in attacking the US dollar via sterling and deliberately creating pressure on the US gold reserves. Fortunately, the gold pool had held firm; and the French Government now found themselves in a position in which they had to choose, in effect, between selling some of the gold which they had acquired or accepting a rise in unemployment, It looked as though Debré, the Finance Minister, had already decided to opt for the former course.[28]

Wilson also remained resolute in his opposition to any form of Association as an alternative to full EEC membership. He told the Irish Prime Minister, Jack Lynch, on 14 February that the German variant of the idea, some kind of industrial free trade area, had no future. The French were already deeply concerned at the likely effect on their economy of meeting, by the middle of 1968, the full force of competition from the other members of the EEC and it was therefore certain that they would strongly oppose any additional competition from the four applicant countries. In any form of Association, the French would undoubtedly demand that we should accept their agricultural policy in order to boost their exports of agricultural products to Britain. Britain would, therefore, be in the unacceptable position of having taken on the obligations of membership of the EEC without any right to consultation on the development of EEC policies and without any final date fixed for when we could assume full membership. The suggestion offered a blind alley, along which we would get nowhere, slowly.

Lynch said that, in general, he agreed with Wilson's assessment of the proposed industrial free trade area, and certainly there would be no attractions for Ireland in a free trade association which did not cover agricultural arrangements. Lynch then asked whether devaluation of the pound meant that the economic benefits of the EEC were no longer important for Britain. Wilson's answer was revealing. It was not so. By strengthening the position of sterling, devaluation had removed one of the main French arguments against British membership. Nevertheless, there was still a strong economic argument for membership: if the new technological industries were to develop fully and to attract the right level of investment, they would need to be assured of the large markets which could only come from membership of the EEC. It was, moreover, impossible to separate the economic argument for membership from the political. As the economic strength of the Community increased so would its political authority.[29]

The communiqué from the de Gaulle-Kiesinger summit on 16 January included the following language: "They [the two Governments] wish the Communities to be enlarged to include other European countries, particularly those who have already applied for membership, once those countries are in a position, either to enter effectively into these Communities, or as the case may be, to link themselves with them in another form. This applies particularly to Britain and means that the evolution already begun by this country should continue. Until this enlargement becomes possible, the two Governments are ready to envisage the conclusion by the Community of arrangements with the applicant countries capable of developing exchanges of agricultural and industrial products between the two parties. Such arrangements, which would include progressive reductions of trade obstacles for industrial products, would be designed to facilitate the above-mentioned evolution and would in any case contribute to the development of relations between the European countries".

German State Secretary Duckwitz was detailed to brief the British Ambassador in Paris on the outcome of the Franco-German discussions. The Germans seemed genuinely pleased with their handiwork. The Declaration embodied, so Duckwitz claimed, the first real concession which the French had made. It had been won by a hard fight, particularly between Kiesinger and de Gaulle. Pompidou and Couve de Murville had seemed more flexible. The essential point was that the French Government had agreed to discussions on the German proposal for some kind of free trade area which would have an agricultural content. The mere fact that the Six would be sitting together with Britain and the other candidates and talking about measures to be adopted would be a kind of institution in itself. The Germans' idea was not so much actually to bring into being a kind of free trade area but to get into a negotiation with the French in the hope that at some stage it would be possible to convert it into one for entry into the Community. The Germans considered that the French agreement to discuss their idea was a real concession. Britain now had an opportunity to put her foot in the door and it was up to Britain to decide whether she wished to take it. De Gaulle, according to Duckwitz, had gone so far as to say that it would be a great advantage for Europe if Britain could become a member of it both politically and economically. These were the General's own words, spoken with much emphasis. De Gaulle had in fact admitted that Britain was European. Britain must, however, prove that she could enter Europe on the same conditions as all its other members and she must make great efforts to fit herself to do so. De Gaulle had admitted that there had been certain developments in the United Kingdom already in the right direction.

Reilly asked whether the Benelux proposal had been discussed and Duckwitz replied that the French had made it absolutely clear that they would have nothing to do with it. The General had rejected it with a gesture as if he were sweeping it from the table. Duckwitz thought therefore that the proposal for a meeting of ten governments to consider the Benelux proposals should now be regarded as replaced by the discussions contemplated on the German free trade area proposal.[30]

Palliser greeted the news from Paris, in a note to Wilson, with what he called "very qualified optimism". The French had been obliged to withdraw to what, in wartime, had been known as 'a prepared position'. Those who had withdrawn presented this as a skilful tactical manoeuvre on their part; but those who were attacking knew that they had gained a position of potential advantage. The tactical advantage in this case, for Britain, was slight.[31]

Reilly, who had been the recipient of the German analysis of their own achievement, gave the Germans short shrift. "It looks", he wrote the following day. "as though the Germans have done the French a considerable service. They have broken the isolation which the French were finding increasingly uncomfortable. They have queered the pitch for the Benelux proposals. They have joined with the French in a public reaffirmation that so far as both countries are concerned it is to be business as usual again in the Community; and they have made it more difficult for the Dutch and Italians to maintain their boycott on technological progress at Six.".

In return, the French had given very little. What was offered was something which had been freely discussed in the French media beforehand as something which de Gaulle would regard as a harmless gesture to enable the Germans to retreat without undue loss of face from their position of outright support for early British membership. These were, as one French commentator had put it that morning, French ideas dressed up in German clothes. If, Reilly argued, these ideas for an interim commercial arrangement were to find favour, the French would contend that the British had finally come round to their original advice to seek a relationship less than full membership and that the formal maintenance of an application was therefore purely academic. One source in the German delegation had told the Embassy that the French had been solely concerned to play the issue out to the Greek Calends and that the purpose of French tactics was to outflank the Benelux proposals. Kiesinger, according to this German source, had been desperate for some semblance of agreement with the French and in no mood to do battle. The most that could be said for the Germans was that they had persuaded the French to use in a formal declaration language more positive than ever before i.e. that they wished for the enlargement of the Community and, in particular, the entry of Britain.[32]

To Reilly, Jean Monnet, who had already shown himself nervous of British pressure on the Germans, said that he was perplexed by the outcome of the talks in Paris. But his main concern once again was that the Germans not be rebuffed. He was very anxious about the threat of a new German nationalism, which de Gaulle was encouraging. The German Ministers were weak men but, apart from Kiesinger, he believed that they, and especially Brandt and Strauss, and many important German parliamentarians, genuinely wanted Britain in the Community.[33]

In public, the British Government kept their own counsel about the Franco-German Declaration, remaining hopeful that the Benelux proposals could be kept alive. Others were similarly cautious. Even Fanfani, who in private was angry with the French and Germans and who blamed the Germans for obtaining nothing but empty words from de Gaulle, told the British Ambassador in Rome that he had decided to say nothing.[34]

Frank Roberts had spent the weekend in Brussels and had called on many of the key players in the Commission, NATO and the Belgian Government. On his return to Bonn he called on State Secretary Lahr. He felt obliged, he said, to tell Lahr that the Paris communiqué had left a pessimistic impression on nearly all of the important people he had met in Brussels. Lahr would have noted, however, that the British Government had not contributed to this gloomy mood, having refrained from any official comment.

Lahr responded that it was as ridiculous to claim that Kiesinger had achieved a great victory as to attack the Germans for having given way all along the line to the French. Lahr was, however, personally convinced that a real change for the better had taken place. The points had now been moved and the European train could move out of the station and in the right direction. He thought that Pompidou above all, and to a lesser extend Couve, had brought home to de Gaulle that the French could not hope to play the kind of role in Europe that they wished to play if their policies drove all their partners together against them.[35]

The official private French line – that nothing of substance had been changed by the Franco-German Declaration – was borne out by comment in the French Press. In the case of André Fontaine, Foreign Editor of *Le Monde*, the confirmation of French methods was also critical. Quoting de Gaulle as having said "I only respect those who resist me, but I cannot tolerate them", Fontaine described de Gaulle as being utterly convinced of his own infallibility. In Western Europe, although de Gaulle could not get his own way, he could prevent what he did not want, for example British accession. De Gaulle could achieve this because France's partners had taken seriously, and probably with justification, French blackmail about the destruction of the Community and because the German Government would not compromise its good relations with Paris for the sake of London. Kiesinger's visit to Paris was, said Fontaine, a masterpiece of French diplomacy. The French had succeeded in presenting as a concession to the Germans an agreement which in reality represented German acceptance of the French position. No wonder spirits were high at the Elysée. But Fontaine questioned the longer-term wisdom of French policy and tactics, arguing that many Germans were infuriated by their Government's docility towards French policy and that the German habit of lavishing praise on de Gaulle, as well as the steady increase in Germany of neo-Nazis, were equally sinister.[36]

Fontaine was no friend of the Gaullist Government but the Embassy in Paris were told separately by a reliable source in the French Foreign Ministry that, before the talks with Kiesinger, de Gaulle had issued just one *mot d'ordre* to his Ministers. It was that if the Germans formed a common front with the Four against France, this would mean the "automatic and immediate end of the Common Market". The French had taken good care to leak this to the Germans and, when it had had the desired effect and the Germans had made it clear that they had no intention of forcing a showdown, de Gaulle had agreed to the Declaration as a face-saving device for them. De Gaulle, according to this same source, regarded the result of the talks with great satisfaction. Kiesinger had not sided with the Four against France, and he had made a number of critical remarks about 'Atlanticism' which, the French thought, had encouraging implications. The French no longer felt in danger of isolation. Some officials, including the French Ambassador in Bonn, doubted German sincerity. But the present mood at the Elysée was, for the time being at least, euphoric.[37]

Wilson, for his part, favoured a measured and unemotional reaction to the Franco-German Declaration. The British Government's stance was that, if a proposal arising out of the Declaration were put to them by the Six, they would of course consider it. At the same time, they did not want to lose sight of the Benelux proposals, which they had publicly accepted but which the French were inclined to dismiss as redundant.

When the EEC Foreign Ministers met on 29 February, Brandt, more robust than Kiesinger on these issues, suggested that the European Commission might be asked to suggest ways in which the Benelux, Italian and Franco-German plans could be combined. Brandt tabled a list of eight principles, which drew a picture of a commercial agreement involving linear reductions in tariffs, to be negotiated with the four candidate countries and in conformity with GATT, which would provide an intermediate solution with the aim of facilitating the entry of the candidate states.

Brandt's proposals had the effect of once again lining up the Five on one side and the French on the other. When the UK Representative to the EEC, Marjoribanks, took soundings of all his EEC colleagues the following day he found all of them, bar the Frenchman, of the view that the discussion in the Council had gone better than they had expected. They thought that real pressure was now being exerted on the French; that Brandt had gone a long way towards forcing the French either to agree with, or veto, an eventual proposal for a free trade area; and that the French Foreign Minister might well have to seek authority to go along with Brandt's eight points if the French were not to be isolated. At the same time, most doubted whether Couve would be given such authority. Couve had at no stage directly attacked the German presentation in the meeting, but his own contribution had demonstrated the gap between French and German positions.[38]

It was a few days before the French reacted. On 8 March, the French Ambassador in Bonn called on Kiesinger on instructions. According to State Secretary Duckwitz, in conversation with Roberts, the Ambassador had expressed the French Government's "strong displeasure" at the German eight-point programme. The Ambassador had gone so far as to say to the Chancellor that the action taken by the Federal Government misinterpreted the agreement reached between the

Chancellor and de Gaulle and that "the spirit of Paris" was now in danger. To Duckwitz, the French Ambassador had said that Couve de Murville was furious with Brandt and could not understand the haste with which the Germans were proceeding in the matter, when it was something that called for very careful thought and would take a very long time.

Separately, Brandt told the British Ambassador that the French, and in particular Couve, had clearly supposed their German partners to be more stupid and gullible than they were. It was after all the French who had spoken of an arrangement and, whatever they might have said later, they had clearly given the Germans to understand in Paris that they were prepared to go along with the kind of eight point programme subsequently worked out by the Germans. It was too much to be accused now of going back upon what had been agreed in Paris when it was in fact the French who were doing just that. Brandt said that he did not intend to be influenced by these rather obvious French tactics and would present his points as a German proposal, leaving it to the French to take upon themselves the onus of rejecting them and so once again making themselves alone responsible for any further setback.

Duckwitz told Roberts that Kiesinger had been irritated by Ambassador Seydoux, who was clearly being held on a tight rein by de Gaulle. Duckwitz was in no doubt that the French were in fact going back on what had been agreed in Paris and that the Foreign Secretary's warnings to that effect had, not entirely to his own surprise, been fully justified.[39]

The EEC Council of Ministers on 10 March was, according to the Belgian Foreign Minister, "another bad meeting and the atmosphere . . . almost as strained as on 29 February or 19 December. The Five and the Commission in their different ways had all played their part in seeking to advance the common cause, but the French attitude had been cold and uncompromising. Brandt had been justifiably irritated when the French in effect told him that he had quite misunderstood the French position. Couve de Murville was increasingly irritated to find that the Five had not accepted the French veto of 19 December and that, on the contrary, at each Council of Ministers meeting the problem of British adhesion was on the table". Harmel went on to suggest that perhaps the best next step would be for the British Government to take the initiative and to ask the Six what stage must be reached in the reestablishment of the UK balance of payments position before the Six would accept that we were qualified to begin negotiations for membership.[40]

Not surprisingly, this idea did not find favour in London, where Balogh advised Wilson that it "would not only not embarrass the French but is more likely to play straight into their hands" and Palliser agreed: "Let us by all means irritate the French if we gain something by doing whatever causes the irritation; but not otherwise . . . Surely Harmel is back to front".[41]

On the same day, Reilly called on Couve de Murville at the latter's suggestion. Couve launched off about the "passion, carried to a point of absurdity", with which subjects concerning France were now treated in the British Press. There seemed, he said, to be an obsession in Britain that the French were always responsible for everything that went wrong.

Reilly replied that, if this was so, it was a regrettable consequence of the French Government's action, of the effects of which the French Government had been given clear warning. Couve complained that the British never went to the heart of the matter, which was simply that Britain's economic difficulties made it impossible for her to join the Community at the present time. And now, Britain was forever trying to work against France and to get the Five to combine against France as well. He could not see where this would get us. De Gaulle's death would not change anything.

Reilly, perhaps with the courage of someone whose time in office was coming to an end, responded that, if criticism of the French Government's attitude was so bitter in the UK, it was largely because nobody there believed that the French argument, based on Britain's economic difficulties, was a genuine one. The British Government knew that if that argument was removed, other objections to British entry would be found.

Couve then accused the British Government of rejecting the ideas in the Franco-German Declaration and of colluding instead with the Benelux to come up with proposals which were bound to be refused by the French.

Reilly dealt with this lie too. Britain had no responsibility for the Benelux paper. Nor had Britain rejected the ideas in the Franco-German paper, if only because no proposals had been made to Britain. The British Government would consider any proposals made to them by the Community. After some further argument, Couve conceded that this was so and that the position of the British Government on this matter had been reasonable.

Towards the end of the discussion, Couve said that there had been much talk of technological cooperation with Britain. But France, quite apart from the rest of the Community, already had a lot of such collaboration with Britain, and no doubt there would be more. Reilly said he was not so sure. When Couve evinced surprise, Reilly said that the climate was unpropitious for new cooperative projects. Couve denied that the French Government had done anything to make it so, to which Reilly responded that the French Government had taken a decision which now dominated relations between France and Britain. Couve said that this might be so but there was no change in the French position on British accession and no early prospect of one.

Reilly commented to the Foreign Office that this had been as tough an argument as he had ever had with Couve and that, while Couve had not been personally disagreeable, his line had been hard throughout and especially at the end. But Couve had also left Reilly with the impression that he was very put out by what was happening in the Community. There was no sign of give on Couve's part but he must, thought Reilly, at least realise that things would not now go as easily for the French as they had hoped.

After reading these reports, Wilson agreed with Palliser that Reilly had given as good – if not better – than he got.[42]

On 15 March, George Brown resigned as Foreign Secretary and left the Government, thereby bringing an end to his front line political career. The immediate issue (Wilson's alleged failure to consult him over the calling of a special

Bank Holiday) was only the proximate cause. Wilson had defeated Brown for the Labour leadership. Wilson was thoughtful and methodical; Brown insightful but mercurial. His alcoholism made him erratic, monstrously behaved and often publicly embarrassing. He had threatened resignation before. On this occasion, Wilson seized the opportunity to accept.

The Government's course on Europe owed a huge amount to Brown's conviction and leadership. He carried weight within the Labour Party and, as a European idealist, with Britain's would-be partners within the EEC. He took the edge off their scepticism about the genuineness of Wilson's conversion. He indeed helped persuade Wilson to choose the European path and to carry the overwhelming majority in the Cabinet with him in doing so. But that course was now set and, in choosing Michael Stewart to return as Foreign Secretary, Wilson selected someone of almost equally strong, if less emotionally based, European convictions.

Whether, had George Brown stayed in the Government, Labour would have turned against Europe after 1970, is an imponderable. Brown would, by his own claim, have strongly advised against going to the country at the moment Wilson chose. Beyond that it is futile to speculate. But in the list of British politicians who led Britain to EEC membership, Brown remains one of the most prominent and influential.

The Council of Ministers had asked the Commission to make proposals as to how to carry forward the various ideas (Franco-German Declaration, Benelux and Italian plans) about which the Member States had quarrelled in March. The Commission duly did so on 2 April in a document which the British Delegation in Brussels characterised as "unsatisfactory". The document represented, they said, a tardy realisation by the Commission that it was unwise to undertake to provide an opinion to the Council at short notice and in the present political climate. In an attempt to find some common ground for agreement in the Council, French arguments had been given prominence and used to reach conclusions which leant more to Couve's thinking than to that of the Five. In particular, the document, which had nonetheless provoked abstention within the College by the French Commissioners, did not provide any credible mechanisms for binding the existing Community and the applicants together and thus to lead to full membership. The Commission had shied away from the task of proposing practical means of working towards membership.

On the plus side, the document did present an outline of proposals which were much more complex and far-reaching than anything the French had thus far shown willingness to accept. It was for that reason that the French Commissioners had abstained. The Dutch Commissioner dissented because of the lack of any automaticity about membership at the end of the preparatory period.[43]

The ill omens for the meeting of the Council scheduled for 5 April were reflected in a speech which the German Chancellor made to the Bundestag on 2 April, when he confirmed that there were significant differences between Germany and France on the issue of enlargement. Frank Roberts saw the speech as firmly dissociating the Federal Government from French policy. It was clear that Kiesinger's dissatisfaction with the French had deepened and that some of the prevalent

German anger with the French Government had found its way into Kiesinger's speech. Hitherto, Kiesinger had invariably said that he favoured British entry and had then added a 'but'. On this occasion, the 'but' had been dropped.[44]

The ill omens were an accurate predictor for the mood when the Council met on 5 April. The French Foreign Minister made it plain that France was proposing an arrangement with the candidate countries which would have no direct link to their possible accession. The other Member States refused to accept this. Couve threatened that, if others insisted on what he termed an all-or-nothing approach then it was obvious what the result would be. Couve's intervention was greeted in silence. After further exchanges the Germans asked for a suspension. State Secretary Duckwitz, who was leading the German delegation, telephoned Kiesinger for instructions. But the latitude he was given did not go far enough for the rest of the Five. The Italians made clear that, if the Germans were now prepared to make only a general declaration linking any commercial agreement with the applicants to their eventual accession then this would have serious consequences for the relations between the two delegations. Duckwitz went back to the telephone and, this time, came back with agreement from Bonn to reaffirm the position as established by Brandt at the February Council i.e. making a clear link between any commercial agreement and enlargement. Indeed, when the Council reassembled Duckwitz, speaking with some emotion, restated the wish of the German Government to see the accession of the candidate states and the start of negotiations as soon as possible. He reaffirmed the German position – that the text of any commercial agreement must clearly state that the arrangement was agreed with a view to the enlargement of the Community. He put the question to the French Government: did they still wish to facilitate an arrangement of this nature? If the answer was positive then the Commission should be asked to work out something on those lines. Couve, Duckwitz insisted, should answer this question. But Couve did not answer it saying, instead that he was not going to read the Franco-German declaration again. It was for the United Kingdom to bring itself to the position of being able to accede. The one thing the Council were not agreed about was whether negotiations should be opened and the question was therefore what should be done in the waiting period. As Chair of the meeting Couve then proposed remitting the issue back to the Committee of Permanent Representatives (COREPER), the standard face-saving device, then as now, when Ministers could not reach agreement.

Rey, the Commission President, affirmed the Commission's formal position as contained in their Opinion on British accession. They had confined themselves on this occasion, as requested, to the so-called waiting period. In doing so, they had not neglected the Franco-German Declaration, although the Commission had had some difficulty in reconciling French and German views. But they also had to take account of proposals from other delegations and of views in other parts of the Community. Couve retorted that the Council would take note of Rey's declaration. France would certainly do so.

After some further exchanges, Couve reluctantly accepted that any issue could be raised in COREPER, provided it was also accepted that the French view had already been made clearly known.[45]

The net effect of all this activity without action was that the months slipped by without an effective progress from the perspective of Britain and the other candidates.

It was nearly three weeks after the Council before Couve and Brandt met – in Bonn for regular consultations under the Franco-German Treaty. Brandt took the opportunity to warn Couve that lack of progress on the question of British membership would have unfavourable effects on the work of the EEC. Brandt was not invoking the possibility of a boycott but feared unfavourable effects as an inescapable result. Brandt pressed Couve on the link between accession and the other work of the Community, although Couve scored an important point when both men agreed that the development of the Community must not be prejudiced, thus rendering Brandt's warning rather hollow.

Perhaps more significant, because surprising, was an intervention, in the middle of the talks, by Kiesinger who appealed "to our French friends to interpret the Franco-German declarations concerning the possibility of British entry in a generous manner". He also appealed "to others not to reject a real step forward on grounds of dogma. If we wish to make progress we must also make compromises and here is a compromise which would reward the whole of Europe".

The German Government publicised Kiesinger's appeal at a press conference, urging acceptance of the German approach as a starting point. The spokesman denied that the German Government thought the British Government was being dogmatic.[46] And two days later, in response to a message from Brandt, the new Foreign Secretary, Michael Stewart, confirmed the position of the British Government: "Our position remains unchanged. We will certainly be interested in any proposals that are put to us by the six Community governments and will consider them carefully. But you will understand that until such proposals are put forward we cannot comment. Meanwhile, I am glad to see that you hold that any arrangement should help to facilitate enlarging the Community".[47]

Lest there was still any doubt, a few days later, in a speech to the European Movement in Luxembourg attended, exceptionally, by the Grand Duke as well as by the Luxembourg Prime Minister and other Ministers, the President of the Commission, Jean Rey, stated plainly that it was the Six, by reason of their lack of unanimity, who were preventing Europe from playing its proper role in the world. The one dissenting member had a perfect right not to agree with the opinion of the Five and of the Commission but no country had the right to remain set on one course without attempting to find a compromise. It was essential to solve the present crisis and paralysis in Community affairs.[48]

One member of the British Cabinet was ready to suggest a less patient British approach than had been implied by Stewart's message to Brandt. In a minute to Stewart on 6 May, Tony Crosland, President of the Board of Trade, suggested that the Franco-German declaration looked like leading nowhere. For Britain, any agreement resulting from it must provide for eventual accession. That in turn ruled out French agreement. So it seemed unlikely that the Six would be able to put forward any serious proposals based on the Franco-German ideas. Crosland went on to propose that, in the context of the Government's desire for ultimate entry into the EEC, they should commission a study in order to re-assess the possible courses open to them: "I think that the study should start from the assumption that it will be a considerable time before we are able to start negotiating for entry into the Community [and] consider what course might meanwhile be most compatible with the need to keep our sights firmly fixed on future entry, while at the same time missing no chance of any liberalising of European trade which might meanwhile be obtainable. Such a study should take into account the desirability of showing our EFTA partners that our stance is not entirely immobile . . ."

Stewart consulted Wilson before replying that he hoped to bring his considered views to Cabinet before long but that in the meantime a study by officials "might be premature".[49]

The Foreign Secretary's considered views were not long in coming, taking the form of a draft Cabinet Paper, approved by Stewart himself, and then sent to Palliser at No. 10 for consideration by the Prime Minister before it was circulated. At the core of the paper was the assessment that the Franco-German initiative was getting nowhere ("The process of establishing the sterility of the German approach continues."). It seemed probable, the paper argued, that either no proposal would emerge or, if it did, it would involve agreement among the Six on French terms which Britain would have to turn down. Instead, Stewart suggested, the British Government should take an initiative, building on the Benelux proposals, involving (i) consultation with the Community; (ii) joint action in science and technology; (iii) cooperation in the aid field; (iv) European defence cooperation; (v) political consultation; (vi) British views on the future development of the Community. On this last point Stewart thought it should be an objective of British policy, while she was prevented from joining, to do what she could to prevent the Community from developing. If this crippled, and even undermined, the Community, that would be preferable to its development without Britain.[50]

Stewart acknowledged that the proposals which the British Government was able to make in the prevailing circumstances were "somewhat deficient in practical content". Nonetheless, Wilson, advised by Palliser, agreed with them.

Wilson and Stewart met alone on 13 May to discuss the paper. According to Wilson's subsequent account to Palliser he had advised Stewart to include in the paper a reference to monetary problems and to the possibility or otherwise of some form of European monetary cooperation. The paper should also include the possibility of alternatives to membership of the EEC, e.g. NAFTA. This was not because the Prime Minister favoured alternatives or regarded them as practicable: quite the contrary. But he thought that, if there were no such reference, if only in dismissive terms, the possibility of alternatives would certainly be raised in discussion and could prove to be something of a red herring.

Wilson thought that it would also be a mistake to lay too much emphasis in the paper on Britain's desire to prevent the Communities from developing until she could join. This comment too did not indicate dissent from the substance. But if it became known that a paper setting out this objective was being considered, it could be very damaging to Britain's policy. For similar reasons, Wilson advised deletion of the last sentence of the draft paper which suggested that, if Britain did not take an initiative "our friends in Europe may well give up hope, and acquiesce in the further development of the Community on lines acceptable to France. This could mean the eventual terms of membership becoming unacceptable to us". Stewart agreed to these changes.[51]

In the event, the Foreign Office paper never made it to Cabinet. It was taken first by the Official Committee on European questions where, as Palliser reported to Wilson, it "received fairly rough handling". Palliser thought that the most telling point which could be made in favour of the paper was the one which the Prime Minister himself had made: to stand aside in dignified withdrawal, from a position of strength, was one thing. But when one's position, whatever the underlying realities, could be presented by opponents as one of weakness, such a posture would seem merely timid and defensive. If we did nothing, we should probably move backwards rather than stand still; and we should certainly not move forward.[52]

However, when the paper was considered by the Ministerial Committee on the Approach to Europe (which Stewart chaired) on 21 May, the Committee also had in front of them a minute from Crosland which concluded: "I have grave doubts whether an early initiative on the lines proposed by the Foreign Secretary would help us with our primary objective of restoring our economic strength; I fear it would lead to difficulties with our EFTA partners and, for different reasons, with the Germans; and I do not believe that it would bring us nearer to ultimate membership of the EEC . . ."[53]

Colleagues on the Ministerial Committee agreed with Crosland, obliging the Foreign Secretary to sum up that, while no member of the Committee considered that there should be any weakening in the Government's determination to pursue the long-term objective of securing membership of the EEC, the general view of the Committee was that, in view of the uncertainty of the German attitude and over future developments in France, it would be premature to launch an initiative in July; and that the desirability of doing so in the autumn was also open to doubt. He would accordingly reconsider the proposals.[54]

Later that morning Stewart was obliged to confess to Wilson that his paper had been in a minority of one in the Committee and that his approach had been attacked both as containing inadequate substance to carry conviction and as being wrong in terms of timing, given particularly the present situation in France. Wilson and Stewart agreed that it would be "inappropriate" to try to bring the paper to Cabinet.[55]

Palliser subsequently commented to Wilson that, as the Prime Minister himself had remarked, not all the arguments advanced against Stewart's paper derived wholly from considerations of foreign policy. That said, it was probably also true, as Lord Chalfont had told Palliser, that this very open clash between the Foreign Secretary on the one hand and virtually all his colleagues on the Committee on the other, would not have arisen if George Brown as Foreign Secretary had been disposed to allow more regular discussion in the Committee on his European approach in the first place.[56]

The 'present situation in France' which Ministers had adduced as one reason for not proposing a British initiative was of course the events of May 1968. On

20 May, the British Embassy in Paris reported to London that strikes had spread to almost all sectors of the French economy, that the nub of the crisis was increasingly political and that, as a member of Pompidou's cabinet had told one of the Embassy staff, the Government was not in full control. The crisis had caught everyone unawares and was still in a way incredible. This fact had greatly contributed to Government waverings between violence and appeasement.[57]

An internal Foreign Office minute of the same date judged that the crisis was the most serious threat to the Gaullist regime in its ten years of power, including Algeria, and that "wrongly handled, the situation could become revolutionary". Student riots early in May, dealt with by needless police violence, had caused public sympathy to swing towards the students and had led to trade union action and then the occupation by workers of around a hundred factories in all parts of France. Around two million workers were on strike and the transport system was at a standstill. De Gaulle had been on a State Visit to Romania when the trouble started. He returned early but let it be known that he would not advance the date of an address to the nation previously arranged for 24 May. Whatever now happened, the Foreign Office minute advised, the events of the previous ten days had damaged the prestige of the French Government, and of de Gaulle himself, to a degree unimaginable before the riots. "It is hard to believe", the memo concluded "that things can be the same again".[58]

From Paris, Reilly, who had recently been touring the French provinces, reported that during de Gaulle's absence in Romania he seemed almost forgotten. A view often expressed to Reilly outside Paris was the direct opposite of what a British observer might think, namely that de Gaulle's foreign policy had been highly successful, but that he had done nothing for France internally. In fact, Reilly said, to anyone travelling widely in France as he had done, the great progress made in the past ten years in many fields leaped to the eye. But modernisation, both in agriculture and industry, had hurt many people and this was a major factor in the general malaise which the Embassy had discerned and reported for many months. But Reilly's strongest impression was of a very widespread feeling in France that the country had had enough of being ruled in the paternalistic and authoritarian spirit which had characterised the Gaullist regime. Reilly suspected that it was that feeling which now represented de Gaulle's greatest problem.[59]

On 24 May, de Gaulle broadcast to the French people promising reform and a referendum. But the broadcast was lacklustre and the situation remained unstable. So much so that, five days later, Reilly telegraphed to London that if de Gaulle was forced to resign the question might arise of his leaving France, at least for a period. Reilly imagined that, in those circumstances, de Gaulle would try to go to Switzerland or Italy. "I cannot see him returning to Britain if he has any choice in the matter", Reilly concluded. [60]

On the same day (29 May), the Embassy reported that the French Government appeared to be in a state of disintegration and that Ministers who had arrived at the Elysée that morning had found that the Council of Ministers had been cancelled and that de Gaulle had left.

The tension and sense of impending collapse was reflected in Michael Stewart's report to Cabinet on 30 May, when he told his colleagues that it was possible that de Gaulle would resign that day, and probable that he would do so before the Referendum fixed for 16 June. The present situation was explosive and the possibility of an extremist Government could not be excluded.[61]

On the following day, having been to Baden Baden and assured himself of the loyalty of the French army, de Gaulle broadcast again to the French people, deferring the promised referendum and calling legislative elections. "The General's will has not failed", Reilly reported. "His resolute decision has put an end to yesterday's feeling of a disintegration of power … In fighting language very different from his apathetic style on 24 May he has challenged the Communists and those to the left of them and with his contemptuous reference to 'discarded politicians' who might form a Government with the Communists he has burnt any bridges that could remain with the left."[62]

By 31 May, the Embassy were telling London: "The last 24 hours have been de Gaulle's … Public order seems fully assured. The morale of the Paris police was clearly raised by General de Gaulle's declaration and the Gaullist demonstration. The movements of troops around Paris, including tank manoeuvres, are well publicised."[63]

As the dust settled on the French crisis, in which the British Government again maintained tactful silence while providing assistance to help the position of the Franc, attention turned again to the question of how to take forward Britain's candidature.

In a conversation with the Danish Prime Minister, Hilmar Baunsgaard, in London on 17 June, Wilson confirmed his view, which Baunsgaard shared, that the idea of a trading arrangement, proposed by the Germans in the light of their discussions with the French Government, was unlikely to prove fruitful. Wilson also confirmed that the British Government were not planning any initiative of their own, given the French situation and the fact that new Governments were only just being formed in Italy and Belgium. It was, he added, in any case difficult to see with whom such an initiative could be taken.[64]

On 25 June, Commission President Jean Rey was in London, against a background of concern on the part of the British Government that special measures taken by the EEC to help France economically should not be allowed to become contagious. Rey took the point, adding that he thought it would also be understood by the new French Finance Minister, Couve de Murville, "whose long practice in saying no to France's negotiating partners should provide useful training for the need to say no to the French protectionist lobby". Rey thought that recent events in France made it necessary to hold a full review of EEC policy, including a reappraisal of the position on negotiations for new members. The Community could not continue on the present basis of no negotiations, of French aggression against the dollar and of continuing French opposition to Britain. One thing at least was certain, according to Rey. The French argument that it was the weakness of the British economy that prevented the extension of the Community had now been completely demolished. It would be abundantly clear that, in her own crisis, France had been obliged to turn for help, not only to the Commission, but also to Britain and the United States. It would be impossible for the French to continue to maintain their previous stubborn attitude. The Commission therefore intended to make a major effort to reopen the whole question in the autumn. It was not for Britain, but for them, to take the initiative.

Wilson confirmed that the Government's position on membership was entirely unchanged. He concluded from Rey's remarks that Britain could only await patiently a renewal of activity on the continent in support of the British application. If the delay became too long the danger was less of British opinion becoming impatient than of its becoming bored. Hitherto, the British Government had not experienced great difficulty on this score and had been able to stand firm on the position that their decision to apply for membership, which remained totally unchanged, had been approved by the largest majority in British Parliamentary history. Wilson added that he could not deny that the Government had faced considerable temptations during the French upheaval a few weeks earlier. But they had resisted those temptations. The British Government desired stability in France. Equally, they hoped for a change of heart and of policy there. But chaos, or a Communist takeover, in France were clearly not in the interests of her close neighbour across the Channel. As he had sought on a number of occasions to make clear to President de Gaulle, European unity and cooperation depended on France and Britain working together and could not be achieved as long as they failed to do so. But this general approach was not very exciting for British opinion and it could become difficult for the Government to hold it for too long.[65]

Wilson took the lead once again in resisting the temptation to play the anti-French card when he saw a telegram from the UK Mission to the UN in Geneva recommending that Britain take the lead in opposing recent French trade measures (incentives to exporters, quota restrictions and the administrative surveillance of imports) in the context of discussions in the GATT. Wilson minuted: "We should think very carefully indeed before getting into the lead, both on foreign and economic grounds. There are plenty of others. We paid a heavy price last year for taking the lead against France in the NATO row of two and a half years ago".[66] His view was echoed in advice from Reilly in Paris who thought it likely that France's EEC partners would accept the measures with varying degrees of docility, with the risk that "we may find ourselves at the opposite end of the see-saw from the Five with the French sitting comfortably in the middle".[67]

The Prime Minister's view prevailed and on 4 July, the Foreign Secretary reported to Cabinet that the French Government's measures would leave the Kennedy Round untouched and that the French Government had announced their intention to comply fully with their engagements under the EEC and the GATT. The EEC were likely to give the necessary approval. The British, Stewart concluded, were not in a position to criticise the French measures and to do so would not help.

Stewart also told Cabinet that, in the elections held under the promises that de Gaulle had made at the height of the May crisis, the Gaullists and the Independent Republicans had achieved an overwhelming victory while all the other parties had been defeated. It was possible that Pompidou might be replaced as Prime Minister. French policies were unlikely to change, in particular with regard to NATO and to the British application to join the EEC. But France's power to carry through her policies might have been weakened as a result of the May disturbances.[68]

With the Summer holiday in Europe coming up, by the time the EEC resumed business in September, almost a year would have elapsed since de Gaulle's veto – a year in which absolutely no measurable progress had been made in advancing the British cause. Could the British Government have gained by accepting the Franco-German declaration at face value and seeking to build on it? The course of the discussion within the Community, and not least the disagreement between France and Germany about what each had meant by the declaration, suggests, rather, that the British Government's fear that anything short of negotiation for membership would be time wasting and productive of no clear outcome had been correct.

Against that background, the discussion which Stewart held on 9 July in Bonn with the German and Belgian Foreign Ministers had a wary familiarity to it. Harmel suggested that the first meeting of the Council of Ministers in September should be devoted entirely to the question of enlargement. Brandt agreed but then said that Kiesinger's meeting with de Gaulle at the end of September was likely to diminish the importance of the Council. Brandt acknowledged that the German ideas for a free trade arrangement had gone nowhere. He thought there might have been a small shift in the French position but the shift, if it existed, had been so small that the idea had come to look like a substitute for membership. He regretted that the idea had thus been made to look like a move in the wrong direction or, as Harmel had put it, a French trap.

Harmel then said that he had been re-reading the Brussels Treaty and wondered whether the WEU could not be used in some way to fill in the interval between the present time and the opening of negotiations to enlarge the Community. Both Brandt and Stewart thought the idea a good one, though of course it was only new to the extent that it represented a reversion to the situation before the false start of the Franco-German Declaration.[69]

On 15 July, a somewhat repentant Jean Monnet met Wilson in Downing Street. He had been over-optimistic in his assessment of de Gaulle's intentions and now felt, he said, obliged to be cautious in his forecasts. He had now reluctantly concluded that there was no hope of a change of heart by de Gaulle. The vote for the Gaullists in the recent French election was not a positive vote for the General but one cast by those who feared either chaos or Communism. De Gaulle's own attitude would not change. The Germans could not be expected to go to the point of breaking with France over the British application. Moreover, the Germans remained suspicious and somewhat sceptical of Britain and British intentions. It was difficult to establish any particular reason for this attitude. It was more a general state of mind. Wilson agreed that German suspicions tended to go beyond the facts.

Monnet said that too much importance should not be attached to the French economic measures. The only reason why de Gaulle and Couve de Murville (who, after a brief spell as Finance Minister had become Prime Minister following the elections) supported the Common Market was because they both believed that a return to protectionism would be the worst thing that could happen to France. The French Government had been obliged to take the steps in order not to be overwhelmed by the recent crisis. But he was confident the measures would not last long. Wilson commented that it was difficult to believe that Couve would pursue any policies other than those dictated to him by de Gaulle. Monnet agreed. Indeed, the reason why Pompidou had been dismissed as Prime Minister after the election was precisely because he had been gradually becoming an independent centre of power and this had become intolerable to de Gaulle.[70]

At lunch with Palliser on the same day, Monnet waxed gloomy about Germany. He felt that time was gradually running out for Germany. It had been paradoxically of great value to the West and to Europe that all the men in charge of German affairs, politicians as well as officials, during the past fifteen years had been themselves involved in the last war. But they were gradually giving way to a younger generation who had either not known the war at all or had been children during it. The present generation understood, even if they resented, the attitude of veiled superiority, if not downright hostility, towards Germany which continued to characterise both the French and the British approach to Germany. But the new generation could not understand it and thus resented it even more than their elders. They would not come to power until the election following the 1969 election. But if there had not been by that time a fairly radical transformation in the attitude towards Germany of her leading Western partners, Monnet foresaw a major upsurge of potentially dangerous nationalism in Germany at the time of that subsequent election.[71]

Wilson and Stewart were due to meet on 20 July to discuss European policy. What Stewart had in mind was essentially, so Palliser told Wilson, a diplomatic campaign "to protect and cover our economic position, while also preserving our political and economic future in Europe". Palliser thought Stewart's approach was basically sound but "lacking a certain dynamic". Palliser thought that, unattractive though the prospect might be, given that he would not be the favourite personal contact of either Palliser or Wilson, it might be time for another meeting between the PM and the German Chancellor. Wilson assented to both propositions, and doubtless to Palliser's conclusion that "the plant of continental confidence in Britain's choice of the European option is still very tender and needs a lot of watering. If I may put it that way, no one can water it more effectively than you!"[72]

When they met the next day, Wilson said that he agreed with what he understood to be Stewart's view, namely that Britain's application for full membership remained on the table, and there was no weakening in it, but that in the meantime the Government should not indulge in any gimmicks. Stewart agreed while pointing out that if Harmel's idea of cooperation within WEU surfaced in more concrete form in September the Government would have to respond. Wilson agreed. We should do nothing to discourage Harmel's efforts. But he also thought that Kiesinger needed some attention, probably in the form of a meeting in October or November, following Kiesinger's meeting with de Gaulle in September.

Stewart expressed concern at the growing scepticism in Europe at the Government's technological initiative i.e. the proposal to establish a European Technological Centre. The Government's decision in April drastically to curtail their involvement in the European Space programmes had "much disturbed" Britain's European partners. Wilson said that it had always been clear that, in speaking of a British technological initiative, the Government were not referring to costly cooperative ventures in space. Stewart agreed but, he added, the technological initiative always seemed to change its shape when one tried to grapple with it. He and Wilson agreed that the project of a technological centre also seemed to be running into difficulties.[73]

Preoccupied as the Government was with the fate of its European policy, it had other foreign policy concerns as well. They were summed up in a candid brief prepared by the Foreign Office for a meeting between the Prime Minister and John Freeman, a prominent and distinguished journalist and broadcaster, who had been appointed as British Ambassador to the United States. "The United States", the Foreign Office wrote. "is our most important friend, ally and trading partner. At the same time, America represents a danger to us in some fields, particularly through its ability to dominate technological research and development, to compete in overseas markets and to use its commercial power to take over British industries. We no longer consider that our relations with the United States have a 'special' character. This phrase, coined after the last war, really referred to the relationship resulting from the Anglo-American monopoly of that time. The phrase is harmful in the context of our application to join the Common Market. The Americans themselves do not set store by it. In fact there has been a recent tendency in the US regretfully to write Britain off because we seem to them to be failing to fulfil our part in maintaining world stability in the defence and monetary fields . . . The Americans do not object to our plans to join Europe and many believe that a more united Europe (including the UK) would strengthen the Atlantic Alliance. But they deplore our withdrawals from East of Suez [and] . . . many Americans resent our unwillingness to support the war [in Vietnam]."[74]

Trouble was looming in Central Europe where, as Cabinet debated on 18 July, "the Soviet Union was clearly hoping to intimidate the present Czechoslovak Government or to promote its overthrow". If those tactics failed then, Cabinet concluded, the Soviet Government might use force. If they did so there could be no question of intervention by the Western powers and the case would probably be taken to the United Nations.[75]

A change of Ambassador in Washington from a career to a political appointee was about to be matched by a similar change in Paris as Christopher Soames, former Conservative Cabinet Minister, prepared to take over from Patrick Reilly.

Soames and Stewart were as big a contrast in background and personality as any two politicians could be. Soames was big, extrovert and wealthy, the owner of two race horses, a large cellar of fine wine, a Bentley as his private car. He was completely un-bookish, but he was also smart, with an astute political brain and the ability to project himself as the powerful personality he was. As Churchill's son-in-law, and speaking good French from his time as junior Defence Attaché in the Embassy after the war, he was well placed to make his mark in France. And he did. When he walked into a room he filled it. People stopped what they were doing to pay attention. When his official Rolls Royce stopped at traffic lights in the Paris streets, people would come up wanting to shake his hand. He and Mary Soames made the Embassy a place where leading French men and women wanted to be seen.

Stewart was a true son of the Labour Party, intellectual, quiet, superficially unimpressive, speaking with something of a lisp, cautious where Soames was bold. Two men of such contrasting backgrounds and temperaments might have hit it off. They did not, and the reasons were as much of substance as of personality.

The first sign of difference came in a minute which Soames wrote to Stewart on 24 July, called 'Britain and Europe'. It was now evident, Soames wrote, that Britain was not going to succeed in battering her way into the EEC in the teeth of French opposition, even with the help of her friends. The Germans were determined not to antagonise the French and no other Member State had the strength, even if they had the will, to force the issue. These facts in turn led Soames to conclude that it would be pointless to expect any early negotiation to flow from the British application until, for one reason or another, there was a change of heart on the part of the French Government. While it was fashionable to think that de Gaulle would retire before long, there was no evidence to that effect. So, if Britain could not become a *de jure* member of the EEC then, Soames advised, she should at least seek to become a member *de facto* in as many ways as were practical. In Soames's view there was some substance in de Gaulle's assertion that Britain could pursue more European-oriented policies, and there were three promising policy areas where she could do so: monetary, defence (where Soames hoped that nuclear matters would not be excluded) and technology, including both civil and military procurement. Was it impossible to conceive of a British initiative to try to arrive at a European view on international monetary matters? Old men – especially de Gaulle – did not change their fundamental beliefs. But if Britain took initiatives which were demonstrably and irrevocably European it would be possible to face de Gaulle with the dilemma of appearing to turn down every idea and initiative aimed at a European voice, or of going along. "At all events", Soames concluded, "I am convinced that HMG's European policy should be for itself to seek to outflank French resistance rather than to use others, who anyway lack the strength, to meet it head on".[76]

This was not what the Foreign Office wanted to hear, and they duly prepared for the Prime Minister a brief for a meeting between him and Soames which, as Palliser put it, was "a little discouraging and governessy". For an eager political animal, to whom the Government had just offered a challenging Embassy, the tone was exactly the wrong one to use. Fundamentally, Palliser advised, Soames was right in aiming to pursue policies which would confront France with the awkward choice of turning something down and appearing to be un-European, or of accepting it even if it was unwelcome. Of course Soames would find the French difficult to pin down in this way because they were canny fighters. But the objective was the right one. The Foreign Office note ticked Soames off, by implication, for considering Britain's European policy 'too exclusively in terms of Anglo-French relations'. But Palliser, by contrast, detected in Soames's minute to Stewart a feeling (which he had doubtless picked up from his talks with officials and Ministers in the Foreign Office) that European policy was considered in the FO too exclusively in terms of getting the Five to beat France into submission which the Five would never do.[77]

When Soames and the Prime Minister met on 30 July, Wilson was sympathetic to Soames's proposed approach. Wilson agreed that there might be openings for fresh British initiatives, possibly in the monetary field, during the next six months. He did not rule out the long term concept of a fully European currency. Britain would be prepared to move at least as fast in this respect as anyone else in Europe. But in the shorter term he thought that any steps in the currency field would essentially be pragmatic ones. In any event any initiatives taken by Britain should have real substance and not merely be gimmicks. At present, Wilson told Soames, the Government were responding positively to, for example, the Benelux proposals. But this simply meant that we were marking time while facing in the right direction.

Soames referred to the suggestion in his minute that Britain might take the initiative toward a more specifically European component of the Western defence system. Here Wilson was more sceptical. It was not clear what this might mean. Nor would it necessarily commend itself to the French Government whose purpose seemed to be to disengage from the Western system of defence as far as was possible. De Gaulle had displayed no more than a passing glimmer of interest in the nuclear aspects of defence and had certainly never said anything to suggest that an Anglo-French cooperative effort in the military nuclear field would either be welcome to France or facilitate British membership of the EEC. On the other hand, Wilson did think that there should be considerable potential for cooperation in the civil nuclear field and particularly in the production of enriched uranium.

Soames sought Wilson's views on the public stance he would take. He would naturally take the utmost care over his public utterances but he hoped it would not be misunderstood if, for example, he tended on occasion to indicate the need for greater independence by Britain from the United States – more particularly since he was personally convinced of the need for this, especially, for example, in monetary matters. Wilson agreed. He had himself referred in his Strasbourg speech in January 1967 to the danger of Europe becoming industrial helots of the Americans. Any speech by the British Ambassador in Paris would tend to attract attention and, if it expounded the Government's European policy, was liable to be criticised in Parliament and elsewhere by the opponents of that policy. This did not cause him concern.[78]

Soames's conclusion that French policy was unlikely to change while de Gaulle remained in power was swiftly confirmed. When the EC Council of Ministers met on 30 July Michel Debré made his first appearance as the new French Foreign Minister. He was very friendly, a big contrast to his predecessor. But French policy on Europe had not changed. The only change, so Davignon (Harmel's Chef de

Cabinet) told the British Ambassador in Brussels, was in the arguments Debré had deployed. Where Couve had maintained that it was for economic and financial reasons that Britain was not fit for membership, Debré had taken his stand on the position that the adhesion of the United Kingdom and the other applicants would fundamentally change the nature of the Communities and France was opposed to this. It had also been clear that the French were not interested in the German ideas for a trade arrangement with the candidate countries and Davignon thought that the proposition was effectively dead.

Davignon added that Debré had spoken in very bitter terms about the British attitude to European space projects and CERN. He claimed that he had himself with great difficulty persuaded the General to go along with the CERN project and now the British had let him down.[79]

Then, as Western Europe snoozed on its August beaches, Soviet tanks rolled into Prague, brutally suppressing the Prague Spring in what Downing Street, in a statement of 21 August called "a flagrant violation of the UN Charter and of all accepted standards of international behaviour. This is a tragedy not only for Czechoslovakia but for Europe and the whole world". Cabinet was called for the following day and Parliament was recalled for 26 August.[80]

When Wilson discussed the crisis with the Foreign and Defence Secretaries on 22 August, Healey argued that the first reaction of the United States suggested that the Americans might be a bit more cool in their reaction to the invasion than the Europeans and that, if there were such a difference of emphasis, Britain should be on the side of the Europeans. Wilson showed some sympathy for this view and anyway thought that the Government should consider whether the crisis did not give the Government an opportunity to get a little closer to France and possibly to advance thereby Britain's broad European policy. Wilson acknowledged that the initial reaction of the French Government, in a statement issued on de Gaulle's clear authority, was fairly objectionable (it attributed ultimate responsibility for the Soviet invasion to the Yalta Agreement). But there had been other indications of a possible French willingness to work more closely with Britain in handling the crisis.[81]

Wilson reverted to the idea of getting closer to the French when he and Stewart met later in the day. Wilson thought there might be advantage in his sending a personal message about Czechoslovakia to de Gaulle who was now witnessing the breakdown of his Eastern policy. While, Wilson said, he had no illusions about de Gaulle's general attitude, there might be some small benefit to be gained from indicating to him, at a time when his prestige, both internally and externally, had suffered a series of heavy blows, that the British Government attached importance to his views on a matter of European concern and that we were not simply in cahoots with the Americans about it. Clearly, Wilson thought, the prospect of de Gaulle doing any serious rethinking of his European policy must be regarded as extremely remote. But if recent events were causing any such reconsideration, a gesture in the European context by Britain might conceivably be of some value. The Prime Minister also commented that at least one useful dividend of the crisis should surely be to make de Gaulle realise (even if he would not admit it) the need for a strong NATO. This could be important in the context of a possible French withdrawal from the Alliance in 1969.

The Foreign Secretary advised the Prime Minister the following day that "at a time when General de Gaulle has clearly suffered the reversal of so many of his hopes it might seem patronising for these to be rubbed into him quite so quickly". Wilson accepted the advice and no message was sent.[82]

A revealing insight into de Gaulle's general thinking was given on 26 August to Patrick Reilly when Reilly paid his farewell call on Maurice Schumann who, in the post-election reshuffle, had been appointed Minister for Participation i.e. social affairs. Reilly had known Schumann well for a long time and Schumann talked freely. Reilly said that he saw no prospect of British accession to the EEC while de Gaulle remained President which, Reilly assumed, barring accidents, he would do at least to the end of his existing mandate. Schumann replied that he was not so sure. After 30 June, Pompidou had shown him a letter which he had written to the General (not a very modest letter, Schumann added) in which Pompidou had referred to a conversation in which the General had told him that he regarded him as his successor. Pompidou had said that in these circumstances, he thought it would be best for him to withdraw from the Prime Ministership in order to be available for the Presidency when the need arose. Schumann said that the General did not reply to this letter, at least for some time; but he did discuss it with those people to whom Pompidou had, with de Gaulle's knowledge, shown it, including of course Schumann himself. De Gaulle had said that the position about a Presidential election had now changed, since the Opposition had no valid candidate and the Gaullists had, in Pompidou, a candidate who was bound to win. De Gaulle apparently regarded this as an argument for allowing Pompidou to leave the Prime Ministership and reserve himself for the Presidency in due course. Schumann had said in reply that there was no reason why de Gaulle should not go on as President for a long time, and had quoted the example of Dr Adenauer. De Gaulle had replied that he was inclined to think it unlikely that he would live to complete his mandate. It was true that he felt fine at present, but his family were not long-lived and his brother had died suddenly here (presumably at the Elysée). De Gaulle had then added that if something could be achieved over 'participation', the job with which Schumann was now tasked, then that would make rather a good moment to retire. Schumann commented that of course this language did not mean that, when it came to the point, de Gaulle would in fact decide to withdraw before the end of his mandate. It did, however, show that he was giving thought to the possibility.[83]

Reilly called next on Debré, the new Foreign Minister. Debré reiterated what he had said to his EEC colleagues a month earlier: the entry of Britain would mean that of Denmark, Norway and Ireland and, in time that of Spain, and perhaps even Sweden. The EEC would become something quite different. He had nothing against this personally, since he was no ardent champion of the EEC. The fact remained that such an extension of the EEC would mean major changes in its policies. Therefore, his view was that before enlargement of the EEC could be considered, the Six should agree among themselves on all outstanding matters:

agricultural, transport, energy, fiscal policy etc. A common fiscal policy was essential. There would be no Common Market without one. The adoption of the value added tax throughout the Community was indispensable.

Reilly responded that the British Government did not believe that the changes necessitated by enlargement need go nearly as far as M. Debré seemed to think. Debré brushed this aside. The present discussions were not serious. The only way to make progress was for the Six to take among themselves all the decisions on common policies which were now outstanding. Reilly said that he must therefore conclude with sadness that, as he left France, there was no prospect of early progress with the British candidature. Debré did not reply but, Reilly thought, "his whole attitude indicated that I was right".[84]

Debré was enunciating what was to become a subtle but significant change in French policy, one that was to be pursued by Pompidou when he eventually became President. At the time, not surprisingly, this was far from clear and it looked to the British as if, just as they had feared, as one set of arguments against their membership was knocked down, so another hurdle was erected in its place.

The Foreign Secretary said as much the following day to the French Ambassador in London, Geoffroy de Courcel. Courcel had, perhaps rashly, asked for an interview in order to learn the Foreign Secretary's views before returning to Paris where he would be seeing Debré.

Stewart told Courcel, one of the best qualified and least liked of the Ambassadors France has sent to London since World War II, that when he had talked to the previous French Foreign Minister it had seemed clear that the great French objection to opening negotiations had lain in the British economic situation. M. Couve de Murville had said that it would be clear enough when the time came that the objection had been removed, and then negotiations could begin. Now, however, M. Debré seemed to be raising a quite new point, namely that the Community must settle its own internal policy problems before there could be any question of enlargement. The special mention Debré had made to Reilly of fiscal issues, meaning that all members must introduce the Value Added Tax, seemed to be imposing yet another new condition. Since, as General de Gaulle himself had said, the EEC was a dynamic organisation, and there would always therefore be outstanding problems, then it seemed that those problems could always be made into a reason for delaying negotiations with new applicants.

Courcel said that there must be a limit to enlargement. Four applicants was enough already. But the French had always said that Europe would be better balanced with the United Kingdom in. Stewart said that the Czech crisis had surely underlined the need for British entry: here was a way of strengthening Europe without offending French susceptibilities about military talks. Courcel said this was no doubt true, but the economic difficulties were formidable.[85]

French tactics were uppermost in the Foreign Secretary's mind when, later on the same day, he met the Dutch Foreign Minister, Joseph Luns, one of Britain's staunchest and most outspoken supporters. Stewart told Luns that the French were using one argument after another to prevent British entry. There were two possible reactions to this. One was to despair, which would be wrong. The other was to find a stronger position, ready for the time when the tide turned and the French were no longer set on disrupting the Community. The biggest single factor, Stewart thought, was the attitude of the Germans. He did not doubt that they wanted to see the Community enlarged but if they were forced to choose between helping Britain or pleasing the French, they would always decide to please the French.

Luns said that he agreed entirely with Stewart's analysis. Kiesinger would not be willing to have a row with France. He had told Kiesinger and Brandt that he was astonished that a small country like the Netherlands could take a strong line with France and still maintain good bilateral relations whereas Germany apparently could not. The Germans explained it by blaming the division of Germany. Luns expected Kiesinger soon to press for a new initiative among the Six consisting of regular meetings to exchange views on political subjects (i.e. going beyond those matters which were Community issues as such). The Netherlands would reject such a proposal. Luns also had some reservations about Harmel's idea of using WEU as a vehicle for discussion. He did not think that using WEU would achieve very much. The Dutch wanted to stick to the Benelux proposals but the Germans disliked them, the Italians were wavering and the Belgians were looking for ways out.

Stewart said he was very appreciative of all Luns's efforts to help and was particularly glad to hear of the Dutch reaction to Kiesinger's proposals for political consultations among the Six. Luns said that about a fortnight previously, the Germans had proposed a meeting of the Six to discuss the crisis in Biafra. The Dutch had replied that, if the Six were going to discuss Biafra then the British and Scandinavians should be there. That had killed the idea. Luns had recently asked Brandt if there was any point in the Netherlands maintaining an Embassy in Bonn since all the decisions were taken in Paris.[86]

As far as those decisions taken in Paris were concerned, it was more than clear that there was no visible shift in French policy. The Italians claimed to find Debré even more intransigent than his predecessor, Couve de Murville. Debré had told the Italian Foreign Minister that he was not prepared to have any substantive discussion of British accession until the British Government had put their economic house in order and until they showed greater independence of the United States and became more European-minded; nor was it good enough for Britain to accept the Treaty of Rome as it stood. The Community had gone beyond the Treaty of Rome during the last ten years and what the Six had built, e.g. the Common Agricultural Policy (CAP) should be accepted by new entrants as far as possible without modification. Debré had ended by telling Medici that he would take an equally negative line with Brandt and Harmel.[87]

On 9 September, de Gaulle gave a press conference which demonstrated that his world view was, if anything, more entrenched than ever. Harking back to France's exclusion from Yalta, the result, he said, of an understanding reached between Washington and Moscow, de Gaulle said that he could not accept that the fate of Europe should in effect be decided in the absence of Europe. Since his return to power in 1958 he had not ceased to labour to put an end to the regime of two blocs. "It is for this reason", de Gaulle continued, " that, whilst maintaining close relations with all west European countries and even transforming our old hostility towards Germany into cordial cooperation, we have progressively detached ourselves from the NATO military organisation in which Europeans are subordinated to Americans. It is for this reason that, whilst taking part in the Common Market, we have never agreed to a supra-national system for the Six which would submerge France in an organisation without a national identity whose only policies would be those transmitted to it from across the ocean. So also, the same desire to avoid the risk of Atlantic absorption is one of the reasons which has so far caused us to postpone, to our great regret, the entry of Britain into the present Community".[88]

On 12 September, Wilson discussed with Stewart the ideas for the conduct of European policy which Soames had put in his minute to the Foreign Secretary, the centre piece of which was, as Wilson himself had put it, that "while we continue to invest the Citadel, we should also consider a number of outflanking initiatives: political, monetary, technological, civil, nuclear etc."[89]

Wilson reverted to his metaphor with Stewart. We should continue to invest the Citadel. In other words, we were standing at the main gate awaiting entry. Our application for entry was in and remained in. That was the centre piece of the Government's European policy. But the Government should be considering what other possible initiatives it could take. These should not of course be presented as in any way directed against France, or indeed as other than designed to include France within their ambit. But, given de Gaulle's attitude, they should be designed, not only to increase his isolation but also to help ensure that the potential resistance to British entry by the post-de Gaulle regime in France should have been weakened as far as possible beforehand. If de Gaulle were succeeded by a Pompidou or a Debré there must, on present form, be a risk of a further period of veto. The Government's purpose should be to pursue initiatives designed to lessen that risk.

Wilson was clear that not much progress could be made at present on the technological front but the Government should perhaps consider taking a more positive attitude on the political front. He had been considering, in this context, whether the Government might not try to launch the Fouchet Plan again in some form. He realised that this plan for inter-governmental cooperation in foreign and defence policy had in the past not had much appeal to certain of France's partners, such as the Benelux countries. But so many of their hopes had been disappointed since the Fouchet Plan that they might now welcome something on those lines on British initiative. Moreover, the advantage of an approach of this kind would be that it would be logically very difficult for de Gaulle to oppose it. Overall, Wilson said he was impressed by the need for some fresh political impetus to be given to Britain's European approach so as to outflank the embattled positions, such as the Benelux ploy which, while valuable, had not so far led to much progress.

Stewart agreed that the Government had to recognise that Britain could not join the EEC as long as de Gaulle remained in power, and that she might not be able to do so until some time after his disappearance from the scene. Equally, the more the Government succeeded in emphasising how ridiculous de Gaulle's policies and opposition were, in the general context of European interests, the more difficult it might be for a successor regime to adopt an equally rigid line.

Wilson noted that Kiesinger's attitude seemed to have evolved in the light of the Czech situation. Kiesinger was concerned about the likely attitude of the Americans and, as a result, more convinced than before of the case for a stronger form of political cooperation in Europe, including Britain. Wilson and Stewart agreed that a meeting with Kiesinger would now be timely. It would be desirable to try to get the Germans to realise how little their special relationship with France was helping their policy towards the Soviet Union and Eastern Europe.

Stewart referred to his own recent visit to Romania where he had earlier reported that he had "found Ceausescu himself a less impressive figure than I had expected . . . He is no latter-day Tito. He is first and foremost a party boss. His speech is peppered with well-worn Communist generalisations which he gives every impression of believing; and when, in discussion, he found himself on weak ground he tended to retreat behind a dialectical smokescreen."[90] Now, Stewart said that he would arrange for the Germans to be given an account of his talks in Romania about the German problem and would underline to them that de Gaulle's visit to Romania and his allegedly close relationship with the Romanians had had no effect at all on the Romanians' excessively hard line towards Germany.

Wilson thought that, in addition to the political field, there might be scope for action in the monetary field. He had always regretted what he regarded as the premature winding up of the European Payments Union (EPU) and he remained of the view that some EPU-type arrangement could be helpful now. There might be a widening of the Bank for International Settlements. Stewart noted that Soames had talked in terms of a united Europe taking over from Britain the reserve currency function of sterling. Wilson said that this had now been done to some extent through the recent Basle agreement. It had been noticeable that the French attitude to Basle had been relatively satisfactory. He thought that there were possibilities of progress in this area which should be considered.[91]

It might be thought that such a clear indication of direction from the Prime Minister would have led to at least a shift in compass direction on the part of the Foreign Office. But the story of the next several months was one in which all the key players (Britain, Germany and France) stuck closely to their preferred scripts.

The French were predictably the most consistent. Reilly paid his farewell call on de Gaulle on 10 September. De Gaulle was, in personal terms, characteristically courteous, commending Reilly for the work he had done in Paris and acknowledging that "much that had been dreamed of and much that Reilly himself had desired had not been achieved". Nonetheless, de Gaulle claimed, Britain and France had never been so close as they were now and he cited the Jaguar and Concorde projects and the prospect of Airbus and the Channel Tunnel in evidence. "Of course there was the Common Market", de Gaulle added, with an expression and gesture as if this was a matter of secondary importance. It was economic, he said, as if that counted for little. He knew, of course, that the British bore France "a small grudge over the Common Market affair", but he indicated that he thought the British would get over it in time. Whatever the differences between the two countries, there were many important matters where they agreed such as Czechoslovakia where they had acted together.

Reilly felt bound to say that the Common Market difficulty was not something that could be easily dismissed. It was a much graver affair than the President seemed to realise. After all, what was at stake was not just the Common Market. It was Europe. It was the future. The fact was that the future was blocked. Reilly recalled that de Gaulle had referred in his most recent press conference to what he had called the risk of Atlantic absorption. Reilly had, he said, never really been able to follow the President's thinking on this issue, nor what exactly he was asking of Britain. What was the criterion by which he would judge that the British had reached a point at which they were qualified to enter the Common Market?

De Gaulle replied that his criterion was that Britain should follow a policy that was really European. For instance, in monetary affairs it was not right that either France or Britain should have a currency that was tied to the dollar. Britain had a currency that was still threatened. France had one that was not as strong as it had been, but it was free of the dollar. Britain's was not because it was a reserve currency. Then there was the military field. In all sorts of ways Britain was tied to the Americans. Then in foreign policy, to take the Middle East, he knew that the British really agreed with France "that the Jews were going much too far and needed a lesson"; but the British would not say so because of the Americans. Then in Europe, if Britain came into the Common Market, she would bring the Americans with her. It was difficult enough already to keep the Germans, the Italians and Benelux under proper control. If Britain came in too with her present policies Europe would be submerged. Of course, if Britain and France could agree, that would be quite different. Britain and France were the only two countries that counted. But, alas, they did not agree.

Reilly, choosing his words with exquisite care, said that the General's conception of a European policy seemed to him to be very special. It was essentially the policy of France. It was not the policy of France's partners. De Gaulle agreed but dismissed Reilly's point as irrelevant. The "poor Germans", he said, had no alternative but to look to the Americans. As for the Italians, they were little better. Wagging his finger at Reilly, de Gaulle said that Britain was quite capable of doing what was needed if she wished to. He had sometimes thought that the British were going to take the necessary decisions. Mr Eden was the person who had come nearest to doing so. Just once or twice, Mr Macmillan too had seemed on the brink. Even Mr Wilson had seemed to catch a glimpse of what was needed. When it came to the point of action, however, the British Government never took it.

Reilly said that, even if Britain did what the General was asking in the political field, which he was bound to say he believed to be impossible, he could also not help fearing that Britain would then find that all the economic difficulties would again be raised. De Gaulle said that it was of course true that there were still real economic difficulties but he made it clear that he considered the essential point was that Britain should take the right political decisions.

Reilly said that there seemed to him to be a contradiction in French policy. France wanted Britain to come nearer to Europe. Yet, all the time, French policy pushed Britain further away. De Gaulle admitted this. But there was a contradiction in British policy too. The British said that they wanted to come into Europe but never did what was necessary to make this possible. One should never make a foreign policy to please public opinion. The right course was to adopt the right policy. Public opinion would then follow.[92]

On 12 September Debré gave a speech at the UDR Party Conference in which he restated the French Government's view. Enlargement would not be a question of moving from the Europe of Six to the Europe of seven but to ten or twelve. France would not jeopardise the effort it had made towards European independence while she did not feel that the will existed on the part of the applicants to accept a common policy.[93]

The *Financial Times* reported Debré's speech with the comment that it had made clear that the French Government remained as opposed as ever to Britain joining the Common Market. Indeed, the paper thought that the prominence given to the claim that Britain might threaten the Continent's independence seemed to confirm that the Czechoslovakian crisis had made de Gaulle even less inclined than ever to see the Common Market enlarged or reinforced.[94]

Some days later, in answer to questions at a Diplomatic Press Association lunch, Debré went even further. He said that France's conception of the organisation of the Common Market was not that of the Treaty of Rome, with its political ideology which France rejected. It must, rather, be conceived as a large economic whole with, in addition, an orientation towards European political independence. Consequently, the move to 10 or 12 members posed the question whether such a move was aimed at achieving such complete independence. France would not allow the substance to be abandoned for the shadow or allow centrifugal forces to disperse what had been laboriously put together. To pass from six states to ten or twelve would at present be a leap into the unknown in which all that had been achieved would risk being destroyed. France had no objection to the study of enlargement but that could only be done at Six and by unanimous agreement and would take many months. Debré also cast doubt on whether British membership of the EEC would help Europe to achieve technological independence, implying that Britain was too dependent on American technology.

In reporting the speech and questions, the Paris Embassy noted that the line was even harder than before. In particular, Debré's statement that the risks in enlarging the Community were so great that no-one should desire it, directly contradicted the Franco-German Declaration of 16 February, as well as the Treaty of Rome. The statement that France rejected the political ideology of the Treaty of Rome was blunter than anything said even by de Gaulle in public.

"If there were any doubts about the French Government's continuing hostility towards British membership of the Common Market they were laid to rest today by M. Michel Debré", wrote Paul Lewis of the Financial Times.[95]

The next day, the Embassy in Paris reported that the official version of Debré's replies at the previous day's luncheon, issued by the Foreign Ministry, omitted altogether the comment by Debré (reported by *The Times* and heard by the Embassy's own staff member who was also present) that Britain's involvement with American technology would constitute a hindrance to European technological independence.[96]

Wilson regarded Debré's criticisms on this score as "particularly impertinent" given the extensive dependence of France on American technology. He called for a list comparing British and French technological dependence on the United States[97] and deployed the arguments when he saw the Belgian Foreign Minister later on 18 September. Debré's utterances seemed, said Wilson, to have been harder, if that were possible, than those of his predecessor, though Wilson added, with characteristic perspicacity, that this was no doubt somewhat illusory and simply reflected the difference in temperament between the two men. Wilson said he sometimes wondered whether the French Government held a monthly competition for the best reason for keeping Britain out. This month's contribution certainly deserved no prize. After the previous arguments about the dangers of widening the Community and changing its nature, about the British economic position (on which during recent months the French had presumably been arguing with their tongue in their cheek) and about Britain's excessive Atlantic associations, Britain was now being told that her technology was too involved with that of America. But Britain at least had her own computer industry. France did not. Britain made her own aero-engines. France operated under American licence. When the French had competed with Britain in a tender for the generation of Belgian electricity by nuclear power, it had emerged that the French were committed to an American system. The argument was sterile. What was needed were European arrangements that would enable Europe so far as possible to shake itself free of any such domination.[98]

On the following day, the Foreign Secretary summoned the French Chargé d'Affaires, M. André, to seek clarification of Debré's remarks, telling him that "one reason was being put forward after another why we should not enter the Community and why it should not be enlarged. This seemed to be a tragedy when events in Eastern Europe had shown so clearly the need for closer cooperation in Western Europe. I deeply regretted the estrangement this caused in our relations".[99]

This remonstration, extremely mild even by the generally civil standards of diplomacy, produced a characteristic French response. "If this offensive", wrote the London correspondent of *Le Figaro*, "is typical of British diplomacy in preparation for 'après-Gaullism' the task of Christopher Soames will not be made any easier".[100]

So far as Germany was concerned, on 26 September Wilson sent a message to Chancellor Kiesinger designed, in the words of the Foreign Secretary, to encourage "the Chancellor to conclude that, if he cannot make progress towards wider integration with the French, he should seek the means of making progress without them".

Wilson's message was calculated to flatter. It expressed admiration for the steadfast attitude which Kiesinger had taken throughout the crisis "precipitated by the Soviet Union's brutal intervention in Czechoslovakia". It went on to say how the Prime Minister was "increasingly impressed with the fundamental identity of views between our two Governments" and their close agreement on the lessons which Western Europe must draw from those events. Britain, Germany and their partners should now be seen to take a broader look at the problems of Europe so as to seize the psychological opportunity which the Czechoslovak crisis had undoubtedly created for giving a firm impulse to the move for greater unity. If arrangements in which unanimity was essential proved impossible because of the reluctance of one country, then it would be necessary to move onto other proposals where participation of all members of the Community was not essential. Wilson hoped that Kiesinger would take the opportunity of his forthcoming meeting to explain to de Gaulle the dangers of allowing the present impasse to continue.[101]

The prospects appeared, briefly, to be relatively bright. When the EEC Council of Ministers met on 27 September there was "an impressive display of cohesion among the Four and, eventually, of unity on the part of the Five which forced Debré to deny categorically that there was any French willingness to admit a link between enlargement of the Community and its internal development or, consequently, to allow the proposed commercial arrangement, arising from the Franco-German declaration, to be seen in the context of accession. It was, according to the British delegation in Brussels, perhaps too early to say that the commercial arrangement was now dead but the discussion had at least enabled Brandt to return to Bonn before the Kiesinger/De Gaulle meeting with a clear picture of the extent of French opposition to German ideas on the trade arrangement.[102]

When, however, the new British Ambassador in Bonn, Sir Roger Jackling, delivered the Prime Minister's message to the German Chancellor, there was no detectable change in Kiesinger's approach. He was determined to pursue the goal of British accession. All the indications from Paris were that the French were still opposed. He was very conscious of the strength of public opinion in Germany on the issue but he was reluctant to contemplate pushing things to the point of a break with France.[103]

"I think", Wilson wrote in green ink on seeing Jackling's letter "we are being taken for a ride and I'm getting fed up with this a[rse] l[icking] attitude of ours".[104]

Reports of the meeting between Kiesinger and de Gaulle did nothing to dispel the doubts. On 28 September, the German Press Agency, reflecting joint Franco-German official guidance, issued a report which said that the German Chancellor had assured de Gaulle that the Federal Government would view a European policy without France as destructive for Europe. It was agreed, the Agency report went on, that the German and French Governments would seek to activate policy in Europe through what de Gaulle described as preferential cooperation. The two Governments would look again at a commercial arrangement with Britain, which might facilitate Britain's eventual accession even though France continued to oppose any automatic link between a commercial arrangement and British entry.

On German television, Kiesinger claimed that some progress had been made. Though the French attitude towards present British entry was unchanged, there

was scope for useful interim action. Kiesinger emphatically repeated his opposition to the view that Europe should be strengthened with Britain and Scandinavia
even if France would not cooperate: Europe could only be built with France. It
was left to the leader of the FDP, Hans-Dietrich Genscher, to comment that the
German Government must face the possibility of action for European unity
without France.[105]

Reporting from Paris bore out the view that once again France had prevailed
over Germany. The British Embassy suggested that before the Bonn meeting
Paris commentators had been unusually nervous about the outcome and were
speculating about what they described as a new tone of German self-confidence
discernible in recent Franco-German exchanges. Some commentators had
suggested that this was the moment when the French Government would be well
advised to take account of the views of the Five on British accession. But, the
Embassy now reported, the apparent success of de Gaulle in Bonn as well as
the brutal torpedoing by Debré of the latest German ideas to facilitate British
membership, had transformed the picture. The general impression conveyed by
the French Press was that de Gaulle had won yet another round over Kiesinger
whom he had successfully frightened into abandoning any attempt to speak up for
Britain. He had done this by a mixture of cajolery and threat and, most effectively
of all, by threatening to leave the Common Market if Germany ganged up with
her other EEC partners to work for British entry or for greater cooperation with
Britain. The only note of reserve was struck by *Le Monde* whose editorial concluded
that grievances were piling up against France among the German public and
parliamentarians and that these would "prevent a true flowering of Franco-
German cooperation".[106]

Wilson commented on this telegram: "See my note on previous telegram (in
fact the Jackling letter). In view of their vulnerable position and early elections we
should start playing German politics".[107]

When Jackling called on the German Foreign Minister on the evening of
30 September he found Brandt, as he reported by telegram that night, "most
disturbed" as, he said, was Kiesinger, by the tone of the Press coverage of the talks
with de Gaulle. ("I bet they are" wrote Palliser in the margin of the telegram,
eliciting from Wilson the response: "Yes. Why don't we start putting the fear of
God into Kiesinger? We could.")

Brandt said he had never seen Kiesinger so upset by Press reactions and the
way his remarks had been taken out of context. The Chancellor had, for example,
said something to the effect that Europe without France was unthinkable. This
had been interpreted as meaning that the Federal Government would only move
in agreement with France. In fact, the Chancellor had used this phrase in the
same sense as it he had said that Europe could not be built without England.
(Marginal comment from Palliser: 'Why not say so then?'). Brandt had sought to
assure Jackling that the meeting had not changed anything very much and that
Kiesinger had "spoken very firmly indeed to General de Gaulle on the need for
progress in Europe". Brandt admitted that de Gaulle had indeed implied that
France might withdraw from the EEC, although Brandt professed not to believe

it and intimated that the threat had had no influence on the talks. Nonetheless, Germany must continue to try to work with France. Geography and history, and the ties developed between the two peoples, made this necessary.

Jackling told Brandt that the reports of the Franco-German meeting were bound to give the impression that the Federal Government placed their concern for Europe and the Alliance in a position secondary to that of their relations with France. Brandt, unsurprisingly, assured him that this was a complete misunderstanding.[108]

When a telegram from the British Embassy in Luxembourg arrived in Downing Street, reporting commentators there as thinking that any change in the situation was unlikely while Kiesinger and de Gaulle remained in power, Wilson commented: "Yes. Why should they?"[109]

An account of the Bonn meeting given to the Minister in the British Embassy in Paris, Bernard Ledwidge, by Beaumarchais, the French Political Director, confirmed the Press accounts even though Beaumarchais claimed that they had been too dramatic. The question of enlargement had not been discussed in detail because Debré had already just made clear continued French opposition to it. At the plenary session of the talks Kiesinger had volunteered that he ruled out schemes for cooperation involving the Five without France. This had prompted President de Gaulle's remarks in his reply to the effect that without France there could be no European Community and that France could live without the Community if necessary, although she would regret its break-up. Beaumarchais confirmed that the French Government stood by the Franco-German Declaration of 16 February and were still ready to consider terms of a strictly commercial arrangement between the EEC and applicant countries.[110]

Jackling too, in Bonn, in drawing together the threads of reports and impressions of de Gaulle's visit there, concluded that there had been some movement backwards in that the Germans had reverted by implication to the French thesis underlying the Franco-German Joint Declaration, namely that despite the impossibility of enlarging the Communities, the work of strengthening the Community must go forward and that the only satisfactory basis for that was the closest possible Franco-German collaboration in all fields. In Jackling's view, German professions that they were encouraged by the French confirmation of the declaration lacked conviction. In his talks with de Gaulle, and subsequently, Kiesinger had emphasised the priority which the relationship with France enjoyed in German policy making, the impossibility of building Europe without France and the danger of, as well as his personal opposition to, any action directed against France. The Chancellor had, said Jackling, been at pains to explain that his remarks did not imply that he refused to take any step forward without France but he had certainly given that impression. There was a growing body of German opinion which felt that some willingness to progress without France must be demonstrated if any progress was in fact to be made. The German Press had been extremely critical and, whilst this was unlikely to have any effect on Kiesinger's policy, it would affect the political parties who were getting increasingly election-conscious. There were important groups within the two coalition parties which were calling for a clearer definition of the Government's European policy over the whole field and were critical of the impression which Kiesinger had given of selling out to the French. Jackling suspected that Brandt was personally sympathetic to that view.[111]

While there was no change in either French or German positions, which in practice tended to reinforce each other because greater French intransigence tended to produce greater German subservience, the question remained whether the British Government could adapt its polices in the way the Prime Minister and Foreign Secretary had agreed when they met on 12 September.

Inside the Foreign Office, the principal motivator of British European policy was the Head of the European Department, John Robinson, brilliant, robust to the point of roughness, single-minded and uncompromising. In a minute to Pat Hancock, the Under Secretary responsible for European policy, Robinson analysed the discussion between the Prime Minister and Foreign Secretary. The Prime Minister's views, Robinson believed, were very much those which officials in the Foreign Office had been advocating since the French veto. Two factors had, however, prevented the Government from building on the Benelux proposals. The first was Germany and the second was majority opinion in the Cabinet. At the end of January the Foreign Office had achieved a position within WEU where all present except the French had been prepared to envisage meetings to consider exactly the kind of consultation and cooperation the Benelux had proposed. But then, in mid-February, came de Gaulle's meeting with Kiesinger and, since that meeting, the Germans had been maintaining their preference for a trade arrangement. The Germans preferred this approach because it was their object to avoid having to make a choice between France and Britain. The German approach of a trade arrangement would never get anywhere and that in turn meant that it would never get the Germans to the point of trouble with France. Until it was possible to expose France's position in relation to the trade arrangement idea, Germany was not likely to contemplate action on the lines the Prime Minister was suggesting.

The Foreign Secretary, Robinson reminded his readers, had circulated to the European Committee a paper advocating the preparation of an initiative but it had got nowhere. Even the Chancellor of the Exchequer, Roy Jenkins, had not been prepared to support it. In the light of that reaction, the answer to the Prime Minister's latest suggestions must depend on a judgement of the likely reaction of other Ministers to a revival and intensification of the Government's European efforts. If they stood by their opposition of the previous May then a further meeting of the Ministerial Committee would only serve to limit the Foreign Secretary's freedom of manoeuvre and should therefore be avoided. If, on the other hand, Ministers were prepared to agree and prosecute vigorously action of the kind the Prime Minister was proposing – which was essentially the implementation of the Benelux proposals – then that was what the Foreign Office had been advocating since the end of 1967.

At present, Robinson argued, the Foreign Office was trying to develop the tactical position in the Community to the point where Germany would have to admit that France would not agree to anything worthwhile on trade arrangement lines. But that was a purely tactical operation. In substance, what was being attempted was to ask the Five to block the development of the Community, and to define its sphere of action as narrowly as possible so as to leave the widest possible field of cooperation with Britain. That would lead inevitably to confrontation with France. To succeed in getting the Five to that point, Britain would have to show that she was ready for action with them which would at least replace in importance for them what they hoped to get out of cooperation with France on a Six basis. To achieve that would involve showing readiness to lead in Europe in the direction of political union, and defence and technological coordination. The first two would involve some delay and limitation in practice on Britain's own actions. Technological coordination would involve Britain in having a greater regard for the views of other European countries on ELDO and CERN.[112]

Wilson's meeting with Stewart had demonstrated that he was willing to go quite a long way down a path which, if not that of political union, was certainly more daring than any trodden by any Government previously, notably in suggesting the revival of the Fouchet Plan as well as willingness to undertake far-reaching monetary cooperation. What is surprising is how little was done to follow up on what the Prime Minister had proposed. Maybe, in believing that the Prime Minister's suggestions were what the Foreign Office was doing anyway officials felt that no specific response was called for. Certainly, it was only after three months that the Foreign Office responded to the Prime Minister's suggestion for a revival of the Fouchet Plan and, even then, only after he had reminded them that they had failed to do so. But, even if there had been a more efficient response to the Prime Minister, the quandary identified by Robinson would have remained: detaching the Germans from the French sufficiently to allow for the Five to cooperate meaningfully was more about the fundamental German attitudes than about finding specific projects. In that respect, Robinson was right: what Wilson was suggesting was an evolution of the Benelux plan and the German Government had allowed themselves to be ridden off their support for that plan at the first whiff of a Franco-German alternative, even though it had become rapidly evident that the French had absolutely no intention of turning the Franco-German suggestions of a trade arrangement into an acceptable political reality.

Thus, in practice, what the Foreign Office did was to fall back on the Benelux plan even though they knew that it would not detach the Germans from the French and with the added factor, as Palliser warned Wilson in a minute of 4 October, that attachment to the Benelux plan carried the danger of "the Foreign Office tending to get again into a posture, in association with Benelux, of isolating the French and thereby inevitably isolating the Germans too. If we allow ourselves to go down this road, we shall progressively part company with Italy, Luxembourg and Belgium; and at the end of it only we and Joe Luns will be hand in hand. Not an adequate basis for a European policy".[113]

The Foreign Office were clear in their view that British ability to 'play German politics' as the Prime Minister had suggested was very limited indeed. The present position, the Foreign Office correctly analysed, was that the French were succeeding in frightening the Germans, and the British were not. The Germans were truly frightened of what de Gaulle might do to them if they stopped toeing his line: recognition of East Germany, withdrawal of troops from Germany, or even leaving the Common Market. Britain's ability to frighten the Germans would depend on threats or hints of threats to withdraw troops or to abandon the commitment to defend Berlin. But, the Foreign Office argued, it would be dangerous even to threaten such things. They would not be in the British interest and to threaten them would be a bluff which might be called. British troops were stationed in continental Europe not only to defend Germany, but to defend Britain. To recognise East Germany (a regime heartily disliked by Britain) or to withdraw from the commitment to the defence of Berlin would involve a big row with the rest of the Alliance, not least with the Americans.

So, the Foreign Office concluded, the only realistic pressure was to go on proposing, and even in some cases engaging in, forms of European cooperation which the Germans would have to reject because of French pressure. But Britain's first object should be to try and bring the Germans along, even though the indications of success were not particularly good. Of course, insofar as Britain possessed a big stick, the best person to wield it would be the Prime Minister when he went to Bonn in January.[114] The Prime Minister saw this letter and ticked it.

The Foreign Secretary was in New York at the UN General Assembly in mid-October and various contacts took place between the EEC Foreign Ministers, and with Stewart. Stewart, in a message to Wilson, said that it was clear to everyone except the Germans that the trade arrangement approach was dead. The Belgians were now proposing that there should be an exploration of the scope for closer cooperation on a European basis in foreign policy and defence. Denis Healey had had separate discussions with the German Defence Minister, Schroeder, which had revealed considerable reluctance on his part to consider multilateral talks on defence, whether inside or outside WEU. Kiesinger, however, to whom Healey had also spoken, had been much more forthcoming and had promised to speak to Schroeder accordingly.[115] Harmel believed he had Debré's assurance that France would not object to a procedural discussion when WEU Ministers met in Rome later in the month. But Debré had equally made it plain that he would oppose decisions of substance being taken at that meeting. Stewart drew the conclusion from all this that irritation with French obstruction was running high in the Five and he was, he said, in no doubt that the present was a favourable moment for Britain to resume a more active role in European affairs. [116]

For the Prime Minister, however, what was proposed was, as he said to Palliser, "not a great deal more than a minuet – albeit one that is moving us closer to our objective".

Wilson agreed with Palliser that, while the advice of the Foreign Office about the scope for pressure on the Germans was broadly right, there was a tendency to be a little too soft with the Germans. What Palliser had in mind was not kicking the Germans in the teeth but, rather, the exercise of political guile. Resurrection of the Fouchet Plan, as the Prime Minister had suggested, was part of that and Palliser had put the Foreign Office on notice that the Foreign Secretary should be briefed to speak on the subject when he next met the Prime Minister. Palliser expected the Foreign Office to pour some cold water on the idea. Equally, Palliser thought that the Foreign Office had failed to address, save by critical implication, the Prime Minister's suggestion that "we should start playing German politics". The problem was to create for Kiesinger a situation in which the attractions of snuggling up to de Gaulle were outweighed by the political criticism which built up within his own party as a result. That in turn meant exploiting the criticism and those who were doing the criticising. Palliser proposed inviting men like Strauss, Barzel, Birrenbach, Schroeder and other of the CDU/CSU top brass to visit Britain. The Government, not surprisingly, had better relations with the SPD than the CDU. Relations with the CDU should be strengthened so that people who sympathised with the British position could be infiltrated round Kiesinger. A senior Labour politician with good contacts in the CDU but outside Government should be used to take this forward. Now that the Labour Party had accepted Jean Monnet's invitation to join his Action Committee for Europe, greater use should be made of Monnet himself given his first-class contacts with the top Germans in politics, industry and the unions. With all this the Prime Minister agreed.[117]

Despite disturbing signs that the German Government were having second thoughts about their preparedness to cooperate within WEU if the French did not play ball, those fears were not borne out when Foreign Ministers of the WEU met in Rome on 21 October. As usual, the French Press contained the most detailed and tendentious reports, clearly based on official French Government briefing since *Le Figaro* and *Le Monde* gave virtually identical accounts. The atmosphere, the newspapers claimed, had been most unpleasant and France had been taken by surprise. There had been a clear conspiracy against France and an attempt to show her up once again as the obstacle to all progress. What Harmel had put forward in Rome had borne no resemblance to what had been agreed between him and Debré in New York. France had been confronted without warning with a cut and dried scheme containing three new elements – the creation of a special working group, the establishment of a permanent secretariat and the extension of collaboration to non-Member States of WEU. It was clear, the two newspapers reported, that the British and Dutch had worked on their Belgian colleague and *Le Monde* accused Stewart of conducting in the wings a policy of 'all or nothing' by hotting up the Harmel plan. France had offered a concession by being ready to agree to collaboration between Britain and the Six in the field of foreign policy and to a study of measures to be taken in this sense before the next WEU meeting. But there could be no question of using such suggestions as a means of circumventing decisions already taken in Brussels with regard to the enlargement of Europe, or of adulterating the projects for political cooperation between the Six.[118]

Needless to say, the British account of the meeting was somewhat different. "The French Delegation were throughout completely negative on substance and offensive in tone", wrote the Foreign Secretary in a telegram in his name sent from Rome. This had become clear at a meeting of officials on the Sunday night when the French had accused the Belgians of bad faith and objected to their proposals. The bad atmosphere had continued, uninfluenced by successive attempts by Belgium and Germany to make things easier for France. At the end, the summing up by Medici, the Italian Chairman, had fully exposed the French responsibility for the outcome. So resentful were the other delegations that they had been willing to meet with Britain and without France (Five + Britain) on the evening of 22 October. However, when Medici proposed the appointment of a special group of the six on the lines of the Harmel mandate, only the Dutch supported while the Germans, Luxembourgers and Belgians all felt they must consult their Governments.[119]

The new-found boldness of the Five proved short-lived. When, at a diplomatic reception in London on 28 October, Lord Chalfont told the Luxembourg and Belgian Ambassadors that the British were going ahead with their plans to organise a meeting with the Five in the margins of the forthcoming Brussels meeting of NATO, in accordance with the understanding reached in Rome, both men reacted with apprehension. The Belgian Ambassador cited revived interest in the possibility of a trade agreement (to which the French were now giving a new wind as a response to the WEU meeting) as a possible reason why Harmel was now having second thoughts.[120]

The Germans, who had being trying for months to breathe life into the moribund idea of a trade agreement, took fresh heart from this renewed French interest and sent a formal aide-mémoire to the US Government outlining their proposal. They received from the Americans a rather tart reply: "The US Government notes the German Government's view that its proposal for a trade arrangement between the EEC and other European countries is a political rather than a trade policy question . . . The consistent support given by the United States for European unification has always been based on a broad political assessment of our common interest. The creation of a strong united Europe would improve political relations in the Atlantic area and enhance the security of the free world. The trade arrangement . . . is not clearly linked to, and indeed has no demonstrable connection with, the enlargement of the Communities or, for that matter, the broader process of European unity . . . The arrangement could not be considered even a modest concrete step in the process of the unification of Europe. The drastic enlargement of discrimination against the United States and other third countries which would result from such an arrangement would thus provide no compensating political advantage. It would weaken public support in the US for European unity with adverse consequences for Atlantic relationships . . . The effects of a trade arrangement would be deeply divisive between Europe and the United States at a time when both our countries are seeking to strengthen the Atlantic area. . .Consequently, the United States Government finds a preferential trading arrangement with no clear link to membership or to European unification objectionable from a political, as well as a commercial, point of view".

"Very good statement", Wilson commented. "We ought to have a similar one on EEC agricultural policy".[121]

The US Secretary of State, Dean Rusk, who was in Brussels for a NATO meeting, told Stewart on 14 November that he had informed Brandt that the American reply had been personally authorised by himself. When Stewart met the

Foreign Ministers of the Five later in the day, Brandt referred to the American note and argued that it provided an additional argument in favour of a clear link between the trade arrangement and full membership. He suggested that, even if a juridical link could not be found, a timetable expressed in years perhaps could be.[122]

Rusk meanwhile helpfully piled on the pressure, telling the European Commission that "in horse parlance, it was no use asking the United States to pay the price without getting the horse".[123]

If Brandt was committed to the cause of enlargement, Kiesinger remained lukewarm. Nearly two months passed before he replied to Wilson's friendly September message, itself an indication of his priorities. Kiesinger's message, when it came, was cordial but bland and non-committal. One sentence in the letter ("Europe can neither be built up without France nor can it dispense with the cooperation of Great Britain") hardly put Germany's view of the two countries on an equal footing. It even contained a hint that Britain should not be awkward by asking for more than Germany and France were willing to concede.[124]

Christopher Soames, meanwhile, two months into his Paris appointment, was taking a fresh political view of how to tackle French opposition to British accession. Hitherto, he argued in a letter to the Foreign Secretary of 15 November, the Anglo-French diplomatic war over the Common Market had meant total war across the board. But there was an element in the French Government which wanted to find issues on which France could cooperate with Britain and other European countries. This element might just catch the ear of de Gaulle. On the British side, Soames argued, nothing had been lost by the Harmel proposals but they were, in truth, nothing more than another tactical move in the five-year old war. Britain had not lost anything by them but they were certainly not destined to be the vehicle of progress. Soames recommended, instead, that the British Government should seek discussion on specific issues, with the emphasis on the issue rather than the forum. Soames had been told that Debré had reported to de Gaulle on the talk he and Soames had had on 30 October and had suggested that it would be worth having talks to see if a common view could be achieved on subjects such as the future of South East Asia after a Vietnam settlement, Africa and the Middle East, i.e. subjects outside Europe but important to Europe. De Gaulle had replied that the British would not be persuaded to call off the guerrilla war about European affairs but if Debré wanted to try talking to the British he was at liberty to do so.[125]

Four days later, Soames was at a meeting with the Foreign Secretary and officials to discuss the issue (the Diplomatic Bag went daily between the Paris Embassy and the FCO so that a letter written by Soames on 15 November would have been seen by the Foreign Secretary the following day). The meeting was inconclusive.[126] Stewart was still wedded to the Harmel proposals and went so far as to give Soames "a gentle rebuke" for not carrying out his instructions "too faithfully" on one or two occasions.

This in turn reflected, not just the unsurprising tension between two politicians of opposing Parties and drastically different temperaments, but the difficulty which the Foreign Office has always had in recognising that a political appointee is not only bound to operate differently from an official but that part of the rationale for making a political appointment in the first place is to change the way the game is played. Harold Wilson had seen that clearly when he had picked Soames for the job, telling Palliser that it was, at that moment, a job for a politician and a politician who was pro-European, and adding: "My money is on Soames".[127] The Foreign Office was very explicit in its instructions, rarely setting the objective and then leaving the Ambassador to work out the tactics or have the discretion to duck and weave to achieve it. Moreover, as events were shortly to demonstrate all too starkly, suspicion of de Gaulle was, with good reason, so deeply embedded in the Foreign Office psyche that any apparent overture would be seen as a trap to be avoided rather than as an opportunity to be explored.[128]

On 25 November, Soames told the Foreign Office that his doctors had diagnosed heart trouble and had advised him to cancel all social engagements for a month. Soames himself attributed the problem (which was in fact a mild heart attack)[129] to stress[130] but he was in no way laid low. In reply to a letter from the Prime Minister expressing sympathy and advising him to take things easy and to go away for a spell, Soames replied in manuscript that, were he to go away, he would "be pawing the ground after a few days". Palliser had been to Paris to talk to Soames. "As he will have told you", Soames wrote, "I have no confidence in the Harmel proposals getting us anywhere. Though plainly we must go through the motions now that we are embarked on that course, my private feeling is that the sooner they are over and buried the sooner will we be able to launch out on more worthwhile approaches – and monetary matters will, in the first instance, figure largely in the early months of next year. Would it be inconceivable to achieve a European view prior to talking with the Americans? If it were possible to achieve this, and flowing from a British initiative, then I believe that much else would follow. Europe, including France, is longing to end these political quarrels. What we need is to find a 'casus pace' (forgive my Latin grammar but you will see what I mean) . . . The General has said he would like to have a talk with me in January and I would hope to have a talk with you – or failing that with Michael [Palliser] who will know your thoughts – before then . . ."[131]

On 26 November, André Fontaine writing in *Le Monde*, asked why the Dutch, Belgians and Italians continued to oppose the Fouchet Plan which might help to bring to an end the little cold war raging between France and Britain. Had the moment not come to make a place for Britain in Europe's ideas of political union?[132]

"What thought are we giving to the Fouchet plan?" Wilson asked. "It is some months since I raised it". When the Foreign Office replied some ten days later, using arguments which Palliser described to Wilson as "deplorably negative; they write as if nothing had changed in Europe since this plan was first launched", the Foreign Office "doubted whether anything would be gained in present circumstances in trying to relaunch the Fouchet Plan or even a variant of it". The first and second versions of the Fouchet plan had been regarded as unsatisfactory by the Five, not least because they contained no provision for majority voting or for any supra-national elements. The alternative produced by the Five, with its "strong flavour of supra-nationality caused, and might still cause, certain difficulties for us. We therefore doubt whether it would be wise for us to give currency to a French plan which still shows no sign of being acceptable to the Five". The time for an initiative, so the Foreign Office argued, was when it became clear (as it might well, they thought, at the beginning of February when the WEU was due to meet) that Britain was dealing with the Five without France.[133]

Inspired by Palliser, and on the basis of a draft which Palliser provided, Wilson sent a minute to the Foreign Secretary on 17 December voicing his disappointment in the Foreign Office outlook. Of course, Wilson argued, the Government might find some of the supra-nationality which the Five had wanted difficult but the thinking underlying the Harmel plan showed that the ideas of those who used to be convinced Federalists showed that they expected to have to accept a great deal less than they had wanted six or more years earlier. When the WEU met in February in Luxembourg it could well be that no progress would be made on the Harmel Plan and that Britain would not be in a situation in which the Five were clearly separated from the French. Surely, Wilson contended, all present indications were that the Germans had absolutely no intention of letting such a situation arise. Since he (Wilson) was due to meet Kiesinger immediately after the WEU meeting he felt that he must be in a position to develop some new ideas to the German Chancellor. Of course these must not be called the Fouchet Plan. They must be differently devised and dressed up. Was it not possible to find something to discuss with the Germans which would both keep up the momentum and at least be difficult for France to turn down out of hand? If so, it should surely also be welcome to Italy and the Benelux. "The Harmel minuet", Wilson concluded, "will have served a useful purpose by keeping our approach to the forefront of European affairs for a considerable period. But the dance must go on even after Harmel has ended".[134]

Stewart replied three days later, implicitly accepting that the Harmel plan had run its course. He agreed that the Government should expect France, at the WEU meeting in the New Year, to make it clear that she could not agree to the Harmel proposals. At that point, the Government must be ready with new ideas. Stewart was arranging a conference of British Ambassadors from the main posts concerned with European policy to take place on 20 January. Thereafter he would circulate a paper to Ministers. One possibility would be to propose to the Six and any other European country interested a treaty providing for cooperation in foreign policy and defence. The Foreign Office were preparing a draft.[135]

There remained, however, a difference between the Foreign Secretary, on the one hand, and Chalfont, Soames and, to an extent, the Prime Minister on the other.

In a minute of 19 December to the Foreign Secretary, Lord Chalfont had expressed himself bluntly: "If we continue to commit ourselves obviously to a policy designed, however we may present it, to outflank the French, to paralyse the Common Market and to evolve new frameworks for political, military and technological consultation, we shall face the real possibility that it is we, not the

French, who will be isolated." Chalfont was in favour of a major British initiative, in concert with Germany and, if possible, with France, to set up effective machinery for European political consultation. He saw this as consistent with the ideas which Soames was formulating in Paris.[136]

Soames, so Palliser reported to Wilson on 23 December, after spending a day at the Paris Embassy, was in an unhappy and frustrated mood, despite being in much better health. Soames's relationship with Stewart was not a happy one. He felt that the Foreign Office, confronted as they saw it with a choice between isolating the French and seeking to find ways of getting nearer to them, had consistently chosen the former course. And those plans had come, or in the case of Harmel, would come, to nothing because it was impossible to isolate the French so long as the Germans refused to break their own relationship with France – a refusal which, Soames judged, they were bound to persist in. What Soames wanted was to be allowed to re-open the dialogue with France and to be allowed to probe in fairly substantive fashion at his first meeting with de Gaulle in the New Year. Soames, Palliser believed, wanted authority to hint at the possibility of a nuclear defence relationship between France and Britain and Palliser had warned him that he saw no chance at present of his being allowed to do so. But that was not the only possible issue. Soames did not accept that he, as a political animal, had been appointed to Paris to possess his soul in patience and give cocktail parties until de Gaulle died.

Palliser thought that Soames's despair at the rigidity of the Foreign Office was a bit exaggerated but that it had some truth in it. The efforts of Soames and Chalfont might help to stir the mixture a bit but the Prime Minister might need to give a hand with the spoon as well. Wilson, while agreeing with Palliser that nuclear defence could not be a subject of conversation with the French, declared himself as having "a lot of sympathy with Soames's view".[137]

In early January 1969, the Foreign Office produced a draft of a Cabinet paper on the future of European policy which was prudently sent to No. 10 Downing Street for consideration. The core of the paper was a proposal for a 'treaty of union states' in Europe, preceded by a trial period during which efforts would be made to harmonise foreign and defence policies to an increasing degree. The Foreign Office argued that, for such an initiative to commend itself to German public opinion (which was thought vital if the Germans were prepared to contemplated any initiative which might not command French support) it would "have to make it clear that we are aiming at a federal, or at least confederal Europe . . . We should not have to commit ourselves to practise any of this from the outset. But we would have to indicate convincingly that this was the road on which we proposed that Europe should advance . . ."[138]

In submitting the draft to Wilson, Palliser commented that, without the federal ideas, the broad approach had much to commend it, not only to the Five but also to France. Wilson himself commented that the paper had failed to examine the Fouchet Plan as such or to propose a form of the Fouchet Plan sufficiently unfederal to make it difficult for the French to be totally negative. He wondered whether the plan would be more attractive to the German SPD than to the CDU and, therefore, whether it might give Brandt some electoral advantage. Wilson agreed with Palliser's view that to put forward federal or confederal ideas was unwise: "Very wrong timescale. Also more repugnant to the French. And to PLP [Parliamentary Labour Party] with their fears of nuclear integration. NPT would allow a federal – though not confederal – Europe to inherit our (and France's) nuclear status" (a reflection of the legal advice Wilson had received on the point).[139]

Like Wilson, the Foreign Office had by this point come to the conclusion that the forthcoming meeting of WEU Ministers in Luxembourg was unlikely to produce results. Fortuitously, Professor Altiero Spinelli, one of the EEC's leading and lifelong champions of federalism, had been in London on a mission of unofficial sounding to discover what the likely British attitude would be if the Italian Government were to take a major initiative in the political/defence field. Spinelli had it in mind that the Italians should propose the establishment over a number of years of a full-scale Community (not simply a Council of Ministers) with a Parliament and a Commission to cover foreign policy and conventional defence. Without an assurance in advance of British support, it was clear that the Italian Government would not take the initiative but that, with British backing, it would be impossible for the German Government to abstain.

In the view of the Foreign Office, such an initiative would fit with what they themselves had had in mind but it would be much easier for the British Government to respond to an Italian initiative than to take one themselves. "We should no doubt be able to avoid a commitment to a federal structure in a political/defence community, just as we have been able to avoid it in accepting membership of the European Communities", the Foreign Office advised. "But", they continued, "we should have to recognise and accept that, at the end of a transitional period, foreign and conventional defence questions would be subject to some sort of majority vote". Against this background, the Foreign Secretary proposed that he should tell the Italian Foreign Minister, Signor Nenni, when they met in Luxembourg, that he was personally very interested in Spinelli's ideas and looked forward to working out a broad identity of view. In parallel, Stewart proposed that he should indicate to Brandt that, if the Luxembourg meeting failed to take a really significant step towards closer political cooperation, then the British and German Governments must do so in the Declaration of Friendship which was to be signed by Wilson and Kiesinger in Bonn later in the month. The underlying idea was that, if the Germans were not prepared to go far enough, then Wilson should refuse to sign.[140]

All this commended itself to Wilson who wrote that he very much agreed with the line the Foreign Secretary was taking both in his general strategy and in its detailed working out, especially in what Stewart was proposing to say to Nenni and Brandt.[141]

But much more dramatic events were soon to overtake the British Government in the form of what became known as the Soames Affair. On 5 February Soames went to see de Gaulle. De Gaulle rehearsed many of his familiar themes. Soames told him that he thought it difficult to find a period in Anglo-French history, other than when the two countries were at war, when relationships had been worse. The General, Soames told him, had repeated almost word for word the arguments Soames had read in the records of meetings from Macmillan onwards. Was he not failing to take into account that many things had changed since then? If it was Britain's desire to become an American satellite, why then was Britain trying so hard to participate in the creation of a European economic and political entity?

De Gaulle replied that the fact remained that, whereas France had succeeded in achieving a totally independent position, this was not so in the case of Germany, Italy or the Netherlands, and certainly not in the case of the United Kingdom. The whole essence of a European entity must be an independent position in world terms and he was not yet convinced that it was possible for Britain to accept that. Did that mean, Soames asked, that de Gaulle thought it necessary for Britain to leave NATO? De Gaulle replied that he was not looking for that, but in his view, once there was a truly independent Europe, there would be no need for NATO as such "with its American dominance and command structure".

The two men then went on to talk about the European Community. De Gaulle foresaw it changing, and wanted to see it changing, into a looser form of a free trade area with arrangements by each country to exchange agricultural produce. He would be quite prepared to discuss with Britain what should take the place of the Common Market as an enlarged European Economic Association, but with a small inner council of a European Political Association, consisting of France and Britain, Germany and Italy. But it was necessary first to have political discussions between Britain and France to find out whether the two countries saw things sufficiently in common. Over the centuries, de Gaulle said, it had been the rule and not the exception for Anglo-French relations to be bad, a relationship between rivals, not allies. It was only a common fear of Germany which had, exceptionally, brought the two countries together in the twentieth century. That fear no longer existed and with its disappearance had also disappeared the one spur which had enabled Britain and France to work together. Fear of Russia was not the same thing because it affected so many others, especially the United States, that it did not provide a specifically Franco-British bond. Could the two countries now achieve what they had never achieved or even tried in the past, namely a real cooperation based, not on a common fear, but on a genuine desire to build something in Europe together? He would like to see talks between the two countries on economic, monetary, political and defence matters to see whether they could resolve their differences. His proposal would be secret until a decision was taken to have talks. If talks took place then the fact would of course be public. De Gaulle asked that his proposal be transmitted to the Prime Minister and Foreign Secretary.[142]

In reporting the meeting to London Soames said he was inclined to believe that de Gaulle had proposed talks with an open mind and was not writing off in advance the possibility of their leading to a new Anglo/French entente. De Gaulle had many worries about the present weakness of France and the rise of Germany, and had admitted to a certain fear of Russia. The idea he had expounded to Soames of a larger and different organisation than the existing Common Market harked back to ideas that had been in his mind at the end of the war, and had then been shelved. Soames recommended that the next step should be for him to probe matters further with Debré and also to sound out others close to de Gaulle.[143]

Palliser, in putting Soames' telegrams to the Prime Minister, advised that de Gaulle should not be turned down flat and that, in any case, Soames should be authorised to probe further with Debré. "Playing poker with the General, though fascinating, is not always a profitable enterprise", Palliser wrote. "But on the present occasion my hunch is that there may be something genuine underlying the old man's thinking. And we should be well advised not to ignore the possibilities it might conceivably open to us".

Wilson was of the same mind. Palliser wrote to the Foreign Office on 6 February that the Prime Minister had said: "We should follow this up: we must be careful not to rebuff him and we should have in mind the possibility that, given encouragement, this could be escalated to higher level meetings – first the Foreign Secretary, then possibly myself".[144]

The reaction of the Foreign Secretary, who was in Luxembourg, was one of profound suspicion. He sent a telegram of instruction to Soames on 6 February telling him that he would be discussing the implications of the conversation with the Prime Minister before the latter's visit to Bonn. He might ask Soames to come to London. In the meantime, Soames was to take no action with Debré, or to explore de Gaulle's views further in any other way.

But Debré had meanwhile asked to see Soames two days later on 8 February. Stewart instructed Soames to confine himself to saying that he had reported his conversation with de Gaulle to London and had so far received no reaction. Stewart concluded that "I should not like the French to get any impression of particular interest or lack of interest on our part".[145]

What Soames was not privy to was a separate telegram of 6 February from Stewart to Wilson in which Stewart's suspicions of de Gaulle (doubtless aided by his suspicions of Soames) were given free rein. It would, Stewart believed "be dangerous to make any response to de Gaulle's approach which could be interpreted as positive or as showing interest. He has given us his terms of reference: the disappearance of NATO; the destruction of the existing Communities; and a four-power political directorate in Europe. This is not a basis for discussion as far as we are concerned, nor even for probing his intentions further." Stewart went on to recommend that Wilson should tell Kiesinger of de Gaulle's approach when he saw him in the following week. Others of Britain's partners should also be informed. "Whatever we may ultimately decide to do", Stewart concluded, "there will be advantage in showing de Gaulle that we are not to be moved by the first puff of wind".[146]

Had Soames seen this telegram he would undoubtedly have intervened to provide a corrective, not least on two points where Stewart's telegram distorted what de Gaulle had said. De Gaulle might have implied a four-power directorate but he had never used that word. Nor had he posited the disappearance of NATO as part of his putative scheme. He had, in response to a question from Soames, said, as often in the past, that the creation of a truly united Europe would render NATO in its present form unnecessary.

Soames called on Debré in the evening of 8 February. Debré told Soames that de Gaulle had telephoned him twice about his conversation with Soames, once immediately after it had happened and again on the evening of 8 February before Soames's call. Soames told Debré that he had thought it wise to make a factual record of his conversation with the President. He had shown it to Tricot, the Secretary General at the Elysée. Tricot had told him that there were some points which the General had not reported to him but that he would show the report to the General and ask him if there was anything in it with which the General disagreed. He would then inform M. Debré who would discuss it with Soames at their meeting. Debré replied to Soames that he had indeed heard from Tricot that the General had seen the account and that there was nothing in it with which he disagreed.

Debré went on to outline his thinking. He personally had been absolutely convinced by his experts that it was not possible for the Treaty of Rome to function realistically if Britain and others were to join. So that was one thing that the French Government would be glad to discuss with the British: how did both Governments see the future economic structure and shape of Europe? It might well be that the Treaty of Rome would prove to have been just a stage in the economic development of Europe. There was also the question of the political development of Europe. Here again Debré suggested bilateral talks on political questions which would be separate from, but could run in parallel with, the economic talks. De Gaulle had told him that Soames had raised the issue of the confidentiality of these talks. Debré's proposal was that the first few talks should be in the strictest secrecy until it was clear whether or not the seeds of agreement could be seen. It would then be for each Government to consult with friends and partners. De Gaulle had asked Debré to repeat that if the time came when the Prime Minister or Foreign Secretary wished to come to Paris, he would gladly have such discussions.

"Up to then", Soames reported, "bearing in mind your telegram from Luxembourg, I had remained commendably quiet". But when Debré had finished Soames reverted to a point he had raised with Debré when the issue of bilateral talks had first been mentioned by Debré himself the previous October. Did Debré see these talks as being a genuine attempt to resolve the differences between the two Governments about the future economic structure and political purpose of Europe? Debré replied that he wanted Soames to understand that in his view there was grave peril in the fact that France and Britain seemed to be vying with each other to woo Germany. This was extremely dangerous for both countries. He personally therefore regarded it as in France's interest to reach an accord with Britain and he recommended that Soames put this in balance against any pessimistic impression he might have drawn from de Gaulle's words or demeanour.

Soames told London, in reporting his call on Debré, that he read the situation as being that talks between the two Governments had been in Debré's mind for some months but that he had first to sell idea to the General so that de Gaulle would take it up as his own, which he had now done. The ball was therefore now in the British court. Soames proposed that, accompanied by his second-in-command, Bernard Ledwidge, the Minister in the Embassy, he should come to London to expand orally to Stewart and the Prime Minister on these important conversations.[147]

It was of course the middle of the weekend. But on Sunday 10 February, Palliser sent a memo to Wilson, who was at Chequers, recommending that on balance, and despite the risk of a leak and speculation, Soames should be allowed to come. But for that to happen the Prime Minister would need to say so fairly soon to Stewart "whose instinct I suspect will be against it". Palliser also commented that "the very hard line . . . sent to you by the FCS from Luxembourg reflects, I think, the continuing reluctance of the FCO to face the fact that European unity is meaningless unless all three of the big Europeans i.e. Britain and France and Germany form part of it".[148]

But the die was already cast. On the previous day, Stewart's Private Secretary, Donald Maitland, had sent Soames a telegram, following consultation with Stewart himself. "Your conversation with Debré", Maitland wrote, "added little to what you heard from the General and we remain anxious to show caution in this matter . . . [The Foreign Secretary] fears . . . that if you and Ledwidge were to come here now . . . your journey might give the French ideas which we would rather they did not entertain and would inevitably give rise to public speculation which would cause trouble with the Germans on the eve of the Prime Minister's visit to Bonn." Instead, Stewart had instructed Pat Hancock (the Under Secretary responsible for European matters in the Foreign Office) to fly to Paris the following day to discuss matters with Soames. Hancock would be attending a briefing meeting with the Prime Minister the following morning before flying to Paris and would be accompanying the Prime Minister to Bonn.[149]

When Wilson and Stewart met in Downing Street on the Monday morning to discuss the Prime Minister's impending visit to Bonn, Stewart told Wilson that he had decided that it would not be appropriate for Soames to return to London. The two men "agreed that . . . it would be desirable to inform Dr Kiesinger (and the [other] Governments of the Five) of the French approach; and to tell the French that this was being done. It could be made clear to Kiesinger that we were not disposed to return a flat negative to the French proposal. But if we entered into talks with them, we should do so in consultation with the Germans (and our other European allies) and we would make clear at the outset that we did not accept General de Gaulle's approach to NATO or his concept of seeking some alternative arrangement to the EEC . . . It was agreed that a brief should be prepared for the PM's use on General de Gaulle's proposal; and that the talking points should lay particular emphasis on the disruptive approach to the EEC inherent in General de Gaulle's attitude".[150]

Hancock's visit to Paris did nothing to reassure Soames. He showed Soames a piece of paper recording the decisions taken in London on what would be said by the Prime Minister to Kiesinger and more generally to the Five and to the Americans. "I would strongly urge you", Soames wrote in a telegram after Hancock's visit, "to reconsider both the form of words and the timetable proposed which, as they now stand, would amount to a betrayal of General de Gaulle's confidence . . . This is tantamount to rebuffing the French in a way which I fear could have long term adverse consequences".

Soames proposed instead a form of words for the Prime Minister to use in private and in confidence with Kiesinger, couched in much more general terms and revealing none of the detail of what had passed between Soames and de Gaulle and Debré. Soames proposed that the Prime Minister say to Kiesinger that, while by no means sanguine about the likely outcome of such talks, he nonetheless thought it right to pursue the issue further through diplomatic channels in order to see what was in French minds. If it looked as if anything was going to come out of the talks the British Government would keep the German Government informed.

Soames suggested that, if the Prime Minister agreed to talk to Kiesinger on 12 February on the lines he had suggested then he, Soames, should be authorised to see Debré on 11 February to tell him that the Foreign Secretary and the Prime Minister were interested in the French Government's initiative and wished him to have further discussions with them; that the Prime Minister would be talking privately to the German Chancellor in general terms about the initiative and that the British Government proposed to inform the Benelux and Italian Governments on the same basis. Crucially, Soames argued that this timetable would enable him to inform the Prime Minister of Debré's reaction before he saw Kiesinger.[151]

Hancock's own record of his meeting with Soames described him as being very upset and determined to come to London at once. Hancock had told him that "this could not be agreed to". Soames had set out why the course of action proposed in London would kill the French approach dead at the outset. What was the use of his mission in Paris? There had followed "a long argument about this and about the duties of an Ambassador. Mr Soames took it pretty well".

Hancock was shown by Soames the record of his discussion with de Gaulle that he had, in effect, cleared with the Elysée. Hancock confirmed in his report that the record agreed with the telegrams which Soames had sent. Hancock went on to report that Soames was likely to telegraph his views and recommendations, as indeed he did.[152]

Palliser on the same day had already put to Wilson his sense of unease at the way in which the Foreign Office were treating Soames. He had, he said, "seldom read a telegram which pours colder water on an Ambassador from a greater height" than the one Maitland had sent dismissing Soames' meeting with Debré as of little consequence. Palliser feared that Soames might "do something foolish" i.e. resign. He was after all a rich man and not used, as Hancock had put it at the No. 10 meeting, to 'accepting that he is now only an Ambassador'. A resignation could be embarrassing for the Prime Minister though not, Palliser suspected, for the Foreign Secretary "who finds himself in any case little in sympathy with Soames". Palliser thought that the Prime Minister might need to have a discreet word with Stewart about the need to handle Soames differently. "I entirely agree", Wilson wrote, "and I too reacted badly to Hancock's remark. I meant to pick it up but was diverted".[153] Separately, Palliser advised Wilson to consider whether, in the light of Soames' advice, he wanted to go as far in informing Kiesinger and others of de Gaulle's approach as had been recommended by the Foreign Secretary and, if he did so wish, whether the Prime Minister's relationship with de Gaulle would be able to stand the strain.[154]

Wilson and Stewart discussed their tactics the following day and Wilson decided to test the atmosphere when he got to Bonn before taking a final decision. "The more I have thought about this since you left for the airport the more convinced I have become that you should not leave Bonn without telling Kiesinger the whole story", Stewart wrote in a telegram to Wilson, who had by then arrived in Bonn. Stewart went on to deal, as he saw it, with the issue of a breach of confidence, arguing that it was the French who had done just that by proposing secret bilateral talks on matters which vitally affected the interests and security of their partners in the Six and fellow allies in NATO. The French anyway had more respect for those who looked after their own interests and who spoke plainly. Nor, Stewart argued, was he suggesting that no reply at all should be given to de Gaulle. On the contrary, Soames should be instructed to tell Debré that the Government would be glad to express to the French their views on the important issues they had raised. "I most earnestly advise you to accept the procedure I have outlined".[155]

With characteristic efficiency the Foreign Office had sent a warning telegram to its Embassies in EEC capitals containing an account of Soames's meeting with de Gaulle and instructing Ambassadors to expect a trigger before passing the contents to their host Government.

On 12 February Wilson spoke to Kiesinger who, so Dennis Greenhill, the Permanent Under-Secretary at the Foreign Office who had accompanied Wilson to Bonn, reported by telegram "showed no real surprise about de Gaulle's line on NATO, which he said was what the Germans had heard on NATO from the General many times before. But Kiesinger was obviously shaken by what de Gaulle had said about his preference for a looser association to take the place of the European Communities".[156]

That same day British Ambassadors in EEC posts were sent the trigger to inform the Governments of the Five of de Gaulle's initiative. And Soames was instructed to seek an interview with Debré where he was to tell the French Foreign Minister that the British Government regarded the proposals put forward by President de Gaulle as significant and far-reaching. It was, however "too much to ask" that Britain should not tell Kiesinger and Britain's other partners. The British Government rejected de Gaulle's views on NATO and maintained their position on entry into the EEC. Nevertheless, on these understandings, the British Government were prepared to have discussions with the General provided other partners were fully in the picture. If Soames was accused of a breach of faith by Britain he was to respond that any charge of breach of faith could not be levelled against *Britain*.[157]

Stewart followed up with a personal message to Soames which anyone who had ever had anything to do with Soames should have known would be seen as what it was: crass, patronising and ignorant of the impact of the decisions which Stewart had taken on Anglo-French relations. "Our reaction to these proposals is not all you would have wished", said Stewart. "I do not believe that in the longer run the reply I am now asking you to return to Debré will damage either our policies or your position in France. On the contrary, I am convinced that both will benefit. If, as I hope, the French are willing to have talks on the clear understanding we have laid down, I will want your advice as to how they should be handled. At this stage we shall be able to derive the maximum advantage from your foresight in getting an agreed record of your conversation with de Gaulle . . ."[158]

The Foreign Office's instructions did not reach Soames until 8 o'clock at night, by which time Debré was unavailable. Rather than wait until the next day, Soames called on Alphand, the Secretary General at the French Foreign Ministry who, unsurprisingly, reacted badly. Alphand reminded Soames that the French leadership had specifically asked that their proposition should remain secret, at least until the British had decided whether or not to agree to talks. The British Government might at least have told the French Government of their intention to inform other countries before actually doing so. Soames reported that this latter charge was, to him, "most wounding", given that what Alphand was criticising was the very action Soames had advised his Government not to take. To reinforce his point, Alphand went to his safe and took out a document which Soames got a glimpse of and saw was a memorandum from de Gaulle to Debré reporting his conversation with Soames. Alphand read out a passage from the document in which the General had said he had made it clear to Soames that he attached great importance to his proposal being kept secret between the two Governments at that early stage.[159]

Once British Embassies around Europe had briefed their host Governments, it was only a matter of time before the story of 'the Soames Affair' became more widely known. In response to leaks which began to appear in Paris the Foreign Office, on 21 February, took the unprecedented step of briefing the Press. Without clearance from Number 10 the Foreign Office gave journalists a comprehensive account of Soames's conversation with de Gaulle. This provoked a predictably furious public reaction from the French, which in turn provided the backdrop for a meeting between Soames and Debré the following evening, the first time the two men had met since things had gone badly off track.

Debré, contrary to his usual custom, had a note taker with him. He began by saying that the two of them were meeting '*sur un champs de bataille*. It was for him, he said, a matter of great personal sadness. Debré reminded Soames that, from the moment he had presented his credentials as Ambassador, he had made it clear that he saw as the purpose of his mission an endeavour to reach a better understanding with France; that he himself had early on proposed that the two Governments should have bilateral talks and that, while the British Government had not at that time wanted them, he had understood that it was Soames's intention to do his best to mend fences. Debré described the background to Soames's meeting on 4 February with de Gaulle. On that occasion the General had told Soames frankly and privately of his views,, adding that he felt that Soames's was something of a special mission. He, Debré, had subsequently gone over the ground with Soames. Up to that point he understood everything that had happened. He even understood that Mr Wilson might have thought it right and necessary to tell Kiesinger something of the conversation. But from then on he failed totally to understand what had happened. The General had spoken to Soames in the greatest confidence and had made it clear that the talks should, at least to begin with, be in secret. But there had followed '*diffusion, déformation et sensationalisme*'. For instance, when de Gaulle had talked of his distant hopes of seeing the day when European defence forces could be of a size and power to be able to defend Europe, this had been presented to others as a French desire to bring down NATO. And so now, Debré concluded, 'we find ourselves on a field of ruin'.

Soames, who must privately have shared Debré's sentiments, was nothing if not a real professional. He explained that the British Government had always hoped that the information they had passed to other Governments would remain in Government circles. Indeed, on the same day others were informed, Soames had seen Alphand and told him that the British Government were prepared to have talks. What was the response of the French Government?

How can we possibly talk, Debré replied? Did Soames see himself having another talk with President de Gaulle now? He added that he knew that many in London had been hoping for a long time that the General would soon go and would be followed by a Government of a different persuasion. This was an illusion. We now found ourselves on a field of ruins, Debré said again. There was nothing that could now be done. The book had been opened in good faith on 4 February and closed on 22 February.[160]

The story dominated the Press on both sides of the Channel with a tendency to see the incident as an all-time low in Anglo-French relations. It was exacerbated by the fact that the French Government had announced their refusal to take any further part in meetings of the WEU until the rule of unanimity was honoured and the organisation was no longer used to promote British interests.

In London, a Conservative backbencher secured a Standing Order debate on the Soames Affair and Stewart was obliged to make a full statement of the Government's position. On the eve of Richard Nixon's first visit as President to London, this was embarrassing, but the Conservative front bench could scarcely put themselves in a position of siding with de Gaulle and, in the Division, the Government won the vote comfortably. Stewart had similar support within Cabinet.

On 11 March, Soames sent to Wilson a letter setting out the lessons of the affair. Soames thought it was "the greatest pity" that he had not been allowed to come home to talk to Wilson and Stewart since, had he done so, he would have sought to persuade both men to act somewhat differently. "As I see it", Soames continued. "the General handed me a cup which I handed on to Whitehall. It may have been full of peace or poison. This, only time and discussion would have told. I saw it as the beginning of what you wanted me to achieve when you sent me here. So of course I was dismayed when it was deliberately smashed to pieces."

Soames went on to seek Wilson's view: did the Prime Minister want him and his Embassy to encourage those in France who still wanted to try again? It would be worse than pointless for the Embassy to seek to do so if, in its heart of hearts,

HMG did not wish to enter into a dialogue with France. If the answer was 'no' then we should have to carry on 'bashing the French', as Hancock had put it to Soames on 10 February. From all that the Prime Minister had said, Soames assumed the Prime Minister's answer would, however, be 'Yes'. And so, he argued, it should be for, in Soames's judgement, such rigid positions had now been taken up, and the degree of mistrust was such, that an Anglo-French dialogue was an essential precursor to any negotiation.[161]

On 18 March, Palliser wrote to Maitland at the Foreign Office that the Prime Minister's "own answer to Soames's main question would certainly be 'Yes'".[162] The Foreign Office told Soames by telegram two days later that "the short answer to your main question (whether you should encourage those in France who want to get a dialogue going with us) is 'yes'. You made our position clear to Alphand on 12 February and I repeated it in my [Stewart's] letter to Debré of 24 February. In a phrase, our position is that we would like to talk bilaterally with the French provided our partners are fully in the picture."[163]

In the following week, Soames returned to London for talks with the Prime Minister and Foreign Secretary. Wilson's visit to Germany, at the start of the Soames Affair, had been reasonably satisfactory, concluding in a joint declaration which affirmed German support for British accession. But Kiesinger's own subsequent meeting with de Gaulle had shown, as Kiesinger put it to the British Ambassador in Bonn, that the General felt very bitter about his treatment by the British. On the WEU, de Gaulle had been very hard. He was no longer interested. When Kiesinger said that he had hoped that the Luxembourg meeting would mark a step forward to improved political cooperation, de Gaulle indicated that, as far as he was concerned, political discussions might continue there, but France would not be a party to them.[164]

Soames endorsed the assessment that de Gaulle was feeling very bitter personally. There was, he told Wilson and Stewart when they met, a general mood of sadness, as well as considerable bitterness, in the Elysée. This did not mean that the idea of an Anglo-French dialogue might not be revived on the French side. Some of Soames's French contacts believed that de Gaulle was in too bitter a mood to be willing to talk to the British. Others disputed that. What was certain was that distrust of Britain was now so great within the French Government that there could be no question of negotiations for British membership of the Common Market taking place without a prior Anglo-French dialogue. To seek too rapidly to restore relations would court a rebuff so, for the time being, the water must be allowed to flow under the bridge. Soames welcomed the initiative taken by the Foreign Secretary in seeking a bilateral meeting with Debré when the two men were in Washington together within the next few weeks. It was important for Stewart personally to convince Debré of his own willingness for talks to take place between the two Governments.[165]

There was more than a hint in what Soames said at that meeting that the idea of an organisation different from the EEC was still in the air. Soames at one point remarked that "if by some miracle the General were suddenly to invite Britain to negotiate for entry on the basis of HMG's acceptance of the Treaty as it stood this would surely embarrass HMG, particularly in the agricultural context. He fully accepted that nothing should be done that ran counter to the interests of Britain's friends in Europe and that was no doubt relevant to any consideration of possible alternatives to the Common Market.[166]

Pat Hancock, one of the main Foreign Office authors of the tough response to de Gaulle's initiative, was about to depart for Rome where he had been appointed as Britain's Ambassador. In a valedictory minute, Hancock examined the idea of a different kind of Europe. "It is true", he said, "that the impetus behind the EEC has been failing and that the present CAP is becoming unworkable. But we should not lose sight of the fact that there is one difference between the EEC and any alternative form of western European organisation. That difference is that the EEC exists and that the other forms of organisation do not exist. We have to deal with what exists". Hancock was clear that if Britain pursued her present policy of seeking EEC membership as, in his view, she should, that would continue to be at the expense of her relations with France. The right course for Britain was to keep her EEC policy in repair in the expectation that France would get weaker and would have to toe the line in the end. This was not flogging a dead horse. The horse was alive, but could not at present be run. In short, Hancock concluded, "I think that the Government have nowhere else to go and must stick to their guns".[167]

"Mr Hancock's minute of 2 April is *'magnifique'*," wrote Sir Denis Greenhill, the Permanent Under-Secretary in a minute to Lord Chalfont, "but is it really *'la guerre'*?" Greenhill's opposite number at the Treasury, Sir Douglas Allen, had told him that Britain's economic situation meant that it would be at least two years before she could contemplate joining the Common Market. The problem with waiting for de Gaulle's opposition to fade and Britain's own economic position to improve, Greenhill believed, was that support in Parliament and the country for the Government's present European policy could drain away and, more importantly, the opportunity for a constructive European policy both economically and politically involving a wider European grouping than the Six would be lost. For this reason, Greenhill said, he would like to see the search for a new organisation pursued, at first very privately and internally. If Britain were following a new, wider economic road a lot of obstacles at present existing to political progress would be removed, not least the opposition of the French and the hesitation of the Germans.[168]

Palliser had just left Downing Street on a posting, effectively arranged between Soames and himself, as the Minister in the Paris Embassy. In his place had come Edward (Teddy) Youde. Youde, a China expert and hero of the Yangtse incident, was later to become Governor of Hong Kong. He was a man of skill and real charm, but he had just returned from a posting in the UK Mission to the United Nations in New York, so had been uninvolved in the politics of Britain's EEC application.

"I think you will be familiar with Mr Hancock's views on Europe", Youde said, in putting Hancock's and Greenhill's minutes to the Prime Minister. "In short, he advocates a continuation of our present policy; but asserts that this is not compatible with good relations with de Gaulle; and that we ought nevertheless to continue with our policy even at the expense of our relations with France. I detect in Sir D Greenhill's minute a growing belief that we ought to be considering whether we ought not to look further to see whether there is some more constructive move we can make".

Wilson, who had acknowledged to Soames that the Government's handling of the Soames Affair could have been done "with greater refinement", commented "We've paid enough price for this nonsense. When does Hancock go to Rome? More power to Denis's elbow. We should review in the light of meeting with Soames and first step following, namely [Stewart's] meeting with Debré".[169]

That meeting, in the French Ambassador's Residence in Washington, turned out to be polite but uneasy. Stewart made clear that he believed both Governments had been trying to act in good faith. He still hoped that talks could take place. Debré said that 'the line was down for the time being'. Stewart should understand the importance which de Gaulle had attached to his ideas and his disappointment that they should not have been considered in the spirit in which they were made. Debré did not think that sufficient time had yet passed to make it possible for the two sides to begin to exchange ideas. Debré also expressed French dislike of the fact that 'the WEU was being used against them'. But Stewart felt after the talk that, while Debré had been ill at ease throughout, he did seem to want normal relations with Britain.[170]

Debré had referred to the significance of the forthcoming referendum in France on regionalisation and senate reform. When Wilson saw the telegrams reporting Stewart's conversation he wrote: "Presumably Debré is right in stressing the referendum. Presumably we should wait for that and then perhaps have a further meeting of FCS and Soames. All this confirms my view before, during and after the event that we were taken for a ride by that oaf Hancock".[171]

Michael Stewart, in his autobiography, described the Soames Affair as "the only occasion on which Harold and I seriously disagreed on foreign policy".[172]

Wilson, in his own published account of the Labour Government, said that he felt at the time "that the Foreign Office were going beyond natural and justified caution. The way they wanted me to handle it in Bonn seemed designed to discredit the French with their EEC partners, and at the same time present ourselves as a rather priggish little Lord Fauntleroy who had resisted the General's anti-EEC blandishments". Wilson thought that the Foreign Office had ignored his own wish to present to Kiesinger a low-key account of what had transpired with de Gaulle and claimed not to have known until his return to London from Bonn that the Foreign Office had set in train steps to give a full account of the de Gaulle/Soames meeting to all Britain's EEC friends.[173]

Two of those closest to Soames, Bernard Ledwidge, the Minister in the Paris Embassy, and Alan Campbell, Soames's Head of Chancery, later gave published accounts of the Soames Affair.

Ledwidge thought that the Foreign Office's public response when leaks of the Soames interview with de Gaulle began to appear in Paris was "extraordinary". Rather than content itself with giving the British version of the proposals, or of refusing to comment at all on the grounds that the conversation had been confidential, the Foreign Office had taken "the unprecedented step of issuing the full text of Soames's account of his discussion with the General, and describing it as an agreed record. Such treatment of a confidential diplomatic exchange with a foreign Head of State is perhaps without precedent in British history. It was accompanied by guidance to the Press to the effect that de Gaulle seemed to be contemplating the break-up of both the EEC and NATO, whereas it was British policy to strengthen both organisations." Anglo-French relations, according to Ledwidge, sank to a nadir. Soames's mission seemed to be in ruins and he thought seriously of resigning, something confirmed by Wilson in his account.[174]

"Soames", in Campbell's account, "was mortified over the whole incident . . . When at last the General had made a move forward, the British Government had sharply rebuffed it. He was angry with himself for not insisting on going home at once to talk to Wilson and Stewart and get them in a less anti-French frame of mind. He was angry with the Foreign Office for the way he thought it had bungled the affair . . . He reflected bitterly that if George Brown had still been Foreign Secretary he would have handled the matter in an entirely different way. He realised that he had overestimated the political backing available to him from the Prime Minister and also that he had failed to see how dangerous it was for him and the present Foreign Secretary to be on such entirely different wavelengths. Campbell's account confirms that, not only had Michael Stewart had no hand in proposing that Soames should be appointed to Paris but that he "was thought indeed to be unenthusiastic about the appointment".[175]

There is no doubt that the Foreign Secretary and the Foreign Office could, with cooler heads, have kept open the door to dialogue with the French while saying enough to their partners in the Five to avoid charges of duplicity. Their actions and reactions were undoubtedly coloured by previous experience of de Gaulle but also by the continuing hope that somehow the Five could be brought to stand firm with Britain against France. Wilson was harsh in his judgement of Hancock but Wilson himself could have stood more firmly by the objections which he rightly entertained about the course the Foreign Secretary was advocating. And if Hancock was wrong to have closed his mind to the possibility of dialogue with the French he was surely right in thinking that there was no more realistic alternative for Britain than to stick to the basic course she had embarked on; and that alternatives to EEC membership were not realistic.

At the moment when minds in London were turning to the possibility of some organisation wider than, and different from, the European Community, there was an assumption that de Gaulle would be in power for a few more years at least. But then the French people delivered a 'no' in the referendum on constitutional change. De Gaulle had said that, in the event of a 'no' he would resign and on 28 April 1969 he did just that.

A very different chapter was about to open.

* * * *

7   The start of negotiations: 1969–1971

"His final decision to stake his future on the outcome [of the referendum] was characteristic hubris or, as many people now think, a death wish. It may nevertheless turn out to be the last great service he has done France, in that it should make possible an orderly transfer of power". Such was Soames' verdict from Paris on de Gaulle's departure.[1]

"Your resignation is an event which touches the world", Wilson wrote in a message. "I speak for all my fellow countrymen in expressing the deep respect we feel for you who have for so long embodied the courage and dignity of France".[2]

On the same day, the Foreign Secretary told Cabinet that Pompidou looked to be the most likely successor to de Gaulle. He would certainly enjoy the support of at least 47% of the French electors who had voted for de Gaulle in the referendum. Sudden changes in French policy were unlikely, but change would nevertheless come. The whole concept of de Gaulle's policies was so contrary to the general trend in Europe, and indeed to France's own best interests, that it was unlikely that it could be continued by anyone who did not hold de Gaulle's special position or exceptional hold over public opinion.[3]

Stewart was right in predicting no early changes in the French approach. While it seemed probable, so Stewart wrote in a minute to Wilson nearly two weeks later, that Pompidou would be elected President on the following Sunday, it was too soon to speak with confidence about his position on individual international issues. It was reasonable to assume from Pompidou's public statements that the veto of principle on negotiations with Britain would now be withdrawn. Against this, Pompidou's recent statements had tended to cast fresh doubt on Britain's European convictions and Pompidou had been careful not to commit himself to the proposition that full membership was the right form for Britain's association with Europe. Pompidou could be expected to drive the hardest of bargains. But the departure of de Gaulle, and of the personal attitudes that had given the edge to the differences and frustrations of the past ten years, meant that a line could be drawn under the account. Britain should give no appearance of wishing to visit the sins of de Gaulle on Pompidou. Stewart advised against an early British overture for talks with the French since this might give the French Government an occasion to try to extract a price for opening negotiations on British accession. But the Government should respond positively to any signs from the French that they wished to open a dialogue. Once agreement had been reached on the opening of negotiations it might be expedient to have bilateral exchanges with the French. With all this Wilson was in complete agreement.[4]

With elections pending in Germany, Wilson invited Willy Brandt to dine with him in London on 16 June. Youde reported to Johnny Graham (who had succeeded Maitland as Private Secretary at the Foreign Office) that Brandt had commented that Kiesinger might have some initial difficulty with Pompidou because Kiesinger had made some remarks appearing to favour Pompidou's main rival for the Presidency, the centrist politician, Alain Poher.

Brandt had been much impressed by a speech by Pompidou on French priorities in foreign policy in which he had said that Franco-German relations should set an example but that they did not need to be preferential. Brandt thought that this was exactly right and that relations between the two countries might now become more relaxed. Brandt thought that the biggest substantive difficulty for Britain would be over the relationship between the Common Agricultural Policy and British entry. Debré had told him that a Government of the centre in France would have to be even harder on the CAP than the Gaullists. The French would want a firm commitment to the continuation of the CAP.

Wilson asked Brandt if he thought Britain would be wise not to press too hard on accession until the autumn. Brandt agreed that the British should not try to rush things but he equally hoped the British Government would not leave the improvement of her bilateral relations with the French too long.[5]

Pompidou defeated Poher (his main rival for the Presidency) by a large margin in the second round of the Presidential elections and signalled a clear change of tone in his appointments to the new French Government, which made the Government look tougher in internal matters and more liberal in foreign, and in particular European, ones. "No one expects the lightweight, Jacques Chaban-Delmas [the new Prime Minister] to have a mind of his own", Soames commented. But it was significant that the orthodox Gaullists, who had wanted Debré to remain as Foreign Minister, had not got their way and Debré had been moved to Defence, albeit with the position of second in the Government hierarchy by way of compensation to him and reassurance to them. In exchange, Soames thought, the appointment of Maurice Schumann to the Foreign Ministry, the retention of Lipkowski as his Secretary of State (equivalent to British Minister of State) and the appointments of Giscard d'Estaing to be Minister of Finance and of Duhamel to be Minister of Agriculture, all gave the Government an undeniably European stamp. This did not, Soames warned, automatically mean a more flexible attitude towards Britain's candidature. What was clear was Pompidou's intention to be boss.[6]

Stewart had called a meeting in London of Britain's Ambassadors in EEC countries and, wisely in the light of earlier events, arranged a separate meeting with the Prime Minister and Soames to discuss tactics with the French. The three men met against a background of a changing mood among British opinion. In the House of Commons, Wilson and Stewart agreed, although the anti-European lobby was not significantly larger than in the past, the 'cool lobby' i.e. those who lacked enthusiasm, was growing. Because Britain had been knocking on the door of Europe for so long, some MPs had lost interest. On the Opposition Front Bench there was also a tendency not to say too much on the European issue for fear of raising issues which would affect the unity of the Conservative Party. Heath, for his part, seemed to be devoting more interest to the development of Europe politically rather than economically.

Significantly, Soames secured authority to make it clear to the new French Foreign Minister that "if the French were ready to talk to us, we were ready to talk to them". Soames could even invite Schumann to visit London if it was certain that he would accept.[7]

Soames called on Schumann on 11 July. Schumann quickly made clear that, for the French Government, the principal prior condition for opening negotiations was that the existing EEC members should first reach agreement on ending the EEC's own transitional period and moving, by the end of 1969, into the 'definitive period'. In other words, the French wanted prior agreement on the definitive financing arrangements of the Community, including, and especially, of agriculture.

Schumann added that, as one who wished to see the entry of Britain into the Common Market, he felt that it would be counter-productive for Britain to 'bousculer' (badger) too much on enlargement while negotiations among the Six were still continuing on ending the EEC's transitional period.

Soames made all the polite noises he had been authorised to make and Schumann responded in kind, saying that he would like to see bilateral talks take place on a range of subjects. He had not wanted to raise the subject himself at his first meeting with Soames for fear that the British would think he was trying to fob them off or divert them from the objective of joining the Common Market. Soames in turn stressed the importance for the British Government of negotiations beginning. The British Government had their own political problems. If nothing happened and little was said, the Government would find it harder to deal both with those who would accuse the Government of cooling in its European aspirations and those who were cool already.

"I regard this as no bad start", Soames told London. "I would guess . . . that the French Government have decided, as indeed we thought they would, to trade agreement to open negotiations for a 'temporary definitive arrangement on agriculture'." "I do strongly urge", Soames concluded, memories of his previous treatment at the hands of Michael Stewart fresh in his mind, "that the details of this conversation be not, repeat not, given to the Five. I would suggest that in communicating with them we confine ourselves to saying that M. Schumann and I had a general talk over the whole field of Anglo-French problems, including Europe, and we regard it as a good beginning".[8] This time round his advice was heeded.

What Schumann had implied was made more explicit when the Dutch Foreign Minister, Dr Luns, called on Wilson in Downing Street on 16 July. Luns believed that the French would be keen to get the agricultural policy of the Community definitively fixed before British entry.[9]

Luns later told Wilson that, once the French had agreed to negotiations they would be hard but they would no longer be able to impose a political veto. The French were, however, still suspicious that the British might be intent on undermining their legitimate preponderance in Europe. Wilson asked whether Luns thought the French might not be willing to contemplate an interim arrangement among the Six on agriculture, leaving definitive arrangements to be discussed as part of a negotiation with Britain. Luns thought this most unlikely. The potential of the British market for French agricultural produce was important to France but this factor would be outweighed by the political disadvantages for France of bringing Britain into a discussion of the CAP. In general, Luns took the view that there was no need for the British to take some new initiative on entry to the EEC. It would be better to take the line that the British application was on the agenda to be dealt with by the Six. Wilson confirmed that this was exactly the position he had taken both in official discussions and in Parliament.[10]

It was against that background that the Foreign Secretary told Cabinet on 22 July that, as the prospects of negotiations being opened had now become considerably greater, so the opponents of entry in Britain had become correspondingly more vocal. That in turn had created doubts elsewhere in Europe about the wholeheartedness of Britain's candidature, though Stewart drew comfort from the fact that an Early Day Motion in the House of Commons opposing British membership had attracted little support. Nevertheless, it would be damaging if the idea that the Government were not serious about their application were to take root. It was the Government's settled policy to seek membership and nothing should be said by Ministers that might be taken as implying that our candidature was not a genuine one.

The doubts to which Stewart had referred found some echo in Cabinet itself with Peter Shore (Secretary of State for Economic Affairs) and Fred Peart (Lord President) arguing that the situation had changed considerably since the original decision had been taken in 1967 and that there should be an up to date appraisal of where Britain's interests now lay and of how negotiations should be conducted. The price Britain might have to pay could be too high and the Government should not seek membership of the EEC at any cost.

Denis Healey (Secretary of State for Defence), one of the original opponents of membership, argued that there was no need for any "agonising reappraisal" for the time being. This issue would not become a live one until 1970 given the imminence of the elections in Germany and the internal crisis within the EEC over the future financing of the CAP. In any event, Healey argued, the Opposition might well split over Europe, with Heath in confrontation with Enoch Powell.

Economic developments, Wilson said in his summing-up, including the devaluation of sterling and developments within the EEC itself, notably in regard to the CAP, which was still in the melting pot, confronted the Government with problems even more difficult than those which had faced them when the original decision had been taken in 1967. There was no need for any reappraisal of policy at the present time. The application to join the EEC remained on the table and the various problems on which decisions might later be taken were being studied. Meanwhile, it was of the greatest importance that policy in regard to the EEC should be considered and decided on collectively in Cabinet; and that individual members of the Government should refrain from statements reflecting Departmental interests rather than Government policy.[11]

As Cabinet was meeting, so was the Council of Ministers of the EEC. Schumann was guardedly more positive than any French Foreign Minister had been in the past, enabling Luns, who was in the chair, to "pay homage to the eloquence and European sentiment of Schumann". But the meeting, as the UK Delegation reported, left many questions unanswered. The French had given little ground on matters of substance and had firmly established their proposal for an EEC summit – at Six – at the expense of Brandt's idea of a summit at which the candidates would be represented. Nevertheless, Marjoribanks believed that a clear, though certainly not decisive, step had been taken towards the opening of negotiations. The French had aroused expectations which they could not now dash without jeopardising their own objectives in the field of agriculture. They had agreed to the Commission's Opinion on accession being updated and to discussions which would lead either to a revelation of the emptiness of their new fair words, or to a gradual definition of the conditions under which negotiation might be opened. The attitude of the Five, and of Brandt in particular, would not have given the French reason to hope that they could side-track discussion of enlargement until they had achieved what they wanted on agriculture.[12]

The British Government were contemplating the possible start of negotiations for accession to the EEC against a background of deteriorating public support for the enterprise and increasing concerns about the balance of payments costs of membership for Britain.

One of Wilson's advisers, Andrew Graham, an Oxford University economist and later Master of Balliol College, had been attending a small Whitehall group which was reviewing the economic costs of entry to the Common Market. Graham reported to Wilson's Principal Private Secretary, who in turn showed Graham's paper to the Prime Minister (who read it without comment). Graham argued that, as a result of the devaluation of sterling and, even more, of the growing agricultural surpluses in the EEC, the direct balance of payments cost to Britain of EEC membership had risen, potentially to the order of £400–£600 million. As a result, industrial costs would also rise, as people tried to compensate themselves for the higher cost of food. The total effect on the balance of payments could thus be of the order of £1,000 million. The underlying problem, Graham argued, was how to actually get and maintain a balance of payments surplus of £500–£1,000 million a year out of which to pay for membership of the EEC. The United Kingdom had been struggling for twenty years with the smaller problem of merely maintaining a balance. Even if this feat could be achieved, would the UK consumer really feel that butter at eight or nine shillings a pound was worth economies of scale which might not in practice materialise from EEC membership? "Accepting the CAP", Graham concluded, "is exactly identical to giving aid – only it is to the French farmer rather than to the underdeveloped world and it may be doubted whether the former is the best use of our resources . . ."[13]

Wilson, along with the other main Political Party leaders, was due to speak at the Guildhall on 29 July at a pro-European dinner. Wilson, rightly sensitive to the changed public mood, focussed in his speech on the political benefits of membership. He spoke cautiously and sceptically about any commitment to political union or any other form of federalism. He acknowledged that his words would be a disappointment to many in his audience. But his speech was very far from being a pledge of 'thus far and no further'. "The immediate task of this generation", he said, "is to work, as we are pledged to work, for that degree of political unity which is within our immediate grasp. That is *our* task in the months and years that lie ahead of us. But we are not here to legislate for the views, still less prejudice the views, of those young people whose personal identification with the ideals and aspirations of a wider Europe is one of the hopes of all of us here tonight. They will choose their own course. They will fashion the institutions they think right for the Europe of which they will be a part. Our duty is to create something on which they can build".

The Conservative leader, Edward Heath, according to Wilson's account of the evening, used his speech, not just to reiterate his pro-European philosophy, but to give voice to some worries about the costs of membership and the weakening of Britain's national identity. While not doubting Heath's European convictions, Wilson began to think that Heath was "engaged on an uncharacteristic anti-Market manoeuvre".[14]

The Foreign Office felt it necessary to address these issues in a Guidance telegram sent to its European posts on 1 August. It drew comfort from the fact that the speeches of the three Party leaders at the Guildhall demonstrated all-party support for the Government's European policy. This should put into perspective the recent revival of criticism among "a small number of vocal backbenchers in the House of Commons". Some of these criticisms related to the Government's attitude towards supra-nationality and a federal European state. In making these criticisms those concerned were confusing supra-national powers and responsibilities in the Community institutions, on the one hand, with the federal idea, on the other. The Government had acknowledged that membership of the European Communities involved acceptance of a good deal that was supra-national. But membership did not, the Foreign Office said, involve federal obligations, though the Guidance made no attempt to define what the distinction was between 'supra-national' and 'federal'. Accession, as the Prime Minister, had pointed out, would not of itself involve the acceptance of political obligations going beyond those in the Treaty of Rome. The Government were prepared to go as far and as fast as her European partners in the future political development of the Community.

As to the suggestions from opponents of the Government's policy that the economic cost of entry would now be much higher than was thought in 1967, and that HMG should publish estimates (a call to which Heath had lent himself at the Guildhall), the Government's position was clear: no sensible estimate could at present be made. The House of Commons would be given "all full information as soon as it is meaningful to give it".[15]

Wilson and Stewart were sufficiently concerned to agree that Stewart should, at the Labour Party conference, "put the Government's case for our application to join the EEC in my speech in forthright terms". They also agreed that there was a need for clear statements by members of the Government on EEC policy. Indeed, Wilson subsequently told Stewart that he had it in mind to call all the junior Ministers together after the Party Conference to "exhort them about the general principles of Ministerial conduct". He might also use his planned forthcoming Ministerial changes to emphasise the Government's commitment to Europe.

Wilson was also clear that he wanted the work of revising the estimates of the costs of EEC membership to be done "without restriction or inhibition" but the work should be properly coordinated under the Cabinet Office and there should be no private enterprise by individual Departments. So far as the CAP was concerned, the costs should be calculated on a wide range of assumptions, including of price reductions which "the Six, for their own internal reasons, might probably decide to adopt". Wilson also conjectured that, as a result of devaluation, British exports must have risen since the 1967 estimates "much more than anyone would have thought likely two and a half years ago". The recent movements in exports to the Common Market "might lead to quite different calculations about the net movement of our trade against the background of a phased reduction of tariffs."[16]

French attitudes remained ambiguous. In August, the distinguished journalist Cy Sulzberger had run a series of articles in the *International Herald Tribune* which, though this was not publicly known, had been based on a long private interview with President Pompidou. "Despite a less acerbic attitude towards London", Sulzberger wrote, "there is not much more chance that Britain will enter the Common Market under Pompidou than under de Gaulle. Paris insists that the Market's crucial agricultural policy must be fixed before the British application is even considered. Thus the vital question of prices for farm products would be settled without London's participation. It is apparent that Pompidou simply does not think Britain can afford to pay the price of accession or that it will wish to do so".

Michael Palliser, now Minister in the Embassy in Paris, forwarded the articles to London but with a caution: while the articles reflected what Pompidou probably believed, there was nothing in what the President had reportedly said which need change the view reached in the British Government that the fundamental veto against British entry was no longer there.[17]

Nonetheless it was undoubtedly with residual French scepticism in his mind that, at the end of a first meeting between Stewart and Maurice Schumann in New York in September, Stewart "took Schumann alone into a neighbouring room. I asked him if the French Government were (a) against our entry; (b) reluctant but ready to accept it as inevitable; (c) positively in favour. He said he could assure me that his Government were positively in favour". "All in all I am well satisfied with my first contact with him", Stewart concluded in a message to Wilson.[18]

A few days later, at the Labour Party Conference in Brighton, Wilson dealt with his own sceptics by seizing on some apparently critical remarks about the EEC by Heath and on a comment by Heath that the Government's decision to apply for membership in 1967 had done the British case a great deal of damage. With his unerring gift for the inconvenient fact, Wilson quoted to his Party Heath's unequivocal welcome in 1967 for the British application. "Now", Wilson went on, "nearly three years and one Powell speech later, it apparently was the wrong decision".

Having neatly set up his audience, Wilson was able to deliver the message to which they might otherwise have been less receptive: "if they, the Six are ready for negotiations to begin, we are ready. If, in these negotiations, we achieve terms satisfactory for Britain, on the lines we have outlined, then negotiations will succeed ... It is the common interest of us all to achieve economic unity. But if this cannot be achieved, we can stand on our own feet. At a heavy price for Britain, no doubt, but at a heavier price for Europe, and at a devastating price for Europe's influence in the world".[19]

The Cabinet, when it met on 25 September, heard from the Foreign Secretary that, while it was clear that the French precondition for enlargement was an agreement among the Six on the CAP, the view of other EEC Foreign Ministers with whom Stewart had discussed the matter was that no more than a temporary agreement would be possible pending British entry and consideration of the plan for a reformed CAP prepared by Commissioner Mansholt.

In general, Cabinet felt that the Government's negotiating position had improved since the 1967 discussions in that the British economy was stronger while the self-confidence of the Six had declined. Wilson commented that the Government's continuing commitment to accession was dependent on the achievement of satisfactory terms. The economic position was now strong enough to allow Britain to carry the initial burdens of membership but Britain was also strong enough to stand on her own feet if membership on acceptable terms proved impossible.[20]

The British negotiating position was given a further boost when the European Commission, on 2 October, published their revised Opinion on the applications for membership. The Commission had been asked to update their 1967 Opinion but, according to the British Delegation in Brussels, they had to all intents and purposes produced a new document and one which was considerably more favourable to Britain's candidature than its predecessor. In particular, the Commission, unlike in 1967, were now recommending that negotiations should be opened 'as soon as possible'. Again, by contrast with 1967, the revised Opinion in no instance found any serious difficulty for the Community's enlargement in either the economic and financial state of the United Kingdom or in the dissimilarities between British and Community policies. The main disappointment in the Opinion was that it nowhere recognised that it would be patently unfair to expect Britain to bear over half of the burden of the CAP. The Commission did, however, acknowledge that the cost of the CAP could be a grave difficulty for the applicants and that it was a problem with which the Six must deal.[21]

Despite the generally improving prospects for the British candidature, Christopher Soames, who was a politician to his fingertips, had clearly picked up on both the unpopularity of the EEC among the British public, which was evident from the opinion polls, and the effect this was having on senior politicians. Soames invited Edward ("Teddy") Youde, Wilson's Foreign Office Private Secretary, a Cabinet Office official and John Robinson of the FCO to lunch in London on 6 October, essentially to make three points. There was now a tide in Europe which, if taken at the flood, would lead to Britain entering the Community; clearly it would not be easy to undertake a negotiation in what might prove to be a General Election year in Britain but the absence of fundamental differences on Europe between the Party leaderships ought not to make that insuperable; he wanted to be assured that it was still the Government's intention seriously to seek and pursue negotiations. He did not want another Soames affair. He had been sent to Paris to get over the barrier which the French had erected to British membership and now that the barrier had fallen (as Soames was convinced it had) he was anxious not to find himself out ahead of the field with the Government and Parliamentary opinion failing to follow him into Europe.

Youde relayed all this to Wilson who minuted that Youde could let Soames know privately his "strong favourable reaction" to the propositions that negotiations could be held despite an election and that the Government intended seriously to pursue negotiations.[22]

Wilson's reassurance was timely for on 10 October Soames had his first audience of President Pompidou, whom Soames found to be in "confident, relaxed and friendly mood". Indeed, Pompidou spoke for about twenty minutes without pause. The President thought that bilateral relations between France and Britain were "still basically satisfactory. Europe of course remained a source of friction. But he was optimistic about the future. He had neither the desire nor the intention of using any veto. As soon as the Community had moved into its definitive period (i.e. resolved the financing of the CAP), and Pompidou believed it was possible to do this by December or shortly thereafter, then there should be negotiations with the candidates. While the President did not think it would take long for negotiations to be opened he thought that the negotiations themselves might take a pretty long time."

Pompidou went on to say that, while it would not of course make any difference to him whether there was a Labour or a Conservative Government in office in Britain, it would be important to the Six that they should be dealing with a Government which would have some time in power.

Soames assured Pompidou that he need have no anxiety on this score since both the present Government and the Opposition were convinced that Britain's destiny lay in Europe and were determined to do all they could to bring about the opening of negotiations and their successful fruition. Soames hoped the President was not implying that negotiations should wait until after the British General Election. There would be quite a strong tide moving in Europe in the early part of 1970 and it would be a great mistake not to catch it. Pompidou said that he took Soames's point but went on to make comments which implied scepticism about the real desire of Britain for membership. He had, the President said, studied the resolution on Europe approved by the Labour Party Conference. It seemed to be much hedged around with qualifications. Moreover, there seemed to be a powerful current of public opinion in Britain that was opposed to membership.

Soames, according to his own account of the conversation, "responded energetically". The President should look at the categorical way in which the Prime Minister, Stewart and George Brown (who, though out of the Government, remained Deputy Leader of the Party) had reaffirmed the Government's European purpose. Soames could assure the President – and he had had this at first hand from the Foreign Secretary – that the Government remained as resolute as ever in their application and in their desire for the earliest possible negotiations. The Conservative Party had also reaffirmed its support for membership by a very large majority. In Britain, what mattered was the declared policy of the two main parties in the country "not the kerbside collections of the opinion pollsters". The President said he noted all this and hoped that Britain, for her part, would leave the Six to work out their own common position and not try to encourage divisions between them.

Soames thought his interview with Pompidou was "on the whole encouraging". One thing the President had sought to do and succeeded in doing was to make it clear where the power lay in France. And that was very clearly with him as President.

There had also been a significant change at the top in Germany. In the elections in September, the CDU/CSU had emerged as the largest party but the FDP, with 30 seats, voted overwhelmingly to accept an offer from the SPD (who had 224 seats) to form a coalition and, on 20 October Willy Brandt was elected as Chancellor by the Bundestag. Walter Scheel became Foreign Minister, offering the prospect, as Stewart had told Cabinet earlier in the month of "greater German enthusiasm for our entry into the EEC", as well as a more determined search for a better relationship between the Federal Government and the Soviet Union.[23]

Wilson had of course had a polite exchange of messages with Brandt when the latter won the election but Wilson's message had made no mention of Europe. In London, the German Ambassador (Blankenhorn) advised Con O'Neill at the Foreign Office that the British Government needed to make the need for early progress on its application clear to Brandt at the highest level. Brandt would of course be most reluctant to endanger German relations with France but this would be nothing like so exclusive a preoccupation for Brandt as it had been for Kiesinger. On the subject of British membership, Brandt was in a much stronger position than his predecessor. There would be no opponents of British membership in the new German Cabinet. Blankenhorn advised that the essence of the matter was that it was essential that the forthcoming summit of the Six should decide that, come what may, negotiations for British membership should open in the first half of 1970.[24]

Within two days Wilson had written to Brandt. The British Government and the British political parties had, Wilson wrote, kept a remarkable faith with Europe over the past two frustrating years. The British had high hopes that the Summit of the Six in The Hague would open the door to negotiations with Britain and fix a date for their start. Wilson hoped that Brandt would use "the immeasurably stronger position" he had in Community affairs to deliver that result. "On my side," Wilson said, "I can assure you that there will be no change in policy and no weakening in our determination to open negotiations as soon as possible on terms that are fair for all; and see them develop in our common interest . . . It would be a blow to the hopes we have all set ourselves if the Summit passes with progress on other fronts but not on this".[25]

Brandt replied almost by return, quoting from the statement which the new German Government would make to the Bundestag: "The enlargement of the European Community must come. The Community needs Great Britain as much as the other applicant countries. In the chorus of European voices the voice of Great Britain must not be missing, unless Europe wants to inflict harm on herself. We were gratified to note that the decisive voices in British policy continue to be convinced that Great Britain in turn needs Europe." In this spirit, Brandt concluded, he would support, not only the Community's internal development, but equally the applications for membership.[26]

When the British Ambassador in Bonn, Roger Jackling, called on Brandt three days later, Brandt described himself as still somewhat sceptical but not pessimistic about the prospects. He thought there was some sign of movement on the French side and, in any case, he intended to make matters clear to the French in friendly but firm fashion.[27]

The British Government continued to gird itself for a negotiation. William Nield, in a minute of 20 October to the Cabinet Secretary, Burke Trend, noted the need for urgent completion of the work on the cost of joining the EEC which the Prime Minister had promised to give to Parliament and the public before the end of the year; for a survey of the Government's European strategy over the next six to twelve months; and for the preparation of negotiating positions. The Cabinet Office, on the basis of Whitehall work to that point, was making "a guess" of a total balance of payments cost of membership of between £620 and £950 million, as compared with a figure of about £500 million a year given by the Prime Minister in the House in May 1967. This was partly due to the devaluation of sterling but by far the most important factor was the escalation of the total cost of the CAP to $2,500 million a year (compared with the estimate of $1,300 made in 1967). The Commission's estimate of the cost of the Community's agricultural budget by the mid 70s was $3,600 million.

Nield went on to spell out the dilemma for the Government: "We obviously cannot afford to accept the CAP without some ceiling on the UK contribution, and this is increasingly recognised in Europe . . . Changes in estimates of commodity prices and production do not alone make sufficient difference to produce a plausible and acceptable lower figure. But what will be the consequences of indicating publicly that with a ceiling we could limit the total cost of entry to about £500 million? The latter figure could well then be interpreted as our negotiating objective. This would be a very different situation from that in 1967 when the

Prime Minister indicated that entry might cost us £500 million if we could secure no improvements through negotiation . . ."[28]

Trend forwarded the minuting to the Prime Minister, asking for a meeting. When the three men met on 24 October Wilson asked Nield to prepare a scheme which would involve a series of prices for each of the main agricultural products as well as various assumptions of limitations on the British contribution to FEOGA (the agricultural support budget of the EEC) in relation to GNP. The paper on agriculture (if there was more than one White Paper) or chapter (if one White Paper would suffice) should contain a detailed scheme while others could be 'essay' papers in more philosophical mood e.g. on Britain's industrial competitiveness depending on whether she entered the Community or stayed out.

Significantly, Wilson was clear that the possibility of a General Election was not a reason for delay in seeking the opening of negotiations. The Government should be ready to begin as soon as the Six were ready. But the Prime Minister thought it unlikely that negotiations would be completed and entry achieved before an election took place.[29]

On 21 October, the Foreign Secretary had addressed a meeting of junior Ministers in Downing Street, enjoining them to refer to the Government's firm policy on EEC membership and to remove misconceptions: "Too many people still have a mental picture of western Europe as a war torn continent, in almost every economic way inferior to ourselves. That is, of course, a totally imaginative picture now. There is also unawareness of the results for the world if this country were to commit a 'volte-face' if we did not go ahead with negotiations". It was important, Stewart said, that it was not just FCO Ministers who spoke on the subject, for it was the policy of the whole Government.[30]

At the end of October, the Prime Minister himself sent a minute to all Ministers on the same theme. The Foreign Secretary reiterated the appeal at Cabinet on 6 November.[31] At the same time, the composition of the Ministerial Committee on the Approach to Europe was revised though its chairmanship (the Foreign Secretary) and its terms of reference ("To exercise general supervision of the negotiations with our applications for membership . . . and to report as necessary to the Cabinet") remained unchanged.[32]

The date for the summit meeting of the Six had been fixed for the first two days of December. By mid-November the British Government had a clearer, though by no means certain, sense of French intentions. Stewart told Wilson when the two met on 12 November that "the danger was that there could be an agreement on agricultural finance which the French would insist could only be changed by unanimity (i.e. the French would have a veto)." Wilson thought that the French might press for negotiations among the Six on the agricultural/financial Regulation to be completed before a date was fixed for negotiations. They might also seek agreement that the Community should establish a joint position on negotiations before these began.

The two men also discussed the preparations for the White Paper on the economic effects of the United Kingdom joining the EEC. Wilson said that it had been suggested to him that this might take the form of a Green paper but he was much against this. A Green Paper was for the purpose of promoting public discussion on policy to which the Government were not necessarily committed and from which they could withdraw without loss of face. A Green Paper would give the impression that the Government's policy on Europe had changed since 1967 and that the policy was now open for reconsideration. Both Wilson and Stewart were strongly of the view that the document should be in the form of a White Paper.[33]

At meetings in Bonn a few days later, when Stewart met both Brandt and Scheel, it was made clear to him that the German Government saw no alternative to an agricultural finance agreement being reached by the Six by, or shortly after, the end of the year in a definitive form. The Germans regarded this as inevitable if the French were to be induced to agree to the opening of negotiations.

On 17 November, the Foreign Office instructed its Embassies to make no reference to these conversations but to continue to stress the disadvantages of a definitive settlement on agricultural finance between the Six in advance of negotiations for British entry. "The reasons for maintaining our line on this point (even though we can now no longer have much confidence of gaining it)", the Foreign Office argued, "are (i) the need to maintain pressure on the French through the Five for maximum adaptability in the event of enlargement of any agreement on agricultural finance which they may reach; (ii) the fact that other Community Governments (especially the Italians) have not yet given way over a definitive Regulation; (iii) the risk that, if we appear to accept as inevitable a definitive agricultural finance settlement, the French will use this fact to increase pressure on their Community partners for further concessions; and (iv) the need on our part to be able to point afterwards to the fact that we had warned the Community of the consequences of a definitive agreement. This last point has a double importance: before negotiations begin we may be obliged to take up a public position about the Six's agreement; and when the negotiations start we shall want to be able to make full play of the fact that we had fairly warned our friends in the Community of the difficulties arising from a definitive settlement".[34]

President Pompidou was the first speaker when the EEC Summit opened in The Hague on the afternoon of 1 December. The President asserted France's determination to maintain and develop the Community. However, (a) what had already been achieved must be "jealously preserved". Completion must take place according to the timescale laid down; (b) it was urgent to develop Community action, particularly as regards cooperation in economic and monetary policy. A list of precise and realistic objectives should be drawn up, and he would have proposals to make; (c) "the candidatures of Great Britain and the three other countries must be approached in a positive spirit but without losing from sight the interests of the Community and its members". Negotiations should be prepared among the Six so that a Community position could be defined. They should be conducted in the name of the Community and in the spirit of the Community.

Brandt spoke next. "The German Parliament and public expect me not to return from this conference without concrete arrangements regarding the Community's enlargement. I want to say that without Britain and the other countries desirous of entry, Europe cannot become what it should and can be . . .

The candidates should be given to understand that we think it possible to start negotiations next spring". Brandt set out a procedure for the Six to reach common positions in the negotiations. He also proposed that the Foreign Ministers of the Six be instructed to draft an agreement for the gradual development of political cooperation (foreign policy cooperation) among the members of the Community, and this on the assumption that the Community would be enlarged. Brandt said that the German Government was willing to proceed along the road to economic and monetary union "in a sober and realistic fashion".

That opening discussion had little in it that was new and there was a feeling of disappointment among the delegations of the Five that Pompidou had not been more forthcoming. The Dutch Chairman, Prime Minister de Jong, admitted in his press conference that evening that not much progress had been made, though Luns added that the delegations of the Six were agreed that there should be a financial regulation and that this should not be such as to make it impossible for negotiations to open with the candidates. The regulation should also be capable of being altered in the course of negotiations; in other words, it should be negotiable.

Luns's view was contradicted by the French spokesman who said at a separate press conference that what had been agreed was that there should be a financial regulation and that it should be in place by the end of the year. It would be definitive. Such a definitive regulation could be adapted, but only by agreement of the original parties. No one, according the French spokesman, had contested the necessity of maintaining unanimity.[35]

Over a dinner hosted by the Queen of the Netherlands that evening, Ministers continued their discussions informally. Walter Scheel, the new German Foreign Minister, said to Schumann that there seemed to be no really new features in what Pompidou had said. Schumann denied this claiming that, for the first time, Pompidou had not only said that France was in favour of enlargement negotiations in principle, but that she wished them success.

Whether because Schumann reported back to Pompidou on the mood of disappointment, or because one of Brandt's crucial private interventions with Pompidou (not widely known about at the time) had already taken place, Pompidou spoke in more concrete (and conciliatory) terms when the session resumed the next morning. The need to close the previous day's session had, Pompidou said, prevented him from developing his thoughts. He then set out a six point plan for the EEC: economic integration; monetary cooperation; technology; developing countries; social policy (by which he meant the harmonisation of the policies and practices of Member States in the social sphere); political cooperation (the Community should not separate its members from their US friends or indeed from anyone else but frequent meetings of the Foreign Ministers were called for). Pompidou concluded: "We are willing to go through these problems in a progressive spirit, notably with regard to the candidates".

Pompidou made a second intervention during the course of the day. He wished, he said, to convince his colleagues of his good intentions with regard to enlargement. He was not hostile to enlargement; on the contrary, he was in favour and he thought that the decisions necessary for reaching a common position could be taken in the shortest and most practicable timescale. If this were done there would be no need to have a specific date for the opening of negotiations.

The final communiqué stipulated, as the French had required, that the Community would "pass from the transitional period to the final stage. . . . and accordingly lay down a definitive financial arrangement for the CAP by the end of 1969". The wording on enlargement reflected French refusal to accept any suggestion of a starting date for negotiations in the communiqué. Instead, the communiqué itself noted that "insofar as the applicant states accept the Treaties and their political finality, the decisions taken since the entry into force of the Treaties and the option made in the sphere of development, the Heads of State or Government have indicated their agreement to the opening of negotiations . . ."

In the end, disagreement on the issue was resolved by a classic piece of Community compromise. The Dutch chairman, de Jong, put a formula to the delegations, based on words used by Pompidou, and proposed that this form of words should be used by all the national delegations in their press conferences. The formula was that all were of the opinion "that the difficult problems mentioned in the communiqué, problems which should be solved before the start of negotiations, could be decided in the first half of 1970, and probably earlier, and that negotiations could start immediately thereafter".[36]

"The significance of the Summit meeting", Nield wrote in a note for the Prime Minister, "is that it marks no more and no less than the first small breach in the dyke of French obstruction to both the development and the enlargement of the Community".

Nield attributed the breach to three main causes: the personality, position and performance of Brandt, who had done well for Britain, being openly friendly to the United Kingdom where Kiesinger was covertly indifferent, if not hostile; the weakened position of France following the May 1968 disorders, the fall of de Gaulle and the devaluation of the Franc; and the position taken at the summit by the Community as a whole. But Nield also advised caution. Whilst there had been the first breach, there was a long way to go before the dyke was down. The settlement of Community policy was still under discussion and, while Britain had a major interest in it, she was still a third party. The stagnation of the Community and the obstruction of de Gaulle had left Britain with a ten-year syndrome of being 'unwanted' by a Community whose problems had in recent years been more in the public eye than its achievements. The image of a not very good club with a high subscription and expensive meals persisted. Even if the Community had been a public triumph, Britain's own problems in respect of membership would be great. The Government were, in effect, asking the public to look beyond the price of butter tomorrow to the position of Britain and Europe in the last three decades of a twentieth century dominated in all fields by America, Russia and perhaps China.[37]

Nield had intended his minute to be used by the Prime Minister as a speaking note at Cabinet. But Wilson was too canny to expose so much front. He allowed the Chancellor of the Duchy of Lancaster, George Thomson, who had been put in charge of European matters in the autumn reshuffle, to make the running and

Thomson concentrated on the achievement of a mid-1970 deadline for the opening of negotiations and on the 'outstanding' performance of the German Chancellor "whose firmness and consistency in discussion had contrasted very favourably with the performance of previous German Governments".

Cabinet as a whole agreed that "the results of the meeting both, politically and economically, were as good as could be expected".[38]

Wilson remained only "moderately" (the word he inserted into a draft message of thanks to Brandt)[39] encouraged even after a special visit to London by Dr Paul Frank, who was sent by Brandt from the German Foreign Ministry to brief Wilson and Stewart on the meeting in The Hague.

It was clear from Frank's account that the outcome of the meeting had indeed been touch and go. On day one, the Dutch Prime Minister had spoken in a way which suggested that enlargement was the main issue to be discussed. This had almost led to a French explosion. So Brandt had intervened to suggest that the way forward would be for the three main issues (completion, future development and enlargement) to be taken as a whole. There had also been two private meetings between Brandt and Pompidou at which Pompidou had said that he gave his word of honour that negotiations would begin during 1970. Brandt had told Pompidou that he could not go back to Germany with that indefinite a position, and at a further conversation the more forward formula was worked out.

Frank also spoke of the importance for Brandt of cooperation on monetary and economic policy. The Prime Minister assured Frank that the British position had always been that the British Government was prepared to go as far and as fast as her European partners.[40]

That there was a high agricultural price for Britain to pay for the opening of negotiations became even clearer when the French Finance Minister, Valéry Giscard d'Estaing, visited London on 4 December. In advance of the visit, the Foreign Office sent to the Prime Minister the Paris Embassy's Leading Personality Report on Giscard. These reports were a compendium, prepared annually by every British Embassy in the world, on the leading figures in their country. They invariably contained a pen portrait of the top men and women written by the Ambassador himself. Of Giscard, the British Embassy in Paris wrote: "M. Giscard's greatest personal assets are his intelligence, energy, originality and practical ability and experience; and his greatest shortcomings are lack of popular appeal, due to his arrogance, coldness of manner and the silver spoon he allows too obviously to stick out of his mouth. He has most influence among the traditional middle class, the administration, the professions, and the student world, to which he represents the better aspects of Gaullism. He is well-disposed towards Britain and has gradually moved to a position of support for the British EEC candidature. He is now one of the supporters of British membership of the Communities within the French Government. He speaks fair English".[41]

Giscard told Wilson that Pompidou had told him that the results of the EEC summit had been broadly in accord with what the French had wanted. There had been some misunderstanding of the French attitude among her EEC partners but Pompidou felt that a basis of trust had now been established. The French, Giscard said, had insisted on the need to complete in the current year an agreement on the agricultural financial regulations and agricultural policy. The French supported the proposal that all agricultural levies and all customs duties should be devoted to the common EEC agricultural fund. These two sources of funding would, however, still leave a 30% shortfall in the funding of total expenditure under the agricultural fund, amounting to between $600 and $750 millions. Different keys, Giscard suggested, could be used to calculate the contributions needed from the Member States to meet this shortfall. But, in substance, the use of different keys, for example GNP or population, would not lead to significant differences in the final figures.

The Prime Minister pointed out that under the proposed system the highest contribution to the fund would come from those countries with the highest imports. This appears to have made little impact on Giscard who replied that a financial solution on the lines he had described was important to France, not only financially but politically, because the EEC had not been a good bargain for France industrially, and they relied on the agricultural sector to offset this.

Giscard said he would not seek to make any estimate of the probable length of the negotiations but there would be two main items: agricultural policy and monetary problems. Monetary cooperation would become more urgent. Wilson replied that the UK had always made it clear that she was prepared to go as far in monetary matters as her European colleagues, not excluding a common currency.[42]

That view was consistently held. When, in February 1970, the Chancellor of the Exchequer, Roy Jenkins, visited Paris, he told Giscard that some people had suggested that the United Kingdom might find difficulty in movements towards monetary union because they might disturb Britain's relations with the United States. This was not true, Jenkins said, in any sense. He did not believe that the United Kingdom would have any difficulty in moving as far and as fast as any member of the Six. That Jenkins knew precisely what moving as far and as fast as any member of the Six might mean was not in doubt. For when Giscard said that, in due course, there might be only two currencies of any importance – the European currency and the US dollar – Jenkins did not demur and confirmed that the British Government "did not want to reserve the monetary field from the Community, and we were prepared to move far in this field".

When Wilson saw a record of the conversation, he minuted: "Yes. Interesting. Chancellor seems to me to have given all the right answers".[43]

That the financial regulation which the EEC was about to adopt would be enormously damaging to Britain was no news to officials. On 12 December, Nield briefed No. 10 that "the Six appear likely to agree in meetings next week on a definitive agricultural regulation which would make it impossible for us to join the Community unless it was very substantially modified, and correspondingly diffi-cult to negotiate adequate modifications". Nield advocated intervention with the Five even at the risk of being told that a regulation of this kind was the price of getting negotiations started.[44]

In parallel, at the Foreign Office, Con O'Neill briefed the Foreign Secretary. "Only Britain and Germany are likely to be substantial net contributors to the Fund".

O'Neill also warned Stewart that "the sort of arrangements the Six are now discussing could lead, if unmodified, to our having to make a net contribution three and a half times that of Germany.[45]

The proposed lobbying telegrams were authorised for issue by the Prime Minister. It is not clear how much influence, if any, they had on the final outcome of the Community's negotiations. The agreement reached in the Council of Ministers on 22 December made no reference to enlargement. The overall outcome was described in a Foreign Office note sent to No. 10 on 8 January. In what the Foreign Office called "an extremely complicated agreement", the French had secured their prime objective: the payment of agricultural levies to the Community. But the agreement also made provision for the repayment of 10% of those levies to the levying countries, an important concession. The Five had also secured an additional transitional period; the establishment of a country's GNP as one of the elements in calculating its contribution (directly during the transitional period and through Value Added Tax thereafter); a tight rein on changes in the share to be paid for by each country for at least the next eight years; and some increase in the role of the European Parliament, to which the Netherlands and Italy in particular attached importance.

There were, the Foreign Office argued, still too many uncertainties in the agreement for it to be possible to assess the consequences for the United Kingdom. Three points were, however clear: changes would have to be agreed unanimously. But the agreement now reached could not be applied to an enlarged Community without important changes, if only because of the need to renegotiate the basic financing key on which the whole agreement was constructed. No principles had been laid down for the definition of this key; a very great deal would depend on whether the narrow limits placed on annual variations in the share of expenditure paid for by each country continued after 1977. Nothing was said about the post-1977 period.

It was also important, the Foreign Office concluded, that the Six had given themselves in effect a further substantial transitional period in agricultural finance. This would have helpful implications for Britain's own prospects because it strengthened the case for Britain having a long transitional period, at least in agriculture; and because, in the course of such a period, important changes could take place in the operation of the CAP itself.[46]

The Prime Minister's Christmas recess reading had been the draft of the Government's proposed White Paper ('Britain and the European Communities: An Economic Assessment'). The aim of the White Paper had always been to set out the facts and figures of the costs of membership. But Nield, in submitting the draft White Paper to the Prime Minister on 19 December, suggested that the draft also needed "a rather longer and much stronger piece on the political advantages of joining, not only to counter-balance the generally adverse and partly quantified general economic sections, but also because the political advantages were given in 1967 as a major reason for applying for membership". Wilson was not persuaded, writing in the margin: "Not certain. Should be as factual as possible, not argumentative". On a separate slip of paper, Wilson wrote: "I like this draft but am worried about the idea of a political introduction".[47]

When Wilson met Nield and the Cabinet Secretary, Burke Trend, a few days later, the Prime Minister pronounced the White Paper "an impressive document". But he repeated that he did not favour a long introductory passage on the advantages of entry, since "to do so would give the opponents of entry the opportunity of saying that we were seeking to disguise the economic effects by vague political arguments. To argue the political case at length would also change the nature of the White Paper, which was to give facts". The Prime Minister suggested instead the insertion of a short paragraph which could simply refer back to statements made in the House or in one of his own speeches on the importance of the political arguments for Britain's entry into the EEC. Such an approach would also be consistent with his thought that any debate in the House should be on a 'take note' motion; and the attitude of the Government would be that it could not come to any conclusion on the issue until it was clear what the terms of Britain's entry to the EEC might be.[48]

Was Wilson hedging his bets on membership, as one German newspaper, the *Muenchner-Merkur*, suggested when the White Paper was published on 10 February, arguing that the White Paper made it difficult to believe in the Prime Minister's enthusiasm for the Common Market? He must realise, the paper said in an editorial, that "only the anti-Marketeers would profit most from publication. Those in Western Europe who thought that Britain's entry to the EEC had been decided already should not be quite so certain".[49]

Le Figaro was perhaps closer to the mark. Noting that the higher estimate of the cost to Britain of joining the EEC would present ammunition to the anti-Common Market factions in Britain, the paper concluded that the White Paper would be a weapon that Wilson would not fail to use during negotiations with the Six.[50]

The evidence of the documents about discussion of the White Paper itself and of the Prime Minister's attitude to enlargement at that time suggests political caution on Wilson's part. He was certainly tacking in an unfavourable wind. But there is no evidence that he was harbouring doubts about the destination.

For a start, the Government had promised a factual White Paper. Wilson wanted its objectivity to be accepted by those who read it and he told Cabinet on 3 February that "the White Paper deliberately avoided setting out the political and other arguments for and against membership. The introduction of such arguments would undermine the objective – even pessimistic – assessment contained in the draft". Nonetheless, in his presentation to Cabinet, Wilson was at pains to play down the "theoretical" range of cost to the balance of payments of between £100 million and £1,000 million annually. Neither the top nor the bottom of this range represented a realistic estimate. He thought it might be reasonable to assume that the eventual cost might, at the end of the transitional period, be of the order of £700 million a year, compared with a similar estimate of £500 a year which had been indicated to Parliament in 1967. The increase since 1967 was partly due to sterling devaluation and partly to the escalation of the cost of CAP. But it was only necessary to assume a very small increase in the annual rate of growth of Britain's GDP as a result of entry into an enlarged Community in order to provide the additional resources required to meet the cost of membership over a long transitional period.

Wilson also told Cabinet that he would arrange to see the Directors General of both the BBC and ITA "and explain to them that the Government did not consider it appropriate for this important issue to be made the subject of confrontation on TV between the advocates and opponents of UK membership of the EEC."[51]

What seems clear is that Wilson wanted to get the figures into the public domain without reopening an argument within the Labour Party, Parliament or the public about the fundamental issues. He wanted to have the political argument on the back of the outcome of the negotiations, not on the basis of prior speculation on worst case scenarios. Equally, it had never been his position that the political advantages of joining (more decisive though they were, in his view, than the economic ones) were of themselves overwhelming. That there could be an economic price which Britain simply could not afford to pay was clear from the submissions officials had made before Christmas about the risks of the EEC's impending agricultural/financial settlement.

For those reasons, in presenting the White Paper to the House of Commons on 10 February, Wilson spelled out that "Britain's application for membership has been made and that is not in question . . . Until the outcome of [the] negotiations is known neither the Government nor Parliament will be in a position to take the final decisions. The negotiations will take place against the background of Britain's economic progress, and particularly of the improvement in our balance of payments and in the strength of sterling . . . These facts create a situation in which the Government and Parliament can take their decisions in full confidence that on fair terms we can stand and profit by the far more competitive situation that entry into the Market implies. But equally they create a situation which leaves no-one in doubt that should the negotiations not lead to acceptable terms for entry, Britain is and will be strong enough to stand on her own feet outside . . . The Government will enter into negotiations resolutely, in good faith, mindful both of British interests and of the advantages of success in the negotiations to all the members of an enlarged Community. We have made it clear that if the negotiations produce acceptable conditions for British entry we believe that this will be advantageous for Britain, for Europe and for Europe's voice in the world . . . Failure of the negotiations would involve a cost for Britain, a cost for Europe, and a diminution of Europe's influence in world affairs."[52]

That Wilson's presentation was taken then at face value seems to be borne out by Edward Heath's low-key and supportive response from the Opposition benches. When Jeremy Thorpe, for the Liberals, congratulated Wilson "on his consistency in keeping as many options open at the same time as is possible, apart from a definite commitment to open negotiations", Wilson replied that Thorpe had "got it about right. There are no options open at all in respect of the decision to open negotiations and to approach them in a determination that they should succeed if the price is acceptable".[53]

Further evidence of Wilson's position at the time comes from both public and private events. On 11 January 1970, Hugh Cudlipp, Chairman of the Mirror Group of Newspapers, and one of the most powerful newspaper chiefs of the time, organised a non-attributable press conference on Europe, involving Wilson, Stewart and Thomson. Wilson referred then to the "few important subjects for negotiation", among which the CAP and its financing were paramount. In the negotiations, Britain would be concerned about the length of the transition period, the allocation of burdens and the ultimate future of the CAP itself. In monetary matters, Wilson said, Britain would not be backward and he quoted both Roy Jenkins and Jim Callaghan as being in support of a European currency. As to future integration, Wilson said that human progress was based on the progressive derogation of sovereignty. The important questions were to whom sovereignty be ceded and for what purpose. Organisations such as NATO, EFTA and the UN were "calculated derogations of sovereignty". One had to calculate whether the advantages were greater than the sacrifices. In his view, all these arguments about sovereignty had ceased to be valid thirty years ago.

On the issue of the use of majority voting in the Community, Michael Stewart said that the Treaty of Rome obliged Member States to institute Qualified Majority voting. Britain must accept no more nor less, though the Treaty of Rome indicated where the future lay. We were talking about a living thing, and not a geometrical problem.

In reply to a question about what limits the British Government would place on Europe's political development, George Thomson replied: "We would not use the word 'never'. In all this talk of harmonising the objective must be 'uniting'."[54]

When Wilson visited Washington at the end of January, he did so against a background in which, as the British Ambassador, John Freeman, had warned him "the present US Administration were not as committed to our European venture as President Kennedy had been. President Kennedy had been prepared to contemplate the US paying an economic price with equanimity in return for the political gain . . . Kissinger had asked him to produce 'five good reasons' for our joining the Communities".[55]

When Wilson and Nixon met at the White House on 27 January, Wilson told the President that "it was probably true that President Pompidou remained opposed in principle to the entry of Britain to the EEC. On the other hand, it was perhaps unlikely that he would actively seek to frustrate it, since he would now regard it as the price he would have to pay for preserving the CAP which was essential to the French farmer. Moreover, he did not suffer from the same psychological inhibitions as his predecessor in relation to the Atlantic community".

As regards Britain's own application to join the EEC, Wilson continued, "it remained true that the economic argument was finely balanced – as our forthcoming White Paper would shortly show. But the case for our membership on political grounds was a strong one; and in the eyes of the French it would be reinforced by their growing fear of a revanchist Germany. For these reasons we were cautiously optimistic about the outcome of the negotiations".

On 29 January, Wilson was invited to attend a meeting of the National Security Council (NSC). He was the first foreign leader ever to be invited to do so.

Wilson told the meeting that, on the EEC, the British Government well understood the difficulty for the United States. He asked the Administration to try to understand the UK problem and the wider interests involved in it. It was equally true for the United Kingdom and for the United States that it was worthwhile putting up with a certain amount of economic difficulty for the greater political unity which could follow.

For his part, the President said, as he had done in his meeting with Wilson two days earlier, that he favoured a strong Europe, economically, politically and in the end in defence, and with Britain included in that Europe. It would, in his view, be entirely healthy to have Britain in Europe "bringing a dimension of our common thought and background into the counsels of Europe".[56]

The same thought was expressed even more clearly in a document submitted by the President to Congress on 18 February. In *US Foreign Policy for the 1970s: A New Strategy for Peace*, the Administration affirmed that "in the third decade of our commitment to Europe, the depth of our relationship is a fact of life. We can no more disengage from Europe than from Alaska . . . We have no desire to occupy such a position in Europe that European affairs are not the province of the sovereign states that conduct them. Intra-European institutions are in flux. We favour the definition by Western Europe of a distinct identity, for the sake of its own continued vitality and independence of spirit. Our support for the strengthening and broadening of the European Community has not diminished. We recognise that our interests will necessarily be affected by Europe's evolution, and we may have to make sacrifices in the common interest. We consider that the possible economic price of a truly unified Europe is outweighed by the gain in the political vitality of the West as a whole . . ."[57]

Wilson had been in Ottawa prior to his visit to Washington and, after his return to London, the British High Commissioner, Sir Colin Crowe, wrote to Wilson's new Foreign Office Private Secretary, Peter Moon (Teddy Youde having left Downing Street following a heart problem) to say that a number of the correspondents who had attended the Prime Minister's press conference in Ottawa had grumbled afterwards about Wilson's references to speeches made in the House of Commons or to White Papers published in the United Kingdom, on the grounds that they could not be expected to recollect them or to look them up.

Moon showed Crowe's letter to Wilson. The Prime Minister's reply was characteristic. His action had been deliberate: "I always refer back to speeches when I want to kill a question, which I did (a) to avoid pre-empting Washington talks and (b) to prevent feedback on things not new but [which] would be given a new twist".[58]

The Government faced a number of difficulties. Their commitment to membership of the EEC had been taken primarily on political grounds but the case for entry had to be rooted in economic argument and the figures given in the White Paper were not favourable. It was this determination to join, combined with an underwhelming economic argument that in part accounted for an opinion poll finding early in 1970 that 72% of those questioned were against Common Market membership but that 76% believed that Britain would nonetheless eventually become a member. Roy Jenkins explained the anomaly by arguing that "people generally do tend to believe that what the country's political leaders are committed to is likely to come about in the long run. Furthermore, it has often been the case that when a majority think that something is likely to occur this presages a movement of opinion in favour".[59]

Wilson reiterated the Government's commitment in talks with the German Chancellor, Willy Brandt, at the end of February. He told Brandt that the Government would be entering accession negotiations in the determination to succeed. The White Paper had inevitably been deficient in that it could only deal with the economic aspects. But, as he had told Brandt's predecessor three years earlier, the overriding arguments in favour of membership were the political ones and it was these, in particular considerations of the role which an enlarged EEC could play in the world, which had converted him to seeking membership. The British Government intended to go into the negotiations with the political aspect in the forefront of their minds.

Brandt told Wilson that, in the previous week, the Finance Ministers of the Six had discussed ideas (a plan would be too big a word) for the development of the Community into an economic and currency union. But no-one in Britain need fear that progress on this aspect would advance too far before negotiations for enlargement started. There had in any case been a change of thinking on political integration since the early days of the Community. It was now generally recognised that, as things stood in Europe, it was better not to concentrate on a supra-national form of federation, but on organised qualified consultations in the political field, going beyond bilateral action. Roy Jenkins, who was present at the meeting, confirmed that "the developments in the Community in the monetary field posed no difficulties of principle for Britain and were in general welcome to her".[60]

Despite these brave words, the difficulty of negotiating for entry was increasingly apparent. Britain's Ambassadors in EEC countries were brought to London for a strategy meeting in March. George Thomson set the scene by telling the Ambassadors that the lesson of the Government's recent White Paper for the "intelligent uncommitted minority" was that the short-term economic disadvantages of membership were quantifiable whereas the medium-term advantages were not quantifiable. At the end of the day, it would be necessary to make a historic political judgement on whether the consequences which would flow from entry would be preferable to those which would flow from Britain's exclusion. That was not a question which could be answered by calculations made in a little black book. The Government were determined to negotiate toughly but in good faith.

Christopher Soames set the tone of the subsequent discussion. The French, having secured their national interests in a definitive financing deal at EEC level "were stressing the need for *communautaire* solutions because such solutions were basically in the French interest." The conclusion which Soames drew from this, and which was largely supported by the other Ambassadors present, was that the Government should also seek *communautaire* solutions rather than ask for derogations. It might, he argued, be easier to tell Parliament that the Government had secured a ceiling to the British contribution. But he did not think we would get one. An alternative would be to aim for an assurance that the movement of agricultural prices and production during a long transitional period would be such that the British contribution after the end of that transitional period would not be excessive.

It took Sir Con O'Neill, rather more than either Thomson or the Foreign Secretary, to inject a note of political realism. Community finance was, he said, the crucial issue. The meeting had been told by the Ambassadors how the Governments of the Six were attired in the white sheets of Community purity and would seek to find *communautaire* solutions to the problems of the negotiations, and not solutions involving exceptions. The advice might be good but, for this problem, it would be very hard to carry out. The figure of £670 million for the cost to Britain of the EEC budget was mentioned, but then virtually dismissed, in the White Paper. But it was not correct to dismiss it so lightly. The Government could not simply disregard the upper end of the scale of possible costs. Once automaticity applied, at the end of the transitional period, Britain would be in severe difficulties over Community finance unless some modification of the application of the system to Britain was agreed. It was true that the Germans paid a big share of Community costs. But if the system were applied without modification to Britain, Britain would have to pay a much larger share. If Britain's share of the costs were to approach £670 million, the other members of the Community would secure an enormous net benefit in terms of the resulting reduction in their own contributions. In terms of gross contributions, because of Britain's patterns of trade, she might have to contribute something like 40%, rather than the 20% which was the right share by the standards of comparative GNP. In terms of net contributions, taking account of the benefits which EEC countries received from the agricultural fund, Britain might well be paying something like 80%. This would be manifestly unjust. The French would naturally want to hang on to the benefits which they received. If they and others were prepared to accept an arrangement whereby they did rather better than they did now, instead of enormously better, then the problem could be solved. At The Hague, the possibility of adaptation of the Community finance system had been accepted. The British Government would have to cling to the possibility of such an adaptation, even though it would need unanimous agreement.

Sir William Nield from the Cabinet Office reinforced the point. If the costs of entry proved to be at the upper end of the White Paper scale, that would call for a transfer of resources from Britain to the EEC which would inhibit the growth to which Britain was looking forward as a consequence of accession. If that extra growth was to be severely inhibited, then it would be wrong for Britain to join the Community. Whether or not Britain could afford to join would depend on the solution of the Community finance problem. No country in the world could afford a burden of the size which might fall on Britain.[61]

This discussion is interesting for two reasons. Firstly, it provides early evidence that the issue of an equitable British EEC contribution predated by almost a decade the advent of Margaret Thatcher, to whom the single-minded search for a solution is usually uniquely attributed. O'Neill and Nield had recognised, as

Thatcher later did, that wrapping the national interests of the other EEC Member States in a *communautaire* flag was an issue of shared national self-interest, dishonestly disguised, not one of principle and that, while to attack such an approach would lay Britain open to accusations of nationalistic self-interest, that did not undermine the basic case in justice and equity for radical change. Secondly, the tone of the meeting suggests that the Ambassadors found it hard to see beyond the face value of the claims of the EEC Member States. Sir Roger Jackling appeared to take at face value that the Germans were becoming increasingly *communautaire* in their attitude. It would, he argued, be hard to persuade the Germans that Britain had serious and genuine difficulties over finance and he supported what he described as Soames's "plea" that the British Government should seem *communautaire* in the negotiations. The dichotomy evident at that meeting between the Ambassadors, scarred by years of exclusion from the EEC and finally on the threshold of acceptance, and officials at home with a harsh domestic opinion to satisfy, was one that was to characterise the pursuit of British EEC policy for years to come.

The difficulty in being *communautaire* (too readily interpreted at home as a synonym for over-accommodating) was of course compounded in a situation where, according to a Europe-wide opinion survey published in March, only 19% of Britons were in favour of EEC membership, against an average of 64% in favour of British accession in the EEC itself, including 69% in favour in Germany and 67% in France.[62]

Shortly after the meeting of the British Ambassadors, Nield put to the Prime Minister a paper which proposed a negotiating strategy based on three propositions, propositions which Wilson "very much liked". These were: (i) that the 1970 White Paper had demonstrated that acceptance of Community policies, and especially of the financial arrangements as they stood, would impose a balance of payments cost which was not viable in terms either of economics or equity; (ii) that entry on such terms would in fact excessively disadvantage both Britain and the Six and that an economic and monetary union (the solution favoured by the Commission) would only serve to convert a national balance of payments problem into a regional resource allocation problem of equal gravity and equal drag on the development of the enlarged Community generally; (iii) that the only way to overcome the problem was to see how the balance of payments cost could be reduced (a) by general means, e.g. a formula limiting national shares of the cost, and/or a spreading of the cost on the basis that the higher the cost the longer the transition period, and (b) by an item by item reduction of the cost by means which were *communautaire* i.e. which would bind the enlarged Community together and not divide it.

Such a strategy, Nield suggested, would keep all of the Government's options open, and none of the options should be closed until all had been squeezed dry. The bulk of the problem lay in the costs of the CAP and its financing and only very substantial reductions in the cost of the CAP would help the United Kingdom. So the focus of the strategy must be on agriculture and the Government's dual objective should be to reduce both its total cost and Britain's share of that cost.[63]

Officials were busy preparing negotiating briefs, ready for a June start. At the same time came the first indication of the rift that was to dog Labour in opposition. Given that a General Election in the Government's fourth year was usual and that Labour were far ahead of the Conservatives in the polls, speculation in Britain about the imminence of a General Election was rife. So it was perhaps not surprising that, on 25 May, Peter Shore, Minister without Portfolio in the Cabinet, should make a speech which implied, so the Foreign Secretary told Cabinet the next day that the Government "no longer wished, or intended, to make a real effort to join the EEC." Stewart, who would undoubtedly have cleared his line in advance with Wilson, went on to say that Shore's speech had been at variance with the Government's official policy and would create an unfortunate impression of divided counsels within the Government which could not be other than damaging to the prospects of success in the forthcoming negotiations.

Shore was apologetic on process (he regretted that he had not consulted Stewart before making the speech) but, on substance, he "could not accept that it would necessarily have damaging results". Its most critical passage, dealing with the balance of payments impact of membership, had been agreed in principle with the Foreign Office and the rest of the speech "merely drew attention to the undeniable fact that the EEC was not simply an enlarged free trade area but was a Community which involved its members in a commitment to a closer and more intimate relationship with fellow members than with outside countries . . . It could not be maintained that it was wrong to remind public opinion of this essential fact".

Wilson reaffirmed to Cabinet both the Government's policy and the need not to allow any "impression to be created that they were prepared to treat a major issue of national policy as the subject of mere party political controversy in the period before the forthcoming General Election". Shore was instructed to "seek an early opportunity to put his speech in better perspective, making it clear that it remained the Government's declared purpose to join the EEC if acceptable terms could be obtained".[64] Shore did so, in a rather grudging way about five weeks later.[65]

In the meantime, the speech was seized on in the House of Commons by opponents and supporters of EEC entry alike. Wilson was not to be drawn into direct comment on Shore's speech but he made clear to Willie Hamilton (a Labour opponent of entry) that "we are extremely anxious to get in, if we can get the right terms, and that we will proceed to negotiate with full determination to that end". In reply to the Liberal Leader, Jeremy Thorpe, who cited Shore's speech as casting the Government in the role of 'Mr Facing-Both-Ways' on Europe, Wilson said: "We are negotiating to get in with determination and, if the terms are right, we shall put a proposition to that effect before the House".[66]

In what turned out to be the final weeks of Harold Wilson's Government, the evidence that the Prime Minister and other senior Ministers were preparing seriously and single-mindedly for negotiations for EEC accession, and were doing so with every intention of a successful outcome, is plentiful. This evidence is not unimportant in the light of what transpired when Labour were in Opposition and of frequent assertions that Wilson was always half-hearted about EEC membership.

On 7 April Wilson and Roy Jenkins held a meeting in London with the Swedish Prime Minister, Olaf Palme. Jenkins told Palme that there was a new momentum within the Six towards some form of monetary union, to be achieved by the end of 1978 or 1979. Jenkins himself thought the date a little optimistic and that it might slip into the 1980s. Such a move would have political implications. A move towards monetary union could mean the end of the exchange rate adjustment as an instrument for dealing with economic disparities within the Community. If the theory became practice, this would entail a high degree of economic coordination to support monetary cooperation, and this in turn raised the question of what degree of political control there should be. The move towards monetary union might thus impose a faster pace on political integration than would otherwise be the case. It was not necessarily the case that the monetary union argument was propounded only by those who favoured a close degree of political cooperation. France, for example, seemed to favour monetary union. Politico-monetary considerations might thus tend to replace politico-military considerations as the central issue of international policy over, say, the next five years.[67] Wilson did not gloss what Jenkins had said in any way. He subsequently reported to Cabinet that the Swedes "were strongly in favour of British membership of the EEC".[68]

On 27 April, Wilson met the Luxembourg Foreign Minister, Gaston Thorn, in London. Thorn referred to the work on economic and monetary union being undertaken by the Luxembourg Prime Minister, Pierre Werner. Wilson replied that the British Government were ready to play their part in this field. He had long thought that closer monetary cooperation was essential if there was to be greater unity.

Wilson went on to ask whether Britain's entry into the Common Market was now widely accepted in the rest of Europe. Thorn thought that it was, including in France. There were, however, some doubts about the British readiness to go as fast as others on political integration. Wilson said he thought the British Government were ready to go as far and as fast as the rest of the Six would wish to, but he believed that a supra-national political federation was still a long way off.[69]

On the following day, Wilson met the Economic Committee of the TUC. He told them that the Government's decision on entry into the Common Market would ultimately depend on the terms that could be obtained. It was true that if the terms were crippling the effect would be to nullify the dynamic advantages of entry. But on better terms of entry there could be important dynamic advantages. There would be a continuing balance of payments cost but the faster the growth rate the easier it would be to absorb that cost and, in any case, reducing the balance of payments cost to Britain was of course a matter to be dealt with in the negotiations.

Wilson went on to spell out some of the obligations of membership. Britain had to accept the constitution of the EEC. There was no question, however, of a total loss of sovereignty and of absorption into a single unit. A federal Europe might come in time. But that was not what was involved in acceding to the Treaty of Rome. Nor was it a present reality.

That Wilson was already seeking to establish for himself an adequate degree of negotiating room is evidenced by his telling the TUC that "on the one hand we could accept a balance of payments cost of £20 million. On the other hand, we certainly could not accept a balance of payments cost of £2,000 million. In between was what might be called the negotiating belt". Wilson concluded by reverting to give examples of what he saw as the dynamic advantages of entry.[70]

On the same day, Michael Stewart sent to Wilson the draft of an article he was submitting to the July issue of *Foreign Affairs*. The focus of the article was European integration for which, Stewart believed and wrote, the field was a very wide one. At the end of the day, members of the European Community would have to be prepared to accept its full political, military and economic obligations. It would be very much a second best if some European countries were to abstain from integration in certain fields. It was impossible to predict what institutions would be needed for this European integration. They would have to grow pragmatically.

Stewart acknowledged that, largely because of anxiety about a rise in food prices, there was a fluctuating majority who answered 'no' to the question 'do you want Britain to join the EEC?' But the leadership in every walk of British life, as well as the younger generation, were decisively in favour of British entry. Public opinion could be expected to take a more positive attitude when negotiations had started and looked like succeeding.

Wilson had only one adverse comment on the article: the implication that a Western Europe, integrated for every purpose, might be taken to mean that the Government favoured such integration for defence. That seemed to go beyond what the Government had said. Stewart made that passage of his article less specific.[71]

The final piece of evidence of the position of the Labour Government on the eve of the General Election is in the minutes of the first session of the Ministerial Cabinet sub-committee on the EEC negotiations which met under George Thomson's chairmanship on 11 May. The meeting looked at three options for dealing with the huge balance of payments problem with which Britain was threatened by the EEC's financing arrangements: to insist on a reshaping of the EEC's arrangements; to seek a specially favourable arrangement for the UK; or to accept the EEC's arrangements but to adopt some of the Community's own devices to find a tolerable solution. The sub-committee considered that, while it looked as if either of the two first courses would not be acceptable to the Six, it was not necessary or indeed desirable to define British objectives before the British problem had been exhaustively examined with the Six. Thus, the Government were clearly prepared for a detailed negotiation on what was recognised as by far the most difficult issue that needed to be resolved.[72]

Cabinet met on Sunday 17 May to be told that Wilson had decided to ask the Queen to proclaim the dissolution of Parliament for 29 May, with the General Election to be held on 18 June.

Since the three main parties all supported Britain's accession to the EEC, Europe was not an issue in the campaign, although the position taken by some

Conservative candidates in their individual election addresses was to become a problem for Heath later on. The Election Manifestos of both the Labour and Conservative parties had relatively little to say about Europe. The Labour Manifesto noted that negotiations for accession were due to start in a few weeks' time. "These will be pressed with determination with the purpose of joining an enlarged Community provided that British and essential Commonwealth interests can be safeguarded". The manifesto claimed that, unlike the situation in 1963, Britain would be negotiating from a position of strength and would be able to meet the challenges and realise the opportunities of joining an enlarged Community. But Britain's economic strength meant too that, if satisfactory terms could not be secured in the negotiations, Britain would be able to stand on her own feet outside the Community.

The Conservative Manifesto was more evenly balanced as between the pros and cons of membership, pointing out the short-term disadvantages of accession and the fact that "obviously there is a price we would not be prepared to pay . . . Our sole commitment is to negotiate; no more, no less. As the negotiations proceed we will report regularly through Parliament to the country. A Conservative Government would not be prepared to recommend to Parliament, nor would Members of Parliament approve, a settlement which was unequal or unfair. In making this judgement, Ministers and Members will listen to the views of their constituents and have in mind, as is natural and legitimate, primarily the effect of entry upon the standard of living of the individual citizens whom they represent".

The Conservative Manifesto was clearly designed to placate all those with doubts about membership. In addition, in a speech in Paris in May, when it was becoming increasingly clear that an election was to be called, Heath had said that the EEC could not be enlarged without the "full-hearted consent of the peoples and Parliaments" of the applicant countries. Heath later argued that anyone who knew the British constitution should have known that he was referring only to approval by Parliament and that he was not hinting at the possibility of a referendum. But the fact remained that he had referred to "peoples *and* Parliaments" rather than to the people *through* Parliament. His words were to return to taunt and haunt him.[73]

The opinion polls consistently put Labour ahead throughout the General Election campaign but, on the day, the Conservatives won with a convincing majority of 31 seats, when combined with Unionist support. The reasons for Wilson's defeat were various but Europe does not appear to have been among them. Subsequent suggestions that the Conservative politician Enoch Powell, who had come out against British membership of the EEC in 1969, had made a significant contribution to the successful outcome for the Tories remain unproven and disputed. Powell was a popular and populist figure and it may be that his popularity helped boost Conservative turnout in some constituencies, whilst complacency probably depressed the Labour turnout. But there is no evidence that anti-European feeling contributed to Wilson's defeat and Heath's success.

The most significant fact about the new Government, from a European perspective was that its Prime Minister, Edward Heath and its Foreign Secretary, Alec

Douglas-Home, had been intimately involved, as Lord Privy Seal and Foreign Secretary respectively, in Britain's first attempt to join the Community. Both men were committed, by personal as well as political conviction, to achieving British accession. Heath put Home in overall charge of the impending negotiations and appointed Anthony Barber, as Chancellor of the Duchy of Lancaster, to conduct the policy and negotiations on a day to day basis. This was an exact mirror of the arrangements under Wilson.

In a manuscript note which he wrote for himself before the first meeting of the Cabinet, Heath placed the EEC immediately after the Queen's Speech in his list of priorities.[74] Heath told Cabinet that he and Home thought it advisable for the Government to accept the invitation from the Council of Ministers of the EEC to be represented at a formal ceremony on 30 June to mark the opening of the accession negotiations. Cabinet would be asked to approve the text of the statement which would be made by the Government at the meeting. Cabinet would also have to decide whether the Government could prepare a negotiating position in time for the first substantive negotiating session on 21 July or whether to seek a deferral to the autumn.[75]

When Cabinet met two days later there was a general feeling that the Government's opening statement as drafted was "too elevated and diffuse" and that it needed to focus more clearly on the Government's negotiating objectives. These should include fisheries as well as agriculture "in order to anticipate the possibility that the Council of Ministers on 29 June would make some move towards the development of a Common Fisheries Policy which, by leading to changes in international fishery limits, could be seriously damaging to UK interests". This was agreed. Cabinet also agreed that the first negotiating session should be on 21 July provided that it was confined to the establishment of official working groups to examine the facts in relation to Britain's negotiating issues.[76]

On 26 June, on the recommendation of the Cabinet Secretary, Heath established a Cabinet Ministerial Committee on the Approach to Europe, chaired by the Foreign Secretary.[77] The first official note submitted to the Committee by the Cabinet Office Secretariat on 29 June was a reworked version of the one prepared for Labour Ministers. It set out the difficult areas for negotiation: Community finance (and the British share in particular), New Zealand exports, access for Commonwealth sugar, the CAP. A separate paper set out in detail the costs to the United Kingdom of the EEC's financing arrangements, advising that "no country can be expected to carry a regular burden on its balance of payments of the order of £430 million per annum for the purpose of financing Community activities". The paper went on to advise that "our participation in the Communities' budgetary arrangements in the circumstances foreseen in the preceding paragraphs would impose a burden on the United Kingdom in the late 1970s which would be both intolerable and inequitable, as compared with other members". But, the paper continued, while it could be argued that Britain should seek changes in the financing arrangements during the negotiations, it was equally clear that this would not be achievable. The European Commission's latest Opinion on accession had said in terms that "the accession of new members to the Communities implies acceptance on their part, not only of the Treaties, but also of the decisions which have been made since the Treaties came into force".

After setting out the arguments in detail the paper concluded, just as similar advice to the previous Government had done, "that we are likely to get further with the Six, and especially the French, if we seek alleviation in the application of Community rules to us rather than challenge those rules as being unsound or inappropriate to our case . . . Rather we should demonstrate to the Six that the unrestricted application to the enlarged Community of the financial arrangements agreed by the Six in December 1969 would place an intolerable and inequitable burden on our balance of payments . . ."[78]

The new Government accepted the official advice. Anthony Barber told Cabinet that the British opening statement for the negotiations had been revised and was intended "to strike a balance between, on the one hand, the need to demonstrate to the . . . European Community our goodwill . . . and our intention to negotiate in earnest for membership and, on the other hand, the need to avoid allowing domestic public opinion to suppose that we were adopting an approach to the negotiations which was too enthusiastic and insufficiently hard-headed".[79]

When Douglas-Home made the opening statement in Luxembourg on 30 June he made the new Government's position clear: "If I appear to labour this point", he said, "it is only because, unless a solution is found, the burden on the United Kingdom would become intolerable and no British Government could contemplate joining. Moreover, without such a solution, the whole basis of stability and confidence, essential to the further development of the Communities, would be lacking". Douglas-Home also made clear, however, that the Government shared the "determination of the Six to go into new spheres of cooperation beginning with economic and monetary matters, but at the same time laying the foundations for a new method of working together in foreign policy and defence. In all these problems, we should seek to achieve solutions which are Community solutions. We welcome the moves which you have already made towards closer economic and monetary integration, and are ready to play our full part . . . We, no less than you, will want the institutions to match those objectives".[80]

The Foreign Secretary's reference to economic and monetary cooperation was given some substance by a Treasury paper on the subject submitted to the Ministerial Committee on Europe on 8 July. At that stage, thinking within the Community was in practice limited to two issues: the obligation to engage in prior consultation about economic policy changes; and the acceptance of broad numerical guidelines for the conduct of economic and monetary policies. The paper noted that any difficulties associated with these ideas were at present theoretical. The UK might be called upon to confirm that she too had "chosen the option of monetary union". In the light of statements already made by Ministers of the present and previous Administrations that should, the paper asserted, "cause no difficulty". What such a choice would amount to in practice would be easier to gauge by reference to the rate of practical progress made by the Six than by reference to the theoretical proposals which had been put forward. There was no reason overall to suppose that Community measures in this field would apply more stringently to Britain, as a member, than to other members. To the extent that such measures as the Community might agree on turned out to be ineffective, the problems associated with them would not arise. To the extent that they did turn out to be more or less effective, the United Kingdom would be able to influence the economic decisions of other members of the Community as a whole, as a counterpart to accepting Community influence on British economic decisions. The central issue was thus not technical, but political.[81]

A more immediate preoccupation was how to engage with the Six at the opening of the formal negotiations on 21 July. Anthony Barber's advice to the Ministerial Committee, which was subsequently endorsed by Cabinet as a whole, was that the British delegation should propose work on several subjects in parallel. The British Government had been advised "by friends in the Community" to avoid concentrating on either the easier or more difficult of the subjects, but to take some of each. The aim of this approach was to avoid setting all the difficult subjects to one side and, at the same time, to tackle some subjects on which early progress could be seen to be made. Nor should work to establish the facts focus solely on the budgetary issues since this would give the impression that the Government were interested only in the costs of accession, which would get the negotiations off to a bad start and be bad for public opinion on both sides of the Channel. Moreover, the more emphasis was placed on the budgetary questions, the greater the risk that the Six would seek to turn a solution to the issue into a precondition for considering anything else.

Against this background, Barber came up with a list of topics to be considered in parallel by the negotiators: the Community's budgetary arrangements and the consequences of the CAP for agriculture and food in an enlarged Community; dairy products; sugar; the Common External Tariff; the European Coal and Steel Community (ECSC); Euratom; and the preparation of the necessary (and time consuming) translations into English of the relevant Treaties and Community decisions.

Barber sought and obtained from Cabinet discretion to play his hand in accordance with circumstances on the day. Heath, summing up, promised Cabinet an opportunity to consider the Government's main negotiating objectives before the substantive negotiations themselves began.[82]

The new Government were in no doubt of the importance of the French Government in the negotiations and Douglas-Home paid an early visit to Paris, telling Cabinet on 16 July that a cordial Maurice Schumann had indicated that the French were disturbed by the position of preponderance which the German Government were acquiring within the EEC. Schumann had given the impression that the French Government were now more alive than hitherto to the advantages of British membership of the Community as a possible counterweight to German influence.[83]

Two weeks later, Cabinet was wrestling, as had its Labour predecessor, with the problem of Concorde whose costs, Cabinet was told, would, if the project were continued, be some £250–300 million more than if it were cancelled. That was always assuming that the French Government did not take the British to the

International Court, in which case, so the Attorney General, Sir Peter Rawlinson, advised, the possibility of an award against Britain of up to £230 million could not be completely excluded.

Against that background, a number of Cabinet members argued that cancellation without the agreement of the French Government might not only be financially costly but might also seriously damage Anglo-French relations in general as well as the prospects for the EEC negotiations.

The Prime Minister summed up, with devastating accuracy, that "there appeared to be little prospect that Concorde would prove an economic success. The costs of continuing were substantial in relation to the reduction in public expenditure for which the Government were aiming. But the risk of adverse repercussions for relations with France and for the EEC negotiations was also very real". So, a decision was postponed.[84] When the issue was looked at again in September, Heath concluded that there was no practical alternative to continuing with the project until March 1971 in order to allow the current programme of tests to be completed and evaluated.[85]

The Foreign Office had been hard at work on a paper for the Foreign Secretary on Anglo-French relations which Denis Greenhill, the Permanent Under-Secretary, submitted to Douglas-Home on 2 September. "The British and French", the paper opened, "while they nourish a healthy mutual respect, actually like each other about as well as cat and dog". The work of rapprochement would be an uphill struggle, rather than a labour of love and would have to be based on a sober calculation of interest rather than on any natural affinity. The task was not helped by the fact that recent studies showed that France's GNP might be as much as 50% greater than that of the United Kingdom by 1980. If so, the United Kingdom would find itself dealing with France from a position of substantial inferiority, and would be confronted by two Western European powers (France and Germany) of substantially greater economic power than herself. Britain would need to have good relations with both.

The paper drew encouragement from the fact that the "quasi-mystic conceptions of France's destiny" promoted by de Gaulle had already been abandoned which meant in turn that the myths and taboos which stood in the way of better relations would lose their hold. On balance, it seemed likely to the paper's authors that the French, mindful of the need to find a counter-weight to the growing power of Germany, had decided that Britain should be admitted to the EEC provided that essential French interests could be safeguarded. But the price was likely to be high.

The paper also noted the short term attractions of the French concept of a '*Europe des nations*' but thought that the logic of British policies and of Britain's longer-term ambitions for Europe pointed towards the British interest lying in a considerably greater degree of integration at European level. Sectors of French opinion would probably follow suit.

Heath read the paper and thought it "a good paper but, like all such papers, it lacks precision; and 'encouragement' in many cases means more money! The possible future economic comparison is startling. I much agree that it is counterproductive to try to force the NATO issue [the issue of re-integrating France into the NATO command structure]: we should let the 'English speaking world' win without boasting, or even drawing attention to it".[86]

Among the issues which British officials were now examining in depth was that of the legal order in the European Community. What that legal order would mean had already been the subject of debate and would continue to be technically, conceptually and politically difficult. A bright and rather uncomfortable light was shed on the issue in a speech given to the British Chamber of Commerce in Brussels on 16 September by Pierrre Pescatore, the Luxembourg member of the European Court of Justice.

The British were well aware, Pescatore said, that adopting the Community system as a whole would mean the absorption, with the acceptance of the EEC Treaties, of a whole body of case law by which many notions and rules of Community law had been interpreted and developed. But the implications of this had not yet been fully realised in Britain. Pescatore went on to quote from a statement made in 1962 by the then Lord Chancellor, Lord Dilhorne, and repeated by Dilhorne as late as 1967. "I venture to suggest", Dilhorne had said, "that the vast majority of men and women in this country will never directly feel the impact of the Community-made law at all. In the conduct of their daily lives they will have no need to have regard to any of the provisions of that law. Nor are they at all likely ever to be affected by an administrative action of one of the Community institutions. With few exceptions, the obligations under the Community law will fall directly only on industrial and commercial concerns, long-distance carriers and persons or firms engaged in the export of agricultural products".

Pescatore continued: "I think it only fair to say that such views rest on a misunderstanding of the reality of Community law as it has been defined by the Court [of Justice] in numerous decisions which show that the rules of the Common Market are the concern, not only of Governments, but also of private persons, whether they are individuals or corporations. The Court, in its findings, has made quite clear that rights conferred to, and obligations imposed on, individuals by the Treaties themselves, as well as by the Community regulations, have to be protected and enforced by the internal tribunals of Member States. This means that judges all over Great Britain, whatever their rank in the judicial hierarchy, will have the power and obligation to ensure the implementation of Community law in the national sphere. They will have to consider that Community law will be, in the United Kingdom, part of the law of the land. More than that, as has been stressed on several occasions by the Court, European law claims precedence over the rules of national law. This new combination of direct impact with priority of Community law . . . will require a fundamental revision of some deep rooted habits of political and legal thinking in Great Britain. There is no point in concealing this fact".[87]

Although some of these legal issues, and their far-reaching implications, were to play a considerable part in scepticism and hostility towards the European Community as time went on, they were not, as Pescatore's speech (and the fact that it was appended to a Whitehall legal analysis) showed, widely known about at the time even among legal experts. The drivers of British opinion were, according to an opinion poll carried out in September for the Conservative party, and reported to Heath by his Political secretary, Douglas Hurd, much more prosaic. In late 1970, public opinion had veered markedly against membership, compared with the situation four years earlier. In 1966, 70% of adults questioned had been in favour of joining. Four years later only 33% were in favour while 53% were clearly against. In 1966, 28% were strongly in favour of joining and 7% strongly against. In 1970, 10% were strongly in favour and 26% strongly against. Men tended to be more in favour than women. In the political parties, Conservative Party supporters were only marginally more in favour than Labour supporters, and Liberals were more hostile than either Tory or Labour.

Few of the hostile majority were moved by issues such as support for the Commonwealth or fear that Britain would lose her identity in the EEC. Only 3% were worried by these issues. Equally, few were persuaded by the attractions of a passport and customs-free Europe. The main driver of hostility was fear of a sharp rise in the cost of living. 80% believed that prices would go up faster if Britain joined and there was no compensatory confidence that there would be an equivalent rise in prosperity. However, a majority of people would be in favour of joining if they could be sure of being better off in the end. 62%, including 60% of Conservatives, wanted a referendum before joining.[88]

How to influence public opinion was just one issue tackled in a whole range of negotiating papers prepared by officials for Ministers at this time. A meeting under Sir William Nield's chairmanship in the Cabinet Office revealed the classic dilemma: the opponents of membership "were being allowed to dominate the media", according to some, while others thought that at a time when the Common Market per se was not thought newsworthy, the opponents of Government policy tended to secure more coverage than did the Government's supporters. Officials, and later Ministers, drew the conclusion that the information effort should concentrate on factual information until the crux of the negotiations was reached, at which point "a short concentrated campaign would offer the anti-marketeers least opportunity".[89]

Of more immediate concern were economic, agricultural and fisheries issues. Financing issues aside, officials knew that the Government would have to have what they hoped would be "a discussion in depth, not a negotiation" on the sterling balances – preferably after substantial progress had been made in negotiating the renewal of the Basle arrangements, together with the Sterling Agreements. Officials knew too that they would have to discuss the Community's plan for EMU, though here the first official doubts about how far Britain should commit herself began to emerge. Britain's opening statement of 30 June had made clear that she accepted the objectives of the Six and, since then, the Chancellor of the Exchequer had welcomed them. But, according to the negotiating brief prepared by an interdepartmental group of officials "we should try to limit ourselves to this but if we are pressed further we should say that we are following their work [that of the Six] with close attention, and look forward to full discussion with them as soon as they are ready – which may be by the end of the year. Meanwhile, there would be scope for playing things long e.g. by asking for their own views on matters on which they may be finding difficulty in reaching agreement"[90]

Britain's indebtedness would also be an issue. At the end of June 1970 outstanding short and medium term indebtedness was $3,506 million. The concern of Britain's potential future partners, according to a Treasury note, lay in the extent to which that might represent a burden on the balance of payments which would in turn limit the extent to which the United Kingdom could accept the costs of entry. The UK negotiators would have to convince the Six of Britain's determination and ability to achieve a healthy balance of payments surplus.[91]

The problems of agriculture were familiar; those of the Common Fisheries Policy, then in discussion among the Six, were new. A detailed account of the issues and the negotiations is given in Sir Con O'Neill's comprehensive history.[92] In short, the EEC members were on the point of adopting a Common Fisheries Policy (CFP) designed in the interest of the Six and paying scant heed to the interests of Britain, Ireland and Denmark – all significant fishing nations. Britain had put down a marker at the opening of the negotiations in June. In October, the British tabled in Brussels a memorandum which recalled that the British Delegation had already made clear that a willingness on the part of the Six "to take note of statements made or documents submitted by the applicant states" fell short of the request by Britain for proper consultation. Total fish production in a Community of Ten would, the British pointed out, be four times that in the Six, and the pattern of trade both within the Community and with third countries would therefore be radically altered. In the United Kingdom alone, British landings of fish for human consumption (of the order of 900,000 tonnes in 1969) exceeded landings for the same purpose by the fleet of any other member, or applicant for membership, of the Community. Given that 40% of that total tonnage was caught by the British inshore fleet "the great interest of the United Kingdom in the evolution of a Common Fisheries Policy becomes clear". As it was, the new EEC policy and associated regulations would immediately introduce a new regime which, in the view of the British, a view shared by the Norwegians, would be neither appropriate nor even workable in a Community of Ten. Politely, perhaps too politely, the British Delegation pointed out that the United Kingdom "would be particularly concerned to ensure that any measures which might be proposed for the waters of any Member State exposed to the risks involved in intensive exploitation were non-discriminatory in fact as well as in form" and went on to "underline the difficulty of forming a view on how the proposed common policy will actually operate without first discussing that policy on a wider basis than the present membership of the Community".[93]

Heath himself was as focussed on the United States as on Europe, with an impending visit by President Nixon. He held a meeting on 30 September with the Foreign and Defence Secretaries which, in the light of subsequent developments, sheds interesting light on his view at that early stage of his Administration. Although UK-US relations were, Heath thought, still good at some levels, the close relationship which had existed between the previous Conservative Government and successive US Administrations had not been maintained. The attitude adopted by the Labour Government over Vietnam might have played some part. The Americans might also have concluded that Britain's status in the world had declined and that they needed in consequence to pay less attention than previously to British interests and to British advice. Heath thought that the new Government's decision to retain a British military presence in the Far East had been welcomed by the Americans and might do something to redress the balance; but too much reliance should not be placed on that since the military effort the Government intended to maintain in the Far East would be far smaller than the one Britain had deployed before the rundown began. At the same time, Heath thought, there was no alternative candidate for the position which Britain occupied in relation to the United States and no other power whose modes of thought were so close to their own or with whom they found it so easy to work.

The Foreign Secretary commented that the problem was compounded by the uncertain division of responsibilities between the White House and the State Department. It was difficult to determine where responsibilities began and ended, and decisions appeared at times to be taken arbitrarily and without full consultation within the Administration. President Nixon frequently communicated, not only with the Prime Minister, but with Douglas-Home himself, through his special adviser on foreign affairs, Dr Kissinger; and on occasion the White House had asked the British Embassy, in so many words, not to inform the State Department of discussions held with them.[94]

In the event, Heath and Nixon had a satisfactory meeting, culminating in a lunch at Chequers attended (at her own suggestion) by the Queen. Heath's own view of the visit was that Nixon wanted "to put fresh life and meaning into the concept of the special relationship which has become a little tarnished in recent years. I think that he genuinely wants to be close to us . . . I think I can best summarise my impressions by saying that the President is a cool, clear-headed and pragmatic man, who is basically well-disposed towards us and will do all he can to help us; but that, in the last resort, he will put American interests first, will expect us to act similarly in our interests and will respect us all the more if we do".[95]

Meanwhile, the tenor of the newly opened accession negotiations in Brussels and Luxembourg was one of "modest progress" according to the report given by Geoffrey Rippon to Cabinet on 29 October. Iain Macleod, the Chancellor of the Exchequer, had died suddenly of a heart attack in July. Anthony Barber had been promoted to replace him, an appointment which Harold Wilson cruelly described as "the only thing Mr Heath has ever done to suggest that he has a sense of humour".[96] Barber's place as Chancellor of the Duchy of Lancaster and day-to-day leader of the British delegation had been taken by Rippon, Member of Parliament for Hexham and an experienced lawyer. Rippon reported, to his probably bemused colleagues, that the meeting with the Six on 27 October had managed to resolve problems about the effects of the CAP on the market for pigmeat and eggs; on supplies of liquid milk; and on future arrangements for the Annual Review of the prospects of the agricultural industry. Agreement in principle had been reached that the United Kingdom's dependent territories – apart from Hong Kong – would become Associates of the enlarged Community. Rippon had told the Six that Britain could accept the Community's Common Commercial Policy. British papers had earlier been tabled on the major problems to be negotiated: imports of sugar from developing Commonwealth countries and of dairy produce from New Zealand; and the size of Britain's contribution to the EEC budget. The fact-finding stage was therefore now over and Britain had been asked to table her proposals for resolving all the major outstanding problems by the end of the year.

There was no discussion in Cabinet and Heath concluded that "the Cabinet would no doubt be satisfied with the progress which had been made, and would wish to consider at a fairly early date the general situation and outlook for the negotiations as a whole".[97]

In a separate written report to Heath the next day, Rippon complained that "the Community's procedures are even more wooden than they were in 1962. Only the Chairman is allowed to speak while we are present, and he can neither agree to, nor comment on, anything we say, however trivial, without prior agreement within the Community or an adjournment. This in turn means that the Community tends to progress – or regress – on the basis of elaborately worked out texts. On substance, I think I can say: so far so good. For the next stages, we should have no illusions about the difficulties. The French may sometimes misjudge their interests and play the diplomatic game for its own sake. But they will fight hard and effectively for what they judge their interests to be, and none of the Five or the Commission seems able to stand up to them in the end. The vital question for us is what political price they attach to the consequences of success or failure. Either could be costly for them, as it could for us. If they opt for success, the big issues can be settled fairly quickly, at least in the next eight months. I remain an optimist".[98]

In a separate report to the Prime Minister, William Nield put his finger on the nub of the problem with France. The Conference in The Hague the previous December, called by Pompidou, had marked the end of General de Gaulle's veto on the development of a Community of Six of which de Gaulle had explicitly disapproved. "This was clear", Nield wrote, "from the very terms M. Pompidou used for the tripartite French plan for the development of the Community, which the conference adopted: completion, deepening and enlargement. Since the conference, the French have pressed hard for the first two of these objectives, and the results are clear e.g. new common policies on financing, wine, fisheries and now the Werner Plan. But the third aim, enlargement, was made conditional on the achievement of the other two; and on the acceptance of the results by applicant countries. In sum, France now accepts that she is not powerful enough to go it alone and that her aim must be to use a strengthened Community as an instrument of French policy. Her success to date in this policy has re-established her position in the Community and her confidence".[99]

The knowledge that France remained both the lock on, and the key to, the negotiations took Rippon to Paris on 9 November for talks with the French Foreign Minister, Maurice Schumann. There were, Rippon told Schumann, only four major problems: New Zealand dairy products, sugar, transitional arrangements and Community finance. He wanted to get away from the whole idea of the negotiations being a series of demands and counter-demands. We had to settle things between friends and allies. It would be a mistake to regard the problems over New Zealand dairy products and Commonwealth sugar as British problems. They were rather an aspect of the Community's relations with the outside world. He did not like to think what would happen if the negotiations failed. There would certainly be a period of sour relations between Britain and the members of the Community but at the end of it we would have to take things up again.

Schumann, who gave very little away during the meeting, responded that the negotiations represented a great chance for Britain. So far as Europe was concerned, they represented a risk but it was a risk that the French were ready to take for political, more than economic, reasons. Rippon replied that the British were ready to take the same risk for the same reasons.[100]

Heath set out his own view in a message to the German Chancellor, Willy Brandt, on 2 December. He was pleased with the way the negotiations had begun and with the evident wish of all concerned to tackle the main problems seriously and quickly. But Heath feared that the more rigid the Community's position became on any given problem, the more difficult it would be, at the end of the day, to reach a compromise of the sort Britain would be able to accept. "I can give you my firm assurance", Heath wrote, "that the British Government will not waver in its commitment to enter the Community provided that we can agree terms which I and my colleagues can recommend to Parliament in good conscience and with a fair prospect of securing Parliament's approval. But we must be able to convince Parliament that the terms of entry are fair. This involves putting to them an agreement which we can demonstrate to be beneficial to the enlarged Community as a whole, including the United Kingdom".[101]

Heath made no mention of the value of a meeting between himself and Brandt, though this had been a significant element of a letter earlier in November from the British Ambassador to Bonn, Sir Roger Jackling, to Sir Denis Greenhill. The letter was also sent to No. 10 though whether Heath saw it is not clear since, unlike Wilson, he was not much given to commenting in the margins of papers.

According to Jackling, the coming year would see the German Government occupying their traditional place in the ups and downs of Britain's EEC policy, not as the key to the negotiations, for that role would remain with France, but as the major question mark. It was still the case that German influence could never be decisive within the Community against the determined will of France. But the views of the Federal Government were likely to impact on those of the French Government. The balance of power in Europe had now tilted further to Germany's benefit, with her clear economic preponderance and with the changes from de Gaulle to Pompidou and from Kiesinger to Brandt. Brandt had told the journalist Henry Brandon some weeks earlier that he thought a rescue operation might be needed at some point in the first half of 1971 in order to ensure that Britain's EEC negotiations succeeded, and that he was ready to undertake it. But Jackling did not take this as a cheque in the bank and he recommended a bilateral meeting between the Prime Minister and Brandt, not least as part of Britain's balancing act between Germany and France. Moreover, Jackling argued, a Prime Ministerial meeting would cast a beneficial shadow ahead of its actual occurrence.

During the couple of months before it took place, the fact that it was impending would ensure that the Germans approached problems involving British interests more than usually positively.[102]

An early meeting with Pompidou did happen. General de Gaulle died suddenly on 9 November 1970 at his home in Colombey les deux Eglises where, at his own behest, he was buried after a private funeral. A formal Requiem Mass was, however organised by the French Government at Notre Dame Cathedral in Paris on 12 November. It was attended by the Prince of Wales, the Prime Minister and three former Prime Ministers (Eden, Macmillan and Wilson). The French Government, so Heath told Cabinet on the following day, had been gratified by the high level of British representation at the Mass. There had been little opportunity for political discussion with those attending but a number of them had congratulated Heath on the manner in which the British Government were dealing with the problems with which they were confronted.[103]

Nonetheless, Heath did have a short one-to-one meeting with Pompidou of which Heath, who was a meticulous record-taker of such meetings, wrote an account. "The President made a complimentary reference to the tribute I had paid to General de Gaulle on French television. He then referred to the changes which had taken place, especially in Britain, since we last met in the spring. I said that I was glad that relations between our two countries had improved and that we were working together in so many fields. The President endorsed these remarks . . . This gave him as much pleasure as it gave us. He hoped there would be an opportunity for fuller discussion before long."

So much was a routine exchange of courtesies. But then, so Heath recorded, Pompidou said that he had something to show him, and produced from a tray on his desk a copy of that day's *Le Monde* opened at a page bearing an advertisement headlined '*L'Amérique commence à Londres en VC10 BOAC*'. The advertisement vaunted London, and BOAC, as the fastest, most luxurious way of getting to the United States. Pompidou, having produced the advertisement for Heath's inspection, made no comment on it, and nor did Heath. There was a pause, after which Heath said he hoped the President would visit Britain, something which The Queen would welcome. Pompidou said he would be pleased to do so.

Heath commented: "Although this was a brief encounter, I was struck by the change in President Pompidou's demeanour. There was none of the scepticism I had noticed when we last met in the spring. At one point he acknowledged the European orientation of our policies".

Heath did not speculate on Pompidou's motives in producing the advertisement from *Le Monde*. But Pompidou must have meant something by it: whether as proving the traditional French view of Britain as a Trojan Horse for the Americans, or a sign of what France could expect from Britain as a competitor, since BOAC were inviting French travellers to go to London to take a plane to the United States rather than use Air France from Paris. Or just as something that had amused him and caught his fancy. Long after the demise of BOAC and the VC10 (Britain's last great airliner) the advertisement sits to this day on the No. 10 file, as an enduring, trivial and tantalising scrap of Anglo-French history.[104]

On 18 November, Geoffrey Rippon was back in Paris for a meeting with Jean Monnet, at which the great European idealist demonstrated that he also had a hard-headed view of national interest. Rippon explained to Monnet (and Robert Marjolin whom Monnet had brought in to work with him) that the vital issues in the negotiation were really very simple. Britain was ready to accept all sorts of things but the essential requirement was some sort of guarantee that a disaster to Britain's balance of payments, which everyone said would not happen, did not in fact happen. The British Government's calculations showed that the risk was considerable, and fears in Britain were very real. Monnet immediately rejected any notion of a guarantee. So Rippon suggested a review clause instead and hoped that Marjolin, who was to prepare a report for Monnet's Action Committee for the United States of Europe, would emphasise in his report the danger of Britain being asked to accept an excessively big share of Community finance. Marjolin said that this would be very difficult to do. Changes in the basic mechanism of Community finance "could not be contemplated". The best Britain could expect was a transitional period with, possibly, a further three years of special protection. Rippon said that, so far as he was concerned, he must be in a position to say to Parliament and to the country that, whatever transitional arrangements were made, they did not represent a transition to disaster. Monnet repeated that there was no possibility of a special guarantee for Britain alone. This would involve making the system more expensive for others. Any such proposal by Britain would make it impossible to conclude the essentials of the negotiation by July.

If anyone had doubted the Foreign Office assessment that the French had successfully wrapped their national interest in a respectable Community flag, the comments of Monnet and Marjolin would have disabused them.[105]

Despite Monnet's rather unhelpful view, which was a harbinger of very tough negotiations to come, Heath had been right to detect a real change in French attitudes emanating from the President himself. When Christopher Soames called on Pompidou on 20 November, the President expressed satisfaction at the similarity of view between the two countries on the Middle East, though he added that he would not like to read too much into it. One of the reasons for it was that Britain and France were both very conscious of their weakness and this tended to draw them together. Soames replied that, while that might be true in general, neither country was much weaker in relation to the world than they had been five years earlier. But five years previously, many more differences had divided them than was now the case. The fact that negotiations had opened, with the best of political intentions, for the enlargement of the Community had a lot to do with it; and one thing which was quite certain was that the outcome of the negotiations was going to make all the difference to relations between France and Britain across the board. The back of the negotiations should be broken in six months. Did the President regard this as a political reality?

"He had plainly been waiting for this", Soames recorded. "He leant forward onto his desk and spoke with great vigour. Schumann was going to be in the chair for the next six months and one thing he was determined should not happen was for the negotiations to become a battle between Britain and France . . . The last thing France wanted to do was to drag her feet. We should tackle some of the major topics before the end of December and therefore before France was in the chair. He wished to be clear that he wanted these negotiations to succeed".

Soames referred to the fact that there had been a lot of recent talk about the role of sterling. Pompidou replied that what he did not like was the reserve role of sterling. He reminded Soames that de Gaulle had said to him shortly after his return to power in 1958 that one of the troubles about the Common Market was that it was going to bring France into conflict with Britain. Pompidou himself now felt that when Britain came in it was going to bring France into conflict with the United States. There could be only one reserve currency and that was the dollar. The last thing he wanted was to have a monetary war with the United States. Europe needed the Americans for her defence and he did not want to create any more difficulties with them than was inevitable anyhow with the Market being enlarged. He saw no role for another reserve currency, whether it was sterling or a European currency. It would be wrong to seek to create a European reserve currency.

Soames referred to Press comment that the French Government saw the reserve role of sterling as giving an undue competitive advantage to Britain and that this was the reason for the French Government wanting to see that role abandoned. Pompidou said that he wanted to assure Soames that this was certainly not his view; indeed he saw the reserve role of sterling much more as a disadvantage. He thought it would be necessary to have talks in depth about this issue in the context of the negotiations.[106]

Soames followed up his conversation with Pompidou by getting members of the Embassy staff to talk to Pompidou's advisers at the Elysée about the issue of sterling. Raimond and Bernard confirmed that the last thing Pompidou wanted was a monetary war with the United States. The question for discussion with Britain, therefore, was how the reserve role of sterling could gradually be phased out. What worried the French was not so much the reserve role of sterling as such but, rather, the policies of economic management which the role forced onto Britain. The French were reluctant to import into an economic union the liability of having to accept and support such policies because of events in Hong Kong or some other remote part of the world over which the Community had no control. Nor was it in Pompidou's mind to peddle the argument that the British economy was too weak for it to enter the Community. For Pompidou, the key issue was how to avoid the entry of sterling into the EEC leading *ipso facto* to the establishment of a new European reserve currency aligned against the dollar.[107]

Two conversations – the Foreign Secretary with his Canadian opposite number, Mitchell Sharp, and the Prime Minister and Chancellor with Giscard d'Estaing – at the end of November appear to show that the new Government was no more committed to institutional integration than was its predecessor, perhaps marginally less so. On 26 November, Sharp told Douglas-Home that he had the impression that both the French and the British Governments were reluctant to move very far or very fast in the direction of establishing common political and financial institutions. His own view, however, was that once countries had started on the road towards such institutions it was very difficult to turn back.

Douglas-Home said that the Six had decided to move rather slowly on institutions. Until 1973, they would be in a period of 'cooperation'. It was their present intention to move from 'cooperation' into 'integration' during the period between 1973 and 1980, but he thought progress might well be a good deal slower than that. He could not see countries with the history and traditions of Britain, France, Italy and Germany adopting common institutions at all easily. Some form of national veto in the Council of Ministers would probably be held in reserve for a long time to come.

Con O'Neill, who was present, said that the Werner Plan for Economic and Monetary Union went into the institutional question very thoroughly. His own view was that there might be some reluctance among the Six even to accept a general commitment. In any case, by the time the Werner Plan moved into its second phase, in 1973, Britain hoped to be a member of the Community with a say in the way it developed. It was impossible at this stage to forecast the form that development would take. He himself thought it unlikely that integration would have gone as far as the Werner Plan envisaged by the end of the decade.

Sharp said that the introduction of a common currency would inevitably involve common institutions and common economic policies. This would create a new situation and the European currency would be competing with the dollar as a reserve currency. In the free world, only Canada, Japan and the under-developed countries would be left outside the two power groupings. The new European currency would of course be much more stable than sterling had recently proved to be.[108]

On the same day, Giscard d'Estaing told Heath and Barber that, on the basis of the Werner Plan, he thought that the EEC would move into joint monetary action in 1971. The first stage would be joint action of a technical nature to reduce market fluctuations. There would be expressions of good intentions for the future, but these would be on vague terms. The Germans might try to insist on formulating more definite aims, but he doubted whether the French and other members of the Community would agree. This might well seem to be a rather limited degree of progress in European cooperation; but he believed that it was better that cooperation in these matters should emerge as a gradual process than that it should be forced.

Heath agreed that the right course was to work through the first stage suggested by the Werner Report and see where that led before taking final decisions about the second stage. Giscard then changed tack slightly, arguing that progress towards joint cooperation and joint action in this field was inevitable.

Giscard went on to say that he thought the negotiations for British accession would take longer than the British hoped. Barber thought this could pose a problem in terms of handling British public opinion, which was already uncertain since they saw membership as a leap in the dark. Heath added that, after two unsuccessful attempts to enter the Community, British public opinion was disillusioned and perhaps sceptical about anything emerging from a third attempt.

The French Ambassador, Courcel, never a man to question his own judgement, disagreed. British public opinion was, in his view, more frightened than sceptical. And there had been very little attempt by the British Government to influence public opinion in the matter. Heath said that, after all that had passed, there would be little point in conducting a campaign to influence public opinion on the subject until it was possible to demonstrate the result of the negotiations. If agreement were reached, a treaty would be signed and the Government would put it to Parliament for ratification. At that point it would clearly be important to have a major public relations exercise.[109]

That public relations exercise would have to extend to the Conservative Party according to what Heath described as "a very good paper" written by Tufton Beamish, MP, Chairman of the Conservative Group for Europe in the House of Commons and forwarded to Heath by his Chief Whip, Francis Pym.

"Unless urgent steps are taken to reverse the present trend", Beamish wrote, "we may well have the ironic situation where the veto is imposed, not by any member of the Six, but by the British electorate. Public and Parliamentary opinion may well be so strongly against, and so highly organised, that even if the terms are favourable, as they look like being, the Government may risk defeat in the lobbies. In that event the present leadership of the Party would be at risk. This, I believe is what Enoch Powell is waiting for, and it explains his recent tactics. If the Labour Party, returned to office with its present balance of Social Democrats and Marx-influenced left-wingers, under the present leader, there would be no brake on their effort to destroy private enterprise such as is incorporated in the Treaty of Rome. In the June election, in constituencies where the Tory candidates held strong anti-Market views, they did not hesitate to make this their platform although it conflicted with the Party's pro-Market policy. It is strange to find the left wing of the Labour Party, including all the crypto-Communists, in unholy alliance with the Tory anti-Marketeers, most of whom are on the right wing of the Party. Now the impression has gained ground, both in the country and in Parliament, that there is no clear official policy, and that it is perfectly acceptable for a Tory MP to defy the Government pleading, of course, 'conscience'. This impression is strengthened by the fact that it is at present not the intention to use either Government resources or the Party machine actively to further the pro-Market cause, or to counter the harm being done by anti-Market propaganda, much of which is based on special pleading, jingoism and emotion".

Beamish drew attention to the latest NOP poll findings showing that 61% of the electorate were against membership, with only 24% in favour. During the first round of negotiations Beamish, as chairman of the Foreign Affairs Committee had, he said, confidently promised the Chief Whip that close to 90% of Tory MPs would go into the 'Aye' lobby. Today, Beamish guessed that the number would not exceed two thirds and certainly not more than three quarters. What most worried him was that many former enthusiasts now preferred to be uncommitted, either because they were not sure the terms would be good enough or because they dared not risk losing favour with their constituents. Some had promised to demand a referendum before any decision was taken. Others maintained that the issue of entry should be determined after the next General Election.

According to Beamish, the Labour Party was even more divided. The Labour Europe Committee claimed more than a hundred supporters but Beamish was "reliably informed" that not more than 50 would vote for entry on fair terms. So the Government, in those circumstances, could not be sure of a majority. Wilson, according to Beamish, had never been genuinely in favour of going into Europe and it would therefore be in line with his own convictions on the subject, his dedication to nationalisation, and his obvious desire to keep in line with popular public opinion, to take all possible steps to return to power as the champion of the anti-Marketeers: "we must remember who made him Leader of the Labour Party".

Beamish went on to recommend a concerted campaign to convince the public ("there is much enthusiasm to be tapped among younger voters") and among Government MPs.[110]

Managing French opinion, especially at Government level, was an equal preoccupation. In early December, Soames delivered to Chaban-Delmas, the French Prime Minister, an invitation that had been long pondered in London, namely to visit London in February 1971 for the England v France rugby match and to stay over for talks at Chequers.

Soames, in a letter to Greenhill, said he thought that Chaban-Delmas would "see little difficulty" about accepting the invitation. But Soames added that he suspected (almost certainly meaning that he had been so tipped off) that Pompidou might have expressed some doubts to Chaban about the British initiative. Pompidou's own visit to London in 1966 had not been a happy one; he might suspect the British of trying to get at his Prime Minister; and there might be a personal factor, as illustrated by a recent French cartoon showing Chaban, following a recent visit to Poland, as a much bigger figure than Pompidou and as saying "J'ai mis mes pas dans ceux du Général".[111]

In the event, Chaban-Delmas did decline and the reasons advanced in the satirical French newspaper, *Le Canard Enchaîné*, were unusually interesting, according to Michael Palliser, Soames's deputy in the Embassy. These were Pompidou's wish to put his name to 'the great Anglo-French reconciliation', his 'good understanding' with Heath, the fact that 'it goes without saying' that British entry to the EEC was part of Pompidou's policy, and the likelihood that the Queen would be invited to visit France in 1972.[112]

As the year neared its end, Cabinet was asked to wrestle with the vexed issue of the United Kingdom's likely contribution to the EEC budget once she became a member. On 8 December, Nield sent the Prime Minister a brief for Cabinet that week. Britain could, said Nield, reasonably expect a transitional period of eight years in all from 1973, and a provision for a review of the budgetary arrangements. The European Commission had just proposed that the British financing 'key' should be either 22.5% or 25% after the first five years of membership. At the end of the transitional period i.e. in 1981 if Britain got the eight years for which she was aiming, the Government would have to hand over 90% of UK levies and duties collected at British ports of entry and up to 1% of VAT. So long as nearly all of the Community's budget was spent on agricultural support, it was inevitable that Britain would pay far more into the Community budget than she could hope to get back from Community expenditure. Britain's pattern of international trade and, in particular, her low level of agricultural self-sufficiency meant that arrangements which suited the Six were extremely disadvantageous for her. On the latest estimates, Britain's net contribution to the budget (i.e. the result after netting off receipts against gross contributions) would reach £184 million by 1977 and £230 million in 1980. Thereafter, unless some alternative arrangement had been reached, Britain would become subject to the full rigour of the Community's definitive arrangements and her net contribution would reach an annual total of £470 million.

It was, Nield pointed out, only *after* Britain had joined the EEC that she would have an opportunity to try to change the Community financing system permanently in her favour. Britain would then need to seek to move the enlarged Community in the direction of more sensible and less expensive agricultural policies and perhaps to promote Community policies in other fields from which Britain would be a net beneficiary. In the last resort, Britain would "simply have to refuse to pay" her assessed contributions, but Nield thought it unlikely that matters would come to such a pass.

It was likely, Nield warned the Prime Minister, that in Cabinet the Chancellor of the Exchequer would emphasise that the size of the British contribution would be a very heavy price to pay for entry. He might even suggest that Britain would have to devalue. In any event, the net result of the size of the British contribution to the EEC budget would be a significant rise in public expenditure from 1975 onwards.

On the other hand, Nield pointed out, these costs of entry were very small in relation to Britain's GNP of about £40,000 million a year (in fact about 1% of GNP) and would be very readily offset if the dynamic effects of entry enabled Britain to achieve a faster rate of economic growth than if she remained outside. "Unfortunately", Nield added, "it remains almost entirely a matter of judgement (or an act of faith) to decide whether there would be a dynamic response to entry".

Nield went on to make the 'negative' argument to which all advocates of British EEC membership have had to have recourse over the years i.e. not so much to stress the advantages of going in as the disadvantages of staying out. No clear alternative economic strategy to entry had yet been presented, Nield pointed out, and the likelihood was that Britain would find herself virtually isolated in a world in which the major economic blocs were tending to become increasingly protectionist. They would be, and already were, settling the rules of international trade without regard to Britain's interests. In such circumstances, Britain would probably be forced within a few years to try again to get into the EEC, although by then the difficulties would have become greater (because more common policies would have been adopted at EEC level and Britain would be obliged to accept them as the price of membership) and the Six would probably be even less inclined to grant reasonable terms, especially if by then they had made substantial progress towards economic and monetary union. Moreover, the immediate economic effects of a failure of the negotiations would in themselves be serious. If it became known that Britain had given up her attempt to join the Community because she believed she could not afford the price of entry, she could hardly expect there to be much confidence internationally in her ability to be economically successful on her own, and sterling might come under extreme pressure.

"It thus remains a matter of judgement, on which the economists can offer no useful guidance, whether the stiff price we should undoubtedly have to pay for entry into the Common Market is worthwhile. But taking into account the marginal increase in GNP required to pay the price of entry and also the long-term economic costs of exclusion from the Community, the case for entry seems well worthwhile on economic grounds alone. When the political consequences of entry and exclusion respectively are brought into the balance, the case seems overwhelming, even at the sort of price we must expect to have to pay". The Government, Nield concluded, would be able to say in January that its case for entry was the same as that of the previous Administration, namely that it considered that there were dynamic effects to be gained from entry and that these would be more than sufficient to pay the cost of entry; and if, contrary to the Government's expectation, the benefits in the end proved insufficient to cover the costs, the enlarged Community would undoubtedly be obliged to review the financial arrangements.[113]

In predicting the discussion in Cabinet, Nield did perhaps overlook one new element. The negotiations in Brussels were already engaged. At this stage, Britain had to have an eye to the endgame but the only decision to be taken was on the opening positions for the negotiations. Whether or not the outcome was acceptable was a decision for the future. Thus, at Cabinet on 10 December the Foreign Secretary (who, as a former Prime Minister was not someone to be gainsaid easily) concentrated on the budget contribution key Britain might reasonably expect to end up with at the conclusion of the negotiation (not lower than 17%) and on the opening bid that Britain might therefore make in the immediate future.

In the subsequent presentation, Rippon pointed out that if he eventually secured agreement to a contribution key for Britain of 17% that would probably represent a balance of payments cost to the UK of £460 million in the sixth year of membership, compared with the European Commission's already published estimate of £470 million. Rippon went on to point out that, even if the economic advantages from membership turned out to be only half as much as Roy Jenkins, as Chancellor of the Exchequer, had suggested to the House of Commons in February, they would still provide sufficient real resources to meet the estimated costs, which were, incidentally, substantially less than those suggested in the Labour Government's White Paper.

Rippon thus, more or less subtly, implied to his colleagues that a pro-European Conservative Government could hardly jib at terms which were likely to be better than those considered acceptable by a supposedly less European Labour Administration.

Heath was able to sum up that "it was not necessary for the Cabinet to reach a final decision at this stage on the question whether we should be prepared in the last resort to accept the terms . . . A more detailed examination of all the relevant factors would be required before it could be decided whether the balance of payments burden implied by such terms would or would not be a tolerable one. It was not, however, suggested that the burden would so clearly be intolerable that no useful purpose would be served by continuing the negotiations".[114]

One week later, on a visit to Washington, Heath deployed to President Nixon an almost identical point to the one Wilson had made a few months earlier, namely that "although the economic arguments on balance were probably in favour of our joining the EEC, the political arguments were far stronger. Did not the President agree"? Nixon did agree: "Now that Western Germany was being actively wooed by Moscow, British political leadership in Europe was becoming increasingly important, provided that Britain proved able to pay the economic price of entry. The British were essentially a competitive people although, like others, they needed a jolt from time to time. That was what entry into the Communities should give them". Heath agreed but added that the initial enthusiasm and momentum of the original approach of 1961 had largely died away. The British Government would have to exert themselves to recreate the sense of conviction that entry into the EEC would be to the long-term advantage of the United Kingdom and would give British industry a fresh chance to prove its worth.

Nixon said that anybody who doubted the truth of that assessment should consider the alternative if Britain did not succeed in entering the EEC. In that event, it would not be so much a question of economic damage to the United Kingdom (the British could always look after themselves all right) but rather a question of the political damage to Europe as a result of the loss of British leadership and of the stimulus which that leadership would provide to Europe to realise its full potential in world affairs. It was of course precisely that revival of political power in Europe which some elements of American public opinion viewed with alarm. But Nixon did not share their apprehension since he believed that a division of world authority between the two great power blocs would be unhealthy in the longer term and that a proper concept of the balance of power – and the balance of power was still essential to the maintenance of world peace – called for the creation of a strong political and economic entity in Europe. That was not to say that some of the protectionist policies of the EEC did not confront the US Government with a considerable problem. In particular, if the impression grew up that the United Kingdom was moving towards agricultural protectionism as part of the approach to Europe, the effect on the farmers would be devastating, and the political difficulties in the way of any further liberalisation of trade on the part of the US Government would be virtually insurmountable. Heath sympathised. What the British Government were changing was the system of agricultural support, not the level of support. The cost of support was being transferred from the Exchequer to the consumer. Things could of course be different if and when Britain entered the EEC and was obliged to move towards the EEC's higher prices. But, once Britain was a member, it would be open to her to seek to moderate EEC prices by means of the annual price reviews.[115]

On the next day, at Camp David, Heath (accompanied only by Burke Trend on the British side) raised with Nixon the possibility of Anglo-French nuclear collaboration. The French Defence Minister, Debré, had indicated to Lord Carrington, the British Defence Secretary, that the French might be interested to explore the possibility of Anglo-French nuclear collaboration, while hinting that Britain's relationship with the United States might be held to prevent France from taking the initiative in this matter. Heath thought that, on the whole, it was unlikely that this question would become a serious issue in the context of the EEC negotiations. But, if Britain succeeded in joining, France might then propose some kind of joint nuclear arrangement. Might this provide an opportunity to bring France closer to NATO again?

Nixon's reply, as recorded by Trend, was forthcoming: "You should feel that you have a great deal of running room on this . . . I would tend to be quite outgoing in this respect". Nixon saw this as being a period of opportunity as far as Anglo-French collaboration was concerned but, if the opportunity was not seized, it might slip way again. The US Government would sympathise with any reason-able proposition and Nixon said that he "would not be too conservative or miss a chance".

Henry Kissinger, who was present, intervened at this juncture to remind Nixon that this was a very sensitive issue in relation to Congressional opinion. The US Government would need to know in very great detail what the British Government's intentions were if the President was not to find public support for his European policy evaporating. 90% of that support would be liable to be alienated by any suggestion of Anglo-French nuclear collaboration.

Nixon thought that those who reasoned in that way were living in a different world. The crisis was "rushing down on us" and any step which would help to create a position in which the Soviet Union would find themselves confronted by a strong and united Europe should surely be welcomed. He favoured "bold action" provided that it was carefully and precisely worked out. The alternative of a divided and quarrelling Europe was something which he found totally unacceptable.

In a footnote to his record, Trend wrote that Kissinger had, after the meeting, again stressed the domestic risks to the President. This was a matter in which both the British and the Americans must proceed with extreme caution. Any approaches should be addressed to him direct and there should be no discussion with the State Department or the Pentagon without Kissinger's prior knowledge and concurrence.[116]

On Heath's return to London thoughts were turning to the start of 1971 and the crucial phase of the negotiations. The French, so Nield reminded Heath at the turn of the year, would be in the chair for the first six months. During the previous few weeks they had "again demonstrated their capacity for intransigence both on crucial subjects in the negotiations and also within the Six on the Werner plan". At home, the negotiations could be expected to receive much more intensive polit-ical attention. The British delegation would be negotiating on the whole range of problems, major and minor, with a view to breaking the back of the negotiations by July. There might conceivably need to be a summit to break a deadlock in the negotiations arising from French intransigence. In the debate scheduled for the

New Year in the House of Commons the Government would be able to present a satisfactory progress report on the last six months. The Opposition's official line was still to enter if the terms were right. But the anti-Marketeers would present dire forebodings of the cost and consequences of entry and perhaps the need for a referendum. But none of this (and Heath agreed) required the Prime Minister's intervention at this stage.[117]

Somewhat (and characteristically) more upbeat was a letter from Soames to Douglas-Home of 4 December: "I have dined with Giscard since his visit and was pleased to be told that he had not only much enjoyed the visit, but had also been greatly impressed by the sense of purpose and team spirit which he had derived from his talks with British Ministers. For the first time, he had gained the firm impression that HMG had decided beyond peradventure that Britain should join the EEC. I believe he was sincere in what he said (which is by no means always the case). To judge from the communiqué put out after the meeting of the Council of Ministers here on 2 December, Giscard seems to have given a favourable account of his talks in London. I would think that he now judges our entry into the EEC as inevitable and has decided to back it. This is good on two counts. Firstly, because on this issue his influence in Cabinet here should be a very helpful factor. Secondly, he is highly ambitious and he does not lightly back a horse unless he is pretty confident it is going to win".[118]

Another Frenchman with a significant influence on the negotiations was in London early in January 1971. At a meeting over dinner at Chequers with Heath, Deniau, the French EEC Commissioner, said that the likely final level of the British contribution to the EEC budget must be between 20 and 25%. It was, he warned, necessary to think, not in terms of national economic interests, but in Community terms and in terms of the Community system. At the same time, he recognised that, unless contributions were broadly proportionate to national economic activity, intolerable political strains could be created. This suggested that Britain's contribution ought to be somewhere between that of France and Germany, though Deniau made no reference to the money France would recoup through the CAP and Heath reminded him that Britain's GNP was now smaller, and increasing more slowly, than that of France.

Deniau concluded the conversation by "reminding" Heath that de Gaulle's veto of Britain's candidature in 1963 "had been imposed from below; it was not just the General's whim" though he did not explain how he arrived at this version of events. But he gave Heath, and his Principal Private Secretary, Robert Armstrong, the impression that "he did not seem to believe that the French Government at the top was now opposed to British entry" and that, while British entry had been "impossible" in 1963, it was possible now.[119]

Deniau had a more detailed conversation with Geoffrey Rippon the following day, in which Rippon told him that the four points of greatest importance to Britain in the negotiations were (a) the fact that Britain wanted to join the Community and that, while it was natural for existing members to take up negotiating positions, it would help if these could be tempered by expressions of a desire to have Britain in; (b) the need to do something which was visibly equitable for New

Zealand. The British Government had limited the area of negotiation to New Zealand dairy products, and a generous solution to this problem was politically necessary; (c) the need for a fisheries policy which took account of the interests of Britain and the other candidates and not just those of the existing members. Acceptance of the Fisheries Regulation as it stood would, in the view of the British fishery industry, lead to the invasion of British coastal waters and the denudation of stocks of fish and shellfish. Unlike other Member States which had a coastline, Britain still had fish. The British policy of conservation, and British exports to the Community, would both "risk disaster" if the Fisheries Regulation was applied in its existing form. Many of the most European-minded of British MPs had constituencies in which this was a red hot political issue; (d) the need to show that Britain was not shouldering an unfair burden through its contribution to the Community budget.[120]

On the budget, there remained a wide gap between the British Government and the Six. The British wanted to start at a contribution rate to the budget of about 3%, rising to 15% at the end. The Six wanted Britain's contribution rate to start at around 12% and go up to a significantly higher end figure.

On 22 January 1971, the British Ambassador in Bonn called on Brandt and Scheel, on instructions from London, to make the British case on the budget and to point out that, while the existing EEC members could reasonably wish to avoid incurring an extra financial burden as a result of British membership, the reality was that, if the UK paid a budget share of 15%, every other EEC member would pay about a fifth less. What Jackling was too polite to point out was that the existing members had doubtless done their sums and had deliberately sought to maximise their financial advantage at British expense.[121]

Jackling's call on Brandt had been designed to influence the German Chancellor before he travelled to Paris for talks with Pompidou, and it evidently had some impact for, on 27 January, Brandt sent Heath a message in which, he said, he had suggested to Pompidou that "Britain should make a bearable contribution to start off with, gradually working up to the full contribution; and I advocated the possibility of making a corrective adjustment in accordance with internal Community regulations during a further period of three years after the completion of the five year transitional phase". Pompidou, Brandt reported, had not been willing to take a final position on these issues.[122]

From a separate briefing given to Jackling by German State Secretary von Braun on the same day, it was clear that, for Pompidou, a key issue was the importance of Britain giving full Community preference in the agricultural field from the very beginning. In other words, Britain would have to start importing French agricultural products. Deniau, the French EEC Commissioner, was, so von Braun reported, "said to be far from satisfied with the answer he had been given in London on this." Deniau had clearly given the French Government a privileged briefing on his talks with Heath and Rippon. Overall, however, and despite German Press reports that the German Government had moved smartly towards French positions, von Braun thought that the prospects for enlargement had not deteriorated. The French wanted it but had their own interests much in mind.[123]

The extent of those French interests was highlighted in a note on the negotiations prepared for Heath, at the Prime Minister's request, by Nield. Even with the correctives of which Brandt had spoken, which would give Britain some protection until 1980, the kind of British share of the EEC budget of which the European Commission were talking would mean that in 1981 Britain would be a net *contributor* to the EEC budget to the tune of £470 million, making her massively the largest net contributor to that budget, whereas France would be a net *recipient* from the EEC budget to the tune of £320 million. "Our claim to the Community", Nield wrote, "that our financing proposals, plus the additional burden just described, plus our debt repayment obligations, constitute something very close to the maximum burden we can be asked to assume, even allowing for a favourable dynamic effect, is thus fully justified. But the Community line remains that we must accept their regulations; that our claim for a review clause would open up the renegotiation of their own regulations . . . that actually we intend to break up the present Community regulations at the end of, if not during, our transitional period". Thus, Nield reasoned, it was clear that the financial arrangements tailored to fit the circumstances of the Six did not fit Britain at all, but the Six would not renegotiate the CAP or their financial arrangements to make the terms for Britain any easier. The British Government's only course, therefore, was the one they were following: to try to limit the size of Britain's gross contribution to the EEC budget through the percentage key, and/or by seeking higher receipts from the budget to balance out the high contribution, and to negotiate a review clause. The British position was, however, open to the "Morton's fork attack" that either Britain would do well enough economically to be able to afford to join or, if she did not, that she had no business joining because she could not afford to.

Nield ended by suggesting that, if the logjam was not broken by March then it might be necessary to turn the scheduled May meeting into a meeting of Heads of Government.[124]

On the back of Nield's minute, Heath held an informal meeting with Douglas-Home, Barber and Rippon on 31 January to discuss the state of the negotiations. Robert Armstrong, who had seized the overriding political importance of this issue for Heath and was therefore taking the lead on it within Downing Street, was also present. The sense among those at the meeting was that the success or failure of the negotiations would be determined by three main issues: Community financing, arrangements for New Zealand and sugar. The meeting was more sanguine than Nield had been about the prospects on Community financing, believing that an acceptable outcome was negotiable. But it was decided that Rippon should offer no concessions at the meeting with the Six, due on 2 February. "He would seek to dispel any impression that, because the British Government saw no alternative to entering the EEC, they were likely to be prepared to accept any terms that might be demanded of them".

On New Zealand, the Ministers agreed that "we should be doing reasonably well by New Zealand, and ought to satisfy British public opinion, if we were able to secure guaranteed outlets for 75% of New Zealand's butter production".[125]

It is noteworthy that those present at the meeting made no bones about the fact that they saw no alternative to joining the EEC. A Foreign Office paper, whose conclusions Rippon and Douglas-Home 'broadly' agreed with, and which was sent to Heath at this time, argued that failure of the negotiations for entry would be a severe blow to Britain's international standing and prospects. There could be short-term palliatives but they would fall far short of being a substitute for membership.[126]

In the event, Rippon's meeting with the Six produced what he described to Cabinet as "a useful clarification of views"[127] but little more.

A meeting between Heath and German Foreign Minister Walter Scheel on the following day was more significant. Scheel thought that a compromise on the issue of the British budget contribution would have to be found. He was convinced that the French Government were determined to see the negotiations with Britain succeed. It was, he argued, impossible to calculate what Community costs would be in the distant future. The important thing was British readiness to accept the Community's own resources system in the end. Heath agreed that this was the key point. His own approach to Community affairs had always been that it was not a question of negotiating with the Community, but of finding common solutions to common problems. What was needed was recognition of the problems and deter-mination to find solutions. It was incomprehensible to him that solutions could not be found and he thought the Commission's attitude difficult to understand. Looking at GNP, Britain was well below Germany and France and it was forecast that, at the end of the decade, French GNP would be double that of Britain. This gave him no pleasure but it was a fact; a fact the Commission appeared to have overlooked completely. A further factor was that the Community members had had twelve years to take advantage of the dynamic effect of the EEC. Britain, by contrast, would be starting from scratch. Taking Britain's contributions to the budget on the one hand, and her receipts from it on the other, it looked as though Britain would get very little back on the agricultural side. British agriculture had already been reorganised and it anyway represented only a very small part of the British economy. Nor was it yet clear what was going to be available in terms of EEC money for regional development. It would be damaging to the Community if Britain came in on terms which compelled her to pursue deflationary policies which held down her growth. Britain's balance of payments position was currently strong, as was sterling. There were, however, large debts to pay off and there were large payments across the exchanges. The budget argument was fundamentally about whether Britain started with a large contribution or made a large jump at the end, Heath argued. He suspected that the French feared that, if Britain were allowed to make a slow start, so as to reap the dynamic effects of membership, she would then ask for renegotiation at the end. The British Government had no such intention.[128]

That conversation is revealing. For, as Nield's paper had made very clear, the key issue for Britain was not so much the way in which the British contribution to the EEC budget started and grew (though both were important) as the final outcome in 1981 when Britain would be at risk of making the biggest net contribution of any Member State, despite a relatively modest performance in terms of GNP. Yet this did not come through as Heath's major preoccupation, perhaps because the main adverse impact would only be felt some years into the next Parliament.

Lurking in the background to these issues was the growing sense that most of them boiled down to an Anglo-French standoff. John Robinson, Head of the European Department in the Foreign Office recorded in late February a conversation he had had over a weekend with a French official whom he knew well. Unusually for an internal Foreign Office minute, this one was seen by both Rippon and the Prime Minister.

Robinson's French contact had told him that there was a sharp difference of view between Pompidou and Giscard d'Estaing on the question of the role of sterling. For Giscard, as for most French officials, there was only one issue: Britain must so apply the Community rules on capital movements that there was no discrimination in favour of sterling area countries against other Community countries. But for Pompidou there was a less clearly defined fear that somehow the role of sterling would mean that EEC members would wake up one morning and find themselves in the sterling area. These anxieties stemmed from Pompidou's fear of 'being done'. He was not a tough banker, but for that very reason he acted (indeed over-acted) the tough banker all the time. Nor did he want to be thought by French public opinion to have failed to strike a tough bargain in French interests. Robinson was dismissive of Soames's acceptance of Pompidou's declared view that his sole concern was to avoid conflict with the United States. In Robinson's long conversation with his unnamed French colleague, not a word had been said about US susceptibilities.

Robinson concluded that, in his judgement, the most significant comment made by Pompidou thus far was his remark in December to Hargrove, the Paris correspondent of *The Times*, that, while it was true that what was happening in Brussels boiled down to a Franco-British negotiation, it would be unwise to present it in that way because, if the negotiation did not succeed, it would only make the breach worse. Robinson, who was a hard-boiled negotiator, recommended that British negotiators had nothing to lose by giving the impression from then onwards that the negotiations were indeed a Franco-British negotiation: "If we are playing to win in these negotiations, we have every interest in making the French fear that, if the negotiations fail, the breach will be very bad indeed".[129]

That was not Heath's way of working. Nor that of Soames. And a meeting between the two men in the House of Commons on 1 March showed that, while they were hugely different personalities, they shared a sense that Pompidou was a fly who would be caught with more honey than vinegar.

Pompidou had told Soames that the issue of the financial arrangements for Britain might be put aside while other issues were discussed. Heath was intrigued by this and also picked up on Pompidou's remark to Soames that Community preference was more important than the British financial contribution, at least in the early years. There was still a big gap between British and EEC positions on Community finance and Soames advised against getting into a position where concessions were dragged out of the British negotiators piecemeal. What was needed was more of a package approach to the two questions.

Heath asked Soames for his view on how these matters should be resolved: at a Summit of the Ten, with Pompidou in the chair and with the outcome carefully prepared in advance; or in a talk between himself and Pompidou with the negotiations being concluded thereafter at Ministerial level in Brussels? Soames was clear (and he had talked to Michel Jobert, the Secretary General at the Elysée before coming to London) that the bilateral meeting was the way to go. A summit of the Ten risked being unproductive. He was sure Pompidou would want to settle the main outstanding issues himself with the Prime Minister. Pompidou would not take the initiative and it would be up to the Prime Minister to do so. Heath agreed that Soames should, on his return to Paris, see Jobert again, tell him that Heath agreed with Jobert that an understanding between himself and Pompidou would be an important element in the negotiations and that a meeting between the two of them, which might discuss other topics besides British accession, should be envisaged.[130]

Soames's view was not universally shared. A note from Nield on 5 March firmly recommended a final 'crunch' Summit of the Ten as both inevitable and desirable. A bilateral talk with Pompidou could help prepare the Summit but was "an optional extra". In putting Nield's minute to the Prime Minister, Armstrong noted that his view was "widely held in the European team".[131]

But Soames had not left the ball passed to him by Heath sit idly at his feet. He went to the Elysée to see Jobert on his return to Paris and the two men took up the issue of a bilateral meeting without any mention of an alternative option. Jobert said that a point for consideration was "how much of a crisis atmosphere was desirable for the holding of the meeting". Jobert's own view what that "the best situation would be one that was short of a crisis, but where there was a sufficient degree of impasse for people to appreciate the need for a meeting". The meeting should be well prepared in advance. The French Foreign Minister should not be told since, if the Quai d'Orsay got wind of it they would create many difficulties.[132]

The meeting which in due course did take place between Heath and Pompidou has rightly been seen since as a turning point in the negotiations for British entry. But it is interesting to note, not just the realisation of the need for preparation, so that a success could be anticipated, but also the degree of contrived theatricality which was envisaged from the outset.

Another light was shed on the Anglo-French scene in a conversation between Davignon (Chef de Cabinet to the Belgian Foreign Minister) as he and Nicholas Barrington, one of Douglas-Home's Private Secretaries, walked round St James's Park on 10 March. Power in France, Davignon argued, was now centralised even more than it had been under de Gaulle, and Pompidou had the mentality of a small trader who wished to sell his overcoat for as much as possible. The only way to persuade him that it was hardly worth selling at all was to put the British arguments to him directly at a meeting with the Prime Minister. It would be a good idea, Davignon believed, if such a meeting could take place fairly soon before the French position had hardened, as it might, in future discussions within the Six.

Davignon thought a summit of Heads of Government would not take place for the simple reason that Pompidou did not want one since such a meeting, under his chairmanship, would put the responsibility on him, and his whole style of government was to evade responsibility. On the other hand, nor would he want to play second fiddle to the Italians when they took over the Presidency of the EEC Council of Ministers in the second half of the year.

In putting the note to Heath, Peter Moon, Heath's Foreign Office Private Secretary, commented that he found some difficulty in reconciling the argument for a Paris meeting with the view that President Pompidou wanted to evade any appearance of responsibility for the outcome of the EEC negotiations.[133] Moon had a point. Davignon, assuming he was accurately reported, might more correctly have surmised that Pompidou, in the chair of a Summit, would be inhibited by that responsibility from putting the French national case without compromise whereas a bilateral meeting (whose contents were much less likely to become public since there would not be ten participants to leak them) would give him much greater freedom of manoeuvre, while still allowing French negotiators to play hardball in Brussels subsequently were that what French interests appeared to dictate.

Although Soames was now clearly working for a bilateral meeting between Heath and Pompidou, Heath himself was still undecided. At a meeting in mid-March with Douglas-Home and Rippon, at which Nield from the Cabinet Office and O'Neill from the Foreign Office were present, there was no discussion of a ten-power summit but equally no commitment to a meeting with Pompidou (for which April then seemed the likely timing). No decision could be taken until after the negotiating meeting with the Six the next day, or perhaps even until Heath had met Brandt in Bonn in early April. There was no point in a meeting with Pompidou unless he was prepared to do business and on that score reports remained conflicting. Yet a meeting could provide a means of enabling the French to climb down from some of their more extreme positions.[134]

Rippon was obliged to report to Cabinet later in the week that, since the Six had been unable to reach agreement among themselves on a common negotiating position on Commonwealth sugar, New Zealand dairy products and the UK contribution to EEC finance, no progress had been made at the meeting between British negotiators and the Six on 16 March. The failure of the Six to agree was due to French intransigence and it was "no bad thing", in Rippon's view, that the French had isolated themselves in this way: it was France against the Five, not France against Britain. Nonetheless, the French Foreign Minister, who was in the chair, had conceded that the EEC side should make proposals to the British on Community finance as soon as they could, a shift from the previous French position that the Community should sit tight and wait for the British to improve their opening offer. Rippon had also won agreement to additional negotiating meetings in May. In the meantime Heath would be visiting Germany and he, Rippon, would be visiting the Netherlands and Italy.

This lack of progress caused some dismay in Cabinet since, it was noted, those in Britain who were opposed to entry were now convinced that no acceptable terms could be negotiated and the morale of those who were in favour of entry had been dampened as a result. Unless early progress could be made in the negotiations, the battle for public opinion could be lost. On the other hand, it was also recognised that French tactics were plain: to adopt an extremely hard line now in order to extract the maximum concessions from Britain. So, whatever the problems of morale and public opinion, the Government must not be rattled into making unnecessary concessions.[135]

Similar thoughts about their own public opinion were in French minds. In a conversation in mid-March with Crispin Tickell of the British Embassy in Paris, Jean René Bernard, one of Pompidou's senior advisers at the Elysée, said that the fact that Pompidou was ignorant of Britain did not mean that he did not want Britain to join the Community. On the contrary, he was anxious for the negotiations to succeed and was planning on the assumption that they would. Failure would be a disaster for France and Europe and a catastrophe for Britain. The French, who were everybody's scapegoat, would be blamed for failure. Bernard thought it was already clear that the essential issues would have to be decided by the British and the French. He was sure that the British had a shopping list. Tickell said that was not the way Heath envisaged such a meeting. It was of course open to the President and Prime Minister to deal with each other through their respective Foreign Ministers, but Bernard indicated that Schumann did not have Pompidou's confidence to that degree. Alternatively, Tickell suggested, the negotiations could continue on their course in Brussels. Bernard was clear: a bilateral meeting between Pompidou and Heath would be necessary if the negotiations were to be successfully concluded. Pompidou did not face a problem, as Heath did, with either his Parliament or with public opinion. But he was subject to pressure from vested interests who would be very ready to reproach the French Government if those interests were sacrificed. For Pompidou, the best way in which he could convince the French, and in particular French industrialists, of the advantages of British entry, was to demonstrate some tangible gain. The gain Pompidou had in mind was access to the British market for French agricultural produce. Hence the French insistence on Community Preference. This was more important to the French than anything else.

Heath, who saw Tickell's record, commented: "Very interesting and it rings true". To Peter Moon's written comment that there were clearly a number of advantages in a bilateral meeting from Pompidou's point of view, not all of them to Britain's advantage: to break the logjam; to extract concessions; to reduce the pressure on France from the Five; to demonstrate that French policies were not damaging to Anglo-French relations; Heath commented "Quite".[136]

The French were also doing their own version of 'soft cop/hard cop'. While the Elysée were giving positive signals of Pompidou's desire to see the negotiations succeed, in Brussels the French remained isolated in their intransigence among their EEC partners as Schumann's chairmanship of the Council of Ministers came in for renewed criticism for its partisan nature. Rippon, however, in a minute to Heath on 17 March, said he thought Schumann's position, however insensitively handled, was part of a deliberate strategy: "The French are now constructing the best negotiating position for themselves in preparation for the crunch [in Brussels] and also, no doubt, for any bilateral meeting with us. The French fear that if they make concessions to their partners before the crunch they will have to pay a second time when the crunch comes with us. And they are right. They may also want to demonstrate to us the ineffectiveness of the Five in order to strengthen their position in talking to us". All in all, Rippon did not think the impasse a bad scene-setter for Heath's imminent meeting in Bonn with the German Chancellor, Willy Brandt.[137]

Britain's Ambassador to the EEC, Sir James Marjoribanks, in his Valedictory Despatch on retirement from Brussels in the same week felt able to say that "in the 1980s our present worries about joining the Community will, I am confident, seem as unreal to us as their early doubts and hesitations now seem to the founder members", but that thought would have brought little comfort at the time and was to prove equally unreliable as a prediction of the future.[138] Indeed, the French added fuel to the flames and gave serious cause for concern to Heath when, without warning, their Ambassador to the EEC raised, in the weekly meeting of the Committee of Permanent Representatives on 18 March, the whole issue of the position of sterling, thereby apparently putting it at the front of the negotiating agenda, rather than treating it as a matter for sensitive and private handling.

The Chancellor of the Exchequer was not unduly dismayed, commenting in a minute to Heath that these moves did not of themselves provide any evidence that the French were trying to disrupt or delay the negotiations. The French attitude remained, Barber thought, as enigmatic as ever and the latest development afforded no firm evidence one way or the other.[139] Heath on the contrary thought that "it is the way the French have done this, and the forum in which they chose to raise the question, which almost makes it a hostile act".

The French Ambassador, Geoffroy de Courcel, as egregiously disingenuous as ever, told Rippon a few days later that the French Government much regretted that there had been a leak of what had been said in the Committee of Permanent Representatives. They were themselves entirely innocent of any responsibility for it.[140]

Rippon, like the Chancellor of the Exchequer, was inclined to take a cool view of what had happened. It might well be, so he told the Prime Minister, that Pompidou's decision to raise the question of sterling in this way reflected his realisation that the negotiations generally were reaching their crucial phase and that he had to make his position clear now if he was to do so at all. The Dutch had told Rippon that their conclusion was that the statement showed that the French were coming to terms with the fact that the negotiations were condemned to succeed.

"Agreed", wrote Heath, "but we cannot be certain about French motives".[141] A few days later, when Heath met the Board of Shell, he told them that it would be unwise to assume that the French had acted other than deliberately. It had always been recognised that capital movements would have to be dealt with in the accession negotiations, but that the position of sterling should fall outside. He did not think that this was a deliberate attempt by the French to wreck the negotiations, but there was a danger that this would be the unintended effect of French determination to make the most of their negotiating position, without sufficient regard for longer term considerations.[142]

Despite the setback to mutual confidence, the minds of Heath and his closest Ministerial colleagues were increasingly focussing on a meeting with Pompidou. Rippon saw to the heart of the issue, telling Heath: "Whatever the date of the meeting, you would have to convince Pompidou that Britain and France could work together in Europe. Putting over this conviction would be more important than anything else, and [would] recall the meeting between Adenauer and de Gaulle at Bad Kreuznach in 1958, which laid the foundation for subsequent Franco-German cooperation".[143]

When Soames called on the Secretary General at the Elysée on 27 March he took Jobert to task for the failure of the most recent negotiating meeting in Brussels. Jobert asked airily what else Soames had been expecting. The vital meeting would be the talk between the President and the Prime Minister. In the President's view, all of the main subjects were already pretty well ripe for discussion by the two men and "it was important not to remove too many leaves from the artichoke before their talk took place".

Soames and Jobert then danced around the subject, Soames insisting on keeping Community preference for the bilateral, Jobert insisting on keeping sugar for the two leaders to discuss so that, in Soames's view, Pompidou could make a concession to Heath on sugar while hanging tough on New Zealand dairy produce.

Jobert then set out his view of the endgame. June was the right time for there to be a complete package. If the Prime Minister and President met as early as April, there would be two months left during which officials would try to reopen matters which had been decided in Paris and this was a danger which should not be run. The best solution, in Jobert's view, was to have a meeting more or less as late as possible and Jobert took it as read that "once they met, they were condemned to succeed". After the bilateral summit, there could be whatever Ministerial meetings were necessary in Brussels in June to put the seal on what had been agreed in Paris.

"As I got up to leave", Soames wrote to the Foreign Office, "Jobert repeated two points to me: firstly that there was no doubt in his or the President's mind that when the meeting with the Prime Minister took place, it was imperative that it should succeed; and secondly 'too many leaves should not be removed from the artichoke before these talks' ".[144]

By the time Soames met Heath and Douglas-Home in London two days later all the talk was of the tactics for the bilateral summit. Soames had secured the position for which he had striven – a good example of an issue where a determined and skilful political Ambassador could make the weather in London as perhaps an official could not. And Soames had learned the pitfalls vis-à-vis both the Elysée and the Foreign Office from his experience over the Soames Affair.

Soames' position was, in addition, stronger under a Conservative Government than it had been under Labour. George Brown had done Soames something of a favour, after Soames had lost his seat in the House of Commons in 1966, in giving him an important political post. Soames was viewed with suspicion as a Tory toff by some in the Labour party, not least by George Brown's successor, Michael Stewart.

By contrast, while Soames and Heath were not buddies, they had served together in the Cabinets of Macmillan and Douglas-Home and both shared a vision of Britain's European vocation. Soames and Douglas-Home represented new and old money respectively in the Conservative Party but both men, unlike most of their officials, knew what it meant to 'brown a covey' and Douglas-Home, recumbent on a *chaise longue* in the Ambassador's Residence on the Faubourg St Honoré, reading the racing page of the *Daily Mirror*, felt entirely at home with an Ambassador who owned two race horses whose fortunes occupied a fair proportion of His Excellency's time.

At the meeting in London, the Prime Minister, Foreign Secretary and Soames agreed that there was a danger that, if it was known that the Prime Minister and Pompidou were to meet at the end of May, this could hold up progress in Brussels in the meantime. If there was no progress then, that in turn posed the danger that the meeting with Pompidou would take place in a crisis atmosphere. To avoid these twin dangers, the May meeting of the Six might be used to settle some of the minor items in the negotiations; or for some 'loosening up' of all or most of the items. British agreement to a meeting with Pompidou should be conditional on the French agreeing to handle the May meetings with the Six so as to avoid an atmosphere of crisis.[145] A further point was raised when Heath and Douglas-Home met with Rippon two days later. Public opinion in the Five would not much like it if it looked as if the British were doing a direct deal, over the heads of their own Governments, with the French. It was agreed that no such *appearance* should be given. The best course, therefore, would be to take no final decision until after Heath had held his meeting with Brandt.[146]

That Pompidou placed importance on a meeting with Heath was clear from a meeting he held on 3 April with the editor of *The Times*, William Rees-Mogg. According to the paper's Paris correspondent, Charles Hargrove, it was evident that Pompidou still harboured doubts about the sincerity of the intentions of the British, apart from Heath whom Pompidou explicitly excluded from his expressions of scepticism. According to the President, entry into the Common Market would involve a profound change in British habits and British thinking. What for him was the heart of the artichoke (clearly a favoured analogy) was the question of Community preference. The Common Market was a Community of countries which had abolished customs barriers between them and which imposed a penalty on those who chose to go on purchasing from outside. The whole purpose of its mechanism was to encourage member countries to develop their trade with one another. Pompidou sometimes had the impression that even those people in Britain who wanted her to come into the Common Market regarded it as some sort of free trade area with, in one corner, something called the CAP which they saw as a device concocted by France. In fact, the CAP was part of the essential mechanism of the Community. It was important that people in Britain should appreciate that what they were joining was not a free trade area but a Community, with its common standpoint and its rules. Of course, one could conceive of other kinds of organisations to which Britain might belong, but it was the Common Market that Britain wished to join. The Common Market was not merely an organisation of countries which made the free circulation of fridges and motor cars possible across the frontiers. It was something more. This, British opinion must appreciate. Pompidou agreed with Rees-Mogg that once the decision had been taken that Britain should come in, there would be a sort of psychological shock which would mean that Britain would become converted to the idea and prepared to live with it, whereas it had not been before. This would require, said Pompidou, an effort, just as it had for the Six when they signed the Treaty of Rome. And that effort should also be such as to ensure that Britain gradually assumed the financial burdens of the CAP in such a way that, at the end of the transitional period, the gap was not too wide between it and full membership in financial terms and the British did not then say that they could not meet the financial obligations of membership. For, in those circumstances, the Community would have to face the problem of how to get Britain out, and that would lead to the break up of the organisation.[147]

On the same day, Pompidou made similar remarks to the Belgian Ambassador in Paris, M. Rothschild, who gave a record of the meeting to Soames. Pompidou said that there was still uncertainty in his mind about British attitudes and intentions. First, it sometimes seemed as if the British were still hankering after the free trade concept and were reluctant to recognise the implications of the Community. If Britain came in, would she then seek to dilute the Community into a free trade area? Paradoxically, Pompidou then went on to express a fear that the British might prove too integrationist and try to insist on an extension of the practice of majority voting.

Pompidou also made no secret of his preoccupation with developments in Germany. For him, it was monetary policy, rather than anything achieved so far within the Community, that was most likely to integrate Germany within Western Europe.[148]

Germany had been much on Heath's mind as his visit to Bonn approached and he asked Rippon to let him have a note of the main points he might seek to get across. The Germans, in Rippon's view, tended to sit on the fence hoping that time, at no cost to themselves, would resolve Anglo-French differences. The most important point to get over to Brandt would be that the back of the negotiations must be broken by the end of July and that, while the French did not want the negotiations to fail, they might nonetheless do so as a result of miscalculation. It would be inadvisable to put pressure on Brandt to have a showdown with Pompidou but Brandt was well placed to explain, as a fact of negotiating life, the consequences of delay and of failure. What Heath should rub in, since it was consistently overlooked within the Community, was the extent of the very great efforts made by Britain to move towards the Community and its policies. These included acceptance without qualification of the Treaty of Rome, the CAP and the direct incomes (the own resources) system. In addition, Britain had also introduced agricultural levies, taken a decision on VAT and instituted a publicity campaign on Europe.[149]

Heath, in his autobiography, described Willy Brandt as "one of the most perplexing personalities with whom I have had to deal" but readily acknowledged the "full support", Brandt had given him in the negotiations for British accession.[150] When they met in Bonn on 5 April 1971 they did so with only interpreters present. Later, as Brandt's command of English improved, they would meet alone.

In Bonn that April, the two men saw eye to eye on the importance of timely success. When Heath asked Brandt how he had managed to persuade Pompidou at The Hague to accept enlargement, Brandt was modest in claiming responsibility. He had exchanged letters with Pompidou before the summit and "on the evening of the first day, we had a little private discussion", but Brandt added that, of course, Pompidou must have made his mind up before then. Since then, Pompidou had told Brandt that, having taken that decision, he wanted the negotiations to succeed and Brandt drew hope from that. Brandt advised that it would be better for Britain to go for a deal under French chairmanship of the Council of Ministers, even if the clock had to be stopped, as the Community had done before. There were still some in France with doubts about Britain, for example Debré, who feared that the United Kingdom would be an outpost in Europe of the United States. Pompidou's views were more balanced, though he was concerned about the position of the French language in the Community if Britain joined. Heath was willing to give an assurance that British representatives in the European Commission would be able to speak French and he had, he told Brandt, always made it a condition for members of the British Delegation in Brussels that they must be familiar with French and German, have Commonwealth experience and have served in several British Government Departments. French fears for their language were, he thought, genuine ones.[151]

If Brandt thought, as he commented to a member of the British Embassy staff in Bonn, that "he felt he had achieved with Mr Heath a more informal and easy-going relationship than he ever has with either Pompidou or Colombo"[152] it would, on the face of it, be harder for Heath to achieve the same with Pompidou.

"Pompidou has never been – and is not now – enthusiastic about our entry", Soames wrote in a letter to Greenhill on 21 April. Pompidou, Soames argued, was no European visionary panting for political unification. He was a cautious, hard-bargaining, reticent Auvergnat with limited imagination and no talent for grandeur. But Pompidou, Soames was convinced, had accepted that on balance it was right and necessary for Britain to come in and it was equally right for Heath to think in terms of a personal meeting with the President. The French were expecting the Prime Minister to make the first move. But they were realists and, while the President wanted the Prime Minister to come to Paris, he knew full well that Heath would not "go to Canossa". This meant that there must be a favourable build-up to the meeting and not a crisis. The meeting of the two leaders was a card which could only be played once – for success or failure. As Lloyd George had rightly said, "it is dangerous to try to cross a chasm in two jumps". Thus, the gap between the negotiating positions of the two sides must be narrowed before the meeting. The artichoke must be prepared. But not stripped. As to the leaves on the artichoke, Soames found it difficult to believe that a package deal could be arrived at unless the British Government were prepared to move on Community finance, to concede the principle of full Community preference from the start and to enter into some kind of undertaking in principle with regard to the future of sterling. In return, the French would have to move on finance, on sugar and a long way indeed on New Zealand.

So much for the artichoke. What about the sauce, asked Soames, for whom matters of food and drink were ever a high priority? In Soames's view, the Prime Minister would need to stress that, for Britain, joining the European Community was but the beginning of a road which must lead to closer political – and eventually defence – collaboration for Europe, as also to the emergence of a Europe which would be far more independent of the United States politically, financially and industrially than was currently the case. Heath would also be wise to reassure Pompidou that Britain shared his view of the essential role of the nation state and that Britain would not seek to challenge the de facto rule of decision by unanimity: Pompidou was afraid that Britain would bring with her a number of client states, servile to British wishes and that, in addition, the Dutch and others among the Six would tend to gravitate into the British orbit. Finally, it would be necessary to help Pompidou over the language hump.

In a separate paper, Soames argued that Pompidou's refusal to date to authorise any significant shift in French negotiating positions had given heart to the anti-British parts of the French Foreign Ministry. From the Quai d'Orsay had "re-emerged, one after the other, all the old stage props" from the era of Couve de Murville: the Trojan Horse, the danger of a new iron curtain in Europe if the Community enlarged, the price the Americans would extract for acquiescence in the increased trade discrimination against them implicit in enlargement, the inevitable disappearance of the French language in what would become an English-speaking Community, and the likelihood of the Community itself disintegrating into an Atlantic free trade zone.

Soames also picked up on the frequent pleas from Britain for the French to be more demonstrative about wanting Britain to enter the EEC. The French were, he said, genuinely puzzled by this aspect of British behaviour. It was fundamental to the French approach that the British were *demandeurs*, and gestures of spontaneous goodwill towards the other party simply did not exist in the French negotiating repertoire. For the French, this was a marriage contract in which the business side had to be settled between the lawyers before the ceremony. The French could see for themselves the British Government's difficulties with public and Parliamentary opinion and the pressure this put on the Government to secure a quick decision. It would be untrue to the French character if they did not see this as strengthening their own bargaining position.[153]

Two days later, Soames was in London for a meeting with Heath and Rippon as a result of which he was authorised to float with Jobert at the Elysée, and subsequently propose, a meeting between Prime Minister and President. Soames was also instructed to find out how far Pompidou would wish to reach at least the basis of an agreement with Heath so that the negotiations could be brought to the point of certainty at the Ministerial meeting due in Luxembourg in June. The British, Soames could say, did not expect finally to dispose at the May meeting of any of the main outstanding issues, but they did think it important to show some visible progress on each of them: on sugar and Association for the remaining Common-wealth countries; on New Zealand; on Community finance and on Community preference in agriculture.[154]

On receiving his instructions, Soames saw Jobert the following day. Once Soames had been able to assure Jobert (and through him, Pompidou) that sugges-tions in the British Press that Heath wanted to play things long were mistaken, agreement was reached that the President might in effect cancel the visit which his Foreign Minister, Schumann, was due to make to London on 20/21 May and use those dates instead for Heath's visit to Paris.

Soames went to see Jobert again later on the same day (which was easily done since the Embassy and the Elysée were only two doors apart in the Faubourg St Honoré) to be told that the President accepted the outline plan.[155]

Meanwhile, back in London, the egregious Courcel, just back from a visit to Paris but, fortunately, not in the loop on the prospective bilateral summit, was berating Rippon for the failure of the British Government, as seen from Paris, to show themselves sufficiently Community-minded in the negotiations. The British were giving the impression by their proposals on the EEC budget that they wanted only to put one toe in the water rather than go in, as the French now were, up to the neck. Rippon gave this contention short shrift. Courcel went on to express the hope that the state of British public opinion would not make it impossible for the British Government to accept the compromises which would eventually be necessary if an agreement was to be reached. What a pity it was, Rippon replied, that Courcel felt unable to make in England the sort of warm and friendly speeches being made by Mr Soames in France. Why did he not take the opportunity one day to make a rousing speech expressing his Government's wish to see Britain join the Community and expressing appreciation of British acceptance of the Treaty of Rome, the CAP, the direct income system and so on, and declaring the need for Britain, France and the other members of the Commu-nity to make a new Europe together? To this, Courcel made no answer.[156]

In fairness to Courcel, he was not an unfaithful conduit for a vein of opinion in Paris which stretched to the President himself. At the end of that same week, Pompidou gave a lunch for about eight senior French political journalists, one of whom, from *Le Monde*, gave Michael Palliser a record. "I am naturally less opti-mistic than I was two or three months ago", Pompidou was reported as saying, "because the English have not progressed by an inch and because they are putting forward, on the contrary, every week new questions – sugar, butter and now pears, for which they seek a special regime. Yet, while these details are being discussed, the essential point is being forgotten, that is the question of whether England is now ready to play the European game, whether she has really renounced the idea of entering in order to upset everything, whether with regard to currency, finan-cial participation and political understanding she is ready to prove herself a loyal partner. Every day one discovers new difficulties, new objections. This is logical as the final day approaches. With Mr Heath, I should naturally not be able to continue this dialogue of the deaf; we shall not be able to continue for much longer to avoid each other; but nothing has been fixed as regards a meeting.[157]

On the British side, suspicions were further aroused by a paper which Jobert gave to Soames on 4 May. It had been approved by the President and was in two sections, the first consisting of points to which the President attached the greatest importance and the second comprising matters of lesser importance.

Soames immediately spotted that there was no mention of the British contribution to EEC finance or to New Zealand or to sugar, in other words of any of the issues to which the British Government attached most importance. Jobert's response was that Pompidou felt that if he and Heath could reach an understanding on the points in the French paper then all the rest would follow. The principal items on Pompidou's list were, in order of importance: the operation of the institutions. In particular, did the British Government accept that even for those decisions capable of majority decision, discussion should continue until unanimous agreement had been reached when the very important interests of one of more partners were at stake? In other words, did Britain accept the so-called Luxembourg agreement which had helped end the French boycott of the EEC institutions in 1965? The future of the pound. What was the British Government going to do to bring about the progressive reduction of the sterling balances? Community Preference. Did the British Government subscribe, unambiguously, to the immediate application of Community Preference in its entirety once she joined the EEC? What did the British propose for the future of the French language within the EEC institutions?[158]

Soames returned to London straightaway to see the Prime Minister, Foreign Secretary and Rippon. Douglas-Home said at the outset of the meeting that a bilateral discussion restricted to the items which Pompidou had suggested could be dangerous. The Prime Minister would be pressed to make concessions on sterling and Community preference which the French could make public while getting no commitment in return on items of British concern beyond being told that they should be handled in Brussels. It was agreed that Soames should ask for the addition of two items to the agenda: the role of the enlarged Community in the world and the decisions needed to ensure a successful outcome to the enlargement negotiations in June. The addition of the first item would enable Heath to introduce into the discussion the consequences if the negotiations failed. The second was self-explanatory. Soames should propose a new item for the agenda: "The decisions necessary to ensure the early success of the negotiations for enlargement of the European Communities. What are the French Government's views on the main outstanding issues, and what understandings can now be reached between the President and the Prime Minister to facilitate the resolution of the main outstanding problems at the Ministerial Meeting on 21/22 June?"

Soames was instructed to make clear that, unless Pompidou was prepared to agree, in detail, solutions to Britain's problems in the negotiations – as well as to his own – the British Government would see little or no advantage in a bilateral meeting.[159]

Soames played this quite difficult hand with characteristic acumen. When he saw Jobert again on 6 May, he began by saying that the Prime Minister wanted to use his meeting with the President to talk to him about the future of Europe in the broadest sense, touching on economic, political and defence questions. Jobert immediately said that this was what the President wanted too. He, Jobert, was convinced of Heath's European view and convictions, which he had heard him expound with great sincerity when they had met in Spain some time ago (they had met while both were on holiday in Marbella in 1960, when a dieting Heath had been accosted in the hotel restaurant by Jobert with the words 'I do not know how you expect to deal with de Gaulle when you eat so little food').[160] He, Jobert, honestly believed that Heath and Pompidou were two of the most European leaders in Europe and, from what he knew of the beliefs and aspirations of the two men, he was sure they would have a good and effective dialogue.

Soames then said that, in his earlier talks with him, Jobert had impressed on him how important it was, from both the British and French standpoints, for the meeting to be a success. For this, it was necessary that there should be a meeting of minds on a broad front, though of course the fruits of the meeting would only become evident at the later Ministerial meeting in Brussels. On this basis, agreement between the two men was reached.[161]

Soames followed up a day later with a further letter to Greenhill. Pompidou, he had said in his earlier letter to Greenhill, was no visionary. But, at the same time, he did want to put a hallmark of his own on European history and, so far, he had not yet found one. Pompidou was well aware that his predecessor had achieved considerable resonance with the French public with his grandiose fantasy of a Europe stretching from the Atlantic to the Urals and his assiduous cult of the myth of French might. Pompidou had so far put little or nothing in place of de Gaulle's vision. So far, he had done no more than open the door, like a reluctant concierge, to four prospective new tenants and follow them around muttering that, if they signed the lease, the furniture must not be moved. Pompidou needed to be persuaded that, if the deal went through, the value of the premises would be enormously increased and that he would go down in history as the man who pulled it off for France.

Soames thought that the first step in this direction had to be reached in a fairly cosmic perspective, with Heath telling Pompidou that Britain wanted to join the Community because she saw it as the beginning of a great enterprise on which Britain and France fundamentally saw eye to eye. This would lead the Prime Minister naturally into an exposition of his own conception of a united Europe with a distinctive personality of its own, free of economic, political, military or monetary vassalage and deriving its cohesion from the voluntary interlocking of nation states pursuing common objectives. The objective would be to persuade Pompidou that British accession provided an opportunity to add a valuable and genuinely European ally, rather than the risk of Atlantic dilution of the Community, and to enable Pompidou to see himself as a man of vision. It could be said of Pompidou, as Macaulay had once said of Dryden, that his imagination resembled the wings of an ostrich: it enabled him to run, though not to soar. He needed to be shown that he could fly, but he would need to shed ballast first. The difficult concrete issues were ultimately negotiable. What would be more difficult to get at would be the residual legacy of mistrust and disbelief about Britain which Pompidou had inherited from de Gaulle and which was, in any case, what he instinctively felt. Those feelings were being assiduously worked on by those on both right and left who were opposed to British entry and Pompidou was not unaffected by their arguments. What Pompidou would need to hear from the Prime Minister was that his fears and misgivings were unfounded. If Heath could convince Pompidou that Britain's European policy stemmed from a desire no less deep than his own to see an effective and really independent Europe then Britain would "be in the straight and not very far from the post". It would be no easy task to dispel these suspicions from the mind of a man who was in any case of a mistrustful nature. But Heath had two important assets in his favour. His own European sincerity was regarded in France, even by Britain's opponents, as unimpeachable. And Pompidou held him in esteem and believed he was a man with whom he could do business.[162]

On 6 May, Heath had had an opportunity to sound out Brandt, who was on a visit to London to speak at an anniversary dinner of *The Guardian*, on some of these matters. Brandt was alert to the most sensitive issues for Britain and broached with Heath what Brandt described as the emotional issue for Britain of New Zealand. Heath confirmed that there was "great emotional steam" behind the support for New Zealand in Britain, based partly on the fact that New Zealand had built her agricultural economy on access to the British market, but partly also on the fact that New Zealand had sent her men to serve alongside British troops in both World Wars. Britain wanted a satisfactory solution, not because she wanted to keep New Zealand in her grasp, but because it was impossible overnight to change the pattern and orientation of the economy of a country. In fact, New Zealand had made a big effort to diversify her markets but had faced the ironic situation of finding that, because of the CAP and its subsidies, it was possible for the French to sell their butter in South East Asia more cheaply than could the New Zealanders.

Brandt immediately 'got' the issue in a way which would have been inconceivable in a French politician. Securing a satisfactory arrangement for New Zealand was, he said, clearly a point of honour for Britain. But, in his view, it was also a test of credibility for an enlarged Community. If the Community could not find a solution for this relatively small problem, the enlarged Community would not command confidence in other parts of the world either. The CAP had been a serious mistake. The Treaty of Rome had not required such a policy. But it was now impossible to turn back the clock and to undo it.

Brandt went on to talk about Pompidou's views of the nature of the European Community and its institutions. Pompidou's view was not as extreme as that of de Gaulle and it should be possible to find a common position with the French. Brandt thought that the founders of the EEC had been over-sophisticated in thinking that the European Commission could become a kind of Government of the Community. Pompidou would accept that the Commission should remain independent; but the change of balance that had been envisaged whereby more power would be given to the Commission and less to the Council of Ministers would not now happen. For a long time to come a European Government would have to include a large element of coordination among those who held national responsibilities. His own view was that Foreign Ministers should continue to be the members of the Council of Ministers. He did not favour the idea of special Ministers for Europe. But the meetings of Foreign Ministers in the Council would need careful preparation, politically as well as technically.

The French Government were, according to Brandt, still reluctant to see the further development of the European Assembly. It had been given some additional competence already and it would be better to develop it on those lines than to introduce direct elections to it. Heath said that he shared that view.

Heath asked Brandt whether the Luxembourg Agreement (the Luxembourg Compromise) on voting arrangements was working satisfactorily. Brandt thought (and in this his judgement bore out the advice officials had given to British Ministers at the time of its negotiation) that more importance had been attached to the Agreement than it really contained. It had always been the position that on a question which was vital to one particular country, a decision would not be pushed through in the Community against that country's wishes. There had been some issues, not of such a vital nature, which had been decided by majority vote and there would be more. It was essential in a Community of the kind that had evolved that, if a matter was regarded as of vital interest of one member, a decision should not be pushed through against that member's wishes; but it should also be made difficult for a Government to invoke this sort of 'necessity' saving clause except where its vital interests really were involved.

Heath agreed and recalled that Monnet had said to him many years previously that being in a Community meant not overruling any one country on a point of crucial importance to the national interests of that country. This was not a matter just of rules. The fabric of the Community would not stand the strain which overriding vital national interests might impose on it. Brandt suggested that to make this sort of point clear could help in presenting entry into the EEC to British public opinion.[163]

Against a background of slow but not insignificant progress in the negotiations in Brussels, preparations continued for the bilateral meeting between Heath and Pompidou. An announcement had been made by both Governments on 8 May 1971 that the two leaders "consider that a meeting to discuss matters of common interest would now be useful" and that Pompidou had accordingly invited Heath to Paris.

On 9 May, the Germans took a decision to float the DM. The basic cause, the Treasury advised Heath, was the weakness of the dollar. The Swiss franc and Austrian Schilling had been revalued, and the DM and Dutch guilder had been allowed to float upwards, at least temporarily. The Germans, the Treasury noted, had been both determined to float and to obtain Community agreement to their doing so. They had succeeded, albeit against the wishes of the French and Italians, who were now 'cross'. The Dutch were unhappy at being pushed into action which they would have preferred not to take and were cross with the Belgians for not floating with them.

These movements, the Treasury believed, would help British competitiveness. Overall, however, instability and disturbance in the international monetary system were disadvantageous unless they promoted useful reform; but at present there was no clear vision as to what that reform might be. Closer to home, their defeat by the Germans could make the French more favourable to UK entry to the EEC as a counterweight to the Germans, a point which the French Press had also been making. But it could also make the French less inclined to compromise over Community financing. As far as economic and monetary union was concerned, the first move towards narrowing exchange rate margins had been postponed and progress generally set back temporarily. French hostility to the United States and to the dollar would intensify.[164]

On 20 May, Heath flew to Paris. In his autobiography, Heath describes the anxious expectation of the Press when he and President Pompidou entered the Salle des Fêtes in the Elysée at the end of two days and eleven hours of talks, which had gone on into the late afternoon of the second day. "It was obvious from the looks on their faces that the majority of the media believed . . . that we had found it impossible to reach agreement". Heath had not, he wrote, confided even in Douglas Hurd or Michael Wolff, his political advisers, "to their evident annoyance".[165]

That the Press were in the dark is not surprising since the preparations for the summit had taken place between the Elysée and Number 10 and with great discretion. But there is some poetic licence in Heath's claim that his advisers were in the dark. Heath and Pompidou had, it is true, held four meetings over two days on their own, apart from the presence of interpreters. But, on the British side, the interpreter was Michael Palliser, number two in the Paris Embassy, and he had conveyed at least the mood music, which was positive from the start, to his colleagues. Moreover, when Heath and Pompidou met at the start of day two, they had already set officials to work on an agreed record of conclusions and on a separate final communiqué. The previous evening, at a formal dinner at the Elysée, both President and Prime Minister had, in the words of Soames's subsequent formal Despatch on the visit, "in their exchange of toasts lifted enough of the blanket of silence which they had, by mutual consent, imposed on the results of their conversations until these were concluded, to reassure the assembled company that good progress was being made . . . M. Pompidou felt able to say that on many of the essential points, and notably the general conception of Europe, including its organisation and objectives, his and Mr Heath's views were 'sufficiently close for us to be able to continue without pessimism'. The Prime Minister, for his part, said he believed that the negotiating problems could be settled to the satisfaction of all the partners concerned".

Soames also noted in his Despatch that it was exceptional, except during a State Visit, for the President to go out for a meal at an Embassy but Pompidou was happy to lunch at the British Embassy on the second day of Heath's visit. These arrangements were, said Soames "quickly noted by the Press of a country which, despite its claims of civil egalitarianism, in fact observes the nuances of protocol and social relations with an attention which recalls Byzantium". So a public signal was given in the middle of the talks that things were going well. And Soames felt able to say in his lunchtime toast, as he would not have done if there had been any *froideur* in the talks, that Heath's visit was "a historic event for Europe and the world". The President, doubtless gruntled by the specifically Auvergnat nature of the menu and by Soames's cellar, on which he spent significant sums from his even more significant financial resources, spoke in reply of "this mark of the renewal of confidence and warm feeling between our two countries".[166]

A little poetic licence on Heath's part does not distract from either the significance of the meeting or his achievement. It was, as Soames recorded, a "unique experience" to see the President of the French Republic and the British Prime Minister seated together at a table in the room at the Elysée where, eight years previously, General de Gaulle had pronounced his first veto on Britain's application. Pompidou played up the sense of drama: "Many people believed that Great Britain was not, and did not wish, to become European, and that Britain wanted to enter the Community only so as to destroy it or to divert it from its objectives. Many people also thought that France was ready to use every pretext to place in the end a fresh veto on Britain's entry. Well, Ladies and Gentlemen, you see before you tonight two men who are convinced of the contrary".[167] That statement was all the more noteworthy given that Pompidou had been one of those people who had harboured persistent suspicions of British motives and intentions.

The actual records of the talks were, at the insistence of Heath and Pompidou, held very tightly at the time within both Administrations. They reveal an impressive performance on Heath's part. He set out, exactly as Soames had advised, a historical vision of Britain's place in the world in general, and in Europe in particular, which was heartfelt and compelling. He had briefed himself exhaustively on the issues and had the details of the key British negotiating issues at his fingertips – rather more so than Pompidou who, when asked by Heath to explain a technical point on the British budget contribution that he had just made, was forced to admit that he could not explain it but would get one of his staff to do so to someone on Heath's delegation.

On the big picture, Heath said, right at the start of his first meeting with Pompidou that, whereas once only Europe had counted, now it was a world dominated by two super powers, the United States and Russia, which would probably be joined by a third, China, before the end of the century. European countries could not hope to exert influence unless they were united, with a strong economic base of comparable size to that of the United States and the Soviet Union. It was, Heath continued, sometimes said that Britain only sought partnership with the United States. But there could not, even if Britain wanted it, be a satisfactory partnership between two powers one of which was barely a quarter the size of the other. His own purpose was to see a strong Europe, which could speak with a single voice after a full discussion in common of the world problems affecting it, and could then exert influence in different parts of the world. He did not regard it as healthy that world affairs should be settled between the two super powers. With this exposition, Pompidou readily agreed.

Pompidou, for his part, was anxious to pin down Heath on the issue of the EEC's institutions. France's partners sometimes regarded her as obsessed with the subject. This was because they believed profoundly, in the light of their past history and that of their partners, that there could be no normal progress in

Europe without respect for national feelings and vital national interests. The French were convinced that, if vital interests were at stake, whatever theoretical dispositions might be taken (a reference to majority voting) there must be unanimous agreement on the conclusions reached i.e. the country concerned must give its assent. This had produced a crisis in the Community in what had been known as the policy of the empty chair and the meeting in Luxembourg. France had made clear the very firm interpretation she placed on the text agreed in Luxembourg and he (Pompidou) had had it incorporated in the annotated agenda of his meeting with the Prime Minister in the hope of obtaining Heath's complete agreement to it. This was not a matter of such legal importance as was sometimes thought. Clearly – and he could speak only for France – if some unacceptable decision affecting vital French interests were taken, France would not allow it to be imposed on her. But there was no point in deliberately organising a state of permanent crisis within the Community. It was preferable that everyone should know that if vital interests concerning Britain, Germany or Italy (just as much as France) were at stake, then any decision in the matter must be unanimous. This was, in any case, the way things had worked so far; but there were constant efforts by certain countries, especially some of the smaller ones, to bypass the Luxembourg understanding. France was resolutely determined to stick to that understanding and hoped that Britain would be prepared to do likewise. It seemed to him to conform to the British 'genius' and to the Prime Minister's own thinking.

Heath expressed his complete agreement with Pompidou. When, in 1960, he had told Jean Monnet of the concern which people in Britain had about the majority voting provisions of the Treaty of Rome, Monnet had replied that, in a Community of old established states such as those in Europe, it would always be impossible for the other Member States to overrule any single member which felt its vital national interests to be involved. Indeed, if such an attempt were made, the Community would, so Monnet, believed break up. Thus, since all members were concerned to preserve the Community they would, according to Monnet, be obliged to recognise that they could not overrule the vital interests of a member. This was, Heath explained, a significant element in the willingness of the British Government to accept the Treaty of Rome, its regulations, its institutions and its voting arrangements.

On the substantive outstanding issues in the negotiations for British accession, the two men reached positions which were summarised in a secret note which Armstrong sent to the Foreign Office and other Departments on 24 May.

On economic and monetary union, Heath had made it clear that Britain would join fully in the economic and monetary development of the Community, accepting the consequences for British policies.

On New Zealand, Pompidou had indicated that for him cheese represented a greater political problem than butter and the two men had agreed to see whether butter and cheese could be dealt with separately. Pompidou was prepared to contemplate the possibility of a transitional period of five years, over which guaranteed access for New Zealand butter degressed by a small amount and guaranteed access for New Zealand cheese degressed to a very low figure, followed by a review at the end of five years.

On EEC finance, Heath and Pompidou agreed that the method of dealing with the problem of Britain's contribution to the Community budget which had been proposed by the Community on 12 May provided an acceptable framework. Under this proposal, a notional British contribution to the EEC budget would be calculated for each of the years of the transition but, in order to determine the sum actually payable in each year, this notional contribution would be reduced by a proportion which became progressively smaller during the transitional period. Rippon had already told Cabinet on 18 May that, provided the sums corresponding to these proportions were themselves reasonable, this approach could provide a satisfactory solution. Rippon reported on the same occasion that sugar had also been satisfactorily sorted.[168]

Figures for Britain's budget contribution, according to Armstrong's note, would be for discussion in the Brussels negotiations but Pompidou had indicated his awareness of the need to ensure that the initial contribution did not impose too heavy a burden on the British balance of payments. The separate agreed record of Conclusions of the talks has Heath telling Pompidou that "the problem was simply one of transition".

On the Common Fisheries Problem, Pompidou said that the French Government would be prepared to consider whether the EEC Fisheries Regulation should be adapted to the needs and circumstances of an enlarged Community.

Armstrong's note did not refer to the sensitive subject of sterling but the agreed record of conclusions noted that Heath had agreed "to work towards an alignment of the external characteristics of sterling with those of the currencies of the other members of the enlarged Community" and to work for "an orderly and gradual reduction of official sterling balances in the framework of progress towards economic and monetary union in the enlarged Community".[169]

Referring to his joint press conference with Pompidou at the Elysée, Heath described it over a quarter of a century later in his memoirs as "a wildly exciting moment" and "an historic occasion".[170]

Heath spoke almost as dramatically when he reported to the House of Commons on 24 May. He was, he said, "confident that the divisions and suspicions which have so hampered relations between Britain and France in recent years have now been removed". Britain could approach both the final phase of negotiations and the development of Europe thereafter in a spirit of confidence and partnership, with the prospect of "a degree of unity, and thus of peace and prosperity, in Western Europe which our continent has never seen before, and which would be of profound significance for Britain, for Europe and for the whole world".

Wilson, who must have found it galling that the General Election had snatched from his grasp the prize for which he had striven, offered no congratulations but posed instead some characteristically pertinent questions. The mood within his own Party anyway allowed him little room for manoeuvre and, by contrast with today, when a Government statement is often matched by a response of equal length from the Opposition, brief and pointed questions from the Opposition benches were then the norm. Interestingly, Wilson at no point included in his follow-up (which covered defence, New Zealand and Britain's budget contribution) anything on economic and monetary union where Heath had told the House that he had said to Pompidou "that Britain looked forward wholeheartedly to joining in the economic and monetary development of the Community". Insofar as there was acrimony between the two Party leaders it was over Heath's refusal to spell out how and when Parliament would be consulted on the outcome of the negotiations if they were concluded, as hoped, in June. The Opposition, and some of the anti-Europeans on Heath's own benches, suspected that the Government were planning to bounce something through without MPs being given adequate time for reflection.[171]

All that was for the future. And, while Heath's predictions for Europe as a whole were to be buffeted by events, his comments about Anglo-French relations have stood the test of time. Soames said it somewhat more fully in his Despatch on the Paris visit: "I conclude this Despatch with a reference to the subject which remains, for this post, our paramount preoccupation. It is a truism to say that, since the withdrawal from power of General de Gaulle, and perhaps even before it, there has been an improvement in Anglo-French relations from the nadir of December 1967. This, grudging at first and almost fatally undermined by the 'Soames affair', has since acquired an encouraging momentum as the months have passed . . . Now that the process of *rapprochement* has received the seal of approval at the highest level, we can again talk about the *entente cordiale* without embarrassment".[172]

****

8 Good thing, bad thing? The terms of entry and a country divided: 1971–1973

Heath reported to Cabinet on his talks with Pompidou on the same day he made his statement to the House of Commons. In congratulating the Prime Minister warmly on his success, Cabinet agreed that it would now be necessary to adopt a more positive policy on the presentation of the issues involved to public opinion, especially to the younger generation, and that further consideration should be given as to how best to go about it.[1]

Clearly, one way of handling the issue was to let certain sleeping dogs lie. Since 1970 there had been on the Government's table the question of whether to legislate (or encourage a Private Member's Bill) in order to clarify the doubt that existed as to whether a Roman Catholic could legally become Lord Chancellor. On 24 May, the day Heath reported on his Paris triumph, one of his Private Secretaries wrote, on his instruction, to the Home Office: "The Prime Minister feels that, particularly at the current stage of the negotiations for our entry into the EEC, the time is inopportune for an initiative on this".

Yet, the issue did not so easily go away. A month later, there was a Parliamentary Question on the subject from Lord Norwich. The Government decided to answer by not answering i.e. by asserting what Lord Norwich's question was presumably designed to elucidate, namely that it was clear that there was some legal doubt on the matter. Heath was reminded by one of his Private Secretaries that he had already determined that "the time seemed inopportune to consider this, since people might be prepared to attribute it to the Treaty of Rome".[2] EEC membership as a combination of the end to a thousand years of history and an attempt to overturn the Protestant Reformation was not far from the surface of some anti-European sentiment.

Continental reaction to Heath's visit to Paris was mostly favourable, only the Belgian and Dutch Heads of Mission in London expressing disappointment to the Foreign Office, on behalf of their Governments, that Heath had come down on the French side over the institutions of the Community and majority voting.[3]

Reaction in Paris was also positive, if slightly less breathless than on the part of Heath and his associates. Following the meeting of the French Council of Ministers on 27 May, the Government spokesman told the Press that there might yet be difficulties for the Brussels negotiations which had not been settled and which would have to be. But President Pompidou had noted with pleasure the evolution of thought which was taking place "particularly in Britain".[4]

This businesslike approach on Pompidou's part was reflected in a television interview which he gave in Paris a month later, after the conclusion of the enlargement negotiations. Attributing to de Gaulle pro-British sentiments which would have come as a surprise to British viewers, Pompidou said that as far back as 1958 de Gaulle had told him that what bothered him about the Common Market was that it would cause trouble between the British and the French. Ignoring the self-fulfilling nature of this prophecy over the ten years of de Gaulle's rule, Pompidou laid firmly at the door of the British Labour Government the failure of the approach towards Britain, through Soames, which de Gaulle had made in the last months of his Presidency. Pompidou had, he said, realised at the same time that France's partners no longer wanted to make progress within the EEC, progress which Pompidou defined as "renewing and settling for good, if I may say, the CAP". For that reason he had put "the deal" clearly to France's partners at the summit in The Hague: "and I achieved, on the one hand, a definitive agricultural settlement in return for, on the other, the opening of negotiations with Britain".

Pompidou went on to say that he had put four questions frankly to Mr Heath. Did Heath accept what was the very basis of the Common Market for agriculture: Community Preference, whereby "we feed ourselves in the first place from within the Community"? The Prime Minister had, said Pompidou, confirmed in the clearest possible way that he did.

The second question had been on the rule of unanimity, to which France attached the greatest importance. This meant that when a country believed that a capital issue was at stake, no one else had the right to impose upon it the will of the majority. A unanimous agreement must be reached. Here too, the British Government had made clear that they agreed and had confirmed their agreement publicly.

The third question had been monetary. Sterling enjoyed a special status as a reserve currency. It enjoyed privileges. Within a Community, it was obvious that all must be on an equal footing and, consequently, the British currency must be like all others. Here too Heath had assured him that this was indeed how he saw things and that progressively sterling would become a currency like the rest and would accordingly take part in what the Community were trying to create – a European monetary union.

Pompidou's fourth question had been probably his most important one, namely whether Britain had really decided to become European; whether "Britain, which is an island, had decided to moor herself to the continent and if she was therefore ready to come in from the wide seas which had always drawn her." Mr Heath's explanations had demonstrated that his views were similar to France's conception of the future of Europe and were consistent with what he had been saying for the last twenty years. Of course, Pompidou continued, there should be no illusions. A lot of effort would be needed to handle a Community of nine or ten, all the more so as that enlarged Community would have to take account of "British traditions, administrative habits, ways of thought and special commitments in certain fields, as in defence, for example". France would make it her duty to be vigilant "and she will be, believe you me". Moreover, she had the geographical advantage of being in the centre and therefore indispensable. But, Pompidou, concluded, subject to these cautions, he was hopeful.[5]

French 'vigilance' had of course already extended to the concluding stages of the enlargement negotiations. Heath and Pompidou had discussed the political parameters of eventual deals in a number of areas and had given a clear signal that they wanted the negotiations to be brought to a successful conclusion. But the devil lay in the unresolved detail and on that detail would hang the acceptability or otherwise of the outcome to Parliament and the British people.

One issue, sugar, had been agreed even before Heath and Pompidou met, and the acceptability of the deal to the member countries of the Commonwealth Sugar Agreement (CSA) was confirmed at a meeting in London in early June. At the end of it, the CSA members expressed themselves satisfied with the Community's readiness to offer them a choice of forms of Association with the EEC or a trade agreement, as well as with the United Kingdom's contractual commitments to all the CSA member countries up to the end of 1974. As regards arrangements after 1974, the CSA Governments and the British Government accepted as a "specific and moral commitment" the Community's assurance of a secure and continuing market in the enlarged EEC. Wilson was later to attack the agreement as no more than the expression of a firm purpose of intent on the part of the EEC rather than as a clear and unequivocal guarantee.[6]

Another issue was close to resolution: the role of sterling. On 24 May, Armstrong had written to Ryrie, a senior Treasury official, to say that, in his talks with Pompidou, "the Prime Minister accepted that, with British entry into the EEC, it would be appropriate in the context of progress towards economic and monetary union to work towards an alignment of the external characteristics of sterling with those of the currencies of other members of the enlarged Communities". This in turn meant that Britain would "work for a gradual and orderly reduction of official sterling balances in the framework of progress towards economic and monetary union in the Community".[7]

Armstrong wrote again to Ryrie on 3 June, referring to the Prime Minister's undertaking to Pompidou that the British Government intended to take measures which would "tend to stabilise the level of official sterling balances between 30 June 1971 and the date of our accession to the EEC". The Prime Minister hoped, said Armstrong, that "those who manage our affairs in this regard will carry out an operation to put us in the best possible position on 30 June for the purpose of being able to satisfy this requirement with least difficulty and embarrassment".[8]

In fact, by early June, the British Government were ready for Rippon to make a statement, at a meeting with the Six on 7 June, undertaking "to discuss after our entry measures to achieve a progressive alignment of the external characteristics of, and practices in relation to, sterling with those of other currencies in the Community in the context of economic and monetary union, a progress in which we are ready to take our full part. In the meantime we should manage our policies in relation to the official sterling balances in a way which would be consistent with these longer term objectives". As a result of discussions with the French Government it was expected that "the French Presidency will be able to indicate that this statement disposes of sterling and associated matters". Britain's Embassies in EEC capitals were instructed to prepare the ground with their host Governments over the weekend.[9]

All would have gone according to plan but for the intervention of the European Commission who, as Rippon reported to London, had been directed by Raymond Barre, French Commissioner, "to widen the discussion before the Community had heard my statement, and even circulated a detailed paper in an attempt to reach a compromise between what Barre thought were French views and those which had been expressed by other Member States." After Rippon had made his statement and had withdrawn to allow the Community to consider it, Giscard d'Estaing, from the chair, said at once that he could accept what Rippon had said. This was greeted with some laughter from other delegations and some indignation from the Commission. Barre told Rippon subsequently that the British statement amounted to "zero plus zero plus zero" and he could not understand why Giscard had agreed it.

Mission accomplished, but Rippon cautioned that London "must recognise that the Commission (not only Barre) feel that some deal has been done behind their backs and, since we shall need the Commission's goodwill in the next two weeks if we are to be able to reach satisfactory agreements on fisheries and New Zealand it will be important to give them the impression that we still look to them to play an essential role in the final stages of the negotiations". Rippon also worried that the Five, especially the Germans, to some extent shared the Commission's feeling of having been left out of things.[10]

The Foreign Office shared these apprehensions and, on 11 June, instructed its Embassies in the EEC to say that the British Government looked to all Governments in the Community and the Commission to play their part in achieving a satisfactory outcome. Sterling had been raised essentially by the French alone and was not a matter covered by the Treaty of Rome or by regulations or directives. The outstanding matters in the negotiation, including Community finance and New Zealand, were in a different category altogether. Although they had been discussed between the Prime Minister and Pompidou "there was no attempt to reach agreement or understanding in detail, it being recognised that the right place to resolve these matters was in the negotiating conference in Brussels and Luxembourg". Britain needed a better offer on New Zealand than the one that was on the table. As to Community finance, while the British Government "can certainly move well above 3% as our opening bid, it is going to be essential to get a first year figure well below the 11.5% figure of which the French are talking".[11]

More precise instructions were sent to Soames for use with Schumann.

Soames had called on Schumann on 10 June. Schumann said that he had read with the greatest care the record of Pompidou's meetings with Heath and "it was evident that nothing had been agreed between them" on the main negotiating subjects. This was unfair, although Douglas Hurd, who had been in Paris with

Heath for his meeting with Pompidou, had recorded in his diary on the first evening of the talks: "It emerges that the great men have got through the agenda in high good humour, without settling anything of importance".[12]

Now, said Schumann, the time had come for plain speaking if the negotiations were to be ended at the next Ministerial meeting. On New Zealand, Schumann continued, what the French would have liked to do was to have given New Zealand a lengthy transitional period before reducing her dairy exports to zero. But he had put this to the New Zealand Deputy Prime Minister, Marshall, who had said that he could never accept any arrangement which involved a rundown to zero over however long a period. So Schumann was thinking instead of an agreement which would involve a rundown of New Zealand exports over a five year period to a percentage figure to be negotiated, with a review at the end which would be subject to unanimity. In his view the unanimous view among the Six as to what the correct percentage figure should be was 50%.

Soames expressed surprise. The Dutch, for starters, had suggested a figure of over 60%. Schumann dismissed this as simply a tactical counter to the French proposal of zero percent. Of course, Schumann added, if the French agreed even to 50% this would be a considerable sacrifice on their part. Such a sacrifice for France would have its implications for the agreement on Community financing of agriculture. If the Community were to have to agree to 50% as the figure for New Zealand dairy exports (expressed as 'milk equivalent') then the French could not come down below a figure of 9% of the EEC budget as Britain's first-year contribution (compared with the 3% offered by Britain). It was thus that he saw a financial package being struck.

Soames begged to differ. Marshall had told him that even the Dutch proposal of 60% would not do. The New Zealanders could not take a reduction of 40% in their dairy industry. As to Britain's financial contribution, Schumann was absolutely correct in accepting that the figure for Britain's contribution had to come out at lower than 10% but Soames saw no reason to suppose that 9% would be acceptable. Soames added "that the New Zealand question was, from a political point of view, even more important to us than the question of our financial contribution, although it was the latter which put the financial burden on the United Kingdom. It was sufficient to say this for him to realise how vital it was politically that a satisfactory arrangement for New Zealand should be arrived at."[13]

The ingenious Cabinet Office had worked out that, provided Britain contributed 3% of the EEC budget in 1973, and the other three applicant countries contributed between 1.5% and 2%, enlargement would cost the Six precisely nothing in that year. In other words, every advance on 3% represented a net financial gain to the existing members of the Community. These facts also meant that the cost in 1973 of the difference between what the French were now proposing for New Zealand butter and what Britain had in mind (somewhere in the high 70% range), would be covered by an additional contribution of about half a percent in 1973. Thus, a contribution of 3% to the EEC budget by the United Kingdom in 1973 would cover the costs of enlargement. From every 1%

above this, the existing members of the Community would make a significant profit. If Britain contributed 6.5% to the budget in 1973 (the compromise figure which Heath had given implicitly to Pompidou during their discussions) then the gain to the existing members of the Community would be worth at least 3.5% of the EEC budget.[14]

So, on 11 June, Armstrong sent a further telegram of instructions to Soames. He was to see both Jobert ("on the principle that one should always purr when one is pleased") and Schumann. The point of seeing Jobert was of course to mark his and the President's card and to ensure that Schumann and the Quai d'Orsay were not allowed by the Elysée to revert to type. With Schumann, Soames was to cover the three outstanding issues: fisheries, Community finance and New Zealand.

On fisheries, preservation of an exclusive six mile limit was "an essential ingredient in a satisfactory settlement". On Community finance, Soames could refer to the fact that Heath and Pompidou had discussed the need to cover the cost of the accession of Britain and the other applicants to the Community and was then to deploy the facts which the Cabinet Office had brought to light: a UK contribution of 3% in 1973 would be enough to cover the costs of enlargement, with an extra half a percent to cover the difference between the French and British positions on New Zealand. All this would justify an initial contribution "not substantially greater than 6.5%, if excessive burdens on our balance of payments are to be avoided".

On New Zealand, Soames was instructed to say that neither a settlement based on degression to 50% milk equivalent over five years, nor a settlement which involved phasing the butter guarantee to zero over seven years, would be "presentable to the New Zealand Government (or to British public opinion) as satisfactory. We believe that the figure will have to be in the 70s "percent milk equivalent".[15]

Soames saw Jobert on 14 June and "we had a purr-in". Pompidou and Heath had, said Jobert, agreed that the detailed matters under negotiation should be left for Brussels. Pompidou had accordingly told Schumann to go on and do the best he could. Hence the position Schumann had presented to Soames.

Soames explained that his instructions from London were to tell Schumann, broadly, that what he had offered was not anywhere near good enough. Jobert took note and said the President would be seeing Schumann again on 18 June "when he might or might not give him more precise instructions".[16]

In the event, some word almost certainly went from the Elysée to the Quai in advance of the next encounter between Pompidou and his Foreign Minister. For, after Soames had seen Schumann again, the French Economic Director at the Quai, Brunet, summoned Palliser to tell him that the French were prepared to modify their attitude on New Zealand, given its capital importance to Britain. The quid pro quo was that the United Kingdom should be more responsive to the French Government over Britain's initial contribution to the Community budget. The French Government, according to Brunet, could expect serious Parliamentary and public criticism of concessions to Britain over New Zealand. Even more so if they appeared to be conceding too much on the budget. At present, the British were talking of a first-year contribution of 6.5% and the French of 11.5%.

In the French view, the initial British contribution "must not be" lower than 9 to 9.5%. This really was as far as the French could go. The French assessment of the British Government's political priorities, Brunet added, was that New Zealand came first, with fisheries second and Community finance third. The French were ready to help Britain over New Zealand and accepted the need to look again at the fisheries regulation. But only if Britain helped France on the financial contribution to the budget.

Palliser said that he would not quarrel with Brunet's assessment of Britain's political priorities, except to warn against underestimating the importance to the British Government of Community finance. The two men sparred for a bit over New Zealand and fisheries, but with clear evidence that British objectives for New Zealand were not unattainable. The French also advised that fisheries should be taken in slower time, a suggestion which Palliser refused: if the final package was to be tied up at the meeting in the following week in Luxembourg, then it must include an element on fisheries, including the preservation of the six mile limit i.e. allowing only vessels genuinely from British ports to fish within the six mile limit, while allowing the rest of the Community fishing rights within the 6-12 mile limit.[17]

On 18 June, Schumann showed Soames what he described as a formula for which he would try, with no guarantee of success, to obtain Pompidou's approval. He then set out, with much emphasis on how great a French concession it would be, "a sacrifice by France, but one that it was necessary for her to make in the wider interests of a greater Europe, appreciating the moral obligations which the United Kingdom felt towards New Zealand".

Schumann might just have got away with this had he been talking to a political novice, but Soames was a former Agriculture Minister who knew the subject and, more pertinently, had negotiated with the National Farmers Union (NFU), as hard-headed and unsentimental a bunch as any Minister could have to deal with. So, it took Soames about three seconds to point out to Schumann that his offer was in reality more or less the same as the proposal already made by the Dutch and which was simply not good enough.

Schumann tried again. Having gone as far as he had on New Zealand, he would have to ask the British to agree to a first year budget contribution of 9%. Soames told him that, frankly, the French Government would have to do better.

Schumann later telephoned Soames to tell him that the President had agreed to the proposals that Schumann had outlined to Soames earlier in the day. Soames advised him to expect a tough battle in Luxembourg.[18]

Soames had meanwhile again seen Jobert and had come away with the feeling that, after a rearguard action, the French would give the British what they wanted on New Zealand and that it would be possible to knock them off 9%.[19]

Rippon and Ministers of the Six met in Luxembourg on 21/22 June. Rippon was in touch with Downing Street by telegram throughout and received telegraphed instructions from Heath, who consulted Ministerial colleagues, during the two days. Armstrong reported to Heath on the second day: "It is evident that our proposals for New Zealand, on a figure of 71% and a review clause, came as something of a shock to the Six . . . First reactions were gloomy, but after four hours among themselves, they seemed to have accepted our figure . . . Our people were optimistic about reaching agreement on this soon . . . They were then going to break for dinner . . ." Armstrong reported that the Community were expected to make an offer on Community finance which left him feeling that "it should not be difficult to arrive at some kind of agreement on this basis, though the negotiations may go on into the night . . ."[20]

"Well done indeed. I congratulate you most warmly on this splendid result. You have done famously", Douglas-Home telegraphed to Rippon after agreement was reached in the early hours of 23 June.[21]

Rippon returned to the warm congratulations of the Prime Minister and his other colleagues in Cabinet the next day. He had, his colleagues concluded, "succeeded in negotiating most satisfactory terms". The Government should commend the arrangements and not be defensive. They would make it clear that they had accepted the need to make a rather larger first year contribution than otherwise in order to secure satisfactory terms for New Zealand. The absence of an agreement on fisheries (postponed until July) could be defended on the grounds that the final arrangements were dependent on the interests of the other three applicants as well as those of the United Kingdom.[22]

The deal, as Rippon reported it to the House of Commons later in the day, gave New Zealand a guarantee of butter exports amounting to 80% of existing quantities in the fifth year. For cheese, the quantities guaranteed would be reduced to 20% in the fifth year. This result meant that, in terms of milk equivalent, New Zealand would be assured of selling 71% of the present quantity even in 1977. The price level would also be guaranteed to New Zealand at the average of that enjoyed in Britain during the years 1969–1972. It was estimated that this would give to New Zealand prices substantially higher than the average of recent years. There would be a review in the third year.

As to the British budget contribution, agreement had been reached that the annual amount to be paid by Britain would amount to 8.64% of the Community budget in 1973, rising to 18.92% of the Community budget in 1977. Before the end of 1977, the Commission would calculate the contribution which the United Kingdom would have made in 1977 had she then applied in full the EEC budgetary system. On the basis of that calculation, a limitation would be applied to the British contribution for a further two years (1978 and 1979) to ensure a gradual progression to Britain's final contribution. Rippon told the House that Britain could expect to receive payments from the Community budget so the net contribution would be around £100 million in 1973, rising to perhaps about £200 million in 1977.[23]

Reaction in the House, including from Labour's frontbench spokesman, Harold Lever, was moderate though from Peter Shore came an indication of storms ahead when Shore accused Rippon of being "outwitted, out-generalled and out-faced". The love-in had to stop some time, said Shore and agreement had been reached only by abandoning essential British and Commonwealth interests.[24]

Reaction from New Zealand was, the British High Commission reported, generally good, apart from the open hostility of the New Zealand Labour Party

– a factor which was to fuel Wilson's later attacks on the deal Rippon had accepted. Businessmen and officials in New Zealand thought that Britain had done well by New Zealand. A more circumspect reaction came from New Zealand Deputy Prime Minister, Jack Marshall, who had led the New Zealand team in Europe throughout the negotiations. His initial public response was lukewarm, more so than that of the Prime Minister, Sir Keith Holyoake, who saw immediately that, with a deal done, the New Zealand Government had little alternative but to present it as a success. Marshall was probably leant on since he quickly sent a more reflective message to Rippon acknowledging that "the overall package for New Zealand is a good one and in some respects better than we thought could be negotiated". Marshall expressed himself satisfied that the result was "the best you could, in the circumstances, get for us".[25]

The Australian Government, which had been far less proactive than the New Zealanders in lobbying for their (admittedly less critical) interests were more disgruntled. In the face of public criticism by the Australian Prime Minister, William McMahon, that "it is a matter for regret that Britain has not pressed our case with the Six to an outcome satisfactory to us"[26], Heath responded in a letter of 2 July: "We believe that we have secured protection for Australia's interests . . . Your representatives were kept fully posted throughout . . . I really must urge you that it is not to anyone's advantage to belittle what has been undertaken by the Community".[27]

The British High Commissioner in Canberra, Sir Morrice James, sought to put the reaction into perspective. MacMahon's style of Government, he told the Foreign Secretary, was one of "chasing, panting after events without ever quite catching up with them". There was, in Australia, a widespread feeling that joining the EEC was something Britain had to do but there was also a sense in the country of regret. The world seemed chillier and more lonely than it had a fortnight before. Speeches were being made and editorials written drawing the inference that, in a world where Britain sought her future as part of Europe, Australia must henceforth base her relationships on the Pacific and Asia. Trade with Japan was thriving. An offer of military training facilities had been made to Singapore. "But", James believed, "it is all done somewhat against the grain. This is not yet an Asia-oriented country, but a displaced European one, and in a deep sense British".

With characteristic Australian robustness, most Australians, according to James, had seen MacMahon's reaction as a poor display of small-town party politics. "We're whingeing, aren't we?" asked the Speaker of the New South Wales Legislature when James called on him. Sir Morrice James felt it necessary for the benefit of Douglas-Home, his addressee, to add a footnote by way of explanation: "To whinge is a pejorative Australianism meaning to complain unjustifiably, presumably derived by blending 'whine' and 'cringe' ".[28] The Foreign Secretary could probably have told James that the term had in fact arrived in Australia with immigrants from Scotland.

From Canada came a letter from Prime Minister Pierre Trudeau. He was pleased that "some success was achieved in the course of the UK accession negotiations over trade in forest products of interest to Canada and . . . to avoid disruption of trade during the transitional period, particularly in the agricultural sector". But, Trudeau went on, the terms negotiated would nonetheless mean a deterioration of the terms of access of a significant part of Canada's trade to the UK market. Trudeau welcomed therefore the intention of the Heath Government to exert a positive influence on the trade policies of the Community: "We would welcome a greater appreciation by Europeans of their worldwide responsibilities".[29]

Heath would have liked to get clear early approval for the terms Rippon had negotiated. If as large a majority could be won in July as in October, after the recess, why wait? But Heath and Rippon were more confident than Whitelaw, the Leader of the House of Commons. Rippon's own feel for the House was in any case imperfect, *The Times* describing his manner in Parliament as "brusque, bordering on the contemptuous".[30] But the principal reasons for caution were several, including the now clear hostility of the Labour Opposition, potential defections among a number of Conservative backbenchers and the continuing aversion to membership of a majority of the electorate. More time was needed to work on public opinion and, under pressure from the Opposition and from some of its own supporters, the Government decided to have a debate on the outcome before the summer recess, but on a 'take note' motion which would not require a Division. In the autumn would come a debate on the acceptability of the terms negotiated, followed by a Bill.

By now, the Labour Party had turned against membership of the EEC. One key factor was that the shock of their unexpected defeat in the General Election had made the Party, never wholeheartedly behind Wilson in his bid for membership, and veering to the left in opposition, see Europe as a ready stick with which to beat the Government. In tactical terms, this seemed to make all the more sense because of the possibility of making common cause with Conservative rebels. One of the more remarkable and incongruous features of the months of opposition to the European Communities Bill was, for example, the partnership between Enoch Powell and Michael Foot. For its duration, Foot seemed impervious to arguments that he was in bed with someone whose views on other issues he would normally deplore.

At the Labour Party's first Conference following their defeat, in Blackpool in October 1970, a resolution calling for opposition to EEC membership was only narrowly defeated.

In January 1971, John Silkin who, as Labour Chief Whip, had reduced Labour opposition to membership to only 35 votes against in a House of Commons vote on the issue in 1967, himself put down an Early Day motion opposing membership "on the terms so far envisaged". His motion attracted 108 signatures in its first 48 hours, including those of 26 new MPs – half the new Labour intake in the 1970 General Election.[31]

Early in the New Year, Wilson was still telling Roy Jenkins, the leading Labour pro-Marketeer, that he thought the Labour Party could be got to vote officially for entry and that, at the very worst, the leadership could fall back on a free vote. Wilson had earlier rejected a suggestion by Tony Benn that, whatever terms the

Conservative Government might secure, Labour should press for a national referendum on the outcome. Jim Callaghan said at the time that Benn's proposal might turn out to be "a rubber dinghy into which we may all one day have to climb".[32]

Most contemporary observers believed that Wilson's intention in Opposition was to continue to support British accession. However, in the early months of 1971, the situation deteriorated, not just in terms of growing hostility on the part of Labour rank and file, but also in terms of the stance taken by some of Wilson's senior colleagues. In the spring, both Healey and Crosland came out against membership. Healey had been against the original membership bid, though he had gone along with it. Early in 1971, he signed a pro-EEC advertisement which appeared in the *Daily Mirror*, but recanted within weeks. Crosland, who had hitherto been a constant supporter of membership, simply read the way the wind was blowing and decided to shift with it.

Much more decisive was the intervention of Jim Callaghan who, as Chancellor of the Exchequer, had been a stalwart supporter of membership in 1967. Now, on 25 May 1971, only days after the Heath-Pompidou meeting, Callaghan gave a much trailed speech on Europe in Southampton. Anthony Howard, one of the journalists who had received advance briefing on the speech, wrote in *The Observer* that Callaghan was "in a position virtually to determine what Labour's eventual attitude to any Brussels terms will be".[33]

Callaghan had urged the Press to come and listen to his speech, reportedly telling one journalist who had a prior commitment that if he wanted to hear the next leader of the Labour Party, he had better arrange to be there.[34]

The speech itself was a classic Callaghan performance: avuncular, accessible, funny – and deadly.

In an interview with the BBC's flagship news programme, *Panorama*, a few days before the summit with Heath, Pompidou had referred to French as the language of Europe. So, said Callaghan, we must now expect that the language of Chaucer, Shakespeare and Milton must in future be regarded as an import from which the British people would be obliged to protect themselves. "If we have to prove our Europeanism", Callaghan continued, "by accepting that French is the dominant language in the Community, then my answer is quite clear, and I will say it in French in order to prevent any misunderstanding: *Non, merci beaucoup*".

There was much more to Callaghan's speech than that but, as Callaghan had intended, his '*Non, merci beaucoup*' was universally interpreted as Callaghan saying 'no' to the EEC.

Wilson was in Helsinki when the speech was delivered but Callaghan's use of it as a launching pad for his own leadership ambitions was unmistakeable and Callaghan's supposedly private comment to the reluctant journalist that this would be the speech of the next leader of the Labour Party was reported back to Wilson within hours. Wilson thus had defections on Europe from three of his most senior colleagues – and rivals for his job: Callaghan, Healey and Crosland. Roy Jenkins, for his part, tried to assure Wilson that if he stayed true to his European convictions then there could be no question of the Labour Europeans siding with

Callaghan or anyone else against him.[35] But Jenkins too was a rival for Wilson's job and his assurances would have given Wilson no comfort.

Wilson was faced with a situation in which he could take a stand on Europe and, almost certainly go down to defeat, or allow himself to be carried by the tide. And defeat was a real prospect. Wilson had, after all, lost the General Election and his performance as leader since June 1970 had been lacklustre. His preoccupation with his memoirs, and the unprecedentedly large sum he had been paid for them, had made him few friends. Meanwhile, the unpopularity of the Government, as the economy turned rapidly downhill, meant that most Labour Party members wanted to seize any opportunity open to them to bring Heath down. The 'Tory terms' on Europe looked like a golden opportunity to inflict a defeat which, on such a matter of confidence, might provoke a new election. It must be doubtful if the Party as a whole would have allowed Wilson to stand in their way.

Wilson's attempt to head off pressure for a special Labour Party Conference on Europe failed in the National Executive Committee when the proposal for such a Conference was carried by one vote, that of the pro-European, Shirley Williams, who felt strongly that all views should be heard. So, at the special Labour Conference in London on 17 July, Wilson made what Jenkins described as a pedestrian speech which nonetheless "took him quietly almost out of intellectual hailing distance with us. It was like watching someone being sold down the river into slavery, drifting away, depressed but unprotesting".[36] There was no vote but the dye was cast.

On 21 July, in the take-note debate on the outcome of the negotiations, Wilson spoke at great length, seeking to contrast the approach of the Labour Government he had led, on issues such as New Zealand, the CAP, the Community budget and Commonwealth sugar, with the results which the Government had actually achieved. It was barely credible and was made less so as, one after another, the former Ministers who had been prominent in the bid and preparations for negotiation, came out in public to affirm their view that the terms negotiated by the Conservatives were ones they themselves would have accepted had they still been in Government. George Brown's views could be discounted because of his resentment. The same was not true of Michael Stewart, George Thomson and Lord Chalfont; or of their colleagues at the Treasury, Roy Jenkins, Harold Lever and Dick Taverne.

Matters were to come to a head in the Labour Party in the autumn but, from the Government's perspective, at least they now knew where they stood. That some hope had been retained that Wilson might have supported the terms is presumably the explanation for Heath's characterisation as "extraordinary" a copy of a letter from Wilson to Lord Drogheda, dated 26 July, and which Drogheda passed on to Heath. "I recognise", Wilson wrote, "that it is extremely disappointing to anyone who holds the view you have always held when the Labour Party, and I myself, find it difficult to support entry into the EEC on the terms negotiated. The important view throughout has been that what was clearly a project of great potential advantage must be on the right terms, and that Europe must be prepared to move at least as far in meeting us as we must move in their direction. I cannot feel that these terms fulfil that condition or any of the conditions that we laid down ... It is manifest that, to take New Zealand alone, these terms have not been met, and my suspicions can only be aroused by the failure of the Six to agree to them. With all we were told in Europe we had reason to believe that five of the Six would agree to what we were asking. It is clear that it is the attitude of the French that has carried the day: a veto, not on negotiations this time, but on the only terms we could have considered reasonable and fair."

Wilson's letter ended on a characteristically neat, if facile, riposte: "Incidentally, I noted that in support of the views you expressed, you referred to the Russian view, appearing to infer that if we rejected the terms we would be placing ourselves in the Russian camp. No motive could have been further from my own approach, but if this is the argument it will be fair to reply that since the Chinese have come out in favour of our joining the Market, to have followed the attitude you would have wished would have allied us with a still more populous Communist nation". "Both my boss and I", Armstrong wrote in thanking Drogheda for his letter, "thought that the enclosure [Wilson's letter] was a very remarkable communication".[37]

When Crispin Tickell accompanied Rees-Mogg, the editor of *The Times*, to call on Jean-René Bernard at the Elysée on 27 August, Bernard too bemoaned Wilson's performance. He had, he said, never doubted that Wilson would rat. Wilson seemed to have political agility, but not brains. Wilson's present actions would do him great harm in the long run.

When Bernard, making no secret of French concern that Wilson might return to power in 1974, asked whether things were as bad for the Heath Government as they looked, Rees-Mogg reassured him. He was convinced that the Conservatives would win the next election.[38]

Heath, in the meantime, had asked for an analysis to be done "of all the different postures taken up by the Opposition since the conclusion of the European negotiations ... It may never be necessary to use this but I would like to have it handy." Heath's Press Secretary, who had a proper sense of the proprieties, noted that this request had been passed to Hurd, Heath's Political Adviser, for Conservative Central Office to deal with.[39]

At the end of August, the Labour Party published its own 'White Paper' on the EEC negotiations in response to that already published by the Government, a short version of which (3.5 million copies) had been distributed to homes in Britain by the Post Office. The Labour Party document concluded, unsurprisingly, that the Conservatives had so weakened and divided the nation that no confidence could be placed in their ability to lead the country into the EEC. It deplored the fact that VAT and the CAP had been accepted without negotiation. It condemned the failure of the White Paper to project a cost of the terms to the UK's balance of payments. The paper concluded that, if the Labour Party's annual conference opposed the terms, and the two main parties were therefore divided on the issue, the matter must be subjected to the will of the electorate though an immediate General Election.[40] A referendum, as suggested by Tony Benn, had not yet become Labour Party policy.

According to an analysis of the Labour Party document, prepared by Cabinet Office officials for No. 10, the only new departure in the document was "the truly astonishing claim that a Labour Government would have insisted on a total renegotiation of the CAP. This is an attempt to rewrite history of almost Stalinist proportions . . . Never in the period 1967–70 was there the slightest suggestion that the British Government would call in question in any negotiations with the Six the whole structure of the CAP". The author of the Cabinet Office paper went on to note that the Labour Committee for Europe "are likely to be dealing fairly trenchantly with this claim in a press release later today . . . and it may well be therefore that thereafter less will be made of it by Mr Callaghan et al . . . The document . . . is by any standards a very unimpressive piece of work, though part of the explanation may well lie in the fact that authorship was apparently divided between Mr Terry Pitt (strongly anti-Europe) and Mr Gwyn Morgan (strongly pro). It is presumably to Mr Morgan's influence that we owe the occasional interruption of the generally hostile and captious tone of the document by a sentence or two pointing to the advantages of membership".[41] The partisan tone of this minute by a civil servant is a reflection of the almost religious fervour that surrounded the European issue at the time.

A few days later, *The Economist*, with all the signs of having been briefed by Wilson himself, gave a more perceptive analysis of what Wilson was about. "Mr Wilson", the paper wrote, "would now like to soft-pedal the Party's opposition to Europe so far as he can. Labour will go through the motions and denunciations to which it has committed itself. It will make the Government's Parliamentary majority in October as inconveniently small as possible. It may fight the consequential legislation which will drag through Parliament thereafter pretty hard, in the hope of defeating the Government on a detailed point . . . Having outflanked those of the Party's anti-Europeans who hoped to unseat him, Mr Wilson's concern inside his party is now not to split it . . . Europe is not Clause Four. What divides the Labour Party is not something worth jeopardising future elections for. It is, as Mr Wilson said on July 17th, 'an important policy issue, not an article of faith'. He is therefore picking a way along a path which leads neither into Europe, not out of Europe, but towards the next General Election . . . What Mr Wilson's mild and accommodating tactics inside the Party show is that, for the moment, he does not reckon he can bring the Government down on Europe; and that he would prefer to have a whole Party at the end of the day rather than part of one . . ."[42]

With the key vote on EEC membership due in late October, the issue of which Conservative supporters would vote against, and whether the Government could carry its policy with its own supporters alone, was a major preoccupation for Heath. He was against a free vote: the Government's supporters must be expected to support a key part of the Administration's policy. But his Chief Whip, Francis Pym, saw it differently. On 5 October, Pym sent Heath a minute containing his latest assessment. There were, in his estimation, 26 hard-line 'antis' on the Tory benches; 6 were borderline as between voting against and abstaining; 13 were uncertain and 281 would vote in favour. The "absolute blackest" picture was therefore that there would be 45 defectors. A more likely figure was 38, and it could conceivably be as low as 30. On that analysis, the Division could not be won without some Labour votes and or abstentions.

According to Pym, the Labour pro-Europeans, whose morale was high, claimed that between forty and sixty of them would vote with the Government. But their estimates had varied wildly. If the Labour Party imposed a three-line whip, the pressures on the pro-Europeans would be such that only around twenty of them would vote with the Government while a further twenty might abstain. The Liberals were 5:1 in favour. On this speculative basis, Pym believed that the Government might secure an overall majority of 5.

Pym went on to make a new and crucial point. Over the previous two months, with the Conservative constituencies swinging firmly and sharply behind Heath's leadership, all the pressures on Conservative MPs were now to support the Government. Such a strong and favourable reaction had not originally been expected. But it had happened. The result was that "whether you have a three-line Whip or a free vote, the result will almost certainly be exactly the same". The crucial difference was that, if the Government offered a free vote and the Labour Party followed suit, as they would be under pressure to do, then the number of Labour MPs who would vote with the Government would be between 45 and 75, tending towards the higher number. Pym went on to argue strongly in favour of the free vote: "There exists therefore the precise opportunity you need – to spring a surprise that will, in my judgement, serve your Parliamentary end, please the people and raise the whole level of the final stages of the debate to a new plain". Secrecy, Pym concluded, was of the essence. The slightest whisper in the bars at Brighton [at the Party Conference] would blow the whole story.[43]

After some hesitation, Heath accepted Pym's advice, a bold decision on his part and a mark of Pym's adroitness as Chief Whip. Wilson did not follow suit. A few months earlier he had told Roy Jenkins that a free vote would be the ultimate fall-back if the Labour Party could not be brought to continue to support EEC membership. At the Party Conference early in October Wilson had calculated that there would be a vote by 3:1 against entry and that the Parliamentary Labour Party would, narrowly, go the same way. In the event, the Conference rejected British entry by 5:1 and the PLP by nearly 2:1.[44] In this situation, Wilson and the Party managers went back on the semi-undertaking he had given to Jenkins earlier in the year, thus hardening the resolve of Jenkins himself and his allies to take a stand.

When the Division came, on 28 October 1971, the Government had a majority of 112. The Labour rebels contributed 69 positive votes and 20 abstentions (including Crosland). Had all the Labour rebels followed the Party's three-line whip, and had all the Conservative anti-Europeans all continued to rebel, a majority of 112 in favour of EEC membership would have been turned into a majority against of 46.[45]

"It was", David Owen, one of the young Labour rebels later recalled, "the best Parliamentary vote that I have ever cast and I have no regrets whatever for voting as I did. What I do regret, and bitterly, was thereafter voting against the legislation necessary to ensure that entry was enshrined in our law . . . I have no doubt that, immediately after the White Paper vote, we should have said that we would abstain on the subsequent legislation . . . As it was, we humiliated ourselves night after night voting against what we believed in".[46]

With the vote successfully behind him, Heath issued a statement (after several competing drafts had, as is the nature of such exercises, been batted around between his advisers): "Parliament has now decided that Britain should, in principle, join the EEC on the basis of the arrangements which have been negotiated. Today's decision has been reached by a clear majority of the elected representatives of the people – men and women who, irrespective of party political differences, share the conviction that this decision is right for their country. This is the outcome of years of patient negotiation by Governments of both parties. It marks the end of ten years of debate. Now we stand ready to take our first step into a new world full of opportunities. Our historic decision has been made: the British people accept the challenge. Let us show ourselves to that new world as we would wish it to see us – confident, proud and strong".[47]

Messages of congratulation to Heath poured in from across the world, including from Nixon, Brandt and Pompidou. But while Heath did, as the writer Uve Kitzinger put it, collect the glittering European prizes, prizes which, ironically, would almost certainly have been awarded to Wilson in similar circumstances had he won the 1970 election, there was little time for self-congratulation.

The British Government had a number of more pressing preoccupations: to secure an agreement with the Six on fisheries; to prepare a Bill for Parliament on EEC accession; to manage Parliamentary and public opinion and to handle deteriorating relations with the United States.

In August 1971, President Nixon had surprised his allies by announcing, without prior warning, an economic package which included a surcharge on all dutiable imports and suspending the convertibility of the dollar into gold and other reserve assets. Nixon also announced, again without prior warning, that he had accepted an invitation from the Chinese Government to visit Peking.

Heath's strong views formed the basis of instructions to Lord Cromer, Britain's Ambassador in Washington, for a brisk conversation with Henry Kissinger. Heath also gave public vent to his feelings, leading the *New York Times*, under the heading 'Transatlantic Gaullism', to comment that "Now, instead of joint action by the Atlantic nations in the common interest, Britain's Prime Minister sees the United States 'acting drastically' to protect its own balance of payments and trading position. And he calls on the countries of Western Europe to secure their own prosperity and even their own defence".[48]

Nixon's economic measures had a dramatic effect, leading to the collapse of the Bretton Woods post-war monetary system. Small wonder that the minds of European leaders were turning to the idea of a Summit of the Ten, which Heath was actively espousing. He had written to Brandt early in October suggesting that "it would be especially valuable to establish as clearly as possible, at the highest level, the broad lines along which we propose to tackle the problems which face us all; we should be able to outline the future role of Western Europe as we see it in the light of the growing unity of our countries. Such a meeting of the leaders of the Ten . . . could well mark the beginning of a new chapter in the history of Europe". Heath envisaged a meeting towards the end of 1971.[49]

President Pompidou had other ideas. On 22 October, he told Soames that it was the monetary question which should settle the timing of the conference. The German currency, the DM, should, in his view, be revalued by about 5% in respect of other European currencies; but in relation to the dollar it should be revalued by about 10%. The right way to do this would be for the DM to be revalued by 5% and the dollar devalued by 5%. Otherwise, two Marks would be needed, one for internal European trade and one for external trade. This would be an impossible situation. So, there should not be a summit until everyone knew the views of others and it could be certain of success. His present thinking was that the situation would probably not be ripe for a summit before the latter part of 1972 and that it would be necessary to have bilateral discussions first. He envisaged that the new parities would be fixed at the summit itself.[50]

Pompidou's concept of a summit with very concrete economic and monetary outcomes was thus very far from Heath's idea of a more general 'onwards and upwards' conversation.

Another potential source of European friction was also becoming evident to Heath. "I have often expatiated", he wrote in a note to Armstrong and Moon, "on the difficulties which arise in European Community affairs from the 'we' and 'they' attitude. We certainly still have a long way to go to get over this in Britain. Moreover, on reading the telegrams, I realise that the Community, and in particular the Commission, suffer from exactly the same problem; and in some ways seem to realise even less than we do that it exists. They are constantly barging ahead with regulations drawn up to suit themselves and then coming along, more or less with a take-it-or-leave-it attitude, to present them to us. I really think we must muscle in on this machine now in a big way without wasting any more time. Presumably this is best done through Michael Palliser in Brussels . . . There is certainly no time to be lost".[51]

The Prime Minister's views were passed to Rippon who, unlike Heath, had correctly spotted that the problem was endemic. He responded emolliently that it was inevitable that a 'we' and 'they' relationship should have grown up over the past ten years, and that the answer lay in far more continuous and frequent contacts with the Community at all levels; and that such contacts would "give a rapidly increasing number of officials from home departments first-hand experience of dealing with the Community and so make a very effective contribution to the spread of European-mindedness throughout Whitehall".[52]

By late November, the Government had settled the form of its draft legislation to enact the provisions of the EEC Treaties. There were a number of issues at stake. Geoffrey Howe, the Solicitor General, had explained them at a Ministerial meeting on 17 November. The Government's legislation had to include a hard core of certain basic and constitutional provisions: provisions giving effect to Community law in the United Kingdom; financial provisions about expenditure incurred in complying with Community obligations and the arrangements for payments to, and receipts from, the Community; provisions about Northern Ireland, the Channel Islands and the Isle of Man; and a general power to give effect by subordinate legislation to the obligations of Community membership.[53]

At one extreme, the Lord President, Willie Whitelaw, told Cabinet a few days later, it would theoretically be possible to make the necessary legislative changes by a very short substantive Bill, leaving all the detailed modifications to be implemented thereafter by subordinate legislation. That course would be open to criticism on the ground that it would be constitutionally improper to curtail Parliamentary debate on matters of such fundamental importance to the life of the nation. At the other extreme, nearly all the changes immediately required in British law could be made in the substantive Bill, leaving relatively little to be accomplished subsequently by subordinate legislation. But that would result in a Bill of undesirable length and complexity. Whitelaw, acting on the advice of the Solicitor General, Geoffrey Howe, who was the mastermind of the operation, recommended a middle course, whereby the substantive legislation would contain express provisions on the main matters of controversy, with less significant issues to be dealt with in subordinate legislation under general powers in the main Bill. This was what Cabinet agreed.[54]

The provisions, as they would apply to Britain, of the Common Fisheries Policy, remained unsettled. The British Government had some cause for grievance, as Tickell (Rippon's Private Secretary) explained to his opposite number in the cabinet of French EEC Commissioner Jean-Francois Deniau. British Ministers were, Tickell said, quite prepared publicly to say that the agreement by the Six on the new fisheries policy, on the eve of the opening of negotiations with Britain and the other applicants, was no more than a coincidence. In reality, British Ministers felt otherwise and resented the fact that a major obstacle to agreement had been created in that way and on that day.

Monsieur Leng acknowledged that there might have been some, in particular the French, who were not averse to agreeing on something which could always be used as an excuse for obstruction and for whose removal the British might well have to pay.

Tickell, warming to his theme, said that another source of ill feeling arose from the fact that the fishing interests of the candidate countries cumulatively exceeded those of the existing Member States. The candidate countries felt therefore that they had every right to ask for changes in a policy which had obviously been designed for the Six rather than the Ten. The most serious aspect of the problem was the fact that the Community had accepted as a dogma the principle of no limitation of access. Britain, on the contrary, saw no reason to accept that, even as an objective. The fishermen of the candidate countries thought it right to have permanent arrangements which protected their coastlines from competition from any other sources, including those within the Community. They also attached particular importance to conservation. Any deal with the existing Member States by which Community vessels could fish the waters of the candidate countries in exchange for the candidate countries fishing the waters of the existing Community would be totally unfair. There were fish in our waters because they had been protected, and very few in Community waters because they had been overfished.[55]

Heath himself was anxious about the subject. In late November he wrote to Pompidou seeking his agreement that, in the light of the US economic measures, the Six and Britain should aim to harmonise their objectives and positions to the greatest extent possible, even in advance of membership. Separately, Armstrong, on the Prime Minister's behalf, instructed Soames to speak to Jobert about the risk of delay or setback in concluding the negotiations. If the negotiations with Norway broke down over fisheries there would be serious consequences for "Scandinavian relations and links with the West". This was an important matter for Britain too. Fisheries policy was a sensitive issue in a large number of constituencies, and the continuing support of some MPs depended upon the Government being able to present the settlement of the fisheries issue as satisfactory. So a deal with Norway was necessary to keep them in negotiations, but the deal could not be more favourable for them than for Britain.[56]

At the same time, Heath was anxious to sign the EEC Accession Treaty before Christmas and, on 25 November, he wrote to Jim Prior, the Agriculture Minister, warning him against spending "a lot of time on an elaborate process of bids and counter bids over fisheries. We must be prepared to get down quickly to reasonable bids, and we must aim to settle fisheries on 29 November. Attempts to sustain manifestly unreasonable bids are not going to impress the members of the Community." Heath wanted Rippon to be given the authority to settle on 29 November for something "more limited" than the opening bid which he had so far been authorised to make. Prior should consider what such a position might be: possibly twelve mile belts for most of Scotland (the north and east coasts and as much of the waters of the Outer Hebrides as could be secured); part of the coast of Northern Ireland; and the crustacean areas of Devon and Cornwall. Heath proposed that a firm message be sent to the Norwegian Government with a view to settlement on 29 November.[57]

In the event, the meeting on 29 November, under French chairmanship, got nowhere. The French Foreign Minister left early, to keep a date with President Bongo of Gabon. In his absence, the Community, according to a subsequent German account, "had behaved at its worst: with the French deploying legalistic blocking tactics" which, according to the Germans, "helped no-one" but were thought by the French to be "the best way of obstructing progress".[58]

On the same day, Armstrong discussed fisheries with the French Ambassador over lunch. Courcel, whose knowledge of fish was almost certainly confined to what species to put on a diplomatic menu, observed that "he knew that a certain amount had been made of the fact that the CFP had been agreed by the Six after the start of the negotiations. His answer to that was that it would have been open to the Community to delay the start of the negotiations until after the fisheries regulation had been agreed". In any case, the French Government had gone a very long way to meet British desires.[59]

The issue was now serious enough for Heath to chair a meeting of interested Ministers, and for Rippon to address a special meeting of the Conservative Party

Fisheries Committee, where his performance, according to the note of the meeting prepared by an unnamed Government Whip "was the worst I have seen him give, and all the ditherers [i.e. those contemplating voting against their Government] believe he is going to sell out". When one of the Members produced a cutting from a Scarborough newspaper, reporting the Prime Minister as saying, in Scarborough, that he would defend the 12 mile limit, Rippon had responded that Heath had only said this to help him in his negotiations. This was, according to the Whip, "very ill-received".[60]

On 9 December, Rippon told Cabinet that the right to exclusive fishing rights within the six mile limit for ten years from accession had already been secured. After ten years, there would be a review. Provided the review was a genuine one "we should be able, by one means or another, to preserve our vital national interests in the subsequent period". Much more difficult would be safeguarding the present position in the 6 to 12 mile belt in certain areas of the British coastline. The Community had so far proposed that, for the first ten years, and subject to review thereafter, Britain should continue to maintain the present regime around the Orkneys, the Shetlands and an unspecified part of north-east Scotland. Britain would be expected, in those areas, to maintain the existing fishing rights of other Member States. Britain had requested the extension of this special treatment to the Scottish coast from Cape Wrath to Berwick; the north east coast of England to Spurnhead, the south west coast from Sidmouth to Aberdovey; and County Down. Provided part of these demands was secured "we should have done reasonably well in practical terms, having regard to the existing fishing rights of Member States within the existing 6 to 12-mile belt". An additional problem, Rippon reported, was that Norway was now unlikely to settle before the spring so Britain would have to settle before she knew what terms Norway had secured. At the same time, as some of Rippon's Cabinet colleagues noted, British deep-sea fishermen were in favour of Norwegian accession in order to preclude the Norwegian Government from extending their own maritime jurisdiction against other Member States beyond 12 miles. On this unsatisfactory basis, Cabinet "took note" of what Rippon had had to say.[61]

The deal was in the end done in Brussels in the early hours of 12 December. Britain, as Rippon reported to the House of Commons the next day, had retained full jurisdiction over the whole of her coastal waters up to twelve miles. Access to British coastal waters within six miles of the baselines would be limited to British vessels. In areas between 6–12 miles, where the baselines were not in themselves a sufficient safeguard, or where stocks were already fully exploited, the fishing would be limited to British vessels and to those Community members with existing rights to fish. The areas covered in this way out to twelve miles were the Orkneys and Shetland, the North and North-East coasts of Scotland, North-East England from the river Coquet to Flamborough Head, Devon and Cornwall including the Scilly Isles and Lundy Island; and County Down. The effect of all this, Rippon told the House, was that "there is no change at all in the protection now afforded in areas from which 95% by value of the total inshore catch is taken". There was to be a review starting in 1982 of the arrangements which would follow the initial ten-year period.[62] When the Opposition asked for a Parliamentary debate on the outcome, Cabinet agreed that the Government "should not on this account defer our signature of the Treaty of Accession to the Communities, which should be practicable by mid-January".[63]

Had the Heath Government secured a good accession deal overall for Britain? At the heart of the answer lies a judgement as to whether, as all three main Party leaders had concluded, and as the Labour and Conservative Cabinets had agreed, it was essential for the British national interest to get into the European Community. As Lord Crowther put it in the House of Lords on 27 July 1971, "You do not haggle over the subscription when you are invited to climb into a lifeboat. You scramble aboard while there is still a seat for you".

While that was certainly an important factor, neither a Conservative nor a Labour Government would have joined at any price. Even if they had had a mind to, they would have had to contend with a very sceptical public and considerable opposition within their own ranks. A fair deal for New Zealand and an affordable budget settlement for Britain were essential. Equally, neither Heath nor Wilson ever saw Community membership as a palliative. Britain's economic success could be enhanced by membership but would only be achieved by Britain seizing the opportunities which membership offered. They were much more certain of the inability of Britain to play a significant role in the world save as part of a larger organisation.

Both political parties, when in Government, had to start from a harsh reality: the terms of the Common Agricultural Policy had been set to suit France and the whole of the budget was geared to the 90% of it which was devoted to agriculture. Pompidou had insisted on the financing of the budget being settled, on terms hugely favourable to France, before he would allow negotiations with Britain to be opened. The Six as a whole deliberately set the terms of the Common Fisheries Policy before the start of the negotiations with the candidates. At no point between 1963 and 1971 did anyone in Whitehall identify a viable alternative grouping for Britain to join. And the analysis available to both Labour and Conservative Governments suggested that the harsh realities of life outside the EEC would compel Britain to seek entry sooner or later, with every prospect that the terms of membership set by the Six, and especially France, would get harder with the passage of time.

Con O'Neill, who was the senior official member of the British delegation in the negotiations, pinpointed in his Report on the Negotiations the essence of the dilemma that had faced Britain. "There is no doubt", he wrote, "that we bought a satisfactory arrangement for New Zealand dairy products by agreeing to a less than satisfactory one on Community finance". O'Neill also believed that a mistake had been made in not trying harder to stop the adoption of a Common Fisheries Policy.[64]

David Hannay, who participated in the negotiations as a young member of the UK delegation in Brussels, edited O'Neill's Report for publication in 2000. His conclusions were similar. O'Neill had argued that it was not that New Zealand deserved less than Britain had secured for her but that Britain herself had had to pay more in terms of her budget contribution than she would otherwise have done. "This judgement is difficult to contest", Hannay concluded, "given the very clear linkage established in the final stage of the negotiations by the French". But Hannay was equally clear, and all the official papers bear him out, that "the British negotiators cannot be accused of having failed to identify the scale of the problem that would arise once all transitional constraints on the British contribution were removed. The calculations put forward from the British side, although not borne out in every respect by subsequent developments, were a great deal closer to the truth than the less closely reasoned figures put forward from the Community side". But Hannay also believed that the toughness of the five year negotiation from 1979 to 1984 which eventually secured a lasting settlement to the British budget issue "does not encourage confidence that a fundamental change could have been negotiated in 1970–1971".[65]

What the British negotiators did secure was endorsement by the Six of an important statement by the European Commission. The burden of the Commission's response to the British calculations of their likely net budget contribution was that the British had under-estimated the dynamic effects of membership as well as the evolution of non-agricultural policies from which the United Kingdom would benefit. The Commission's statement, in a paper of November 1970, nonetheless acknowledged that: "Should unacceptable situations arise within the present Community, or an enlarged Community, the very survival of the Community would demand that the institutions find equitable solutions". That statement was reproduced in the Government's White paper of July 1971. John Robinson, one of the Foreign Office's senior (and toughest) negotiators referred to the statement at the time as a weapon which, if the button was ever pressed, would cause a nuclear explosion.[66]

As the debates and votes in Parliament in the first half of 1972 were to show, the actual terms of the Treaty, though they were the focus of the Opposition's assault, were less germane to the overall judgement than the gut instincts of supporters and opponents of membership. On one side, supporters of membership judged that it was essential for Britain's place in the world and, on the other, opponents feared that too great a sacrifice of sovereign independence was being required either in absolute terms or in exchange for an uncertain gain.

Just after New Year 1972, Heath invited to Chequers the High Commissioners in London of Australia, Canada and New Zealand. Other guests were Carrington, (the Defence Secretary), Burke Trend, Sir Denis Greenhill and Armstrong.

After all had dined Heath spoke of the profound change in world power relationships which, in his view, would come about as a result of the enlargement of the European Community. The enlarged Europe would be the largest trading bloc ever known, with a share of world trade considerably greater than, and an economic potential as great as, the United States. Heath did not believe that the implications of this change had been fully absorbed either in Europe or in the United States. It implied a profound change in the partnership between the US and Europe within the Western world. The previous August's monetary crisis had forced the United States to an awareness that they could no longer take decisions on their own and expect others to accept the consequences without question. The United States now had to share with others the responsibility for the decisions that would determine the future. A new round of trade negotiations would demonstrate the same point. So, Heath continued, there needed to be a better balance between the US and Europe in a partnership in which Japan must also have a place. The importance of such a partnership was underlined by the developments of the past decade (which Heath viewed with concern) as a result of which the Russians had been able to approach nuclear parity with the United States. Thus, it was no less necessary in the defence field than in the economic field to establish a degree of balance between Europe and America. This would entail a greater European nuclear capacity and better arrangements for cooperation between the United States on the one hand and Britain and France on the other. All this was very much for the future, since the sort of cooperation that might be envisaged could only apply to a new generation of nuclear weapons. But, although this would not become effective for up to twenty years, some of the basic decisions would need to be taken before very long.

Enlargement of the European Community, Heath continued, would also change the relationship between Britain and the rest of the Commonwealth. The new Commonwealth would continue to "make their own decisions and their own mistakes". The old Commonwealth would need some counterpoise for relationships which would otherwise become over-dominant: in the case of Australia, the relationship with Japan and, in the case of Canada, the relationship with the United States. They were most likely to find this counterpoise in Europe and Heath looked forward to ties between Britain and the old Commonwealth becoming stronger as a result.

Heath was listened to largely in silence. But the Canadian High Commissioner, Mr Warren, took issue with the Prime Minister. The economic and military power of the United States, he argued, remained very great and the United States was therefore likely to continue to predominate. He doubted whether Europe could find the resources to match the US in nuclear capacity. He did not therefore see much future in a policy of trying to attain a position where Europe could in some sense match the strength of the US in each field, and thus alter the fundamental basis of the Euro-American relationship. As he saw it, the United States faced great problems, both domestically and internationally, and had suffered some considerable setbacks. This had tended to make them sensitive and difficult. The responsibility was on their partners to help them back into an easier and more constructive relationship; but Warren did not see the fundamental basis of the relationship as liable to change or indeed as being capable of being altered.

When the guests had departed, Heath commented that Warren was not in tune with the thinking of his own Prime Minister.[67] Nearly forty years later, it has to be said that Warren looks closer to the mark in his judgement than was Heath.

The Treaty of Accession of Britain to the European Communities was signed by Heath in Brussels on 22 January 1972. Harold Wilson had declined Heath's invitation to accompany him, arguing that Labour policy made it inappropriate for him to accept Heath's "kind and considerate invitation".[68] The third Prime

Ministerial architect of Britain's membership, Harold Macmillan, accepted the invitation with alacrity, writing to Heath that "it is not common for old men to live to see their hopes finally realised. This is due to your patient and persistent pursuit of the great ideals of European unity, on which you and I worked together almost from the beginning".[69]

If Heath and his predecessors chose this moment to reflect on the course of recent history so did President Pompidou. In early January, Pompidou held an off-the-record fireside chat with a journalist from *Paris Match*. "As the years go by", the journalist wrote, "M Pompidou's taste for silence has grown more pronounced. During a week at Carjac [his holiday home], he has found the sort of quiet that he likes: winter outside the window, a fire in the hearth . . . and above all memories. Memories have danced in his head during this week of rest. Not through a liking for the past, but because of a passion for the future". At the Hague conference, the piece continued, clearly reflecting closely what Pompidou had said in the fireside chat, the President had "decided on his aim – to drag Europe from its former torpor . . . This is an old dream and the opportunity to realise it only comes once . . . This is an exceptional historical situation. The President of the Republic has fixed the means and the time. Firstly, the means: that will be the summit confer- ence of the ten countries of Europe; the time: before the Summer . . . If, between now and then, he has succeeded in convincing his partners one by one, the old continent will no longer be the same at the end of the year . . . Sometimes, he turns over in his mind fragments of conversations which he has had with Edward Heath and Willy Brandt. With the first (Mr Heath) relations are cordial . . . The President knows he can count on the British Prime Minister. Mr Heath has won his battle of Europe. The Labour Party and the opposition newspapers had stopped grumbling by the end of the year . . . Mr Heath in Bermuda discovered that there was a sort of pleasure in talking to the President of the United States no longer as a spokesman of an old nation, but as a possible leader of a new continent. A note in M Pompidou's file sums it up. Britain will be a vital support. She will perhaps be more European than Germany or Italy. Her Prime Minister has the enthusiasm of a neophyte and he feels that he is pulling his country back from decadence.

"With the second, Chancellor Brandt, relations are more difficult. M Pompidou has respect for the leader of the new Germany, but he does not understand him well. One day, on a steamer on the Rhine, Willy Brandt pressed the President of the French Republic once more to support the efforts of the Commission in Brussels. M Pompidou exploded . . . 'Let us not lie to each other. The Brussels Commission can put forward interesting proposals, for example about transport or education. But you know perfectly well that it can do nothing in basic political questions. All that depends on you and me'. The German Chancellor had nothing to say in reply. In fact, the Europe he wants is more free trading, more open to the Atlantic world than M Pompidou's. That is to be expected: Germany exports; France exports little; Germany always feels that the United States is a privileged friend, whereas France thinks that for the US to be the ally of Europe, Europe must be really independent of the US. So there is a tension. But no more than that. The Bavarian farmers keep an eye on him [Brandt]; and behind them, Herr Strauss. A tough opponent. So, if he can be clever and patient enough, M Pompidou is convinced that Herr Brandt will follow him. It comes down to one question. What should be proposed to the nine Heads of State or Government who will meet in the name of Europe in a few months from now . . . Starting from some of the ideas which make him tick, one can draw up a list of the problems which seem to him to be ripe. The Common Agricultural Policy, the only Common Market which really exists. M Pompidou does not want anyone to touch it . . . Then foreign policy. M Pompidou is aware that he cannot go very far in this field . . . In the Middle East, for example, Germany, Britain and France would react differently. So nothing is ripe. On the other hand, vis-à-vis the Soviet Union and the United States, Pompidou thinks that common attitudes are henceforward possible . . . No question of taking up the problems of defence. 'What could I say to Mr Heath on this subject' sighed the President a few weeks ago? 'I would say to him: Leave NATO like us' and he would reply 'You come back into it first'. There is no sense in that. Contrary to what has been written in a lot of newspapers, no talks have been begun about atomic matters between Great Britain and France.

"Finally, there exist the possibilities of agreements in the monetary field. He would like every country in Europe to have suitable reserves of other European currencies. That is not sufficient. Pompidou knows it. He must imagine a minimum of institutional procedure among the Ten. By temperament he does not like that. If he followed his own inclination, everything would be settled by meetings between man and man . . . So it remains to find the machinery which will respect the old national realities and the new European reality. On this point, M Pompidou has not yet found anything. He is looking. For once, he is in a hurry".[70]

Pompidou had let down his guard in the warmth of his Carjac fireside. The *Paris Match* article would have made more comfortable reading for Heath than for Brandt, though Pompidou's somewhat patronising appraisal of both of his fellow leaders was noteworthy. It sparked a reflection from Michael Palliser, who had moved from Paris to head the UK delegation to the EEC. In describing the CAP as the only common policy so far achieved by the European Community, Pompidou had, Palliser pointed out, discounted the Common External Tariff and the Common Commercial Policy. But his remark exemplified both French satisfaction with the CAP and her determination to keep it in being. But of course, Palliser continued, the CAP was certainly not the most advantageous common policy from the British perspective. Britain had to accept it, and her agricultural community should derive some benefit from it, but it should be the aim of British policy to balance the CAP by progress toward common policies necessary for British interests. Britain accepted that the long-term effectiveness of the Community required the achievement of economic and monetary union. But that union would itself have to represent the fulfilment of a number of other common policies. Indeed, there could be some risk to the British economy and to Britain's financial stability if progress in the monetary field was not accompanied by progress towards common policies in such vital (to Britain) fields as those of industry, regional policy and transport. But to state the aim was not the same as achieving it. And there lay the rub. For the achievement of those aims must imply a readiness by all concerned to contemplate some fusion of national responsibility for such policies within a wider form of Community responsibility.[71]

Of more immediate concern for Heath and his colleagues was the issue of whether they could secure a majority on Second Reading for the European Communities Bill, a vote which would be a vote of Confidence as far as the Government was concerned. That the vote on second reading would be a close run thing was clear, not least because the pro-Europe Labour rebels would respect their Party's three-line whip and vote against the Government. Robert Armstrong went so far as to draft a 'Just in Case' statement for the Prime Minister to make if the vote went against him:

". . . I do not believe that this Parliament can sensibly continue, having refused a Second Reading to a measure to put into effect a decision which it took, by so substantial a majority, less than four months ago. I shall need to consider timing, in relation to the completion of essential financial business and so on; but, subject to that, my intention is to ask The Queen for dissolution so that we can proceed to the election of a new Parliament".[72]

As often happens when critical moments approach, housekeeping can provide both a useful distraction and a consoling sense of permanence and stability. Heath and Douglas-Home discussed in January a number of key appointments, notably those of Britain's first European Commissioners, of which there would be two, reflecting the allocation afforded to the larger Member States. The Foreign Secretary minuted Heath on 19 January to propose, as the two men had discussed, that Christopher Soames should be the first of Britain's two Commissioners and that either George Thomson or Dick Taverne (both Labour MPs) should be the second. There was no absolute requirement for a bipartisan requirement of this kind but Heath "was particularly determined that Britain should have two top-rate members of the Commission, and that one should come from each side of the House, to demonstrate the depth of cross-party support".[73] Heath favoured Thomson, who had Ministerial experience and would have led the EEC negotiations had Labour remained in office after 1970.[74]

Heath's attention had also turned to the need for first class civil servants to staff the British Permanent Delegation, and to fill posts in the Commission, in Brussels. On 31 January, Heath sent to Sir William Armstrong, the Head of the Home Civil Service, a minute drafted for him by Robert Armstrong. "I hope", Heath wrote, "that we shall be concentrating a lot of attention on the choice of people to serve in our Permanent Delegation and in the Commission . . . We are both aware of the risks that we have to guard against: the danger that some Permanent Secretaries and Establishment Officers may find postings to Brussels a convenient way of disposing of people whom they find it difficult for one reason or another to place at home; and the fear among some of the liveliest and most desirable candidates that a posting to Brussels may put them out of sight, out of mind, and therefore out of the main stream for promotion. These risks must be avoided . . . I should not in the least mind your letting it be known within the Civil Service that, when my approval is being sought for senior appointments, those whose *curriculum vitae* includes a successful tour in Brussels, whether in our Permanent Delegation or in the Commission, will start with a distinct advantage".

In a separate note to Robert Armstrong, Heath wrote: "I signed your minute to William Armstrong about Brussels staff but I doubt whether what you proposed is enough – yet. When under way it may be all right. I expect I shall have to discuss with him and the sooner the better i.e. when he's ready to stand the shocks".

When Sir William Armstrong replied, Heath was more satisfied than he had anticipated, but he wrote in the margin: "Have to be the best men: any Permanent Under-Secretary who puts forward a dud will be demoted".[75]

New arrangements were also set in place for managing EEC business within the Government and Whitehall, following a lengthy tussle in which the Foreign Office, and indeed the Foreign Secretary, sought to keep control in their hands.

In the autumn of 1971 the Foreign Office, ultimately supported by the Foreign Secretary, had resisted the Prime Minister's proposal to move Geoffrey Rippon from the Foreign Office to the Cabinet Office. A characteristic Whitehall compromise had been reached whereby, as from mid-September, Rippon ceased to be a Minister in the FCO but continued, for the time being, to have the responsibilities in the FCO that he had previously exercised in relation to the negotiations for British accession. Now, in February 1972, Robert Armstrong confirmed to the Cabinet Secretary "the new definitive arrangements" under which the Foreign Secretary would be the Government's representative in the Council of Ministers of the Communities and would chair the Ministerial Committee on Europe which would take Ministerial decisions on EEC policies and, as necessary "on instructions to our Representatives in discussions with the Communities (including all Ministerial meetings with the Communities), except insofar as these decisions have to be referred to the Cabinet".

The task of coordinating the preparation of these policy discussions and instructions would be the responsibility of the inter-departmental European Unit which had already been set up under Cabinet Office chairmanship. The Unit would have direct access to the Prime Minister (and he to it) but would report in principle to the Foreign Secretary as Chairman of the Ministerial Committee.

Rippon's position, as a Minister of Cabinet rank in the Cabinet Office, would be preserved in that he would handle the European Communities Bill in the House; he would take the chair at meetings of the Ministerial Committee on Europe except when major policy issues were being discussed; he would attend the meetings of Ministers in Brussels, except when it was agreed that specialist Ministers should represent their Governments – as, for example, when Agriculture Ministers met. He would supervise the work of the Cabinet Office European Unit.

As a consequence of these new arrangements, officials in the FCO and in the UK Delegation to the EEC would report direct to the Foreign Secretary and not, as hitherto, to the Chancellor of the Duchy of Lancaster (Rippon). Parliamentary questions addressed to the Foreign Secretary on matters connected with the European Communities would, until the end of the interim period, continue to be answered by Rippon.[76]

These Byzantine arrangements have survived more or less intact to this day with two major exceptions. The role of Europe Minister within the Cabinet Office lapsed after the unhappy tenure of the post by John Davies, Rippon's successor, and has not been revived although, under the 1997 Government of Tony Blair, Peter Mandelson, as Minister of State without portfolio in the Cabinet Office, took a close interest in European matters. In principle, the Council of Ministers remains a single entity. In practice, that has become a fiction as specialist Councils have multiplied and the central control over policy exercised by the General Affairs Council (Foreign Ministers) has largely been eroded out of existence.

As the vote on second Reading of the European Communities Bill approached, "spirits in the Whips' Offices rose and fell as voting intentions became known".[77] And not just in the Whips' Office. At Cabinet, on the day of the vote, Heath told his colleagues that "he had advised Government supporters in the House of Commons who might be disposed to vote against the Second Reading of the Bill that evening that the policy exemplified by the Bill had the support of the whole Cabinet and that the Government would therefore regard the issue as one of confidence on which they could not sustain a defeat. The Government must stand or fall together". Maudling then intervened to say that "the entire Cabinet would endorse this view".[78]

In the event, with the Labour pro-Europeans shamefacedly observing their Party's three-line whip, and with fifteen Tories voting with the Opposition, the Government secured the Second Reading by just eight votes.

The Government could breathe more easily, though months of difficult debate, with the Committee Stage conducted on the floor of the House, were to follow. Heath's attention turned to preparing for Pompidou's first official visit to Britain as President. The start was inauspicious. "I have just had a call from the British Ambassador in Paris, who in turn had just had a call from M Jobert at the Elysée", Armstrong wrote in a letter to the Foreign Office on 9 February. "The President of the Republic has spent part of his afternoon completing immigration documents for his forthcoming visit to this country".

It appeared that British officials had sent these documents to the French Embassy in London with firm instructions that they must be filled in by the President and all who were to accompany him to Chequers. Pompidou, ever law-abiding, had filled in his form. Jobert had no intention of doing so. "I prefer to leave to your imagination what the Prime Minister said when this was reported to him", Armstrong concluded. It was evidently not the first time for this kind of "stupid and bureaucratic unimaginativeness". After what Armstrong called "a rather unedifying" spat of blame-passing between the Foreign Office and the Home Office, the matter was resolved.[79]

More significant was the issue of potentially divergent British and French views on European priorities. For the British, as Rippon told Cabinet on 10 February, "it would be of critical importance . . . to seek to influence the future development of Community policies – regional and industrial policies, agriculture, economic and monetary union, and external commercial policies". It was also essential that, in order to keep to a minimum the burden of Britain's budget contributions, the

Government must obtain the maximum return from existing Community expenditure programmes. Rippon also referred to the importance of having top-quality staff to fill senior posts in Brussels and it was this, rather than the other issues he had mentioned, which Heath highlighted in his summing up.[80]

Soames spent some time with Heath on Sunday, a few days later (even though Heath was in the midst of a major dispute with the National Union of Mineworkers). On his return to Paris, Soames wrote to tell Heath that Pompidou's recent meeting with Brandt had confirmed that Pompidou wanted to see Europe set firmly along the road of monetary union. It was easy to see two motives for this: "one is that experience has persuaded him that the CAP could not survive for long without progress on monetary union. Secondly, he sees it as an essential weapon for the economic defence of Europe against the ravages of the dollar. Of all the impressions you will be able to get of Pompidou's thinking during the course of the weekend, I believe that by far the most important and fundamental will be whether his desire for monetary union is essentially the child of the factors I have just mentioned (which have a high content of French national interest); or whether he is coming round to envisaging the sort of Europe you and I would like to see and is pushing monetary union as the realistic approach to it".[81]

In the event, Pompidou's visit, scheduled for the end of February, was deferred at Heath's request because of his preoccupation with the miners' strike. Before the visit eventually took place three weeks late, Pompidou had launched something of a *coup de théâtre*. Towards the end of a press conference on 16 March, the President announced that he proposed to obtain French ratification of the Treaty of Accession by means of a referendum.

Internally, the Paris Embassy reported, Pompidou had chosen his ground well since the referendum would cut across party lines and oblige "even his opponents, if they are pro-European, to vote for the issue, and thus support the man. At the same time, it will neatly separate the Socialist party, traditionally pro-European, from the Communists".[82] The result of all this, the Foreign Office advised Downing Street the next day, "is likely to be that the President will obtain for himself a demonstration of massive popular support which will divide the opposition and thus give a boost to the Government parties with next year's Parliamentary elections in view".[83]

Pompidou's visit to Chequers over the weekend of 18 March was marked by an attempt by Heath to interest Pompidou in nuclear collaboration, a subject that had long been of interest to him and about which he had spoken publicly while in Opposition. Macmillan had tried, in vain, with de Gaulle after Nassau. Wilson had hoped, in vain, to interest de Gaulle in the same direction. Heath had prepared himself for a discussion of nuclear collaboration at his meeting in Paris in 1971 but the French had made it clear that the subject was not up for discussion.

Now, Heath told Pompidou that he had always believed that when the Community was enlarged, and France and Britain once again came closer together, they should seek closer collaboration in nuclear matters. The British Government had been studying the longer term position. They had to think of the next generation of nuclear weapons systems, as far ahead as 1995. If French and British time phasing could be slotted together, there could be useful opportunities for them both. The real key lay in the opportunity that might present itself to France and Britain for phasing together the next round of nuclear weapon development.

Pompidou agreed that he and Heath could discuss the issue. So could their respective Defence Ministers, Debré and Carrington. But that was as far as it could go. Of course, in time, it would become evident that a single economic or political policy required a single defence policy. But some cardinal difficulties arose: the apprehension that would be felt by the Soviet Union at the prospect of any kind of German cooperation in a nuclear force, an apprehension that would be shared by others in Europe; and the attitude of the United States. What Heath did not know, and Pompidou did not reveal, was that the French had embarked on their own private dialogue with the Americans on nuclear matters.

Pompidou said that the five French nuclear submarines that were set to enter into service over the coming five or six years, and the first generation of thermo-nuclear weapons, were now under construction. In such a difficult and expensive area it would obviously be more economic and efficient for there to be a general exchange of information. But a nuclear force could only be independent if it did not depend on sources of supply from outside which could be stopped by someone else. It had to be independent of any external logistics system. The owner of the force had to be completely free to use it. France had paid a great price to satisfy these three conditions and he readily admitted that the result was modest. But they had been forced by circumstances to do things that way and now intended to derive the maximum benefit from having done so. In other words, the French were independent and now that they had paid the bill it was unthinkable that they should sacrifice the result.

Heath, realising that he would get nowhere, concluded that, if asked in Parliament, he would say that these were not matters for discussion at present.

The conversation turned to EEC institutional matters and Pompidou set out what was then the classic French view. At the time of the signature of the Treaty of Rome it had been thought that it might form the embryo of a future European Government. Since 1958 (the year of de Gaulle's return to power) France had been unwilling to accept that view and Pompidou thought that no one in Europe now supported it. Even Dr Luns ("a most authentic type of European") had told Pompidou that no-one now regarded the President of the Commission as the potential President of a United States of Europe. The French thought it illusory to seek to build Europe on the basis of international officials. Europe was an association of states. If, in due course, this association moved towards some kind of European Government, then it should have its roots in the Council of Ministers. Pompidou believed Brandt to be of the same view, even if he preferred to express it less plainly. Other Member States were quite happy to hide behind France but it would be easier if France did not have to be the only plain speaker.

In the French view, Pompidou continued, the decision centre of the Community was the Council of Ministers. The French, of course, had laid down the principle of the rule of unanimity. All this really meant was that on any important matter there must be agreement between the Member States and not an attempt to impose something unacceptable on any of them.

As regards the Commission, Pompidou thought it too inclined to play a political role to which it was not entitled and to behave as if it was a seventh state in a Community of six. It had an important enough role as it was. Its first function was to make proposals and it thus had the dual role of preparation and of encouragement and inspiration towards progress. Secondly, the Commission of course executed the decisions of the Council and managed the Community machine, which had become very large. Thirdly, the Commission had a role of supervision and verification of the actions of national Governments.

Pompidou then gave his views on the European Assembly. He was against a directly elected Assembly and opposed to allowing the Assembly to legislate since this would derogate from the authority of national Parliaments.

Heath readily agreed with what Pompidou had said about the Commission. Its purpose, in his view, was to serve the Council of Ministers and the individual Member States. It did not have a representative role, but it should be as efficient as possible within its sphere of responsibility, which was on the lines the President had described. As to the European Parliament, the British Government had no "present desire" to see it directly elected.[84]

From these and other instances of his views it is clear that Heath's views of the institutions of the EEC were no more integrationist than those of any of his successors as Prime Minister.

Pompidou returned to France and to the campaign for the referendum on enlargement which he had announced and which had been greeted by commentators as a political masterstroke. The British Embassy in Paris, which had shared that view, made no reference to it when they reported, on 24 April, that the result had been a gamble which had not come off. Pompidou was left, after what many saw as a mid-term ballot on his Presidency, exactly where he had started, with 36% of the electorate behind him. Mitterrand had cleverly shot Pompidou's fox by advising his Socialist supporters to abstain. The level of those abstaining or voting blank was 47%, the highest on record. Of those who did vote, two were in favour of enlargement for every one against.

Pompidou, the Embassy concluded, would now be licking his wounds, and might prove more sensitive and difficult to deal with. He had become the prisoner of his own argument (given in a "flat and simplistic" television appearance at the end of the campaign) that a massive vote would have strengthened France's role. Now, Pompidou would be unable to claim that extra measure of influence he was seeking.[85]

In a lengthier report ten days later, Soames wrote that "the referendum seemed to be browning a covey of grouse. But none fell, except that one bird a long way behind got a ricochet pellet through its beak – the British Labour Party – and the man who fired the shot got a sore shoulder which should not be exaggerated".

If Soames' love of shooting metaphors had on this occasion slightly got the better of him, he was clearer in making a few key judgements. At The Hague in

1969 '*on attendait Pompidou mais c'etait Brandt qui arriva*'. This time, Soames thought, with Germany politically distracted and uncertain, Italy likewise and Britain beset with labour problems and Ulster, the prospects for French pre-eminence must have seemed good. But that extra measure of authority which Pompidou had been seeking had eluded him. Some of the magic had been lost.

On the plus side, especially from a British perspective, France was the first member of the Community to have effectively, though not yet formally, ratified the Accession Treaty. The "slow awakening of that Sleeping Beauty the General put to sleep – the sense that France belongs to Europe, not just to herself – has begun".[86]

Heath had followed up his meeting with Pompidou with one, in April, with Brandt, this time at Number 10. Brandt's domestic position was precarious, as he faced a confidence vote in the German Parliament. But he and Heath had been in accord on the preparations for the Summit of the Ten now planned for the autumn. Brandt thought that the Summit would have to reach agreement on three main elements: European monetary union, institutions and external relations.[87]

The British Government's own policy on economic and monetary union was becoming clearer and was spelled out by Rippon at a Brussels meeting of the Six and representatives of the acceding states on 24 April. The British Government, he said, shared the aim of "a progressive move towards economic and monetary union in the enlarged EEC and wish to pay a full part in the development of this aim". Such progress had, in the British view, to be complementary to progress on the reform of the international monetary system.

Within the enlarged Community, the British Government attached importance to parallel development between economic and monetary measures. The Sixties, Rippon continued, were "for the Community the decade of the CAP. The Seventies should prove to be the decade of the Community's industrial and regional policies", with the focus on high technology – aerospace, computers, advanced electronic equipment, electric plant, nuclear fuel and power. The aim should be to "enable the Community to develop industrial units which can compete economically with, and set the pace for, the great firms whose resources are based on the large and integrated home market of the United States and the growing industrial strength of Japan".

Rippon went on to make a strong pitch for an EEC regional policy. The United Kingdom had major regional problems and the British Government therefore wished to play a full part in the evolution of Community regional policies. In the British view, the Summit should decide on the objectives which should guide the development of these new regional policies. The contraction of employment on the land had played a part in the regional problems of EEC countries. But the most acute problems now lay in older industrial areas. The EEC should recognise this as a parallel problem of equal seriousness. At the same time, questions of Community expenditure had, said Rippon to be looked at in the wider budgetary context and with regard to the financial implications for member countries.

Rippon's intervention was a clear statement, firstly that there were British conditions attached to monetary union and, secondly, that Britain was looking for new policies as a means of mitigating her disproportionate share of the cost of the EEC budget.

Other interventions were, according to a note to Heath from Tom Bridges (the new Foreign Office Private Secretary in No. 10), "rather diffuse". But a majority had shared the British view on the need for a Community regional policy. Schumann had intervened towards the end of the debate to repeat his view that progress towards monetary union in 1972 could be hindered if too much attention was paid to regional, industrial or social policies. "This produces a bargaining position", noted Heath, succinctly.[88]

On 1 May, Armstrong instructed John Hunt, who had joined the Cabinet Office and was the as yet uncrowned heir to Burke Trend as Cabinet Secretary, to set work in hand on defining British objectives, in the context of EEC business, for the Summit and on how to achieve those aims. At the same time, Heath asked the Foreign Secretary to prepare a similar set of political aims. These two pieces of work were to be prepared in parallel and coordinated with each other.[89]

Hunt's reply, some days later, was that the British Government should use the Summit: to mark Britain's intention to play a leading role in the formation of Community policies; to revive the idealism of the Community's earlier years and to ensure the adoption of policies in the British interest. That in turn meant a common foreign and a common defence policy; and the maintenance of the present balance between the Council of Ministers and the European Commission, with the Council remaining the principal Community institution.

There would, Hunt advised, be seven main areas of economic policy under discussion at the Summit: EMU; external commercial policies; agriculture; international aid; industrial and regional policy; and environmental policy. Here Hunt reiterated what Rippon had already said in Brussels adding that, while Britain wanted to reduce the cost of the CAP in real terms and make the Community more outward looking, "we must clearly be careful not to revive suspicions, on the part of the French in particular, that we have joined the Community in order to whittle away its identity".[90]

Not dissimilar views were sent to Heath at around the same time by Sir John Partridge, the President of the Confederation of British Industries (CBI), who advocated both industrial and regional policies at EEC level. Monetary union, on the other hand, "should evolve in the process of economic integration and should be regarded as an aim to be achieved only when it can come about naturally".[91]

That Pompidou was not on the same wavelength about the Summit as his partners was becoming ever more apparent. Courcel, who was leaving London to become Secretary General of the Quai d'Orsay, gave lunch to Armstrong on 12 May, reiterating that European monetary affairs would be the main issue at the Summit and responding to Armstrong's pitch for progress on regional and industrial policies by saying that the French Government were "not very enthusiastic".

The British Government was also at variance with Pompidou over the site of a new organisation which both were keen to see set up, namely a Political

Secretariat to service the work of the Council of Ministers, including the closer foreign policy cooperation which both Governments favoured. Pompidou was bidding for Paris as the home of the organisation. This did not appeal to Heath, who favoured Brussels so that the organisation could sit alongside the Commission. Pompidou had gone public on his desire to see the secretariat in Paris and Courcel told Armstrong that the only reason Pompidou wanted the secretariat in Paris was to preserve its role as servant of the Ministers, not as a creator of policy. If it was sited in Brussels, it would mushroom like the Community institutions and try to develop an independent policy role of its own.[92]

On 2 June, at a lunch in Paris in honour of the Belgian Prime Minister, Pompidou told Eyskens that he "would not take the responsibility of inviting nine Heads of Government if the only results of their meeting were to be vague declarations of intent, agreement on minor points or, worse still, badly disguised disagreements".

The Elysée subsequently briefed *Agence France Presse* in some detail. Pompidou had issued a "stern warning" to his European partners. He was "very annoyed" that some of the EEC's Foreign Ministers had "exhumed" the most integrationist projects. He was not prepared to see the focus of the Summit moved away from economic and monetary union. The Political Secretariat must be in Paris. If there was no present crisis, that did not mean that one was not far off. Building Europe was the only way to escape "all servitudes".[93]

"It is clear", the Foreign Office advised, "that President Pompidou has considerably shaken the Belgians. This is not difficult". The underlying factor was the referendum result and the failure of other EEC members to accept the siting of the Foreign Ministers' secretariat in Paris. Hence Pompidou was in a defensive mood and anxious to reassert himself by taking an intransigent line. The advice of the Foreign Secretary was not to react publicly.[94]

On the same day, Soames asked Juillet, at the Elysée, what was biting the President. Juillet said that he could tell Soames frankly, and as a friend, that Pompidou felt he had come a long way over British entry into the Community, and that in domestic political terms he had perhaps come too far too fast. He had the Gaullists breathing down his neck. The secretariat was something he needed badly. The British should help him. When Soames remonstrated that if this was the case it would have been better to have discussed it first rather than stake a public claim in a press conference, Juillet agreed but said that this was Pompidou's manner: he kept things to himself and then burst out with them.

Commenting to London on this exchange, Soames thought that it was mainly domestic considerations that had shaped Pompidou's mood. It was partly the wounded animal syndrome following the referendum and the consequent need both to restore his personal position on the European stage and to take more account of his Gaullist supporters at home. But Soames doubted whether Pompidou really meant to put the Summit in jeopardy since "his prestige was already deeply engaged in it".[95]

It was not just the Belgians who were worried. The Germans too had noted Pompidou's comments with what a Foreign Ministry official called "uneasiness".

The Germans had been accustomed to the growl of thunder from Paris before any major meeting but there was anxiety, reflected in the German Press, that Pompidou might be returning to the more nationalistic policies of de Gaulle.[96]

Heath treated all this quite coolly, telling the Danish Prime Minister, Jens Otto Krag that, on a number of European issues, the British were "somewhere in the middle" among their future partners. On issues such as the evolution of the European Parliament "we should have to see as we went along". On economic and monetary union, the question would have to be tackled stage by stage, emphasising that monetary union would make no sense unless it was matched by economic union, and that economic union in its turn pre-supposed a properly developed and coordinated regional policy. Hitherto, the Community's interest in regional policy had been largely agricultural but the principal British concern was the reorganisation of industry, particularly in the industrially depressed areas of the country.

On the question of the Political Secretariat, Heath said that it would be impossible for both the United Kingdom and for Germany to accept that Paris should become, in effect, the political capital of Europe. If Pompidou insisted, then the British Government might equally have to insist that the Commission or the Council of Ministers should move to London.[97]

Privately, Heath thought that Pompidou's utterances were "part of a characteristic French gambit to achieve a result which suits French interests by a combination of sulks, bullying and wooing". But Heath was aware that Pompidou was letting it be known that he was 'disappointed with Mr Heath' and the Prime Minister thought it politic for Armstrong to have a private chat with Jobert to make clear the limited area of difference between the two leaders and the reason for it.[98]

More serious was the decision forced on the British Government by a run on the pound, fuelled by the domestic industrial and economic turbulence of the previous months. On 23 June, the Government announced the decision to float the pound on what was hoped would be a temporary basis. In a message to Pompidou, Heath said that "these events clearly underline the importance of achieving progress in European monetary cooperation and reform of the international monetary system. We may have to think more radically than we have yet allowed for". Pompidou replied that he was convinced that a regime of fixed exchange rates constituted one of the indispensable conditions for the proper functioning of the Common Market.[99] Apart from some criticism from the French at the lack of prior consultation, the British decision was generally received by her future partners without complaint.[100]

A brighter gleam was the conclusion on 5 July of the Committee Stage of the European Communities Bill without amendment. The Committee Stage had taken over 325 hours, spread over 53 days, 104 Divisions and discussion of over 200 amendments. Every Division was won by the Government with the active complicity of the Labour rebels who contrived deliberate absences at crucial moments. When the Bill received its Third Reading on 13 July, the Government won, by 301 votes to 284. Harold Wilson had told the Italian Ambassador in

London some weeks previously with "unconcealed pleasure" that, with the crucial issues in the House of Commons disposed of, the Opposition could now be more constructive. Wilson also told the Ambassador that he expected George Thomson to be one of the two British Commissioners in Brussels, although neither Heath nor Thomson had said anything to Wilson and caused lasting ill-feeling by their failure to do so until much nearer the date of the announcement some months later.[101]

The issues which had preoccupied the House (apart from the procedural ones which it seemed to crave) were the whole question of sovereignty and the extent to which Parliament would still be able to legislate on matters decided in Brussels.

In their White Paper of July 1971, the Government had argued that EEC membership would not, thanks to the veto, entail any 'erosion of essential national sovereignty'. This claim was based on the existence of a unanimity rule within the Treaty of Rome for many especially sensitive subjects such as taxation, but also on the interpretation which British Ministers gave to the Luxembourg Compromise. At the time of its original negotiation at the end of the French boycott of the EEC institutions in the mid-60s, there had been no doubt in the minds of British officials that the Luxembourg Compromise was just that: essentially a political and not a legal agreement, and in reality an agreement to disagree That in turn reflected the French view, on the one hand, that no Member State's vital interests could be overridden and the view of others, such as the Benelux countries that, where majority voting was the rule under the Treaties, it should be applied. But it was the widespread and sincerely held belief of British Ministers, reinforced by French insistence on the point, that in practice no Member State, especially a large one, would be voted down if its vital interests were at stake. Indeed, British adherence to the doctrine had been one of Pompidou's essential conditions for admitting Britain to membership.

The evidence points to Ministers believing in the assurance they gave to the House, that the Luxembourg Compromise was much more than the unreliable instrument it in practice turned out to be. They also failed to appreciate the extent to which the Community would prove to be dynamic in institutional, legal and political terms. The French view of the Luxembourg Compromise by 1982, when they voted Britain down on the one occasion when a British Government formally invoked it, was not the same as the one Pompidou had adhered to so firmly in talking to Heath ten years earlier.

The issue of the primacy of European Community law had been addressed in the White Paper on the legal and constitutional implications of membership published by the Labour Government in 1967. It was there stated that "*It would be necessary to pass legislation giving the force of law to those provisions of the Treaties and Community instruments which are intended to take direct internal effect within the Member States . . . The legislation would have to cover both provisions in force when we joined and those coming into force subsequently as a result of instruments issued by the Community institutions . . . The constitutional innovation would lie in the acceptance in advance as part of the law of the United Kingdom of provisions to be made in the future by instruments issued by the Community institutions – a situation for which there is no precedent in this country. However, these instruments, like ordinary delegated legislation, would derive their force under the law of the United Kingdom from the original enactment passed by Parliament.*"[102]

Enoch Powell was the most articulate exponent of the argument that this provision proved the illegitimacy of the Government's approach, since Parliament's ability to legislate for the United Kingdom was being fundamentally curtailed. "Had we been sufficiently candid about the implications" Geoffrey Howe asked himself? He concluded "that the technical aspects had indeed been explained, in documents beginning with those published by the Wilson Government in 1967. The electorate *had* endorsed the principle of membership. The final crucial stage could properly be entrusted to Parliament itself. For the very sovereignty of Parliament entitled that body to manage or deploy that sovereignty, on behalf of the British people, in partnership with other nations on such terms as Parliament might decide".[103] In a sense, both Howe and Powell were right: Howe in asserting that the facts and implications of Community law had been explained to Parliament; Powell in recognising that here was an issue which went to the heart of British notions of sovereignty. It proved to be a source of enduring aggravation.

The floating of the pound would have to end if Britain was, by the date of accession, to rejoin the narrow band of fluctuating exchange rates (the 'snake in the tunnel') to which the European currencies had been committed by the Smithsonian Agreement of 1971. In early July, at Heath's request, the Treasury sent to Number 10 their assessment of the EEC's position on international monetary reform, against a background of conviction in Europe, including Britain, that the measures agreed in 1971 were no more than a palliative. The EEC's position on international monetary reform was, said the Treasury, already clear. The common objective was a 'one world' system based on fixed but adjustable parities with general convertibility, including that of the dollar. This involved reducing the role of national currencies as reserve assets, so that the United States could not finance deficits just by adding to her short-term liabilities. France fully supported this position and Pompidou had said over and over again that he did not want a divided world or a major economic confrontation with the United States.

The other elements in French thinking were, the Treasury argued, basically tactical. French insistence on closer monetary cooperation in Europe – the development of a 'Community monetary identity' – was in large part designed to get the Community to combine its bargaining power and speak with one voice. In this they had strong interests to promote: to minimise the cost in terms of trade concessions, of CAP liberalisation, of concessions in the association agreements etc. France's second powerful motive was to have a fallback position in case the international negotiations failed. Narrowing the margins in Europe and establishing a European Fund were the building bricks of a European monetary bloc in case of need, as well as being reasonable first steps towards EMU. But a bloc would be a poor second best for the French. In particular, they were not happy about a bloc floating against the dollar, for they feared that a collective float would go upwards, damaging their competitive strength and impeding the growth of their domestic economy. Hence French insistence on concerting in the EEC effective controls against short-term capital movements, so that if there had to be a collective float, the rates could, they hoped, be prevented from moving up too far.

In all this, the Treasury advised, United Kingdom interests were basically close to those of the French. Britain too did not want to make any undue concessions to the Americans, though Britain differed from France in that some mitigation of the CAP would be in the UK interest and Britain had a stronger interest than did France in trade outside the Community. There was no incompatibility between international monetary reform on the lines proposed and progress towards EMU within Europe. The British problem was not to choose which fixed parity system she liked best. The British problem was that "unless we can rapidly get control of our inflationary problem, we are not capable of meeting the requirements of any fixed parity system at all". In theory, it might, said the Treasury, be an answer for sterling to float perpetually, though this would almost certainly be at the cost of continually escalating inflation. But this would be incompatible with the Government's European policy, for the Community was a fixed parity system. "It is said", the Treasury concluded, "that the motto of the City of Paris is *'fluctuat nec mergitur'*. Pompidou says clearly that the up-to-date translation is 'he who floats don't join'".[104]

Heath's problems were compounded by the hope agreed between Pompidou and Brandt, and conveyed in a letter from Brandt on 7 July, that Britain would soon be able to return to fixed exchange rates. Heath's reply was cautious. Britain had "every intention of returning to the maintenance of agreed margins round a fixed parity as soon as we safely can".

One much more palatable piece of news from the Franco-German summit was that Brandt and Pompidou had agreed that it would not be possible to introduce new institutions at the present stage of the Community's evolution. Brandt had, it seemed, thus got Pompidou off the hook of his insistence on a Political Secretariat based in Paris.[105]

When Armstrong went to Paris on 12 July for his 'private chat' with Jobert (and Raimond) at the Elysée, he and Soames were told even more explicitly that it was very important for Pompidou that Britain should return to a fixed parity by the date of her accession, 1 January 1973. Armstrong assured them that the British Government wanted to return to a fixed parity as soon as they could, but it had to be a fixed parity which they had a good prospect of sustaining. For their part, Armstrong recorded, the French "did not seem to have many ideas about the development of further progress to monetary union, beyond a return to fixed parities and the establishment of arrangements for mutual defence and support for the European monetary system". When Soames and Armstrong suggested that this would amount to no more than protection of the *'acquis'*, with no looking forward, the French view seemed to be that, apart from an early start, on a modest basis, for a European Monetary Fund, and close cooperation between central bank governors, further developments would emerge naturally from the processes and arrangements for fixed parities and mutual defence. The French did not talk at all in terms of a timetable for further progress towards monetary union. The

French accepted as a logical proposition that progress towards economic union would have to march alongside progress towards monetary union. But the Germans, who had put the same proposition to them, had received no clear answer as to what practical measures such progress would entail.

So far as the Summit was concerned, Armstrong's French interlocutors emphasised that it was not enough to enunciate principles. The meeting would have to make a practical commitment to a system of mutual defence of the European monetary system. Soames and Armstrong inferred from this that, if Britain was able to meet the French on this matter, they, the French, would be willing to pay some sort of price in terms of developments on industrial and regional policy. Both men also emphasised that the Summit meeting should look beyond the immediate monetary and economic problems to chart the future progress of the enlarged Community. The British Prime Minister would want to see the conference set a course for wider political cooperation among the members of the enlarged Community.[106]

Soames expanded on what he and Armstrong had been told, and on the Treasury's analysis of EMU, in a letter to Neale at the Treasury on 1 August. He agreed that French enthusiasm for EMU was confined to limited objectives and that they had given but sparse thought to the longer term implications of full-scale EMU. Indeed, when they did look further ahead, they did not much like what they saw, in that full-scale EMU would involve a degree of supra-nationality which went far beyond their existing ideas. There were, Soames thought, two elements in French thinking – one tactical and the other strategic. In the short term were the advantages which EMU would bring them, with the preservation of the CAP top of their list. Secondly, there was a negative aspect. One of the main attractions for the French Government in the creation of a European monetary bastion was that, when this had been accomplished in the limited degree they envisaged, they would hope to be in a much stronger position to impose limitations on their partners' freedom of action over international monetary reform, by insisting on unanimous decisions.[107]

August being traditionally 'the month of the *chargé d'affaires*' i.e. when Ambassadors took to the beach (or in Soames's case the grouse moors), leaving their deputies in charge, it was Christopher Ewart-Biggs[108] who telegraphed the Foreign Office on 18 August on the eve of a visit by the French Foreign Minister to London. Schumann was not, Ewart-Biggs pointed out, an ideal interlocutor for discussions about the finer points of the monetary question. In any case, "the French attitude to monetary unification is conditioned by (a) the need to defend the CAP; (b) the wish to hold France's partners in line with her views on the eventual negotiation of an international monetary reform . . . and (c) the concept of a European Europe. In this there is an undeclared barrier somewhere across the future, in that the French will not want to get carried past a point at which their power of independent decision in their own major interests would be substantially curtailed".[109]

Schumann's visit was unsatisfactory, not least because the issue of the Political Secretariat, which appeared to have been put to bed, was high on his list as an issue which was extremely important to the French. Did the Prime Minister insist on the issue being discussed at the Summit or could it be settled beforehand? Heath replied that he was prepared to discuss the matter anywhere and at any time, but his view was clear. Foreign politics was at the heart of inter-governmental affairs, and the location of the secretariat was of a different quality from that of, say, the Patent Office. The European Parliament was in France and no one questioned that. But if the Political Secretariat was in France as well then each member country of the EEC would have to bid to have a Community institution.[110]

The Foreign Secretary, who had participated in the meeting, accompanied Schumann to the airport and reported back to Heath that Schumann had "reverted to his depressing mood". He could not find enough substance in the discussions he had just had to convince the President that a Summit was worthwhile, although the conversation had confirmed that on EMU there was no significant difference between the two Governments. Douglas-Home concluded that Schuman's attitude was "mostly tactical, that is to put up difficulties so that others scurry around trying to woo the French, and at the end the Summit is held by their gracious permission". The Foreign Secretary went on to suggest that officials should seek to draft a communiqué and see how much substance could be put into it.[111]

In fact, some work on a draft communiqué had already been done and had been shown to the Prime Minister at Chequers by Hunt and Sir Thomas Brimelow from the Foreign Office. Heath had found the draft to be "full of officialese", so the officials were sent away to try again.[112]

On 2 September, Ewart-Biggs called on Schumann. "He was not disagreeable, but he was certainly gloomy", treating Ewart-Biggs to a "long but far from crystal-line dissertation lasting more than an hour", consisting of a version of his talk with the Prime Minister which prompted Heath (unusually for him) to write dissenting comments in the margin of Ewart-Biggs' reporting telegram.

Schumann adduced to Ewart-Biggs some new, and not altogether consistent, arguments in favour of Paris as the site of the Political Secretariat. Paris would be more central to the Community than Brussels if Spain and Portugal were included. At the same time, the importance of relations with Eastern Europe made Paris an obvious choice.

As Ewart-Biggs was leaving, Schumann said that he was as anxious to have the Summit take place as he was worried that it might not. His attitude to the British, as everything in his past had shown, was one of trust and affection. It could not be so, he added, if in what he had said he was being tactical, and there was no need for him to assure Ewart-Biggs that he was not.

It was perhaps something, Ewart-Biggs commented laconically to London, that Schumann at least recognised that that very thought might be in British minds.[113]

A few days later, Heath was in Munich for the Olympic Games (the games that were overwhelmed by a terrorist attack on the Israeli athletes). At a meeting with Brandt, the German Chancellor, who had narrowly survived a no confidence vote in the Bundestag, thought that Pompidou might in the end agree to the Summit taking place. If it did not, then it was the French who would be isolated and recognition of that fact might help persuade the French to agree. If agreement was not possible on the Political Secretariat, then the issue should simply be left open. Heath agreed that the French had to be given time to get out of the public position they had got themselves into.[114]

Heath went from Munich to Balmoral, for the annual Prime Ministerial stay with the Queen. From there he spoke to Brandt on the telephone, telling the Chancellor how much the Queen felt for him and what an unhappy time it had been. Brandt had seen Pompidou and had gained the impression that "our friend is inclined to have the meeting". Pompidou had dropped completely the question of the Secretariat, albeit with a certain degree of bitterness.[115]

By the time Douglas-Home and Schumann saw each other again, at a WEU meeting in Rome on 11 September, Schumann too was "more relaxed and encouraging". There was, Schumann said, now enough substance in the document worked out by Permanent Representatives in Brussels, particularly on economic and monetary matters.[116]

Three days later, Pompidou wrote to his fellow European leaders inviting them to a Summit in Paris on 18/19 October. But he remained grudging. Little by little, Pompidou told a press conference on 21 September, "I saw the idea gaining ground of a Summit destined to celebrate in some way the entry of Great Britain and three other countries into the Community. But we had already drunk champagne in Brussels, I would be perfectly ready to do the same again in Paris, but perhaps it was not quite enough to justify a meeting. So I allowed myself to say so in public". Since then, Pompidou continued, the Chanceries had been working and there was a convergence of views on economic and monetary matters which meant that "holding this Summit was, in the end, useful". Pompidou hoped furthermore that, when all the leaders were round a table "the light of Europe will burn more brightly. And France will not attempt to put it out".[117]

On 25 September, by a majority of 8%, the Norwegian people voted against Norway joining the EEC. Broadly speaking, Oslo and the larger towns returned an overall majority in favour of joining, while the country areas were strongly against, 15 out of Norway's 19 counties voting 'no'. The farmers, the fishermen and the mass of the people outside the large towns, particularly in the north and west, came down solidly against. The 'no' majority was also helped by a higher turnout of voters in the countryside than in the towns. Overall, turnout was nearly 76%.[118]

Whether, had the Norwegians voted after the Danes, a different result would have been obtained, as Christopher Soames surmised[119], is now impossible to assess. Britain's Ambassador in Oslo, Ralph Selby, who had served in both countries, did, however, conclude that "the Norwegians are just not as European as, say, the Danes . . . The Norwegians are more nationalistic, more self-reliant, more introspective and more suspicious of foreigners at large. They still cordially dislike the Germans because of the war. They dislike the Italians because they are swarthy Latins. They are not at all sure that the French like them, or really want them in Europe at all". The Norwegians feared for their fish stocks and for their newly found oil resources. The environmentally conscious young voted 'no'. In what had been a sophisticated debate during the campaign, the pro-Marketeers had not made nearly as much use as had their Danish counterparts of one of the strongest arguments for joining Europe, namely the potential cost of staying out. Nor had they been able to present the opposite, more positive, vision of a truly united Europe for fear of evoking those very fears for the loss of Norwegian sovereignty which they were attempting to set at rest.[120]

Heath, in expressing his sympathy to the Norwegian Prime Minister over the result, said: "You were fighting for a good cause, in the interest both of Norway and of Europe, and I believe that it will in the end prevail".[121]

Informed speculation had been prevalent for some time in the British media that Christopher Soames and George Thomson were to be Britain's first European Commissioners. Soames had had it in mind to return to British front-line politics, but the domestic circumstances were not auspicious for the Conservatives and Heath could not have risked a by-election. In any event, a move to Brussels was a natural one for Soames given his experience, his flair for European politics and his command of French.

Heath, by his own account, ascertained that Thomson would agree to become a Commissioner and noted that "Harold Wilson took no part in these appointments".[122] But it was not, in reality quite that simple. On 26 July, Armstrong told Heath that Thomson hoped the announcement of his appointment could be made on 7 September. Thomson had raised with Armstrong the question of when Heath should inform Wilson and had asked that this be done before Thomson left for Yugoslavia on 21 August. Armstrong, however, advised against telling Wilson "until about 48 hours before the announcement is made; to tell the Leader of the Opposition in the middle of August and make no announcement until 7 September would leave too much scope for leaks".[123]

Given that Heath had offered the job to Thomson on 14 March and that by 12 April the diarist of *The Times* was writing that "well-informed Conservative politicians forecast that George Thomson's future is assured" and that "he has already been tentatively approached with a suggestion that he should become one of the UK's two Commissioners in Brussels"[124], it might be concluded that the Government pot had already exhibited the colours that Armstrong was now attributing to the Labour kettle. Be that as it may, Heath accepted Armstrong's advice.

Thomson subsequently came to the view that the announcement should be delayed until after the Labour Party Conference in early October to avoid the risk that the announcement might drive the Labour Party Conference to a more extreme anti-European position than it might otherwise take. At the same time it was, as Armstrong told Heath on 22 September, "a matter of increasing embarrassment to him [Thomson] that nothing has yet been said to Mr Wilson. He would very much hope that you would find it possible to tell Mr Wilson at an early date, so as to regularise Mr Thomson's position with his leader". Armstrong identified a risk: namely that if Wilson were told before the Labour Party Conference, the matter might leak anyway, with the result that Thomson feared. But Armstrong advised Heath to take the risk. For a start, it was a matter of common and public speculation that Thomson was to be one of the two British Commissioners. Secondly, Wilson would presumably not wish to make life needlessly difficult for himself at his Party Conference. So, it seemed to Armstrong that the time had come for the Prime Minister to write to Wilson. Heath's reply was characteristic: "HW is bound to leak this for whatever nefarious purpose he can – if only to show he knows. Please check with GT that he will not mind it being leaked before the Conference".

Armstrong duly spoke to Thomson, who concluded that, as between the risk of a leak and the embarrassment of Wilson not being told, he would prefer the embarrassment. Armstrong accordingly agreed with Thomson that Heath would write to Wilson (or see him) on 5 October, after the Labour Conference, with an announcement to follow a few days later.[125]

Heath duly wrote to Wilson on 5 October. Unusually for Wilson, who was punctilious about the courtesies, he got his Private Secretary to write to Armstrong two weeks later, acknowledging Heath's letter.[126]

Three years later, when Wilson was back in Downing Street and was considering nominating Soames as the next President of the European Commission, Patrick Wright, Wilson's Foreign Office Private Secretary, advised him that it would be necessary very soon to explain the position to George Thomson. Wright recorded that "the Prime Minister said that Mr Thomson's relations with the Foreign Secretary were very close and he thought Mr Callaghan was the right person to speak to him. There had been some strain between himself and Thomson in the past, and the PM had particularly resented the way in which Thomson had carried on discussions about Europe with Heath without prior consultation with the Leader of his own Party. The PM did not wish to hold this against Thomson, and was prepared to forget the past, but he thought that for this reason Callaghan was better placed to speak to him".[127] The No. 10 files are weighty with reports of conversations between Wilson and Soames during the latter's time at the Commission. There is not a single piece of evidence of a conversation between Wilson and Thomson.

The nomination of Soames and Thomson was well received both in Britain and on the continent. "It would have been easy", Frank Giles wrote in the *Sunday Times*, "for Mr Heath to appoint two safe senior civil servants. But how much more imaginative, and likely to be effective, are the two choices he has announced. For Soames, it can be claimed that he was one of the architects of British entry into Europe . . . George Thomson, as well as being a man universally respected for his personal qualities, was in his time Labour's 'Mr Europe'".[128] The *Daily Telegraph* thought Thomson was taking a considerable risk with his own political career and that he was doing his Party "a valuable service by showing Europe that there are indeed Labour men who are willing to work for the good of the Community".[129] Sicco Mansholt, the President of the European Commission, told Heath that the British nominations would set a high standard for other members of the Community.[130]

These appointments came as preparations intensified for the Paris Summit later in the month. The most difficult question, as Hunt minuted to Armstrong on

6 October, was "the extent to which we are prepared to make concessions to the French on monetary matters in order to obtain their agreement to an effective regional policy". Concessions on monetary policy would, in the Treasury view, be real while concessions by the French on regional policy would be mere words. Hunt did not agree that this was necessarily so. The plan for monetary union within the EEC was based on the Werner Report, prepared by Luxembourg Prime Minister Pierre Werner at the request of the Heads of Government at The Hague in 1969. The report provided for Monetary Union in three stages. The first, already in train through the 'snake in the tunnel' involved a reduction of fluctuation margins between the currencies of the Member States. The second stage was to involve total liberalisation of capital movements, together with the integration of financial markets and banking systems. The third and final stage would involve the irrevocable fixing of the exchange rates between the different currencies of the EEC.

Against this background, Hunt's advice was that Britain should insist on a commitment to the implementation by the end of 1973 (i.e. simultaneously with the start of the second stage of EMU) of an EEC regional policy which took account of the needs of the enlarged Community and in particular of regions of high unemployment and industrial decline. There was, Hunt believed, scope for common cause between the Prime Minister and Brandt given that the Germans wanted to obtain decisions on social policy at the summit and what they wanted and what Britain wanted were "not merely compatible, but closely related".[131]

When Heath saw the Commission President on 8 October, Mansholt told him that Heath would be obliged to play a leading role at the Summit. Only Heath could explain the clear political engagements which were necessary for the future of the Community. If Heath gave a lead, then Brandt and the Dutch, Belgian and Italian Prime Ministers would follow. The first Summit of the enlarged Community was a great historic moment. It must not be an anti-climax. Everyone would be looking to the Prime Minister to give a lead. So far so good. Even better was Mansholt's support for a European regional policy which would enable Britain "to recover . . . some of her outgoings on account of the CAP". Heath did not, however, respond when Mansholt described the ultimate objective as being "a European Government responsible to an elected European Parliament".[132]

As the Summit approached, Pompidou had belatedly begun to play down public expectations but his domestic situation was not altogether comfortable. He had, Soames advised, to impose himself at the Summit in a European role without appearing too European for the Gaullists. Debré and others were known to have been very doubtful about the decision to go ahead with the Summit when Pompidou had, in their view, signally failed to obtain French objectives. From the Centre-Right, Giscard d'Estaing was waiting in the wings while, on the Left, Mitterrand had made overtures to the Communists which opened up the possibility of a left-wing victory in the Assembly elections of 1973 which could threaten Pompidou's position as President.[133]

There was one specifically Anglo-French bilateral matter which Heath was charged with raising with Pompidou in the margins of the Summit. On

17 October, on the eve of the Paris meeting, the Permanent Secretary at the Ministry of Agriculture, Freddie Kearns, advised No. 10 of the "strong suspicion that President Pompidou has more or less instructed the French Agriculture Ministry and French food concerns to thwart approaches by British food firms". The Minister of Agriculture, Joe Godber, had taken the matter up with his French opposite number, Jacques Chirac, and had "got virtually no change beyond a reference to the political difficulty with an election brewing in France". There was a specific bid by the British company Hector Laing which Godber hoped Heath would raise with Pompidou in order to rehearse a wider argument. This was that opposition from France would not stop the British food industry from growing in Europe. If firms were unable to ally themselves with French concerns, they would find alliances in other Member States. Surely large Anglo-French firms were more to Pompidou's taste than leaving unchecked the giant American concerns such as Nabisco.[134]

When Heath and Pompidou met for a bilateral in Paris the following day, Heath said that he understood that greater freedom of capital movement was causing certain problems for M Pompidou. Pompidou said that this was indeed so, and he had asked that Heath should be informed of it. He saw no objection to an inflow of British capital if this was for "genuine investment purposes. But the City of London was proving itself particularly dynamic at present, especially in the processed foods sector. Already, about half of the French food industry was under American control. If the French Government allowed matters to take their course, the other half would very shortly come under British control." Heath made no response.[135]

By the time the Summit was over, Heath felt able to describe it in a statement to the Press as "a splendid result for us all – in Britain, in Europe and the world at large . . . We have shown that this is a Europe for the people. We are concerned about the quality of life, the environment in which we live and work . . . When the things we have set in hand in the last two days come to fruition they will show the advantages the enlargement of the Community will bring – to us in Britain, to Europe and to the rest of the world".[136]

What those things were was explained in a note which Armstrong wrote the following day. This first summit meeting of the Nine had been a historic occasion. There had been differences of view and hard negotiation but the underlying atmosphere had been one of "great cordiality and friendship". Britain's immediate objectives had been achieved. It was accepted that monetary cooperation must be matched by progress in economic cooperation. In particular, the Community had accepted a commitment to a regional policy, with a development fund, to be financed from the EEC budget, to correct regional imbalances and especially those arising from agricultural decline or industrial change. A course had been set for Community developments in the field of external commercial relations, Community aid to the developing countries, social policy, environmental and industrial policies and on political cooperation. These agreements had covered both principles and specific commitments to turn principles into reality.

"My instructions end here", Armstrong wrote, "but no account would be complete without a reference to the fact that the Prime Minister enjoyed a considerable personal success ... He has quickly established a position of personal authority in the Community's counsels".[137]

On 25 October, Heath told Cabinet that the Summit had been a remarkable achievement and the United Kingdom could be well content with the results. Britain had achieved the objectives she had set herself some six months earlier: a balanced approach to economic and monetary union; a date for the introduction of a regional policy which would take account of the needs of the enlarged Community; progress on industrial policy and the removal of non-tariff barriers; a Community energy policy; a common and positive approach to the next multilateral trade negotiations; progress on political cooperation. The one area where the Government had not achieved their objectives was in that of aid policy where the aim of alleviating the indebtedness of the hardest-pressed countries had fallen foul of German unwillingness to accept new commitments and of French refusal to agree to any waiver of debt servicing.

The agreements reached, Heath continued, were necessarily expressed in terms of major objectives of policy and much hard work would now be required to secure their detailed implementation. The Prime Minister enjoined Departmental Ministers to ensure that the organisational arrangements in their Ministries "were adequate to this new and additional function and that the staffs involved were equipped with the qualities of temperament and judgement which would be needed in the subsequent negotiations".[138]

Heath had had a slightly harder time of it in the House the previous day. Wilson challenged him, in particular, on two points. The first was whether Heath had got an assurance that the amount of money which would come to Britain in the form of regional development assistance would "match what he has already conceded will go from Britain across the Channel, across the exchanges, to the Community for the European agriculture welfare state". Heath replied that what had been gained was full acceptance by the Community of responsibility for providing the resources for the regional policy. The amounts would be worked out in the Council of Ministers.

What Heath had secured, though it was to have a painful gestation, did become a policy of significant value to the United Kingdom, though the Wilson Government of 1974 was surprisingly slow to realise it.

Wilson's second main point was that Heath had committed himself to a full-scale European Union by 1980, "a concept which has not been defined in the communiqué or in the discussions". What, on behalf of the United Kingdom, did he understand by this concept?

Heath replied: "Our concept of a European Union is the same that this country has always had, which is that in developing institutions one develops them to meet the needs of the organisation concerned ... As for monetary union, it is the second stage on which we are to enter by 1st January, not the final stage".[139]

On the same day in the House, the Foreign Secretary had been asked by one of his own side, Norman St. John-Stevas, whether he could spell out "what is meant by the 'European Union' to which we have been committed by the Community"? Douglas-Home replied: "This is something which has to be worked out in each sphere of the Community's activity over the years. Nobody was anxious at the conference to use labels like 'confederation' or 'federation' and therefore 'union' is a word which will gradually become defined over the years".[140]

It was not quite true that nobody at the Paris Conference had been anxious to define what 'Union' meant. The President of the Commission, "relegated to a place at the far end of the table where it was possible for President Pompidou, by ignoring the sometimes insistent demands of Dr Mansholt for the floor, to demonstrate that their status was not the same as that of the Heads of Government",[141] did press for the ultimate establishment of "a real European Government possessing the necessary powers and answerable to a European Parliament freely elected by universal suffrage". But he was largely overlooked.

Nonetheless, the Heads of Government did make two significant commitments in their communiqué. The first was that *"The Member States of the Community, the driving force of European construction, affirm their intention to transform before the end of the present decade the whole complex of their relations into a European Union"*. The second, contained in the next sentence of the communiqué, was that *"the Heads of State or of Government reaffirm the determination of the Member States of the enlarged Communities irreversibly to achieve the economic and monetary Union, confirming all the elements of the instruments adopted by the Council . . . The necessary decisions should be taken in the course of 1973 so as to allow the transition to the second stage of the economic and monetary Union on 1 January 1974, and with a view to its completion not later than 31 December 1980"*.

During discussion of the communiqué by the Heads of Government, late on 20 October, the only question about the commitment to European Union came from the Danish Prime Minister. According to the British record, "there was a surprise, after it had all been agreed, when Mr Jorgensen said that he was not clear what the agreement to move towards European union meant. Was it a federation, a confederation or something else which they were trying to set up?" "Happily", the British record continues, "he did not ask for a reply and President Pompidou lost no time in winding up the proceedings". It was then after midnight.[142]

As regards economic and monetary union, the Werner Report of 1970 had been clear that the basic essential agreement was "total and irreversible convertibility of currencies, the elimination of margins of fluctuation in rates of exchange, the irreversible fixing of parity rates and the total liberation of movements of capital". Werner allowed for the possibility of keeping "national monetary symbols" but argued that "considerations of a psychological and political order militate in favour of the adoption of a single currency which would guarantee the irreversibility of the undertaking".[143]

The British Government was, of course aware of the report and of the potentially far-reaching implications of a commitment to economic and monetary union. There is no evidence to suggest that either the Heath Government (or the Wilson Government of 1966) rejected the idea of a common currency. But nor did they have the sense that they were committed to a process whose conclusion was inevitable or immutable. Hence Heath's reply to Wilson that the commitment reached at the Paris Summit was to the *second* stage, involving the liberalisation of capital movements. That view was reinforced by the disruptive impact which the Nixon measures and the collapse of the Bretton Woods system had already had on European plans for EMU, and was to be reinforced still further by the impact of the oil crisis of 1973.

What perhaps can be said with certainty is that all European Council Conclusions, of which the Paris communiqué was in practice an early example, would prove to be, one by one, the building blocks in the construction of the European Union. Once something had been enshrined in such a communiqué, it could not be unsaid. Hence Margaret Thatcher's complaint that, in resisting EMU in the late 1980s she "was fighting with one hand tied behind my back" because of the terms of the 1972 communiqué, whose language "may have reflected Ted Heath's wishes. It certainly did not reflect mine".[144]

Domestic discussion and argument continued through the autumn about what form Parliamentary scrutiny of EEC legislative proposals should take after accession, and about UK representation in the European Parliament. On the first point, Cabinet had agreed in mid-July that "the special nature of the Community made it desirable that Parliament should have the maximum opportunity to examine the draft instruments in question"[145] but the precise nature of what form that scrutiny was to take provided fertile ground for Parliamentary inter-party bickering.

As to the European Parliament, the Treaty of Accession gave the United Kingdom an entitlement to 36 seats, to be designated by Parliament. Jim Prior, now Lord President of the Council, told Cabinet on 12 December that if the Opposition agreed to send delegates then the Conservatives would have 18 seats, Labour 17 and the Liberals 1. But it looked as if the Labour Party would decline to designate members given their opposition to British membership as negotiated. And the Liberal party were pressing for an extra place, which Prior was disposed to give them on the understanding that it would have to be ceded if Labour decided, in due course, to show up. In general, Prior advised against trying to fill the Labour seats with either compliant Labour MPs or Peers or with additional Conservative and Liberal representatives. While this would be possible, "it would be invidious to intervene in the Labour Party's internal affairs; and visible empty space might encourage the Labour party to adopt a more cooperative attitude towards Europe rather earlier than they might otherwise have done".

Heath summed up that there was probably no legal obligation to fill all the places available to the United Kingdom. Once the Parliamentary Labour Party had confirmed their position (which they shortly did) the Government should table the necessary resolutions in both Houses. Amendments could then be tabled by backbenchers and "in the circumstances, it would not be practicable for the Government to oppose the designation of additional members by way of amendments provided that the requisite number from each House [12 from the House of Commons and 6 from the House of Lords in the case of the Conservative party] was not exceeded".[146]

Something else of significance had happened during the course of the autumn. The Leader of the Opposition had put his job on the line to prevent his Party from committing themselves to withdraw from the European Community if and when they returned to power.

In May 1972, Wilson had told Benn that he was convinced that the next Party Conference would see a strong demand to commit Britain to withdrawal, a campaign which, Wilson suspected, might be linked to a move to replace him by Callaghan.[147]

By the summer of 1972, Wilson had made up his mind that he would have to resign if the party voted for withdrawal. He told the Shadow Cabinet in the summer that, while they could indulge their consciences on the Common Market it had been left to him "to wade through s**t".[148]

"It was only with the utmost difficulty, including my throwing the leadership itself into the stakes and threatening to resign, that enabled me to carry Conference in October", Wilson wrote to Willy Brandt at the close of the year.[149]

"In all my thirteen years as Leader of the Party I had no more difficult task than keeping the Party together on this issue, particularly in our Opposition years" Wilson wrote in his second volume of autobiography. "On the Sunday before Conference in October 1973 I had to lay my leadership on the line, and make it clear that I would resign and face the Party with the election of a new leader if the NEC recommended Conference to bind us to a policy of withdrawal . . . It was a miserably unhappy period".[150]

Wilson's action persuaded two members of the NEC, Barbara Castle and Joan Lester, to change their votes and the line which the Labour Party in the Parliament had taken (renegotiation of the terms of membership, not withdrawal altogether) was upheld by 14 votes to 11.[151]

It was a measure of Wilson's skill in reading, and riding, the Labour Party that an October 1972 Harris Poll gave him the backing of 79% of Labour supporters. His nearest rival was Roy Jenkins – with 5%.[152]

Edward Heath called the chapter of his autobiography devoted to the EEC 'Fanfare for Europe', after the series of concerts (both classical and popular) and other events which the Government arranged to mark Britain's entry to the EEC. One of them, a 'The Three vs. The Six' football match at Wembley Stadium was watched by 36,500 people and was won 2 – 0 by the 'Three' on the basis of goals scored by Danish and Scottish players.

A special commemorative 50 pence coin (showing, at the insistence of the Prime Minister, the word 'pence', rather than the letter 'p',) was issued. It was based on the existing coin of the same denomination, but showed nine joined hands around a seven-sided coin. It had not followed Robert Armstrong's tongue-in-cheek suggestion that the design on the reverse should "portray the maiden Europe on the back of a large white (John) Bull". More seriously, the Prime Minister had asked for the word 'Europe' to appear on the coin. Baroness Tweedsmuir, for the Foreign Office, disagreed, arguing in a letter of 31 October 1972, that "the use of the word 'Europe' by itself might cause difficulties. As it is the European Community and not Europe which we are joining on 1 January 1973, there could be criticism from the European countries not in the Community if this were not set out more precisely". The Royal Mint advised that the lettering would have to be very small and Heath accepted that no lettering would be preferable to 'Europe' alone.[153]

The cost to the taxpayer of 'Fanfare for Europe' was, as the Secretary of State for Education (Margaret Thatcher) told the House on 23 November, £350,000. On 1 November, Sir Geoffrey Howe had written to Heath's Political Adviser, Douglas Hurd, enclosing a letter from one of his Surrey constituents. "Surely", she had written, "at a time when our economy is at such a low ebb, there are better and more useful ways [than Fanfare for Europe] of spending taxpayers' money . . . May I suggest that we erect a block of old peoples' flatlets (so sorely needed) as a monument to this event . . . or some other useful way for the good of our own people . . ."

As a result of this letter, and with Heath's support and Hurd's engagement, agreement was eventually reached on £100,000 of Government funding for a Europe Chair of Rehabilitation at Southampton University, designed to demonstrate the conviction of the United Kingdom and her fellow members of the Community "that there is need to encourage training in, and development of, rehabilitation of sick and disabled people".[154]

Whatever the merits of 'Fanfare for Europe' (and it seems to have had little impact on public opinion), it was by its nature transient. The Chair of Rehabilitation at Southampton University, by contrast, exists to this day and is engaged, among other things, in research into strokes and Parkinson's disease.

'Fanfare for Europe' was the tip of an iceberg of preparation for the start of membership that had been going on since the summer. From August onwards a special committee, composed mostly of officials but under the chairmanship of Anthony Royle, a junior Foreign Office Minister, had been meeting to carry out a remit from Heath to devise "a special information and educative effort . . . to stimulate greater awareness of the challenges and opportunities" of membership. Individual Departmental plans were drawn up as well as a document, to which all Departments had contributed. Over 34 pages, *'Are You 'Ready?'* described the basics of membership across sectors ranging from agriculture to free movement of pensions and contained a list of contact points across Whitehall.

In addition to a live broadcast of the Covent Garden Gala which was to launch 'Fanfare for Europe', the BBC organised programmes on European culture, interviews with leading European industrialists, schools programmes including a French-language series about the life of young people in a small French town, and a European Quiz. The Reith lectures, by the journalist and commentator, Andrew Shonfield, were to be on the theme of 'Europe – Journey to an unknown destination', a title of greater aptness than was perhaps appreciated at the time.[155]

In late September, Royle's committee circulated speaking notes for Ministers about the EEC: "It has been a long road . . . Now, eleven years later, we are on the threshold and the door is not only open but we know that a warm welcome awaits us. The opportunities of full membership are at last there for us to grasp . . . We must now concentrate on making our future in the Community the success which awaits us all if we make the effort". It is hard to imagine that this document escaped the fate awaiting most such worthy but unusable efforts.[156]

Royle himself was aware of the pitfalls, minuting to Heath on 17 October that "it would be inadvisable to mount a general information effort for the public at large, as they are not likely to be directly and early affected and there is nothing new to say to them that might not be just counterproductive at this stage". Royle hoped that the information which was being targeted on business, industry and the professions would have a useful spin-off effect on the public at large. In addition to the information booklet of useful contacts, of which one million copies were to be distributed free, advertisements were to be placed in the national and provincial Press throughout November and December as a reminder of the imminence of membership, of the need for preparations and as publicity for the checklist. Royle foresaw some criticism but the whole character of the effort could be justified as a practical public service and the total cost should, he said, "be only £275,000". Heath expressed himself well pleased.[157]

Royle's committee concluded its work at the beginning of January 1973. In its final report it counted 270 Ministerial speeches on Europe over three months, a considerable feat of organisation. '*Are You Ready?*' had, in the end, gone to an initial audience of 340,000 and, in total 615,000 copies had been distributed. 75% of the applications for it had been by coupon request arising from the national Press advertisements. Peak demand, stimulated by a period of TV advertising, had run at up to 40,000 a week. The remaining 25% had come from business and industry. The rate of public enquiries about the Community received by the DTI EEC information unit had risen from an average of 150 a week before the campaign to 500 a week at its December peak. The media had responded well to the Government's appeal to them to step up their own coverage. In particular, the general campaign theme of 'Are we ready for Europe?' had been carried in the Press with, for example, a special supplement in the *Financial Times*, TV and Radio programmes and a centre-page spread in *The Sun*. There had been no Parliamentary or Press criticism of the Government campaign and only one letter of criticism from the public. There had, on the other hand, been "a respectable volume of letters of commendation" from industrialists, trade associations, lawyers, journalists, librarians and others.[158]

All of this effort derived from a very clear sense, emanating from Heath himself, that a change of mindset and engagement would be required by Ministers and officials in order to get to grips with the reality of membership.

Following the Paris Summit, Heath sent a minute to all members of Cabinet on 9 November enjoining them "to extend within the British Government familiarity with the techniques which the Community has developed for doing its business. Those techniques are by now second nature to those who conducted the negotiations for entry; for the next stage others will need to learn them". Each Department would have to modify its own organisation. Following the Paris Summit "it is not too soon for us to be defining our objectives, seeing how they will relate to the objectives of our partners, working out how our objectives can be met in the complex bargaining situations in which we shall certainly find ourselves . . . I ask all my colleagues that they and their Departments should give their full support to the considerable expenditure of time and effort that this will require".[159]

When, in mid-December, the Transport Minister, John Peyton, brought to Cabinet the danger that, early in the new year, the Community would try to force through a decision on the weights and dimensions of commercial vehicles which would be damaging for Britain, the Prime Minister used it as a further opportunity to urge Ministers to ensure that their Departments were in close touch with developments in Brussels in these last days before British accession. The Government must be ready to take prompt decisions when necessary and efficient interdepartmental coordination would be particularly important.[160]

On 1 January 1973, Britain formally entered the European Community. "I saw this", Heath wrote years later, "as a wonderful new beginning and a tremendous opportunity for the British people".[161] But, in December, the Chancellor of the Exchequer had had to tell Heath that Britain would have to continue to float the pound beyond the January date of her accession. Even if Britain did return to a fixed parity, she could not take the risk of rejoining the 'snake'.[162] Britain's first year in the European Community was to prove even more challenging than anyone then foresaw.

* * * *

9 The year of living dangerously: Britain's first year of European community membership: 1973–1974

As Sir Laurence Olivier, Judi Dench, Tito Gobbi, Kiri te Kanawa and other stars strutted their stuff at Covent Garden on 3 January 1973, celebrating what Heath called "an appropriately high-spirited and good-natured introduction to Britain in Europe", few could have foreseen the travails that lay ahead. A year which started in bright lights was to end in fuel-starved, strike-ridden, three-day-week candle light in Britain and in ill-tempered tensions within Europe and between Europe and the United States.

The transatlantic year began with President Nixon in a benign mood towards the United Kingdom. The Heath Government had not joined with some of its future partners in condemning the United States for its resumption of bombing in North Vietnam. Nixon, reported to be 'coldly furious', had threatened to cancel his planned tour of Europe. As to those who had criticised the United States, and they included Germany and France, Nixon had given instructions to Kissinger that their Ambassadors in Washington were henceforth to be received only at desk level within the State Department. Paris could forget about hosting the international conference to ratify a settlement in Vietnam.

Britain, so Kissinger told Britain's Ambassador, Lord Cromer, on 16 January, was the exception and Nixon's gratitude to Heath was proportionately great. Even Cromer had been surprised by the intensity of Nixon's rage but the British exception would, whatever the wider complications, help the atmosphere for Heath's forthcoming visit to Washington.[1]

Heath, who was in Washington at the end of January, was the first foreign leader to visit Nixon since the President's re-election. Considerable though the respect was between the two men, and warm as Nixon's hospitality was at a wintry Camp David, Heath found it necessary to counter some entrenched American myths, notably that in defence the Americans were expected by Europe to do too much while in trade and commerce they were granted too little. He urged the Administration to be liberal and far-sighted.

Nixon's principal preoccupation was with the defence implications of the Soviet Union's achievement of nuclear parity with the United States. He was, he said, looking for a new conception of European defence and a complete rethinking of NATO strategy. He wanted to recreate the wartime habit of intimate and deep discussions in a relaxed atmosphere. Heath responded politely but suggested that the US Administration should consider bringing other European Governments into the circle. Nixon agreed to consider the point.[2]

Back home, Britain's first exposure as a member to the European Community's working methods produced a characteristic British response. Douglas-Home used his first appearance at the Council of Ministers in January to make a speech about the need for the Council to reform its procedures and to deal more with policy questions. Schumann contradicted him.

Heath told Monnet at about the same time that he hoped the Council of Ministers would get away from its "terrible habit" of sitting late into the night and that it would focus on major questions of policy and less on minor details of regulations. It took Michael Palliser, Britain's Permanent Representative to the EEC in Brussels, to educate Heath as to the reality. Many of the Foreign Ministers in the Council of Ministers felt that specialist Ministers (Agriculture, Finance and Transport notably) were developing their own closed clubs and that the Foreign Ministers should therefore consider matters in great detail so as to keep an eye on what was going on. In any event, the Council was both legislature and executive: it was not only formulating policy but also making law. It was therefore doing much of the work which in the British system was done by Parliament, as well as the work done by Cabinet; hence its concentration on detail and its long-drawn-out sittings.[3]

A week later, Christopher Soames told Heath that, three weeks into his time as the senior British Commissioner in Brussels, he had been much impressed by the dominance of agriculture in the affairs of the Commission. In Soames's opinion, this was going to have to be changed.[4] In Cabinet the next day, the Chancellor of the Duchy of Lancaster, John Davies, bemoaned the tendency of the Agriculture Council, which had just met, to show too great a readiness to accept higher prices. Foreign Ministers would have to intervene.[5]

Two weeks later, Cabinet directed its dismay towards the recent meeting of Community Finance Ministers, which had "provided further evidence of the organisational weakness of Council meetings". It was particularly regrettable that Permanent Representatives (officials) should be allowed to substitute for Ministers when matters of political substance were being discussed.[6]

The Government's own presentation of European Community issues was not pitch perfect either. Under the heading 'Trouble amid the alien corn', the *Daily Mail*'s Parliamentary sketch writer, Andrew Alexander, wrote on 22 February that "once upon a time, farming was so straightforward. You watched the crops, prayed to some meteorological deity, stood around auction rings looking wary and prodding beasts. Outsiders could understand what it was about". Now, however, with the advent of the Common Agricultural Policy, had come a whole new range of mumbo jumbo. Mr Godber, the British Agriculture Minister, had provided a good example of it the previous day in trying to explain to the House of Commons the concept of 'monetary compensatory amounts'. What Alexander thought Godber had been trying to say was that there would be no increases in prices in Britain as a result of the latest currency developments.

Francis Pym, the Chief Whip, seized on this in a letter to Heath, agreeing with Andrew Alexander. "The language that it appears to be necessary to use in connection with European matters is not comprehensible to anyone who is not totally conversant with the subject". No criticism of Joe Godber was intended, Pym insisted. It was simply that hardly anyone in the House had understood what he meant.[7]

As a consequence of Pym's initiative, Heath sent a minute to all Ministers in charge of Departments on the subject of 'Euro-jargon', asking his colleagues to insist that any Ministerial statements were expressed in language that everyone could understand. It was, the Prime Minister said, "essential for the acceptance of our membership of the European Community that people generally should not feel that their lives are being affected by arcane European policies which they cannot understand".[8]

More serious issues quickly confronted the Government. The unilateral economic measures taken by the US Government in August 1971 had effectively destroyed the Bretton Woods post-war monetary system. It was against that background, and the pressing need for international monetary reform, that the EEC Heads of Government had agreed at their Paris Summit in October 1972 to press ahead with their own plans for Economic and Monetary Union.

On 12 February 1973, in the face of continuing speculative pressures, the US dollar was devalued. The immediate consequences had, so Governments believed, been managed; and sterling, being outside the European currency 'snake', was not in any case under immediate pressure. When a group of senior European Commissioners made an official visit to London in early March the central Cabinet preoccupation before their arrival was not the monetary situation but the siting of the proposed European Monetary Cooperation Fund, one of the features of Stage Two of EMU to which the Community was committed. In due course, the Fund seemed likely to become an institution of major importance. The British Government accordingly favoured siting it in Brussels, alongside the Commission. Others in the Community favoured Luxembourg and, that being so, Cabinet thought they might need to consider throwing the London hat into the ring.[9]

But when Heath visited Bonn at the start of March, the monetary situation had become more critical.

Just before Heath's visit, Willy Brandt had given an interview to the Editor and Deputy Editor of *The Times* (William Rees-Mogg and Louis Heren). In an editorial following the interview, the paper described Brandt as "the only European statesman who has a substantial appeal outside his own country" and thought it "almost inconceivable that he would not be elected as President of Europe against any competitor". To meet Herr Brandt, said the editorial, revived one's faith in the ability of political leadership to combine idealism with common sense. Brandt's success owed most to his determined pursuit of humane and moderate ideas, ideas which, when expressed in power, had proved to be remarkably in tune with the feelings of a modern European nation.[10]

By the time Heath arrived in Bonn, Brandt, the '*Man for All Europe*' as *The Times* had called him, was facing a currency crisis of very big proportions. The subject dominated the discussions between the Chancellor and Heath and the two men came close to agreeing to a great leap forward towards economic and monetary union.

When the two men met in the late afternoon of 1 March, Brandt warned Heath that he would have to break off to go an address the Finance Committee of the Bundestag. Germany had taken in $2.7 billion during the day, an unusually high amount. Brandt had expected the settlement reached three weeks earlier, when the dollar had devalued and the yen had floated, to last for six to eight months. It had in fact lasted three weeks. The Germans were now in the front line and the French, not least with an election approaching, were in baulk. Both men envisaged the need for the Nine to meet in Brussels, with consultations between France, Britain and Germany beforehand. Both men were prepared to take radical action provided it was part of a European decision and taken in the context of a Community policy.

At dinner at Schloss Gymnich later that evening, Heath departed from the prepared text of his speech to say that there were times when political leaders had to take big decisions, on a political basis. Before very long, the Community would be faced with the sort of situation with which free Europe had been faced in June 1940, when Churchill had offered the French common citizenship with the British. There came a time when political leaders had to take great decisions and make a great leap and Europe was near, if not at, that point in relation to their monetary affairs.

After dinner, Heath and Brandt resumed their discussion, with Karl Otto Poehl, then a senior adviser in the German Economics Ministry, and Derek Mitchell, a senior Treasury official, also present. Mitchell said he had been heartened by what the Prime Minister had said over dinner but the money markets (which had been closed) could not stay that way forever. Decisions would have to be taken about methods of intervention and settlement, of support for weak currencies (sterling and the lira, notably), for the pooling of reserves and for the acceleration of other aspects of economic and monetary union.

Poehl followed this with a statement for which he appeared to have authority. After ruling out other courses of action, Poehl said that Germany was in favour of a Community float. If Britain participated, there was likely to be a move out of sterling which could be of the order of six thousand million dollars. If Germany committed herself to supporting Britain, the problem would be eased. If a decision was taken not to go ahead with a common float then the prospect of EMU would be postponed for a long time. Of course, a joint Community float would be only a first step. The next step would be the harmonisation within the Community of monetary policy, interest rate policy and perhaps even fiscal policy. The main question was whether the Community was ready to take such a step.

The Chancellor and Prime Minister held a further, unscheduled, meeting the following morning where they again went over the ground. Mitchell spoke positively of the technicalities of a joint float. The German Finance Minister, Helmut Schmidt, indicated at one point a total lack of conditionality in terms of the support to back up such a float. Heath recapitulated the four options which had been discussed (for the Germans to defend the existing dollar parity; for the Germans to float the DM; for the members of the Community, other than Britain and Italy, to go into a joint float, on the basis that Britain and Italy would come in when they could; a joint float). He had earlier said that this last alternative was the one which would be a major step forward, including the pooling of reserves which would have to go with it.

No conclusion was reached, though there was a discussion of modalities in which Poehl agreed with Mitchell's comment that the Brussels machinery could not run the operation. Poehl thought it would have to be run under the aegis of the European Monetary Cooperation Fund, which would mean that it would be run by the central bankers.[11]

In a minute to Heath during the course of the talks Mitchell had asked the question: "Is any EEC member ready for this in political terms? Do we have the Community institutions to support the massive transfer of sovereignty that is implied? We have hitherto regarded 1980 as an optimistic deadline".[12]

The matter did not end there. On 4 March, the Chancellor of the Exchequer put a series of propositions to his EEC colleagues at a meeting in Brussels. He proposed that for a common float to be practicable and enduring, first, the starting pattern of central rates must be acceptable to each Member State in terms of its immediate economic problems; second, that each member must have an unimpaired right to change its central rate after consultation with the Council of Ministers; third, that all must be prepared to grant support without limits of amount, without conditions, and without obligation to repay or to guarantee; fourth, some, at least, of the support should be interest-free; fifth, the pattern of exchange rates established in connection with a joint scheme should not lead to an immediate increase in food prices for the United Kingdom, and any necessary increase should be spread over a long period.[13]

But the British Government's initiative did not prosper. Monnet, writing to Heath on 7 March, urged that "France, Germany and Great Britain show to themselves and to the world that they are determined to, and can, solve their main problems together within the Community. You may think the proposal Mr Barber put forward meets this essential criteria . . . I think some of the terms and conditions put forward could usefully be reviewed, and correct the impression of 'take it or leave it' which has been created".[14]

Heath replied on 19 March: "For a time I thought that the events of the beginning of this month might provide the opportunity for the major step forward in Community cooperation of the kind we discussed when you came to Chequers. I believe that these events have shown that none of us in the Community is fit enough by ourselves to withstand the pressures of the enormous short-term capital movements which are now experienced, and which reflect the lack of a stable international reserve asset; and that we shall not succeed in re-establishing a lasting stability until we are able to agree upon cooperation and mutual defence of a far-reaching kind and on a very large scale".

It was that idea which the British Government had had in mind in the proposals which Barber had put forward. "I am sorry", Heath continued, "that they created a 'take it or leave it' impression, because we were and are ready to review them with our partners. But it became clear at the meeting in Brussels, and in other contacts, that most of our partners were not yet ready for anything so far-reaching;

and of course these matters have to be discussed against the need for a quick decision that will enable markets to be reopened. Alas, this has not proved to be the moment for the major step forward . . ."[15]

It is hard to say how close Britain and Germany truly came to launching the Community on the fast road to EMU. In the cold light of day, Helmut Schmidt, the German Finance Minister, was one of those in Bonn who had understandable reservations about the extent of the German economic and financial commitment that would have been involved. What is incontrovertible is that never again has a British Prime Minister come anywhere near the audacity in European matters which inspired Heath in that powerful speech in Germany in March nearly three decades before the single currency became a reality.

Heath had assured Monnet that the British Government had set work in hand "so that we are not caught unprepared if and when the opportunity recurs". Sir John Hunt was directing Cabinet Office work on EEC issues prior to taking over from Sir Burke Trend as Cabinet Secretary later in the year. Hunt minuted Heath on 14 March, advising him that the European Commission were due, by 1 May, to make proposals for the second stage of EMU. The Paris Summit had agreed that the second stage should begin on 1 January 1974. Full EMU, Hunt wrote, "is an essential element in complete political union in the Community and, achieved in the right way, would bring all the economic benefits that are expected to flow from completely free movement of goods, services, labour and capital within the Community. But the road is dangerous and, in particular, we have to avoid intra-Community exchange rates being irrevocably locked before the necessary preconditions exist. Full EMU would deprive member countries of many of the policy instruments used to influence their economic performances and to rectify imbalances between them. Thus, either economic performances (growth rates, rates of increase of wages, productivity etc.) must converge to a much greater extent than hitherto or central provision must be made for imbalances to be offset by massive and speedy resource transfers. Failing this, equilibrium could only be restored by inflation in the high performance counties and unemployment and stagnation in the low performance countries. We need therefore a package of second stage measures . . . with as much emphasis on promoting economic convergence as monetary integration; and which will not place undue restraints on our freedom of economic manoeuvre over the next two or three years . . . Full EMU has very big implications, not least over the transfer of economic and political responsibilities from member countries to the Community . . . But the choice is between supra-national economic and monetary policy with pooled reserves and coordinated economic and regional policies, or the continuation of a customs union only. We are committed to the former and it is much in our interests to achieve it. What is at issue is the rate at which we move towards it . . .".[16]

Hunt's description both of the ambition and the obstacles omitted one vital factor: Britain was outside the European currency snake, with no early prospect of re-joining. On 21 March, the Paris Embassy reported that Christopher Soames, in his capacity as the European Commissioner responsible for international trade issues, had called on Pompidou and had been told in no uncertain terms that

Britain must fix her parity. There was, the Embassy argued, an element of tactics in this. Pompidou must have foreseen the line Soames was likely to take on the multilateral trade negotiations, for which the French had no great enthusiasm. What better way to take the wind out of Soames's sails than to attack him on the British position in Europe, for which Soames had no responsibility but on which Pompidou would guess that Soames would be particularly sensitive? Given Soames's earlier involvement in the series of commitments and undertakings about sterling, dating back to the Prime Minister's visit to Paris in May 1971, Pompidou would also have calculated that Soames would be particularly strong in his advocacy in London for a return to a fixed parity.

This element of tactics did not mean, however, that Pompidou was not genuinely preoccupied by the issue. Pompidou, according to the Embassy, no longer thought that things were going the way he thought he had agreed with Heath. In particular, British membership of the Community appeared to be holding up the progress towards economic and monetary union that Pompidou wanted. The next step, the Embassy advised, was to clear up the misunderstanding by direct contact with the Elysée.[17]

The Embassy had advised that the Prime Minister should not make himself *demandeur* for a meeting with the President but John Hunt thought otherwise, telling Armstrong, who passed the advice to Heath, that the British Government were being 'sticky' on so many issues (re-fixing the parity, the siting of the European Monetary Cooperation Fund, steel prices) that it was imperative for Heath to meet Pompidou at an early date in order to re-establish the Prime Minister's European credentials with him, as well as the relationship of personal trust which had been built up.

Armstrong also advised Heath that he could play such a meeting to tactical advantage. Palliser had told him that the currency turmoil had made the CAP almost unworkable. This in turn gave Heath a bargaining card: Britain could abandon her float and re-fix with the Community provided she had a guarantee of very considerable monetary support and of the implementation of a Community Regional policy.[18]

Christopher Soames dined with Heath at Chequers on 25 March and reinforced the message about the forthright nature of Pompidou's disappointment in Britain. The President recognised that no commitments had been given about the timing of re-fixing, but there had been indications that Britain would re-fix, first by 1 January 1973 and then by 1 April. But now there was no date in sight and no prospect of any progress on other Community policies of interest to Britain so long as Britain was outside the monetary arrangement. In general Soames, like Hunt, thought that the British Government were giving the impression in Brussels of hanging back and behaving in a non-*Communautaire* fashion. Of course, Soames said, the Government should not give away essential national interests but they should have in mind "the wider significance for our relationships with the Community of the positions which we took up on individual matters".[19]

A further reason for getting back on side with Pompidou was that he had won the March legislative elections in France with 54% of the vote for the parties of the right against 46% for those of the left. His position as President, able to command a clear majority in the National Assembly, was secure. Pompidou had taken a gamble, beginning in February when the French Government's political managers in desperation, having tried every expedient without success, had gambled on a massive Presidential intervention on French television as a last recourse. On 8 February, the President had told the French people that if, in 1973, the country changed the sense of the vote they had cast in 1969, the result would be crisis. Pompidou, in the view of the British Ambassador, Sir Edward Tomkins, had exchanged the role of *rassembleur de tous les français*, which had served de Gaulle so well, for the direct engagement of presidential prestige behind his Parliamentary majority. "Whether this decision was the right one, will only appear with the election results", Tomkins had concluded.[20] Now, while the Gaullist majority was reduced, it was large enough. The danger of cohabitation between a President of the Right and a Government of the Left, then thought to be insupportable, had been averted.

Other EEC countries were, as was the British Press, taking stock in early April of Britain's first 100 days as a member. Hunt, in a minute to Heath of 12 April, thought that much had gone well. Senior jobs in the Commission had been secured; post-Summit work was well in hand; the Whitehall machinery was working well. Other things had gone less well. Many of Britain's partners felt that her terms for re-joining the snake had been deliberately pitched unacceptably high; the anti-Marketeers remained unconverted and British industry had "yet to show convincing signs" of readiness to take advantage of the commercial advantages of membership. On other areas, Britain had been right on substance, for example on CAP prices, but the issue had been made to look like an Anglo-French confrontation, creating a sense of brashness on which leading British journalists had commented.

Hunt then highlighted something for which Whitehall had perhaps not been psychologically prepared. "We shall", he said, "need to work very hard to obtain support for our views and, above all, to avoid being in a minority of one. The truth is that we are in a perpetual state of negotiation with our partners, and presentation is an integral part of getting what we want".

Hunt went on to criticise the Foreign Office for getting their role wrong. They felt that they ought to have a coordinating role (which properly belonged to the Cabinet Office) and were all too ready to argue about the merits of the policies of Home Departments. What the Foreign Office should be doing, Hunt argued, was advising Whitehall on the negotiability and impact of proposed policies and then, when the policy had been decided, assisting with its presentation and with lobbying on its behalf. "I should like", Hunt wrote, "if the Prime Minister agrees, to encourage the FO to concentrate more on the negotiability of our policies in the Community and on the marshalling of support for them and rather less on marking the cards of Home Departments". Heath did agree, though the issue has never been completely resolved.[21]

In a related minute, which Heath described as "very perceptive", Tom Bridges, his Foreign Office Private Secretary, wrote: "The effect of our policy has been to dissipate a lot of the good will we had with our Community partners on 1 January to no productive result. What is needed is a more deliberate strategy on the approach to the key issues . . . It would help to get the right results if the senior Ministers concerned could establish the key decisions on the central subjects which will fall over the next year or so, the partners who will require persuasion on particular issues, the bargaining counters to use, and a timetable . . . I have the feeling that we are conducting our affairs too much on a continuous tactical level, and not sufficiently in the higher strategic one".[22]

The practical product of this collective angst was Heath's tried and trusted remedy: a visit by Armstrong to Paris on 10/11 April. Armstrong lunched with Jean Monnet who urged that Heath, together with Brandt and Pompidou, should seize the fact that there was a period of about eighteen months to two years without the need for further elections in the three countries to make decisive progress within the Community. Armstrong assured him that Heath had this clearly in mind.

Together with the British Ambassador, Armstrong also went to see Jobert who, following the elections, had been promoted to be French Foreign Minister. Armstrong broached the idea of a further meeting between Heath and Pompidou. Heath knew, Armstrong told Jobert, the importance which Pompidou attached to Britain joining the snake. Heath could explain to Pompidou why his hopes that Britain should have joined before now had been disappointed, as well as the Government's firm purpose of joining in the next few months. It was a matter of confidence and of credibility. There was no point in re-joining the snake at a time when doing so would not be credible and when sterling might be forced out again in short order. But the situation in Britain had become somewhat easier with the decision of the coal miners not to strike and the settlement of most of the outstanding disputes over the implementation of the Government's counter-inflation programme. Much would depend on the nature of the Community arrangements in place at a time, within the next few months, when Britain could come back into the snake. Britain had proposed discussions at technical level with the Germans on issues such as mutual support arrangements, and would like to have similar discussions with the French Government.

As to the sterling balances, Armstrong continued, it remained the British wish to see an orderly and progressive rundown. But the situation had fundamentally changed since the President and Prime Minister had discussed the issue in May 1971. The holders of sterling were not now particularly likely to wish to move into dollars; and it was unlikely that Britain's European partners would be keen to take them on instead. The existing sterling agreements were due to expire in September 1973 and their future should be considered against the background of the Community's own arrangements.

Jobert said that Pompidou understood the British difficulties very well. But it remained his feeling that Britain could not be a full Community partner until she was participating in the Community's monetary arrangements. After his meeting with Soames, Pompidou had said only one sentence to Jobert, to the effect that he had told Soames that there could be no progress on multilateral commercial negotiations while Britain was outside the snake. Jobert hastened to add that the President's point was one of principle, not opportunism.[23]

It was agreed that a visit 'genre Chequers' (which Jobert said had become a new term of art in French diplomatic terminology) should take place, albeit in Paris. When the visit was announced at the beginning of May, the French Press reported it prominently but with somewhat downbeat comments to the effect that the Heath-Pompidou honeymoon was over and that British suspicions of the European Community were once again in evidence.[24]

Commenting on the French scene ahead of the visit, Tomkins described Pompidou's situation as one of "present strength and future uncertainty". The elections in France had scarcely focussed on foreign policy at all. There was little feeling in France against forward movement in Europe. The French people had fewer inhibitions than their Government on that score, but they were indifferent. Europe tended to bore them. They did, however, attach importance to French pre-eminence, prestige and independence.

Translated into French behaviour in Europe, the Embassy believed this would mean that Pompidou would not risk initiatives that could go wrong for him. There would be no leap of faith. Pompidou saw clearly that France's future could be assured only through Europe. But it would be a Europe *à la française* and he would judge British intentions by his own. In sum, Britain would be left with the policies and philosophy she already knew – those of the Auvergnat, down to earth and vigilant in the interest of his territory, cultivating his own garden, calculating in the present, cautious about investing in the future.[25]

If a return by Britain to a fixed parity was the key to renewed confidence between Heath and Pompidou, then the portents on the British side were not wholly positive. On 10 April, Armstrong told Heath that the latest paper from the Chancellor of the Exchequer on the conditions that would be necessary for Britain to join a Community float showed "signs of being a product of unregenerate minds in the Treasury". It would, Armstrong thought, be a little disturbing if the paper provided the basis for talks with the French and the Germans.[26]

Similar doubts were expressed to Palliser by Ortoli, the President of the Commission. He was delighted that Heath and Pompidou were to meet. It was obvious that the future of the Community lay in the hands of Heath, Brandt and Pompidou. But it was difficult, if not impossible, for the three of them to meet since this would raise hackles among the other members. Accordingly, there needed to be a regular pattern of bilateral meetings involving the three leaders. This was particularly necessary at present. The key to the Heath-Pompidou meeting was still the monetary problem. Ortoli had never been in any doubt of the sincerity of Heath's intentions. But he had equally never believed in the sincerity of the British Treasury, where he was convinced that the senior establishment was against re-joining the snake. In consequence, the presentation of the British proposals to the Finance Council had not been successful and had not carried conviction. Since the scepticism about re-joining the snake felt by British officials was fully shared, though for a variety of quite different reasons, by their opposite numbers in Bonn and Paris, this had enabled Treasury officials to ensure that the response to their own proposals was such as to make their rejection inevitable.

Ortoli went on to say that he knew that Brandt had responded positively to Heath during the latter's visit to Bonn; and that Schmidt too had been initially well disposed. But Brandt had subsequently spoken with less authority and resolution to his own people than he had to Heath; and once the experts had been given their head, neither Brandt nor Schmidt had been prepared to fight the battle – more particularly since the German experts had been able to call in aid the alleged lack of conviction with which the British proposition had been put to the Council.

Ortoli said that his doubts about attitudes in Paris did not relate to Pompidou himself but, rather, to Giscard d'Estaing. Giscard's Finance Ministry officials were in no hurry to see the pound back in the snake, not least because they were also in no hurry to see further rapid progress on Economic and Monetary Union, or indeed on those broader aspects of it, such as the regional policy, to which Britain attached importance. And the same was true, Ortoli added, of many German officials too. Nonetheless, Ortoli found Giscard's own attitude something of an enigma. This was unfortunate since Giscard was a man of much influence. Nonetheless, Ortoli continued to believe that the key lay with Pompidou himself.[27]

That the Chancellor of the Exchequer himself harboured significant reservations about joining a Community float (which was now the situation of the currencies within the snake) was evident from a minute he sent to Heath on 14 May, covering official Treasury briefing for the Prime Minister's visit to Paris. "While recognising that there are wider considerations", Barber wrote, "I feel strongly that we should not join until we are confident that it will not prejudice our domestic economic policy and that the amount and conditions of the support arrangements are such as to be an effective deterrent against a speculative attack which might otherwise follow our parity being fixed in relation to the other members of the EEC. We must not find ourselves loaded with debt as a result of our joining . . . I therefore hope that you will be able to avoid mentioning any time for joining . . . I am sure that it will in due course pay us if, at this stage in our private discussions with the Community, we adopt a fairly tough posture".[28]

Heath was hardly in a position to contradict his Chancellor. But the situation for him, on the eve of his visit to Paris, was a tricky one. From Paris, the British Embassy felt it necessary to send a paper called '*Living with the French*', clearly prompted by the feeling that recidivist tendencies were not confined to the French side of the Channel. "In most cases", the Embassy advised, "we shall make faster progress by trying to persuade them to work with us than by trying to work against them . . . This means above all making a conscious effort to promote regular bilateral discussion and explanation of where we stand on the important issues. If we want to carry them with us, we must be prepared to be franker with them that we have been in the past. We should eschew the temptation not to take the trouble of talking to them on particular issues simply because our views are too far apart . . . We should not exclude the use of forcing tactics on carefully chosen issues where we have the power and the intention to carry them to their conclusion. But we should avoid using such tactics as a means of softening up the French. This rarely succeeds and creates an impression of hostility in their minds which increases their mistrust and makes them more difficult on other issues . . ."[29]

With the best will, these precepts were not going to be easy to follow on the occasion of Heath's visit. In separate advice, the Embassy summarised Pompidou's position as being one of looking to Heath for reassurance that:

"We shall rejoin the snake soon;

We are not trying to undermine the CAP;

We share his priorities on the development of the Community – with the first emphasis on money and inhibitions about supra-nationality;

We share his concept of defending the European personality against the Americans."

This litany found its mirror image in the areas of difficulty for Britain as the Embassy saw them:

"The problem of giving him [Pompidou] a precise enough indication of our intentions about sterling;

The proposed review of the CAP, about which he will be defensive;

The idea that we share with the rest of the Community, except the French, that Europe needs to define its relationship with the United States as a matter of political consultation and should work out a common position for meeting Nixon and a common response to the Kissinger speech;

The political need to show willing with the Americans over the trade negotiations. He will want to stand pat and put the monetary problem first."

After this depressing catalogue, Tomkins' telegram ended with phrases written by Christopher Ewart-Biggs, the number two in the Embassy and, since Soames's departure, the undisputed mind and motor of the Paris Embassy. "There are", the telegram concluded, "certain advantages on our side. Pompidou needs us. He knows that France must make her future through the Community and he cannot afford to let it break up. The heart of it is triangular but for him the two sides are not equal. He is more worried about the Germans than about us: in one case it is fear and in the other merely disappointment".[30]

The Embassy had referred to 'the Kissinger speech'. Nixon, within months of his successful re-election, was in trouble. The Watergate scandal had begun. Heath wisely fended off Cromer's advice to send a written message of support, telling Cromer that, on Kissinger's recent visit to London, he had "told him in private that . . . I would like him [the President] to know that he had all my sympathy in his present problems, and we were confident he would find a way out". "I gather", Heath added, "that Harold Macmillan has sent a rather similar message, through Annenberg [the US Ambassador in London] recalling his experiences in the Profumo Affair".[31] Given that the Profumo Affair had directly contributed to terminating Macmillan's premiership, the analogy may not have struck Nixon as being as helpful as it was (presumably) intended to be. In any case, only three days later, Denis Greenhill, whose judgement Heath respected, wrote to Bridges: "I think the Prime Minister would be interested to know that the unanimous view of the American participants in the Bilderberg Conference was that eventually President Nixon would be compelled to resign. They maintained that the cumulative evidence, working on Mr Nixon's temperament, would in the end bring about a resignation. As you know, all this contrasts sharply with what Dr Kissinger was saying".[32]

Kissinger's visit to London, a week before Heath's own visit to Paris, had been preceded, on 23 April, by a speech at the annual lunch in New York of the Associated Press, a speech which, as Burke Trend told the Prime Minister a few days later "was intended to be a major statement of US policy. It was devoted to the importance of reaffirming and reconstituting the Atlantic Alliance in 'the Year of Europe', and in its nature and scope it was clearly designed as a challenge to Europe (and ultimately Japan) i.e. a challenge 'whether a unity forged by a common perception of danger can draw new purpose from shared positive aspirations . . . to lay the basis of a new era of creativity in the West . . . to deal with Atlantic problems comprehensively . . . We can no longer afford to pursue national or regional self-interest without a unifying framework'." The speech had concluded by emphasising the necessity to articulate a clear set of common objectives (the concept of 'one ball of wax') which should be formulated in a new Atlantic Charter to be worked out by the time of President Nixon's visit to Europe towards the end of the year.

Trend's initial reaction to Kissinger's speech was sceptical but, now that it had been launched, he advised Heath against rebuffing it since to do so would foster the isolationist tendencies in America which Nixon's Administration was genuinely trying to resist. At the same time, in view of Britain's obligations to her EEC partners, it would be unwise, Trend believed, for Britain to offer to take the initiative in organising a specifically European action to promote the purposes outlined in Kissinger's speech. The US Government should be responsible for the follow-up "for at least the next round or two". In any event, in the light of Brandt's recent visit to Washington, of the imminent visit there by Jobert, and of work within the Community on the speech, which was already in hand in preparation for a meeting of EEC Foreign Ministers on 5 June, it should be made clear to Dr Kissinger that it must be up to the US to ascertain for themselves the probable reactions of Germany and France to the propositions he had made in his speech. Britain should, however, offer her full support in pursuing those purposes "by whatever means are shown to be the most realistic as a result of further testing of European opinion by the United States and of our own discussions with our European partners". "This", Heath commented, "seems to be the right approach".[33]

When Kissinger visited London on 10 May, he told Trend and Greenhill that the sole motivation behind his speech was the conviction that, although it might not be easily perceptible, there was a profound crisis in the West which would lead, unless real and positive steps were taken to combat it, to a steady erosion of the capital at present shared between the United States and Western Europe. He believed that if the US and the UK could agree on a course of action, Germany would support them.

Trend and Greenhill were not quite as non-committal in their meeting with Kissinger as Trend's earlier minute to Heath had suggested. The United Kingdom, they said, fully accepted Kissinger's analysis of the situation in which the West found itself and agreed that urgent steps should be taken to consolidate the transatlantic relationship. The problem lay in the considerable difficulty there would be in persuading other members of the EEC and NATO of this view. A very careful approach was essential. They suggested that the US Government should come up with some proposals, perhaps after preliminary discussion with the UK, France and Germany. If practical proposals could be tabled, it might be possible to avoid a continuing round of unproductive and multilateral talks.[34]

The 'Year of Europe', which was to prove one of the most ill-conceived of American initiatives and one that provoked the greatest ill-temper on both sides of the Atlantic, was to be one of the main topics of discussion when Heath and Pompidou met. Questions over Nixon's political health were matched by questions over Pompidou's real state of health. On the eve of Heath's visit, the Paris Embassy reported that there had been a renewal of speculation about Pompidou's health, the undoubted visual evidence being "that his face and neck have become swollen over the past four or five months, his colour is high and he has put on weight. There are two unsubstantiated reports that he may be undergoing cobalt treatment for cancer. We understand that his appearance would be medically consistent with a tumour and the accumulation of fluid in the body resulting from it. But the evidence is not at all strong and we were previously told in confidence by the head of SDECE, (one of the French intelligence agencies) who is close to Pompidou, that his appearance was the result of cortisone treatment for rheumatism. The most that can be said therefore at the moment is that there is a distinct question mark over his health".[35]

Christopher Ewart-Biggs, who was never in doubt that Pompidou was other than gravely ill, penned a note for the Prime Minister's attention on his arrival in Paris. A senior journalist from *Paris Match* had dined with the Ewart-Biggs having lunched with Pompidou earlier on the same day. When Tournoux had asked Pompidou what he thought of the Watergate affair, the President had replied: "We all have our difficulties. As for me, I am going to die". Tournoux had taken this to be a bantering remark about the reports in the Press. But, all the same he had found it amazing.[36]

Over two days, on 21 and 22 May, Heath and Pompidou held more than nine hours of talks, with only Palliser and Andronikov present to interpret and, in Palliser's case at least, to produce a detailed record of what had transpired.

The records of the two days of discussions in Paris bear out the Embassy's subsequent description of them as more explanation than negotiation. Heath reaffirmed his acceptance of the CAP, which the British Government would continue to support. But British public opinion was critical, most recently of the fact that, while they were paying a higher price for butter than before accession, butter surpluses were being sold off cheaply to Russian communists. The British people tended to think that their own housewives were more deserving than Russian housewives. Pompidou reiterated his attachment to Community Preference and went on to make what he called a "very French point" about the importance of preserving the countryside and its way of life. It was the small farmer who kept the countryside going. France was not a heavily populated country. She needed to maintain a certain degree of agricultural life and to avoid a system of great estates on the Latin American pattern. That was not the European vocation. Moreover, the small farmer formed part of a politically sensible and moderate social class and it was in the national interest that this class should be kept alive. It must, he believed, be possible to find formulae for achieving this other than straightforward price mechanisms. He agreed that the sale of cheap butter to Russia was an absurd anomaly. One had to remember that the company in France that handled this sale was a communist one. Pompidou added that his concept of the CAP formed part of the French philosophy. The French did not believe that the future lay in the development of giant concerns, whether in towns or in trading or in agriculture. They believed that there would be an increasing need to come back to a more modest rhythm. He intended to say to President Nixon that if there were a transfer of 6–7% of the French population from the country to the towns, the Americans could confidently anticipate the establishment of a Socialist/Communist Government in France.[37]

When the two men turned to monetary matters, Heath explained that the floating of the pound in June 1972 had resulted from sterling being pushed off its parity by largely unjustified external speculation. At the same time, there had been anxiety about the British economy and about industrial unrest and therefore about the prospects for the balance of payments. Between the end of 1964 and 1970 Britain had had the bitter experience of seeing the determined efforts made for four years (1965 to 1968) to defend the sterling parity, as well as the resultant indebtedness, amounting to nearly £4 billion, incurred in ensuring that defence. This had been a millstone and the Government had accordingly decided to let the pound float and to protect the reserves. Since then, the Government had developed a prices and incomes policy on a statutory basis, in which the trades unions had now acquiesced. The British economy was growing at an annual rate of 5%. Investment was growing apace. By the beginning of the next Financial Year there should be a reduction of £235 million in Government expenditure. He therefore considered that the economic position of the country was improving. But Britain must expect a balance of payments deficit in the current year. He wished to return to the Community monetary system. He strongly supported it and regarded it as the basis of Community life. He believed the measures the Government had taken would give the confidence necessary to prevent speculators from trying to push sterling off the selected parity. But he had to choose the right moment.

Pompidou said that, if he tried to put himself in the Prime Minister's shoes, he felt that Heath had chosen the best way of dealing with the problem. He could have tried, by very drastic measures, to hold the parity and to stay in the snake. But to have done so would have condemned Britain to economic paralysis. He had instead played a dynamic card. Heath had no doubt been told that he (Pompidou) would urge him to return to the snake and to a fixed parity. Naturally, he would like this to happen, in the interests of the Community as a whole and of the future of Economic and Monetary Union. But he accepted that the Prime Minister needed first to put his house in order. So, contrary to what the Prime Minister had no doubt been told, he was not so insistent on a return by the pound to a fixed parity. It was first necessary that the dollar problem should be settled.

Until it was, there would always be a currency somewhere under attack. This sometimes produced absurd situations: France was at the top of the snake ("what strange terminology we all employ these days") while the DM was at the bottom. Yet Germany's exports of engineering and capital goods were much higher than those of France and in reality it should be the DM that was high and the Franc low. This showed the extent of the real psychological problem involved in all this speculation.[38]

On the prospective Regional Development Fund, Heath and Pompidou edged towards an understanding. For Heath, "this was of major importance . . . and comparable to the importance for France of the CAP . . . If the Community was to avoid monetary difficulties between the member countries there must be a balanced economy throughout the whole Community". Otherwise, Heath argued, distortions and stresses of various kinds within industry and in agriculture would threaten monetary union.

Pompidou was sceptical. Britain had, in George Thomson, chosen their Commissioner well. He was clearly determined to make France and Germany pay out large sums of money at any cost. Naturally, he (Pompidou) and the Prime Minister could agree that Germany should pay for everyone. But it remained to be seen whether the Germans would agree.

Heath replied to the effect that, for Britain, securing the Regional Fund was the *quid pro quo* for her acceptance of the CAP. In that case, Pompidou said, clearly a solution would have to be found. It could lie in the pace and staging of progress. He would be content if progress were to be made at a reasonable rate. But if the British objective was to start with a huge fund paying benefits simply to Britain and Italy, this would be very difficult for the French Government to accept; nor did he think that they would be alone in taking that view.[39]

Because of the existence of Palliser's detailed accounts, Tomkins waited until 1 June before recording in a Despatch "if only for the history books" his impressions of the Prime Minister's visit. The first importance of the visit, Tomkins believed, was that it helped to establish a pattern. The multilateral negotiations of Brussels did not preclude the need for a web of confidence woven bilaterally among the leaders "and more particularly with the country which is at the same time the most difficult and the nearest and most necessary of our partners". Franco-German relations tended to be cyclical: they moved apart to a point from which they were rescued each time by Pompidou and Brandt at their bi-annual meetings. Each of the Prime Minister's meetings had, similarly, followed a difficult period with the French and had in turn been followed by a better one – though not of indefinite duration. The latest meeting had come at a time when Europe seemed to be losing impetus. The French were professing to believe that Britain's exigencies as a new member of the Community threatened both its structure and its development. On the British side the perception was that the French were making life unnecessarily difficult, often putting themselves in a minority of one in the process.

On the major issues, the meeting had not been, and had not been intended to be, either a negotiation or a confrontation. It was an explanation. "It seems", said

Tomkins, "to have started slowly, with Pompidou unresponsive and less than himself, but to have got much better. Both he and the Prime Minister were at the end well pleased with the way it had gone". Its significance was that it had dissipated much of the mistrust and misunderstanding of British motives with which they had been surrounded. Pompidou had shown more understanding of British positions than the build-up to the meeting had suggested. He did not press the Prime Minister unduly about the pound. He gave more priority to doing something about the dollar. He did not put up the shutters on regional policy or on the prospects of modifying the CAP without detriment to its basic structure – though "he obviously deployed his own arguments to support his wish to limit the extent of the first and to preserve the benefits that France derives from the second". He accepted the need to stick to the timetable of the GATT negotiation, while subordinating it to a return to international monetary order.

The Embassy saw in this something of tactics. It was Pompidou's normal practice to soften up his protagonists by putting out a harder line in advance of such meetings than he generally took at the meetings themselves. Pompidou also had his eye on a meeting later in the year with President Nixon. "There is" wrote Tomkins (or more precisely Ewart-Biggs in Tomkins' name) "a magnificent effrontery in the double claim to be the *interlocuteur privilégié* of Europe both with the Soviet Union and with the United States, in one case because France is the most forthcoming of the Nine and in the other because she is the least: to command the eastern campaign from the front and the western one from the rear".

None of that was to discount the real improvement wrought by the renewal of personal confidence. Pompidou had always put faith in the sincerity of the Prime Minister's European vocation. The meeting had improved the climate of understanding within which the two Governments would seek to work together. Things might slip back "but each time the Prime Minister meets Pompidou the French body bureaucratic receives an injection from the top against the virus of mistrust, and we may hope the effect is cumulative". It had also to be said that, on the French side, the visit had strengthened an *idée fixe* in the Elysée: that the Prime Minister was more 'European' than either his officials or his public opinion.

The French approach towards European construction would, in the Embassy's judgement, remain selective. But Pompidou's attitude also seemed consistent with some uncertainty about where he wanted to go. Doctrine was being eroded by reality. Behind that uncertainty there lay too the shadow over Pompidou's own future. It was only too evident that he had suffered a change for the worse physically. "He is no longer the man the Prime Minister saw so vigorously and effectively in action at the Paris Conference. He is still effective, and still – perhaps more than ever – keeping in his own hands the French power of decision. But his potential for carrying on as before has been seriously weakened. His uncertainties are metabolic as well as metaphysical".

Tomkins' conclusion (and this was very much his own) was that the view prevalent in Whitehall had, prior to the visit, been that the French would stand pat on their immediate desiderata – on sterling, on the negotiations with the Americans, and on the dollar – and would regard these as defining the limits on progress towards European Union. Tomkins believed that the meeting should occasion some review of that view. It was not that there would be some dramatic abandonment of French positions in Brussels, the French being by nature more hardened than the rest of their partners to being in a minority of one. But Pompidou was not well placed to push this to the point of total breakdown even if he wanted to. What the Prime Minister's visit would perhaps have achieved was not so much a substantial increase in the area of common ground between the two countries, as the existence of enough question marks to make a better basis on which to work together.[40]

In his own report to Cabinet, Heath had described his discussions with Pompidou as "full and valuable" – dominated by the issue of European relationships with the United States. He had found Pompidou not prepared at present to take part in any discussions with the US Government on European defence; and he had also been "unaccommodating" about the arrangements for Nixon's proposed visit to Europe, being particularly opposed to any joint meetings between Nixon and representatives of the members of the European Community. Nixon could meet the Presidents of the Commission and of the Council of Ministers but, that apart, his contacts with member countries of the Community should be bilateral.[41] Pompidou had also viewed with reluctance the idea of a declaration of transatlantic principles, and declined Heath's suggestion that he might draft such a document himself.

Heath was due to visit Bonn a week after his talks in Paris. Emerging differences between Britain and Germany on the one hand and France on the other, over how to handle the Kissinger initiative would feature on the agenda. Heath had recognised that "Nixon now needed a resounding success vis-à-vis public opinion in the United States and would attempt to do this in the coming months either by embarking on a systematic search for agreement with Europe, or by increased intransigence in the negotiations". Pompidou, for his part thought it imprudent "to tamper with the existing structure which had proved the test of time and proved its worth. To talk of a new Atlantic Charter was to put the cart before the horse. The form of any new alliance should emerge from the discussion at the end of the day. They should start with practical problems in the economic and monetary field".[42]

The Foreign Secretary's advice to Heath, following a talk with his own opposite number, Walter Scheel, was that the Germans shared British worries about French attitudes on US-European relations.[43]

But both the Bonn Embassy and the Foreign Office were also warning of a more serious emerging issue. In Libya, the Government had given an ultimatum to the foreign oil companies: to allow themselves to be taken over or to have their production stopped. Libyan production represented some 14% of British requirements and 25% of German needs. Meanwhile, the OPEC oil-producing countries were seeking to rewrite the 1972 Geneva Agreement compensating them for the effects on oil prices of dollar devaluations. Cooperation between consumer Governments was essential but, when EEC Energy Ministers had met on 22 May, they had made no progress because of French refusal to make any move towards the development of a common position on oil by the main consumer countries (the Community, the United States and Japan) until the Community itself adopted a policy on the control of oil imports similar to that in place in France. It was vital, said the Foreign Office, to avoid a scramble for oil.[44]

Heath and Brandt met at Brandt's house on the evening of 29 May. Scheel, the Foreign Minister, Schmidt, the Finance Minister, and Leber, the Defence Minister, were also among those present.

In an impressionistic letter to Brimelow following the visit, the Ambassador, Sir Nicholas (Nicko) Henderson, described the scene: "It was a fine evening and we had a drink on the terrace before the PM and the Chancellor went into the latter's study. Perhaps it was the unforgiving light, but the PM said to me afterwards that he had been struck at the first moment by how much older Brandt looked. Personally, I do not see any considerable recent change in appearance except that the Chancellor has got much fatter as a result of giving up smoking.

"While the PM and the Chancellor were talking privately, von Hase [the German Ambassador in London] and I received the other guests and watched young Matthias Brandt, in his early teens, playing badminton on the lawn outside. By 8.15, which was the time for dinner, everybody had arrived except Helmut Schmidt. It had been a matter of astonishment to me that he had ever agreed to come at all, because he has strange eating habits and rarely seems to sit down to table, or at any rate not at the same time as other people. He eventually arrived after we were all in the dining room. He made no apology for being late. He may have thought we were lucky to have him there at all. To the PM he gave initially, I believe, an impression of aggressiveness but this wore off as the evening wore on. He entered carrying, as is his custom, a large leather bag, the sort of elaborate affair you can buy at Asprey's for carrying shaving equipment, but which for him contains pipes, cigarettes, lighter and matches . . . He chain smoked throughout the evening, but it was a chain that alternated between pipes and cigarettes, the pipes all with Dunhill white spots.

"Conversation at dinner was general but not lively. Schmidt was ready for a certain amount of banter. Nothing very serious was discussed, unless you count the character of the Bavarians, which Schmidt depicted so disparagingly that the Chancellor said, albeit laughingly, that this must not be repeated outside the room.

"We did not sit for long at table afterwards . . . The Chancellor and PM sat down next to each other in the main reception area and the rest of the party formed a circle. The following hour produced a most interesting discussion. It did not begin very excitingly, with Scheel giving an account of his recent visit to the Middle East. Brandt, who may well have heard it before and found it dull on first acquaintance, looked ungripped and peered through his brandy glass, apparently in search of different prisms of light. Schmidt, the chain apparently broken, went to sleep.

"The Prime Minister then made a statement in which he described the way that the Middle East situation might develop to the grave disadvantage of the West, given the growing dependence of industrial countries on oil. Schmidt woke up, relit and then entered the arena with a forceful line of argument. He spoke with great confidence, and he did so not only on subjects within the sphere of his own Department, but also on foreign and defence questions. When, later, the subject turned to East/West relations and force levels, he gave his views categorically, with only a passing reference to Leber . . . Scheel meanwhile had dropped into the background with his second cigar and took little further part in the discussion.

"It was fascinating for us outsiders to watch the German political leaders engaging in discussion among themselves. I doubt whether the PM found any of them of any great timber except Schmidt. Schmidt's self-confidence was certainly striking. As you know, he has a health problem – thyroid – and he is under medical treatment. His eyes protrude a bit and he is a bad colour. But he seems to keep going. On the German side he dominated the discussion . . . The feeling I had, and it really was only a feeling, because it was derived as much from grunts and nods as from expressions of opinion, was that Brandt, Schmidt and Bahr [State Secretary in the Foreign Ministry] on the whole believe that the important interests and dangers for the Federal Republic in the next few years lie in the political and economic, rather than the military, field. This does not mean that they will want the Federal Republic to become weak members of NATO. But they will tend to attach less importance than Scheel or Leber to the dangers that may arise from Soviet military strength"[45].

The Prime Minister's comments on the Middle East, to which Henderson alluded in his letter, came after Scheel had said that he did not think that there was any great danger of military action in the Middle East in the coming few weeks. Heath said he thought the danger was of a different character. Hitherto, everyone had worried about the dangers of another war, the possibility of dangerous extension of the conflict, the reopening of the Suez Canal and so on. But none of these was the real issue now. The fact had to be faced that the Russians were in the Indian Ocean and that trade had got used to the Cape route. The underlying danger in the present situation was that the Arabs would before long threaten to stop oil supplies to the United States unless the Americans withheld their support from Israel. Demands, such as those by Libya for 100% participation in oil production, would force countries such as Iran to break their agreements with consumer countries. The Arabs would soon use their commercial position for political means. The Americans, who had an energy crisis already, would face a new dilemma: suspension of their oil supplies, or the use of force. Heath thought it likely that the US Government would turn to Europe, and seek a division of whatever oil supplies were available. Western Europe would find the basis of her industrial power threatened. It was imperative to avoid a situation in which Western Europe was subject to blackmail of this kind.

Schmidt said he drew the conclusion that the oil companies should not be left to operate on their own. The OPEC monopoly was effective, but there was no matching organisation among the oil consuming nations. Heath replied that, in a monopoly situation, the only effective reply was an oligarchy backed by power. But the oil consuming nations lacked the necessary power; they had no alternative sources of energy.

Schmidt thought that Western Europe could face a petrol crisis within eighteen months, or sooner. It was only to be expected that the Arabs would turn the screw on oil prices. The Federal Republic was in a weak position over the supply of energy. He had hoped for some understanding of this general problem within the Community, but the latest reports from Brussels were not encouraging. It seemed that France was confident of her ability to withstand any general crisis because of her good relationship with the Arabs, and he was sorry to say that the British appeared to be taking the same line in Brussels, although their views were expressed in more polite form. He noticed that there was now a growing competition for use of Soviet sources of energy. This was a false approach: oil policy needed to be considered as an urgent item on the international agenda. A particularly disagreeable aspect was the prospect of conflict between the interests of the Western nations.

Heath agreed with Schmidt. There were certain lines of action open to countries within the EEC, such as continuing coal production at prices which, although at present uneconomic, would be fully competitive with oil within a short period. It was also necessary to press on with the development of fast breeder reactors, although they might not be fully productive until 1985. Oil from the North Sea would not be available in quantity for some years. He agreed with Schmidt about the need for a Community policy which embraced the activities of the oil companies. Whatever the French said in Brussels, he had not found Pompidou confident about the French position on energy generally. The real problem was the Israeli view. Israel took the simplistic line: 'Here we are, here we stay'. But this was quite erroneous because the Arab potential threat of pressure and political blackmail had to be taken seriously. Israel must be persuaded to evacuate the Occupied Territories under the terms of UN Security Council Resolution 242, and to give up the position which they had adopted for so long.

Schmidt said that energy was one of the subjects not dealt with adequately in Kissinger's speech. The speech showed Kissinger's lack of understanding of the issues involved. Heath said that part of the difficulty lay in Kissinger's conceptual approach to politics, and his consequent belief that all aspects of the American relationship with Europe needed to be considered together. Nixon and Kissinger genuinely believed in the need for continued American participation in the defence of Europe. But the Administration had to show that the separate issues of money and trade were being handled to the best national advantage of the United States, if the American defence commitment was to be continued. The Americans were, in Heath's view, wholly sincere in wanting to have a fair deal with Europe and were frustrated by their inability to do so and their failure to understand the reasons.

Schmidt thought that the feelings of frustration were shared by many Europeans. The fact had to be faced that the American case on agriculture was different from that presented by the Americans themselves. This did not mean that the Community's existing agricultural policies were anything less than a scandal. Brandt agreed that there was much wrong with the CAP in its present form, but the effects of this were felt more strongly in Europe than they were in the

United States. Heath commented that British housewives could not understand why the price of butter went up when price restraints were operating and why the Soviet consumer should benefit at her expense. He hoped that Schmidt would do something to rectify this state of affairs of which he disapproved so strongly, as did the British. Schmidt countered that he thought Heath was better placed to act himself.[46]

A number of issues were converging, at the year's mid-point: continuing volatility in the money markets as a result of the weakness of the dollar; growing tension in the Middle East, both between the Arab states and Israel and between the Arab oil producers and their customers in the West; and domestic pressure on Nixon because of Watergate, which contributed to American impatience with the Europeans for their failure to accept Kissinger's concept of the Year of Europe.

In early June, the weakness of the dollar caused sterling to appreciate in value against it. But other European currencies appreciated even more and, as a result, sterling, in effect, dropped out of the bottom of the snake, despite the fact that the British banking authorities spent about $60 million on 4 June to try to keep sterling in touch with the snake.

In a letter to Bailey in the Treasury, following an earlier telephone conversation, Armstrong recorded that the Chancellor of the Exchequer had considered whether it would be right to spend yet more money in order to push sterling back into the snake. This might require considerable expenditure and the resulting rate would probably not be regarded by the market as credible. The Chancellor had judged that, in a market situation which was highly volatile and fluid, it would not at this stage be right to spend a great deal of money on trying to push the sterling rate back into the snake.

Armstrong had put these considerations to the Prime Minister who had thought the Chancellor's judgement "was right for today". But the Prime Minister had also asked for the position and the policy to be reviewed from day to day.[47]

Heath followed this up with a minute to Barber on 14 June asking for the present state of the Chancellor's thinking on the time of Britain's rejoining of the snake. While Pompidou had not pressed the issue in Paris, he had nonetheless made it clear that progress on a number of decisions taken at the Summit the previous October – the second stage of EMU and regional policy, for example – would be contingent on Britain being a full participant in the Community's monetary arrangements. It was, Heath continued, an objective "of primary political importance" that a Community Regional Policy should be agreed and established by the end of the year and that the British Government should not be responsible for any delays in the timetables laid down at the October Summit.

Barber replied on 19 June. The markets had been very turbulent, he said. $59 million had been spent on 4 June in an attempt by the Government to lift the rate of the pound, with little effect. To achieve this in existing conditions would mean authorising the Bank of England to spend several hundreds of millions of dollars. It was equally clear that any European Monetary Compensation Fund would not be large enough to provide the massive support necessary to make it practicable for Britain to join the common European float. When Britain did join, the Government must be in a position to convince public opinion at home that the move was a sensible one which would not jeopardise the Government's domestic policies. It would be difficult to pull that off. And to choose a time when there was a prospect of a succession of very bad trade figures would "bewilder our friends and give a handle to our critics". A further related thought disturbed the Chancellor a great deal. According to the forecasts, Britain was unlikely to be able to stay in the snake at a rate as high as the current one. Rather than put itself into debt, the Government would want to change the reference rate on which they joined the snake. But to do so would be seen as a straight devaluation and would be a gift to the Opposition.

Finally, Barber argued, "I believe that most people, including the CBI and the TUC, in our current talks, would think it extraordinary if, in circumstances anything like the present, we were to tie our hands by rejoining the snake". The only realistic course, the Chancellor concluded, was to take stock from time to time.[48]

Commenting on Barber's minute, in a note to Heath, Armstrong summed up its message as 'Wait and See'. Armstrong found it hard to fault the conclusion that the present moment was not the time to go into the snake. But Armstrong did question the implicit Treasury belief that the Prime Minister was concerned to get back into the snake in order to get an acceptable regional policy. The Treasury did not believe that the benefit to Britain of an acceptable regional policy would be sufficiently large to justify the risks of going back into the snake. In taking this view, the Treasury were, Armstrong thought, overlooking the fact that at stake was not just the regional policy but the progress of the Community. The monetary field was the one to which the European Summit had given priority. Thus, the damage that was being done by the delay in returning to the snake was damage to Community progress as a whole. Jean-René Bernard at the Elysée had recently told Palliser that Pompidou had been briefed so firmly by his Elysée advisers not to bully Heath about coming back into the snake that he had failed to make clear the importance which he still attached to Britain coming back in. It might well be, Armstrong continued, that the snake would break apart under the strain caused by the weakness of the dollar. No doubt that was the event for which the Treasury were praying. But there was a case for some contingency planning. Did we let events take their course, and await an opportunity for rejoining the snake, or did we do something to try to create an opportunity?[49]

Heath was also preoccupied by the situation in the United States. With the "Watergate dogs snapping ever more viciously at his heels", as Cromer put it, Nixon had moved to shore up his position by prevailing upon General Al Haig to retire from active service and become General Manager and Overseer of White House business. Cromer, who suffered from the syndrome that affects almost all in similar positions, of devoting so much energy to getting on with the 'ins' that he could not conceive of them as ever being 'outs', believed that Haig's appointment "could represent a very welcome strengthening of the President's ability to govern effectively".[50]

Heath, with his politician's antennae twitching, asked for a fresh assessment from Cromer "of President Nixon's present position and the impact of Watergate on his ability to carry through Congress his policies most important to us, in particular trade negotiations, monetary reform in the IMF and the maintenance of American Forces in Europe".[51]

Heath himself was feeling increasingly disaffected with US policy. When Walt Rostow (former National Security Adviser to President Johnson) and his wife, called on Heath on 18 June, Rostow said that his impression, from his tour of Europe, was that Europe did not see any reason, in the natural course of business, to pull up the Atlantic Alliance by the roots and have a look at it. He did not wish to defend either the substance or the style of Kissinger's Atlantic Charter speech. However, Europe should understand it as a plea from a President who needed help in dealing with isolationist and protectionist pressure within the United States. What the President was entitled to expect from Europe was, on the one hand, recognition of, and a commitment to, a continuing need for the Atlantic Alliance, recognising a community of interest in such fields as energy, environment and policy towards the Third World; and on the other a clear and unambiguous offset agreement to meet the cost of American troops in Europe.

Heath did not "entirely accept" this analysis. For the last 25 years, Britain had been divesting itself, largely to please the Americans, of imperial responsibilities and creating a Commonwealth of independent countries. The result was of little benefit to the UK. America was now going through a similar process. She was no longer number one, either militarily or in economic and trade affairs, though this fact was not yet widely recognised in the United States. The United States had allowed her nuclear superiority to be eroded. Soviet strength was constantly growing and America must not be surprised if the Europeans were apprehensive. In the meantime Europe, in the shape of the enlarged European Community, now existed. The United States could no longer deal with the European countries on the old basis. The creation of the enlarged EEC meant that the Kennedy concept of the twin pillars was now a reality. For the present, the EEC dealt with economic, monetary and trade matters, but had no defence personality. On defence the personality was still the Atlantic Alliance. This meant that the United States could not do a grand negotiation with Europe on the whole range of affairs in a single forum, as Dr Kissinger was proposing. Any attempt to do this would mean the countries of the Community putting their interests at the disposition of non-Community Europeans such as Iceland and Greece. Britain and the other Community countries would not be prepared to put up with this. It was not only the rhetoric and terminology of Dr Kissinger's speech that could be faulted, though references to Europe as a region were not tactful. It was the fact that the initiative had been launched without any attempt at preliminary consultation with Europe. If Dr Kissinger had been floating the idea of a Soviet-American Charter there would have been a tremendous amount of preparation and exploration to see what could or could not be done. In future, the United States was going to have to deal with Europe in that way.

Heath wished that there was more understanding in the United States of the facts of the situation. Europe could do with less preaching about burden-sharing and more recognition of the fact that European countries were providing by far the greater part of the conventional effort in NATO. Britain was contributing a larger proportion of GDP to NATO expenditure than the United States. As to the balance of trade, the United States had a visible trade deficit of $6 billion. Of this, $4 billion was accounted for by Japan; $1.5 billion by Canada and only half a billion dollars by the rest of the world including Europe. Yet Heath constantly encountered in the United States the argument that Europe was one of the parts of the world mainly responsible for the American trade deficit. It was not easy to accept American demands for the dismantling of the CAP to assist the American balance of payments when America itself took action to control exports of food commodities. He would welcome greater understanding of these realities. Rostow said that "he got the message loud and clear".[52]

So loud and clear had Heath been that, on 29 June, Armstrong relayed to him the Foreign Secretary's misgivings about his criticisms of Nixon and Kissinger. Douglas-Home saw the Kissinger initiative as being intended for, and beamed to, the American domestic market. It was a sort of signal that, now that they had sorted out Vietnam, the next problem to sort out was Europe. The Foreign Secretary feared that the PM's line to the likes of Rostow would get back to the White House and upset them. Equally, if reported to the Dutch Foreign Minister or to Jobert, the Prime Minister's comments might inflame anti-American prejudices. In either case, the result could be to make it more, rather than less, difficult to get the transatlantic relationship right.

Heath jibbed at the phrase about 'sorting out Europe', commenting that that was "precisely why it has gone wrong. But I suppose we need not say so though, unless we do, they will go on lecturing Europe in the old-fashioned way they do".[53]

One way or another word did get back to Washington and, on 30 July, an irritated Kissinger told Trend, Hunt and Brimelow that the text on transatlantic relations under preparation by the Europeans (with British leadership and encouragement) would simply present the United States with a *'fait accompli'*. The United Kingdom was putting too much emphasis on building Europe and not enough on the strengthening of the trans-Atlantic relationship. The US Government would make no further move in the Year of Europe; it was now up to the Europeans and the US Government would reserve their position.[54]

In Whitehall, the work of taking forward the British Government's objectives, especially on follow-up to the 1972 Paris Summit commitment to a Regional Development Fund, prompted the Treasury to produce a paper on the longer-term implications for Britain of the evolution of the European Community budget. Community expenditure in 1977 would, the Treasury estimated, come to £2,040 million. By that stage, at the end of the transitional period, the United Kingdom's gross contribution (at a contribution rate of 27%) would be about £565 million. The UK could expect receipts from the EC budget (from the Agricultural Guarantee fund and from the Social Fund) of about £85 million, so her net contribution would be about £425 million. If a Regional Development Fund was set up, the UK would, in the longer term, and given the likely evolution of expenditure, need about 19% of the money from the Fund in order to make a financial return. The financial return test would, however, not be the only one which the Government would need to apply to proposals for new EEC expenditure. In particular, the Treasury argued, EEC-financed expenditure should replace or refinance existing UK public expenditure.[55]

This argument (that EEC expenditure should replace national expenditure) was to prove a long-running running sore in relations between successive British Governments and the European Commission, who insisted on the 'additionality' of EEC expenditure in beneficiary countries. In British domestic terms, it was to reach its climax in the 1980s with the introduction of a Treasury scheme which required those Whitehall Departments that argued for, and accepted, EEC finance, to have their receipts from the Treasury reduced accordingly.

In other areas, while Whitehall worked away on follow-up to the Paris Summit, progress in Brussels was, as John Davies reported to Cabinet in mid-June "difficult and slow". The next few months were likely to prove "a period of considerable frustration".[56]

One such area was reform of the Common Agricultural Policy where the Agriculture Minister, Joe Godber, warned Heath that "it will be somewhat unrealistic to expect that we shall get very far along this road this year. We shall certainly have some allies but, in spite of what President Pompidou told you, all the evidence I have is that the French will be very suspicious of all these proposals and very reluctant to change course. However, you may be sure I shall push matters as far as I can". Godber had invited his French opposite number, Jacques Chirac, to come to Britain for the Royal Show, though he had not managed to persuade Chirac (even then not notably uxorious) to bring Madame Chirac with him.[57]

When Chirac came to Britain, he called on Heath, telling him that he had been impressed by his visit to the Royal Show.[58] But, he immediately added, the French Government remained worried by the British attitude to the CAP. He did not believe that the character of the CAP could be changed, although he did not rule out modification on matters of detail.

Heath replied that France had no reason to worry. A prosperous agriculture was essential for the Community. This could be attained by three means: first, by price support on the levy system; secondly, through the system of Community Preference and thirdly through the level of prices and this last element, which was important for both farm incomes and consumer purchasing power, was what chiefly interested Britain. Large farmers needed less help than small farmers. At any given price level, the returns for different producers were variable. There lay the underlying problem: how could we help the small farmer without giving unnecessary bonuses to the large producers.

Chirac said he could understand this point of view in Britain where only 3% of the population was engaged in agriculture. But the proportion was higher in Germany (8–9%), in France (with 12–13%) and in Italy (22–23%). Because these countries had a large number of small farmers, a Community system designed to produce special benefits for them would be very expensive and difficult to finance. An additional one centime on each litre of milk produced in the Community would require additional finance of 200 million units of account (roughly the same number in dollars). The average income of an Italian farmer was only one quarter of that of the average British farmer. So caution was required. This was not a question of principle, but of money.

Heath suggested that, to bring about increased production, it might be better to help farmers by providing low cost fertilisers and other incentives, rather than relying on the price mechanism. Chirac, however, doubted whether the small producers, who were most in need, were best placed to use these technical incentives. Of course, an alternative was a structural reduction in the number of farmers. But France did not favour this, since the French regarded their farmers as an important factor in maintaining equilibrium in the structure of society. The Germans took the same view. Heath said he was puzzled by this, as far as Germany was concerned. Germany had an industrial manpower shortage but was obliged to import workers from abroad when they could obtain some of the manpower they needed by encouraging movement from the land. The traditional view was understandable in Adenauer's day but not comprehensible when espoused by an SPD Government. Chirac repeated his caution.[59]

At the end of June, Pompidou had been in Bonn, where he and Brandt had discussed the future of political cooperation (for long the EEC code for foreign policy cooperation).While his boss was away in Bonn, Bernard at the Elysée ("on his own, keeping the shop, friendly and discursive") had told Ewart-Biggs that Pompidou, on bumping into Christopher Soames in the corridor (Soames had been visiting Bernard) had immediately launched into the question of political cooperation. The President's point was that this was for Governments, and not for the machinery of the Community. If Sir Christopher Soames were the British Foreign Minister then Pompidou would have been glad to see him handling it, but he was not and it was not for the Commission to do so. According to Soames's separate account, Pompidou had said to him: "*Retournez à vos places*".

Speaking of the May meeting between Heath and Pompidou, Bernard thought that both men had shown '*pudeur*' in the conversations. They had held back rather than getting down to brass tacks. Ewart-Biggs said that he had the impression that on the French side there was not much hurry – about the pound, about EMU, about replying to Kissinger, and so on. Was this a change of policy? Bernard said it was more a question of what could or could not be done. The French were anxious to see Britain back in the snake, even though the problem of the dollar was more important than that of the snake. When Ewart-Biggs asked him whether the return of the pound would help advance the EMU programme, Bernard was "vague and easy-going". It was a matter of definition. One day would be the last day of 1973 and the next the first day of 1974. There was no magic about what happened from one day to the next. The important thing was to have the political will to tackle the obstacles. It was not really the French who were dragging their feet over EMU but the Germans "who were chary about having to pay out a lot of money to the rest of us".[60]

On Pompidou's return from Bonn, the new Secretary-General at the Elysée, Edouard Balladur, told Tomkins that, while the Germans believed in political cooperation for its own sake, the French did not. Political cooperation should be directed at some specific objective. Meetings should be between Ministers and Ambassadors, acting on instructions from their Governments. Meetings should not be in Brussels unless there was good reason.

A further point of disagreement between Pompidou and Brandt was that Brandt favoured a summit meeting between Nixon and the Heads of Government of the EEC countries. He also seemed to favour a NATO Council meeting at Head of Government level. Pompidou had said he would have none of this. The Europeans could not appear as vassals summoned before their American liege lord.

When Tomkins asked about progress on the implementation of the 1972 Summit programme, Balladur said that both France and Germany agreed in principle that the timetable should be adhered to, but in practice this made little sense. Progress towards the second stage of EMU would be pretty meaningless if the preconditions had not been met. Neither the fiscal harmonisation nor the re-establishment of order in the European monetary system, which had both been agreed on, had come about; nor did they seem likely in the near future. There was no point in the French and Germans asking the British and the Italians to return to fixed parities if they were unwilling to defend the pound or the lira. Equally, if the British considered that it was in their interest to go on floating, they could not expect progress in other fields. Did this mean, Tomkins asked, that Europe would simply have to go on drifting or was another attempt not needed to pull it together? Balladur's answer was not very clear: the Europeans must do what they had said they would do, even if that meant sacrifices all round.

Tomkins concluded, in reporting to London, that on what were, for the French, the essential points – a European position of independence (not to say mistrust) vis-à-vis the United States; a preoccupation with the implications for Western Europe's security of the American/Soviet agreements on disarmament matters; and an equal preoccupation with the American wish to redefine the European/US relationship – it was clear that the French still saw a wide gap between German inclinations and their own.[61]

Heath rather impatiently told the Dutch Foreign Minister, Max van der Stoel, on the same day that the Community's Finance Ministers and Central Bank Governors "should stop theorising and work out machinery for progress towards EMU". In Heath's view, that did not mean accepting that progress had to be only by small stages. It remained his view that the dollar crisis at the beginning of March had presented the Community with a great opportunity to take a stride forward in this direction, and that opportunity had been missed[62].

A sure sign of the tetchiness of the times came in a note from Armstrong to Heath at the end of June. On one side, said Armstrong, stood the FCO, believing that "we are in the presence of a new outbreak of Gaullist bloody-mindedness: a reviving regret that they let us into the Community and a determination to obstruct the progress of Community development, to hold fast to the benefits to which the Community has brought to France and make sure these are not eroded". On the opposing side were Hunt and Palliser, and others in the European Unit in the Cabinet Office. They recognised that the French Government could be expected to pursue French interests with great determination. But then we had been pursuing our interests with equal determination. And, seen from the French side, the British must be thought to have had a certain amount of success: there was to be a review of the CAP; a result satisfactory to Britain had been reached in the preparation of a Community position for multilateral trade negotiations; George Thomson was making a pretty good running on regional policy; we had largely won our point on food prices; and we had resisted pressures to come into the snake.

It would not be surprising, Armstrong thought, if the outbreak of francophobia in the Foreign Office was matched by a recrudescence of anti-British sentiment in the Quai d'Orsay. Nor was it surprising that the French Foreign Minister, speaking to the National Assembly, desired to show himself as good a defender of French interests as the British Foreign Secretary and other Ministers claimed themselves to be when speaking to the House of Commons.

The point of fundamental importance, as seen by Hunt, Palliser and Armstrong, was that "those who matter most in the French Government wanted us in, and still want us in, and that the improvement in Anglo-French relations has been so striking that it is strong enough to withstand the strains created by divergences on a wide range of individual issues. As in the previous history of the Community, positions are irreconcilable until the last moment; but at the last moment they are always reconciled and cheerfulness breaks out again. This . . . calls for qualities of patience and a strong nerve". "Very interesting", Heath commented. "The FCO is wrong again".[63]

Palliser himself was, of course, a son of the Foreign Office and the view attributed to the Foreign Office was less that of the Foreign Secretary and the top official echelon than that of its exponent at the meeting Armstrong was describing, John Robinson. Robinson had performed brilliantly as a key member of the British negotiating team for accession but he was direct, driven and knew he was right. Under the leadership of Con O'Neill, his ferocious energy and genius had been channelled and directed to brilliant success. Now, whether he was right or wrong, he would have enjoyed challenging any Whitehall tendency to complacency. And, judging by Armstrong's response, he had produced a result. The overall Foreign Office view was closer to that of Palliser and Brussels and Tomkins in Paris, though Robinson's viewpoint had sufficient resonance for the point to have to be argued.

The one aspect of Whitehall that was not working was the arrangement whereby John Davies, as Chancellor of the Duchy of Lancaster, had day to day responsibility for EEC issues within Whitehall. Contrary to original expectations, Hunt reported in a minute of 6 July, both the Foreign Secretary *and* Davies had attended most meetings of the Council of Ministers. The basic problem was not so much that there had been "a good deal of sideways glances as between FCO Ministers and Mr Davies" as that Davies's performance had been the main problem and that the Foreign Secretary had not felt able to leave British representation to him. This was not to suggest that everything had gone wrong; quite the contrary. But there had been no feeling of reliability. Davies himself, for a variety of reasons including his own frequent travels, had made very little impact on Whitehall coordination. In one respect indeed according to Hunt, "coordination has been marginally harder by having a Minister (or at any rate this Minister) because his colleagues often feel that they must argue with him when they would accept a central view worked out by the inter-departmental unit known to have access to the PM".

After setting out the pros and cons of various options, Hunt concluded that, although the idea of having a 'State Secretary' in the FCO, while keeping the official coordinating machinery in the Cabinet Office, was a tempting one, he recommended that Heath should go for another senior Ministerial appointment within the Cabinet Office. In that event, it would be very important to have someone who would gain the confidence of the Foreign Office at the negotiating table. Geoffrey Howe would be the outstanding candidate, if he could be spared.[64]

In the end, Davies survived in office until the General Election of February 1974 although a prevailing view of him was summed up in a piece in the *Sunday Telegraph* of 2 September 1973 in which Graham Turner wrote that "John Davies is variously assessed as a total disaster and quite pathetic and that, supposed to sell Britain to Europe and vice versa, he had done neither".[65]

Success for Ministers hangs a lot on having either a Department at their disposal, or the ear of the Prime Minister. Davies had neither. As a late-comer to politics from business, he was not at home in Whitehall or Westminster. When Labour returned to office in 1974, with Callaghan and Wilson determined to keep European matters firmly in their hands, the job as devised for Davies was abolished. Roy Hattersley became Minister of State in the FCO with responsibility for European matters, under Callaghan. That has been the pattern since.

A more general stocktaking, from different angles, as the summer holidays approached confirmed the sense of dissatisfaction and lack of direction in European policies and politics. At Cabinet on 26 July, Davies reported that the Commission had been obliged to propose a supplementary budget for the year because of additional CAP expenditure which resulted from earlier policy decisions by EEC Ministers. It would, he believed, have an adverse effect on Parliamentary and public opinion towards the Community at a critical juncture in the roll-out of the Government's counter-inflationary policies. It was already difficult to point to the benefits which had resulted from British accession as an offset to the more evident disadvantages. The supplementary budget would cancel out the improvement in the British net contribution which had been expected. Although British industry was beginning to benefit from access to the larger market, and the Government had been successful in some Community negotiations such as the CAP price fixing, the total outcome to date was less than satisfactory.

Heath, summing up, said that the balance of advantage to the UK from membership of the Community should be kept under careful review; and an attempt should now be made to assess it in quantitative terms. In view of the financial implications, it would be necessary to adopt a determined attitude toward the negotiations with the Community on the CAP and the Regional Development Fund.[66]

Three days later, the *Sunday Times* carried a report headlined 'Britain heads for disaster in Europe, say civil servants'. The report claimed that the evidence of seven months of membership was that the Community was a disaster for Britain. Heath wanted to know who the source was. "Both Sir John Hunt and I", Armstrong replied, "have the impression – it can be no more – that the origin of what Mr Fay wrote may have been in Press briefings by the Chancellor of the Duchy of Lancaster earlier in July. You will remember that at one stage he was depressed about the prospects and resentful of the French; and there is reason to believe that this attitude was reflected in talks which he had with some journalists . . ."[67]

From Paris came advice from Tomkins that "in this month of July. Anglo-French relations are like the weather – rather damp and disappointing". But, argued Tomkins, the sign of bad old habits reasserting themselves on both sides was no cause for despondency – only for a renewed determination, which he knew a great many Frenchmen shared, to make a success of the new bilateral relationship within the Community. "Enlightened self-interest impels the two nations in this direction; but so does a certain exasperated admiration which their citizens feel for each other".[68]

In a letter to Oliver Wright, Tomkins was in no doubt that France needed a strong Europe. If the French were at present in a difficult mood it was primarily because important avenues to progress were blocked, notably by the division of EEC currencies into those in the snake and those outside it, and by the dollar crisis. It was the latter factor that conditioned all of French attitudes to the United States: "As the dollar softens, so we harden", as Brunet had put it. The Germans, as Henderson had reported from Bonn, were not prepared for confrontation with the French, and Britain could not succeed in a confrontation without them. It was in any case significantly difficult to beat the French by using a blunt instrument. "I strongly urge a positive approach on our part on the pragmatic lines suggested above. I am strengthened in my view by recent positive signs on the French side. It is noticeable that at a time of pessimism and doubt, with monetary instability and divisions in Europe prominently discussed and commented upon, they have not reacted by blaming the British. The Americans have been very strongly criticised. There is no pretence that Franco-German relations are good". Only by working with the French, and not against them, could the British Government have its hopes for Europe realised. "Interesting – and convincing", was Armstrong's verdict in putting Tomkins' letter to Heath.[69]

Nicko Henderson had, as Tomkins mentioned, advised London that he could "not really say the Germans are in any mood for a decisive confrontation with the French. They are very conscious that the Community cannot survive without France, let alone develop into a Union. Even though they may be losing some of their guilt complex, I do not believe that they feel like a showdown . . . Just because the French are such a nuisance, the Germans are bound to pay more attention to them than to anyone else – galling though this may be to the British". The Germans, while understanding that Britain needed to pursue her own objectives "are at times inclined to believe that, by what seems to them an excessively determined pursuit of our national interest – something that in itself they see as entirely understandable – we are making it more difficult for the Community as a whole to urge the French along successfully in the development towards a European identity".[70]

Henderson and Palliser were both of the view that progress to the second stage of EMU depended on Britain joining the snake and that the British Government had failed to follow up with the Germans the possibilities of monetary cooperation which Heath and Brandt had discussed in March.[71]

As a result of that advice, but only a month later, Heath did write to Brandt proposing a renewal of discussions about the idea of unlimited support to underpin the snake.[72] That initiative was to be overtaken by events. In the meantime, on 3 August, Heath had written to Pompidou and Brandt suggesting that the three of them should meet to try to sort out a view on what action Europe should take on the Year of Europe. Not surprisingly given the likely adverse reaction from other EEC members, both Brandt and Pompidou were wary, preferring to leave it to the regular meeting of EEC Foreign Ministers in September to sort things out.[73]

Throughout the early summer, work had been going on to find a basis for a common European Community response to the Kissinger initiative of the 'Year of Europe'. The initiative was proving to be a catalogue of accidents and misunderstandings.[74] The responses to the Year of Europe, to the October Arab-Israel war and to the subsequent Arab oil embargo were to have significant implications for the European Community and for Britain's place within it.

On 30 July, Trend and Brimelow met Kissinger in Washington, expecting a discussion about the progress being made in the European consultations on Kissinger's initiative. But Kissinger allowed no opportunity for discussion and spent the entire meeting complaining bitterly about European and British behaviour. He found the procedure whereby the Nine agreed a common position and then transmitted it to the United States unacceptable and insulting. The Year of Europe was over. It was no good for the Europeans to respond as a Community. That way of working would have implications for bilateral Anglo-American relations.[75]

Richard Sykes, the number two in the Washington Embassy, reflecting on Kissinger's hard line, attributed it to vexation, pique and the shadow of Watergate and, also, to the impact of British membership of the EEC. Whether the Anglo-American relationship was called 'special' or 'natural', in the eyes of the Americans it had been qualitatively different from that which they enjoyed with any other country. Of course, Sykes, continued, US behaviour did not always match the regard in which they held the relationship (Suez being the prime example) but the Americans had got into the habit of relying on the British and of expecting to discuss things before either party took major action. To find Britain discussing matters with her European partners before discussing them with the Americans had come as a traumatic shock, however implicit it might always have been in Britain joining the EEC in the first place. Subconsciously, the Americans had always regarded the British as a close relative, whereas other Europeans were only friends, or at best cousins. In addition, Nixon might well be thinking that even the British might now assess him as going under because of Watergate and his reaction (via Kissinger) was accordingly all the more violent and emotional.[76]

The French Foreign Minister, Michel Jobert, chose, that August, to take a holiday, with his wife and son, at the Imperial Hotel in Hythe. This manifestation of profound eccentricity provided an opportunity for Heath to invite them all to lunch at the home of his close friends Lord and Lady Aldington, Knoll Farm in Kent. Heath recorded the meeting in a number of detailed minutes, and in a more personal letter to Armstrong. The Joberts had, said Heath, "appeared somewhat straight-laced when they arrived – particularly Michel in a dark brown suit – despite the fact that I had sent him a message to say that I would be in seaside clothes and hoped he would be quite informal – but they all thawed after a time. Janie [Aldington] took the son in tow and knocked a croquet ball around. Toby [Aldington] slothed around the garden with his [Jobert's] wife and he and I talked for some two hours during which he became very relaxed. He told me at least three times how horrified President Pompidou had been to arrive at Heathrow in a country suit only to find me standing looking rather formally respectable. This had obviously weighed with Michel heavily in his choice of attire for Knoll Farm. We managed to get them to Knoll and back to ... Hythe without anybody knowing ..."[77]

On his own situation, Jobert said that he had not wanted to become Foreign Minister and had told Pompidou that he would rather go out and run some big industrial concern. But Pompidou had overruled him. Jobert went on to complain that he had lost de Beaumarchais (to London as Ambassador) and been landed, in exchange, with Courcel (now the Secretary General at the Quai) whom he found unbelievably and intolerably slow. Courcel had asked for an hour a day with him. Jobert has pronounced this quite impossible and had suggested an hour a week instead. He (Jobert) was now trying to get this down to twenty minutes a fortnight, though Courcel invariably stayed for an hour. Courcel put him thoroughly on edge so, when he wanted a peaceful evening, he just refused to see him at all.[78]

On more substantive matters, Jobert told Heath that the French were now deeply worried about the Germans. There were three possibilities open to Germany: to move further to the East; to become purely Atlanticist; or to develop as part of the European Community. At present, they showed far more inclination to move to the East or to become Atlanticist than to identify with Europe. Jobert added that the French were also very worried about the impact on Europe of all the sweetness and light between the two super powers, which was one of the reasons why the French would have nothing to do with the conference on mutual balanced force reductions (MBFR). Heath said in response that he shared the sense of the vital importance of locking the Federal Republic into the European Community and "the developing European entity". The British assessment of the size of the Soviet Forces was different from that of the Americans. Heath could not help having the suspicion that the US Government were producing an assessment which would justify them making an agreement at the MBFR conference for their own Congressional reasons. This was something of which the Europeans had to be very wary.[79]

After talking about Germany, Jobert went on to tell Heath of a plan on which he was working to help bind Germany into Europe. He had already mentioned it briefly to Pompidou who had asked him to produce a paper. This he was engaged on at the Imperial Hotel, Hythe, and Jobert produced some written notes from his pocket. He wanted Heath to know what he had in mind "but trusted that I would not pass it on to the Foreign Office at this stage". The idea was to make an immediate move to get Europe speaking with one voice on political issues, in particular with the Americans. This would require the appointment of a spokesman for the Nine and, if Pompidou, Brandt and Heath could all agree "the rest of the Nine would have to fall in with the idea". "Maybe", Jobert added, "there was an Italian Prime Minister", though he could not remember his name, who could also be brought into the plan.

Jobert would propose to Pompidou that the first spokesman of the Nine should be Brandt. This would have the double objective of forcing the German Chancellor to represent what the Nine agreed upon, instead of just the Federal Republic's views; and also of pleasing the Americans, who looked particularly towards the Federal Republic as their spokesman. This would be for the period of a year. The German Chancellor would then be followed by the British Prime Minister and then the French President. No doubt, Jobert added, some arrangement could then be made for a representative of the small countries to follow, and this process could be repeated. The spokesman could be backed by a small secretariat, which might well be in London with a French Secretary General. Jobert would present this arrangement as being temporary – to deal with the European-American dialogue. But, like so many provisional arrangements, it might well last much longer and become the basis of a future political structure. Jobert invited Heath to think it over and let him have his comments.[80]

Only a week later, Armstrong and his wife had lunch with M Jobert and his wife and son at the Quai. Jean Monnet was the only other guest. Armstrong had three quarters of an hour alone with Jobert before lunch. Jobert told him that he had put to Pompidou the idea he had outlined to Heath but the President had said 'no', declining even to read Jobert's memorandum. Later, he had said he would reflect on the matter but Jobert wanted Heath to know that, for the present at any rate, Pompidou had squashed it.

The second message which Jobert wanted Armstrong to convey to Heath was that Pompidou was expecting a considerable revival of interest in institutional development among other members of the Community, in particular in the issue of direct elections to the European Assembly. When Jobert had told Pompidou he would be seeing Armstrong, the President had said: 'Tell Mr Armstrong to tell the Prime Minister that, if he supports me in resisting the pressures for such developments, I will support his position on regional policy'. Jobert emphasised that these messages were for the Prime Minister only and were "on no account to be passed to the Foreign Secretary or to the Foreign Office. Once anything got into the hands of the diplomats, it was half way across Europe before you knew where you were". Jobert added that his relations with Armstrong and Heath were "*un autre circuit*".[81]

A preoccupation with institutional issues was to become regular displacement activity in the European Community when faced with a lack of substantive will to make progress. Monnet was, at the time, touting his own version, which he put to Heath at Chequers on 16 September 1973. His proposal was that the nine Heads of Government of the EEC should constitute themselves into a "provisional European Government which would meet not less than once every three months and would be able to take decisions". Heath, according to Armstrong's record, "saw much force in Monnet's analysis of the problem, and considerable virtue in his proposal". But Heath doubted the need for so formal a body and did not greatly favour the title 'Provisional Government', "which would frighten some people". Heath preferred 'Supreme Council' and thought that the Heads of Government should meet more often than every three months.

Monnet left behind a note in which he proposed that the Provisional European Government would, within six months, set up a commission for the organisation of the European Union. That commission would recommend the precise shape of the project which would then be submitted for ratification by the Member States. Monnet himself gave no prescription as to what form the eventual European Union would take, beyond stipulating that the Provisional European Government would not interfere with the operation of the existing institutions.

On 21 September, Monnet telephoned Downing Street to report that "Brandt could not have been more emphatic and definite. He liked the proposition". On 24 September, Monnet rang again to tell Armstrong that Jobert has reported Pompidou as being "very much interested". But Pompidou had not reacted one way or the other on the proposal itself, beyond commenting that, although Heads of Government should indeed meet several times a year, "they need not meet too often". Pompidou also had reservations about the idea of appointing a commission to work out plans for European Union.[82]

Armstrong was heartened when, at a press conference on 27 September, Pompidou said that what had been defined at the October 1972 Summit led beyond economic problems and inevitably into the political field. The essential precondition of a European Union, Pompidou said, was a European policy, and if that required "from time to time, at not too frequent but at nevertheless regular, intervals, handling by those responsible at the very top, by them and by them alone, then I am in favour". Armstrong immediately wrote to the Foreign Office asking the Foreign Office News Department to say that the Prime Minister welcomed what Pompidou had said and that he would be very ready to take his part in the sort of development Pompidou had indicated.[83]

When, however, John Davies proposed to make a speech explaining what European Union would mean, Heath wrote on the draft: "I am never happy about such pieces. They always do more harm than good". He especially disliked the reference to true Union involving integration in every sphere and asked that everything in the speech about European Union be deleted. He also asked for a reference to 'legal harmonisation' to be deleted. A reference to the responsibility of the European Commission for external trade negotiations was, Heath insisted, to be qualified by a stipulation that the Commission were 'operating under the authority of the Council of Ministers'.

Armstrong wrote to Davies' Private Secretary instructing Davies, on the Prime Minister's behalf, "to make a different speech on this occasion; perhaps one which deals with the progress of the Community to date and the way in which we are dealing with our problems in a Community context". The speech was duly turned into something mundane, safe and uninteresting.[84]

Davies was not so discountenanced that he failed to return to the charge, urging Heath, in a minute of 2 October that work was needed "to create a more favourable climate of opinion, to restate our expectations of future benefits, to deal firmly with the fallacious arguments put forward by our opponents, and to take full advantage of the good news".[85]

Davies suggested the establishment of a Cabinet Committee to oversee this work but the Foreign Secretary had doubts as to whether Davies was the man to chair it and the Prime Minister had considerable doubts as to whether to proceed on the lines proposed at all.

Davies had copied his minute to other interested Ministers and Geoffrey Howe, now Secretary of State for Trade and Industry, commented on 16 October that what was surely needed was "a methodical analysis of the reasons for the current disenchantment here with the Community . . . It is, for example, probable that the reasons for current disenchantment are not limited to the popular association of the EEC with high food prices, but spring from a more general feeling that things nationally are not going well. This inevitably rubs off on one of our main achievements – our entry into the Community. There is a sense of post-honeymoon disillusion, a feeling that entry has not been followed by immediate and tangible benefits. This analysis could well lead to the conclusion that a full-scale campaign on the 1972 basis would be wrong . . . A suitably low-key campaign could, on the other hand, be increasingly effective."[86]

Francis Pym, the Chief Whip, was characteristically forthright. "Despite various attempts I have made earlier", he wrote, "I remain thoroughly fussed at our consistent failure apparently even to try to sell Europe and the advantages of our joining a European Community to the British people . . . One never hears any trumpet blown in its favour except by the PM from time to time . . . The pro-Europeans on the Labour side are getting dismayed and depressed at our seemingly total silence . . . I know that John Davies is most effective on the subject at public meetings but it is a far bigger task than one person can cope with. Can we plan a campaign, coordinated or directed by a senior Minister? There is plenty of good will in the Party but we are wasting it by apparently failing to give a lead".[87]

Heath did in the end agree to the establishment of a group of senior information specialists from the key Whitehall Departments, as an information strategy group under the chairmanship of his own Chief Press secretary, Robin Haydon. Heath himself, at the Conservative Party Conference in Blackpool in mid-October, said that "of course, we are not satisfied with the European Community as it stands today", and went on to refer to the Government's efforts to secure changes in the CAP, better budgetary control and the establishment of a Regional Development Fund.[88]

Wisely, Heath decided not to use a detailed line on the advantages of the CAP, prepared for him, at Douglas Hurd's request, by the Cabinet Office. Its author, Mr D A Evans, had done his best with unpromising material, but thought it necessary to append a health warning: "In the first place, we must be careful not to make a silk purse out of this sow's ear. The fact is that the CAP is to our disadvantage financially and is a long way short of perfect as an instrument for managing Community agriculture. We want to see changes made and we should be weakening our hand if Ministers now took to praising the CAP in public. The whole field is full of pitfalls".[89]

A similar Cabinet Office note of 10 October on EEC achievements 'so far' since British accession provided similarly thin pickings, though it did note that, thus far in 1973, the monthly rate of exports to the rest of the EEC was 22% higher than for the second half of 1972. A CBI survey of fifty big companies showed that they expected to spend nearly 27% more in the three years 1973–1975 than had looked likely at the same point a year earlier. Many of them had increased their investment programmes for 1973 by around 15%. The available figures also showed an increase both in UK investment in the EEC and in EEC investment in the United Kingdom. The first global loan to the United Kingdom from the European Investment Bank had just been negotiated and was worth £3.5 million. By the end of the year, Britain would have submitted claims on the European Social Fund worth £32 million, with every expectation of gaining a substantial proportion of that sum.[90]

Heath's main concern was to use the Party Conference speech to further the idea of more frequent meetings of EEC Heads of Government. Pompidou, like Heath, had the bit between his teeth on the idea of some kind of supreme council. On 10 October, a few days before Heath's Party Conference speech, Pompidou told Tomkins that he did not have in mind meetings like the Paris Summit. He wanted to reduce the number of participants, other than the nine principals, to an absolute minimum. The meetings would not be those of a kind of European executive but, rather, gatherings at which common understandings were sought on political matters so that the various Governments could give a push to things when necessary. Pompidou believed that the inertia and obstructiveness of national bureaucracies was an obstacle to the successful development of the Community. Brandt had just sent him a letter (having himself met Heath only a few days earlier) in which he said that all the difficulties in the Community could be overcome if there was agreement between Britain, France and Germany. Pompidou had, however, one word of warning. If the three principals were in agreement, this was bound to have a powerful effect on the affairs of the Community but a tripartite directorate would be a mistake. It would cause endless trouble with the other members. He had had the same argument with Kissinger: it was not possible to act as though some countries mattered and others did not and Europe could not be constructed by ignoring the interests of the small powers.

Pompidou, described by Tomkins as "fat but . . . in very good form", had made it clear that he wanted to help Heath politically because he admired him and considered him an irreplaceable asset for Europe. Pompidou himself, according to Tomkins, was giving the political development of Europe higher priority than before and was showing less interest in economic and monetary integration. His aim was to organise the Nine into adopting a common attitude in world affairs that was distinct from that of the Americans.[91]

A similar message was given to the junior Foreign Office Minister, Anthony Royle, by the French Europe Minister, Jean de Lipkowski, who told Royle that Pompidou hated Harold Wilson and was determined to put together a package which would help Heath. On important issues, Lipkowski said, one could not now put a cigarette paper between French and British attitudes. The French Government were, Lipkowski added, deeply suspicious of the Soviet Union. The new Soviet Ambassador in Paris had recently lectured Pompidou for twenty minutes on Soviet policies. Pompidou had felt it necessary to remind him that the Ambassador's last post had been Prague which, like Paris, was an ancient European city. But Prague was now under the Soviet heel. The Ambassador could not speak in Paris as he had in Prague and Pompidou wanted to hear no more such nonsense from him.[92]

Heath's enthusiasm for Pompidou's initiative on meetings of EEC leaders, a central theme of his own Party Conference speech, was not wholly shared in Whitehall. The Foreign Secretary had written to Heath on 5 October suggesting that more meetings at Head of Government level were a good idea "provided the meetings are not too frequent". Douglas-Home was also worried that if the President of the Commission was not invited (as Pompidou seemed to have in mind) there would be a flaming row.[93]

Brandt too was concerned. He wrote to Heath on 25 October, recalling with pleasure "the talks we had in the pleasant atmosphere of an English country house [Chequers]" as "a gratifying memory". Brandt had followed up his and Heath's discussion of Pompidou's initiative. Pompidou was gratified that both Brandt and Heath agreed with it. But Pompidou clearly intended to confine the meetings he had in mind to political cooperation. Brandt, on the other hand felt it unrealistic to have meetings of the Heads of Government at which Community business was not discussed. Such meetings should not change the Community's structure. Nor should they be allowed to serve as a pretext for lack of action in the Community's institutions. They should, rather, give an impetus to the overall work of European unification, regardless of what Brandt saw as an artificial distinction between Community business and Political Cooperation. Heath agreed and wrote in the margin of Brandt's message that he would try to persuade Pompidou when the two of them met at Chequers in November.[94]

Whitehall, perhaps exhibiting the inertia of which Pompidou complained, was in no hurry. Nairne had told Armstrong that "there might be some inclination in official circles to adopt a low profile" on the Pompidou/Heath initiative. Armstrong had stressed in reply that this was not the way the Prime Minister saw it. Having taken the initiative at Blackpool, following on what Pompidou had said, Heath did not now want to see a vacuum. He should be given proposals for follow-up that very week.

Hunt, who had just taken over from Trend as Cabinet Secretary, agreed with the course of action Armstrong had called for "against the advice of the European Unit". There was a difference of approach between Brandt and the PM on the one hand and Pompidou on the other. But the reality was that, even if a summit was ostensibly directed to Political Cooperation, it was unrealistic to think that it would not in practice discuss Community affairs as well. There was no point in having a theological argument with Pompidou on the role, or even the presence, of the Commission or to lobby on the subject, as had been proposed in Whitehall. That would look as if the UK was lobbying against the President when the effort should be focussed on carrying him with us.[95]

All Prime Ministers and their Cabinets have to be expert jugglers. In 2003, detailed discussions were held between the Prime Minister and the Chancellor of the Exchequer on the vexed issue of whether or not Britain should join the European single currency even as British and American armed forces were invading Iraq. In the autumn of 1973, argument continued about the shape of EEC summits, the size of the Regional Development Fund and the fall-out from the Year of Europe, even as the Middle East blazed in the Yom Kippur war between Israel and her neighbours and as the Western world faced the war's aftermath in the form of an Arab oil embargo directed at Western consuming nations.

The Arab-Israel war exacerbated the already considerable tensions between the United States and Europe. The European Community countries were more even-handed as between Israel and the Arab world than was the United States and more attached to the implementation of UN Security Council Resolution 242 and its call for the withdrawal from occupied territory. When Britain, in mid-October, refused to act as the United States' stalking horse for a Security Council resolution linking a cease-fire explicitly to a final settlement of the dispute, Kissinger berated Cromer for Britain's failure over the past three years, as Nixon had put it, to stand with the Americans when the chips were down. Kissinger threatened, almost in retaliation, the massive military resupply of Israel, prompting Cromer to say that 'Europe would not be content to go without Middle East oil because of American actions'.[96] A few days later, when news reached the Middle East that the US had supplied extra weaponry to Israel, the Saudi Arabian Foreign Ministry told European Community representatives in Jeddah that, if the Nine did not bring pressure to bear on the United States to be more even-handed, Saudi Arabia would cut back her oil production. The following day, 17 October, the OPEC member countries announced that their oil production would be reduced by 5% per month until the Israelis had withdrawn from the occupied territories and the legal rights of the Palestinian people had been recognised.[97]

Britain and France were in a happier position than some of their partners, being in effect privileged over other EEC Member States because they were perceived to be more friendly to the Arab cause. The Dutch, by contrast, who were seen to be more sympathetic to Israel, were faced with an embargo on approximately 58% of their oil imports. The Germans were also at a disadvantage. However, when the Council of Ministers met on 6 November, the British and French agreed that the best way to ensure the continued flow of oil was, despite Dutch and German requests to the contrary, to say as little as possible about European consumer solidarity. "We must", wrote the Head of the Foreign Office's Energy Department, "resist short term collective or collaborative approaches which would either set at risk our supplies from the Arab world or prejudice our full employment at a later stage of the benefits of North Sea Oil".[98]

This was a view shared by Heath and Pompidou in a comparatively short discussion of the issue during their two days of talks at Chequers on 16 and 17 November. The two men spent a great deal of time discussing their plans for European Summits aimed at promoting Political Cooperation, i.e. a common foreign policy, with no evident sense of incongruity over the fact that, however good the reasons of self-interest, they were the principal cause of the lack of European solidarity in the face of the oil crisis and its damaging impact on two key Member States. Both men agreed that they were indeed the beneficiaries of a more or less privileged status on oil supplies compared with the United States, Japan "or even other European countries". Pompidou was opposed to an intervention with the Arabs in favour of one or more Community countries. This was not because he did not well understand the position of the Dutch and indeed of the Germans. But he felt that, as long as no progress had been made in peace negotiations, any such action was more likely to result in their being attacked by the Arabs and treated by them in the same way as other countries, than in agreement by the Arabs to restore the position insofar as the Dutch and Germans were concerned. Heath agreed. Pompidou saw the answer as lying in the diversification of energy sources, whether geographically or technically. This meant the rapid development of nuclear power. Of course, he added, the United Kingdom was in the most favourable position of any of the Nine because of its reserves of coal and because of the North Sea.

Heath did not respond but instead looked forward to the signature of the Channel Tunnel agreement between the two Governments the following day. Pompidou commented that hitherto, virtually the sole link between the Continent and Britain had been called 'Heath'.[99]

Heath made another determined attempt to interest Pompidou in Anglo-French defence cooperation. He sometimes felt, he said, that however he raised the matter, the French Government suspected that a means was being sought of bringing them back into NATO by the back door. This was not the case. The British analysis suggested to them that, if the two Governments so desired, France and Britain could cooperate at a later stage in the development of nuclear weapons. Could the President conceive of circumstances in which Britain and France, while retaining the right of independent action which they both now had, could cooperate with the United States on the basis that all three had equal access to all available information, in regard both to weapon development and to intelligence and early warning – or did the President rule this out? Pompidou replied that the French nuclear programme ran until 1980. Thereafter, he excluded nothing. What happened would depend first on Europe itself, then on the attitude of the United States and finally on what had happened in the meantime in respect of the Soviet threat. The Russians were constantly talking peace, but their military strength was increasing at an alarming rate.[100]

Heath argued that the Nine should formulate a common policy towards the relationship between the Community and the Soviet Union and the countries of Eastern Europe. That would help to keep the Federal Republic of Germany integrated within the Nine. Pompidou agreed. But one should have no illusions. If one day there was some kind of fundamental trend in Germany for reunification at any price, there would be a risk that everything would break apart. He was wholly confident in the determination of Brandt to pursue his present policies. But the East Germans, the GDR, were arguing that the Federal Republic had treacherously abandoned the concept of the German Reich and wished to integrate Germany into some kind of 'European jelly'. The GDR, they argued, represented the real Germany. If they persisted in that argument what might happen one day in a crisis? There was a German reality which could bestir itself one day and would take no account of what had been decided by any Government. France and Britain were fortunate enough to be very old nations living within well-defined frontiers, with no particular ambitions or desires. The German reality was uncertain. He had no mistrust of Brandt. On the contrary, he said, but Brandt was not eternal. It was salutary to remember that only ten years had separated Herr Stresemann[101] from Adolf Hitler.[102]

More time was spent by Heath and Pompidou on EEC institutional matters than on any other topic. Pompidou clearly feared that his original idea of meetings of the EEC Heads of Government had been distorted. He still considered that the participants should be confined to the nine Heads of Government. But the trades union of Foreign Ministers had got hold of the situation. He had been told that Sir Alec Douglas-Home had said he would rather be in Scotland than in Copenhagen. But others did not see it that way. In Italy, for example, Signor Moro, the Foreign Minister, did not regard his Prime Minister as better qualified than he was. The Belgian Foreign Minister spoke of his own Prime Minister in affectionate, but decidedly superior, terms. The Dutch claimed that their constitution was at stake. Others thought it would be difficult to exclude the Commission. His initial concept had been of the family meeting, for example as it used to be in the past in order to give its blessing to the desire of the youngest daughter to marry her suitor, but not to discuss the marriage contract, the menu of the wedding breakfast or similar mundane details. He saw two dangers. One was that the Heads would leave the meeting chanting 'Europe, Europe' at the top of their voices, rather like a stage army in a musical comedy singing 'Onward, Onward' without actually moving from the stage and that, in short, the only outcome would be vagueness and ambiguity. The second danger was that the meeting would find itself expected to cope with matters within the responsibility of the Council, the Permanent Representatives or the Commission and which did not really justify a meeting of Heads.

Heath fully agreed but he had been told that when their senior officials met they had seen grave difficulties about that kind of meeting. But then officials had a vested interest in a more fully attended meeting. Heath did, however, favour the maintenance of good relations with Ortoli, as President of the Commission, by inviting him to part of any meeting. He might, thought Pompidou, be invited to dinner and to attend the second day.

Heath thought this would reassure some of the smaller countries, concerned for the protection of their interests. Pompidou said that when he had recently seen the Dutch Foreign Minister the latter had indeed referred to a 'directorate of the three great powers'. Pompidou had told him that the tradition within the Community, and especially the rule of unanimity when a country's major interests were at stake, provided the necessary reassurance against any fears of the three larger powers imposing their views on the others. The trouble was that the Dutch still thought that France was living in the age of Louis XIV and Spain in that of Philip II. They sometimes also seemed to think of England in terms of William and Mary. He had also told the Dutchman that it would be a mistake to think that Europe consisted only of the Benelux countries. 'Plus Ireland', added Heath. The Irish continued to think in historical terms analogous to those ascribed by the President to the Dutch.

Pompidou continued that it would be wrong to accept that any purely Community organisation must inevitably be run by the Benelux because the French would not want it run by the British, who would not want it run by the Germans, who would not want it run by the French. The Community must be genuinely *communautaire*, representing the nine member countries equally. The key question was whether the Nine recognised that the European continent did not at present play the part internationally that it could and that others were seeking either to use it or to ignore it; whether they wished their continent to play a major role in all fields; and whether they were prepared to draw the necessary conclusions. It was a conclusion in this respect that he sought from the summit meeting. They must stick by whatever they agreed to and not go away afterwards saying privately to third parties, as had happened with the recent declaration on the Middle East, that they did not really mean what they said to each other.[103]

Heath continued to be preoccupied with securing a large Regional Development Fund of at least 3,000 mua (or roughly the same in dollars) for the first three years, with a minimum share for Britain of 25%. He made some headway with Pompidou at Chequers, although he secured no commitment, or even comment, from Pompidou on the figures.[104]

The Foreign Secretary, however, was uneasy about the Government's tactics. The British Government, he wrote to Heath and Barber shortly after the Chequers weekend, had decided to demand a fund of 3,000 mua for the first three years, including 750 mua in 1974. Britain wanted the largest possible RDF provided she secured a return of at least 25%. But in reality, Douglas-Home believed, the Government would be very content if it could achieve the figures that the Commission had proposed, namely a fund of 2250 mua, with 500 mua in the first year. Sir Michael Palliser's best guess was that Britain could expect to get something like 300 to 350 mua in the first year, with a promise of substantially greater sums in the following two years. Those figures were realistically closer to the likelihood that the Germans could eventually be brought reluctantly to agree to a fund in the first year of between 200 and 300 mua. If, the Foreign Secretary argued, Britain were to put its high-figure demands on the table in Brussels as planned on 21 November then, in the debate in the House of Commons on

26 November, the Government would have set itself up for criticism and disappointment when the more modest likely outcome was achieved. A better tactic would be to go hard for the Commission's proposals.[105]

Barber commented in response that "it seems to me that we shall never achieve very much in the Community if we are always inhibited from asking for what we want by the fear that we shall not get it and this will be interpreted as a defeat".[106]

Barber's view prevailed (not surprisingly given that the higher British figures had already been given to Brandt by Heath) and, in any event, George Thomson, the Commissioner responsible, told Nairne on 27 October that the high British bid was helpful. It would have been wrong to set British sights any lower. He himself hoped that the British share might rise to as high as 29% over the three-year period. It was vital for Britain to be ready with suitable projects to draw down her share of the Fund once it had been agreed.[107]

Heath immediately instructed the Ministers concerned to "be ready with a large batch of applications for assistance from the Fund, so that the cash can start to flow to this country as quickly as possible, and to be seen by the regions to be related to specific projects".[108]

At about the same time, Anglo-US relations lurched further downhill. On 24 November, Kissinger told Cromer that "if European behaviour towards the United States continued as at present, a public confrontation could not be avoided". Kissinger's particular fury was directed at the fact that the EEC had proposed to the Japanese a bilateral EEC/Japan declaration when it was known that the United States was pressing for a trilateral Declaration. This represented yet another deliberate Franco-German attempt to forge European unity by distancing Europe from the United States. That was just one example. Jobert's speeches were another.

When Cromer ventured the not unreasonable comment that the British Government could hardly be blamed for Jobert's speeches, Kissinger riposted that if no other member of the European Community ever opposed the French, then the French would succeed in setting the tone for Europe. Kissinger then said out of the blue that his sadness in the case of the British was that the special relationship was collapsing. Britain's entry into the EEC should have raised Europe to the level of Britain. Instead, it had reduced Britain to the level of Europe. Up until the end of July that year, the United States had not treated Britain as a foreign country. Now it was different. The party was over. The US would never have embarked on the Declaration if they had thought it would lead to the present troubles. But these were anyway only symptomatic of something deeper. Europe simply did not seem to appreciate that the present Administration was the most Atlanticist that the United States would ever have. If Europe could not cooperate with the United States now, it would never get another opportunity. In the past, the UK and the US, and the Germans and the US, had been able to agree on common positions and carry the Alliance along. This was no longer possible: first the US and the UK no longer had the closeness which they had enjoyed two years earlier; and secondly, the Germans were unreliable. The Alliance had no firm base any more. The French were being allowed to dominate European thinking on the Atlantic relationship and were seeking to build Europe up on an anti-American basis. So far, the United States had refrained from public attacks on France, but this restraint could not continue. But he felt bound to observe that the French could not do what they were doing without the tacit help of the United Kingdom. Objectively, the United Kingdom made it possible for France to pursue its policies. The UK provided the political competence. Britain no longer counted as a counter-weight to France in Europe. France had made the cold blooded assessment that it could drive the UK to share in the construction of Europe on the basis of coolness towards America, in the belief that the Americans would not retaliate. This was the worst decision since the Greek city states confronted Alexander.

"This was a very difficult session", Cromer reported. Even allowing for the extent to which Kissinger spoke for effect it would, Cromer advised, be unwise to underestimate the seriousness of his assessment and the degree to which he believed that Europe was taking an anti-American turn.[109]

Heath offered no immediate recorded comment but the Foreign Secretary decided to respond in a message to Kissinger sent on 28 November which was placatory but robust, arguing that "there is really nothing in my view which justifies the fear that US/British relations are collapsing" and seeking to "restore the old intimacy".

On one issue the Foreign Secretary was clear and firm. "In the Middle East", he said, "we and many others, on the basis of our own independent judgements, have been convinced for a very long time that there could be no peace except on the basis of Israeli withdrawal from occupied territories. We have said so year in year out since 1967; but the US, which was the only country in a position to put the necessary pressure on Israel, did not feel able to do so . . . It would be dishonest if we did not insist, as the European Declaration in fact did, that the issue of Israeli withdrawal cannot be fluffed any longer. Possibly you feel that we have bent to Arab blackmail. All I can answer is that three years ago I laid down in a public speech in considerable detail our ideas on a Middle East settlement. We have not deviated from that one iota. If there is peace at all, I believe it is bound to be on that pattern. We have tried time and again to persuade the American Administration of this, but we failed. That has been America's decision, but I do not really think our attitude is one for condemnation when events are likely to prove us about right".

The Foreign Secretary then turned to Europe. The Nixon Administration had, he said, consistently supported the aim that Europe's trading policies should be outward-looking and that Europe should put itself in a position to talk with one voice. Britain could not deliver Europe but the Government had worked hard since British accession in January towards those objectives, and with a good measure of success. It might indeed be that the European response to Kissinger's April speech had "seemed almost culpably slow. But, frankly, it caught us on the hop. First, the 'one ball of wax' concept was one which was not acceptable to a lot of Europeans and, secondly, our Community machinery for rapid response simply was not there". Douglas-Home hoped that continuous contacts (and he hinted at the damage done by Kissinger's secretive and mistrustful working methods) would enable the Administration to be informed of the direction of European policy and allow for Europe to take account of American comments. Thus could the damage of the past six months be repaired and confidence restored.[110]

Heath does not appear to have seen his copy of the message until 2 December (the day on which he initialled it as read). In Washington, Lord Cromer woke up on 30 November to an Associated Press report from London that "offended British officials are meeting Henry Kissinger's criticism of European behaviour during the October Arab-Israeli war with biting attacks on his style of diplomacy . . . letting loose a cascade of complaints almost unprecedented since World War II".[111]

That afternoon, Larry Eagleburger, Kissinger's Special Assistant, telephoned Cromer to remonstrate on Kissinger's behalf. Cromer, having given Kissinger "about an hour to get his feet back on the ground", telephoned him and advised Kissinger not to give credence to what looked "like bar-room stuff". Cromer said he was sure the reports could not have come from official sources. Kissinger found this hard to believe. "Your people only gossip on instructions", he said.

In reporting to London, Cromer apologised on Kissinger's behalf for his "display of prima donnish behaviour: Kissinger at his worst. It is really quite intolerable that we should be exposed to this, but it a fact of life and we must do the best we can".

Then Cromer added a rider: "Since dictating the above, Eagleburger has again telephoned me on Kissinger's instructions. Kissinger wished me to know that he had heard from a very reliable source that the story" (which had been carried in the *Washington Post*) was "the direct result of a backgrounder which the Prime Minister gave yesterday in which he made some very uncomplimentary remarks about the Secretary of State. Kissinger therefore wondered what would be the purpose of his coming to the United Kingdom".[112]

After an apologetic message from the Foreign Secretary, Kissinger simmered down and the Foreign Office, who had themselves been caught unawares, pieced together the story and relayed it to Cromer. At an off-the-record dinner on 28 November (the day of the Foreign Secretary's first firm but placatory message to Kissinger) Heath had said that, although "people on the other side of the Atlantic seemed unable to understand it, the Europeans were at last getting their act together". It was wrong to imagine that the Americans could have a Year of Europe without any prior consultation. He did not believe that the United States would ask for 'A Year of China' without consulting the Chinese. Yet the Year of Europe had been launched without a single word. The enlarged Community had only been in being since January. Apparently, Dr Kissinger did not like having a Dane speak for Europe in Washington. Well, he would have to get used to it. Whoever was Chairman would be speaking for Europe.

Asked about the Middle East, Heath said that the United States had assured everyone that they could deal with the Israelis but there had been another war despite those assurances. Dr Kissinger apparently felt that Europe should fall into step behind the United States but he could not expect Europe to follow lamely because Europe simply would not do it. It was no good expecting the Europeans to follow the American lead if they did not agree with it.[113]

In reporting Heath's outburst, the *Washington Post*'s London correspondent, Bernard Nossiter, attributed much of Heath's irritation and frustration to the fact that his "high hopes of convincing the British public that entry into the Common Market would give Britain a new and glorious role to play on the world stage" had turned to ashes. The latest opinion poll, Nossiter reported, showed that only 29% thought that EEC membership was helpful to Britain. 44% thought membership hurt British interests, and the remainder could not decide.

Nossiter went on to describe the Paris Conference of 1972 as all-but-forgotten, its timetable for "something called Union" already derailed. The second stage of EMU, which had been due to start at the beginning of 1974, was now lost in the mists of time. As a result, the one big New Year's present which Heath intended to give to the British public, a hefty Common Market fund for depressed areas like Belfast and Glasgow, was disappearing. The "canny French" had linked the fund to the achievement of the second stage of EMU. Along with the Germans, the French now planned to endow the Fund with little more than token contributions.

Even more embarrassing, Nossiter argued, was the Common Market's public betrayal of its custom union signified by the announced decisions of Britain and other EEC members to observe the Arab oil embargo against the Dutch. Heath, according to the article, was known to blame the Dutch for their difficulties. But for the man on the street, the episode demonstrated that the Community's rule for the bigger states was 'me first'.

Finally, wrote Nossiter, some of the rancour reflected a curious Gaullist streak in Heath. Some of the General's thinking had rubbed off on Heath. De Gaulle believed that European identity (an abstraction which Heath used and which carried a 'Made in Paris' label) depended in part on a mix of hostility and friendship – but above all independence – from the two super powers. Heath was behaving in much the same way. De Gaulle believed that France was the only plausible leader of the Common Market, one reason he blocked British entry. Heath seemed to think that Britain could now fill that role.[114]

Heath's biographer, Philip Ziegler, cites Kissinger's view that Heath "actively sought to downgrade" the Anglo-US relationship, as well as Nigel Lawson's judgement that Heath "was obsessively pro-European and almost equally anti-American".[115]

Heath did not consider himself anti-American, rather the contrary, and the record bears out that he sought a constructive relationship. But American policies, both monetary and Middle Eastern, contributed to Heath's domestic economic problems. He was especially irritated by Kissinger who, in Heath's view, affected to support the development of the EEC as an ally of the United States and as a counterweight to the Soviet Union and to China, but in practice operated to divide them. Kissinger maintained exclusive bilateral relations with each, seeking, in particular, to drive wedges between the British and the French.

Heath correctly saw that the United States would become increasingly preoccupied with its Pacific interests – Japan and increasingly China – and that the old

European powers on their own would be puny and of little global account in a world of superpowers. By contrast, operating as a Community, the countries of Europe would have economic, and corresponding political, clout.[116]

Heath may have over-estimated the extent of that clout but he knew that in defence terms the United States would remain indispensable to the Europeans for as long as he could see.

Heath's frustration is understandable. It was compounded by Kissinger's working methods, particularly while he was National Security Adviser, pursuing White House policies which were separate and different from State Department policies. Officials in London could not discuss with the US Embassy the issues which Kissinger was pursuing behind the back of the American Secretary of State.[117]

What is harder to understand is that Heath allowed himself to give vent to his frustration in public, and to American journalists. What Heath said was bound to be reported prominently and it would have taken just one phone call from the American Embassy in London to just one of those present to establish that the author of the criticisms was Heath himself. While Kissinger was the prime author of the disaster that the Year of Europe turned out to be, Heath also made his own contribution.

The Copenhagen Summit in December was supposed to be the occasion for setting in place the ideas on European governance which Pompidou, Heath and Brandt had been developing and discussing. But the Arab oil embargo was much closer to the minds of other leaders as the date approached. "Hitherto", Hunt advised Heath on 10 December "we have concentrated on securing every available barrel of oil for the United Kingdom, against the resistance of the oil companies, whom we have threatened with reprisals if they divert supplies intended for the UK by the Arab producers".[118]

"We fully recognise the gravity of the threat posed by the oil crisis", the Foreign Office told its European posts in a Guidance telegram on the same day. "We have never imagined that we could insulate ourselves from this problem, which has been aggravated in Britain by the current coal situation. We too have already imposed severe measures to restrain domestic demands on oil. But in our view the political factors are the most important. We believe that if the Arab states saw that their embargo was being openly frustrated, this would provoke them to reduce further oil supplies to Europe, thereby increasing the Community's economic difficulties. In these circumstances we judge it essential to continue to resist public declarations of Community solidarity which could only add to our problems . . . The objective of Community solidarity can be pursued best in the political field".[119]

The Foreign Office telegram was, as far as Britain's domestic situation was concerned, an understatement. The Government's dispute with British coal-miners was getting worse. The miners were operating a go-slow which threatened to turn into an all-out strike. This, together with the Arab embargo, prompted Heath, on 13 December, to announce to the House of Commons, and later that day to the British people on television, that in the New Year industry would be put on a three-day week.

Meanwhile, Heath's hopes of securing a deal at Copenhagen on a Regional Development Fund were fading. When Foreign Ministers met on 3–4 December to prepare the Summit, the Dutch complained of British and French reluctance to back any concrete measures to deal with the oil embargo and the Germans threatened to block progress on issues of importance to Britain, such as the RDF.[120] National pressures were unravelling Community solidarity.

Heath described the Copenhagen Summit of mid-December as "the worst Summit I have ever experienced".[121] This was mainly, in his view, down to the fact that four Foreign Ministers (from Algeria, Sudan, Tunisia and Abu Dhabi) descended uninvited on the meeting, kept the Foreign Ministers of the Community from their beds until 3 in the morning and distorted the rest of the summit by making it inevitable that what remained of the following day was taken up with hearing a report of what the Arab envoys wanted and deciding what to say and not to say about it in the communiqué.

The Summit did agree that Heads of Government should henceforth meet three times a year. But on energy and the RDF there was no progress. Douglas-Home responded to German stalling on the Fund by refusing to go further in the debate on European energy policy.

In a speech in London on 13 December, Kissinger had proposed the establishment of an Energy Action Group to prepare a programme for collaboration in all areas of the energy crisis. Kissinger engaged the German Government in its support. Heath did try at the Summit to persuade Pompidou to agree to a favourable reference to the initiative in the Summit communiqué. But the French President refused, seeing this as another attempt by the United States to make Europe dance to their tune.

On the day after the Summit Heath telephoned Brandt. "I just rang up really about, as you may have expected, the RDF, because it is, for us at any rate, a political crisis unless we can get the Fund started on the substantial level which we have been discussing . . . If this does not materialise, then I am afraid it will turn really very bad indeed. But we did try to help yesterday with the energy side of things". Brandt was accommodating but did not think that Germany could agree to the sums of money the Commission were proposing.[122]

Heath, however, remained adamant, himself setting the objectives for the next round of negotiation at Foreign Minister level in the week after the Summit. "I will not", Heath said, "settle for less than 25% of the total funds . . . There must be a three-year commitment . . . We shall not settle for less than the figures we have ourselves proposed . . . We will not be prepared to settle for any text . . . which prejudices the Commission review . . . We will not be prepared to consider a fund benefitting three countries only, whatever totals may be on offer in such a context".[123]

In a separate message to the Foreign Secretary Heath instructed him "to stand firm on our stated position. A derisory sum of the kind mentioned by the Germans would be fatal for both economic and political reasons. If necessary we shall have to 'put back the clock' at the end of the year until we get a satisfactory solution. We shall not obtain what we want from the Community unless we stand up and fight".[124]

In a situation of impasse in Brussels the Foreign Secretary and Heath spoke on the telephone. Herr Apel, State Secretary in the Foreign Ministry, who was the German negotiator, had refused to budge and, according to Douglas-Home, was linking progress on the RDF to progress on EMU and energy. Douglas-Home had warned him that that was a weapon Britain too could use and Heath agreed: "Well, we won't move an inch on energy in setting anything up or doing anything because regional development is just as important to us as energy is to the Germans . . . They have got to produce the full amount – the full amount, that's what it's got to be".[125]

That the situation was serious was demonstrated by a phone call from Jean Monnet to Armstrong, wringing his hands about the impasse in Brussels.[126] The discussion in Cabinet the next day showed that, as the year drew to its close, the Community was indeed being held up at Anglo-German gunpoint. Heath reported that discussions at the Copenhagen Summit had been unsatisfactory because of the German Government's unwillingness to agree to an RDF on the scale necessary. The Foreign Secretary added that he had subsequently been obliged to refuse formally to agree to a resolution of the Council of Ministers setting up a Community Energy Committee because of German unwillingness to move towards the European Commission proposal on the size of the Fund.

In subsequent discussion in Cabinet the point was made that "although our refusal to agree to Community action on energy might be argued to be out of proportion to the problem of establishing the RDF, it should be remembered that it was the German Finance Minister, Herr Schmidt, who in the first place had made a link between progress on energy and the move to the second stage of EMU. It was right for us to make a strong response to the German attitude. Success in Community negotiations depended on being prepared to press with determination for national objectives. Unless we did so we would never play an effective and decisive part in Community affairs or achieve benefits for the United Kingdom".

Heath summed up that "the Cabinet was agreed that the establishment of an RDF of a satisfactory size on reasonable terms was our prime immediate objective within the Community and we must be prepared to press this objective with the greatest determination".[127]

Despite this fighting talk, there was also a realisation that the situation could not be allowed to continue. Palliser was accordingly despatched from Brussels to Bonn to work out with Henderson what might be the next steps. It was a mark of the seriousness of the situation that Henderson opened his telegram containing their joint view (sent in a personal telegram for Douglas-Home and Heath) with the words: "We start from the assumption that HMG want Britain to stay in the Community but that a satisfactory outcome on the Regional Fund is of crucial importance to the Government's pursuit of its European policy". Failure to reach agreement on the Fund at the next scheduled meeting on 7 January would, the two Ambassadors argued, if it were accompanied by Britain's continuing veto on further progress over energy, weaken support for the United Kingdom elsewhere in the Community and thus diminish the prospects of securing a satisfactory outcome on the Fund itself. Of course Britain could make things difficult for other countries too, e.g. on the CAP. But the picture of the Community falling apart in squabbles of that kind would make it increasingly incomprehensible to British opinion. Palliser and Henderson recommended that, with a little flexibility on the British side, and careful private negotiation with the Germans, it should be possible to "arrive at something which is politically acceptable and will enable us to show considerable advantage to Britain".[128]

Nairne recommended this course of action to Heath (who had gone to Chequers for Christmas), Heath spoke to the Foreign Secretary and the latter invited German Ministers to come to London in early January.

A healthy bucket of cold-water realism was thrown over the whole issue in late December by Derek Mitchell of the Treasury who sought to put the RDF into perspective. "In financial terms", Mitchell wrote, "what is at stake over the RDF is not very significant. We have emphasised this repeatedly. At best – that is to say even if the Community were to accept our present proposals *in toto* – the net gain from the RDF in the long run would only go a small way towards offsetting the net cost of Community membership, which arises mainly from the CAP. The fact is that, in doing battle over the RDF, we are promoting the interests of Italy and Ireland more than of the UK, because it is now clear that the Fund will be distributed in a way which will give Italy a very much larger share than the UK, and Ireland a much larger one in proportion to her size and contribution. What we are asking of the Germans, however, is a very substantial increase in their net contribution to finance the RDF . . . If the Germans are to be made to pay, the main pressure will have to come from us again. But we shall not be the main beneficiary and the cost to Germany will not be commensurate with the benefit to us. It seems only prudent to weigh the benefits against the damage which we may do to our own interests, both in the short term and in the longer term, through a major and continuing confrontation with the Germans over this question . . . A continuing conflict between the two Governments could encourage them [the Germans] to make difficulties about multilateral credit, for example through the IMF, and the damage which could be done in this way could greatly exceed any possible financial gain through the RDF."

Mitchell then made his most important point. "In the longer run, we hope at some stage to secure some modification of the Community's budgetary arrangements to relieve us of some of the heavy and growing burden of our net contribution to the budget. This will be extremely difficult for all sorts of reasons, including political ones, and the Germans will not be the only, or even the primary, obstacle. But we shall only be able to get an improvement in our position if the Germans pay more. Of course this is not an immediate issue. But a reform of the Community's financing system might bring the UK much larger benefits than the RDF – because we ourselves would be the main beneficiaries – and we should not lose sight of this long-term point of view, both in stepping up antagonism between ourselves and the Germans, and, to the extent we succeed in dragging more money from an unwilling Germany for the RDF, in stepping up their resistance to any further increase in their net contribution to the EEC budget". This perceptive and, in the rather febrile atmosphere of the moment, brave, letter was seen by Heath, though his views on it are not recorded.[129]

The issue rumbled on, unresolved, through January 1974. It was complicated by an invitation from President Nixon to an International Energy Conference in Washington. At Cabinet on 17 January Heath said that the establishment of an RDF on satisfactory terms remained a prime objective. That objective should be pursued vigorously within the Community and the Government should "for the time being maintain the link with the development of an internal Community energy policy".[130]

After Cabinet, however, the Foreign Secretary sought some attenuation of the hard line. In a minute to the Prime Minister, Douglas-Home argued that when the Government had first made the link between Regional Policy and Energy Policy in December it had caused the Community a salutary shock. Now, Britain's partners would like to see the establishment of the Energy Committee which, but for the British linkage, had been agreed in principle at Copenhagen. Douglas Home advised against accepting that next step but counselled against blocking preparations for the Washington meeting. The Government should, he argued, block all other formal decisions on a Community energy policy but allow the preparation of a common EEC position for the Washington energy conference, as well as preparation by the Permanent Representatives of positions which could be useful for the future. In other words, proposals would be prepared but not formally adopted until the Council of Ministers had adopted the RDF. To this, Heath agreed.[131]

There were other signs of what was to become a prevailing British caution over European matters. Germany had, from 1 January, taken over the Presidency of the Council. Oliver Wright, the Political Director at the Foreign Office, attended a meeting of Political Directors in Bonn on 11 January. The German chairman announced that the Presidency would propose to the Council of Ministers on 14 January the establishment of a Council ad hoc working group of senior officials to prepare by the end of April a preliminary report, for submission to the next Summit meeting, on the issues on which the Paris Summit had called for progress. Wright felt it necessary, as he reported to London, "to put down a firm marker about the possible speed of advance without pouring too much cold water". It was right that there should be the political impulse from the Summit to accelerate the work on European Union. But the political impulse had to go in double harness with a sober appraisal of the economic realities in the countries of the Community. Given the complicated nature of the process of convergence between nine very different countries, there was bound to be a large gap between the political impulse and the economic reality. The pace of advance should not therefore be too fast: we must be cautious.

Bridges showed the telegram to Heath with the comment "The Germans show signs of wanting to go too fast". Heath himself did not comment.[132]

On 21 January Hunt minuted to Nairne, correctly concluding that the French decision, just taken, to float the Franc was widely regarded as having put paid to early progress towards EMU. "Thus all gloom ahead". But, Hunt thought, maybe this was the time for Britain to take the initiative in giving a new direction and emphasis to the Community. Hunt's prescription was notable for its inclusion of "much less emphasis on harmonisation for harmonisation's sake"; and a slow-down on talk about EMU. "Implicit in all this", he added, "is some soft-pedalling of the Commission's role and greater cooperation between Governments".[133]

Nairne responded on 25 January after a brainstorming with his colleagues in the Cabinet Office's EEC Secretariat. Talk had focussed principally on the current issues of monetary affairs, the energy crisis and the RDF issue. Any initiative would have to be directed in the first instance to Paris and Bonn – at a time of strained relations between them. Nairne agreed that the Commission was not the body to look to. The Brussels view was always first in the public domain because that was where the Press corps were situated. But the Brussels view was frequently and quickly trumped by action and comment from Community capitals. It was a fact of life that the Commission's role had been weakened, possibly for many years to come. It had failed to adopt a high profile on the three issues which Nairne had mentioned. Ortoli had signally failed to perform the role of high-level entrepreneur in which he had cast himself when he called on Heath the previous September.

Nairne did not think there was enough in Hunt's minute to form the basis of an initiative. "We would need to have the right substance and the right timing, and I do not think that either are to hand at present".[134]

Palliser addressed the malaise in a Despatch of 25 January 1974 on Britain's first year in the Community. Where had things gone wrong, he asked? Disagreement on specific issues, such as EMU and the RDF was part of it. But the Council of Ministers had also seen a resurgence of national feeling among the original members in parallel with the inevitable self-assertion of the new ones. Agreement was more difficult among nine than among six. Indecisive and chaotic meetings, presented dramatically by the Press, had disillusioned public opinion. In Britain, there was a growing disaffection with Europe. The main cause of disarray lay in the disparate reactions of the Member States to the energy crisis. Britain, France, and in some degree Italy, were in a different situation politically vis-à-vis the Arabs from their partners and, in consequence, in a different position economically in regard to oil supply. The result was that, probably for the first time since 1945, the smaller countries had found themselves, if reluctantly, lined up with Germany in a virtual confrontation with France and Britain. In addition, 'Community solidarity' had seemed to mean, for several of Britain's partners, solidarity with them but virtual independence from Britain on their part in their political words or deeds. One outcome had been blame attributed to Britain as much as France for prejudicing the Community's relations with the United States. "And, in fairness", Palliser added, "I suppose one must ask 'were we quite blameless'? Could we have played the hand in some way differently, and even perhaps with more silence and discretion"?

There was in Brussels, Palliser believed, a widespread view that "we are all condemned to succeed". But if there was one lesson from the last quarter of 1973 it was that "if we do not succeed, then we are most certainly condemned". Crucial to success was cohesion and for that to happen there had to be a basic understanding between Germany, France and Britain. All too often in 1973 it had looked as if the three partners could manage one or other variant of a *ménage à deux*, but not a *ménage à trois*. Yet somehow that had to be achieved and to find concrete expression in specific areas of policy, notably, for 1974, energy policy and the relationship between the European Community and the United States.

The fact that the first year of British membership of the European Community had coincided with a series of daunting economic trends was, Palliser believed, at the root of the growth in disaffection with the Community evident in Britain throughout the year. Opinion in the six original Member States, acclimatised by over a decade of uneven, but essentially successful, European cooperation, saw no reason to blame the Treaty of Rome and all its works. For their part, Denmark and Ireland had the solace of significant net receipts under the CAP to compensate them for disappointments over other European questions. But in Britain, the gathering storm had led those with no confidence in the prospects of fair gain from EC membership to take a jaundiced view of the unfolding scene in Brussels, ample confirmation as they saw it of their initial distaste for the whole enterprise. Britain had had a defensive role in resisting the adoption of policies and decisions inimical to her interests, and in trying to prevent British Government decisions from being attacked as inconsistent with the spirit of Britain's commitments. The British had discovered that it was not all plain sailing to 'join now and negotiate later'. Britain had had to use her elbows to get to the bar alongside the Six. But concentration by all members on their national interests had led to neglect of the Community interest, because Member States had not been ready to distinguish between the two. And indeed, the national Governments of the Nine, except perhaps for the Benelux countries, showed little tendency to accept that such a distinction even existed.[135]

On 7 February 1974, Cabinet discussed the guaranteed price of milk to be set under the 1974 annual farm price review. It was doubtful if the kind of settlement that would be acceptable to the farmers could be paid within Community rules. The Prime Minister summed up that the Minister of Agriculture should press the Commission for a derogation for the UK.

But Heath had something more momentous to tell his colleagues. Following the breakdown of discussions between the Government and the TUC, and the decision of the Executive of the National Union of Mineworkers to call a national coal strike, he had decided to seek a dissolution of Parliament so that the country might express its views in a General Election on 28 February.

Never again, following that election, was Heath to have the direction of national or European affairs. When Margaret Thatcher won the General Election of 1979 Heath's hopes, such as they were, of being appointed Foreign Secretary were disappointed. Her offer, instead, to make Heath British Ambassador in Washington was treated with the scorn it probably deserved.

Heath became after 1975 the embodiment of a certain idea of Europe, and of Britain's place within it, increasingly seen to be at variance with the stance adopted by all the British Governments that followed. He was the most European of Britain's Prime Ministers by instinct and conviction. He embraced the bold ideas of Economic and Monetary Union, and of European Union more broadly. But his views and policies in practice do not emerge from the record as so significantly different from those adopted by his successors. He believed, not in a Europe of the institutions so much as a Europe of nations, led by the three biggest members. He had some of the difficulties all his successors had of turning that idea into reality when faced with British domestic opinion and priorities. He was prepared, over the RDF, to hold the Community to ransom and to do so over the impact of the Arab oil embargo, arguably an issue which cried out for solidarity.

The entente which Pompidou and Heath had fostered and nurtured was to remain an enduring, if fragile and fractious, one. In one of the last scenes from the Heath Government, at the Energy Conference in Washington in February 1974, the French found themselves at loggerheads with their European partners and Britain found herself siding with the United States against France. Oliver Wright, who was there, told his French opposite number that "those who argued in Whitehall that British interests were best pursued through the Community would now find their position significantly weakened".[136] Within days of the Conference, Heath was gone. Within a few weeks more, Pompidou was dead.

Heath never succeeded, as he had vowed, in winning the wholehearted consent of the British people to the European project. It was to fall to Harold Wilson, his hated nemesis, to attempt that task.

* * * *

10 Renegotiation and Referendum: 1974–1975

Harold Wilson was perhaps fortunate that, after losing the February 1974 General Election, Edward Heath spent a fruitless weekend seeking a deal with Jeremy Thorpe's Liberal Party. It meant that when it became obvious that it would fall to Wilson to form a minority Government, the fact that Labour had secured a smaller percentage share of the vote than the Conservatives and that the Government would be vulnerable to being outvoted in the House of Commons, was less relevant than the clear evidence that there existed no feasible alternative. And, as the new Foreign Secretary, Jim Callaghan, told Britain's assembled Ambassadors on 20 March, "the Government would not be brought down while the anti-Marketeers in the Conservative party thought that it was set on a really fundamental renegotiation".[1]

The new Government was committed by its manifesto (at ten pages, one of the shortest ever and a third the length of the Tory equivalent) to re-negotiate the terms of Britain's membership of the European Communities. It was pledged to secure:

Major changes in the CAP;
New and fairer methods of financing the European Community budget;
Resistance to proposals for EMU which would lead to increased unemployment;
Retention of national Parliamentary powers to pursue effective regional, industrial and fiscal policies;
Better safeguards for Commonwealth and developing countries;
No harmonisation of VAT which would require Britain to tax necessities.

In the event of a successful re-negotiation, the "people should have the right to decide the issue through a General Election or a Consultative Referendum". If those two tests were passed (a successful renegotiation and the expressed approval of the majority of the British people) then the Government would be "ready to play our full part in developing a new and wider Europe".

If renegotiation did not succeed, then the Government would not regard the obligations of the Accession Treaty as binding. They would then put to the British people the reasons why they found the new terms unacceptable, and consult them on the advisability of negotiating Britain's withdrawal from the Communities.[2]

Implicit in these undertakings was the notion that the Government would have to make a judgement about whether renegotiation had or had not succeeded. But there was no specific commitment to a Government recommendation to the people. Nor had any decision been taken as to whether the form of consultation would be a referendum or a further General Election, although Wilson himself had spoken several months earlier of the possibility of a referendum. Public expectations lay in that direction and, by the end of April, Wilson was talking to the New Zealand Opposition leader about "the issue which would be put to the nation in the referendum".[3]

At his meeting with Britain's Ambassadors from EEC countries on 20 March, Callaghan said to them that he had told Wilson before the General Election that, if he came to the Foreign Office, he would want to be in overall charge of renegotiation, subject to the control of the Prime Minister and Cabinet. He could not, however, say at this stage whether he would prefer the result to be that Britain should stay in the Community or not. If, after renegotiation, the Government felt that the Community corresponded with British interests and the realities of European relations with the United States, then Britain should stay in; otherwise she should not. The aim must be to reach a conclusion by the end of the year.

While Callaghan professed agnosticism about the outcome of the negotiations, it was self-evident that no Government would embark on a negotiation with the object of failing to achieve its aims.

On his arrival at the Foreign Office as the new Foreign Secretary, Callaghan had sent for Michael Butler, the Foreign Office Assistant Under-Secretary responsible for European Community matters. He had read overnight the briefing paper on Europe which Butler had prepared for him. He thanked Butler warmly for it. Fears of an immediate posting to Tirana began to fade in Butler's mind as Callaghan spoke. "They tell me, Michael" Callaghan continued, "that you really care about Europe. Well, that's all right as long as you remember that I really care about the Labour Party". That was the basis of an understanding. Without it ever being spelled out, it was believed in Whitehall from the beginning that Wilson and Callaghan wanted a successful negotiation. It was equally known that Tony Benn (Secretary of State for Industry) and Peter Shore (Secretary of State for Trade) did not.[4]

One of the questions which the Ambassadors addressed was whether renegotiation could be accomplished without amendment of either the Treaty of Accession or the Treaty of Rome. Michael Palliser, the UK Permanent Representative to the EEC in Brussels, pointed out that to amend either would require the unanimous agreement of all the Member States and a special inter-governmental conference. A lot could be achieved without Treaty amendment and he advised against raising the issue unless and until it became necessary to do so.

Callaghan said that he would like a preliminary view by 1 April on whether Treaty amendment would be necessary. Whether or not he would actually say so to his colleagues in the Community was another matter. They must not be allowed to think that renegotiation was not a fundamental question. He had the impression that the French thought that Britain could be bought off by a few months' grace on food prices. Nobody must think that this would be enough.

Britain's Ambassador in Paris, Edward Tomkins, took his cue to say that the French did indeed hold the key to renegotiation. They could say 'no' and, as everyone in Britain knew, they frequently did. Callaghan again responded true to form. If, he said, the French wanted a showdown, they would have one. Now that Britain was in the Community, she was no longer in the position of *demandeur*. If the British Government did not get what she wanted the Community would not go forward. The Government was not playing from a weak hand and he would not go along with the French. They would have to adjust to him. De Gaulle had been right in thinking it was against French interests to let Britain into the Community. He [Callaghan] thought French policies were appalling, especially towards the United States, and he hoped other Member States would be prepared to speak up against them.

Other Ambassadors said their piece. From Bonn, Sir Nicholas (Nicko) Henderson said that Germany regarded reconciliation with France within the European Community as vital, second only in importance to the Atlantic Alliance. German leaders were afraid that, if there were no European Union, dynamic forces of extremism in Germany, of both Left and Right, would get out of hand. If Chancellor Brandt was supine towards France it was because he did not believe Europe without France was possible.

Henderson's argument clearly resonated with Callaghan. Having experienced war in Europe, it was, he said, of great importance to prevent Germany breaking away. A relationship to meet the German requirement must be worked out, but whether it really required a Common Agricultural Policy and Economic and Monetary Union, he did not know. He personally wanted to know what sort of Europe the other members were aiming at. It was very important for people in Britain to know whether the Community was serious about EMU and European Union. If those matters could be left out of account then it might be possible to do a deal on such matters as the CAP.

Callaghan's mind was already turning to the issue of Britain's contribution to the EEC budget, which the Foreign Office had identified as the issue which, above all others, could, as Michael Butler put it, be dynamite in the Community. What mattered was the net position on payments, and for Britain both sides of the balance were wrong. Britain might expect to get back 8% of the Community budget. But, after the transitional period (during which Britain's budget contribution was limited) Britain could expect to pay into the budget up to 25% or even 27%, amounting to an outflow of up to £700 million per year. This was not reasonable for a country with a low growth rate and a low GNP. At present, Germany was by far the biggest contributor, with Britain next. France was a small contributor. The big gainers were Denmark, Netherlands and Ireland. As Britain's contribution increased, the other countries would all be better off, with France becoming a net gainer.

According to Butler, the expenditure side of the budget did not seem to offer very good opportunities for improving Britain's net position, though some sums might be had from the CAP, Social Policy and a Regional Development Fund. On the contribution side, an external energy tariff would have "much charm".

When North Sea Oil was fully on stream, Britain would import little crude oil and therefore a tariff would cost very little to Britain, but a great deal to other Member States who would continue to be net importers. An alternative idea was for a Revenue Sharing Fund, by means of which each year contributions and receipts would be evened up so that everyone was in balance overall. Such a scheme would be more attractive than an energy tariff to the Germans, and would not be bad for France, but it would hit the small countries, particularly the three who were presently the big net beneficiaries. It would be more difficult to negotiate than an energy tariff. Neither scheme should require Treaty amendment.

Henderson doubted whether either scheme would prove negotiable with the Germans. Palliser advised a less than head-on approach. It should be based on drawing the attention of Britain's partners to the fears of the previous Government that the existing financial arrangements might turn out to be intolerable, and to the marker which had been put down, and accepted by others, in the accession negotiations. Those fears had now been realised. The Government should present the general case first, rather than producing precise remedies. There was a distinction between justice and the *juste retour*, and it should be made clear that it was the first, and not the second, for which Britain was asking.

Turning to EMU and European Union, Butler said it was right to be sceptical. The Werner Plan for EMU had been dangerously over-ambitious. Present Community ambitions were much more modest. Officials would be recommending that the Government agree to a second stage of EMU in the near future. The same considerations applied to European Union. Work was only just beginning and would start with no more than an attempt to define the questions to be answered.

Nicko Henderson, whose unhappiness with the Labour Government's sceptical approach seeps out of his interventions, said that the political arguments for British membership of the Community could not simply be put on one side. He could not see a feasible future for 50 million people belonging neither to Europe nor to the United States. Britain could not become like Norway or Sweden; her interests in the world at large were far too great. Nor did he believe that the United States would welcome a United Kingdom which was outside Europe. If Britain withdrew from the Community, her influence would be virtually nil for a generation. If Britain wanted concessions on the economic aspects of membership she could not at the same time block progress towards a political union which other members wanted.

Palliser added that, if Europe fell apart, there would be no hope of maintaining Britain's existing defence arrangements. The political weight of Europe could only be realised if it put forward its full and united economic strength. The other members regarded themselves as having paid once for British membership. They would see no point in making concessions if they thought that, at the end of the day, Britain was going to pull out in any event.

Trade Secretary Peter Shore joined the meeting and flagged up an issue which was to be one of the most divisive ones within the Government during renegotiation. Automatic changes in the Common Commercial Tariff were due at the end of the year. It was inconceivable, Shore said, that the Government could introduce an Order to effect them, as the previous Government had done. Callaghan was out of the room. No one commented.[5]

The discussion with Ambassadors clearly had some impact on Callaghan because the following day, in Bonn, he told his opposite number, Walter Scheel, that, while he could not rule out the need for amendments to the Treaty of Accession, he did not want to start from that position; and that he hoped, as regards renegotiation, "that things would turn out right".

From the German perspective, the one welcome change arising from the change of British Government must have been the loss of all-consuming interest in a Regional Development Fund. The new British Government did not want to appear committed to the same objective as its Conservative predecessor and, in any case, a Fund would be small compared to national regional aid. Moreover, if the Government pressed for a large Fund, that might weaken their claim for a more comprehensive solution to the British budget problem. Accordingly, when Scheel raised the issue Callaghan said that it could be argued that there were two possible approaches: either a large agricultural contribution and a large RDF in return, or a small RDF and a small contribution to the CAP. But he was not sure that it made sense for the British housewife to subsidise the French farmer (via the CAP) while the German taxpayer subsidised regional development in South Wales (via the RDF).[6]

From other elements of Callaghan's visit, including a call on Brandt, it emerged that the Germans had been taken by surprise by the extent of British renegotiation requirements. German Government circles were reported in the German Press to be "alarmed by Callaghan's announcement that the Labour Government prefers cooperation in a loose customs union to being closely bound in a political and economic European union".[7]

Van Well, the German Political Director, told Henderson that Callaghan's visit had left the Germans "very pensive". They had not realised the full extent of the problems that the Community were facing. The meetings with Callaghan had caused consternation on the German side. Scheel ("very disturbed") and his team had sat up until 2 o'clock in the morning discussing the situation "in the gravest way".

Henderson also reported that he had been able to tell his Community colleagues in Bonn that Callaghan had told Brandt that he would not conduct the negotiations with the intention of getting out of the Community. But Callaghan had pointed out that the verdict of the British people, if sought now, would be unfavourable. Callaghan had said that, whatever doubts the British Government had about the European Community, it was 100% in favour of the friendliest possible relations between its main members, including, of course, Germany and France. However, cooperation between the countries of Europe must be conducted, Callaghan had insisted, without any tinge of anti-Americanism. Good transatlantic relations and good relationships within Europe were not incompatible. Callaghan believed this was a more traditional type of British foreign policy.[8]

All in all, Callaghan probably thought he had got the balance about right: Britain's partners had to see that the Government meant business; opinion at home, not least within the Cabinet, had to see that Callaghan was pursuing the manifesto agenda vigorously; and Britain's key partners needed to conclude that, while there was a price to be paid for satisfying Britain's demands, the prize would be her continued membership which, for almost all of them, was a desirable objective. What had disturbed the Germans, however, was the fact that their six-month Presidency of the Council of Ministers, which had begun in January, would be overshadowed by the British issue and, more profoundly, that Callaghan's perception of the European project as a business arrangement was a far cry from their own commitment to the eventual aim of European Union. Oliver Wright, who had been with Callaghan, told Nairne that Nicko Henderson had been left feeling gloomy. Wright's own view was that, provided Callaghan did not go out of his way to publicise in Europe his agnostic views about the Community, there was a reasonable prospect of establishing "something of a pragmatic partnership with the Germans".[9]

From the perspective of Wilson and Callaghan, there were two main aspects to renegotiation: the external negotiation with foreigners and the internal management of a divided Cabinet. Wilson had constructed his Cabinet carefully. He had within it a majority of people who were either pro-Market (with Roy Jenkins and Shirley Williams prominent among them) or (as with Healey, Callaghan, Crosland and Peart) leaning in that direction, while keeping their options open. The anti-Marketeers (Foot, Benn, Shore, Castle, Hart and Varley most notably) were formidable but in a minority.

Part of the purpose of Wilson in allowing Callaghan clear leadership of renegotiation was to keep the reins in their joint hands. It cannot, in addition, have been far from Wilson's mind that Callaghan, one of the main authors of his European misfortunes in Opposition, would be the person most painfully exposed if things turned out badly in domestic, especially Labour Party, terms. Moreover, if Wilson was to manage the balancing act in Cabinet and Party successfully, he would have to be slightly distanced from the negotiating fray.

An immediate issue was that Peter Shore, as Secretary of State for Trade, would have a role in Brussels in the negotiations. On 7 March, Shore wrote to Wilson recalling that "when we spoke about my role in the EEC negotiations you said that you wished me to take the lead among the economic Departments concerned in this question. I should be grateful if you would confirm this and, further, whether you would agree to set up an appropriate committee". Of course, Shore continued, the Foreign Secretary might wish to chair the committee when he was in London but when he was away Shore assumed that the Prime Minister would want him, Shore, to chair it.[10]

This was not what Wilson had in mind and he spoke to Shore again, prompting Shore to write "to confirm my understanding of our conversation this afternoon about my role in the EEC renegotiations. This was that you wished me to accompany the Foreign Secretary at Council meetings and that, in his absence, I would normally accompany Mr Hattersley to such meetings".[11]

This was closer to what Wilson and Callaghan wanted. Shore would attend Council meetings but either Callaghan, or Hattersley, as Minister of State in the Foreign Office, would lead, even though Hattersley was not a Cabinet member. What was less clear was whether Shore would attend all meetings of the Council at Foreign Minister level or only those which were to discuss trade and tariff policy. Callaghan was prepared for a little ad hoc flexibility, based on the agenda, but was absolutely clear that "I intend to go myself to as many of the Foreign Ministers' Councils as I can, but I suppose there will be occasions when I will have commitments elsewhere. When that happens, Roy Hattersley, with his special responsibilities for Europe, will take the lead in the Council".[12]

After a bit of prodding from Callaghan, Wilson himself wrote again to Shore on 25 March confirming that he had agreed with the Foreign Secretary "that you should accompany him (or, in his absence, Mr Hattersley) to Council meetings when matters of trade and tariff policy are being discussed. Let us see how things develop on this basis."[13]

Wilson established two Ministerial committees to handle renegotiation: a Committee on European Community Strategy (ECS) and a Committee on European Questions (EQ). ECS was chaired by the Prime Minister. It included the most senior members of the Government, some, but not all, of the Ministers directly concerned with European questions and some of the main supporters and opponents of membership of the Community. The most notable absentee from the membership was Tony Benn, though he was often invited to attend. The Committee was thus designed to allow all shades of opinion to be heard, while ensuring that its decisions would tend towards continued membership of the Community.

EQ was chaired by the Foreign Secretary and intended to deal with ongoing European Community business although, over time, it came to handle many renegotiation issues. It had a subordinate official-level committee called EQO. The Cabinet Office European Unit, under Patrick Nairne, reported to the Foreign Secretary but also had a direct line to the Prime Minister. The Unit dealt with much of the day-to-day coordination of renegotiation and made recommendations about tactics. There was within Whitehall no formally constituted renegotiation team as such.

Because of the divided views among senior Cabinet members, officials found themselves, to an unprecedented degree, navigating in tricky waters. Loyalty to the views of an individual Minister had, in some cases, to be weighed alongside fidelity to the overall policy of the Government as a whole. More was done by personal contact, in corridors and on telephones, and less committed to paper, than usual in Whitehall. One official described a sensation of "walking a tightrope and living in dangerous times".[14]

Callaghan's first formal statement to the Council of Ministers on Britain's negotiating requirements was scheduled for the beginning of April. His text would have to be approved by Cabinet, which was also confronted by two other pressing issues, not directly related to renegotiation but with a potential impact on it: Concorde and the Channel Tunnel. Denis Healey, the new Chancellor, wanted

Concorde scrapped. The country, he told Cabinet on 14 March, confronted an economic situation which might well be the worst which had ever been faced in peacetime. Inflation was running at 10%; the balance of payments deficit was at around £1,500 million; the borrowing requirement was £4,000 million; and growth had come virtually to a halt. Proposals on how to end the Concorde project would be brought to Cabinet shortly.[15]

A week later, Healey told Cabinet that the economic arguments for cancelling Concorde were overwhelming. It would be impossible to avoid very heavy losses on its production, sales and operation. Others agreed. But there were two main worries. Firstly, a unilateral decision to cancel Concorde would gravely damage the Government's commitment to real consultation with the trade union movement; and, secondly, the legal risks of unilateral withdrawal could, so the Attorney General advised, carry a heavy financial penalty. The French attitude to cancellation was not clear. Healey believed that the French Government, like the British, faced strong financial pressures in favour of cancellation. Others believed that the French Government might still favour the further development of the aircraft and the quest for additional orders. Wilson concluded that the current mood of most in Cabinet was towards cancellation but that there was insufficient information to enable a decision to be made.

Labour had wrestled with the Concorde issue when last in Government, as had their immediate Conservative predecessors. The Channel Tunnel scheme had been initiated under the previous Labour Administration. In Opposition the Labour Party had not opposed the scheme in principle, but had attacked it in practice, especially the emphasis on road traffic as against through rail services, and the proposals for the terminal at Cheriton. Labour, Tony Crosland, the Secretary of State for the Environment, told the new Cabinet, were committed to a fundamental reappraisal of the project. He proposed that the existing Phase II should be allowed to continue while a review, of a more fundamental kind than the Tories had envisaged, was undertaken. Again, the issue was deferred.[16]

At this stage in the life of the new Government, the focus was on three elements in the renegotiation: the possibility of an empty chair; the need, or otherwise, for Treaty change; and the most important priorities in the negotiation.

There was no real argument in favour of the politics of the empty chair. It would have meant a series of separate bilateral negotiations with the other Member States and an inability to influence key negotiations on normal EEC business. As early as mid-March therefore, Ministers agreed that Fred Peart should play a full part in the annual CAP price fixing which was then under way. They also agreed that it would be preferable to attain the Government's objectives by securing changes to Community policies than by seeking changes to the Treaties, although that option was not ruled out.[17] The negotiating priorities had not yet been established, beyond all those laid down in the General Election Manifesto. But the importance of Britain's adverse budget position had been made very clear at Callaghan's meeting with British Ambassadors and he himself highlighted it when reporting to Wilson on his visit to Bonn. The Germans had been very friendly. They were even sympathetic. They were, however, unenthusiastic since "if we are to pay less, the Germans among others will have to pay more". Callaghan also noted the undoubted fact that the Germans had a vision of a uniting Europe, even if they were not very precise about what they meant by it.[18]

Ahead of Callaghan's first meeting with his EEC colleagues at the Council of Ministers on 1 April, the omens were mixed. Fred Peart had secured an early success at the Agriculture Council, including special arrangements in the price fixing to meet the British need to avoid increases in prices of basic foodstuffs in the shops. The Government was helped by the fact that the world price of foodstuffs had increased so that the cost of food under the CAP looked more favourable than at the moment of accession. Peart was able to tell Cabinet that much good will and sympathy had been shown for the British position by the European Commission and by other members of the Council. Wilson made a point of offering Peart the congratulations of the entire Cabinet on his success.[19]

Relations between the British Government and the United States also took an early turn for the better. On a visit to London, Henry Kissinger told Wilson that the Americans had been unhappy when the Heath Government "seemed to be deliberately detaching itself in its relations with the United States in order to emphasise and strengthen its alignment to the rest of the Community".

Wilson agreed that Heath had leant too far towards the French Government, though he understood the argument that the French had been the key to British entry. Now Britain was in the Community, there would be less need for the French Government to play games. For its part, the new British Government "would not want to kick the US Government in the teeth; on the other hand it would not wish to appear to be excessively pro-American".

Kissinger was content with this. The US Government was not anti-French and did not want to see intra-European confrontations. Equally, they did not want an inward-looking Europe defining its position by reference to opposition to the United States.[20]

Emollient sentiments about France were not echoed across the Channel, but nor were the French Government declining all discussion. On 17 March, the French Foreign Minister, Michel Jobert, told Gaullist members of the National Assembly that there was no legal basis for the British renegotiation. Respect for the Treaties was fundamental. The six founder members of the Community had made sacrifices for Britain. France would defend the *acquis communautaire*. In the face of difficulties, she would "keep her feet firmly rooted in the agricultural soil". But Jobert also said that, while there could be no change in the Treaty of Rome, adaptations to the conditions in force for this or that country could be contemplated.[21]

By coincidence (or perhaps design) Callaghan was absent (seeing Kissinger) when Cabinet on 28 March discussed the statement he proposed to make to the Council of Ministers three days later. This enabled Wilson to say that the text could not be finalised by Cabinet and effectively left Callaghan some room for manoeuvre within a general agreement that the Foreign Secretary should set out the Government's position "on the lines proposed".

Wilson also instructed Ministers to allow their officials to participate in the continuing business of the Community.[22] He followed up with a minute to all

Ministers in charge of Departments reminding them that the Government had decided that an empty chair policy would be against their interests and that the Government would renegotiate from within the Community. Callaghan had told the House of Commons that the Government would be "unable to carry forward further processes of integration which could prejudice the outcome of the negotiations". Any cases of doubt should be submitted to the Foreign Secretary, copied to the Prime Minister.[23]

Callaghan's statement to the Council of Ministers in Luxembourg on 1 April was robust. It sounded, Roy Hattersley wrote later, "as I am sure he intended it to sound – deeply antagonistic to Britain's continued Common Market membership".[24] The *Financial Times* termed it "blunt to the point of rudeness".[25] Hattersley was reminded of what Michael Foot had said of Callaghan in the House of Commons: "The Right Honourable Member for Cardiff South always does everything on purpose".[26] When Palliser accompanied Callaghan to a meeting with Ortoli, Callaghan treated the Commission President with gratuitous and embarrassing roughness.[27]

The British Government and the British people questioned, Callaghan said, whether all was well in the Community. They were deeply concerned about the dangerously over-ambitious plans for EMU. Major changes were needed in the CAP. Trade access for Commonwealth countries, including New Zealand, was not good enough. The EEC allowed itself the indulgence of needless disagreement with the United States. Fundamental changes were required in the Community budget. The system resulted in massive subsidies from Britain to the other members of the Community. That was not acceptable. What Britain was asking for was not charity but a fair deal. The image of the Community in Britain was not good. But, Callaghan also said, Britain would negotiate in good faith and, if successful in achieving the right terms, the Government would put them to the British people for approval. The converse was also true. But he was not hoping for a negotiation for withdrawal. He would prefer a successful renegotiation from which the right terms for continued membership would emerge.

Only Jobert made an actively hostile statement in response, warning Britain that it was for her to adapt to the EEC and not for the EEC to adapt to Britain. Others were more nuanced, in private, if not in public. Callaghan told the Press that he had not expected Jobert "to cast rose petals in my path". Nor did he take a grave view of the refusal voiced by the Irish Government to contemplate any fundamental changes in the CAP: "I have read the Treaty of Rome and it seems to me that you can have almost any Common Agricultural Policy you like".

Did the Foreign Secretary, Callaghan was asked, see any problem about successive British Governments negotiating Treaties that had been signed and ratified? Indeed, said Callaghan, he saw very considerable difficulties. Treaties were to be taken very seriously. But as he had pointed out in the meeting, in a democracy even a Treaty must rest upon popular consent. There was no popular consent in Britain at the present time. After the renegotiation it would be possible to see whether such popular consent existed. Then, the Treaty would rest on a sure foundation. Asked under what circumstances he could envisage Britain pulling out of the Common Market, Callaghan replied: "That is not the basis on which we are beginning, is it"?[28]

When, three days later, Callaghan reported to Cabinet, he said that he had found the Germans generally helpful, though they had made it clear that they would oppose renegotiation of the European Community Treaties, partly on the practical ground that the changes would have to go through the German Parliament and partly because such changes would set a precedent for any other country which was dissatisfied with Community arrangements. These reactions, said Callaghan, confirmed the Government's view that the best approach would be to attempt, if possible, to achieve their objectives by modifying Community policies without changes in the Treaties.[29]

The day after Callaghan's statement to the Council, on 2 April, Tony Benn noted in his diary: "Came back at about 10 o'clock to hear that President Pompidou had died. This is very important for Concorde".[30]

Samuel Pepys, when his brother died of the plague, noted how swiftly mourning gave way to the returning rhythms of daily life. The Foreign Office, in its internal account of renegotiation, attributed to Pompidou's death a useful breathing space and a change in the atmospherics of renegotiation. The suddenness of the news did indeed take the world, and the French people, by surprise. But Pompidou had for a long time (certainly since 1972) been suffering from multiple myeloma, a malignant and lethal deterioration of the bone marrow. All this time, as the Paris Embassy reported, "eaten away from inside his frame, bloated by cortisone and increasingly immobile, subject to such bouts of pain that his staff now say he was sometimes in tears, still keeping the power of his mind, his pragmatic and often trenchant lucidity, though now more prone to irritation and oscillations of temperament, Pompidou had refused to admit that he was gravely ill." Only at the last meeting of the French Council of Ministers, six days before his death, had he spoken for the first time about his health. And even then, he gave no indication of his true condition though, said Christopher Ewart-Biggs, "his Ministers watched him with pity as well as with their customary apprehension".

Pompidou's behaviour had shown almost heroic courage and tenacity. But it was, as the Embassy expressed it, a frightening thought that a man could be secretly and mortally ill and yet have so much power. Yet, if he wanted to stay in the Elysée he could only have done as he did and keep his illness to himself, even if, towards the end, the pressure of public criticism as the President became less and less publicly visible drove his staff to resort to medical bulletins about innocuous complaints which, though perhaps true as far as they went, lied by omission.

Pompidou died before he could prepare the ground for his succession. He left no political testament. The Fifth Republic had been formed around the concept of a natural leader. Now there was no obvious such successor. France's future seemed painfully uncertain. Yet, Ewart-Biggs concluded, the very description of Pompidou's death showed that it was not, as with the General, the great oak falling.[31]

In the House of Commons on 3 April, both Callaghan, and Alec Douglas-Home for the Opposition, paid tribute to Pompidou. In Callaghan's case, the tribute was polite and pro-forma. Douglas-Home spoke in more personal terms of how he and Heath had for more than a year watched Pompidou's "indomitable courage as illness closed in on him. He never for one moment allowed the frailty of the body to undermine his sense of duty to France, to the French people and to Europe".

Turning to Callaghan's performance in Luxembourg, Douglas-Home asked whether it was right of Callaghan to start to threaten that, unless he got all he wanted, he would break up the partnership. Callaghan replied that "if good diplomacy led to the nature of the bargain that was struck by the previous Government, then perhaps a little rougher diplomacy will not come amiss". In any case, Callaghan added, it would not be for the British Government to break up the Community. That was a decision for the British people to take.[32]

The Prime Minister, accompanied by Edward Heath and Jeremy Thorpe, flew to Paris on 6 April for Pompidou's funeral. As Thorpe put it two days later in a 'thank you' letter to Wilson, "I don't think that any other country in the world would have combined its Prime Minister and the Leaders of two Opposition Parties in one plane. Such is democracy at its best."[33]

President Pompidou had something of a working funeral. Nixon, en route to Moscow, so forgot himself in front of an enthusiastic crowd outside the American Embassy Residence, which was a neighbour of the Elysée, as to proclaim it "a great day for France".[34]

In a private meeting with Wilson, subsequently minuted by the Prime Minister, Nixon told him that Kissinger had been wrong to call for the Year of Europe, just as he had been wrong to propose the Washington Energy Conference. On the Year of Europe, "I did say", Wilson wrote, "that perhaps, being wise after the event, this was not a very successful initiative, but I naturally did not say that Watergate was as good an explanation as anything else". On the Energy Conference, Wilson disagreed with Nixon. It accorded with his view that the EEC was far too small a parish to deal with the energy problem. He had supported an OECD approach, which was fundamentally the Kissinger position, and it was necessary to think, in the energy context, about Australia, New Zealand and Japan, as well as Europe, and no less importantly, about the Third World too.

The two leaders had talked about Atlanticism. "I said", Wilson recorded, "that I had a daily press conference in the Election. A different American journalist came each day and asked me, sometimes Callaghan, whether we were Atlanticists or Europeans. Both of us gave a strong Atlantic tinge to our approach to world affairs. Differentiating NATO from the purely EEC problem, I went on to say that, on the last occasion a new American journalist asked me this question, I said first that I was an Atlanticist, always have been, but more fundamentally I was a Seven Seas man because of my feelings about the Commonwealth".

"Throughout the conversation", Wilson concluded, "from the moment when he first shook my hand to the time he left me outside the British Embassy [next door to the American Residence] to which he had insisted on conducting me, with perhaps more regard for his internal position than for mine, it was Christian names throughout. There was no reference by either of us to Watergate though he made a tangential and identifiable reference to the subject when he said something about his internal difficulties which he described as 'a load of crap' "[35]

Wilson was in fact so concerned about being shown on television with Nixon that, unusually for him, he gave an interview to the BBC in order to get the shots of him and Nixon off the television screens.[36]

On 23 April, Callaghan attended an informal meeting of EEC Foreign Ministers, under German chairmanship at Schloss Gymnich, the castle that, for years afterwards, gave its name to such informal 'Gymnich meetings'. It was an opportunity for Callaghan to pose the question: What was meant when the Community members talked about European Union?

Heath had asked the same question a few months earlier, not in Callaghan's existential terms, but in terms of the institutional implications of the project. A retired British diplomat, Sir Bernard Burrows and a small team had been commissioned to report and, after the General Election, Callaghan agreed that their work could be completed.

Burrows' report ("rather better than I expected", according to Nairne) set out the implications of both European Union and Economic and Monetary Union in some detail. European Union, Burrows found, had not been precisely defined. Some thought it should be supra-national, with the European Commission acquiring the powers of a European Government. Others saw it as an inter-Governmental project in which ultimate powers would be retained by representatives of national Governments meeting together and with a strong commitment to unification of policies and the acceptance of more integrated structures for implementation. The present institutions of the Community were, however, barely capable of carrying out their existing tasks which were a long way short of those which would fall on them if Union was achieved. Burrows found it hard to envisage a practicable Union without greater use of majority voting or without an increase in the powers of the European Parliament. But any such increase would probably not be acceptable to public opinion without direct elections.

Burrows also found it impossible in practice to draw a clear distinction between European Union and EMU. He noted that the creation of a fully undistorted market in the Community would require the harmonisation of financial and economic policies which could otherwise cause distortions. The need for economic management on a Community scale would weaken the use of national regulators. External factors might well press the Community to common action in new fields, such as energy. On the other hand, there were obstacles to Union, especially Union of a supra-national kind. The French were highly reluctant to transfer power to an integrated Community system. There was a more general reluctance to undertake financial burdens which were disproportionate to the benefits to be received. National economies were different and, in some cases, divergent. Union would not necessarily reduce that divergence.

That astute observation led Burrows to note that full EMU, involving the fixing of exchange rates, could create disequilibria between different areas of the Community since it would remove, or render less effective, the normal powers of Governments to compensate for differences of performance by varying exchange rates, taxes and rates of interest. It would therefore be a precondition of EMU, Burrows concluded, that the Community should have the resources, and the power to use them, to prevent and correct these disequilibria, unless and until the degree of economic convergence made this unnecessary.

Institutionally, Burrows thought that full EMU would require a Community Treasury and central banking system, a quick-acting mechanism to operate political control over these administrations, and adequate powers of Parliamentary control. From the point of view of efficiency, the control of economic and financial measures of this magnitude would require a highly centralised authority. It would also presuppose an unprecedented exercise of political will on the part of the EEC Member States if they were to adopt, over a wide range of Government policies, the kind of integrated system which appeared to be required.

Unfortunately, and no doubt because of the policies and prejudices of the new Government, Nairne sent the report to John Hunt but decided otherwise to give it no circulation.[37]

Now, at Schloss Gymnich in Germany, when Callaghan put to his eight colleagues his question: what was meant when people talked of European Union, he received eight different answers. The Irish Foreign Minister, Garret Fitzgerald, had not been at the Paris Summit, so he did not know. He did, however, know that the word 'Union' had unhappy connotations in what he politely called "English-speaking circles". Van der Stoel, the Dutchman, said that nobody had a very clear idea. Scheel said they all had different ideas. Jobert claimed that Pompidou had invented the phrase on the last day of the Paris summit as a term of hope, to paper over a lot of differences. Thorn (Luxembourg) said that they had put a label on a bottle; now they had to consider the contents. Moro (Italy) favoured a federal union, as did the Dutch. Ortoli (President of the Commission) said that the key question was: What powers would a Union have? Would there be a common currency? If so, there would have to be one Finance Minister. Would there be a common defence? If so, there would have to be one Defence Minister. Would there be a common foreign policy? If so, there would have to be one Minister of Foreign Affairs. The alternative was inter-governmental cooperation. The choice was between cooperation or integration.

Jobert thought that Callaghan was in danger of falling into Cartesian logic. The plain fact was that British farmers and British industry were already experiencing the benefits of Community membership. The task now was to clothe the skeleton. He saw the existing Community as a plinth. It could not be touched. Meanwhile, something else should be created alongside it and eventually the two would merge.

Ortoli disputed Jobert's version. How could two different systems exist side by side? If the Community did not develop it would wither away.

Callaghan said that public opinion was at a different stage of development in different Community countries. There might be value in having a Green Paper and a proper public debate. And who would then decide: the Council of Ministers or the European Assembly? For his part, he thought it would have to be the Council. Scheel agreed. Governments might retain full sovereignty in some areas and relinquish it in others, and the Union would consist of those areas of activity transferred to European Ministers responsible to a European Parliament.

Jobert intervened again. There was a system, and it was working. If progress was to be made towards Union, it would have to be the work of Governments. If progress was to be made by 1980, it would have to be flexible. A Federal Union could not be imposed on powerful neighbours and emphasis on defence would arouse powerful opposition. There would have to be a long transition period. Questions like a common currency were too abstract; that was the wrong way to start.

Scheel said that if the economies of the Nine were not made to converge, they would inevitably diverge. But he thought convergence had been close. Callaghan disagreed. Paraphrasing Roy Campbell he said that he could "see the bloody harness. But where's the bloody horse?"[38]

Callaghan thought that the task of reporting on this whole issue was not one the Commission should take on. Scheel said it was not clear whether there should be one report or many. The Nine would have to decide at their next meeting.[39]

On Callaghan's return to London the European Coordination Committee (ECS) met in an extended session, in effect, but not in name, Cabinet.

Bernard Donoughue, the new Head of Wilson's Downing Street Policy Unit, who was present, thought it extraordinary that a Labour Cabinet needed to be reminded, as Callaghan did in his opening remarks, that the fact must be faced that the EEC existed and was acknowledged to exist by the rest of the world. On balance, therefore, Callaghan hoped he could negotiate what the Government wanted while still inside the EEC.

The anti-Marketeers (Shore, Benn, Hart and Foot), seated together at one end of the table, reportedly looked stunned. Foot spoke of the implications of EEC membership for the sovereignty of Parliament. Healey thought that Defence and Energy were both critical policy areas where, come the autumn, Britain's negotiating strength would be greater because the crisis in Europe would be more severe. Jenkins said that any quick decision to pull out would be 'very grave'. Benn made what Donoughue called "a very demagogic speech".[40]

The main significance of the meeting, as the Foreign Office saw it, was its definitive conclusion that Britain would not adopt an empty chair policy but would negotiate from within, step by step; that there would be no premature confrontation and no Treaty amendment if it could be avoided. The notion of Britain leaving the Customs Union, put forward by Shore in a long speech (during which Healey fell asleep) was rejected. It was agreed that, on the budget issue, there should be bilateral discussions with other Member States. The meeting also accepted Fred Peart's assumption that world prices would not on the whole be much lower than Community prices. The meeting also accepted Callaghan's judgement, based on his discussions at Schloss Gymnich, that the commitment of other EEC Governments to European Union was of such a general nature as to pose of itself no threat to British independence. Callaghan was able to point out that the discussion demonstrated that continued membership of the Community did not in practice imply a commitment to European Union by a given date.

Thereafter, the subjects of Union and EMU never really became an issue in renegotiation. Almost without a struggle, Wilson and Callaghan had thus gained some vital ground.[41]

They had also gained some time. The next meeting of the Council of Ministers was due to take place on 7 May, between the first and second rounds of the French Presidential elections. Cabinet therefore agreed, as ECS had done before it, that the next substantive presentation of the British case should be held over until the Council on 4 June. Before that meeting Callaghan would come back to Cabinet with negotiating proposals covering the EEC budget, the CAP and the Commonwealth. The Community might, said Callaghan, anyway be facing a major crisis of confidence resulting in part from economic difficulties exacerbated by increased oil prices. The Italian Government's decision a few days earlier to introduce an import deposit scheme in the light of severe balance of payments difficulties, had caused real shock in the Community. It underlined the inability of the Community in its present form to deal with the major problems which confronted it. It also reinforced a general feeling that the time had come for a re-examination of the Community's role, future prospects and objectives, on a more realistic basis than had so far been apparent.[42]

Some of that predicted turmoil was soon evident. On 6 May, Willy Brandt resigned as German Chancellor, following a spy scandal. On the same day in Brussels, the Italian import deposit scheme ran into strong criticism. It was seen by other member Governments as being in conflict with the CAP and with the principles of the Customs Union. Both Foreign and Agriculture Ministers devoted much of their Councils on that day to the scheme. However, as Callaghan told Cabinet later in the week, it had been recognised that at the end of the day the Italian Government had had no option but to take strong measures in the face of a critical economic situation and that the Community had no option but to accept what had happened.

The Community, according to Callaghan, was now entering a period of reappraisal, quite apart from Britain's own aims for renegotiation. The recent changes in leadership in the three major Member States, together with the economic and monetary difficulties which all members currently faced, could lead to a major transformation by the autumn. Renegotiation might then take place against a changed background of Community thinking both on internal matters and on relationships with other countries. This could be to the Government's advantage in renegotiation and in the shaping of the future of Europe.[43]

A bigger change in the Government's renegotiation fortunes came with the changes of leadership in France and Germany. In France, Valéry Giscard d'Estaing, was a man of the Right, but not a Gaullist. He had had a Gaullist rival (Chaban-Delmas) in the first round of the Presidential elections, in which Mitterrand, with the Right split, came through ahead. In the second round, a run-off between Mitterrand and Giscard d'Estaing, the latter won with a majority of fewer than half a million votes.

Giscard would not prove a pushover for the British. But he had favoured British accession when still a Minister in de Gaulle's Government. He did not have

Pompidou's dislike of Wilson, which was part political distaste for Socialism, part poor personal chemistry, part loyalty to Heath and partly the hope (which Heath in Opposition sought to foster) that the Labour Party might soon lose office and be replaced once again by a Heath-led Government.

With Pompidou, died what the Foreign Office considered to be the doctrinaire, grudging and unresponsive attitude of his Government, leavened by the waspish tongue and mischievous intelligence of Michel Jobert. It was replaced by the more open approach of Giscard and what the Foreign Office saw as the professionalism of the new French Foreign Minister, Jean Sauvagnargues, a career diplomat.[44] Nonetheless, Sauvagnargues was to prove as obdurate from the British perspective as Jobert had been.

Confronted with significant economic problems of his own, Giscard saw the British problem as one to be dealt with and disposed of. He preferred an accommodation to keep Britain in, provided the price was acceptable to France, to the disruption of Britain leaving altogether. He was not a man Wilson would get close to, as Heath and Pompidou had been close. That was not his temperament, or Wilson's. But the British leaders found him a professionally satisfactory colleague.

The change from Brandt to Helmut Schmidt was also welcome. The Labour Party had close links with the German SPD. Brandt had, under Wilson's last Government, unlocked the door to enlargement for Britain. But Brandt was mercurial and sometimes messianic. Schmidt was a friend of the Labour leaders and, by contrast with Brandt, politically slyer, more realistic and more practical – and therefore easier to work with. Schmidt shared some of the British impatience with the European Community, as illustrated by his comment at a Brussels press conference in October 1975 when he said that he and Giscard, as Finance Ministers at the time of the Paris Summit of October 1972, had both thought that "pontificating and proclaiming the European targets for the day after tomorrow (1980)" had been "European cloud-cuckoo-land".[45]

It was helpful, if unflattering, to the British that both Schmidt and Giscard saw the British problem as a sideline. For them, the real questions were energy, inflation, unemployment and the institutional development of the Community. Renegotiation should be got out of the way as soon as possible.[46]

That all was not well in the Community was confirmed by Ortoli, the Commission President, when he visited London on 13 May. There were, he told Wilson, increasingly questions about what Europe really meant. Political changes in Member States had slowed down the Community's work. Renegotiation was an added factor. He hoped and believed that solutions to Britain's problems could be found without Treaty change. The Community was much more flexible than was commonly supposed and the Treaties, which were often portrayed as a straitjacket, allowed considerable freedom for development.

Wilson raised the budget issue and his concern at the probable extent of Britain's commitment to the Community budget by 1979. The UK was the world's largest importer of agricultural produce and the Community's own resources system had especially adverse consequences for those heavily dependent on food imports. No Government could move faster than the people it represented, and he had to face the fact that, although British public opinion was divided, the number of people dissatisfied with the terms of entry was larger than the number in favour of staying inside on present terms, or of those who wished Britain to leave.

Ortoli thought that the advent of new leaders in France, Germany and Britain created a fresh opportunity to decide the future of the Community, if there was the political will from Britain to do so. If there was no interference with the Treaties the area of negotiation was within the margin of Community flexibility.

Wilson commented that he believed the British people would welcome a referendum, not because they were hostile to the Community, but because they resented the fact that they had not been consulted hitherto. Ortoli said that if agreement had been reached over the renegotiation this would imply that the British Government supported the outcome. Wilson said, and this was the first recorded occasion on which he said it, that, in those circumstances "we should commend the outcome to the electorate".[47]

During the lull in collective consideration of renegotiation within the Community, two senior British officials, Butler and Bailey, from the Foreign Office and Treasury respectively, had embarked on bilateral consultations on the budget issue. Only the French had refused to see them pleading, not unreasonably, the political interregnum in France.

Butler and Bailey carried with them a paper designed to establish that the United Kingdom was, at all times, going to be a large net contributor to the EC budget and that by 1977 that contribution would exceed Britain's share of Community GDP. There was no realistic hope of Community policies filling the gap. The British team outlined two alternative approaches. The first would be a scheme by which each Member State's budget contribution, as a proportion of the whole budget, would be related to its share of total Community GDP. The second scheme would provide for countries with below average GDP to have their gross contributions to the Community budget brought into line with their share of GDP. The British favoured the second scheme since it would not interfere with the own resources system and would involve no *juste retour*.

The principal difficulty which the British negotiators encountered was that none of the other member Governments accepted the forecasts on which the British schemes were based. This was hardly surprising. To accept the forecast would mean accepting that a solution had to be found. And any solution would involve Britain paying less and every other Member State paying more.[48] The Commission were at least sympathetic, although Ortoli had told Wilson in London that he had reservations about some points in the British approach. For example, it was not clear to him whether France and Germany would continue to expand, following the oil crisis, as rapidly as had been assumed, and the assumption about the growth rate of the British economy was also open to doubt; he hoped Britain might grow faster.[49]

Callaghan reported to Cabinet on the state of progress on 16 May. On the budget, for tactical reasons, more emphasis had so far been placed by the British team on persuading her partners of the need for a change in the British contribution than on the detail of a solution. Bilateral meetings had also been held with

Commonwealth countries. The overall impression was that the Commonwealth approached the Government's ideas on renegotiation with no sentiment and that hard bargaining was to be expected, especially on the issues of better access to the UK and other Community markets and of securing remunerative prices.

On the Regional Development Fund, Callaghan reported the view of the Ministers concerned that the Government should be ready to continue to discuss the proposed Regional Development Fund, partly because the Fund might be of value to the United Kingdom and partly because the establishment of a Fund was an important objective for the Italian and Irish Governments; it would be tactically unwise to forfeit their good will during renegotiation by blocking progress. However, final British agreement should be conditional on a satisfactory outcome on the budget.

Ministers meeting in ECS, Callaghan reported, had also considered Regional Aids. The British Government was committed to an interventionist regional aid policy and would require assurances about the way in which the Treaties and the Community rules might be applied to the Government's industrial measures and, in particular, to her policies for steel. He would flag these issues in the Council meeting of 4 June.[50]

A week later Cabinet discussed Concorde once again. Tony Benn, the Minister responsible, agreed that Concorde should never have been started. It would be convenient if the project could now be stopped "without unpleasant and expensive consequences". But the new French President had made it clear in his election campaign that cancellation would be unacceptable to the French Government. The United Kingdom had already spent £545 million on Concorde and the cost of cancellation, plus damages if the French took the British Government to court, could bring the amount to over £800 million. On the other hand, to complete the existing programme of 16 aircraft might cost only a further £90 million spread over five years. The alternative was to lose the highest engineering skills that had been lavished on the project. Supersonic travel was here to stay. Further orders were possible, notably from Iran. The cancellation of the project would "gravely damage both the reputation of British engineering and our credibility as a reliable partner in collaborative ventures".

Most of Cabinet agreed with Healey in wanting to cancel the project. But they equally feared that the cost of rupturing the project unilaterally might be so high as to make the completion of the 16 aircraft already on the stocks the better course. Accordingly, Wilson concluded that "it would be preferable for the project to be cancelled if the consent of the French Government – however reluctant – could be secured; but that, if they did not consent, we should not withdraw unilaterally from the project but should complete the programme to build 16 aircraft. The next step would be to explore the views of the French Government".[51]

The Council of Ministers on 4 June would be the first for the new French Government. How to handle both France and Germany, and the implications for Britain of Franco-German cooperation, were a significant British preoccupation. As Ewart-Biggs put it in a minute to Tomkins in early June, the British and French were at cross-purposes. The French wanted to give life to the Community. They intended to keep the Community going even if Britain were to leave it, though they would prefer Britain to remain. "The circle out of which we must break", Ewart-Biggs argued, "is thus that we make our European intentions dependent on their sympathy to our needs and they make their sympathy to our needs dependent on our European intentions". In Ewart-Biggs' judgement, the basic requirements for an understanding with the French were, for Britain, that the French should accept such corrections to the Community system as could be represented as a successful outcome of renegotiation and, for the French, that they should be satisfied that, if Britain obtained those corrections, the British Government would recommend to the British people that the country should remain in the Community and subscribe to its objectives, including European Union, and play a full part in European construction. Neither requisite looked at all feasible. It must be assumed, Ewart-Biggs thought, that "Giscard would not want to help a Labour Government, uncertain about Europe, to keep out a Conservative Government committed to Europe".

That analysis was correct. Ewart-Biggs was also correct in his assessment that the French would hope that British demands would become reduced and attenuated as they trickled through the slow machinery of the Community. He was wrong in thinking that part of that attenuation would have to mean acceptance by Britain of an approach "based less on reducing our net contribution, or interfering directly or indirectly with the system of own resources, than on trying to extend and develop Community arrangements in such a way that the British economy receives more financial benefit from them". But Ewart-Biggs did acknowledge that Regional Policy, on the scale anyone in the Community was prepared to contemplate, would help Britain very little. Maybe, he concluded, it needed "some sort of quantum jump proposal of the kind we once made about getting back into the snake. But our present European posture is scarcely conducive to any such thing".[52]

The picture from Bonn provided only slightly more comfort. For the Germans, according to Henderson, painful though it was for him to have to admit it, their relationship with the French was "more important politically and economically to the two countries than the relationship of either of them with the United Kingdom, particularly in our present state of economic and political instability and indifference towards Europe". The danger, as Henderson saw it, was that the British Government might overestimate Britain's importance. It was not that the Germans were unsympathetic to the British budget inequity. But the Germans were biding their time in the expectation of a fresh General Election in Britain before very long. And any financial help from Germany in a European Community context would only be forthcoming on the condition that it formed part of progress towards European political and economic union. That approach would be an essential part of the programme of the new German Foreign Minister, Hans-Dietrich Genscher (a powerful figure as Leader of the FDP, the SPD's coalition partner). The Germans would also avoid doing anything which could involve a quarrel with the French. On the contrary, the crisis in the world economy and the consequent crisis in the Community, made it essential for Germany to purchase French cooperation, and Britain was unlikely to be able to demand a higher price. The German Government would, so Henderson advised, be very concerned if they thought that the British Government were likely to leave the Community. But they were convinced that the British interest lay in remaining within the Community and that, unless irrationality prevailed, Britain was bound to stay in, if not out of any belief in the idea of Europe, at any rate from the hard calculation of where Britain's own national interest lay.[53]

The smaller Member States were, meanwhile, watching with apprehension. Early in June, Palliser received a visit from his Danish opposite number in Brussels, Ersboell, "one of the shrewdest and most intelligent of my colleagues" (and destined to go on to be a highly successful Secretary-General of the Council). Ersboell's own view, shared, he understood, by the Foreign Ministers of the Benelux countries who had met to discuss the matter, was that the French and German Governments would want to give some fresh impetus to the Community. It could not just stand still, or wait to see how renegotiation went. In the absence of progress, the Community would slip backwards. None of these smaller countries was happy at their renewed dependence on the two large Continental powers, of which they had always hoped that British membership of the Community would relieve them. But given the present British attitude, they saw no alternative to moving in whatever direction the French, and more particularly, the Germans saw fit to lead. The Benelux Ministers, in particular, were torn between their desire, for Community reasons, to support a fresh initiative in the economic and monetary field, and their apprehension at the extent to which they then risked increasing subjection to the economic power of the Federal German Government.

This latter feeling was, said Ersboell, reinforced by the domineering tone adopted by the Germans in meetings of the Finance Ministers of the so-called 'little snake' countries, dominated by Germany. Schmidt's tone and manner had been unhappily reminiscent of an earlier age. He had been impatient of any argument. Any harmony was imposed from the top, and the smaller countries were decidedly unhappy. But they had nowhere else to go. The Benelux at least would feel obliged to follow wherever Germany and France might lead.

Denmark was in an even unhappier situation according to Ersboell. She too was dependent on Germany while being politically much less committed to the Community. The risk was of a two-tier Community. In the first would be those countries, including Germany, France and no doubt Benelux, who were prepared to move relatively fast towards economic and political union within an integrated Community. The second class of member would comprise those for whom some kind of trading arrangement would no doubt have to be devised but who would not be expected to take part in real economic or political integration; nor of course to get the benefits of economic and monetary support from the first class members except to the extent that this suited them.

Palliser, who had always found Ersboell very well informed about German thinking, took Ersboell's warnings seriously. Nonetheless, he told Ersboell that he believed France and Germany would play the hand very carefully and try not to get too far out in front. All in all, it seemed to Palliser that greater, and perhaps more real, dangers could flow from a possible failure of the British renegotiation and the consequent withdrawal of the United Kingdom from the Community, with the repercussions that would have, not just on Denmark and Ireland, but also on a future smaller Community dominated by France and Germany with the likelihood of tensions and dissensions between it and the countries on the periphery. Ersboell agreed but he felt that it would be a mistake to underestimate the pressures there would be on both France and Germany to give fresh impetus to European unity and to be ready if necessary to concentrate that effort amongst those countries that seemed really ready to make it.[54]

These analyses were stark. The immediate reality was more ambiguous. The new French Foreign Minister, Jean Sauvagnargues, returned to Bonn, where he had been Ambassador until his elevation, at the beginning of June to say his diplomatic farewells. There, he told the Press that Franco-German cooperation must be the driving force of West European cooperation and integration and that close understanding between France and the Federal Republic would set an example to which others could also attach themselves at any time. On the other side of the coin, the Germans took the opportunity to impress on Sauvagnargues the importance, in the interest of giving the Community a new lease of life, of at least going along with the idea of the Commission being authorised to study, and report on, the Community budget as a prelude to deciding how to deal with the British demands.[55]

A few days later, Renato Ruggiero (then Director General for Regional Policy in the Commission; later Director General of the WTO and Italian Foreign Minister) told a member of George Thomson's Cabinet that he in turn had been told by René Foch, a member of Giscard d'Estaing's so-called 'Brains Trust' and someone who was close to the new President, that Giscard had no intention of turning his mind seriously to the problems of the Community until October. His current view of the problem of British renegotiation was that the best way to deal with it was to ignore it. He would then be in a position to bypass the British by making an initiative in the autumn designed to appeal to the other members of the Community. Ruggiero thought that an approach of that kind would certainly not succeed. To his mind, there were two immediate problems facing the Community: the Italian crisis and the need to find a solution to the British renegotiation. If the right kind of action was not taken in respect of those two questions then any political initiative would be doomed to fail.[56]

Renegotiation was, for Wilson and Callaghan, just as much a matter of internal juggling as of external negotiation. In mid June, Tony Benn, whose capacity for disingenuous naiveté was inexhaustible, sent to Wilson a letter saying that he thought the Prime Minister might like to see the motion he had proposed for the 26 June meeting of the Labour Party's National executive Committee (NEC). He had, he said of course, also sent a copy to Jim Callaghan, the Chairman of the Labour Party "for information". The resolution was for a special two day Labour Party Conference to consider the outcome of renegotiation, once it was concluded. It stipulated that the Party should be free to reach its own view (i.e. separately from the Government) on whether Britain should stay in the EEC or withdraw and that individual members of the Party (i.e. including Ministers) should be free to speak for or against continued membership "in accordance with their own personal convictions, since the idea of freedom of choice on this issue is implicit in our pledge to consult the people and let each elector join in the decision".

Callaghan, who was in Ottawa, sent Wilson a telegram saying that he was inclined to send Benn a message saying that he did not propose to have Benn's motion placed on the agenda of the NEC for June on the grounds that neither Callaghan or Wilson would be present and that, since the matter was not urgent, it could wait until the July meeting – or even later.

Wilson replied that he had had ninety minutes with Benn and had told him that he should not be proposing motions for the NEC without the agreement of the responsible Minister. Benn in turn accused Wilson of "wanting the Party to die when we were in Government". Wilson had responded that there was no conceivable hurry. There was little chance of renegotiation being concluded before an election. Benn was therefore envisaging a situation that was probably at least eight months away. Wilson agreed with the way Callaghan proposed to reply.

Benn persisted. On 3 July Wilson sent him a minute telling him that his actions in tabling a motion "profoundly affecting the work of another Minister, without prior consultation with him and without his prior approval" had been interpreted by the Press in exactly the way Wilson had forecast. "I do not", Wilson wrote, "regard this as acting as a member of a team".

The Prime Minister continued that he had also learned from the Press that Benn had been elected to chair a Party committee to monitor renegotiation, and that this committee would include named members of the Government. Wilson supported the idea of an NEC committee. But, in the interests of the NEC and the Government it should not include Ministers: "We simply cannot have one Minister, by virtue of his membership of the NEC, acting in a monitoring, invigilating role on the work of another Minister, who is himself acting on the instructions of the Cabinet".

A week later, Wilson told Callaghan that he had decided to instruct that no Minister should attend, or in any way facilitate, the work of the Committee. Callaghan replied the next day: "Having seen that the full Transport House document on my supposed attitude to renegotiation was reproduced in full in *The Spectator* yesterday, and having read in *The Guardian* yesterday that Peter Shore is alleged to have complained forcefully about my renegotiating attitude at a Party meeting yesterday, I now realise that you were much wiser than me in your doubts about the usefulness of the Monitoring Committee that I originally proposed . . . As regards Peter Shore, it is quite intolerable that a fellow member of the Cabinet, who has been associated with me in every meeting of the EEC, should attend a Party meeting and, if the reports are true, criticise strongly what is being done in the name of the Government. He cannot even attempt to explain his actions. As you know, I am not prepared to go on like this and the situation must be cleared up".

Callaghan had copied his minute to Shore, who put out a statement making clear "that I made no attack on Jim Callaghan or on his handling of the renegotiations". Shore followed up with an aggrieved minute to Callaghan: "I very much regret that you chose to circulate such a minute without first checking with me. To use your own words, it is quite intolerable to be attacked by a colleague in this way".

There the matter rested. But when, in November, Benn voted in favour of an NEC resolution criticising the Government of which he was a member for conducting a naval exercise with South Africa, Wilson, despite a series of ingratiating and slithering responses from Benn, insisted on, and secured, a written statement from Benn that he accepted "the principle of collective responsibility as applying to all Ministers, and hence all the requirements that flow from it". Joe Haines, Wilson's Press Secretary, lost no time in briefing the Lobby on this outcome.[57]

In the midst of these Party manoeuvrings, all of them played out damagingly in the media, Wilson was preparing for a visit to Bonn where, he was advised, "the German attitude towards renegotiation has so far been cool but not hostile". Apart from the German dislike of the term 'renegotiation' (and Wilson was advised by the Foreign Office to assure Schmidt, as Callaghan had already assured Genscher, that the fact that the British used the term did not mean that the Germans had to as well), they had other priorities. Schmidt, as German Finance Minister, had been shown some budget forecasts by the Conservative Government and had clearly been surprised and impressed by the fact that already in the first year of her membership Britain was the second largest net contributor to the EEC budget. But if Schmidt was going to give Britain something on the budget, the Prime Minister might need to give him an assurance that the British Government were willing to take part in further discussions about economic, monetary and political union, in a constructive spirit. Schmidt, for his part, would have to realise that "in the United Kingdom the word 'Union' is as much a red rag to the anti-market bulls as it is a banner for the pro-Europe crusaders".[58]

As it turned out, Wilson, on this occasion as on others during renegotiation, preferred not to get into the nitty gritty of Britain's requirements. He and Schmidt had an hour alone. As Wilson later told the plenary session, he and Schmidt had spent a good deal of time on political and party matters. On Community matters, their discussions had been of a general kind. Wilson had, though, told Schmidt that he fully understood that other EEC Governments were asking themselves which British Government they would be dealing with in six months' time and that it followed that a conclusion to renegotiation could hardly be expected before the end of 1974 or early 1975. Wilson said that he had also confirmed that the British Government had entered the negotiations with the desire to make them succeed.

On the aeroplane home[59] Wilson told his officials that the only matter he had discussed privately with Schmidt that had not been disclosed in the plenary session was the triangular relationship between Britain, France and Germany. Schmidt had been at some pains to explain to him that all three countries had an essential voice in Community affairs and that it was the three Governments concerned who really mattered. Wilson had drawn the inference from Schmidt's remarks that he should not be afraid that the French President and the German Chancellor would settle everything between them. Schmidt had also encouraged Wilson to see the French President before long. Schmidt had paid "a marked personal tribute to the Foreign Secretary, whose manner, style and friendliness had, he said, created a very favourable impression".

In a discussion about oil prices and prospects, Schmidt had said that the German Government saw Britain as a member of OPEC in due course. Wilson had replied that there was a simple answer to that: it would depend on the terms. Would the British Government seek to renegotiate them afterwards, Schmidt had asked? This was, Wilson commented "a remark made in jest, to outward appearance at least".[60]

The French Government too had concluded that there could not be any real progress in renegotiation before the British General Election, so Christopher Soames told Wilson some days later. Wilson confirmed that this was also Schmidt's view and he thought it realistic. Even if there were to be no British election in the meantime, the Prime Minister did not expect to see renegotiation concluded until early 1975.

According to Soames, both Giscard and Schmidt were thinking of a Community summit. Schmidt was pressing for an early date – say October. Giscard wanted something rather later. In Soames's view it was extremely important that the British General Election should precede the summit since no move on renegotiation could be expected before the election. If the election had been held before the summit, Wilson might hope to use the occasion to conclude renegotiation or get close to an outcome. Both Schmidt and Giscard would go to the summit with the intention of getting something out of it (though it was not clear what that something might be). It was important that the Prime Minister should get something too: the satisfactory conclusion of renegotiation. In a conversation with Michel Poniatowski, French Minister of the Interior, Soames had been told that it was not a question of whether something would have to be done to meet the British needs, but of how and when. From a European point of view Soames was very anxious that Britain should not be on the touchline for too long, while the Community made progress in other ways.[61]

Three meetings between Wilson and other EEC leaders at this time show a shift in the way Wilson was managing expectations. On 25 June, he told the Belgian Prime Minister, Leo Tindemans, that the number of people in Britain who were undecided about Britain's membership of the EEC was growing. This change (from outright opposition) was taking place because people were finding the Community more interesting, and they welcomed the signs of fresh thinking evident within it. The degree of flexibility Fred Peart had found among his Agriculture colleagues had been noted with satisfaction throughout the country. The negotiations had started well and much goodwill had been shown by Britain's partners. He himself had been surprised to find that so much change could be envisaged within the Community without alteration of the Treaties.[62]

Later the same day, Wilson told the Danish Prime Minister, Poul Hartling, that his Government thought the terms of accession agreed by Mr Heath had been crippling. But, apart from the totally committed 'pros' and the totally committed 'antis', the largest single group of people in Britain would be in favour of remaining in the Community, provided the terms were right. He was glad that it now looked as if the British Government could get all they needed by way of renegotiation without the need to alter either the Treaty of Rome or the Treaty of Accession. He expected the attitude of the new French Government to be more pragmatic than that of the old one. President Giscard would look at all his problems "with a clear mind, uncluttered by ancestral voices from Colombey les deux Eglises" to see what was in the best interests of France and of Europe. Wilson expressed satisfaction with his discussion with Schmidt the previous week.

In response to a question from Hartling, Wilson said that he had always thought a referendum more likely than a General Election, which could not easily be confined to a single issue. One possibility was a referendum at the same time as a General Election but it looked more probable that the referendum would come after the election.[63]

Wilson's third meeting was with Luxembourg Prime Minister Gaston Thorn. Wilson told him that he "firmly believed that by the sensible and civilised processes of negotiation the problems we had raised could be solved". He recognised that the prospect of another election in Britain might affect the attitude of others. But people abroad did not realise that the image of the Community when Labour took office was horrible. There was the appearance of constant interference in British affairs; the butter mountain; the absurd threat to British beer, with accompanying jokes with sexual overtones about male and female hops. In some ways the Community had become a music hall joke. Even the British Press, which was solidly in favour of Europe, had been hard put to find good words to say about the Community. But things had now changed. He had to admit that President Pompidou's death had contributed to this. Labour policies were communicating themselves to the country. There was a new and fresh atmosphere.

Wilson confirmed to Thorn that if renegotiation was successful and Britain secured the right terms, then she would play her part as a full member of the Community. The prospects for a successful outcome to the referendum were now improving. Big emotional issues were involved. Britain did not have a written constitution. Her links with Commonwealth countries were close. All this had to be taken into account.

Thorn wanted to know if another British Government would engage in yet another referendum. Wilson said the answer was 'no'. He did not believe so. Once the British people had voted on the question, it would be settled for good.

Thorn said there had been a debate in the Council of Ministers that morning about the use of majority voting in the Council. Callaghan had said that he was against it. The French line had been that it was better not to talk about it but in effect to practise it. Wilson said that Callaghan had been right to speak as he did while renegotiation was in progress. But perhaps the French had been right too.

Thorn went on to speak about the Luxembourg Compromise. It had not been an agreement to respect unanimity but an agreement to disagree. Many things had been read into the agreement which were not there. It had been used to justify the principle of unanimity even on minor issues. Wilson remarked that one could hardly use UN Security Council techniques within the Community. Thorn said that he hoped that, as the years went by, and with a successful renegotiation, a sort of Cabinet would come to exist in which unanimity would only be expected on vital national issues. Wilson drew an analogy with the working of a Cabinet in a Parliamentary democracy. When the British were in on something they did their best to make it work.[64]

On the following day, Wilson and Callaghan met the new French Prime Minister (Jacques Chirac) and Foreign Minister (Jean Sauvagnargues) in Brussels. Chirac wanted to raise three issues: Concorde, the Channel Tunnel and "the problems raised by British policy towards Europe".

On Concorde, Chirac made clear that the French remained committed to the project. On the Channel Tunnel the two Prime Ministers agreed that work on the financial and technical aspects should continue.

Chirac said that the third problem concerned the Common Market. The position of the new French Government was no different from that of its predecessor. It was extremely attached to the *acquis communautaire* in all its aspects and especially those concerning agriculture. The French Government were very anxious that there should be no further challenge to the *acquis* in this field.

Wilson replied that there were members of the Labour Party, and indeed of the Cabinet, who would like the United Kingdom to pull out of the Community, but that was not the policy of the Government; nor had it been the policy on which Labour had fought the election. He and his colleagues were, however, concerned about the terms of entry, which were in certain respects economically burdensome and even crippling. They were not seeking to negotiate with Britain on one side and her eight partners on the other, but were discussing matters from Britain's normal place at the negotiating table. The British aims in renegotiation would not require changes in the Treaty of Rome and he was hopeful that it would be possible to meet British requirements without touching the Treaty of Accession either. He hoped for a result which would help Britain and help the Community as a whole. Callaghan added that for him the most rewarding aspect of Community work had been in the field of political cooperation. He would much regret it if, because of over-emphasis on the economic aspects of cooperation, it was not possible to continue and intensify political cooperation.

Chirac replied that he felt bound to say that he did not think it reasonably possible to envisage any kind of renegotiation. He hoped for the sake of Europe that the British Government would see that the British presence in the Community was essential both for the United Kingdom and for the Community".[65]

Wilson did not report to Cabinet on his discussion with Chirac on EEC matters beyond the fact that "on the CAP Chirac had expressed much concern, but seemed to have nothing new to say". On the Channel Tunnel, it was clear, Wilson said, that the new French Government had decided that the project must take a lower priority, and Chirac had been clear in asking the British Government to join them in deferring progress on it.

On Concorde, so far from being prepared to limit the programme, Chirac had spoken in terms of producing 200 aircraft. Wilson had set out the very strong economic arguments against the project. But Chirac was dead set against cancellation and had gone on to dismiss with contempt the environmental arguments against Concorde and had, instead, enlarged on its political, technological and economic benefits.

Chirac had made it clear that a final decision would rest with the President but Wilson thought it necessary to prepare for his own meeting with Giscard on the premise that, if the project had to proceed, it should do so on the basis of 16 aircraft only.[66]

A week later, Cabinet held a stocktaking on renegotiation on the basis of a report from the Foreign Secretary. Callaghan said that, while he was following closely the programme set out in the Labour Party Manifesto, it would be unrealistic to expect in any negotiation to achieve all the original objectives. At the end of the negotiation the Government would have to decide whether the package of changes that could be agreed was such as to make it better for the country to remain a member or withdraw. Renegotiation was inevitably a long process, delayed by the death of Pompidou and the resignation of Brandt. It was also now clear that other EEC Governments would not be prepared to make real progress in advance of the UK General Election.

The best progress so far, Callaghan continued, had been on matters concerning the Commonwealth and developing countries. Commonwealth apprehensions about British membership of the Community had diminished over the previous eighteen months and (partly because of high commodity prices) there was no desire to return to traditional trading patterns. The Commonwealth saw the EEC market as offering new opportunities and regarded the Labour Government as a friendly spokesman within the Community. Recent decisions indicated that the Community might in future be less of a rich man's club.

By contrast, Callaghan could report little progress on renegotiation of the Community budget. On 4 June, at his first Council meeting, Sauvagnargues had resisted the establishment of a Commission study of the problem, but had found himself isolated and had eventually given ground. The UK contribution was clearly inequitable but the other Member States would be most reluctant to agree to changes. A formula under which each member paid according to its ability seemed a reasonable request. It would be fair and, since it would be self-correcting, it would undermine the case of those other members who argued that it was not justified because Britain would be more prosperous in the future.

Callaghan set out the position on the Regional Development Fund, on regional aids and on the issue of European Union. On the latter, the Community was now attempting to discover what the different Member States meant by the concept. There was no danger to UK sovereignty from this work. Britain was a party to it and could control both its pace and its content.

The sceptics within the Cabinet said that, in pursuing their renegotiation objectives, the Government should have regard to the unpalatable terms of the Treaty of Accession and, in particular, the imposition on the United Kingdom of a written constitution which detracted from the powers of Parliament. The Treaty had been signed against the wishes of the majority of the British people. The

Government had rightly decided against the empty chair approach but the pressures of ongoing business and the need to preserve a good climate for renegotiation had weakened the Government's bargaining power. There was a risk of not being taken sufficiently seriously.

Time on 2 July having run out, Cabinet resumed its discussion on 4 July. The sceptics pursued their argument. Continued membership on the terms which now seemed likely to be obtained could be gravely damaging, particularly in regional and industrial policy. Power had passed from member Governments to the Community and continued EEC membership on this basis would raise constitutional issues of the greatest importance.

Callaghan was criticised for the change of tone between his opening statement on 1 April and his more conciliatory statement to the Council of Ministers on 4 June. While the question of the sovereignty of the British Parliament and the British people remained a major element in the renegotiation, these issues had received only insignificant treatment in the most recent Luxembourg speech. As a result, there had been a collapse in the Labour Party's confidence in the Government's determination. If the Government's supporters felt that the Party's objectives had been modified in order to make renegotiation easier, there would be serious political consequences and the likelihood of a renewed split. Consideration should be given to adopting a more aggressive line. The Government should challenge the principle of the own resources system. Serious studies should be undertaken of the alternatives to EEC membership based on a free trade grouping including the Irish Republic, Denmark and the other EFTA countries.

The pro-Marketeers countered on similarly predictable lines. Callaghan's 4 June speech had set out all the negotiating objectives. Other Governments were unlikely to make significant concessions until the Government had obtained a working majority in a General Election. Nonetheless, a coach and horses had already been driven successfully through the CAP by the Government's insistence on national subsidies for certain commodities during the price fixing and by their refusal to apply permanent intervention arrangements for beef. The New Zealand Government were satisfied with the British proposals for improved arrangements for dairy products up to 1982. By avoiding an over-nationalistic approach the Government had secured private assurances of cooperation from other EEC Governments. The notion of sovereignty, meaning the ability of any Government alone to determine its own destiny or pursue effective policies, was dangerously overstated. There had been swift and radical changes in the situation. Commonwealth Governments now supported continued British membership. The facts would show Community membership in its true perspective. The ultimate decision should be taken on an informed basis and in the light of the external factors affecting British prospects in the world.

Wilson described what had been a valuable discussion. Cabinet would need to continue to review progress collectively from time to time. Renegotiation had been launched on a basis consistent with the manifesto and with the policies on which the Labour Party had fought the last election. There had been little progress so far and there would be serious difficulties in securing the results the

Government wanted. It was not to be expected that other Community Governments would commit themselves until they were clearer about the political situation in the United Kingdom. At the end of negotiations, members of the Cabinet might take different views about the results but at the present stage it was essential that the Government as a whole should maintain a unified and coherent stance consistent with its past commitments and the manifesto. Renegotiation was likely to start in earnest after the Community's summer break and was unlikely to be concluded before the end of the year or the early months of 1975. If there were to be an election in the autumn it would be necessary for the Government's manifesto to mention the timescale of the renegotiation and the way in which the British people would be consulted on the results.[67]

On 19 July, the Prime Minister and Foreign Secretary travelled to Paris to meet the new President. Edward Heath had, shortly before the visit, made a speech in which he appeared to suggest that the United Kingdom's EEC partners should go slow on renegotiation pending a fresh election in Britain and the return to power of a Conservative Government. Wilson had been advised by Soames, who in turn had been advised by a well placed French friend, to address this issue head on, which he did by saying in his opening remarks that he realised that it would be unrealistic not to take account of the possibility of a General Election.[68]

Giscard acknowledged the point but thought it might result in a very difficult problem if renegotiation was still taking place when a possible European Summit was held towards the end of the year.

Callaghan made an emollient statement on the progress of renegotiation. He hoped renegotiation would succeed. In the meantime, Britain was playing her full part in the continuing work of the Community. She hoped to achieve her objectives without any Treaty amendment. In some areas changes of approach were already coming about through the pressure of events; and British objectives were thus converging with other developments in the Community. Britain could survive outside the Community, but it would be a blow to the development of a European personality if that happened and the Community ought to try to avoid wrenching itself apart. The problem was to make the economic considerations fit the political objectives.

Giscard pointed out that renegotiation was a multilateral, and not a bilateral, matter. He did not see how the Community could contemplate any change in the principles of the Common Market, principles which the French themselves had at times experienced difficulty in living up to. The Community was a single homogeneous whole for agriculture and industrial products. Thus Germany contributed more than France to the Community budget but the French had a trade deficit with Germany. It was necessary always to consider the whole. The French did not seek high agricultural prices. What they wanted was a united and regulated market. Similarly, they had not invented the own resources system which was of immense importance to the smaller countries even though costly to France. He did not see how Britain could seek to keep the principles and benefits of a Common Market and avoid the consequential obligations.

After some further exchanges, Giscard said that he had felt bound to refer to the relationship between the principles of the Treaty of Rome and the consequential obligations which flowed from them in order to explain the French attitude. But he was equally anxious to find a solution to enable the United Kingdom to stay in the Community. There seemed to be a general wish among the other members of the Community to make progress towards a united Europe. It would be more difficult to achieve this while Britain retained misgivings about membership, but nevertheless France felt that the effort should be made. He hoped Britain would not try to stop the bus while she was deciding whether to get on or get off.

Wilson asked whether the President was implying that renegotiation ought to be completed before the Community Summit at the end of the year. Giscard replied that if there was a Summit at the end of November or early in December it should have two purposes. The first was to give some content to the meaning of European unity; but it ought also to make some modest practical steps forward on the political and economic sides. Unless that progress was to be frustrated, either the United Kingdom would have to take her decision by then or some formula must be found to enable the rest to go forward while the United Kingdom was left free to take her decision later. Which did Wilson favour?

Callaghan made clear that if the French Government decided to take an initiative the British Government would be glad to consider it and would be present at the discussions. They did not envisage a discussion among the Eight alone. The British Government would contribute to the discussion and the result could well affect the ultimate decision of the British electorate. Wilson and Callaghan said that if a Summit were to be held they would prefer it to be held during the French Presidency and hoped that the French proposals would be as specific as possible.[69]

Wilson had held a private discussion with Giscard before the joint discussions, and dictated his own record of the talk. "President Giscard d'Estaing greeted me warmly, and asked me to sit down beside him on the settee. Part of the discussion was in English but (at one point) he later brought in Andronikov when things got a bit technical . . . He went straight to Concorde. I spelled out very strongly our views on its non-viability . . . I said we were not prepared to have any further development. I thought there should be an exchange of letters setting out the terms for a break and also the basis on which we could consult if there were a surprising breakthrough on orders.

"On Europe, the President spoke at somewhat greater length . . . He was rather firm on the idea that we ought to get the renegotiation out of the way in time for a Summit decision on his 1980 objectives and thought this would mean by the end of October. I told him that was unrealistic, and I also told him my presumption – as in Bonn – that little progress would be made as long as Britain had not had the expected General Election. He confirmed this. His argument that we should get renegotiation out of the way in time for a November-December Summit was much harder than the formulation we got in the wider meeting later; but he clearly wants to have a Summit while France has the Presidency.

"He referred to political unity as well as economic unity. I asked what he meant . . . Giscard said 'confederation'. I asked him whether he meant a confederation on the lines of the North German Confederation of the 1840s, and he simply replied 'on the lines of the Swiss' . . . I asked him how far he would go in having a single European Minister e.g. would there be one Minister of education – and referred to Belgium. He said that might be so since perhaps education was one of those questions that could be dealt with in individual countries on a local authority basis . . . We discussed our relative inflation problems . . . He expressed his hopes about getting inflation down to 7% and a total payments balance by the end of next year, which the Chancellor has of course more than once ridiculed . . . My meeting with Chirac was quite short and very friendly."[70]

When Hunt asked Wilson whether Giscard had given him any idea what he meant when he talked of Europe going forward since, according to Hunt, it was clear that French officials did not know the answer, Wilson replied: "Unity, as he defined it, without any doubt including monetary unity".[71]

Overall, the Prime Minister's visit to Paris was encouraging. Wilson had set out to make it clear that he wanted to avoid a confrontation between France and Britain. He had sought to impress on Giscard that renegotiation was for Britain a political problem and that the British Government was negotiating with a successful outcome in view. Whereas Giscard's predecessors would probably have spent time berating Wilson for attempting to undermine the principles of the Community, Giscard was content merely to say that the principles must be respected.[72]

By contrast with earlier French practice, there was an absence of official briefing of the French media, a factor which, on this occasion, according to Tomkins, had led to coverage that was rather more negative than it deserved to be. That, thought Tomkins, would nonetheless suit the French Government quite well. The French were against renegotiation. They did not want to let it be thought that Anglo-French relations could be really cordial, and certainly not on a par with Franco-German relations, while the '*hypotheque britannique*' (British sign-off) hung over the Community. But Tomkins was sanguine, and more than sanguine on the outcome on the bilateral issues, telling one senior Elysée official that "the arrangements on Concorde and on the Continental Shelf were in fact very important. These were problems which could have caused considerable strains in Anglo-French relations and which had indeed been under discussion between British and French Governments for a long time. It was a remarkable achieve- ment to have disposed of them so quickly and so simply. If this result had been achieved by Heath and Pompidou, it would have been acclaimed as a great act of statesmanship".[73]

Giscard himself seems to have sensed some of this. He took the unusual step of replying to Wilson's bread-and-butter thank-you letter after the Paris visit. "I am firmly convinced", he wrote, "that Great Britain and France have every interest in having close cooperation on the many bilateral issues which concern our two countries. I am also convinced that our two countries doing more together is fundamental to the successful construction of a united Europe, a Europe which will make it possible for our economies to be more efficient and will offer a new generation the hope of a big-picture political future. On all these questions, which are vital for the future of Great Britain and of France, I shall always look forward to knowing your thoughts and views, and equally happy to let you know mine".[74]

One event did mar the generally improving atmospherics. On 20 July, Turkish armed forces invaded Cyprus. Britain was a guarantor power. All of Callaghan's energies had, in the immediate aftermath, to be devoted to the issue. Because of Cyprus, both Callaghan and Hattersley were unable to attend the Council of Ministers, the last before the summer break, on 22 July. The British delegation was therefore led by Peter Shore. Shore prevented agreement being reached in the Community on a negotiating brief for the trade negotiations on commodities. He also opened up the whole question of Energy policy, in contravention of the brief that had been agreed inter-departmentally in Whitehall. His behaviour brought to the fore the whole issue of Britain's commitment to the principles of the Community and tested the tolerance of Britain's European partners. The issue reverberated in the Continental Press. It was generally accepted in Whitehall that it had been a serious mistake to allow Shore, the only Cabinet Minister opposed to British membership who regularly attended meetings in Brussels, to represent the Government on his own. Shore did not in fact ever again represent the Government on his own in Brussels.[75]

Wilson was concerned enough to send a minute to Armstrong seeking a report "not only because there may well be challenges from the Opposition (as well as in any subsequent radio or TV or Press interviews), but also because it is alleged that it was this action which caused the Home Secretary [Roy Jenkins] to erupt, and some of his friends to express anxiety".[76]

Nairne duly reported, highlighting a number of procedural issues which had contributed to the outcome, and Wilson indicated that he would focus on those in dealing with any further criticisms. According to a separate note by Nairne, Callaghan "views the situation calmly recognising that the political impact within the Party may not necessarily be unhelpful to the renegotiation task". Nairne's own view was that "within the Community we shall certainly have hurt our cause by adding to the difficulties of those who are ready to do what they can to help us".[77]

That view was shared by Christopher Soames who spoke to Bridges in Number 10 at the end of August to express the view that what had happened in the Council on Shore's watch had been very sad. "Don't let it happen again", had been Soames's injunction. He quoted Davignon as saying that "The trouble with this Government in Britain is that you cannot take the word of its senior men".[78]

Not that Peter Shore was easily cowed. On a visit to Australia and New Zealand in early August he made a barnstorming speech in Wellington which, with few caveats, looked forward to the day when the British people "can face the future without any necessity of joining a particular trading bloc". At press conferences, he was similarly outspoken, prompting Wilson to send him a message in which the iron fist was characteristically concealed in a velvet glove: "You are getting very good coverage for your visit, and in particular your Australian speech got tremendous and enthusiastic coverage in the Express [i.e. you are being praised in the newspaper most hostile to the Labour Party]. Some of your recent press conference statements, however, in New Zealand are coming back in somewhat stark form. This may be due to selective reporting but they seem to be totally hostile to any question of Britain remaining in the Market on almost any terms, together with an apparent certainty that a referendum, whatever the terms, would prove negative. You can imagine this is causing reactions and could well cause counter statements and a fresh debate here. I shall be glad if you will ensure that your answers are in accordance with the usual statements we have authorised and have all been using".[79]

On his return, Shore reported to Wilson and other Ministers on his visit. But he struggled to extract from it the conclusions for which he had striven. He had found Australian Ministers "far more introverted than I had expected . . . For the most part the Australian Ministers appeared not to care strongly one way or the other whether we remained a member of the Community or whether we withdrew . . . New Zealand is not as fortunately placed as Australia. Here, both Ministers and businessmen are frankly very concerned about the restrictive nature of the CAP. They were firmly in favour of Britain being able to control its own external trade relations; equally, with their usual courtesy, they did not press their views too hard".[80]

In mid-August, Nairne sent to Bridges and Armstrong "a personal review of how things look on the renegotiation front". At a meeting of the European Unit in the Cabinet Office at the end of July there had been general support for Sir Oliver Wright's view that Britain's stock was not high. Nairne thought that the Government's best negotiating card might be that only Britain could take herself out of the Community. There were those in Paris and Bonn who were saying that the Community should not strive to keep Britain in. It was still fair to forecast "an adequate harvest" on the CAP, and in the fields of trade and aid, despite Peter Shore's speeches in New Zealand. As to Regional Policy and the handling of steel, the extent of the Government's difficulties would depend more on internal British decisions than on the Community. Cabinet would have to sort out the approach to regional aids at the start of September. If it proved possible "to take all these matters slowly enough, we should get by at the end of the day".

Nairne believed that the budget question remained the core of the problem and there the British interest might lie in quickening the pace. It seemed likely that the Commission report might do little more than acknowledge, in a general way, that Britain's GNP prospects justified the Government's complaint that her budget contribution would be unjustifiably high in a few years' time. More than that would be needed. When the time was ripe, harder lobbying in EEC capitals at top Ministerial level would be required. Germany was then likely to be the key, if only a way could be found of turning the key in the lock. This could be the crucial element in the whole renegotiation. Schmidt needed to be persuaded that Britain must have a concrete and substantial response to her budget case if the British Cabinet was in its turn to be persuaded that renegotiation had succeeded. But Schmidt in return would ask for clearer evidence of the Government's commitment or vocation to constructive progress towards a unified Europe, and that could be difficult to provide with a referendum in prospect. If the Germans could be brought round, then they in turn would need to be encouraged to bring along the French, who would want a favourable Community climate for the proposed Summit.

On the domestic front, Nairne thought that Benn would not willingly allow his colleagues to finesse their way through the regional and industrial policy field. For his part, Shore had spoken predictably in Australia and New Zealand. The referendum question continued to darken. The Prime Minister's answers to Robin Day on 1 August had provided further evidence that the Government might not be ready to commend any result of renegotiation to the British voters. (Wilson had been asked whether the Cabinet would make a collective recommendation to the British people and had replied: "That is still to be decided. We shall wait until we have seen the result of the negotiations. We shall then decide our attitude . . . we may decide that this could be left to a free vote of the British people as a whole". Wilson also acknowledged that, while the issue had not been decided, it was possible to have members of the Cabinet "going on different sides").[81] Nairne concluded that "the commitment to a referendum could wreck the results of renegotiation", however satisfactory; but it would be premature for officials to assess how the risks might be minimised.[82]

At the start of September, and the resumption of business within the European Community which then, as now, put its quarrels on ice during the August heat, Cabinet twice discussed the Government's approach to regional aids. Callaghan opened the discussion, pointing out that, in his statement to the Council of Ministers on 4 June he had said, with the full authority of the Cabinet, that the Government accepted that the coordination by the Community of the rules under which Member States gave regional aids was useful and that the UK would take part in the working party on the subject in order to ensure that the needs of the UK were safeguarded. Ministers had so far been unable to reach agreement on two alternative approaches. The first, proposed by the Secretary of State for Industry, Tony Benn, was for a challenge to the Community rules and much looser rules allowing each Government effectively to follow its own requirements, after consultation. This approach implied a need to amend the Treaty of Rome. The second approach, as proposed by Roy Hattersley, the Minister of State in the Foreign Office, was to accept the Community rules but argue for a framework of implementation which allowed Member Governments to discharge their domestic responsibilities while avoiding action which would have unacceptable consequences for other Member States. Callaghan, as chair of EQ Committee, where the matter had been discussed, favoured Hattersley's approach, as did a majority of the other committee members.

Benn, in response, argued that "the question was not whether the Community was or was not likely to take a reasonable line towards our regional policy needs, but whether we could accept that the Commission rather than the UK Parliament should have the power of decision in the field of regional aids".

In the absence of sufficient time, the discussion was resumed in Cabinet five days' later. Opinion once again divided on pro- and anti-EEC lines. Benn's supporters argued that the acceptance of Community rules would mean that "however generous the rules might be . . . in the last resort the authority of the

EEC Commission might prevail over that of Parliament". The Election Manifesto had committed the Government to the retention of the necessary powers by Parliament. Any departure from that principle, such as that represented by Hattersley's proposals, would be widely interpreted as a retreat and abandonment of the Government's objectives.

The majority of Cabinet, however, sided with Callaghan and Hattersley. Wilson summed up that "the Cabinet were agreed that the Government must be free to follow the regional policies they required. The majority felt, however, that this was compatible with having rules on state aids and that, indeed, the establishment of the right rules would be in the British interest. They therefore favoured the tactical course recommended by Hattersley".[83]

On 14 September, Wilson was in Paris for an informal dinner of EEC Heads of Government. It was a dinner at which the Heads were unaccompanied and Wilson subsequently wrote his own record. They had, he noted, all agreed that there should be regular summits, which would be informal, routine, working meetings. Giscard had suggested that there might be three or four of them each year, with the aim of reviewing progress and giving instructions about future work. Preparation, it was agreed, should rest with the Presidency, supported by a small international secretariat.

Schmidt had proposed a fundamental review of the CAP. There was general support, although Giscard was equivocal and the Dutch and Irish leaders expressed some concern.

Schmidt had also expressed strong criticism of specialised meetings of the Council of Ministers. He wanted all of them abolished, with all subjects dealt with instead by Foreign Ministers. There was no conclusion.

The prospects for achieving Economic and Monetary Union by 1980 were discussed and largely written off. There was some talk about re-forming the snake but those suggestions were barely followed up.

Schmidt made a strong attack on the Commission as being bureaucratic, too costly and over-staffed. Wilson quoted the examples of Commission interference which had been particularly ridiculed in Britain "and this went down well". Ortoli did not speak in reply.

The three Benelux Prime Ministers spoke about Political Union, but in rather a perfunctory and ritualistic way. According to Wilson's account, Giscard at one point suggested altering the Luxembourg Agreement but did not explain clearly what he had in mind. There was, however, some support for the view that the Luxembourg Agreement was too rigid, and possibilities of more flexible interpretation were discussed. No decisions were taken. Wilson said there could be no progress on this issue until there was a majority Government in Britain and the results of renegotiation were known. Wilson also touched on Regional Aids, recognising the need for some rules, but arguing that they must be flexibly applied and leave adequate freedom for Governments to meet national and local needs.

Wilson concluded his note with the comment that it had to be remembered that "all of us had a pretty vague idea of the purpose of Saturday's meeting", but he found the atmosphere "quite encouraging in that it was a very practical and down-to-earth meeting – much less sanctimonious than other gatherings of the same kind I have known. There were few routine phrases, and the approach was quite iconoclastic: there was no genuflection to sacred cows".[84]

Wilson dictated a rather longer record of his own intervention. He had set out the "consistent approach of the Party I led, and of the previous Labour Government and the present one, from 1966 . . . and I set out the basis on which we had fought the 1970 election, where the final decision would depend on the outcome of the negotiations . . . I stressed that our position meant exactly the same if the terms were right and did not cripple our ability to play a full part in the Community and solve our own economic problems: we could still see advantage in EEC membership in terms of the broader technological base and also the political advantages which I had stressed in the 1967/70 period".

Wilson had explained that, because of renegotiation, the British Government could not get involved in discussions about political union. Even so, the British Government "would not stand in the way of further Community advance if that were the wish of our colleagues during that period". The realism of the speeches Wilson had heard (he spoke sixth out of the nine participants) and their concentration on immediate and threatening economic and financial problems underlined the view that Wilson had brought with him to the meeting. It would not be possible, Wilson had argued, to look at the distant mountains of 1980 because of the swampy territory in the immediate foreground. He cited as examples national and international economic problems, oil, recycling of oil money, inflation, dangers of recession, a shrinking of world trade, etc. Wilson then dealt with some of Britain's particular concerns, including the CAP, regional aids and the budget. He attacked the excessive bureaucracy of the Commission, its tendency to interfere and thus to cause great local resentment. He illustrated his point with a now-familiar litany about petty rules on beer, bread and eviscerated chicken.[85]

At a separate meeting in Brussels two days later, EEC Foreign Ministers discussed Giscard's plans for regular meetings of Heads of Government: the European Council. Hattersley represented Britain in Callaghan's absence and reported that the division of opinion round the table "was not in fact between the pragmatists and the idealists but between the large countries and the small, with the latter not disguising their fear of domination by the former". "I was", Hattersley continued, "forthcoming in my own response to Sauvagnargues' ideas. But I was at times uncomfortably conscious of a feeling on the part of the others that Britain was not really part of the process under discussion. This was never stated but there was an implicit, if disguised, assumption that Britain would not be there when these developments were realised. There was also the slightest hint that if Britain is going to leave the Community 'twere better done quickly'".[86]

It is surprising that, two days after the Paris Summit, Wilson found time to dictate any records. For, on his return to London he had, on 15 September, announced that there would be a General Election on 10 October, hence Callaghan's absence from the Brussels meeting of Foreign Ministers.

Labour's October 1974 Election Manifesto did not spell out the objectives of renegotiation. Instead, it referred back to the earlier manifesto, adding that the

Labour Government had, within a month of coming into office, started the negotiations on the basis of that manifesto. It was too early to judge the likely result of
"the tough negotiations which are taking place". But whatever the outcome in
Brussels, the decision would be taken in Britain by the British people.

The manifesto contrasted Labour's concern for democratic rights with the
refusal of the Conservative and Liberal Parties to endorse the right of the men and
women of Britain to take this unique decision. The Labour Party pledged that
within twelve months of the October election the British people would have the
final say, which would be binding on the Government – through the ballot box –
on whether to accept the terms and stay in or reject the terms and come out.

The overall tone in regard to Europe was quite positive and the manifesto
contained one of those devices which politicians love whereby an improbably
extreme threat is described along with a commitment to prevent its occurrence:
"Labour is an internationalist party and Britain is a European nation. But if the
Common Market were to mean the creation of a new protectionist bloc, or if
British membership threatened to impoverish our working people or to destroy
the authority of Parliament, then Labour could not agree".[87] It is perhaps a
measure of the relative insignificance of Europe as an election issue that Wilson's
foreword to the manifesto made no mention of Europe or of renegotiation.

The tenor of the electoral times was clear from the transcript of a telephone
conversation on 19 September between Fred Peart, who was at an Agriculture
Council in Brussels, and Wilson (in Number 10). The issue under discussion in
Brussels was sugar. The European Commission had put forward some proposals
on access to British markets for Commonwealth sugar which were helpful to
Britain. Peart reported to Wilson that he had said he "would look at their proposals
carefully" [Community-speak for 'well done']. "Bring them [the proposals] back
here", was Wilson's response. "That's right. You bring them back here. Don't say
anything too nice about them ... Because at the campaign committee this
morning it was the general view, coming partly from the anti-marketeers, but the
pro-marketeers didn't object, that after you get back somebody should make the
big point: 'Who the bloody hell are they to tell us where to buy our sugar from?'
So don't say anything that would make that more difficult". Peart replied that all
he would say in public was that the Commission had made a proposal, that the
British Government would look at it and that he (Peart) had opened up discussion
with Australia.

"But", said Wilson, "when the campaign starts one or two of us may say the
other thing, you see ... It's what I'm trying to do – it's to say that we are telling
the people the facts in this Election ...".[88]

In an interview on the BBC's *Nationwide* programme on 27 September Wilson
was much clearer than he had been in speaking to Robin Day at the start of
August about the basis on which the British people would be asked to give their
verdict on renegotiation. *Nationwide* featured what was at the time a notable innovation: viewers were invited to submit their questions in writing in advance and,
suitably sifted, a selection was then used by the interviewer. "Will the Labour
Party", Mr Tomlyn of Morpeth wanted to know, "adopt a definite policy of 'In'

or 'Out' on this subject"? Wilson replied that the British people would decide by a vote of the British people. When the negotiations were complete – when it was known what the terms were – "the Government will of course consider it and the Government will decide whether to recommend the country to accept entry on those terms or to say with regret that our negotiations have not been successful and we recommend looking for some other solution which does not involve membership". "I don't say", Wilson added, "that everybody in the Cabinet will be equally happy about it. But that will raise decisions for each individual member".[89]

On 10 October, Labour were returned to power in the General Election. Compared with the February election the Labour Party won a significantly larger share of the popular vote and an extra eighteen seats, giving them an overall majority of three in the House of Commons.

Wilson kept his senior Ministerial team unchanged and, within days, Callaghan was seeking the Prime Minister's steer on what attitude he should take at a meeting of EEC Foreign Ministers which was to discuss a European Summit meeting which the French Presidency were now planning for early December. "We now know", Callaghan wrote, "what a December summit will not do. It will not decide on new steps towards EMU. We shall not be faced with a demand that we agree to accept the aim of European Union by 1980 (though the other Governments have not dropped 'Union' as an aim toward which the nine Governments should be working). The Summit will not now deal with Schmidt's CAP stocktaking because the Council on 2 October has put this in hand". The question in Callaghan's mind was how to use the Summit to advance Britain's renegotiation aims. Very rapid progress was needed if the Government was to fulfil its election pledge to settle the issue through the ballot box within a year. On the CAP it would be very difficult to get results before April or May 1975. On most other issues Callaghan could see "a reasonable chance" of making sufficient progress in the course of planned Community business. That left the budget and Callaghan was clear that "what we have to do is to use the December summit as a lever to get acceptance in principle to the kind of solution to our budget problem which we need". In return, the other Member States would "no doubt want us . . . to meet them by accepting a greater degree of commitment to progress towards European unity (whatever that may mean) than we have been prepared to give so far".

The Commission's report on the budget was due before the end of October and Callaghan thought that "if we start pushing now, there is a reasonable chance that we might get a breakthrough at a December summit meeting". Callaghan therefore proposed to argue at the Council the following day that, now that the British General Election was over, it was time to tackle that most difficult issue, the budget. It would be very appropriate if the December summit were to agree in principle on the sort of solution which should then be worked out in the Council. Callaghan also advised that Wilson should have meetings with Schmidt and Giscard in the near future on the subject, since they held the key to the success of renegotiation, especially on the budget: "Both of them run their Governments in a very personal way; and we need to soften them up and, if possible, reach some kind of understanding with them privately about the budget". Callaghan recognised that Wilson had told him that morning that "you would prefer to keep these matters within the negotiating channels where they have been so far. But I hold the view that Schmidt and Giscard will wish to play a large personal part and that at a later stage you will have to come in on things". Callaghan added that, if Wilson did not want to do it, he was prepared himself to go and talk to them. If so, that should be before the Party Conference scheduled for November, and would leave it open to the Government to invite Schmidt to attend the Party Conference as well.

Wilson commented: "Most of this was drafted before our talk this morning . . . I do not want to invite Giscard but would be prepared to invite Schmidt, perhaps timed in relation to Conference (immediately before, or just after)".[90]

Callaghan returned to the charge. On 23 October, he sent Wilson another minute. A decision was needed pretty soon, he wrote, as to whether or not to add renegotiation to the agenda of the Summit. There could be little doubt that Giscard's wish for a successful summit would give the British Government additional leverage for getting acceptance in principle of the kind of budget solution they needed. Since the Prime Minister had told Callaghan that he wanted him to pursue the renegotiation through existing machinery, the Foreign Secretary had not raised the issue at the 15 October meeting of the Council. But he now sought Wilson's agreement to tell other Member Governments that Britain would be seeking at the summit a decision in principle on the budget question.

Callaghan went on to rehearse the substantive arguments behind the British case. At ECS on 25 April two possible methods of tackling the problem had been considered, one based on bringing gross contributions to the Community budget into line with shares of Community GNP and the other on compensating any Member State with GNP per head below the Community average for any net contribution. It had been agreed, Callaghan recalled, that the latter would be best, but that it might be necessary to fall back on the former. Bilateral official talks had since shown that the idea of compensation for the UK's net contribution was most unlikely to be negotiable. On the other hand, there was at least a chance that the Government might secure agreement to an arrangement by which the impact of the Community budget on Member States with below average GNP per head should be kept under review, and that a refund should be arranged if such Member State's gross contribution exceeded its GNP share. If soundings of Schmidt and Giscard showed that there was a reasonable chance of getting the Germans and the French to agree to such a solution, and if Cabinet colleagues agreed, then it should be possible to go for endorsement by the Summit of the principle that Member States with below average GNP per head should not bear a disproportionate share of the burden of financing the Community budget, and get the Summit also to ask the Council to settle as expeditiously as possible the means for giving effect to the principle – either through the solution of a refund bringing gross contributions and GNP shares into line, or through any other equally effective solution which might by then have emerged.[91]

Tom Bridges replied on the Prime Minister's behalf the next day. The Prime Minister's view was that, if he and Callaghan were to raise renegotiation at the Summit, it could not be on the basis of the budgetary issue alone. "The Prime

Minister is sure", Bridges wrote, "that if he is to take up renegotiation with his colleagues in Paris, he would need to do so on the basis of all the renegotiation issues set out in the February manifesto and repeated in the Secretary of State's statement of 1 April. On this understanding, the Prime Minister would not object . . ."[92]

Wilson and Callaghan took stock on 25 October. Wilson reiterated his view that there was more to renegotiation than the budgetary item alone. Callaghan agreed but pointed out that the budget was in a special category since its efforts were measurable and did not involve qualitative judgements. Callaghan read out the first tentative draft of a possible conclusion by the Heads of Government about the budget. This had been drafted by Michael Butler and read:

*"In the light of the discussion Heads of Government have had about the reaction of Member States to the world economic crisis and bearing in mind the need to promote convergence between the performance of the economies of Member States if the Community is to work properly, they agreed that Member States with below average GNP per head should not bear a share of the burden of the financing of the Community budget disproportionate with their share of Community GNP and requested the Council to consider and to settle as expeditiously as possible the means for giving effect to this princ*iple".

Wilson thought this "a good effort if we could achieve it". The Prime Minister also thought that it would be necessary to have some discussion in Cabinet before the Summit.[93]

On 28 October, Roy Hattersley discussed renegotiation with Finn Gundelach, the Danish member of the European Commission, responsible for Internal Market issues. The Commission had just produced their report on the Community budget. It confirmed that there was a problem. It showed that the British share of the Community budget would exceed the British share of Community GNP in 1977 and that the British economic growth rate up to 1978 would be much lower than the Community average.

Against that background, Gundelach advised that discussion of the budget in the regular Council of Ministers would involve interminable delays. The battle of dogma would have to be fought and won at the Summit. When the own resources system had been set up the intention, Gundelach said, had in fact been to ensure that national contributions were broadly in line with each country's share of the Community's GNP. The connection between budgetary contributions and GNP was implicit in the Commission's report. Once it was made explicit, there was bound to be a row, principally with the French, whose objections would purport to be ideological, but would in fact be material, and with the Dutch, whose objections would be genuinely ideological. This row could only be resolved by Heads of Government. It would be a fond hope to expect progress at the November Council of Ministers. There, the French would complain and the others would hedge. None of the Eight would take the subject seriously until they had heard a firm assurance from the Prime Minister that he wanted Britain to remain in the Community and would work to achieve that. Once they had heard that, the eight Governments would examine seriously what counterpart they could provide in order to make it possible for Mr Wilson to keep Britain in the Community. If, on the other hand, the Prime Minister were merely to say that Britain's continuing membership was to be left to the British people to decide, the Eight would not tackle the budget problem seriously.[94]

A similar message was given to Wilson on the same day by Christopher Soames. The Summit, Soames told Wilson when the two men met in Downing Street, would not be the place for detailed negotiations, but it could be the occasion on which the framework and parameters for subsequent negotiation would be determined at the highest level. Quite apart from that, a good Summit, which was seen to be dealing practically with problems which affected the lives of ordinary people, would be a bonus when the time came to present the results of renegotiation to the British people. The other Heads of Government would be looking for an indication of the Prime Minister's thinking both on the outcome which he wanted to see from the renegotiation and on the attitude of his Government thereafter.

Wilson thought that the Summit might be too large a forum, and perhaps in any case too early in time, to make the sort of progress which Soames expected on renegotiation, though the subject would no doubt come up for discussion. As to his own position, it was what it had always been: if the terms were right, he would recommend staying in. It was too early to say what those terms would be, though this was not just a question of the Community budget, even if that might well be the issue on which to concentrate in any discussion at the Summit.[95]

An early November assessment by the Cabinet Office, undertaken at the Prime Minister's request produced the following summary of progress in renegotiation:

CAP: A reasonable hope, through the CAP stock take, of satisfactory results. More
   generally, the CAP was likely to be better value because of continuing high
   world prices;

Community Budget: Serious negotiations scarcely begun;

EMU: No likelihood of early movement towards full EMU or European Union. It
   might, however, be necessary at the Summit to agree that further discussion
   of European Union should take place in 1975;

Regional, Industrial and Fiscal Policies: Reasonable prospects of agreement on a new
   set of rules for regional aids and of acceptance of a greater degree of flexibility
   in respect of national regional and industrial policies generally;

Capital Movements: An existing derogation permitting the UK to impose broadly
   the same exchange controls as applied before accession was likely to continue;

Sugar: Favourable prospect of being able to obtain Community agreement to an
   offer in excess of 1.4 million tons for imports from Commonwealth producers;

New Zealand: Reasonable hope of securing extended arrangements for NZ access
   at fair price levels for NZ butter. Cheese would be more difficult;

Aid: Decisions already taken by the Community already went a substantial way
   towards meeting UK objectives of a generous EEC aid policy;

VAT: the current position was expected to continue, enabling the UK to resist any
   unacceptable new proposals.

Wilson commented: "There is a hint – no more – that, as with sugar, the manifesto demands are a little outdated, because of world shortages for e.g. New Zealand products, and that since prices are higher abroad than in the EEC (which may only be temporary) there is less need for, or even practical hope of, reaching objectives which were related to longer term, hopefully more normal, situations".[96]

Nairne's minute was more a prediction of likely outcomes than a snapshot of the then state of the negotiations. Any such snapshot would have been somewhat darker. A senior French official had described the British ideas on the budget as treading on every possible Community toe. At the Council of Ministers on 11 November, the Germans and Belgians showed willingness to consider a solution to the British budget problem. The French were completely hostile. A meeting between Callaghan and Genscher in Bonn on 11 November was thought by Henderson to have been "a disaster".[97]

In London, Peter Shore had begun to agitate on the question of the tariff changes which Britain was scheduled, under the terms of the accession Treaty, to make on 1 January 1975. Under these provisions, Britain was to make a further move towards the Common Commercial Tariff against third countries together with a further 20% reduction in the tariff on imports from the rest of the Community. In a minute to Wilson of 1 November, Shore proposed that the Government should make the further reduction in tariffs on imports from the Six, but not implement the next move towards imposing the Common Commercial Tariff on third countries. He argued that this "would carry us a step further towards the goal of European free trade while avoiding tariff increases on goods from the Commonwealth and other third countries which it is in our interest to avoid". "No doubt", Shore concluded, "some will argue that it would constitute a breach of the Treaty and would have adverse consequences on our whole relationship with the Six. But, on the other hand, there have been occasions in the past when Community obligations have been delayed"[98].

Callaghan was the first to make the argument Shore had predicted. Shore's proposal, Callaghan argued, "would call in question the transitional arrangements which are the core of the Treaty of Accession. We could simply ignore our obligations. But this would alienate the other Member States and undermine our chances of securing our renegotiation objectives".[99]

On 8 November, Healey wrote to agree with Callaghan.[100]

On 13 November, Peart wrote, also supporting Callaghan: "I completely share the views expressed by Jim Callaghan. A standstill on all further tariff moves is not unattractive; but by running counter to the obligations of the Treaty of Accession, we would appear deliberately provocative in Brussels, at a time when our renegotiation aims are being received with some sympathy and we are beginning to make some progress . . . For my own particular sector, moreover, I should draw attention to the underlying assumption that the pursuit of a total or partial standstill would bring about significant benefit to consumers. In the case of the vast majority of foodstuffs, a tariff change of 20% of the difference between EEC and UK tariffs (often only one or two percentage points) would have only a marginal effect on retail prices. Our economists estimate the overall effect on the Retail Food Index would be about 0.1%".[101]

When Ministers first discussed the issue, in mid-November, Wilson appeared to side with Shore and concluded that the Commission could be asked to delay implementation of the tariff changes, and that the issue should come to Cabinet if the Commission refused.[102]

Shore reported back on his discussion with the Commission in a minute to Wilson of 25 November. He had met Ortoli, Soames and Gundelach. Their reaction had been negative on all points: legal, political and practical. "However", Shore wrote, "I was encouraged that the discussion on all points remained friendly and I am confident that in presenting our case to the Member States themselves, it will be possible to deploy the political arguments on our side with greater force and effect". Shore proposed that he should do just that at the Council of Ministers of 2/3 December.[103]

Immediately after the Labour Party Conference, on 29 November, Callaghan returned to the issue, sending Wilson a "personal note". He had, he said, looked carefully at what the problem raised by Shore meant in practical terms. First, if the Government decided to make the move it was required legally to make on 1 January the net effect would be to reduce UK duties as a percentage of total imports by 0.2%. As regards food, if the whole of the increased duty on third country imports were passed on (which was most unlikely) the effect would be to increase the individual's expenditure on food by 0.3p per head, or 15p per year. Thus the saving to British consumers by not making the 1 January move was negligible in real terms.

Secondly, Callaghan continued, the effect on the developing countries was also negligible.

Thirdly, as regards the developed countries of the Commonwealth and South Africa (which was in the same preference area) the 1 January moves would increase the duties on food by £8 million. Here, the most important produce was New Zealand lamb, but Cabinet had already asked Peart to see what could be negotiated with the Community on lamb. And, in any case, the burden was likely to fall almost entirely on New Zealand rather than on the British consumer because lamb was sold by auction in the United Kingdom before duty was assessed.

Callaghan's conclusion was that the gains in real terms from holding up the tariff move were out of all proportion to the problem the Government would create for themselves both in law and in terms of relations with other Community countries. In any event, the Eight would not agree.[104]

Shirley Williams (Secretary of State for Prices and Consumer Protection) minuted in similar vein.[105]

The Attorney General also gave his Opinion and Armstrong summarised it in a minute to Wilson of 29 November. In brief, the Attorney General had concluded that the law, as it stood, required the implementation of the tariff changes. The changes would happen automatically on 1 January 1975 unless Parliament had before then passed legislation. A decision not to implement the changes could lead to major difficulties in the courts, a high degree of confusion amongst traders and little, if any, advantage at the end of the day.

Just in case those arguments were not enough, Armstrong, who knew the character of the Prime Minister, added: "If the Secretary of State [Shore] was expected to launch this proposal at the Council on Monday, it is almost inconceivable that you should not have given Chancellor Schmidt some advance notice of it at Chequers on Sunday". Armstrong also pointed out, as Shore's minute of 25 November had not, that the three Commissioners whom Shore had called on had made it clear that there was no possibility of the Community as a whole accepting what Shore was proposing and that they had advised him in the strongest terms against putting his proposal to the Council of Ministers.[106]

Wilson did not raise the issue with Schmidt. He discussed it with Callaghan after Schmidt had left Chequers. Wilson told Callaghan that he was more inclined than formerly to take a longer–term view. He was more interested in going for the possibility of the longer-term benefits to trade with the Commonwealth that might be available from renegotiation than in the very small and short-term benefits that a delay in the implementation of the 1 January 1975 tariff changes would produce. The fact of having implemented the tariff changes would not make any long-run difference if Britain eventually came out of the Common Market. In that case it would presumably be necessary to reverse engines on tariff changes and on much else.[107]

When Ministers discussed the issue again on 2 December, the discussion turned against Shore.[108] Wilson summed up that the majority took the view that Britain should honour her treaty obligations on tariff changes. However, it might be best if Mr Shore, at the Council meeting later that day, were to make a statement pointing out that a strict interpretation of the manifesto should have held to a postponement of the tariff changes but that the British Government had given careful consideration to the matter and had decided not to ask for a deferral. Such a statement was accordingly made though, according to Donoughue, Shore called a press conference immediately afterwards at which he roundly denounced the European Community.[109]

This entire episode was, the Foreign Office concluded, probably the closest run thing (apart from the final decision in Cabinet on the overall outcome) in the whole Government consideration of renegotiation.[110]

Wilson's apparent sympathy for Shore's position in mid-November and his eventual conclusion on the issue two weeks later are partly attributable to the Labour Party Conference, which had been postponed to the end of November because of the timing of the General Election. Wilson had been nervous about it, and with cause. An Emergency Conference Resolution from Sheffield, Brightside demanded 'complete safeguards', in other words a much tougher approach than the one the Government were accused of pursuing. Callaghan, as Party Chair, was obliged to sit through anti-Market speeches demanding "fundamental renegotiation, not acceptance of the Treaty of Rome and of the Treaty of Accession. We must tell them where to get off in a good and proper voice". Despite a plea from the anti-Market leader of the National Union of Mineworkers, Joe Gormley, to Conference to vote against the Sheffield motion and "to get this damn thing out of the way", the Resolution was passed.

But the next day was better. Helmut Schmidt had accepted Callaghan's invitation to address the Conference. Schmidt spoke in English, with humour. He acknowledged the faults of the Community, said that Germany shared Britain's misgivings and was critical of the CAP. But Europe needed Britain and Schmidt pleaded with his British comrades, on grounds of Socialist solidarity, not to leave the Community.[111]

It was a tour de force, especially given the recalcitrant Party mood at the time. It was rumoured that Schmidt had received 25 drafts from leading members of the Labour Party.[112] He certainly received suggestions from Jim Callaghan and sent Callaghan his own draft for comment. It was probably at Callaghan's suggestion that Schmidt "made some good jokes, quoted Shakespeare, spoke flatteringly of the Labour Party's historic contribution to trade unionism and the welfare state", and appealed to the Labour Party's traditional internationalism. The threatened walk-out did not materialise and Schmidt was warmly applauded.[113]

Schmidt spent Saturday night at Chequers and discussed the European situation with Wilson, Callaghan and Healey. Schmidt wanted Wilson to make clear to his European partners at the Paris Summit that he and his colleagues would be willing to advise the British people in favour of remaining in the EEC provided Britain could get favourable terms. Schmidt thought that Wilson needed to reassure his fellow leaders, and particularly the French President, that he himself wanted Britain to stay in the EEC. So far, this had not been clear and there was a danger, in France and Italy, and in the southern part of Germany, of people saying that, if the British did not really want to stay in the Community, then probably the best course was to let them go and not try too hard or offer too many inducements to keep them in.

Wilson accepted that he would have to respond to the points that Schmidt had put to him. Schmidt had asked whether British Ministers were prepared to put their weight behind acceptance of British membership at the end of the day. So far as he was concerned, the answer was 'yes'. Admittedly, the country, Parliament and the Cabinet were divided. But his own view was what it had been ever since 1966. It was the same view as that of Macmillan. Macmillan had applied for membership in order to see what terms he could get. He had concluded that, on the terms that were available, membership was advantageous for Britain. But he had been frustrated by General de Gaulle's veto. His own position, Wilson continued, was that, on the right terms, British membership was good for Britain and good for Europe too. If, on the other hand, the terms were crippling, he could not advise Parliament or the British people that Britain should stay in; but he saw no reason why the terms should be crippling.

Wilson went through some of the issues, of which the budget was, he said "one of the more important". It was important for Britain's financial viability that her share of the EEC budget should not be inequitable. But he recognised that this would not become a real problem for another three years and that it could in any case be self-correcting if Britain's economic performance improved. He would therefore be prepared to accept a formula, rather than a sum of money, as a satisfactory outcome. But other issues were even more important if the British people were to be satisfied. One of these issues was Parliamentary sovereignty. Another was the right of national Governments to pursue their own regional policies without having to seek permission from Brussels. A third was access for Commonwealth, and particularly New Zealand, food products to the British and Community markets.

Wilson continued that he would like to see the whole operation of the Community made more political. He was appalled by "the moles of Brussels". He would like to see the long-term development of the European Community more under the control of the politicians and less under the control of the jurists, theorists and bureaucrats in Brussels.

Wilson then repeated that he was absolutely prepared to give, both to Schmidt and to Giscard, the assurance that Schmidt had sought on his position in relation to continuing British membership: if the outcome of the renegotiation produced terms of membership which were satisfactory, continuing British membership would be good for Britain and good for Europe, and he would be prepared to put his weight behind acceptance of continuing British membership.

Schmidt welcomed what Wilson had said. He wanted Britain to remain in the Community because he had come to believe that the pragmatic British approach was a necessary element. There were many people on the Continent who felt that, if the sea got rough, they could rely on the tenacity of the British. Wilson could count on the Germans, Dutch, Danish and probably the Irish in every field where he wanted to replace bureaucratic processes by political decisions made by political animals.

Schmidt had, he said, noted with interest Wilson's reference to the similarity between his own position and that of Harold Macmillan. There was, however, an important difference. When Macmillan was negotiating, his object was to find out the terms upon which British membership might be attainable. Today, the position was that Britain was a member, had signed a treaty and had ratified it. That made a great difference, for the French as well as for the Germans. He understood the need for the British Government to take a particular line for public opinion. But the Prime Minister must understand that Britain's partners in the Community were inclined to ask what sort of partner this was, which sought to find out what improvements were possible in the terms and thus called in question the validity of its ratification of a treaty. The British Government were walking a very narrow line. If they asked for changes in the treaties, they could not expect to get very far. But it was a different thing to try to achieve changes in resolutions defining policies within the treaties (as indeed the German Government was trying to do with the CAP). The British Government needed to make its position clear. It had, for example, taken seven months from the time when the present British Government took office before the Community knew what the British Government had in mind on the budget question.

Wilson replied that, from the time of British accession at the beginning of 1973, British public opinion had been disenchanted and even bored with the

Community. Schmidt had talked about Britain signing the Treaty. Indeed Britain had signed the Treaty. But it was the previous Government that had done so. It was an article of the British constitution that no Parliament could bind its successor. When Mr Heath had signed the Treaty he had not had the country with him; he did not have, as he himself had said he would have, the full-hearted consent of the British people. Wilson said that he could not accept the argument that, because the Treaty had been signed by Mr Heath, the present Government was bound by it. The present Government was trying to tread a middle path, between outright rejection of the Treaty and outright acceptance of the terms negotiated by Mr Heath.

Schmidt concluded that his record entitled him to say that the British Government did not need to convince him of the desirability of continuing British membership of the EEC. The problem remained that he still did not know what the British Government needed in order to be able to recommend continuing membership to the British people. He needed to be told. Wilson promised to send him a detailed paper.[114]

Britain's Ambassador in Bonn, Nicko Henderson, had been present both at Chequers and at Central Hall, where Schmidt had addressed the Labour Party. In a letter of 4 December to Oliver Wright, Henderson gave his impressions. Schmidt had been met at Heathrow by Roy Hattersley. "There were hold-ups on the Cromwell Road where rubbish was piled up on pavements as a result of a labour dispute in the cleansing department of the Kensington Borough Council. Upon arrival outside the Central Hall, Westminster, the Chancellor was greeted by hostile posters, boos, angry faces and shaking fists . . . The delegates, preoccupied by a debate on Clay Cross, paid little attention to the arrival of their distinguished visitor".

Henderson described how, after the speech, one former and one present Labour Cabinet Minister had said to him that Schmidt's performance was "the most brilliant they had ever heard at a Labour Party Conference". A widely held, and much expressed, view amongst those present, Henderson concluded, was that if any single speech could have made a difference to opinion and events Schmidt's should have done so.

Henderson's impressions of the talks at Chequers were not especially optimistic. There had, he thought, been a serious attempt to understand and narrow differences, with no attempt to score debating points. It was difficult to be sure what impression the Germans had of the visit. Henderson thought that the Chancellor had found it useful – though certainly exhausting. The speed with which Schmidt had telephoned Giscard afterwards, urging a meeting between the latter and the Prime Minister, suggested that Schmidt perceived the importance of engaging Wilson's personal interest in the renegotiation issue. In all, Henderson thought that Schmidt had drawn a "certain reassurance" about Wilson's attitude.

Henderson had been struck by the private discussion Wilson had had with officials at Chequers after the Saturday meeting with Schmidt. The Prime Minister had indicated that two things were uppermost in his mind. The first was that he thought it had been wrong to focus so much attention on the budget. He did not think that any general budgetary formula that could be obtained would be of any use in winning votes among the British people. There was of course no possibility of getting hard cash in the short term, and the Government were not seeking to do that. But it must be possible for him to be able to show the British people that he had got better terms than the Tories had done.

It was, Henderson wrote, pointed out to the Prime Minister that the British people were benefitting in many ways from Community membership, particularly over food prices. But Wilson dismissed this. He did not think Britain had done as well over sugar as if she had been able to make a five-year agreement herself. When pressed about what he would like to get in the way of new terms, Wilson said that he attached great importance to obtaining duty-free access for New Zealand butter and Australian produce. New Zealand and Australia were of great importance to the British people, he said. Wilson did not dissent when Joe Haines said that it would be essential for the Government to be able to say that, as a result of their renegotiation, they had brought about a reduction in the price of food for the British housewife. Haines said this was what the public minded about. Wilson said at that point that, of course, if he could cancel the Channel Tunnel that also would do a great deal of good.

Henderson observed that, apart from the position the Prime Minister had taken over the budget, which was not in line with the one the Foreign Secretary had been pursuing or that officials had been working on for a long time, Wilson also showed that he had his own ideas about the forthcoming Summit. He did not seem to go along with the idea that the December Summit should come to anything in the nature of a decision in principle about the budget, or, indeed, about any other aspect of renegotiation. As he saw it (and as he said later to Schmidt), he thought it was premature to try to decide these things in December. He envisaged the necessity for a special summit in the spring on renegotiation.[115]

Inside No. 10, Bridges commented to Armstrong that Henderson's letter seemed to underrate the effect of the visit, adding: "I certainly hope so".[116]

In fact, the Chequers meeting was more significant than Henderson allowed, less perhaps for a change in Schmidt's attitude than for an apparent shift in that of the Prime Minister. The day after the Chequers talks, during the Ministerial discussion on the tariffs issue, Armstrong passed Donoughue a note saying: "We have had an extremely interesting and (for those who think like you and me) very heartening weekend. HW showed more of his hand than ever before – perhaps because he had the conference behind him". Later in the day, Donoughue reported Wilson as being "on splendid form. Something has recharged his batteries – possibly getting Conference behind him". On the following day, when Bernard Donoughue and Joe Haines discussed renegotiation with Wilson, the Prime Minister made it absolutely clear by his approach that he wanted the United Kingdom to stay in the Community.[117]

Henderson would have been unaware of a significant telephone conversation between Wilson (who was still at Chequers) and Callaghan shortly after Schmidt had left. Wilson told Callaghan that, as a result of their discussions with Schmidt he was feeling a good deal happier about the possibility of an acceptable outcome to the renegotiation. Following Schmidt's departure he had been going through the party manifesto and had come to the conclusion that "a successful outcome was not all that impossible".

Wilson went through the issues. On the CAP, there was a fundamental stock-taking already under way. In addition, it would be necessary to "get something which corresponded to the manifesto commitment on access to the British market for food from outside the Community".

On the commitment to seek new and fairer methods of financing Community expenditure, Wilson thought that the point to concentrate on was the sentence in the manifesto which stated that the UK would be ready to contribute only what was fair in relation to what other countries were contributing.

As to the manifesto commitment not to increase unemployment for the sake of a fixed parity, Wilson noted that this was now Community orthodoxy. In private discussion, Schmidt had strongly discounted the possibility of any early move to EMU.

On the manifesto commitment on the retention by Parliament of those powers necessary to pursue effective regional, industrial and fiscal policies: regional policy seemed to present no difficulty; nor did fiscal policies because the Community was not seeking to interfere with them. On industrial policies, there was no suggestion that the industrial policy now being pursued by the Government was unaccept-able to the Community, though it might be necessary to get something on steel.

As to the manifesto commitment on Commonwealth and developing countries, Britain had done well on Protocol 22 and on Commonwealth sugar and the Government were in the process of settling something which was acceptable to the Asian sub-continent. A little more on New Zealand would help.

Schmidt, Wilson continued, had assured him that nothing like VAT harmoni-sation was on the cards.

Wilson reported to Callaghan that Schmidt was keen for him to talk to Giscard before the Summit meeting and would be phoning Giscard that evening to urge him to agree. Wilson was ready to go to such a meeting. Callaghan warned that Wilson would find Giscard much more theological than Schmidt. In particular, Giscard would stress the need for the Community to be self-supporting in agricul-tural policies. Wilson recognised this but thought the situation might be moving: "We can give him his theology provided we get the gravy". If the Community were ready to agree to some kind of extended derogation or long transitional period on New Zealand dairy products, that would help deal with the difficulty.

Callaghan said that the issues about which he was most concerned were sover-eignty and the Community budget. On sovereignty, the Prime Minister thought it would be necessary to look closely at the wording of the manifesto. It would be necessary to improve the arrangements for Parliamentary scrutiny of possible Community developments and legislation before they occurred. Callaghan was quite sure the problem could be solved provided that some reference to the Luxembourg Agreement, or something on those lines, could be retained.

Wilson and Callaghan then discussed how Callaghan should handle the issue of arrangements for the Summit at the meeting of the Council the following day.

Wilson said that he would like all the documents to be treated as background documents, not draft communiqué documents. Callaghan said that he would take the line that all the documents could go forward, but that the Prime Minister was not committed to any of them: they were circulated to illustrate the positions of the various countries. Wilson agreed and added that Schmidt had made it clear to him that he was not going to read the documents.

Callaghan asked what Wilson would like him to say at the Council meeting on the Community budget. The Dutch, Danes, Italians, Luxembourgers and Irish would go along with the British formula but everybody would nonetheless reserve their position for the Summit. Wilson was at first inclined to leave the subject until after the Summit, but then agreed that Callaghan should take it as far as he could at the Council, and should push the others fairly hard. Wilson said that he would not mind if the question reached the Heads at the Summit, though he was not inclined to suppose that there would be a final answer on that occasion.

Wilson went on to say that there was not much 'magic' in the budget. Between then and the Summit Callaghan should be looking for possible 'magic', particularly on the question of sovereignty, in order to strengthen the case when the issue was put to the British people.[118]

Wilson's meeting with the French President followed his meeting with Schmidt in short order. Callaghan had, as agreed, been to Paris as a kind of John the Baptist on 19 November. On that occasion, Callaghan had done almost all the talking, in an effort to persuade the President of the British case in both political and policy terms. Giscard had given little away, though he had the last (helpful) word when he concluded the meeting by saying that politics was what really mattered.[119]

In preparing for Wilson's visit to Paris, Nairne made a further attempt to engage the Prime Minister's interest in, and concern about, the budget issue. As the Prime Minister had emphasised, he wrote, the issue should not be got out of perspective. But it could prove to be the toughest issue in the discussions in Paris that evening. It required special handling, and could not be deferred, because it related to a major manifesto aim on which success or failure would be particularly clear to see. The Government had to seek to show that they had secured agreement to a new and fairer method of applying the Community budget system. The hurdle would be a high one to cross because any change which would benefit a relatively poor member of the Community such as the United Kingdom was bound to involve a potentially large budget burden for the richer members. That was the main reason why France and Germany were digging in their toes. Unless agreement was achieved at the December Summit to a principle – to the effect that Member States with below average GDP per head should not bear a budget share disproportionate to their share of Community GDP – then it would not be possible by the spring to secure agreement to an actual mechanism to turn the principle into practice.

It was quite likely, Nairne predicted, that the French President would argue that the principle of equity advanced by the British did not arise because the Own Resources system was an essential part of a Common Market and a Customs

Union; and because there was no proof whatever that the United Kingdom would be hard hit; and that Britain had no case and should, instead, honour its Treaty obligations. It would, Nairne recommended, be important to respond firmly, making clear that Britain found itself in the very kind of "unacceptable situation" in which action had been promised during the Accession negotiations and that this matter was one on which progress was required straightaway if Britain's renegotiation requirements were to be met.[120]

When Wilson and Callaghan met Giscard and Sauvagnargues on the evening of 3 December at the Elysée, Wilson, responding to a question about the budget from the French President, sought to place the budget issue in a wider context. The budget was not the only renegotiation issue and too much emphasis had been placed on it. He then launched into his standard speech about access for Commonwealth products and New Zealand butter.

Callaghan sought to bring the discussion back to the budget. The problem was how to find a self-adjusting mechanism which would enable the British contribution to be related to her capacity to pay. Sauvagnargues immediately retorted that the issue had been discussed at the Council of Ministers that morning that there had not been much support for the British case. The Germans had been opposed and so had he. He had had to state categorically that to invoke GDP was to undermine the system of own resources. It seemed to him that, although the United Kingdom accepted the principle of own resources, it paid only lip service to it. Nor did it observe the principle of Community preference which implied the switch from the Commonwealth to the Community as suppliers of food.

Sauvagnargues' account was not entirely accurate. At the Council, only he had been totally opposed to what the British had proposed, prompting Callaghan to say at the end of the Council that the meeting has been subjected to a jet of cold air. Was this the French Government's last word? If so, there was no point in continuing discussion and renegotiation would have to be deemed to have failed.[121]

Now, in the Elysée, Wilson replied that, as far as Community preference was concerned, one had to be realistic and to take account of consumer preference and long-established habits. For example, Britain had been importing hard wheat for generations. To switch to soft wheat would mean that all British bakeries would have to be converted. That could not be done overnight even though some people, like himself, might prefer French bread to the domestic product. It was no easier for the British housewife to give up New Zealand cheddar in favour of French cheeses. But Britain did accept Community preference in principle. Callaghan added that Britain accepted it in practice as well. He went on to say that there had been more support in Brussels for the British case on the budget than Sauvagnargues had claimed and that, had Genscher been present for Germany, there would have been more support still. According to his tally, the score had been 6.5 in favour and 1.5 against.

Giscard, less doctrinaire than his Foreign Minister, said it was difficult to see how it was possible to change the long-term budget structure since the rules did not allow it. The contribution made by each country from VAT receipts, however, bore a relation to GDP and there might be some possibility of flexibility there.

The President went on to say that he understood only too well that the British Government had a problem over the budget. Speaking for France, he would like the United Kingdom to stay in the Community. But this was not a question he could decide. He thought that an attempt should be made to see whether a system of 'precautions and adjustments' could be worked out.[122]

Wilson's report to Cabinet on 5 December on his discussions with Schmidt and with Giscard was cautiously upbeat. He had, he said, emphasised to Schmidt that the Government were not concerned only with the budget issue, but attached great importance to each of the seven negotiating aims set out in the February Election Manifesto. He had now sent Schmidt a message which set out the position.

Wilson said that his visit to Paris had been deliberately handled in low key, but he thought it noteworthy that the French Government spokesman had been authorised after the meeting of the French Cabinet following the visit to stress the good climate in which the talks had taken place.

Giscard, Wilson continued, had been at pains to give nothing away and he had defended well known French views in familiar and somewhat theological terms. The Government should be ready to allow the French some degree of theology provided that they secured the concrete results they required. He had told both Schmidt and Giscard that the success of renegotiation would have to be judged against what was achieved on all the manifesto aims. He had also indicated to them that, while the issue would need to be considered by the Cabinet at the appropriate stage, the logic of the position which he had consistently taken up meant that, for his part, he would be prepared, if all the manifesto commitments were satisfactorily met, to recommend to the British people that they should support the terms obtained.[123]

Wilson's stress on all aspects of renegotiation, and not just the budget, lay in part in the fact that he attributed less importance to the budget as an issue than did Callaghan and Whitehall officials. The very fact that the budget outcome would be so readily measurable also almost certainly contributed to Wilson's desire not to highlight it. In addition, he had told Callaghan that it had no 'magic' as a selling point to the British public. Wilson himself felt that the Commonwealth and Parliamentary Sovereignty would resonate more. He and Callaghan also knew that they would not be able to claim success on every manifesto issue. They would have to be able to sell to Cabinet and the country the *overall* outcome of the negotiations and that in turn implied the achievement of a broad measure of success across several fields. Wilson was seeking a broad platform on which to sell the renegotiation outcome.

The 5 December meeting of Cabinet was the first occasion on which Wilson told his Cabinet colleagues that he would, if renegotiation succeeded, be willing to recommend the outcome to the British people. That statement appears to confirm the impression gained by both Armstrong and Donoughue at the time that Wilson had turned a corner in his own appreciation of the prospects of success. But even if Wilson had turned a corner, he was cross with the pro-Marketeers for saying so publicly. He told Donoughue that he had to keep a balance and contemplated making the speech he was to give to London Labour Mayors on 7 December somewhat anti-European. At the same time, Donoughue found that Wilson had become fascinated by the "Market problem. He sees it as a challenge – to stay in, get the terms and hold the Labour Party together. He never talks of actually pulling out".[124]

In the event, the tone of Wilson's speech to the Labour mayors was balanced but positive. Membership of the EEC on the right terms would, he told his audience, be good for Britain and Europe. Britain had a "real intent to succeed". "It stands to reason", Wilson added, "that, provided we get the right terms – but only if we get the right terms – I shall commend them to the British people and recommend that we should stay in and play our full part in the development of the Community". His own task, Wilson said, was "to get the ball out of the scrum".[125]

On 9 December, Wilson flew to Paris for the EEC Summit which began that afternoon. Callaghan later wrote that Wilson was "experiencing a number of minor indispositions at the time and was not wholly well during the Paris Summit".[126] Certainly, on his return from the Summit dinner on the first evening he played the politician's trick most disliked by civil servants, asking Palliser and Nairne detailed factual questions on issues they could not answer without notice and denouncing them for their failure and for generally being too pro-Market. He was furious, rougher than an embarrassed Donoughue, who was present, had ever seen him.

Later, Wilson, in his bedroom in the British Embassy Residence, told Donoughue that the civil servants "must not think they have captured me and now it is all plain sailing". He was, Donoughue wrote in his diary, delighted with himself. Twenty-four hours later, when the Paris Summit was over, Wilson invited the same civil servants to join him in the Ambassador's Residence for a wash-up session, seeking the views of each of them in turn. That was his indirect way of apologising.[127]

The Paris Summit, the first of what were to become regular meetings of the European Council, was long, argumentative and at times tense. In that respect too, it established the pattern for most future such meetings.

It took the whole of 10 December, and late into the night, for agreement to be reached. Wilson was unwell, suffering from a racing heart, a problem which recurred on his return to London with such severity that he was forced to withdraw from Cabinet on 12 December and to cancel his engagements for three days.[128]

Giscard, in the chair, was described by Callaghan as being scrupulously fair but Sauvagnargues dug in on the French position, refusing to contemplate any change to accommodate Britain's budget difficulty. In the end, with help from Schmidt, who had promised Wilson that he would 'fix it', agreement was reached on a formula which met the British requirement. The Heads of Government agreed "to invite the institutions of the Community to set up as soon as possible a correcting mechanism of general application which, in the framework of the system of own resources and in harmony with its normal functioning ... could prevent during the period of convergence of the economies of the Member States the possible development of situations unacceptable for a Member State and incompatible with the smooth working of the Community"[129].

Wilson had specifically reserved the British Government's position, pending the outcome of renegotiation, on the Summit communiqué's commitment to achieve direct elections to the European Parliament as soon as possible. He had, however, put his name to three other commitments.

On European Union, the Heads of Government had noted "that the process of transforming the whole complex of relations between the Member States, in accordance with the decision taken in Paris in October 1972, has already started. They are determined to make further progress in this direction . . . The time has come to agree as soon as possible on an overall concept of European Union". The Heads of Government asked the Belgian Prime Minister, Leo Tindemans, to prepare a report on the subject, a procedure which, usefully from Wilson's perspective, deferred the issue until after renegotiation and the decision of the British people.

On EMU, the Heads of Government affirmed "that in this field their will has not weakened and that their objective has not changed since the Paris Conference".

Finally, "in order to improve the functioning of the Community", the Heads of Government recorded that "they consider that it is necessary to renounce the practice which consists of making agreement on all questions conditional on the unanimous consent of the Member States, whatever their respective positions may be regarding the conclusions reached in Luxembourg on 28 January 1966".[130]

These commitments were part of the price Wilson and Callaghan had been obliged to pay for Community cooperation on the key renegotiation issues. When Wilson reported to Cabinet on 12 December, he came under attack from Shore, Foot and Benn. "Certain passages in the Communiqué", they claimed, "appeared to commit the Government on a number of issues in terms which were incompatible with the February Election Manifesto and would weaken the credibility of the Government's approach to renegotiation. This was notably the case in relation to majority voting and the Luxembourg Agreement of 1966, to the election of the European Assembly by universal suffrage, and to the reaffirmation of the 1972 Paris commitment to Economic and Monetary Union. The firm retention of the power of veto was essential to the preservation of the sovereignty of the United Kingdom Parliament and represented a crucial safeguard against the EEC overriding the powers of both the Government and Parliament".

Wilson argued that neither he nor the Foreign Secretary had "in any way jeopardised our national interests, or any aspect of Government renegotiation policy as set out in the Election Manifesto." All the points on which agreement at the Summit was recorded should be read in the light of the paragraph of the communiqué which placed on record the basis on which the Government approached the renegotiation.[131]

Nonetheless, the truth was that the only part of the communiqué to which Wilson had made a specific, recorded reservation was the paragraph on direct elections to the European Parliament. When Wilson was well enough to report to

Parliament, on 16 December, Heath lost no time in congratulating him on his commitment to European Union, to EMU and to the renunciation of the Luxembourg Compromise. Heath believed "it is also right that the Luxembourg Agreement, which has always been an agreement to differ, should have been renounced" – not exactly the position he had taken when in Government.

Wilson replied that all that had been agreed was "on the desire to avoid an over-use of the veto on matters which may not be of overall national importance".

He agreed that European Union was a very desirable objective. But it meant what anyone wanted it to mean and, on that basis, he had gone along with it.

As regards EMU, agreeing to the goal was the same as agreeing to the long-term ideal of general and complete disarmament: "I am all for it. But I do not expect it by 1980. That was the phrase I used last week in respect of economic and monetary union. We accept it as a long-term objective, but it was not accepted by anyone as an objective by 1980, any more than total disarmament was, and that was the phrase that I used".

Later, when Heath returned to the charge, Wilson accused him of having signed a blank cheque on EMU: "He did not have the faintest idea what it meant . . . We made EMU a long-term objective. There is not a hope in hell – I mean in the Common Market – as the other Heads of Government have made clear, of EMU taking place in the near future".[132]

Cabinet on 12 December had also discussed one other renegotiation issue. On 27 November, Foot, Benn and Shore had written to the Prime Minister. It was clear, they argued, that, whatever the outcome of renegotiation, Ministers would have very deep convictions "that cannot be shelved, or set aside, by the normal process of Cabinet decision making". The three men believed that, in those circumstances "it would be wise to agree, in advance, that Ministers should have the right to express their convictions publicly in parallel with their accepted right to record them privately in the polling stations".[133]

Now, on 12 December, Foot argued that the issue had become immediate as a result of the Paris Summit communiqué since "its terms suggested that agreement had been reached on issues which had not been the subject of collective consideration by the whole Cabinet, and about which he personally had considerable reservations". The time had come, Foot argued, for an "agreement to differ" on this single issue for a limited period.

Wilson allowed a brief discussion before concluding that all members of the Government were bound by the passages on renegotiation in the two manifestos on which the Government had been elected . . . The collective responsibility of the Government must be maintained on issues arising both in the course of renegotiation and in the continuing work of the EEC during that period. He would arrange for a discussion early in the New Year of "the position which members of the Cabinet might adopt when the results of renegotiation were clear".[134]

When junior Minister Eric Heffer, who was spoiling for a fight, wrote to Wilson on 16 December claiming that the Paris communiqué and the Prime Minister's speech to the Labour mayors had "endangered Party unity and Ministers will now find it difficult not to express their own personal views on this matter", Wilson slapped him down. Cabinet on 12 December had agreed that the collective responsibility of the Government must be maintained. He could only assume that Heffer's minute had been written before his (Wilson's) statement to Parliament on the Paris summit and he invited Heffer to read it.[135]

The following day, Christmas Eve, Wilson replied to Foot, referring to the Cabinet agreement of 12 December and to the prospect of a resumed Cabinet discussion in the New Year, and concluding that "I am sure that the right course in the meantime must be for us to go on as we have gone until now . . . until such time as renegotiation is complete".[136]

But Wilson was to enjoy no sustained Christmas rest. On 29 December, Tony Benn sent an open letter to his constituents in Bristol South-East in which he claimed, among various other criticisms of the EEC, that the Parliamentary democracy developed and established in Britain, and the basic democratic rights which derived from that Parliamentary democracy, which in turn was based upon the sovereignty of the British people, was "fundamentally altered by Britain's membership of the European Community". The letter was issued by Benn to the Press.

Wilson was at his home on the Scilly Isles. He instructed Nick Stuart, one of his Private Secretaries, to write to Benn's office giving it as the Prime Minister's considered view that Benn's statement contravened the Cabinet decision of 12 December.

Benn wrote to Wilson on 2 January 1975 claiming, in effect, that the require-ment on Ministers to remain silent on the grounds of collective responsibility was "completely unreal". He could not "therefore" accept that his letter in any way contravened the decision of 12 December.

Wilson replied on 6 January arguing that his view that Benn had breached the spirit of the Cabinet conclusions was shared by a number of Cabinet colleagues who had "not disguised the indignation they feel". Any agreement to differ would itself have to be a collective decision, not a decision for any one individual. In the meantime, Wilson ended, "it creates an impression of disarray and adds needlessly to the difficulties of the Government as a whole if individual members of the Cabinet jump the gun as you have done". He hoped Benn would refrain from any further pronouncements of this kind until the Cabinet had taken "the decisions which will provide the framework for our collective and individual approach to these matters in future".[137]

At the turn of the year, Michael Foot returned to the charge on the issue of an agreement to differ that he had raised in his letter to the Prime Minister of 27 November. He argued that Wilson had agreed at the Paris Summit to commit-ments, for example on EMU, that "would never in any form have been approved at the Party conference or by any of the bodies which approved our manifestos". The Summit communiqué had, Foot argued, altered the position on collective Ministerial responsibility that had prevailed before.[138] It was clear that the position could not be held for much longer.

On 14 January, the Cabinet Secretary told Wilson that he had obtained the minutes of the Cabinet meeting held on 22 January 1932 at which an 'agreement to differ' on trade matters had been reached. The 1932 situation was different from the 1975 one in that the Government then had been a coalition but in other respects Hunt thought that the precedent was a useful one. In particular, the agreement was a deliberate decision by the Cabinet as a whole and limited to a specific issue. In 1932, the Cabinet had "determined that some modification of usual Ministerial practice is required and has decided that Ministers who find themselves unable to support the conclusions arrived at by the majority of their colleagues on the subject of Import Duties and cognate matters are to be at liberty to express their view by speech and vote".[139]

Formally, no decision had been taken to hold a referendum but, when Cabinet met on 21 January, they had in front of them a paper by the Lord President of the Council, Edward Short, about the conduct of a referendum and Wilson quickly concluded that that was the means whereby the Government's obligation to consult the people would be fulfilled, once the necessary legislation had been taken through Parliament.

Cabinet also agreed to take a decision by the end of March, in the light of the outcome of the renegotiation, on whether the British people should be recommended to vote for continued membership or for withdrawal. Wilson also recommended, and Cabinet agreed that "if at that point a minority of the Cabinet were unable to agree with the majority decision on what the Government's recommendation should be, the Ministers in the minority should be free to advocate a different view during the referendum campaign on the basis of guidelines precluding any engagement in controversy of a personal kind which could impair the unity of the Government".[140]

Wilson announced the decision to the House of Commons on 23 January. He took some raillery over the decision to agree to disagree, and acknowledged that the situation was unique. He agreed with Heath that, constitutionally, a referendum could not be binding on Parliament. "But", he added, "I perhaps pay more attention to the views of the people in the country than [Heath] did, despite his promise, and I express the view that I could not imagine many hon. Members deciding to pit their own judgment in this matter against what has been the decision of the people of the country".[141] The Lord President, Edward Short, put the point more formally and succinctly when he opened the debate on the Government's Referendum White Paper on 11 March and said: "The Government will be bound by its [the referendum] result, but Parliament, of course, cannot be bound by it".[142]

Many decisions remained to be taken about the organisation of the referendum. But the Prime Minister's first concern was to try to maintain discipline within the Government ranks. On 27 January, he sent a minute to all Ministers. The decision Cabinet had taken was that when the Government had announced its recommendations on the negotiated terms then, and only then, Ministers who felt unable to support it would be free to differ publicly. The decision, Wilson wrote, was almost without precedent and had been taken by the Cabinet "in the full knowledge that, if indeed members of the Government are publicly ranged on different sides of the public debate in the referendum campaign there will be great strains upon loyalty among colleagues, and that the risk of damage from those strains to the Government's cohesion and credibility will not necessarily be confined to the European issue". Wilson enjoined on all his Ministerial colleagues the need to "eschew trying to find ways of observing the letter of these limitations but breaching the spirit of them". Nor should Ministers devote time and energy prematurely to the referendum issues but should instead "recognise that the country faces the greatest challenge we have ever faced in peacetime, and that every one of us has a job to do solving the economic and social problems of the coming months". That last passage was an addition by Wilson to a draft prepared by Armstrong, which was itself a redraft of one by Hunt thought by Armstrong inadequately to reflect the Prime Minister's wishes.[143]

Of the remaining renegotiation issues, the two most problematic ones vis-à-vis Britain's partners were the budget and New Zealand. Internally, within the Government and the Labour Party, regional aids, industrial policy and steel were the major headache since all three raised issues of the competence of the Community to take decisions, or to curtail the power of Parliament to do so, in significant areas of domestic policy.

New Zealand was a problem of both substance and politics. In November 1974, the Agriculture Council had agreed to increase prices for New Zealand butter and cheese. But no progress was made on what arrangements would apply to New Zealand after 1977; nor on the establishment of an annual review of prices to which the New Zealand Government attached great importance. New Zealand sought an improvement in the terms of Protocol 18, the protocol to the British Accession Treaty covering New Zealand. Wilson – who claimed 44 relatives in New Zealand – regarded a generous arrangement for New Zealand dairy products as one of his sticking points in renegotiation.[144]

The New Zealand Prime Minister, Bill Rowling, called on Wilson, Healey, Peart and Hattersley in Downing Street on 10 February at the outset of a European tour. Rowling was seeking a number of things: a five-year commitment from the EEC, with a review in the third year; an automatic price rise for New Zealand products as costs rose; and guaranteed access for an annual total of 160,000 tonnes (consisting of 140,000 tonnes of butter and 40,000 of cheese). Wilson readily volunteered that, in his view, "the terms negotiated in relation to New Zealand [were] among the worst of those negotiated by the Conservative Government". But he thought Rowling was asking for a longer term commitment from the EEC on access than the British Government would be able to negotiate. He believed that the most that could be hoped for was to achieve an end to degressivity.

Rowling continued his tour and, on 18 February, Palliser received an urgent invitation from Soames to a meeting with him and Commissioners Lardinois (Agriculture) and Gundelach (Internal Market). Soames told Palliser that the President of the Commission had asked him and his colleagues to express to Palliser the grave concern of the Commission after their meeting with Rowling the previous day. Rowling's requirements were quite unrealistic. The prospects of achieving agreement on anything as specific as that at the Dublin European

Council in March were "infinitesimal". Above all, Soames warned, after the "great efforts the Commission had made to meet the UK's successive renegotiation requirements, the sudden presentation there weeks before the Dublin meeting of these new demands on behalf of New Zealand was likely to lead to dangerous confrontation with other Member States". Soames feared that the British Government would jeopardise the success achieved in renegotiation for the sake of concessions that New Zealand neither needed nor wanted.

Palliser had been Soames' deputy in the Paris Embassy and Soames, even at his most bullyingly booming, was not likely to cow him. Palliser took him up sharply on the suggestion that these were new and sudden demands. Specific demands had been put to the Agriculture Council by Mr Peart on 18 June 1974. The Prime Minister had referred to New Zealand's requirements at the Paris Summit and the Foreign Secretary had spoken of them at the Council of Ministers on 20 January. The three main problems which would have to be dealt with were duration (including the issue of degressivity), quantity and price. None of these was inherently unreasonable. Palliser did not believe that the Prime Minister and Foreign Secretary would expect the Dublin meeting to lay down detailed technical provisions on price or quantities but rather establish clear guidelines on which the review should be based. The Commission should be careful not to inflate the problem.

Palliser succeeded in deflating Soames and reported to London that the meeting had undoubtedly been stage-managed for maximum effect. But its significance, he advised, should not on that account be discounted. Palliser's worry was that the Government could find themselves in a repetition of the bind which the Conservative Government had got into in 1971, whereby some of Britain's partners would use her demands on behalf of New Zealand as an argument to justify withholding agreement to the budget correcting mechanism.[145]

Back in London, Michael Butler and Oliver Wright agreed with Palliser, minuting to Callaghan on 25 February on the dangers for Britain of a New Zealand/Budget trade-off. In their judgement, the budget was the important thing to go for. Privately, Callaghan might well have agreed with them. The budget had always been at the top of his list of priorities. But the outcome to renegotiation had to satisfy the Prime Minister, the Cabinet, Parliament and the country so, not altogether surprisingly, Callaghan ruled that Butler's suggestion was not good enough. He would not accept a situation in which there was a trade-off between New Zealand and the budget. The Government must continue to fight for both. They must be willing to risk a breakdown in the negotiations.[146]

Rowling meanwhile had been received to lunch by the French President at the Elysée and had also found Chirac relatively forthcoming.[147]. Rowling began to say publicly that New Zealand's interests included a strong Europe with a strong United Kingdom within it and that what New Zealand wanted from the Summit was a broad statement of principles.[148] In discussions between British and New Zealand officials, the latter's demands were somewhat toned down.

At the Council of Ministers on 3 March, Callaghan, with New Zealand support, was able to table a new formula consisting of: a price for New Zealand butter of

65% of the intervention price for Community butter; an import quantity of at least 120,000 tonnes of New Zealand butter; access for some New Zealand cheese; and an annual review of prices.

The budget issue continued to be intractable and Denis Healey, in writing to Helmut Schmidt on 3 February, had none of Callaghan's hesitations in saying that "of all the issues Harold Wilson has raised for renegotiation with the European Community, the question of the British contribution to the Budget is the most important from the public and political point of view".

The European Commission had just published their ideas for dealing with the issue and Healey's purpose in writing was to suggest some necessary improvements in the Commission's approach.

The Commission had agreed with the British Government that there should be a corrective mechanism for any country which was contributing to the EEC budget a share which was disproportionate to its share of Community GNP. The Commission suggested as criteria for qualification: a GNP share of below 85% of the Community average; a rate of growth below 120% of the Community average; the existence of a balance of payments deficit; a total budget contribution of at least 110% of the GNP share. Even then reimbursement would be limited to two thirds of the difference between the GNP share and the contribution share. There would be a sliding scale by which the whole repayment due would only be made if the contribution was as high as 130% of GNP.

Healey noted three principal objections to the Commission's suggested budget mechanism. Firstly, under it, no country with a balance of payments surplus could qualify for a budget reimbursement, even if it was clearly paying more than its fair share. Secondly, full repayment would not apply to the first 30% of any excess budget contribution and was then limited to two thirds of the excess, however large it might be. Thirdly, the total repaid would not, under the Commission scheme, exceed the qualifying Member State's total VAT contribution. But, Healey argued, that VAT contribution was a residual and could be very small indeed if levies and duties were higher, or the total budget lower, than foreseen.

Just in case Schmidt should remain in any doubt, Healey concluded with the words: "There is no issue in the renegotiation on which public opinion in Britain puts quite so much weight as this".[149]

Of course, Healey as Chancellor had a different view of renegotiation priorities from that of the Prime Minister. As the Dublin Summit approached, Healey wrote to Wilson noting that the French Government had explicitly linked a settlement for New Zealand with the budget correcting mechanism. On both issues there would, Healey expected, be pressures on the Government to accept less than their full demands. Healey recognised that the Government owed it to the New Zealanders to try to get them what they wanted. "But", he went on, "I hardly need to emphasise that the budget is also a most important aspect of the renegotiation. In substance, we stand to gain substantial amounts from the Commission's proposed mechanism, starting in about 1978 and building up to well over £100 million a year by 1980 and thereafter (assuming that we can get rid of the Commission's balance of payments criterion). These sums will be of direct benefit to the balance of payments and to the Exchequer. And in presentational terms, it seems to me that it would be very difficult to argue that we had succeeded in our manifesto aim if we had to accept any serious weakening of the Commission's proposals, which are already a good deal less than we wanted and will reimburse less than two thirds of our excess contributions. In particular, there seems no possibility of further compromise with the French proposal for a corrective mechanism confined to VAT contributions alone. By comparison, it seems to me that there could be some room for diluting, if necessary, the text of the proposed declaration on New Zealand, provided that we maintain one or two essential points such as the link with Community intervention"

"Noted", wrote Wilson on his copy of Healey's minute, "But not decisive".[150]

Schmidt, in the meantime, had replied to Healey's letter which had reached him "just in time" before a meeting with the French President. Schmidt was pleased that Callaghan had called the Commission's proposal for tackling the budget issue a good basis. Schmidt sympathised with Healey's point about the balance of payments criterion but beyond that he could not help feeling that the British requests for changes to the Commission proposal were so far-reaching that they would make it very difficult to reach a solution on the basis of that proposal, which all had considered constructive. Flexibility on the part of the British, Schmidt felt sure Healey would agree, was necessary if a compromise acceptable to all EEC partners was to be reached.[151]

On 24 February, Callaghan sent to Wilson a minute entitled *Renegotiation: The Last Lap*. In it, Callaghan argued that the practical situation as regards EMU, capital movements and VAT was satisfactory. There were no moves in the offing within the Community which would cause problems for the Government.

Having secured the beef regime the Government wanted, they could not expect Fred Peart to get any further as far as action on the CAP within the renegotiation timetable was concerned. Sufficient progress had also been secured within the renegotiation timetable on the Commonwealth and developing countries. A new Community agreement with the African, Caribbean and Pacific countries (ACP) was in place. Significant improvements had been secured in the General Scheme of Preferences (GSP), as had a liberal Community negotiating position in the multilateral trade negotiations.

As regards New Zealand and the budget, Callaghan's assessment was that all Community Governments wanted a successful outcome but, equally, they all wanted to keep the cost to themselves to the minimum and therefore to limit their concessions. "I think", Callaghan wrote, "that we shall have a pretty tough negotiation in Dublin. There are reasonable prospects of success. But we may need to show our teeth to get what we want". Moreover, to get what they wanted, the Prime Minister and Callaghan would have to tell the other Heads that, if they met the British Government's requests, they would regard renegotiation as completed and would recommend the outcome to Cabinet and, if Cabinet agreed, to the British people. Publicly, Wilson and Callaghan would need to hold to the line that the Community had gone as far as they reasonably could to meet British requirements and that the position must now be discussed with the Cabinet as a whole.

In other words, if they got what they wanted they could say that renegotiation was over but not what conclusion they drew from that. Cabinet and a statement to Parliament would, in the circumstances, have to follow swiftly if the Prime Minister wanted to "get your blow in first before things start to leak".[152]

At the end of February, instructions were sent to Henderson in Bonn to make a high-level pitch on the Prime Minister's behalf about New Zealand. At the same time, Wilson decided to send Armstrong to Paris to discuss New Zealand and renegotiation more generally. The advice from Tomkins in Paris was that all the signs were that the French were going to be very obstinate and impatient with British demands. They might well be thinking of playing off the budget against New Zealand and the best way of dealing with them in this regard would be to isolate them. If Britain could accept the Commission's report on the budget, and the Germans and others could be brought along with it too, that could be an effective tactic. In general, the French wanted to finish with renegotiation at the Summit and the nearer the budget problem could be brought to a solution before the Summit the more difficult it would be for the French to link it with New Zealand.[153]

In a separate telegram Tomkins advised that Giscard's own domestic position was very much stronger than it had been three months previously. He now had nothing to fear from the Gaullists whom Chirac had got under control. The Opposition was more divided than ever. The Government's economic targets were on the way to being met and there was a feeling that the worst of the crisis was over. Unemployment was still a significant problem, but inflation was slowing down, the deficit on the balance of trade was lessening and the public mood showed no sign of agitation. The opinion polls were showing a strong rise in the President's popularity and a corresponding decline in the standing of his rivals.

In those circumstances, Tomkins believed, Giscard would be thinking in terms of a package at Dublin which aimed to give Britain satisfaction over New Zealand, preserved the system of own resources and met German preoccupations about open-ended financial commitments, while relating national contributions in some way to GNP. Giscard was reportedly working on a plan but, said Tomkins, "I fear the truth is that we are going to be asked to accept an arrangement by which, put crudely, he meets us on New Zealand, but only with a very general formula, and we contribute more to the budget than we would under the Commission's proposals". As far as French public opinion was concerned, the British were in the dog house and it would be a good moment psychologically for Giscard to be seen to be defending the integrity of the Common Market "against the seemingly endless British appetite for concessions and special treatment". "I am convinced", Tomkins ended, "that the last thing they [the French] would want to happen is for the United Kingdom to leave the Community, but if we try to subject them to pressure, they could be tempted to call our bluff".[154]

Armstrong visited Paris on 6 March and he and Tomkins had a ninety minute meeting with Claude Pierre-Brossolette, Secretary General at the Elysée.

On New Zealand, the French thought that Britain was being "more New Zealand than the New Zealanders". On the budget, the French disliked the

Commission proposal which was too complicated, too bureaucratic and did not sufficiently respect the principles of Community financing and own resources. The French Government accepted that discussion would be based on the Commission proposal, and that the outcome would be something very like it, but they would have amendments to propose. Giscard did not want a Franco-British confrontation. There had been too much of that already.[155]

German views were not altogether clear. Schmidt had been ill with pneumonia and, although he was recovering, he had been advised by his doctors to stay at home and not go to Dublin. At the Council meeting in Brussels on 3 March, Callaghan had raised the issue of steel. The Conservative Government, he said, had repealed statutory powers which had given the Government the ability to control private investment in the steel industry. The Labour Government needed those powers and if, as it appeared, to reintroduce them would conflict with the provisions of the European Coal and Steel Treaty then, after renegotiation, and if the United Kingdom stayed in the Community, the issue would need to be addressed. Callaghan said that he was "not now proposing Treaty revision", but the issue would have to be addressed at a later stage.[156]

The Germans were reportedly angry that yet another issue had been raised by the British (even though Callaghan had been clear that he did not expect it to be settled as part of renegotiation).[157] On 6 March, Wilson sent a message to Schmidt, devoted mainly to the budget issue. Most Member States, Wilson suggested, now agreed with Britain that the Commission's proposed balance of payments criterion was not relevant and should be dropped. There were strong feelings in the British Parliament on that score.

Wilson took up a point Schmidt had made to him at the time of the Paris Summit: that it was not possible to foresee the exact budget position more than one or two years ahead. Wilson agreed. The amount of the refund the United Kingdom should get would be different each year. British and German officials had, however, been looking at the problem in percentage terms and were now almost agreed about the size of the gap between the GDP share and the budget share as far as both countries were concerned. In the German case the gap was 8% and in the British case around 7%. Given that Britain would be contributing through the Community budget to her own refund, the proposal by the Commission to limit the refund to two thirds of the gap meant that in practice the United Kingdom would recover only just over half of her excess contribution. Wilson would find it very hard to defend such an outcome to the British Cabinet and the British Parliament. Nor could he possibly accept the French thesis that only the inequity arising under VAT contributions should be corrected. He might, however, be able to accept the Commission's suggestion that a Member State's total VAT contribution should be taken as a ceiling on the size of its refund if that made the corrective mechanism overall easier for the French to accept. "I should like you to know", Wilson concluded, "that if this proves to be the case, I shall be ready to let them have their way provided our other terms are met".[158]

Schmidt, clearly on the road to recovery, telephoned Wilson on 9 March. He had, he said, studied the Prime Minister's message and had instructed the German

Embassy in Paris to contact the French. The British should not be afraid that the French would limit budgetary compensation to VAT only. Both he and Giscard would be willing to take account of levies and duties, but in a degressive way, with a cut-off date of 1982. Unlike Giscard, he himself would be willing to agree to an analysis of the situation before the cut-off date was reached. If Britain could agree in principle to an element of degressivity for levies and duties he thought the French might be brought to agree to dropping the two-thirds limitation. As to the balance of payments criterion, there were difficulties for the French and he himself had not made up his own mind on the question. He would await discussion in Dublin. Schmidt also made clear that, while he could understand why Wilson was opposed to an absolute limit on the refund, Germany attached importance to it being kept below 250 million units of account (approximately £125 million).

Wilson did not comment on any of this. He did, however, tell Schmidt that he would make clear in his opening statement at Dublin that he would not be raising any other matters within the timescale of renegotiation. Schmidt welcomed this.[159]

Wilson, Callaghan and their delegation flew to Dublin by RAF Comet on the morning of 10 March. On 6 March, Wilson had briefed Cabinet. New Zealand and the Budget would be the main renegotiation items. He had also given notice of the British Government's need for assured freedom to control private investment in the steel industry. He and the Foreign Secretary would be negotiating strictly within the terms of the Labour Party Manifesto. If sufficient progress was made to bring renegotiation to an end he would say no more in Dublin than that negotiations had gone as far as they could and that he and Callaghan would be reporting to Cabinet. He would not say whether, in his view, the terms obtained were good or bad; nor whether he would recommend the Cabinet to accept them or not. A full stocktaking report would be circulated to Cabinet before the weekend of 15 March. Cabinet would meet on 18 March to consider their recommendation. If they did not reach a unanimous view, then the proposed 'agreement to differ' would start.

There was some attempt by the anti-Marketeers to suggest that Cabinet should, before Dublin, re-open all the renegotiating issues but Wilson had sufficient support to resist this. He summed up that the Cabinet and Ministerial Committees had held a number of full discussions about the conduct of renegotiation and about the Government's objectives in the different sectors. There was no need for further discussion. The time for Cabinet to review the renegotiation package as a whole would come after the Dublin meeting. They would do so on 18 March and reach their decision.[160]

As was to be the future pattern for most meetings of the European Council where national interests on all sides were at issue, the first day of the Dublin meeting was difficult. Discussions continued, with no progress, over dinner. At nearly midnight, the dinner finished and the Heads of Government adjourned for coffee and brandy. Wilson took Callaghan and half a dozen of his advisers into a large lavatory where they discussed the latest position. When Wilson rejoined his colleagues from the other Member States it was after midnight. He had just turned 59 and was greeted with a chorus of 'Happy Birthday'.[161]

Discussion on the first day had begun with New Zealand but Wilson and Callaghan had met strong opposition to their proposals from the Dutch and Danish Prime Ministers, both leaders of countries with strong agricultural interests.

New Zealand was put to one side while the budget issue was broached. Ortoli explained the Commission approach and was promptly, and to the surprise of the British, roundly attacked by Schmidt who complained that Germany was already the largest net contributor to the EEC budget and had economic problems of her own.

Only late on the afternoon of the second day was agreement reached. On New Zealand, the British side had not in the end been able to secure a specific reference to annual reviews of prices and access for New Zealand dairy products, or to linking New Zealand prices to Community intervention prices. But the commitment made to New Zealand was politically generous. The position of New Zealand as a traditional supplier of dairy products to a substantial part of the enlarged Community was recognised. The Commission was invited to make a proposal to ensure the maintenance of special import arrangements for New Zealand. Prices for New Zealand produce would be reviewed periodically and the reviews would take account of the evolution of Community prices, including intervention prices. Arrangements after 1977 "should not deprive New Zealand of outlets which are essential for it. Thus, for the period up to 1980, these annual quantities . . . could remain close to effective deliveries . . . in 1974 and the quantities currently envisaged for New Zealand for 1975". The Community also undertook to develop "an ever-closer cooperation between the institutions of the Community and the New Zealand authorities with the objective of promoting their mutual interest in an orderly operation of world markets".[162]

On 12 March, the New Zealand Prime Minister released a statement expressing pleasure at the progress made in Dublin which opened the way for a better deal for New Zealand. "During my visit to Europe", Rowling added, "the goodwill of the Member States and the Commission towards New Zealand was made very clear to me. I am grateful that the British Government, which raised this issue, has shown such understanding of New Zealand's position".[163]

The budget produced a long wrangle. Schmidt would not budge from his insistence on a ceiling on any refund of 250 million units of account and, in the end, Wilson and Callaghan accepted it. The limit on the refund to two-thirds of the eligible amount was dropped but the United Kingdom was asked to accept that some account would be taken of the balance of payments situation of a potential beneficiary country. The provision that a country would have to have a balance of payments *deficit* to qualify was dropped and replaced by an agreement to the effect that if a country had been in surplus on average over three years then the correction to which it was entitled "shall only affect any difference between the amount of its VAT payments and the figure which would result from its relative share in the Community GNP".[164]

Michael Butler, the senior Foreign Office official present in Dublin, and later architect of Margaret Thatcher's successful negotiation of a lasting budget settlement for Britain, recorded that the German Finance Ministry had briefed Schmidt "to propose conditions for the corrective mechanism which, they hoped and believed, were unlikely to be fulfilled. Mr Wilson nevertheless settled on this basis".[165] "Harold, you must listen to Michael", Callaghan said during a break in the meeting, as Butler sought to persuade the Prime Minister that the German Finance Ministry counter-proposal to Britain's own scheme was carefully calculated to give Britain nothing at all. But Wilson was not interested, went back into the meeting and accepted the German draft.[166]

Jim Callaghan in his autobiography was defensive about the budget deal, but loyal to Wilson whose unwillingness to put up a fight led to a budget deal which did not in practice produce any benefit whatsoever to the United Kingdom. There is always a judgement to be made by the Prime Minister in a negotiation such as the one at Dublin as to whether the moment to strike a deal has come. How far Wilson made that judgement advisedly or from lack of engagement is not clear but the belief of the officials who were with him was that he was bored by the subject and unmotivated. From Wilson's perspective, he had done enough to be able to sell the results of renegotiation to the Cabinet and to the country. The budget issue had never interested him. The two matters which most concerned him in the run-up to Dublin were New Zealand and steel.

On New Zealand, the outcome was satisfactory and enduring. On steel, Wilson made a lengthy statement at Dublin, a statement which today reads bizarrely in economic terms but on an issue which, at the time, he described to Christopher Soames as "a big worry for him".[167]

"The principal problem", Wilson told the other Heads of Government, "relates to control of investment within the private sector. In Britain today, a problem has arisen – in South Wales – where a private firm, not British, not controlled from any member country or countries of the Community, but controlled from outside the Community, seeks to build a new plant . . . When, as part of our fight against inflation, HMG holds back the level of new investment in the public steel sector, it is unacceptable that the private sector should be free to expand where it wants, and by as much as it wants . . . We are not now proposing Treaty amendment. We would much prefer to avoid it . . . There is always the possibility of extending public ownership . . . But it is of vital importance to us that the problem be solved . . . Provided the problem is understood and acknowledged, we are now prepared to leave its solution, in a spirit of consultation and advice, to the future work of the Community if, after the referendum, we remain as a member". The Conclusions of the Dublin meeting recorded that Wilson had made a statement and the matter "deferred to a later stage of Community activity".[168]

Wilson reported on Dublin to a largely uncritical House of Commons. A question asking the Prime Minister to "confirm that he received maximum cooperation and good will from all the other Heads of Government at Dublin, indicating . . . their desire to help him and Britain in tackling the problems involved", was not going to give Wilson any difficulty and he was probably surprised only that the questioner, the new Leader of the Opposition, Margaret Thatcher, had let him off so lightly.[169]

The Continental Press, for its part, expressed satisfaction at the outcome along-side the sentiment that Europe had been subjected to British blackmail. The French newspaper, the *Canard Enchaîné*, printed a cartoon showing Wilson in bed with the nubile figure of Marianne (France's feminine equivalent of Uncle Sam). His head is nestled in her ample bosom and, as the couple make love, Marianne is saying to him "*Entrez ou sortez mon cher Wilson. Mais cessez ce va et vient ridicule.*"[170]

In the Bundestag, the German Foreign Minister, Hans-Dietrich Genscher, claimed credit for the budget deal which, he said, was based on a German proposal, as modified by the French with support from Belgium and Luxembourg.[171]

Cabinet considered the outcome of the renegotiation over two days on 17 and 18 March on the basis of a memorandum submitted by the Foreign Secretary. Cabinet, Wilson told them, would have to form a judgement, not only on the revised terms that had been negotiated, but also on "the present character of the Community". There was, he said, an important distinction between its practical working, which was now more political in approach, and its theoretical and legal basis.

Callaghan described what had been achieved on each of the renegotiation issues in turn. He pointed out that renegotiation had not got seriously under way until the Government had been returned with a majority in October 1974. This had limited the period of effective renegotiation to about four months and it had clearly not been possible to achieve all the Government's objectives within that period. Some would have to be pursued in continuing EEC business.

On day one, there followed detailed comment by Cabinet members on each item of the renegotiation. Wilson's tactic was to follow this detailed appraisal with a discussion and decision on day two on the overall outcome of renegotiation. He hoped that this approach would enable at least one or two of the opponents of membership to air their view but then rally to what he hoped and expected would be the Cabinet majority in favour of the outcome.

So, at the start of the Cabinet discussion on 18 March, Wilson made clear that Cabinet must now reach a decision. His own recommendation in which, he said, he was joined by Callaghan, was that the United Kingdom should remain a member of the EEC. In their view the objectives for renegotiation as set out in the February 1974 manifesto "had substantially been met". The decision whether or not to remain a member of the EEC should take into account, not only the rene-gotiated terms, but the other changes in the working practices of the Community for which the Government could claim some credit. Wilson continued that "while it was not claimed that the objectives set out in the Manifesto of February 1974 had been fully met, there had been considerable and unexpected success in many fields" and the improvements that had been secured were "in marked contrast to the terms obtained by the previous Administration".

Those members of Cabinet opposed to British membership all spoke. The Cabinet, said Benn, was "on the verge of a tragic decision".

According to Michael Foot "policies which had stood Britain in good stead, for example on agriculture and the Commonwealth had already been destroyed" by the EEC.

Eric Varley (the Secretary of State for Energy), whom Wilson had hoped to convert, stood by his opposition to membership but would work for its success if the referendum so decided.

Peter Shore argued that continued membership was "disadvantageous to us materially, to the powers of Parliament and to the unity of the United Kingdom and in relation to the kind of world we wished to see".

John Silkin (Minister for Planning and Local Government) was not satisfied that the minimum objectives of renegotiation had been satisfied. The logic of the EEC pointed it towards the destination of a federal structure.

Barbara Castle thought the basic principles of the EEC contradicted those of the Labour movement. The Council of Ministers was "in effect an institutionalised system of coalition Government and the Labour Party had always been united in opposition to the notion of coalition Government".

Willie Ross (Secretary of State for Scotland) explained in detail why the Government's negotiators had "failed to achieve the fundamental renegotiation to which the Government were committed".

Wilson then asked those members of the Cabinet who had expressed views against the United Kingdom remaining a member of the EEC whether they would be willing to support the majority view or if they wished to exercise their right to differ from the Government recommendation. All the Ministers concerned said that they wished to exercise that right.

The Prime Minister said that "by a significant majority [16 –7] the Cabinet agreed that the United Kingdom should remain a member of the EEC. This would therefore be the Government recommendation and he proposed to make a statement to this effect in the House of Commons that afternoon",[172] a statement which, with a degree of hyperbole, he later told the House was "one of the most important Parliamentary occasions in our history".[173]

John Dickinson, the paper's Political Editor, described the scene in the *Evening News*, one of two London evening papers which appeared each day in successive editions from midday to around 7 p.m. "Mr Wilson was halted for several seconds by cheers, counter-cheers, laughter and jeers. The jubilation was mainly on the Tory side, the grim faces among the Labour backbenchers . . . Having given the broad decision, Wilson launched into an incredible half-hour long statement which he read at a breath-taking 200 words a minute. He appeared mainly to be addressing the Labour Party about its manifesto promised in the last two elections".

Dickinson also gave his readers an accurate breakdown of who had voted in Cabinet against the decision to remain in the Community.[174]

Cabinet had already taken a number of decisions about the conduct of the referendum. On 23 January they had agreed that there would be no ban on opinion polls; that the referendum decision should be by a simple majority; and that the Government should be guided, as far as possible, by normal Parliamentary election practice.[175] On the same day, the Lord President had told Parliament that the preparation of the referendum would be done by a department of the Cabinet Office under his supervision.[176] Work, under Nairne's direction began on

27 January 1975 in a Referendum Unit headed by J R Jameson, an Under Secretary from the Department of Education, assisted by four other officials and two secretaries.[177]

The unit needed decisions on five major outstanding issues: the arrangements for counting the votes and announcing the result; broadcasting arrangements; expenditure by campaigning groups; the form of the question on the ballot paper; and the Government's own information policy. The date of the referendum too remained to be decided.

Following the initial Cabinet discussion on 23 January, work had been set in train on the feasibility of a central count. The conclusion was that such a count would be difficult but feasible. When Cabinet came back to the issue on 6 February, the Lord President of the Council, Edward Short, said that political, rather than technical, considerations were paramount. In discussion, virtually all those Ministers who supported continued membership of the EEC also supported a central count, on the grounds that this was a national issue. Those opposed to membership favoured a regional count, except for Benn who argued for a constituency count. The Prime Minister summed up that "on balance" Cabinet favoured the central count, though Parliament would be able to express its views.[178] This was to prove a controversial issue.

Less controversial were the arrangements for broadcasting during the period of the campaign. There were informal meetings between officials and representatives of the BBC and the Independent Broadcasting Authority (IBA) which suggested that agreement could readily be reached, as it was, on arrangements which mirrored those used in a General Election, but with the two main campaigning organisations taking the place of political parties.

Those two organisations had been, in effect, self-selecting from an early stage. On the pro-Market side was 'Britain in Europe', which acted as a sponsoring and co-ordinating body for a variety of groups which favoured the EEC. Britain in Europe had Roy Jenkins as its President and Heath, Maudling, Whitelaw, Shirley Williams and Jo Grimond among its Vice-Presidents.

The anti-Market side was represented by the 'National Referendum Campaign', a coordinating committee of all the various national anti-EEC organisations. Neil Marten, a Conservative MP, was the chair with Douglas Jay MP as a Vice-Chair. The Scottish National Party was affiliated to the Campaign which, however, refused affiliation to the Communist Party and the National Front. Each of the campaigning organisations was allocated four television broadcasts of ten minutes each. Similar arrangements gave each side forty minutes of radio time on BBC Radio 2 or Radio 4. There was no commercial or local radio broadcasting at that time.

The Government gave grants of £125,000 to each side of the referendum argument. Expenditure by both campaigning organisations was not limited but each was required to include their names and addresses on all printed campaign material and to make a return after the ballot showing money spent to promote their case. In the event Britain in Europe spent £1,365,583. Their opponents spent £133,629. In both cases, those returns included the Government subvention, which accounted for 94% of the expenditure of the 'anti' campaign but only 8% of the expenditure of the 'pro' side.[179]

The fourth issue, the question on the ballot paper, was the subject of an extensive consultation by the Lord President involving a wide range of interested parties. Short presented a number of options. He favoured a brief preamble ("The Government has announced the results of the renegotiation of the United Kingdom's terms of membership of the European Community") and offered alternatives for the question itself, the principal options being: "Do you think that the United Kingdom should [be] [stay] in the European Community?" with boxes marked 'Yes' and 'No'.

The difference between 'be' and 'stay' was important but, curiously, Wilson had not spotted it until Armstrong drew it to his attention. "The Lord President proposes", Armstrong wrote, "to put 'be' and 'stay' as alternatives. This is obviously a very delicate political question. I have been discussing it with Bernard Donoughue. We both think that the form of the question should be as neutral as it can be, consistent with accuracy. We do not think that the question is accurate if the word used is 'be'. We therefore think that the question in the Cabinet paper should be worded: 'Do you think that the United Kingdom should stay in the European Community?'. This is unquestionably accurate. Some of your colleagues will argue that it is not neutral. But we suggest that it should be for them to make the running in Cabinet, on the basis of a formula which is unquestionably accurate".

Wilson commented: "I should leave the alternatives as he [Short] has suggested. I agree there is a point I had not taken. 'Be' could mean 'Should it ever have been?'"[180]

After some debate on 20 February, Cabinet agreed on the version using 'stay' and Wilson summed up that that version should appear in the White Paper on the referendum scheduled for publication on 26 February. The Lord President should indicate in the debate on the White Paper in the House that this version represented the broad consensus of view which had emerged from his consultations, but he should also mention the main variants.

Cabinet also agreed, for inclusion in the White Paper, that the Government would distribute to each household a popular version of the White Paper giving the outcome of renegotiation and the Government's recommendation, as well as an explanation of the mechanics of the referendum. At the same time, but not in the same document, each household would receive a statement written by the campaigning organisations of the opposing points of view on membership of the EEC.[181]

The White Paper on the Referendum was published on 26 February and debated in the House of Commons on 11 March on a Motion for the Adjournment. It was the occasion of Margaret Thatcher's first speech as Leader of the Opposition and she attacked the whole principle of the referendum. In the Division the Government had a majority of 50.

Work had been going on to prepare the Referendum Bill and the debate on Second Reading was held on 10 April. On the previous evening, at the conclusion of a three-day debate, the House of Commons had endorsed by 396–170 the Government's recommendation in favour of continued membership of the Community. Wilson had been most reluctant to allow Ministers, as opposed to Labour backbenchers, a free vote. But when Cabinet discussed the issue on 8 April, the general view was strongly in favour of allowing the free vote. Those Ministers who were known to intend to vote against membership in the referendum would, it was argued, find it difficult to explain in their constituencies a failure to vote in the same sense in the House of Commons. Failure to grant Ministers a free vote would result "in a number of rebels in the Lobby and in animosity and dissention on a scale which the agreement to differ was designed to avoid". Wilson bowed to the majority but secured agreement "that there should be no change in the guideline that Ministers should not speak in Parliament except in support of the Government's recommendation".[182]

Short opened the Second Reading debate in the Commons and announced that, subject to arrangements being made in Scotland, the date of the referendum would be Thursday 5 June. 19 June had earlier looked like being the most suitable date but Short had told the members of the Referendum Unit that the earlier date would have "very great political and other advantages", notably limiting both the damage that would be done to the Labour Party by a prolonged campaign and the potential damage to sterling from continued uncertainty about British membership of the EEC.[183]

Winding up for the Conservatives, Sir Michael Havers repeated their opposition to the principle of a referendum. Eighty amendments to the Bill had already been tabled and, while the Opposition would not filibuster, the Government had, Havers warned, allowed only an "extremely optimistic" four days for discussion. The Bill nonetheless received a second reading with a Government majority of 70 and was referred to a Committee of the whole House.[184]

The most controversial issues proved to be the arrangements for the count and for the franchise. Immediately after publication of the Referendum Bill on 26 March, the Lord President had announced the Government's intention to amend it to make special provision for servicemen to vote, there having been a strong push for this in Cabinet ten days earlier. The Home Secretary wanted to go further, and include officials and others working overseas and British holidaymakers.

After much argument over a number of weeks, Cabinet concluded on 17 April that, in Wilson's summing up, "the electoral register (apart from the addition of peers) and the arrangements for absent voting in the referendum (apart from the special arrangements to be made for servicemen) should be the same as for a General Election". Cabinet rejected proposals for postal votes for those on holiday and others away from home. For those people, the normal arrangements for voting by proxy would apply.[185]

On 22 April, the Government's amendments to make special arrangements for servicemen to vote were approved. There was also strong support from both sides of the House for an amendment to give the vote to all British citizens overseas. That it was defeated was in large part down to the intervention of Enoch Powell who argued that "there is only one safe ground on which we can stand . . . and that it to say that the privilege of voting for the purpose of this referendum is the same as that . . . which is embodied in our electoral law . . . We cannot without confusion or disgrace change it here and now in this context".[186] A further attempt was made by the Opposition (in part because of a campaign strongly supported by the *Daily Telegraph*) during the Report Stage of the Bill on 24 April, but it was readily defeated, not least because many Conservative MPs were absent.

On 23 April, the House of Commons voted by a majority of over 100 in favour of a declaration by counties of the results of the referendum. At Cabinet the next day, Short proposed, and Cabinet agreed, that he should announce in the House that afternoon that the Government accepted the principle behind the vote and would move an appropriate amendment of their own to provide for counting and declaration by counties in England and regions in Scotland.[187]

Despite their objection to the principle of a referendum, the Opposition had in practice cooperated to get the Government's business through both Houses of Parliament. On 7 May, just before the Bill received final approval, John Peyton for the Opposition stood to "remind the Government of how much they are indebted to the Opposition for the exceedingly reasonable, restrained and sensible way in which they received a Bill which was based on a rather unwelcome dodge and device adopted by the Prime Minister in a moment of difficulty for himself".[188] The Bill received Royal Assent on 8 May.

Mr Jameson, on behalf of the Referendum Unit, wrote to Parliamentary Counsel, Mr Rowe, to thank him for all his work on the Bill. Rowe replied by return:

> *Such praise from such a source is more*
> *Than any draftsman bargains for*
> *When playing his accustomed part:*
> *His is a draft and not an art.*
> *It is beyond his humble skill*
> *To influence the voter's will*
> *Or so to draft his little act*
> *That fiction thereby turns to fact*
> *But as the Bill now reaches port*
> *We can agree that it is Short.*

The referendum campaign would be largely in the hands of the campaign organisations. Apart from the legislation to establish the basis of the referendum and the distribution of the popular version of the White Paper and the statements of the two campaign organisations, the formal role of central Government itself was largely confined to the provision of information through the establishment, as laid down in the White Paper, of an Information Unit, headed by a Foreign Office official, Martin Morland, which set up shop in Parliament Street at the beginning of April. The unit, which employed 15 people over a three month period, was, at the peak of interest, answering several hundred enquiries by telephone or letter each day.

The establishment of the Unit was controversial and criticised by anti-Marketeers on both sides on the grounds that the role of the Unit was not an appropriate one for civil servants to undertake. After Second Reading of the Referendum Bill, however, these criticisms largely died away.

One of the first tasks of Morland's unit was to draft the popular version of the White Paper, of itself a matter of controversy since the anti-Marketeers complained that electors would get two pamphlets setting out the case in favour of membership and only one setting out the case against.[189]

Officials prepared a draft and Jim Callaghan had it translated into popular English by Sydney Jacobson, a distinguished *Daily Mirror* journalist and author of two famous *Daily Mirror* front pages in the two General Elections of 1974. The first, in February, appeared next to a photo of Heath and simply read: *"And now he has the nerve to ask for a vote of confidence"*. The other was an appeal to the *Mirror*'s readers: *"For all our tomorrrows, vote Labour today"*.

Callaghan wrote to Wilson on 10 April commending Jacobson's work. It was "persuasive rather than polemical". Jacobson had particularly urged that the popular version should open with a foreword signed by Wilson and this was agreed.[190]

If there had been any doubt as to Wilson's wholehearted commitment to the Referendum campaign, the pamphlet should have been enough to dispel it.

"Dear Voter", Wilson wrote, "We have tried here to answer some of the important questions you may be asking, with natural anxiety, about the historic decision that now faces all of us. We explain why the Government . . . are recommending to the British people that we should remain a member of the European Community. We do not pretend . . . that we got everything we wanted in those negotiations. But we did get big and significant improvements on the previous terms . . . These better terms can give Britain a New Deal in Europe . . . That is why we are asking you to vote in favour of remaining in the Community . . . Above all, I urge all of you to use your vote. For it is *your* vote that will now decide . . .".[191]

It is quite usual, more than thirty-five years later, to hear people who voted enthusiastically to stay in the EEC in the 1975 referendum say that the European Union as it now is, is not what they voted for. The pamphlet was certainly significant for what it did not say. There was no mention of European Union or Economic and Monetary Union, even though Wilson had confirmed his commitment to both at the December meeting of the European Council in Paris. The Government of course believed that both were ill-defined aspirations, not concrete commitments.

The pamphlet did address the issue of sovereignty, arguing that in the modern world even the Super Powers did not have freedom of action and that membership of the Common Market was akin to membership of groupings such as the United Nations, NATO and the International Monetary Fund. As with those organisations, membership of the Common Market also imposed new rights and duties on Britain but it did not "deprive us of our national identity. To say that membership could force Britain to eat Euro-bread or drink Euro-beer is nonsense".

As regards the role of Parliament, the pamphlet argued that "all the other countries in the Market enjoy, like us, democratically elected Governments answerable to their own Parliaments and their own voters. They do not want to weaken their Parliaments any more than we would. The British Parliament in Westminster retains the final right to repeal the Act which took us into the Market on 1 January 1973. Thus our continued membership will depend on the continuing assent of Parliament".

What the pamphlet did not say was that the EEC was an international organisation unlike any of the others to which Britain belonged in that its rules were not static: they changed with the accretion of Community competence involved in each new piece of harmonising legislation and, potentially, with each judgement by the European Court of Justice.

Nor did it point out, save by very indirect implication, that legislation adopted at EEC level was incapable of amendment by Parliament in Westminster. Parliament's only recourse was the nuclear one of abrogating the terms of the Accession Treaty.

The pamphlet was unequivocal in saying that "no new important new policy can be decided in Brussels or anywhere else without the consent of a British Minister answerable to a British Government and British Parliament . . . These decisions can be taken only if all the members of the Council agree. The Minister representing Britain can veto any proposal for a new law or a new tax if he considers it to be against British interests. Ministers from the other Governments have the same right of veto".

The pamphlet did not seek to distinguish between those Treaty articles (then by far the majority) which required unanimous decision-making and those, such as most decisions under the CAP, which were subject to qualified majority voting. The Government's assumption was that the Luxembourg Compromise was the equivalent of a veto, in other words, that if they invoked a very important national interest, they would not be outvoted and discussion would continue until consensus was reached. The first chink in this armour had been evident at the Paris summit, and Heath had been correct when he reminded Wilson that the Luxembourg Compromise was no more than an agreement to disagree. Nonetheless both Heath and Wilson put great weight on that agreement and believed that it was more watertight than it subsequently turned out to be.[192]

Of course, the contrary arguments *were* made in the pamphlet, also delivered to each household, of the anti-Market campaign, which pointed out that "unlike British laws, those of the Common Market – which will take precedence over our own laws – can only be changed if all the other members of the Common Market agree". But the booklet might have undermined its own credibility, even among a sceptical public, by its claim that "the Common Market . . . sets out by stages to merge Britain with France, Germany, Italy and other countries into a single nation". For those who had lived through ten years of de Gaulle and his veto, it must have seemed rather plain that, even after nearly twenty years of the European Community, the nation state was alive and if not well, at least kicking.[193]

There is certainly no justification in a claim that the implications of member-ship of the European Community were concealed. They had all been aired exten-sively during the passage of the European Communities Act in 1971–72. It is equally true that the Government's pamphlet was in no sense an objective anal-ysis. It set out to make the case for continued membership and while it told the truth and nothing but the truth it did not tell the whole truth. Any member of the public who wanted a full and objective analysis of the constitutional and institu-tional issues involved in continued British membership of the EEC would have had to delve in a way which, in the pre-internet era, would have been extremely arduous.

Before the campaign began in earnest, Wilson had to face a special one-day conference of the Labour Party in London. The National Executive Committee (NEC) had decided to support the 'No' campaign and, at one acrimonious meeting, threatened to campaign against the Government. Wilson, in his own words, for only the second time since 1963, laid his leadership of the Party on the line. The NEC backed down, to the extent of deciding to support the 'no' campaign "on the basis of all aid short of war". At the special conference on 26 April Wilson was heard politely as he set out the case for British membership against a back-drop, carefully contrived and constantly in view, which read: '*Conference Advises – the People Decide*', a message that Wilson himself stressed. The Conference voted 2:1 against continued British membership of the EEC.[194]

Immediately after the Conference, Wilson and Callaghan flew to the Common-wealth Summit in Jamaica. What should have been a welcome respite turned out to be, at least initially, highly stressful as Wilson sought (successfully) to head off a last-ditch attempt by Ian Mikardo MP to persuade the NEC to back an active campaign by the Labour Party against its own Government.[195] The Common-wealth meeting did, however, give a boost to the pro-Marketeers. Michael Manley, the Prime Minister of Jamaica, told Wilson as the communiqué was being drafted that, without consulting Britain, the other Commonwealth Heads had decided to add to the text a paragraph declaring that the members of the Commonwealth regarded continued British membership of the EEC as in their best interests. The communiqué also looked forward to "the further development of relations between the EEC . . . on the one hand and developing countries, including the Asian and other Commonwealth countries on the other".[196]

In the campaign itself, Wilson and Callaghan were careful to avoid contrib-uting to the polemical, and sometimes personal and acrimonious exchanges between Ministers on opposite sides of the argument. Guidelines for Ministers, issued on 3 April, had stipulated that "no Minister should allow himself to be put into a situation in which he appears in direct confrontation, on the same platform or programme, with another Minister who takes a different view on this issue".[197]

This provision caused some problems, which were discussed in Cabinet on 15 May. Independent Television were planning, on the Tuesday before polling day, a two-hour televised debate between supporters and opponents of EEC membership. The effect of the 3 April Guidance would, it was argued, mean that the case for continued membership would be presented entirely by members of the Opposition because the opposing view was being expressed by dissenting members of the Cabinet. Wilson agreed and the guideline rule was lifted as from Sunday 1 June to polling day. "Ministers", Wilson enjoined, "should continue to be guided by normal considerations of restraint and good taste, bearing in mind the importance of doing nothing which would hinder the restoration of normal Cabinet solidarity immediately the referendum was over . . . It was important that the views of the Government on continued EEC membership should be clearly presented, and he himself would seek to do this in the public speeches and radio and TV broadcasts he would be making in the period before the referendum".[198]

Wilson did have to deal with "a public brawl" between Benn and Jenkins.[199] Goaded by what Jenkins called Benn's "false, dangerous and reiterated claims", Jenkins had attacked Benn by name and suggested he should resign from the Government if the 'no' side lost the referendum. Jenkins and Wilson had an exchange of minutes, made more irritable on Wilson's part because "I might just as well have not wasted four days preparing speeches for Dewsbury and Long Ditton since, on both occasions, very little appeared in the popular Press whose readers are those I am trying to appeal to". Instead the Press had "exactly as I foresaw when I wrote to you . . . been dominated by the personalities argument". Jenkins' rather condescending response to Wilson ("As you know, I have always thought there were considerable dangers in a referendum campaign") can have done little to assuage Wilson's disenchantment.[200]

From a relatively early stage, Wilson and Callaghan were concerned about the coordination of the Government's case on Europe. Callaghan argued for "a day to day assessment of the way in which the arguments are being received by the public; recommendations about issues which need special treatment and any gaps which need to be filled; coordination of Ministerial participation in television and radio broadcasts; provision of notes on special points for Ministers who require them; and briefing the Press on an unattributable basis".[201]

Callaghan and Wilson discussed the idea on 11 April and "agreed on the need for an organisation of the kind suggested. They agreed that it should be set up as an official group, under the charge of Tom McCaffrey (the Head of the FCO's News Department). The No. 10 Press Office and the Cabinet Office should also be associated with it. It would be under the general supervision of the Foreign and Commonwealth Secretary".[202]

A month later, Wilson agreed to Callaghan's establishment of a small informal group of Ministers to meet daily under his (Callaghan's) chairmanship to coordinate the presentation of the Government's case on a day-to-day basis. The principal members were to be Shirley Williams, Bob Mellish (the Chief Whip), Roy Hattersley and David Ennals. The group would "rely on Tom McCaffrey and Tom McNally [Callaghan's Press Secretary and Political adviser respectively] and I should be grateful if you would allow Joe Haines to attend from No. 10". This too Wilson agreed to.[203]

On 14 May, Wilson sent a minute to members of the Cabinet, clearly directed to the less active on the 'yes' side: "While some Ministers are committed to a substantial number of meetings on the referendum, others have plans for very few, and in certain cases, no meetings at all . . . All Ministers who have not made firm plans should now arrange suitable meetings, and I should like to be notified as quickly as possible as soon as they have done so".[204]

Paradoxically, at that stage of the campaign Wilson himself had no speeches scheduled. Joe Haines and Bernard Donoughue had set up a programme but Marcia Williams had cancelled it on the ground that it was her job, and not theirs, to organise his speaking engagements.[205]

The pace of campaigning thereafter did become more intense. A programme was arranged that had Callaghan and Wilson addressing meetings every evening during the last fortnight of the campaign.[206] Wilson either participated in referendum-related television interviews, or featured in a related TV news item, on 25 occasions, a total on the 'pro' campaign exceeded only by Roy Jenkins.[207]

Away from the campaign, Nairne and the European Unit in the Cabinet Office could not assume that the outcome of the referendum would be 'yes'. They were engaged in "fairly intensive work, within a small circle, on the problems presented by what we have called the modalities of withdrawal . . . The core of the problem may be this: however fast the Government may wish to get out, there is likely to be an inescapable minimum period of negotiation within which we shall be legally tied in a number of awkward respects until a Treaty of Withdrawal has been negotiated and the European Communities Act repealed".[208]

When, however, an outline contingency plan was put to the Foreign Secretary, pointing to "the impracticality of total withdrawal by 1 January 1976", Callaghan commented that this kind of timetable was "far too leisurely for a Cabinet with a 'No' vote. In my view, we should have to begin to act immediately, e.g. on European Communities Act 1972, to restore supremacy of UK sovereignty; to give notice on 1976 budget of no further payments; to begin negotiations immediately – not leave them until October; not to increase tariffs on 1 January 1976 etc."

Nairne persisted in the view that "however fast the Government wished to go, and however ready the other eight Community Governments might be to fall in with their pace . . . it is most unlikely that negotiations of substance could begin until the autumn".[209]

It is hard to put heart and soul into a task you do not believe in; harder still if the eventuality for which you are planning looks unlikely ever to come about. From February 1975 until polling day, the opinion polls gave the 'Yes' camp the lead, ranging from +8 points at the end of February to +34 at the end of May.[210] On the day, 5 June, on a turnout of 64.5%, 67.2% voted 'yes' and 32.8% voted no. Only the Shetlands and the Western Isles, out of the entire United Kingdom, voted 'no'.

According to Gallup, the issues which had resonated in the campaign in persuading people that they were better in than out were: Defence; Britain's voice in international affairs; Britain's position in the world; and the future for Britain's children. The negative issues which resonated were not the institutional ones but Britain's relationship with the Commonwealth and the price British people had to pay for food.[211]

Behind those findings lay some unpalatable economic truths of which, in general terms, the British electorate was well aware. Between 1961 and 1974

Britain's per capita GDP had risen by 88%; that of the EEC Six by 215%. Labour productivity on a per capita basis had risen by 94% in Britain and 243% in the Six. In the four years between 1971 and 1974 Britain's balance of trade had gone from a surplus of over £1 billion to a deficit of nearly £4 billion.[212]

A Harris Poll taken at the end of April showed that all the 'No' campaigners scored negative ratings (excess of like over dislike) with Ian Paisley at the bottom of the league with a rating of −59. The next in unpopularity were Hugh Scanlon on −17 and Tony Benn on −15. The only anti-Marketeers who scored positive ratings were Enoch Powell and Peter Shore (at +2 and +3 respectively).

Of the pro-Marketeers, the field was headed by Jeremy Thorpe at +29, William Whitelaw, Roy Jenkins and Shirley Williams on +25, Heath on +21 and Wilson on +19.[213]

"The historic decision has been made", Wilson told the House on 9 June. "I hope that this House and the country as a whole will follow the lead which the Government intend to give in placing past divisions behind us, and in working together to play a full and constructive part in all Community policies and activities".

Margaret Thatcher, for the Opposition, joined "in rejoicing over this excellent result". "Also", she said "one cannot let this occasion pass without paying tribute to the vision of Sir Winston Churchill and the courage of Harold Macmillan, who made the original application". Only Enoch Powell gave a gypsy's warning. He reminded the House of the words of the Government's pamphlet ("Our continued membership will depend on the continuing assent of Parliament") and concluded that "whether anyone likes the deduction or not . . . this result can be no more final than that of any single General Election".[214]

The *Daily Telegraph* allowed that the referendum was "quite frankly a triumph for Mr Wilson".[215] David Watt in the *Financial Times* proclaimed that "the Common Market issue is settled". The voters had "banished the issue from the centre of British politics". But even Watt sounded a cautionary note. Secession was, he said, "inconceivable *in this generation*".[216]

The champagne flowed inside Number 10 and, a few days later Wilson wrote to Callaghan to confirm "all I said over a glass (or more) together on Friday night. Basically, it was the success of the renegotiations and the way in which you master-minded them that brought about this result."[217]

Within weeks the Labour Party had decided to take up its seats in the European Parliament.[218] Jim Callaghan noted that when, four months after the referendum, the annual Labour Party Conference was held "there was not a single reference to the bitter dispute that had split and divided the Party for fifteen years". "That in itself", Callaghan believed, "was a tribute to the skilful way in which Harold Wilson had managed apparently unbridgeable differences in the Party and kept his Government intact".[219]

Wilson, in Bernard Donoughue's words, "was never warm to things European". But, "as a pragmatist, he knew that a 'Yes' vote was the most practical choice, because to stay in would be less disruptive – politically, economically, industrially – than to pull out".

Even more revealingly, Wilson said more than once to Donoughue that a victory in the referendum for the 'Nos' would empower "the wrong kind of people in Britain: the Benn left and the Powell right, who were often extreme nationalists, protectionist, xenophobic and backward-looking". Donoughue concluded that Wilson "kept Britain in the Community as he always wished; he achieved the terms which his manifesto demanded, and he held together by Wilsonian elastic bands his Cabinet and his Party".[220]

On the morning after the referendum, when the outcome was clear, though not declared, Wilson sat alone with his new Principal Private Secretary, Ken Stowe. The Prime Minister reflected on how long it had taken him to achieve the 'yes' vote for Europe. It had, he said, taken him ten years. "People say I have no strategy, cannot think strategically", Wilson said. The unspoken implication was that he had held fundamentally to the same view since he had first decided in 1965 that membership of the European Community was in the interests of the United Kingdom. He had seen that the only way to win a decisive victory over the anti-Marketeers in the Labour Party was to go beyond the Party to the country at large. And it had taken ten years to achieve it.

Thirty-six years later Stowe wrote: "There was – and is – no doubt in my mind how much this meant to him; which is why it stands out so clearly in my memory".[221]

Britain's relations with her European neighbours, and the resolution of a historic dilemma, were fateful issues for Macmillan, Heath and Wilson. Would any of them have predicted in June 1975 that the issue would dog the footsteps of their successors to this day? They probably would not.

"*The past is a foreign country: they do things differently there*".[222] The past *is* a foreign country. But when one reflects on the issues which confronted those three Prime Ministers, and the recognisably similar ones that have confronted every Prime Minister since, one is bound to ask oneself: did they *really* do things so very differently there?

* * * * *

Notes on principal people mentioned

Acland, Sir Antony
(1930–) Private Secretary to the Foreign and Commonwealth Secretary 1972–75; Permanent Under-Secretary and Head of the Diplomatic Service 1982–86; Ambassador to Washington, 1986–91.

Aldington, Lord (Toby Low)
(1910–85) Conservative MP for Holborn, 1945–50; Director and Chairman of Beaverbrook Newspapers, 1968–77.

Allen, Sir Douglas (later Lord Croham)
(1917–2011) Permanent Under-Secretary at the Treasury, 1966–74; Head of the Civil Service 1974–77.

Alphand, Hervé
(1907–1994) French Diplomat. French Ambassador to NATO, 1952–54, and to the United States, 1956–65; Secretary General French Ministry of Foreign Affairs, 1965–72.

Armstrong, Robert (later Lord Armstrong of Ilminster)
(1972–) Principal Private Secretary to Edward Heath (1970–74) and to Harold Wilson (1974–75); Secretary to the Cabinet, 1979–87.

Armstrong, William (later Lord Armstrong of Sanderstead)
(1915–80) Head of the Home Civil Service, 1969–74;

Balogh, Thomas (later Lord Balogh of Hampstead)
(1905–85) Fellow of Balliol College Oxford 1945–73; Economic Adviser to the Cabinet 1964–1970; Minister of State at the Department of Energy 1974–75.

Barber, Anthony (later Lord Barber of Wentbridge)
(1920–2005) MP for Doncaster, 1951–64 and Altrincham and Sale, 1965–74; Chairman of the Conservative Party, 1967–70; Chancellor of the Duchy of Lancaster, 1970; Chancellor of the Exchequer, 1970–74.

Benn, Tony (Anthony Wedgwood Benn)
(1925–) Labour MP for Bristol SE 1950–60, and for Chesterfield 1984–2001; Chairman of the Labour Party 1971–72; Secretary of State for Industry 1974–75; Secretary of State for Energy, 1975–79

Blankenhorn, Herbert
(1904–91) German Diplomat. German Ambassador to NATO, 1955–58; to France, 1958–63; to Italy, 1963–65; and to the United Kingdom, 1965–70.

Bohlen, Charles E

(1904–1974) US Diplomat. Ambassador to the Soviet Union, 1953–57; to the Philippines, 1957–59 and to France, 1962–68.

Brandt, Willy

(1913–92) Mayor of West Berlin 1955–66; Vice-Chancellor and Foreign Minister of the Federal Republic of Germany (FRG) 1966–69; Chancellor of the FRG 1969–74.

Bridges, Tom (2nd Baron Bridges)

(1927–) Private Secretary to Harold Wilson, 1972–74; Ambassador to Italy, 1983–87.

Brown, George (later Lord George-Brown of Jevington)

(1914–85) Labour MP for Belper, 1945–70; deputy Leader of the Labour Party, 1960–70; First Secretary of State and Secretary of State for Economic Affairs, 1964–66; Foreign Secretary, 1966–68.

Bruce, David K E

(1898–1977) US Diplomat. US Ambassador to France, 1949–52; to Germany, 1957–59, and to the United Kingdom, 1961–69.

Butler, Sir Michael

(1927–) First Secretary British Embassy Paris, 1961–65; Head of European Integration Department Foreign & Commonwealth Office (FCO), 1972–74; Assistant Under-Secretary in charge of European Community Affairs, 1974–76; Deputy Under-Secretary of State FCO, 1976–79; Ambassador and Permanent Representative to the European Community, Brussels 1979–85.

Callaghan, James (later Lord Callaghan of Cardiff)

(1912–2005) Labour MP for South Cardiff, 1945–50, and SE Cardiff, 1950–83; Chancellor of the Exchequer, 1964–67; Home Secretary, 1967–70; Foreign and Commonwealth Secretary, 1974–76; Prime Minister, 1976–79.

Carrington, Peter, Lord

(1919–) Defence Secretary 1970–74; Opposition Leader in the House of Lords, 1964–70 and 1974–79; Foreign and Commonwealth Secretary, 1979–82.

Castle, Barbara (later Baroness Castle of Blackburn)

(1911–2001) Labour MP for Blackburn, 1944–79; Minister for Overseas Development, 1964–65; Minister of Transport, 1965–68; Secretary of State for Employment, 1968–70; Secretary of State for Social Services, 1974–76.

Chalfont, Lord

See **Jones, Alun Gwynne**.

Chirac, Jacques

(1932–) French Minister of Agriculture 1972–76; Prime Minister, 1974–76 and 1986–88; President of the Republic, 1995–2007.

Courcel, Baron Geoffroy Chodron de

(1912–92) French Diplomat. Wartime Aide to de Gaulle. French Ambassador to the United Kingdom, 1962–72; Secretary General, French Ministry of Foreign Affairs, 1973–76.

Couve de Murville, Maurice

(1907–99) French Foreign Minister, 1958–68; Prime Minister, 1968–69.

Cromer, Rowley (Third Earl of Cromer)

(1918–91) Governor of the Bank of England, 1961–66; Ambassador to Washington 1971–74.

Crosland, Anthony
(1918–77) Labour MP for South Gloucestershire, 1950–55, and for Grimsby, 1959–77; Secretary of State for Education and Science, 1965–67; President of the Board of Trade, 1967–69; Secretary of State for Local Government, 1969–70; Secretary of State for the Environment, 1974–76; Foreign and Commonwealth Secretary, 1976–77.

Crossman, Richard
(1907–74) Labour MP for Coventry East, 1945–74; Leader of the House of Commons, 1966–68; Secretary of State for Social Services, 1968–70.

Davies, John
(1916–79) Director General of the CBI, 1965–1969; MP for Knutsford (Cheshire) 1970–78; Secretary of State for Trade and Industry, 1970–72; Chancellor of the Duchy of Lancaster, 1972–74.

Davignon, Etienne
(1932–) Belgian Official and Politician. Foreign Ministry Official, 1959–65; Head of International Energy Agency, 1974–77; European Commissioner for Internal Market, Customs Union and Industrial Affairs, 1977–81; European Commissioner for Industry and Energy, 1981–85.

Dean, Sir Patrick
(1909–1994) British Diplomat. UK Permanent Representative to the UN, 1960–64; British Ambassador to the United States, 1965–69.

Debré, Michel
(1912–1996) French Gaullist Politician. Prime Minister, 1959–62; Minister of Economy and Finance, 1966–68; Minister of Foreign Affairs, 1968–69; Minister of defence, 1969–73.

De Gaulle, Charles
(1890–1970) Leader of the Free French, 1940–44; President of the Provisional French Government, 1944–46; Prime Minister of France, 1958–59; President of the Republic, 1959–69.

Dixon, Sir Pierson ('Bob')
(1904–65) British Diplomat; British Ambassador to Czechoslovakia, 1948–50; UK Permanent Representative to the United Nations, 1954–60; British Ambassador to France, 1960–64 (and concurrently Head of the Official Delegation to the EEC, Brussels).

Donoughue, Bernard (later Lord Donoughue of Ashton)
(1934–) Teacher at LSE, 1963–74; Senior Policy Adviser to Wilson and then Callaghan in 10 Downing Street,1974–79; Parliamentary Under-Secretary, Ministry of Agriculture, 1997–99.

Douglas-Home, Sir Alec
(1903–1995) Earl of Home, 1951–63; Sir Alec Douglas-Home, 1963–74; Lord Home of the Hirsel, 1974–1995); Secretary of State for Commonwealth Relations, 1955–60; Foreign Secretary, 1960–63; Foreign & Commonwealth Secretary, 1970–74; Prime Minister, 1963–64.

Duckwitz, Georg Ferdinand
(1904–73) German Diplomat. Achieved post-war recognition for helping Jews in WW II. Ambassador to Denmark, 1955–58; Ambassador to India c.1960–1965; State Secretary, German Ministry of Foreign Affairs, 1967–70.

Erhard, Ludwig
(1897–1977) German CDU Politician. Vice-Chancellor of the Federal Republic of Germany, 1957–63; Chancellor of Germany, 1963–66.

Ewart-Biggs, Christopher
(1921–76) British Diplomat. Minister, British Embassy, Paris, 1971–76; British Ambassador in Dublin, 1976. Assassinated by the Provisional IRA.

Fitzgerald, Garrett
(1926–2011) Fine Gael MP for Dublin SE, 1969–92; Irish Minister of Foreign Affairs, 1973–77; Taoiseach, 1981–82, and 1982–87.

Foot, Michael
1913–2010) Labour MP for Devonport 1845–55, for Ebbw Vale, 1960–83, and for Blaenau Gwent, 1983–92; Secretary of State for Employment, 1974–76; Leader of the House of Commons, 1976–79; Leader of the Labour Party, 1980–83.

Freeman, John
(1915–) Editor *New Statesman* 1961–65; British High Commissioner India, 1965–68; British Ambassador in Washington, 1969–71.

Genscher, Hans-Dietrich
(1927–) German FDP Politician. Minister of Interior, 1969–74; Foreign Minister, and Vice-Chancellor of Germany, 1974–82 and 1982–92.

Giscard d'Estaing, Valéry
(1926–) French Minister Finance and Economic Affairs, 1962–66, and of Economics and Finance, 1969–74; President of the Republic, 1974–81.

Godber, Joseph (later Lord Godber of Willington)
(1914–1980) Conservative MP for Grantham, 1951–79; Parliamentary Under-Secretary (PUSS), MAFF, 1957–60; PUSS, Foreign Office, 1960–61; Minister of State, Foreign Office, 1961–63; Minister of Labour, 1963–64; Minister of State, FCO, 1970–72, Minister of Agriculture, Fisheries and Food, 1972–74.

Gordon Walker, Patrick (later Lord Gordon Walker of Leyton)
(1907–80) Labour MP for Smethwick, 1945–64, and for Leyton, 1966–74; Secretary of State for Commonwealth Relations, 1950–51; Foreign Secretary, 1964–65; Secretary of State for Education and Science, 1967–68.

Greenhill, Sir Denis (later Lord Greenhill of Harrow)
(1913–2000) Permanent Under-Secretary, FCO, 1969–73.

Haines, Joseph
(1928–) Political Correspondent for the Sun, 1964–68; Chief Press Secretary to Harold Wilson, 1969–70 and 1974–76.

Hallstein, Dr Walter
(1901–82) State Secretary, German Foreign Ministry, 1951–58; President of the European Commission, 1958–67.

Hancock, Sir Patrick
(1914–?) British Diplomat. Ambassador to Norway, 1964–65; Assistant Under-Secretary, FO responsible for European Integration, 1965–68; Ambassador to Italy 1969–74.

Harmel, Pierre
(1911–2009) Belgian Christian Democrat Politician. 1965–66, Prime Minister; 1966–73, Foreign Minister.

Hart, Judith (later Baroness Hart of South Lanark)
(1924–91) Labour Mp for Lanark, 1959–83, and for Clydesdale, 1983–87; Minister of Overseas Development, 1969–70 and 1974–79.

Hattersley, Roy (later Lord Hattersley of Sparkbrook)
(1932–) Labour MP for Birmingham Sparkbrook,, 1964–97; Minister of State, FCO, 1974–76; Secretary of State for Prices and Consumer Protection, 1976–79; deputy Leader of the Labour Party, 1983–92.

Healey, Denis (later Lord Healey of Riddlesden)
(1917–) Labour MP for Leeds SE, 1952–55 and for Leeds East, 1955–92; Defence Secretary, 1964–70; Chancellor of the Exchequer, 1974–49; Deputy Leader of the Labour Party, 1980–83.

Heath, Sir Edward
(1916–2005) Conservative MP for Bexley, 1950–74, Sidcup, 1974–83 and Old Bexley and Sidcup, 1983–2001; Chief Whip, 1955–59; Minister of Labour, 1959–60; Lord Privy Seal, 1960–63; President of the Board of Trade, 1963–64; Leader of the Opposition, 1965–70 and 1974–75; Prime Minister, 1970–74.

Henderson, Sir Nicholas (Nicko)
(1919–2009) Private Secretary to Foreign Secretary, 1963–65; British Ambassador to Poland, 1969–72; to Germany, 1972–75; to France, 1975–79 and to the United States, 1979–82.

Hogg, Quintin (Baron Hailsham of Marylebone)
(1907–2001) Conservative MP for Oxford, 1938–50 and for St Marylebone, 1963–1970; First Lord of the Admiralty, 1956–57; Minister of Education, 1957; Lord President of the Council. 1957–1959 and 1960–64; Chairman of the Conservative Party and Lord Privy Seal, 1959–60; Leader of the House of Lords, 1960–63; Secretary of State for Education and Science, 1964; Lord Chancellor, 1970–74 and 1979–87.

Home, Lord
See **Douglas-Home, Alec**

Hunt, Sir John (later Lord Hunt of Tanworth)
(1919–2008) Second Permanent Secretary, Cabinet Office, 1972–73; Cabinet Secretary, 1973–79.

Hurd, Douglas (later Lord Hurd of Westwell)
(1930–) HM Diplomatic Service, 1952–66; Private Secretary to the Leader of the Opposition (Edward Heath), 1968–70; Political secretary to the Prime Minister, 1970–74; Conservative MP for Mid-Oxon, 1974–83, and Witney, 1983–87; Opposition Spokesman on European Affairs, 1976–79; Minister of State, FCO, 1979–83; Minister of State, Home Office, 1983–84; Secretary of State for Northern Ireland, 1984–85; Home Secretary, 1985–89; Secretary of State for Foreign & Commonwealth Affairs, 1989–95.

Jackling, Sir Roger
(1913–86) British Diplomat; British Ambassador to the Federal Republic of Germany, 1968–72.

Jay, Douglas (later Lord Jay of Battersea)
(1907–96) Labour MP for Battersea North, 1946–83; Economic Secretary to the Treasury, 1947–50; Financial Secretary to the Treasury, 1950–51; President of the Board of Trade, 1964–67.

Jenkins, Roy (later Lord Jenkins of Hillhead)
(1920–2003) Labour MP for Southwark and Birmingham Strechford, 1948–76; SDP MP for Glasgow Hillhead, 1982–87; Minister of Aviation, 1964–65; Home Secretary, 1965–67 and 1974–76; Chancellor of the Exchequer, 1967–70; Deputy Leader of the Labour Party, 1970–72; President of the European Commission, 1977–81.

Jobert, Michel
(1921–2002) French Official and Politician. Director of the Cabinet of the French Prime Minister, 1966–69; Secretary-General of the Elysée, 1969–73; Minister of Foreign Affairs, 1973–74; Minister of External Commerce, 1981–83.

Johnson, Lyndon B
(1908–73) US Democratic Congressman for Texas, 1937–1949; Senator for Texas, 1949–61; Senate Majority Whip, 1951–53; Senate Majority Leader, 1955–61; US Vice President, 1961–63; President of the United States, 1963–1969.

Jones, Alun Gwynne (Lord Chalfont of Llantarnam)
(1919–) 1961–64 Defence Correspondent of The Times; 1964–70, Minister of State at the Foreign Office.

Kaldor, Professor Nicholas (later Lord Kaldor)
(1908–86) Professor of Economics at Cambridge, 1966–1975; Adviser to the Wilson Government, 1964–70 and to Denis Healey, 1974–76.

Kennedy, John F
(1917–63) US Democratic Congressman for Massachusetts, 1947–53; Senator for Massachusetts, 1953–60; President of the United States, 1961–63.

Kiesinger, Kurt Georg
(1904–1988) German CDU Politician. Minister-President of Baden-Wuerttemberg, 1955–66; Chancellor of the Federal Republic of Germany, 1966–69.

Kissinger, Henry
(1923–) US National Security Adviser, 1969–75; US Secretary of State, 1973–77.

Lahr, Rolf Otto
(1908–1985) German Diplomat. State Secretary, German Foreign Ministry, Bonn, 1961–69; German Ambassador to Italy, 1969–74.

Lever, Harold (later Lord Lever of Manchester)
(1914–95) Labour MP for Manchester Central, 1945–79; Paymaster General, 1969–70; Labour Front Bench Spokesman on Europe. 1970–72; Chancellor of the Duchy of Lancaster, 1974–79.

Luns, Joseph
(1911–2002) Dutch Politician. Foreign Minister, 1952–71; Secretary-General of NATO, 1971–84.

Macmillan, Harold (later the Earl of Stockton)
(1894–1986). Conservative MP for Stockton on Tees, 1924–29 and 1931–45; and for Bromley, 1945–1964; Minister Resident in the Mediterranean, 1942–45; Secretary of State for Air, 1945; Minister of Housing, 1951–54; Minister of Defence, 1954–55; Foreign Secretary, 1955; Chancellor of the Exchequer, 1955–57; Prime Minister, 1957–63.

Marjolin, Robert
(1911–86) Senior French Official. Vice President of the European Commission responsible for the Economy and Finance, 1958–67.

Marjoribanks, Sir James
(1911–2003) British Diplomat. British Ambassador to the EEC, Brussels, 1965–71.

Marsh, Richard
(1928–2011) Labour MP for Greenwich, 1959–71; Minister of Power, 1966–68; Minister of Transport, 1968–69; Chairman of British Railways Board, 1971–76.

Marshall, Jack
(1912–88) New Zealand Politician. National Party Member of Parliament, 1946–75; Deputy Prime Minister 1957, and 1960–72; Prime Minister, 1972.

Maudling, Reginald
(1917–79) Conservative MP for Barnet, 1950–74; Paymaster General, 1957–59; President of the Board of Trade, 1959–61; Secretary of State for the Colonies, 1961–62; Chancellor of the Exchequer, 1962–64; Home Secretary, 1970–72.

Messmer, Pierre
(1916–2007) French Gaullist Politician. Minister of the Armed Forces, 1960–69; Minister for Overseas Territories, 1971–72; Prime Minister, 1972–74.

Mikardo, Ian
(1908–93) Labour MP for Reading, 1945–59, for Poplar, 1964–74, for Tower Hamlets, 1974–83, and for Bow and Poplar, 1983–87; Chairman of the International Committee of the Labour Party, 1973–78, Chairman, Parliamentary Labour Party (PLP), 1974.

Mitchell, Sir Derek
(1922–2009) Treasury Official. 1964–65, Principal Private Secretary to the Prime Minister (Douglas-Home and then Wilson); 1969–1972, Minister (Economic) British Embassy Washington and Executive Director of the World Bank and IMF; 1972–76, Second Permanent Secretary for Overseas Finance, HM Treasury.

Mitterrand, François
(1916–96) French Socialist Politician. Minister of 'Overseas' France, 1950–51; Minister of Interior, 1954–55; Minister of Justice, 1956–57; Leader of the French Socialist Party, 1971–81; President of the Republic, 1981–95.

Monnet, Jean
(1888–1979) French Political Economist. 1945–52, French Planning Commissioner; 1950, Author of the Schumann Plan for the European Coal and Steel Community ECSC), the forerunner of the EEC; 1952–55, President of the High Authority of the ECSC; 1955 Established Action Committee for the United States of Europe.

Moro, Aldo
(1916–78) Italian Foreign Minister, 1965–66 and 1970–72; Italian Prime Minister, 1963–68 and 1974–76. Assassinated.

Mulley, Fred (later Lord Mulley of Manor Park)
(1918–95) Labour MP for Sheffield 1950–83; Chairman of the Labour Party, 1974–75; Minister for Transport, 1974–75; Secretary of State for Education, 1975–76; Defence Secretary, 1976–79.

Nairne, Sir Patrick
(1921–) Second Permanent Secretary, Cabinet Office, 1973–75; Permanent Under-Secretary, Department of Health and Social Security (DHSS)), 1975–81.

Nield, Sir William
(1913–94) Second Permanent Secretary, Cabinet Office, 1969–72; Permanent Under-Secretary Northern Ireland Office, 1972–73.

Nixon, Richard M
(1913–94) US Republican Congressman for California, 1947–1950; US Senator for California, 1950–53; US Vice-President, 1953–61; President of the United States, 1969–74.

O'Neill, Sir Con
(1912–1988) British Diplomat. Ambassador to the EEC, Brussels, 1963–65; Deputy Under-Secretary, FO, 1965–68, and 1969–72 as Official Leader of the UK Delegation negotiating British accession to the EEC.

Ormsby-Gore, David (5th Baron Harlech)
(1918–1985) Conservative MP for Oswestry, 1950–61; Parliamentary Under-Secretary of State, Foreign Office (FO), 1956–57; Minister of State, FO, 1957–61; British Ambassador to the United States, 1961–65.

Ortoli, François-Xavier

(1925–2007) French Politician. Director of Cabinet of Prime Minister Pompidou, 1962–66; Minister of Housing and Supply, 1967–68; Minister of economy and Finance, 1968–69; Minister of Scientific and Industrial Development, 1969–72; President of the European Commission, 1973–77; Vice-President of the European Commission responsible for Economic and Financial Affairs, 1977–84; PDG of *Total*, 1984–90.

Owen, Dr David (later Lord Owen of the City of Plymouth)

(1938–) MP for Plymouth Sutton (Labour 1966–81, SDP 1981–92); Under Secretary for Defence, 1968–70; Minister of State at the DHSS, 1974–76; Minister of State at the FCO, 1976–77; Foreign & Commonwealth Secretary, 1977–79.

Palliser, Sir Michael

(1922–) Private Secretary to Harold Wilson, 1966–69; Minister, British Embassy Paris, 1969–71; Ambassador and Head of UK Delegation to the European Communities, Brussels, 1971–73; Ambassador and UK Permanent Representative to the European Communities, Brussels, 1973–75; Permanent Under Secretary, FCO and Head of the Diplomatic Service, 1975–82.

Peart, Fred (later Lord Peart of Workington)

(1914–88) Labour MP for Workington, 1945–76; Minister of Agriculture, Fisheries and Food, 1964–68 and 1974–76; Leader of the House of Lords, 1976–79.

Pompidou, Georges

(1911–74) French Gaullist Politician. Trained and taught as a teacher. No active War service. Banker with Rothschild's, 1953–62; Prime Minister, 1962–68; President of the Republic, 1969–74.

Powell, Enoch

(1912–98) Conservative MP for Wolverhampton, 1950–74; Minister of Health, 1960–61.

Pym, Francis (later Lord Pym of Sandy)

(1922–2008) Conservative MP for Cambridgeshire, 1961–83, and for Cambridgeshire SE, 1983–87; Chief Whip, 1970–73; Secretary of State for Northern Ireland, 1973–74; Secretary of State for Defence, 1979–81; Postmaster General, 1981; Chancellor of the Duchy of Lancaster, 1981–82; Secretary of State for Foreign & Commonwealth Affairs, 1982–83.

Reilly, Sir Patrick

(1909–1999) British Diplomat. British Ambassador to the Soviet Union, 1957–60 and to France, 1965–68.

Rey, Jean

(1902–83) Belgian Politician. Belgian Minister of Economy, 1954–58; Member of the European Commission responsible for External Relations, 1958–67; President of the European Commission, 1967–70.

Rippon, Geoffrey (later Lord Rippon of Hexham)

(1924–1997) MP for Norwich South, 1955–64, and for Hexham, 1966–87; Minister of Technology, 1970; Chancellor of the Duchy of Lancaster, 1970–72; Secretary of State for the Environment, 1972–74; Shadow Foreign Secretary, 1974–75.

Roberts, Sir Frank

(1907–98) British Diplomat. British Ambassador to NATO, 1957–60, to the Soviet Union, 1960–62 and to the Federal Republic of Germany, 1963–68.

Robinson, John

(1925–98) British Diplomat. Head European Integration Department, FCO, 1968–70; Assistant Under-Secretary, FCO, 1971–73; Ambassador to Algeria, 1974–77; Minister British Embassy Washington, 1977–80; Ambassador to Israel, 1980–81.

Rowling, Sir Wallace Edward (Bill)
(1927–1995). New Zealand Politician. Labour Member of Parliament, 1962–84; Leader of the Labour Party, 1974–83; Leader of the Opposition, 1975–82; Finance Minister, 1972–74; Prime Minister, 1974–75.

Rostow, Walt
(1916–2003) US National Security Adviser to President Johnson, 1966–69.

Sauvagnargues, Jean
(1915–2002) French Diplomat and Politician. Ambassador to Ethiopia, 1955–1960, to Germany, 1970–74 and to the United Kingdom, 1976–1981; Foreign Minister, 1974–76.

Scheel, Walter
(1919–) German FDP (Free Democrat) Politician. Foreign Minister, 1969–74; President of the Federal Republic of Germany, 1974–79.

Schroeder, Gerhard
(1910–1989) German CDU Politician. Minister of Interior, 1953–61; Minister of Foreign Affairs, 1961–66; Minister of Defence, 1966–69.

Schmidt, Helmut
(1918–) German SPD Politician. Minister of Defence, 1969–72; Finance Minister, 1972–74; Chancellor of the Federal Republic Germany, 1974–82.

Shore, Peter (later Lord Shore of Stepney)
(1924–2001) Labour MP for Stepney, 1964–74, for Stepney and Poplar, 1974–83, and for Bethnal Green, 1983–97; Parliamentary Private Secretary to Harold Wilson, 1964–67; Secretary of State for Economic Affairs, 1967–69; Minister Without Portfolio, 1969–70; Labour Front Bench Spokesman on Europe 1970; Secretary of State for Trade, 1974–76; Secretary of State for the Environment, 1976–79.

Short, Edward (Ted) (later Lord Glenamara)
(1912–2012) Labour MP for Newcastle upon Tyne, 19511–76; Chief Whip, 1964–1966; Postmaster General, 1966–68; Secretary of State for education, 1968–70; Lord President of the Council and Leader of the House of Commons, 1974–76; Deputy Leader of the Labour Party, 1972–76.

Schumann, Maurice
(1911–1998) French Politician. Minister of Scientific Research, 1967–68; Minister of Social Affairs, 1968–69; Minister of Foreign Affairs, 1969–73.

Silkin, John
(1923–1987) Labour MP for Deptford and Lewisham and Deptford, 1963–87; Chief Whip, 1966–69; Minister for Public Building and Works, 1969–70; Minister of Local Government and Planning, 1974–76; Minister of Agriculture, Fisheries and Food, 1976–79.

Soames, Sir Christopher (later Lord Soames of Fletching)
(1920–87) Conservative MP for Bedford, 1950–66; Secretary of State for War, 1958–60; Minister of Agriculture, Fisheries and Food, 1960–64; British Ambassador in Paris, 1968–72; Vice-President of the European Commission responsible for external Relations and Trade, 1973–77; Lord President of the Council and Leader of the House of Lords, 1979–81; Governor of Rhodesia, 1979–80. Married to Mary Soames, youngest daughter of Winston Churchill.

Spaak, Paul-Henri
(1899–1972) Belgian Politician. Foreign Minister, 1936–38; 1939–49; 1954–58 and 1961–66; Prime Minister, 1938–39; 1946; 1947–49.

Steel, Sir Christopher (Kit)
British Diplomat. British Ambassador to the Federal Republic of Germany, 1957–62.

Stewart, Michael (later Baron Stewart of Fulham)
(1906–1990) Labour MP for Fulham, 1945–1959; Foreign Secretary, 1965–66 and 1968–70; Secretary of State for Economic Affairs, 1966–67; First Secretary of State, 1966–68.

Stowe, Sir Kenneth
(1927–) Principal Private Secretary to the Prime Minister, 1975–79; Permanent Under Secretary, Northern Ireland Office, 1979–81; Permanent Under Secretary, DHSS, 1981–87.

Thomson, George (later Lord Thomson of Monifieth)
(1921–2008) Labour MP for Dundee East, 1952–72; Minister of State, FO, 1964–66; Chancellor of the Duchy of Lancaster, 1966–67 and 1969–70; Secretary of State for Commonwealth Affairs, 1967–68; European Commissioner responsible for Regional Policy, 1973–77.

Thorn, Gaston
(1928–2007) Luxembourg Politician. Foreign Minister and Foreign Trade Minister, 1969–60; Prime Minister, 1974–79; President of the European Commission, 1981–85.

Thorpe, Jeremy
(1929–) Liberal MP for Devon North, 1959–79; Leader of the Liberal Party, 1967–76.

Tickell, Sir Crispin
(1930–) HM Diplomatic Service, 1954–90; First Secretary British Embassy, Paris, 1964–70; Private Secretary to Chancellor of the Duchy of Lancaster, 1970–72; Chef de Cabinet to President of European Commission, 1977–81; Ambassador to UN, 1987–90.

Tindemans, Leo
(1922–). Belgian Christian Democrat Politician. Prime Minister, 1974–78; Foreign Minister, 1981–89.

Tomkins, Sir Edward
(1915–2007) British Diplomat. Ambassador to Netherlands, 1970–72; and to France, 1972–75.

Trend, Sir Burke (later Lord Trend of Greenwich)
(1914–87) British civil servant. Secretary to the Cabinet, 1963–73.

Varley, Eric (later Lord Varley of Chesterfield)
(1932–2008) Labour MP for Chesterfield, 1964–84; Parliamentary Private Secretary to the Prime Minister (Harold Wilson) 1968–69; Minister of Technology, 1969–70; Secretary of State for Energy, 1974–75; Secretary of State for Industry, 1975–79.

Werner, Pierre
(1923–2002) Luxembourg Politician. Prime Ministe, 1959–74 and 1979–84.

Wright, Sir Oliver
(1922–2009) British Diplomat. Assistant Private Secretary, and then Private Secretary, to the Foreign Secretary, 1960–63; Private Secretary to the Prime Minister (Douglas-Home and Wilson) 1964–66; Ambassador to Denmark, 1966–69; to Germany, 1975–81 and to the United States, 1982–66.

Whitelaw, William (later Viscount Whitelaw of Penrith)
(1918–99) Conservative MP for Penrith, 1955–83; Leader of the House of Commons, 1970–72; secretary of State for Northern Ireland, 1972–73; Secretary of State for

Employment, 1973–74; Home Secretary, 179–83; Lord President of the Council, 1983–88; Deputy Prime Minister 1979–88.

Williams, Marcia (later Baroness Falkender of West Haddon)
(1930–) Personal and Political Secretary to Harold Wilson, 1965–83.

Williams, Shirley (later Baroness Williams of Crosby)
(1930–) Labour MP for Hitchin, 1964–74, and for Hertford and Stevenage, 1974–79; SDP MP for Crosby, 1981–83; Shadow Home Secretary, 1971–73; Secretary of State for Prices and Consumer Protection, 1974–76; Secretary of State for Education and Science, 1976–79.

Wilson, Harold (later Lord Wilson of Rievaulx)
(1916–95) Labour MP for Ormskirk, 1945–50, and for Huyton, 1950–83; Parliamentary Secretary to Ministry of Works, 1945–47; Secretary for Overseas Trade, 1947; President of the Board of Trade, 1947–51; Shadow Chancellor of the Exchequer, 1955–61; Shadow Foreign Secretary, 1961–63; Leader of the Labour Party, 1963–76; Prime Minister 1964–70 and 1970–76; Leader of the Opposition, 1970–74.

Notes

Introduction

1 Uwe Kitzinger: *Diplomacy and Persuasion* (Thames and Hudson: 1973) p. 276

1 De Gaulle Says 'No': 1962–1963

1 Record of telephone conversation between Macmillan and Kennedy on 19 January 1963: The National Archives (hereafter TNA), Public Record Office (PRO), PREM 11/4523
2 Harold Macmillan: *At the End of the Day 1961–63* (Macmillan: 1973) p. 365
3 Unofficial Foreign Office translation of de Gaulle's press conference in CMN(O) (63), CAB 134/1517, TNA Meetings and Memoranda
4 *Macmillan: Volume II of the Official Biography 1957–1986*, by Alistair Horne (Macmillan: 1988 and 1989) p. 319
5 PREM 11/4323, TNA
6 Alistair Horne, op.cit., p. 319
7 Harold Macmillan, op.cit, p. 118
8 Harold Macmillan, op.cit, p. 120
9 PREM 11/4528, TNA
10 Ibid
11 Record of conversation; Ibid
12 Terence Prittie: *Adenauer: A Study in Fortitude* (1972) pp. 102–106 and 267
13 Harold Macmillan: *Tides of Fortune 1945–1955*, p. 479, quoted in Prittie, op.cit., p. 268
14 Author's recollection.
15 Minute of 12 September 1962, PREM 11/4522, TNA
16 Rome Embassy telegram to FO of 29 September 1962, PREM 11/4522, TNA
17 Record of conversation of 29 September 1962: Ibid
18 Paris Embassy telegram to FO of 1 October 1962:Ibid
19 Letter of 7 October 1962 from Macmillan to Sir Edward Beddington-Behrens, PREM 11/4415, TNA
20 Quoted in D E Butler and Anthony King: *The General Election of 1964*
21 Macmillan: *At the End of the Day*, pp. 336–337
22 Ibid p. 338
23 Ibid, pp. 347–348
24 Alistair Horne, op.cit p. 431
25 Rambouillet talks record of 16 December 1962, PREM 11/ 4230, TNA
26 D R Thorpe: *Supermac: The Life of Harold Macmillan* (Chatto and Windus: 2010) p. 534
27 Paris Embassy telegram to FO of 21 December 1962, PREM 11/4522, TNA
28 Charles Williams: *Harold Macmillan* (Weidenfeld and Nicolson: 2009) p. 427

29 Alistair Horne: op.cit p. 437

30 Letter from Macmillan to Heath of 26 December 1962, PREM 11/4412, TNA

31 Minute from Macmillan to Tim Bligh of 26 December 1962: Ibid

32 Record of conversation of 11 January 1963, PREM 11/4523,TNA

33 Michael Butler, later UK Permanent Representative to the EEC, was obliged to return to London in 1964 because his activism had irked the French Foreign Ministry, and de Gaulle had complained to Couve de Murville that "Ce jeune Butler s'agite trop". Conversation with author.

34 Cabinet of 13 January 1963, CC (63) 3rd Conclusions CAB 128/37, TNA

35 Washington Embassy telegram to FO of 14 January 1963, PREM 11/4523, TNA

36 Charles de Gaulle: *Memoires (Londres)*

37 UKDel Brussels telegram to FO of 15 January 1963, PREM 11/4523, TNA

38 Ibid

39 Common Market Negotiations (Official) Committee: Meetings and Memoranda; CMN (O) (63) 3rd meeting: 16 January 1963, CAB 134/1517, TNA

40 Paris Embassy telegram of 17 January 1963, PREM 11/4523

41 Paris Embassy telegram to FO of 18 January 1963, PREM 11/4523, TNA

42 Record of conversation of 2 March 1963, PREM 11/4235, TNA

43 Cabinet of 17 January 1963: CC(63) 4th Conclusions CAB 128/37, TNA

44 Message from Macmillan to Heath of 18 January 1963, PREM 11/4523, TNA

45 Bonn Embassy telegrams of 18 and 19 January 1963, PREM 11/4523, TNA

46 Paris Embassy telegram to FO of 19 January 1963, PREM 11/4523, TNA

47 Paris Embassy telegram to FO of 20 January 1963, PREM 11/4523, TNA

48 Bonn Embassy telegram to FO of 21 January 1963, PREM 11/4523, TNA

49 Bonn Embassy telegram to FO of 2 February 1963, PREM 11/4524, TNA

50 Cabinet of 22 January 1963 CC (63) 5th Conclusions, CAB 128/37, TNA

51 PREM 1/4523, TNA

52 Macmillan: *At the End of the Day*, p. 367

53 Conversation between the British Ambassador to Belgium (Sir A Tandy) and Hallstein, PREM 11/4523,TNA

54 Conversation between Blankenhorn and Dixon of 23 January 1963, PREM 11/4523, TNA

55 Washington Embassy telegrams of 26 and 27 January 1963, PREM 11/4523, TNA

56 Telegram from Heath to the FO of 28 January 1963, PREM 11/4524, TNA

57 Paris Embassy telegram to FO of 26 January 1963, PREM 11/4524, TNA

58 Paris Embassy telegram to FO of 24 January 1963, PREM 11/4523, TNA

59 *Les Echos* of 24 January 1963, quoted in *De Gaulle and the Anglo-Saxons* by John Newhouse, p. 241

60 Treasury paper of 24 January 1963, PREM 11/4523, TNA

61 Minute from Macmillan to Maudling of 28 January 1963, PREM 11/4524, TNA

62 Telegram from Heath to Cabinet of 28 January 1963, PREM 11/4524, TNA

63 Cabinet of 29 January 1963, (CC (63) 8th Conclusions CAB 128/37, TNA

64 Telegram of 29 January 1963, PREM 11/4524, TNA

65 Minute of 18 September 1962, PREM 11/4415, TNA

66 Macmillan's diary of 4 February 1963

67 UkDel Brussels telegram to FO of 29 January 1963, PREM 11/4524, TNA

68 The Autobiography of Edward Heath: *The Course of My Life*, pp. 234–5

69 Macmillan: *At the End of the Day*, p. 348

70 Paris Embassy telegram to FO of 7 February 1963, PREM 1/ 4524, TNA

71 Memorandum by Edward Heath of November 1965, quoted in Alistair Horne: *op.cit.*

72 *Le Monde* of 7 February 1963 quoted in Newhouse: *De Gaulle and the Anglo Saxons* (André Deutsch: 1970)

73 Paris Embassy telegram to FO of 7 February 1963, PREM 11/4524, TNA

74 Arthur Schlesinger: *A Thousand Days*, quoted in Horne, op.cit

75 Newhouse: *op.cit.* p. 223
76 Ibid, pp. 225–226
77 Paris Embassy telegram of 3 January 1963, PREM 11/4151, TNA
78 Official British record of the Rambouillet talks, 16 January 1963, PREM 11/4230, TNA
79 Newhouse: op.cit. p. 209

2 Picking up the pieces: 1963–1964

1 Macmillan's national broadcast of 30 January 1963 quoted in *At the End of the Day*, pp. 368–370
2 Message to Macmillan from President Kennedy of 31 January 1963, PREM 11/4524, TNA
3 Telegram from the British Minister to the Holy See, PREM 11/4323, TNA; and Macmillan, op cit. p. 373
4 Record of Conversation between Macmillan and Fanfani on 1 February 1963, PREM 11/4323, TNA
5 Minute from Philip de Zulueta to Macmillan of 4 February 1963, PREM 11/4524, TNA
6 Macmillan's diary of 4 February 1973 quoted in *At the End of the Day*, p. 374
7 When I worked in Paris in the 1970s the Embassy was told by the French internal security authorities that anything said on an open line could, if sufficiently interesting, be taken from the *table d'écoute* and put before the relevant French Minister within twenty minutes.
8 Foreign Office telegram of 7 February 1963, PREM 11/4524, TNA
9 Minute of 11 February 1963 from Maudling to Heath, PREM 11/4524, TNA
10 Foreign Office telegram of 15 February 1963, PREM 11/4524, TNA
11 Letter from Kennedy to Macmillan of 22 February 1963, PREM 11/4524, TNA
12 Record of discussion between US Ambassador David Bruce and Lord Home on 4 March 1963, PREM 11/4524, TNA
13 Record of meeting between Macmillan and Italian Foreign Minister Piccioni on 14 March 1963, PREM 11/4440, TNA
14 Macmillan: op.cit, pp. 374–378 and *Hansard* for 11 February 1963
15 Macmillan: Private correspondence; op.cit. p. 372
16 Cabinet of 28 February 1963, CC (63) 14th Conclusions CAB 128/37, TNA
17 Cabinet of 21 March 1963, CC (63) 17th Conclusions CAB 128/37, TNA
18 D R Thorpe: *Supermac: The Life of Harold Macmillan*, p. 323
19 Macmillan: op.cit. pp. 24–25
20 *Hansard* 3 August 1961
21 Philip Ziegler: *Wilson, The Authorised Life* pp. 132–133
22 Macmillan: op.cit. p. 378
23 *Hansard* of 11 February 1963, vol. 671
24 Ben Pimlott: *Harold Wilson* (Harper Collins: 1993) p. 266
25 CMN (O) (63) Meetings and Memoranda, TNA
26 Bonn Embassy telegram to the FO of 28 February 1963, PREM 11/4257, TNA
27 Despatch to the Foreign Secretary from Sir Pierson Dixon of 18 March 1963 entitled *General de Gaulle and Britain's Future*, PREM11/4524, TNA
28 Minute of 17 July by Bernard Ledwidge, Foreign Office *et.seq*, PREM 11/4811, TNA
29 Letter to Macmillan of 25 March 1963 from Sir Edward Beddington-Behrens, PREM 11/4530, TNA
30 FO telegram of instruction to UKDel Brussels of 29 March 1963, PREM 11/4530, TNA
31 Record of meeting between Lord Home and M. Couve de Murville on 8 April 1963, PREM 11/ 4524, TNA

32 Paris Embassy telegram to the FO of 9 April 1963, PREM 11/4524, TNA
33 Cabinet of 11 April 1963, CC (63) 25th Conclusions, CAB 128/37, TNA
34 Paris Embassy telegram to FO of 11 June 1963, PREM 11/4219, TNA
35 Bonn Embassy telegram to FO of 12 June 1963, PREM 11/4219, TNA
36 Letter of 21 June from Sir F Roberts to the FO reporting a conversation with German Government spokesman von Hase, PREM 11/4254, TNA
37 Paris Embassy telegram to FO of 16 July 1963, PREM 11/4811, TNA
38 Record of meeting on 10 August 1963 between Macmillan and Home and Swedish Ministers, PREM 11/4524, TNA
39 Despatch of 11 February 1963 from Sir Pierson Dixon to Lord Home, PREM 11/4524, TNA
40 Bonn Embassy telegram to FO of 3 March 1963, PREM 11/4524, TNA
41 Quoted in Newhouse, *op.cit.* p. 243
42 Message from Kennedy to Macmillan of 22 February 1963, PREM 11/4524, TNA
43 FO telegram to British Embassy Washington of 27 February 1963, PREM 11/4257, TNA
44 Cabinet of 25 March 1963: CC (63) 18th Conclusions, CAB 128/37, TNA
45 Cabinet of 14 July 1963, CC (63) 44th Conclusions, CAB 128/37, TNA
46 Cabinet of 19 September 1963, CC (63) 54th Conclusions, CAB 128/37, TNA
47 Manuscript minute from Macmillan to Home of 21 August 1963 and Record of talk between Home and Schroeder of 14 August 1963, PREM 11/4259, TNA
48 Telegram from British Embassy Paris to FO of 10 September 1963, PREM11/4811, TNA
49 PREM 11/4811, TNA
50 Paris Embassy telegram to FO of 18 September 1863, PREM 11/4811, TNA
51 Cabinet of 24 September 1963, CC (63) 57th Conclusions, CAB 128/37, TNA
52 Letter from de Zulueta to Wright of 19 March 1963, PREM 11/4151, TNA
53 Minute from Home to Macmillan of 27 March 1963 and minute from Macmillan to Home and Thorneycroft of 17 April 1963, PREM 11/4151, TNA
54 Minute from de Zulueta to Macmillan of 16 July 1963, PREM 11/4151, TNA
55 Minute of 16 July 1963 from Home to Macmillan, PREM 11/4151, TNA
56 Paris Embassy telegrams to FO of 16 and 17 July 1963, PREM 11/4151, TNA
57 Paris Embassy telegram to FO of 17 July 1963. PREM 11/4151, TNA
58 Message from Kennedy to Macmillan of 16 July 1963, PREM 11/4151, TNA
59 Message from Macmillan to Kennedy of 18 July 1963, PREM 11/4151, TNA
60 Paris Embassy telegram to FO of 29 July 1963, PREM 11/4152, TNA
61 No. 10 Translation of de Gaulle's letter to Macmillan of 4 August 1963, PREM 11/4152, TNA
62 Letter from de Gaulle to Kennedy, sent by Kennedy to Macmillan on 6 August 1963, PREM 11/4152, TNA
63 Telegram from FO to Helsinki (where Home was on a visit) of 7 August 1963, PREM 11/4152, TNA
64 Paris Embassy telegram to FO of 7 August 1963, PREM 11/4152, TNA
65 Letter from Dixon to Home (also seen by Macmillan) of 9 September 1963, PREM 11/4152, TNA
66 Record of discussion between Home and Dean Rusk, 26 September 1963, PREM 11/4152, TNA
67 Record of discussion between Home and Kennedy, 4 October 1963, PREM 11/4152, TNA
68 Macmillan, op.cit., p. 475
69 Record of meeting between Macmillan and Hallstein of 27 May 1963, PREM 11/4816
70 Macmillan private correspondence of 11 March 1963, PREM 11/4440 TNA
71 Macmillan, op.cit. p. 475
72 Edward Heath: *The Course of My Life* (Hodder and Stoughton: 1988) p. 252

73 Despatch of 19 October 1963 from O'Neill to Home, PREM 11/5148, TNA
74 Cabinet Conclusions of 31 October 1963, CM (63) 3rd Conclusions, CAB 128/38, TNA
75 Record of meeting between Dixon and de Gaulle of 23 November 1963, PREM 11/4524,TNA
76 Paris Embassy telegram to FO of 25 November 1963, PREM 11/4524, TNA
77 Minute from Butler to Douglas-Home of 18 December 1963, PREM 11/5148, TNA
78 Records of meetings between Douglas-Home and Erhard on 15 and 16 January 1964, PREM 11/5148 and PREM 11/4817, TNA
79 Telegram from British Embassy Bonn to FO of 4 March 1964, PREM 11/5148, TNA
80 Letter from Dixon to Caccia of 6 February 1964, PREM 11/4811,TNA
81 Conversation with the author

3 The labour government: a toe in the water: 1964–1966

1 Despatch of 25 July 1964 from O'Neill to Rab Butler, PREM 11/5148, TNA
2 Paris Embassy telegram to FO of 4 November 1964, PREM 13/305, TNA
3 Paris Embassy telegrams to FO of 4 and 6 November 1964, PREM 13/1042, TNA
4 Cabinet of 5 November 1964, CC (64) 7th Conclusions, CAB 128/39, TNA
5 Cabinet of 19 November 1964, CC (64) 9th Conclusions, CAB 128/39, TNA
6 Cabinet of 24 November 1964, CC(64) 10th Conclusions, CAB 128/39, TNA
7 Oliver Wright quoted in Philip Ziegler: *Wilson The Authorised Life*, page 192
8 Cabinet of 26 November 1964, CC(64) 11th Conclusions, CAB 128/39, TNA
9 Record of discussion between Wilson and Spaak in London on 2 December 1964, PREM 13/732, TNA
10 Cabinet of 3 December 1964, CC(64) 13th Conclusions, CAB 128/39, TNA
11 Record of meeting between Wilson and Schroeder on 11 December 1964, PREM 11/927
12 Cabinet of 11 December 1964, CC(64) 14th Conclusions, CAB 128/39, TNA
13 Cabinet of 18 December 1964, CC(64) 16th Conclusions, CAB 128/39, TNA
14 Bonn Embassy telegram to FO of 12 January 1965, PREM 13/329, TNA
15 Bonn Embassy telegram to FO of 23 January 1965, PREM 13/889, TNA
16 Record of conversation between Wilson and de Gaulle of 29 January 1965, PREM 13/306, TNA
17 Record of meeting between Wilson and Krag of 29 January 1965, PREM 13/1240, TNA
18 Record of meeting between Wilson and Erhard of 30 January 1965, PREM 13/306, TNA
19 Minute from Stewart to Wilson of 12 February 1965, PREM 13/306, TNA
20 *Hansard* of 16 February 1965, PREM 13/306, TNA
21 Record of discussion between Wilson and Bruce of 16 February 1965, PREM 13/2645, TNA
22 Manuscript minute on telegram of 18 February 1965 from UkDel EEC to FO, PREM 13/1240, TNA
23 Cabinet of 22 February 1965, CC(65) 11th Conclusions, CAB 128/39, TNA
24 Despatch of 1 March 1965 from Roberts to the Foreign Secretary, PREM 13/329, TNA
25 FO Steering Brief of 6 March 1965, PREM 13/329, TNA
26 Minute from Stewart to Wilson of 3 March 1965, PREM 13/306, TNA
27 Minute from Sir Burke Trend to Wilson of 19 February 1965, PREM 13/306, TNA
28 Minute from Stewart to Wilson of 12 March 1965, PREM 13/306, TNA
29 Bonn Embassy telegram to FO of 10 March 1965, PREM 11/329, TNA

30 Despatch from Bonn Embassy of 2 April 1965, PREM 13/329, TNA
31 Cabinet of 11 March 1965, CC(65) 15th Conclusions, CAB 128/39, TNA
32 Paper from Stewart to Wilson of 18 March 1965, PREM 13/306, TNA
33 Ibid
34 Letter from Reilly to Sir Harold Caccia (PUS, FO) of 1 March 1965, PREM 13/324, TNA
35 Despatch from Reilly of 18 March 1965, PREM 13/324, TNA
36 Macmillan's diary for 23 November 1961
37 No. 10 Record of meeting on 3 April 1965 between de Gaulle and Wilson, PREM 13/306, TNA
38 Letter of 8 April 1965 from Wilson to de Gaulle, PREM 13/324, TNA
39 Cabinet of 27 April 1965, CC(65) 26th Conclusions, CAB 128/39, TNA
40 Record of meeting between Wilson and Moro of 28 April 1965, PREM 13/306, TNA
41 FO Guidance to overseas posts of May 1965, PREM 13/305, TNA
42 Harold Wilson: *The Labour Government 1964–1970, A Personal Record* (Penguin Books: 1971) p. 105
43 Memorandum prepared for Cabinet on 10 May 1965, PREM 13/307, TNA
44 Cabinet of 13 May 1965, CC(65) 30th Conclusions, CAB 128/39, TNA
45 FO telegram of 13 May 1965, PREM 13/307, TNA
46 Record of meeting of 17 May 1965, PREM 13/307, TNA
47 *Guardian* article and memo from Derek Mitchell of 21 May 1965, PREM 13/307, TNA
48 Note of 21 May 1965 from FO to No. 10 Downing Street, PREM 13/312, TNA
49 Rome Embassy telegram to FO of 26 May 1965, PREM 13/307, TNA
50 Paris Embassy telegram to FO of 25 May 1965, PREM 13/2653, TNA
51 Memorandum from Jay to Wilson of 15 June 1965, PREM 13/904, TNA
52 Minute from Trend to Wilson of 27 June 1965, PREM 13/904, TNA
53 Cabinet of 1 July 1965, CC(65) 35th Conclusions, CAB128/39, TNA
54 Paris Embassy telegram to FO of 30 June 1965, PREM 13/1042, TNA
55 Paris Embassy telegram to FO of 6 July 1965, PREM 13/1042, TNA
56 Despatch from UkDel EEC Brussels to FO of 7 July 1965, PREM 13/904, TNA
57 Telegrams from Paris Embassy to FO of 3 and 8 July 1965, PREM 13/1042, TNA
58 Cabinet of 8 July 1965 CC(65) 36th Conclusions, CAB 128/39, TNA
59 Paris Embassy telegram to FO of 12 July 1965, PREM 13/904, TNA
60 Paris Embassy telegram to FO of 17 July 1965, PREM 13/904, TNA
61 Bonn Embassy telegram to FO of 21 July 1965, PREM 13/904, TNA
62 Telegram from UkDel Brussels to the FO of 2 August 1965, PREM 13/904, TNA
63 DEA paper of 9 August 1965, PREM 13/904, TNA
64 Brief of 16 September 1965, PREM 13/1042, TNA
65 Cabinet of 23 September 1965, CC (65) 49th Conclusions, CAB128/39, TNA
66 Minute from Brown to Wilson of 19 October 1965, PREM 13/904, TNA
67 Bonn Embassy telegram to FO of 22 October 1965, PREM 13/904, TNA
68 Record of meeting between Stewart and Schroeder on 19 November 1965, PREM 13/904, TNA
69 FO telegram to European posts of 24 November 1965, PREM 13/904, TNA
70 Paris Embassy telegram to FO of 25 November 1965, PREM 13/904, TNA
71 Cabinet of 9 December 1965, CC(65) 69th Conclusions, CAB 128/39, TNA
72 Minute from Stewart to Wilson of 10 December 1965, PREM 13/904, TNA
73 Minute from Balogh to the Prime Minister of 13 January 1966, PREM 13/904, TNA
74 Minute from Brown to Wilson of 18 January 1966, PREM 13/904, TNA
75 Minute from Stewart to Wilson of 21 January 1966, PREM 13/905, TNA
76 Minute from Stewart to Wilson of 26 January 1966, PREM 13/905, TNA
77 Telegram from UkDel Brussels to the FO of 30 January 1966, PREM 13/905, TNA
78 Cabinet of 3 February 1966 CC (66) 5th Conclusions, CAB 128/41, TNA
79 Minute from Stewart to Wilson of 3 February 1966, PREM 13/905, TNA

80 Minute from Jay to Wilson of 3 February 1966, PREM 13/905, TNA
81 Minute from Balogh to Wilson of 10 February 1966, PREM 13/905, TNA
82 Minute from Stewart to Crossman of 15 February 1966, PREM 13/1042, TNA
83 Paris Embassy telegram to FO of 21 February 1966, PREM 13/905, TNA
84 Letter of 9 March 1966 from de Gaulle to Wilson (author's translation), PREM 13/1042, TNA
85 Cabinet of 10 March 1966, CC(66) 17th Conclusions, CAB 128/41, TNA and minute from Wilson to Stewart of 15 March 1966, PREM 13/1043, TNA
86 Letter from Wilson to de Gaulle of 14 March 1966, PREM 13/1043, TNA
87 Record of meeting between Stewart and Schroeder of 16 March 1966, PREM 13/905, TNA
88 Letter from the FO to No. 10 of 17 March 1966, PREM 13/920, TNA
89 Extracts from speech by Wilson at the Central Hall, Bristol on 18 March 1966, PREM 13/905, TNA
90 Paper of 5 April, 1966 EO (E) 66 Meetings and Memoranda, Vol1, G110, CAB 134/2705, TNA
91 Note of 25 April 1966 by the Cabinet Secretary, Sir Burke Trend, E (66), CAB 134/2705, TNA
92 Memorandum of 6 May 1966 by Brown and Thomson, Cabinet Committee on Europe: Meetings and Memoranda, E (66) – (67), G/114, CAB 134/2705 TNA
93 Manuscript minute by Wilson of 6 May 1966, PREM 13/905, TNA
94 Minute from Trend to Wilson of 6 May 1966, PREM 13/905, TNA
95 Record of meeting on 6 May 1966 between Wilson and Thomson, PREM 13/905, TNA
96 Text of Brown's speech of 6 May 1966 as circulated to the Cabinet Ministerial Committee on Europe: E (66) – (67), Meetings and Memoranda, G/110, CAB 134/2705, TNA
97 Minute from Brown to Wilson of 16 May 1966 and reply from Wilson to Brown of 19 May 1966, PREM 13/906, TNA
98 Minute from Balogh to Wilson of 16 May 1966, PREM 13/906, TNA
99 Telegram from Bonn Embassy to FO of 18 May 1966, PREM 13/906, TNA
100 Telegram from Bonn Embassy to FO of 18 May 1966, PREM 13/933, TNA
101 Cabinet of 26 May 1966, CC (66) 26th Conclusions, CAB 128/41, TNA
102 Record of meeting between Erhard and British Ministers in London on 23 May 1966, PREM 13/906, TNA
103 Message of 26 May 18966 from Wilson to President Johnson, PREM 13/933, TNA
104 Article in *Le Monde* of 30 May 1966, PREM 13/1044, TNA
105 Minute from Palliser to Wilson of 31 May 1966, PREM 13/906, TNA
106 Letter of 3 June from Reilly to Thomson, PREM 13/892, TNA
107 Despatch from Reilly to Stewart of 22 June 1966, PREM 13/1509, TNA
108 Official paper of 2 June 1966, EO (66) 3, G.110, CAB 134/2705 TNA
109 Minute from Brown to Wilson of 13 June 1966, PREM 13/906, TNA
110 Minute from Balogh to Wilson of 4 July 1966, PREM 13/907, TNA
111 Minute from Crossman to Stewart of 4 July 1966, Ibid
112 Minute from Stewart to Crossman and Jay of 6 July 1966, PREM 13/907, TNA
113 *Cecil King Diary* quoted in *Wilson The Authorised Life* by Philip Ziegler, p. 241
114 *Harold Wilson: The Labour Government 1964–1970 A Personal Record*, pp. 249–250
115 Record of talks on 7 July 1966, PREM 13/1509, TNA
116 Record of conversation of 8 July 1966, PREM 13/907, TNA
117 Minute by Alan Campbell of 12 July 1966, PREM 13/1509, TNA
118 Minute from Balogh to Wilson of 8 July1966, PREM 13/1509, TNA
119 Despatch of 14 July 1966, PREM 13/1509, TNA
120 Letter of 14 July 1966 from Reilly to Viscount Hood, FO, PREM 13/1506, TNA
121 Cabinet Conclusions of 14 July 1966, CC (66) 36th Conclusions, CAB 128/41, TNA

122 Paris Embassy telegram of 27 July 1966, PREM 13/907
123 Minute from Bottomley to Wilson of 26 July 1966 and Wilson's reply of 27 July, PREM 13/907, TNA
124 FO minute of 25 July 1966, PREM 13/907, TNA
125 Letter of 13 July 1966 from Palliser (No. 10) to the FO, PREM 13/907, TNA
126 Minute of 29 July 1966 by Palliser, PREM 13/907, TNA
127 Record of meeting between Wilson and Johnson on 29 July 1966, PREM 13/907
128 Officials' paper of 1 August 1966, Cabinet Official Committee on Europe, EO (66) Meetings and Memoranda/G142, CAB 134/2756, TNA
129 Minute from Balogh to Wilson of 4 August 1966, PREM 13, TNA
130 Minute from Balogh to Wilson of 6 September 1966, PREM 13/908, TNA
131 Interim Report of the Sub-Committee on the Economic Implications of UK membership of the European Communities of 9 September 1966, EO(E) (66) 26, CAB 134/2758, TNA
132 Report of 8 July 1966 from the Cabinet Official Committee on Europe, EO (L) 66 Meetings and Memoranda, TNA
133 Minute of 29 July 1966 from Holland to Wilson, PREM 13/908, TNA
134 Wilson, op.cit., p. 219
135 Pimlott,, op.cit., p. 435

4 Once more unto the breach: 1966–1967

1 Wilson, op.cit. p. 296
2 Wilson, op.cit. p. 296
3 Conversation with author
4 Michael Stewart *Life and Labour* (Sidgwick and Jackson: 1980) p. 190
5 Memo by Brown and Stewart (E (66) 11, E (66) – (67) Meetings and Memoranda, G 114, CAB 134/2705, TNA
6 Minute from Balogh to Wilson of 20 October 1966, PREM 13/908, TNA
7 Brief by Trend for the Prime Minister of 21 October 1966, PREM 13/908, TNA
8 Leader in *The Economist* of 22 October 1966
9 Author conversation with Sir Michael Palliser
10 Cabinet Ministerial Committee on Europe of 22 October 1966, G 114, E(66) 3rd Meeting, CAB 134/2705, TNA
11 Minutes from Trend and Palliser to the PM of 28 October 1966, PREM 13/909, TNA
12 Brown and Jay quoted in Ziegler, op.cit. p. 332
13 Douglas Jay quoted in Pimlott, op.cit, p. 438
14 PREM 13/908, TNA
15 Telegram from Paris Embassy to the FO of 28 October 1966, PREM 13/909, TNA
16 Cabinet of 1 and of 3 November 1966, CC (66) 53rd and 54th Conclusions, CAB 128/41, TNA
17 Cabinet of 9 November 1966, CC (66) 55th Conclusions, CAB 128/41, TNA
18 Record of meeting, PREM 13/910, TNA
19 Minute from Wilson to Brown of 11 November 1966 and reply from Brown of 14 November 1966, PREM 13/898, TNA
20 Minute of 11 November 1966 from Wilson to Brown, PREM 13/1474, TNA
21 Message from Wilson to President Johnson of 11 November 1966, PREM 13/909, TNA
22 Message from Johnson to Wilson of 15 November 1966, PREM 13/910, TNA
23 Paris Embassy telegram to FO of 14 November 1966, PREM 13/910, TNA
24 Bonn Embassy telegram to FO of 15 November 1966, PREM 13/910, TNA
25 Minute from Callaghan to Wilson of 25 November 1966, PREM 13/910, TNA
26 Telegram from Paris Embassy to FO of 24 November 1966, PREM 13/910, TNA
27 Letter from Soames to Wilson, PREM 13/922, TNA

28 Record of conversation between Reilly and Monnet of 1 December 1966, PREM 13/910, TNA
29 Ibid
30 Wilson minute of 18 November and FO reply of 1 December, PREM 13/910, TNA
31 Written exchange between Palliser and Wilson of 7 December 1966, PREM 13/1475, TNA
32 Record of discussion between Callaghan and Debré of 14 December 1966, PREM 13/826, TNA
33 Record of meeting between Brown and Couve de Murville of 14 December 1966, PREM 13/1475, TNA
34 Record of meeting between Brown and De Gaulle on 16 December 1966, PREM 13/ 1475, TNA
35 Paris Embassy Despatch of 22 December 1966, PREM 13/1475, TNA
36 Telegram from Paris Embassy to FO of 4 January 1967, PREM 13/1475, TNA
37 Letter of 5 January from MacLehose (FO) to Palliser, PREM 13/1475, TNA
38 Bonn Embassy telegram to FO of 9 January 1967, PREM 13/1475, TNA
39 Manuscript note by Wilson PREM 13/1475, TNA
40 Record of meeting between Wilson and Bruce of 10 January 1967, PREM 13/1475, TNA
41 Despatch from UkDel EEC of 10 January 1967, PREM 13/1475, TNA
42 Note by the FO of 10 Januaryb1967, EURO (66) 936) Final G103,CAB 134/2814, TNA
43 Telegram from Bonn Embassy to FO of 12 January 1967, PREM 13/1475, TNA
44 Telegram from Bonn Embassy to FO of 16 January 1967, PREM 13/1475, TNA
45 FO telegram to EEC posts of 17 January 1967, PREM 13/1475, TNA
46 PREM 13/1475, TNA
47 Cabinet of 19 January 1967, CC (67) 2nd Conclusions, CAB 128/42, TNA
48 FO telegram of 26 January 1967, PREM 13/1476, TNA
49 Paris Embassy telegram to FO of 26 January 1967, PREM 13/1476, TNA
50 Message from Brown to Brandt of 26 January 1967, PREM 13/1476, TNA
51 Minute from Palliser to Wilson of 26 January 1967, PREM 13/1476, TNA
52 Cabinet of 26 January 1967, CC (67) 3rd Conclusions, CAB 128/42, TNA
53 Telegrams from the British Embassy Rome to the FO of 28 and 31 January 1967, PREM 13/1476, TNA
54 Paris Embassy telegram to FO of 31 January 1967, PREM 13/1420, TNA
55 Letter from O'Neill to Palliser of 3 February 1967, PREM 13/1476, TNA
56 Telegram from Copenhagen Embassy to FO of 6 February 1967, PREM 13/1476, TNA
57 Telegram from Copenhagen Embassy to FO of 9 February 1967, PREM 13/1477, TNA
58 Bonn Embassy telegram to FO of 9 February 1967, PREM 13/1477, TNA
59 No. 10 transcript of press conference by Wilson on 1 February 1967, PREM 13/1704, TNA
60 FO telegram to Brussels of 14 February 1967, PREM 13/1477, TNA
61 Cabinet of 14 February 1976, CC (67) 8th Conclusions, CAB 128/42, TNA
62 FO telegram to overseas posts of 16 February 1967, PREM 13/1477, TNA
63 Bonn Embassy telegram to FO of 16 February 1967, PREM 13/1477, TNA
64 Brussels and Paris Embassy telegrams of 17 February 1967, PREM 13/1477, TNA
65 Bonn telegram to FO of 18 February 1967, PREM 13/1477, TNA
66 Telegram from Bonn Embassy of 18 February 1967, PREM 13/1477, TNA
67 FT article quoted in PREM 13/1477, TNA
68 Record of meeting between Callaghan and Marjolin of 23 February 1967, PREM 13/14121, TNA
69 Record of conversation between Brown and Rostow of 24 February 1967, PREM 13/1478, TNA
70 FO telegram of 1 March covering talks in The Hague on 26/27 February 1967, PREM 13/1478, TNA

71 Cabinet of 9 March 1967, CC(67) 11th Conclusions, CAB 128/42, TNA
72 Paris Embassy telegram to FO of 13 March 1967, PREM 13/2653, TNA
73 Paris Embassy telegram to FO of 20 March 1967, PREM 13/1478, TNA
74 Paris Embassy telegram to FO of 21 March 1967, PREM 13/1478, TNA
75 Cabinet of 21 March 1967, CC (67) 14th Conclusions, CAB 128/42, TNA
76 Cabinet of 6 April 1967, CC (67) 17th Conclusions, CAB 128/42, TNA
77 Minute from Cabinet Secretary to the PM of 13 April 1967, PREM 13/2108, TNA
78 Cabinet of 13 April 1967, CC (67) 18th Conclusions, CAB 128/42, TNA
79 Record of meeting of 13 April 1967, PREM 13/2667, TNA
80 Cabinet of 18 April 1967, CC (67) 21st Conclusions, CAB 128/42, TNA
81 Cabinet of 20 April 1967, CC (67) 22nd Conclusions, CAB 128/42, TNA
82 Telegram from Wilson to Brown of 20 April 1967, PREM 13/2108, TNA
83 PREM 13/1480, TNA
84 Letter from Sir Patrick Reilly to Fred Mulley of 20 April 1967, PREM 13/1479, TNA
85 FCO communication to No. 10 of 24 April 1967, PREM 13/1473, TNA
86 Record of discussion between Wilson and de Gaulle in Bonn on 25 April 1967, PREM 13/1528, TNA
87 Record of meeting between Wilson and Kiesinger in Bonn on 25 April 1967, PREM 13/1528, TNA
88 Record of meeting between Wilson and Monnet in Bonn on 26 April 1967, PREM 13/1713, TNA
89 Letter from Palliser to MacLehose (FO) of 28 April 1967, PREM 13/1480, TNA
90 Letter of 28 April 1967 from Sir Frank Roberts to Lord Hood (FO), PREM 13/1528, TNA
91 Telegram from Bonn Embassy to FO of 29 April 1967, PREM 13/1480, TNA
92 Cabinet of 29 and 30 April 1967, CC (67) 26th Conclusions, CAB 128/42, TNA
93 PREM 13/1481, TNA
94 Cabinet of 2 May 1967, CC (67) 27th Conclusions, CAB 128/42, TNA
95 Hansard of 2 May 1967

5 We shall not take "No" for an answer: 1967

1 PREM 13/1481, TNA
2 Cabinets of 4 and 9 May CC (67) 28th and 29th Conclusions CAB 128/42, TNA
3 Paris Embassy telegram to FO of 11 May 1967, PREM 13/1482, TNA
4 Paris Embassy telegram to FO 0f 12 May 1967, PREM 13/1482, TNA
5 UKDel Brussels telegram to FO of 12 May 1967, PREM 14/1482, TNA
6 Extracts from de Gaulle's press conference of 16 May 1967
7 Paris Embassy telegrams to FO of 16 and 17 May 1967, PREM 13/2646, TNA
8 Paris Embassy telegram to FO of 17 May 1967, PREM 13/2646, TNA
9 Telegrams from the Embassy in The Hague of 17 May 1967, PREM 13/2646, TNA
10 Bonn Embassy telegrams to FO of 17 May 1967, PREM 13/2646, TNA
11 Minute from Palliser to Wilson of 18 May 1967, PREM 13/1482, TNA
12 Minute from Palliser to Wilson of 17 May 1967, PREM 13/2646, TNA
13 Minute from O'Neill of 18 May 1967, PREM 13/1482, TNA
14 Minute from Palliser to Wilson of 22 May 1967, PREM 13/1482, TNA
15 Minute from Palliser to Wilson of 1 June 1967, PREM 13/1906, TNA
16 UkDel Brussels telegram to FO of 2 June 1967, PREM 13/1482, TNA
17 Brussels Embassy telegram to FO of 2 June 1967, PREM 13/1482, TNA
18 Announcement from 10 Downing Street of 23 May 1967, PREM 13/1482, TNA
19 Exchange between Wilson and Jay, PPEM 13/1482, TNA
20 Exchange between Palliser and Wilson of 26 May 1967, PREM 13/1521, TNA

21 Minute of 5 June 1967 from Trend to Sir Paul Gore-Booth (PUS, FO) PREM 13/1521, TNA
22 Letter from Reilly to Gore-Booth of 7 June 1967, PREM 13/1521, TNA
23 Record of meeting between Reilly and Monnet of 12 June 1967, PREM 113/1483, TNA
24 Record of meeting between Marshall and Wilson of 12 June 1967, PREM 13/3202, TNA
25 Record of conversation between Sir Arthur Snelling (Commonwealth Relations Office) and Selwyn Lloyd of 13 June 1967, PREM 13/1483, TNA
26 Letter of 17 June 1967 from Roberts to O'Neill (FO), PREM 13/1483, TNA
27 Record of discussion between Wilson and de Gaulle of 19 June 1967, PREM 13/1731, TNA
28 Record of meeting between Wilson and Johnson of 2 June 1967, PREM 13/1906, TNA
29 Cabinet of 22 June 1967, CC (67) 41st Conclusions CAB 128/42, TNA
30 Message from Wilson to Brown of 21 June 1967, PREM 13/1521, TNA
31 FO telegram of 22 June 1967, PREM 13/1483, TNA
32 Paris Embassy record of conversations between Jenkins and Mitterrand and Giscard d'Estaing of 26 June 1967, PREM 13/2653
33 Cabinet of 3 July 1967, CC (67) 44th Conclusions, CAB 128/42, TNA
34 Statement by George Brown at the WEU Council in The Hague on 4 July 1967, PREM 13/1474, TNA
35 Minute of 4 July 1967, PREM 13/1483, TNA
36 Minute from Palliser to Wilson of 5 July 1967, PREM 13/1507, TNA
37 Record of meeting between Wilson, Callaghan and Debré of 17 July 1967, PREM 13/1507, TNA
38 Paris Embassy telegram to FO of 12 July 1967, PREM 13/1484
39 Statement by de Gaulle at plenary meeting in Bonn with Chancellor Kiesinger on 13 July 1967, as issued by the French Government and carried in *Le Monde*, PREM 13/1490, TNA
40 Letter of 14 July 1967 from Reilly to Gore-Booth, FO, PREM 13/2653, TNA
41 Minute from Palliser to Wilson of 15 July 1967, PREM 13/1484, TNA
42 Washington Embassy telegram to FO of 20 July 1967, PREM 13/1490, TNA
43 Bonn Embassy telegram of 26 July 1967, PREM 13/1484, TNA
44 Paris Embassy telegram to FO of 24 July 1967, PREM 13/1508, TNA
45 Minute from Wilson to Palliser of 1 August 1967, PREM 13/1484, TNA
46 Paris Embassy report to FO of 10 August 1967, PREM 13/2653, TNA
47 Letter from Sir Frank Roberts to FO of 11 August 1967, PREM 13/1521, TNA
48 Bonn Embassy Despatch to FO of 15 August 1967, PREM 13/1530, TNA
49 Letter from Reilly to Jackling (FO) of 21 September 1967, PREM 13/1484, TNA
50 Letter from Day (FO) to Maitland (FO) of 22 September 1967, PREM 13/1484, TNA
51 UkMis New York telegram to FO of 24 September reporting conversation between Brown and Couve de Murville, PREM 13/1484, TNA
52 Cabinet of 28 September 1967, CC (67) 57th Conclusions, CAB 128/42, TNA
53 UKDel Brussels summary of the Commission Opinion on British EEC accession of 30 September 1967, PREM 13/1485, TNA
54 FO Guidance telegram to posts of 3 October 1967, PREM 13/1485, TNA
55 Paris Embassy telegram to FO of 5 October 1967, PREM 13/1485, TNA
56 Paris Embassy telegram to FO of 6 October 1967, PREM 13/1485, TNA
57 Minute from Palliser to Wilson of 6 October 1967, PREM 13/1485, TNA
58 FO telegram to Posts of 6 October 1967, PREM 13/1485, TNA
59 Foreign Office memorandum of 6 October 1967, EURO (67), G103 Vol. VIII Memoranda 1105–119, TNA
60 Bonn Embassy telegram to FO of 10 October 1967, PREM 13/1485, TNA

61 Record of briefing in HM Treasury on 10 October 1967, PREM 13/1503, TNA
62 Record of Press briefing of 10 October 1967, PREM 13/1503, TNA
63 Cabinet of 11 October 1967, CC (67) 58th conclusions, CAB 128/42, TNA
64 Letter from Reilly to FO of 19 October 1967 and Minute from Palliser to Wilson, PREM 13/1486, TNA
65 Bonn Embassy telegrams to FO of 19 October 1967, PREM 13/1527, TNA
66 Bonn Embassy telegram to FO of 20 October 1967, PREM 13/1486, TNA
67 Minute from Palliser to Wilson of 21 October 1967, PREM 13/1527, TNA
68 Record of meeting in 10 Downing Street on 23 October 1967, PREM 13/1486, TNA
69 Minute from Andrews (APS, PM's office) to Burgh (DEA) of 24 October 1967, PREM 13/1426, TNA
70 *The Observer* of 29 October 1967, PREM 13/1527, TNA
71 *Der Spiegel* articles of 30 October and Wilson comment of 9 November 1967, PREM 13/1527, TNA
72 UkDel Brussels telegram to FO of 25 October 1967, PREM 13/1486, TNA
73 Cabinet of 26 October 1967, CC (67) 61st Conclusions, CAB 128/42, TNA
74 Extract from Callaghan's speech on *The Question of Sterling* at the Lord Mayor's Banquet for the City on 26 October 1967, PREM 13/1436, TNA
75 Letter of 26 October 1967 from Reilly to Sir Paul Gore-Booth, FO, PREM 13/1486, TNA
76 Records of exchanges and messages of 28, 29 and 30 October and 7 November 1967, PREM 13/1486, TNA
77 Letter to Palliser from a French official (unnamed) whose contents were passed to the Cabinet Office on 3 November 1967, PREM 13/1513, TNA
78 Paris Embassy telegram to FO of 7 November 1967, PREM 13/1487, TNA
79 FO telegram to European posts of 10 November 1967, PREM 13/1728, TNA
80 Record of meeting with Vanden Boeynants and Harmel of 14 November 1967, PREM 13/2105, TNA
81 Paris Embassy telegrams to FO of 15 and 16 November 1967, PREM 13/1487, TNA
82 Messages from Wilson of 18 November 1967, PREM 13/1860, TNA
83 Minute from Wilson to Jenkins of 23 November 1967, PREM 13/1860, TNA
84 Minute from Wilson to Brown of 24 November 1967, PREM 13/1487, TNA
85 Message of 23 November 1967 from President Johnson to Wilson, PREM 13/2058, TNA
86 Bonn Embassy telegram to FO of 21 November 1967, PREM 13/1487, TNA
87 UKDel Brussels telegram to FO of 22 November 1967, PREM 13/1487, TNA
88 Minute from Palliser to Wilson of 27 November 1967, PREM 13/2646, TNA
89 Paris Embassy telegram to FO of 27 November 1967, PREM 13/2646, TNA
90 PREM 13/2646, TNA
91 Conversation between Wilson and Brown recorded in letter from Palliser to Maitland (FO) of 28 November 1967, PREM 13/2646, TNA
92 Hansard of 28 November 1967
93 Minute from Shore to Wilson of 28 November 1967, PREM 13/1487, TNA
94 Minutes from Balogh to Wilson of 29 and 30 November 1967, PREM 13, TNA
95 Cabinet of 30 November 1967, CC (67) 69th Conclusions, CAB 128/42, TNA
96 Record of a meeting between Brown and Gregoire of 1 December 1967, PREM 13/1487, TNA
97 Brussels Embassy telegram to FO of 4 December 1967 and FO telegram to Brussels Embassy of 6 December 1967, PREM 13/1487, TNA
98 FO record, PREM 13/1487, TNA
99 Minute from Lord Chalfont to George Brown of 2 December 1967, PREM 13/1487, TNA
100 Minute from Palliser to Wilson of 2 December 1967, PREM 13/'487, TNA

101 Records of meeting between Commission President Jean Rey and Brown and Wilson of 4 December 1967, PREM 13/1487 and PREM 13/2104, TNA
102 FO telegram of 4 December 1967, PREM 13/2104, TNA
103 Bonn Embassy telegrams of 6 December 1967, PREM 13/1487, TNA
104 Bonn Embassy telegram to FO of 7 December 1967, PREM 13/1487, TNA
105 Bonn Embassy telegram to FO of 7 December 1967, PREM 13/1487, TNA
106 FO telegram to Bonn Embassy of 8 December 1967, PREM 13/1487, TNA
107 Paris Embassy telegram to FO of 8 December 1967, PREM 13/1487, TNA
108 Bonn Embassy telegram to FO of 14 December 1967, TNA
109 Telegram from the Brussels Embassy (in the name of the Foreign Secretary) of 14 December 1967, PREM 13/1487, TNA
110 FO telegram of 15 December 1967, PREM 13/1487, TNA
111 Bonn Embassy telegram to FO of 15 December 1967, PREM 13/1487, TNA
112 Message of 15 December from Brown to Brandt, PREM 13/1487, TNA
113 FO telegram to Bonn Embassy of 15 December 1967, PREM 13/1487, TNA
114 Bonn Embassy telegrams to FO of 18 December 1967, PREM 13/1487, TNA
115 Minute from William Nield to Wilson of 29 December 1967, PREM 13/1488, TNA
116 Statement from the EEC Council of Ministers of 19 December 1967, PREM 13/1488, TNA
117 PREM 13/1488, TNA

6 To woo or to win: Britain, France and Germany: 1967–1969

1   *In My Way* by George Brown, pp. 131–133
2   Minute from Palliser to Nield of 12 December 1967 and reply from Nield of 14 December 1967, PREM 13/1487, TNA
3   Minute from Brown to Wilson of 19 December 1967, PREM 13/1488, TNA
4   Minute from Benn to Wilson and other Cabinet members of 20 December 1967, PREM 13/1488, TNA
5   Undated paper by officials referenced in Brown's minute of 19 December 1967, PREM 13/1488, TNA
6   Cabinet of 20 December 1967, CC (67) 73rd Conclusions, CAB 128/42, TNA
7   FO Guidance telegram of 20 December 1967, PREM 13/1488, TNA
8   Oslo Embassy telegram to FO of 21 December 1967, PREM 13/1488, TNA
9   Copenhagen Embassy telegram to FO of 22 December 1967, PREM 13/1488, TNA
10 Bonn Embassy telegram to FO of 28 December 1967, PREM 13/1488, TNA
11 FO report of meeting, PREM 13/1488, TNA
12 Bonn Embassy telegram of 3 January 1968, PREM 13/2110,TNA
13 Bonn Embassy telegram to FO of 4 January 1968, PREM 13/2110, TNA
14 FO telegram to European Posts of 9 January 1968, PREM 13/2110, TNA
15 Minute from Chalfont to Brown of 11 January 1968, PREM 13/2110, TNA
16 Exchange between Palliser and Wilson of 13 January 1968, PREM 13/2110, TNA
17 Record of meeting of 6 January 1968, PREM 13/2110, TNA
18 Minute from Lord Chalfont to Brown of 17 January 1968, PREM 13/2110, TNA
19 Minute from Palliser to Wilson of 17 January 1968, PREM 13/2110, TNA
20 Cabinet of 18 January 1968,CC (68) 9th Conclusions, CAB 128/43, TNA
21 FO telegram to Bonn of 22 January 1968, PREM 13/2110 TNA
22 Paris Embassy telegrams of 12 January 1968, PREM 13/2110, TNA
23 Paris Embassy telegram of 24 January 1968, PREM 13/3216, TNA
24 FO Guidance Telegram of 25 January 1968, PREM 13/2110, TNA
25 Washington Embassy telegram of 29 January 1968, PREM 13/2111, TNA
26 Cabinet of 25 January 1968, CC (68) 10th Conclusions, CAB 128/43, TNA

27 FO telegram to European posts of 1 February 1968, PREM 13/2111, TNA and Cabinet of 31 January 1968, CC (68) 11th Conclusions, CAB 128/43, TNA
28 Record of meeting of 10 February 1968, PREM 13/2111,TNA
29 Record of meeting of 14 February 1968, PREM 13/2111,TNA
30 Paris Embassy telegram to FO of 16 February 1968, PREM 13/2107, TNA
31 Minute from Palliser to Wilson of 17 February 1968, PREM 13/2107, TNA
32 Paris Embassy telegram of 17 February 1968, PREM 13/2107, TNA
33 Paris Embassy telegram to FO of 17 February 1968, PREM 13/2107, TNA
34 Rome Embassy telegram of 20 February 1968, PREM 13/2107, TNA
35 Bonn Embassy telegram of 20 February 1968, PREM 13/2107, TNA
36 *Le Monde* article of 21 February 1968 quoted in Paris Embassy telegram of the same date, PREM 13/2111, TNA
37 Paris Embassy telegram of 22 February 1968, PREM 13/2107, TNA
38 UKDel Brussels telegrams to FO of 1 March 1968, PREM 13/2111, TNA
39 Bonn Embassy telegram of 9 March 1968, PREM 13/2112, TNA
40 Brussels Embassy telegram recording views of Foreign Minister Pierre Harmel of 11 March 1968, PREM 13/2111, TNA
41 Minutes to Wilson from Balogh and Palliser of 12 March 1968, PREM 13/2111,TNA
42 Paris Embassy telegrams of 12 March 1968, PREM 13/2112, TNA
43 UKDel Brussels telegrams of 2 April 1968, PREM 13/2112, TNA
44 Bonn Embassy telegram of 4 April 1968, PREM 13/2112, TNA
45 UkDel Brussels telegram to FO of 6 April 1968, PREM 13/2112, TNA
46 Bonn Embassy telegram of 23 April 1968, PREM 13/2112, TNA
47 Telegram from FO to Bonn Embassy of 25 April 1968, PREM 13/2112, TNA
48 Luxembourg Embassy telegram to FO of 30 April 1968, PREM 13/2112, TNA
49 Exchange of minutes between Crosland and Stewart of 6 and 8 May 1968, PREM 13/2112, TNA
50 FO draft Cabinet paper of 10 May 1968, PREM 13/2112, TNA
51 Letter from Palliser to Maitland (FO) of 13 May 1968, PREM 13/2112, TNA
52 Minute from Palliser to Wilson of 18 May 1968, PREM 13/2112, TNA
53 Minute by Crosland of 20 May 1968, EUR(M) (68) 7 G/163, CAB 134/2803, TNA
54 Cabinet Ministerial Committee on the Approach to Europe of 21 May 1968, EUR (M) (68) 2nd Meeting G/163, CAB 134/2803, TNA
55 Letter from Palliser to Maitland (FO) of 21 May 1968, PREM 113/2112, TNA
56 Minute from Palliser to Wilson of 24 May 1968, PREM 13/2112, TNA
57 Paris Embassy telegram of 20 May 1968, PREM 13/2653, TNA
58 Minute of 20 May 1968 from H T Morgan to Lord Hood, PREM 13/2653, TNA
59 Paris Embassy telegram to FO of 22 May 1968, PREM 13/2653,TNA
60 Paris Embassy telegram to FO of 29 May 1968, PREM 13/2653, TNA
61 Cabinet of 20 May 1968, CC (68) 30th Conclusions, CAB 128/43, TNA
62 Paris Embassy telegram to FO of 30 May 1968, PREM 13/2653, TNA
63 Paris Embassy telegram to FO of 31 May 1968, PREM 13/2653, TNA
64 Record of meeting between Wilson and Hilmar Baunsgaard in London on 17 June 1968, PREM 13/2008, TNA
65 Record of meeting between Rey and Wilson in London on 25 June 1968, PREM 13/2104,TNA
66 Letter from Palliser to Croft (Board of Trade) of 1 July 1968, PREM 13/2647, TNA
67 Paris Embassy telegram of 1 July 1968, PREM 13/2647, TNA
68 Cabinet of 4 July 1968, CC (68) 34th Conclusions, CAB 128/43, TNA
69 Record of meeting between Stewart, Brandt and Harmel in Bonn on 9 July 1968, PREM 13/2113, TNA
70 Record of meeting between Monnet and Wilson in London on 15 July 1968, PREM 13/2090, TNA
71 Letter of 16 July 1968 from Palliser to Maitland (FO), PREM 13/2090, TNA

72 Minute from Palliser to Wilson of 19 July 1968, PREM 13/2113, TNA
73 Letter from Palliser to Maitland (FO) of 22 July 1968, PREM 13/2113, TNA
74 Foreign Office brief of 23 July 1968, PREM 13/2158, TNA
75 Cabinet of 18 July 1968, CC (68) 36th Conclusions, CAB 128/43, TNA
76 Minute from Soames to Stewart of 24 July 1968, PREM 13/2641, TNA
77 Minute from Palliser to Wilson of 26 July 1968, PREM 13/2641, TNA
78 Record of meeting between Soames and Wilson of 30 July 1968, PREM 13/2641, TNA
79 Brussels Embassy telegram of 6 August 1968, PREM 13/2113, TNA
80 PREM 13/1993, TNA
81 Record of meeting between Wilson, Stewart and Healey of 22 August 1968, PREM 13/1883, TNA
82 Exchange of letters between Palliser and Maitland (FO) of 22 and 23 August 1968, PREM 13/1993 and PREM 13/1994, TNA
83 Record of meeting between Sir Patrick Reilly and Maurice Schumann of 26 August 1968, PREM 13/2655, TNA
84 Paris Embassy telegram to FO of 29 August 1968, PREM 13/2113, TNA
85 Record of meeting between Stewart and Ambassador de Courcel of 30 August 1968, PREM 13/1994, TNA
86 Record of meeting between Stewart and Joseph Luns of 30 August 1968, PREM 13/2113, TNA
87 Rome Embassy telegram of 31 August 1968, PREM 13/2113, TNA
88 Paris Embassy telegram to FO of 9 September 1968, PREM 13/2114, TNA
89 Minute from Palliser to Wilson of 11 September 1968, PREM 13/2638, TNA
90 Telegram from the Foreign Secretary from Bucharest of 10 September 1968, PREM 13/2638, TNA
91 Letter from Palliser to Maitland (FO) of 12 September 1968, PREM 13/2113, TNA
92 Despatch from Reilly to the Foreign Secretary of 12 September 1968, PREM 13/2113, TNA
93 Paris Embassy telegram of 12 September 1968, PREM 13/2113, TNA
94 FT report from Paul Lewis (Paris Correspondent) of 12 September 1968, PREM 13/2113, TNA
95 Paris Embassy telegrams to FO of 17 September 1968, PREM 13/2113, TNA
96 Paris Embassy telegram to FO of 17 September 1968, PREM 13/2113, TNA
97 Letter from Palliser to the FO of 18 September 1968, PREM 13/2113, TNA
98 Record of meeting between Wilson and Harmel of 18 September 1968, PREM 13/1947, TNA
99 FO telegram of 19 September 1968 to Paris Embassy, PREM 13/2113, TNA
100 PREM 13/2113, TNA
101 Message from Wilson to Kiesinger of 26 September 1968, PREM 13/2113, TNA
102 UKDel Brussels telegram to FO of 27 September 1968, PREM 13/2113, TNA
103 Letter from Jackling to Viscount Hood (FO) of 28 September 1968, PREM 13/2113, TNA
104 PREM 13/2113, TNA
105 Bonn Embassy telegram to FO of 29 September 1968, PREM 13/2113, TNA
106 Paris Embassy telegram to FO of 30 September 1968, PREM 13/2113, TNA
107 PREM 13/2113, TNA
108 Bonn Embassy telegram to FO of 30 September 1968, PREM 13/2113, TNA
109 Luxembourg Embassy telegram to FO of 30 September 1968, PREM 13/2113, TNA
110 Paris Embassy telegram to FO of 3 October 1968, PREM 13/2113, TNA
111 Bonn Embassy telegram to FO of 3 October 1968, PREM 13/2113, TNA
112 Minute from Robinson to Hancock of 13 September 1968, PREM 13/2113, TNA
113 Minute from Palliser to Wilson of 4 October 1968, PREM 13/2113, TNA

114 Letter from David Morpeth (APS, FO) to Palliser of 11 October 1968, PREM 13/2627
115 Telegram from Healey to Stewart of 10 October 1968, PREM 13/1998, TNA
116 Telegram from Stewart to Wilson of 13 October 1968, PREM 13/2627, TNA
117 Minute from Palliser to Wilson of 15 October 1968, PREM 13/2627, TNA
118 Paris Embassy telegram to FCO (the FO and CRO had formally merged on 17 October 1968) of 22 October 1968, PREM 13/2627, TNA
119 Rome Embassy telegrams to FCO of 22 October 1968, PREM 13/2627, TNA
120 FCO internal minute of 28 October 1968, PREM 13/2627, TNA
121 US Government Note given to the Foreign and Commonwealth Office (FCO) on 11 November 1968, PREM 13/2627, TNA
122 Brussels Embassy telegram to FCO of 14 November 1968, PREM 13/2627, TNA
123 UKDel Brussels telegram to FCO of 14 November 1968, PREM 13/2627, TNA
124 Message from Kiesinger to Wilson of 12 November 1968, PREM 13/2114, TNA
125 Letter from Soames to Stewart of 15 November 1968, PREM 13/2641, TNA
126 Letter from Maitland (FCO) to Palliser of 19 November 1968, PREM 13/2627, TNA
127 Author conversation with Sir Michael Palliser
128 Minute from Palliser to Wilson of 19 November 1968, PREM 13/2641, TNA
129 Sir Alan Campbell: *Anglo-French Relations A Decade Ago: A New Assessment*, Royal Institute of International Affairs, Vol. 58. No, 2 (Spring 1982)
130 Conversation with the author in 1972
131 Letter from Soames to Wilson of 27 November 1968, PREM 13/2627, TNA
132 Paris Embassy telegram of 26 November 1968 to FCO, PREM 13/2627, TNA
133 PREM 13/2627, TNA
134 Minute from Wilson to Stewart of 17 December 1968, PREM 13/2627, TNA
135 Minute from Stewart to Wilson of 20 December 1968, PREM 13/2627, TNA
136 Minute from Lord Chalfont to Stewart of 19 December 1968, PREM 13/2641, TNA
137 Minute from Palliser to Wilson of 23 December 1968, PREM 13/2627, TNA
138 FCO draft Cabinet Paper of 7 January 1969, PREM 13/2627, TNA
139 Exchange of minutes between Palliser and Wilson of 17 January 1969, PREM 13/2627, TNA
140 Letter from Maitland (FCO) to Palliser of 1 February 1969, PREM 13/2628, TNA
141 Minute from Wilson to Palliser of 1 February 1969, PREM 13/2628, TNA
142 Paris Embassy telegram to FCO of 5 February 1969, PREM 13/2628, TNA
143 Paris Embassy telegram to FCO of 5 February 1969, PREM 14/2628, TNA
144 Minute from Palliser to Wilson of 5 February 1969 and letter from Palliser to the FCO of 6 February 1969, PREM 13/2628, TNA
145 Exchange of telegrams between Stewart and Soames of 6 and 7 February 1969, PREM 13/2628, TNA
146 Telegram from Stewart to Wilson of 6 February 1969, PREM 13/2628, TNA
147 Telegram from Paris Embassy to FCO of 8 February 1969, PREM 13/2628, TNA
148 Message from Palliser to Wilson of 9 February 1969, PREM 13/2628, TNA
149 FCO telegram to Paris of 9 February, 1969, PREM 13.2628, TNA
150 Record of meeting between Wilson and Stewart of 10 February 1969, PREM 13/2674, TNA
151 Paris Embassy telegram of 10 February 1969, PREM 13/2628, TNA
152 Hancock's record of his discussion with Soames of 10 February 1969, PREM 13/2628
153 Minute from Palliser to Wilson of 10 February 1969, PREM 13/2628, TNA
154 Ibid
155 FCO telegram to Bonn Embassy of 11 February 1969, PREM 13/2628, TNA
156 Bonn Embassy telegram to FCO of 12 February, 1969, PREM 13/2628, TNA
157 FCO telegram to Paris Embassy of 12 February 1969, PREM 13/2628, TNA
158 FCO telegram to Paris Embassy of 12 February 1969, PREM 3/2628, TNA
159 Paris Embassy telegram to FCO of 12 February 1969, PREM 13/2628, TNA

160 Paris Embassy telegram to FCO of 22 February 1969, PREM 13/2628, TNA
161 Letter from Soames to Wilson (copied to Stewart) of 11 March 1969,PREM 13/2641, TNA
162 Letter from Palliser to Maitland (FCO) of 18 March1969, PREM 13/2641
163 FCO telegram to Paris Embassy of 20 March 1969, PREM 13/2641, TNA
164 Bonn Embassy telegram to FCO of 20 March 1969, PREM 13/3216, TNA
165 Record of meeting between Wilson, Stewart and Soames of 26 March 1969, PREM 13/2629, TNA
166 Ibid
167 Minute from Hancock of 2 April 1969, PREM 13/2629, TNA
168 Minute from Greenhill to Lord Chalfont of 8 April 1969, PREM 13/2629, TNA
169 Exchange of minutes between Wilson and Youde of 10 April 1969, PREM 13/2629, TNA
170 Telegrams to Wilson from Stewart from Washington of 12 April 1969, PREM 13/2629, TNA
171 Minute from Wilson to Youde of 14 April 1969, PREM 13/2629, TNA
172 Stewart, op.cit. p. 226
173 Wilson, op.cit. pp. 610–611
174 *De Gaulle* by Bernard Ledwidge, London 1982
175 Sir Alan Campbell: *Anglo-French Relations A decade Ago: A New Assessment*, International Affairs, Vol.58, No 2 (Spring 1982)

7 The start of negotiations: 1969–1971

1   Paris Embassy telegram of 28 April 1969, PREM 13/2655, TNA
2   Message from Wilson to de Gaulle of 1 May 1969, PREM 15/2655, TNA
3   Cabinet of 1 May 1969, CC (69) 20th Conclusions, CAB128/44, TNA
4   Minute from Stewart to Wilson of 13 June 1969, PREM 13/2645, TNA
5   Letter from Youde to Graham (FCO) of 17 June 1969, PREM 13/2749, TNA
6   Telegram from Paris Embassy of 23 June 1969, PREM 13/2655, TNA
7   Record of meeting of 25 June 1969, PREM 13/2641, TNA
8   Paris Embassy telegram to FCO of 12 July 1969, PREM 13/2629, TNA
9   Record of meeting between Wilson and Luns of 16 July 1969, PREM 13/2637, TNA
10 Record of meeting between Luns and Wilson and Stewart of 18 July 1969, PREM 13/2629, TNA
11 Cabinet of 22 July 1969 CC (69) 35th Conclusions, CAB 128/44, TNA
12 UkDel EEC telegram to FCO of 22 July 1969, PREM 13/2629, TNA
13 Minute from Andrew Graham to Michael Halls (PPS at No. 10) of 22 July 1969, PREM 13/2629, TNA
14 Wilson, op. cit. pp. 687–688
15 FCO Guidance telegram of 1 August 1969, PREM 13/2629, TNA
16 Minute from Stewart to Wilson of 10 September 1969 and minutes from Wilson to Stewart of 16 September 1969, PREM 13/2629, TNA
17 Letter from Palliser to FCO of 6 August 1969, PREM 13/2629, TNA
18 Telegram from Stewart to Wilson of 20 September 1969, PREM 13/2629, TNA
19 Wilson, op. cit. pp. 704–705
20 Cabinet of 25 September 1969, CC(69) 45th Conclusions CAB 128/44, TNA
21 UKDel EEC telegrams to FCO of 2 October 1969, PREM 13/2630, TNA
22 Minute from Youde to Wilson of 7 October 1969, PREM 13/2630, TNA
23 Cabinet of 9 October 1969, CC (69) 47th conclusions, CAB 128/44, TNA
24 FCO letter to No. 10 Downing Street of 22 October 1969, PREM 13/2630, TNA
25 Message from Wilson to Brandt of 24 October 1969, PREM 13/2630, TNA
26 Message from Brandt to Wilson of 27 October 1969, PREM 13/2630, TNA

27 Bonn Embassy telegram to FCO of 30 October 1969, PREM 13/2630, TNA
28 Minute from Nield to Trend of 20 October 1969, PREM 13/2630, TNA
29 Minute of 24 October 1969 from Youde to Nield, PREM 13/2630, TNA
30 Minute from Joe Haines (Press Secretary, No. 10) to Youde of 21 October 1969, PREM 13/2630, TNA
31 Cabinet of 6 November 1969, CC (69) 53rd Conclusions, Cab 128/44, TNA
32 Note by the Secretary of the Cabinet of 28 October 1969, EURM (69) 2 CAB 134/2806, TNA
33 Record of meeting of 12 November 1969 between Wilson and Stewart, PREM 13/1631, TNA
34 FCO telegram of 17 November 1969 to European posts, PREM 13/2631, TNA
35 Hague Embassy telegrams to FCO of 1 December 1969, PREM 13/2631, TNA
36 Hague Embassy telegrams to FCO of 2 December 1969, PREM 13/2631, TNA
37 Minute from Sir William Nield to Wilson of 4 December 1969, PREM 13/2631, TNA
38 Cabinet of 4 December 1969, CC (69) 58th Conclusions, CAB 128/44, TNA
39 Message from Wilson to Brandt of 3 December 1969, PREM 13/2631, TNA
40 Record of meeting between Wilson and Frank of 3 December 1969, PREM 13/2631, TNA
41 Extract from LPR sent to Wilson by the FCO on 3 December 1969, PREM 13/3207, TNA
42 Record of meeting between Wilson and Giscard d'Estaing of 4 December 1969, PREM 13/3207, TNA
43 Record of meeting on 28 February 1970, PREM 13/3201, TNA
44 Minute from Nield to No. 10 of 12 December 1969, PREM 13/2631, TNA
45 Submission from O'Neill to Stewart of 12 December 1969, PREM 13/2631, TNA
46 Foreign Office letter to No. 10 of 8 January 1970, PREM 13/3199, TNA
47 Exchange between Nield and Wilson of 19 December 1969, PREM 13/3198, TNA
48 Record of meeting between Wilson, Trend and Nield of 22 December 1969, PREM 13/3198, TNA
49 Bonn Embassy telegram to FCO of 11 February 1970, PREM 13/3200, TNA
50 Paris Embassy telegram to FCO of 11 February 1970, PREM 13/3200, TNA
51 Cabinet of 3 February 1970, CC (70) 5th Conclusions, CAB 128/45, TNA
52 *Hansard*, 10 February 1970
53 Ibid
54 No. 10 Record of Chequers press conference of 11 January 1970, PREM 13/3199, TNA
55 Record of meeting between Wilson and Freeman in 10 Downing Street on 12 January 1970, PREM 13/3545, TNA
56 NSC meeting of 29 January 1970, UK record, PREM 13/3546, TNA
57 Extract from document sent to Congress by President Nixon on 18 February 1970, PREM 13/2550, TNA
58 Letter of 23 February 1970 from Crowe to Moon, PREM 13/2546, TNA
59 Note of press briefing given by Roy Jenkins in Paris on 28 February, 1970, PREM 13/3201, TNA
60 Record of meeting of 2 March 1970, PREM 13/3201, TNA
61 Record of meeting in London of Britain's EEC Ambassadors on 9/10 March 1970, PREM 13/3201, TNA
62 Telegram from the British Embassy in The Hague of 13 March 1970, PREM 13/3201, TNA
63 Minute from Nield to Wilson of 19 March 1970, PREM 13/3201, TNA
64 Cabinet of 26 March 1970, CC (70) 14th Conclusions, CAB 128/45, TNA
65 Press release of speech by Shore on 6 May 1970, PREM 13/3201, TNA
66 *Hansard* for 26 March 1970
67 Record of meeting in London on 7 April 1970, PREM 13/3201, TNA

68 Cabinet of 9 April 1970, CC (70) 15th Conclusions, CAB 128/45, TNA
69 Record of meeting between Wilson and Thorn in London on 27 April 1970, PREM 13/3201, TNA
70 Record of meeting between Wilson and the TUC Economic Committee on 28 April 1970, PREM 13/3201, TNA
71 Communication from Stewart to Wilson of 28 April 1970, PREM 13/3345, TNA
72 Minutes of the Cabinet Ministerial Committee on the Approach to Europe, Sub-committee on Negotiations of 11 May 1970, EURM (N) 2nd Meeting, CAB 134/2809, TNA
73 Edward Heath: *The Course of My Life*, p. 362
74 PREM 15/007, TNA
75 Cabinet of 23 June 1970, CM (70) 1st Conclusions, CAB 128/47, TNA
76 Cabinet of 25 July 1970, CM (70) 2nd Conclusions, CAB 128/47, TNA
77 Note by the Secretary of the Cabinet of 26 June 1970, AE (70) 1, Meetings and Memoranda, CAB 134/2596, TNA
78 AE (70) 4 of 29 June 1970, CAB 134/2596, TNA
79 Cabinet of 29 June 1970, CM (70) 3rd Conclusions, CAB 128/47, TNA
80 Speech by Sir Alec Douglas-Home in Luxembourg on 30 June 1970, PREM 15/062, TNA
81 AEO (70) 16 of 8 July 1970, CAB 134/2599, TNA
82 Memorandum by Barber of 21 July 1970 and Cabinet Conclusions of 16 July 1970, CM (70) 5th Conclusions CAB 128/47, TNA
83 Ibid
84 Cabinet of 28 July 1970, CM (70) 9th Conclusions, CAB 128/47, TNA
85 Cabinet of 17 September 1970, CM (70) 19th conclusions CAB 128/47, TNA
86 Foreign Office paper of 2 September 1970, PREM 15/1560, TNA
87 Speech quoted in AEO (L) (70) 3 of 16 September 1970, CAB 134/2603, TNA
88 Speech quoted in AEO (L) (70) 3 of 16 September 1970, CAB 134/2603, TNA
89 AEO (70) 3rd Meeting, CAB 134/2599, TNA
90 AEO (70) Revise of 8 October 1970, CAB 134/2599, TNA
91 EEO (70) CAB 134/2599, TNA
92 Sir Con O'Neill: *Britain's Entry into the European Community, Report on the Negotiations of 1970–1972* (Whitehall History Publishing: 2000)
93 Cabinet Ministerial Committee on the Approach to Europe: Note by the Secretaries of 8 October 1970, CAB 134/2598, TNA
94 Record of meeting of 30 September 1970, PREM 15/714, TNA
95 Note by Heath of 13 October 1970, PREM 15/714, TNA
96 Harold Wilson: Speech at the Labour Party Conference on 29 September 1970
97 Cabinet of 29 October 1970, CM (70) 34th Conclusions, CAB 128/47, TNA
98 Minute from Rippon to Heath of 30 October 1970, PREM 15/062, TNA
99 Minute from Nield to Heath of 23 October 1970, PREM 15/062, TNA
100 Record of meeting between Rippon and Schumann of 9 November 1970, PREM 15/062, TNA
101 Letter from Heath to Brandt of 2 December 1970, PREM 15/062, TNA
102 Letter of 11 November 1970 from Jackling to Greenhill, PREM 15/397, TNA
103 Cabinet of 13 November 1970, CM (70) 37th Conclusions, CAB 128/47, TNA
104 Telegram from Heath to Douglas-Home of 12 November 1970, PREM 15/062, TNA
105 Record of meeting between Rippon and Monnet in Paris on 18 November 1970, PREM 15/359, TNA
106 Paris Embassy telegram to FCO of 23 November 1970, PREM 15/1560, TNA
107 Letter from Soames to O'Neill (FCO) of 30 November 1970, PREM 15/062, TNA
108 Record of conversation between Douglas-Home and Sharp of 26 November 1970, PREM 15/016, TNA

109 Record of meeting of 26 November 1970, PREM 15/062, TNA
110 Communication from Francis Pym to Heath of 30 November 1970, PREM 15/030, TNA
111 Letter from Soames to Greenhill (FCO) of 2 December 1970, PREM 15/066, TNA
112 Letter from Palliser to FCO of 30 December 1970, PREM 15/066, TNA
113 Minute from Nield to Heath of 8 December 1970, PREM 15/062, TNA
114 Cabinet of 10 December 1970, CM (70) 45th Conclusions CAB 128/47, TNA
115 Record of meeting between Heath and Nixon at the White House on 17 December 1970, PREM 15/161, TNA
116 Record of meeting between Heath and Nixon of 18 December 1970, PREM 15/161, TNA
117 Minute from Nield to Heath of 30 December 1970, PREM 15/062, TNA
118 Letter from Soames to Douglas-Home of 4 December 1970, PREM 15/1558, TNA
119 Record of meeting between Heath and Deniau on 3 January 1971, PREM 15/364, TNA
120 Record of meeting between Rippon and Deniau on 4 January 1971, PREM 15/364, TNA
121 Bonn Embassy telegram to FCO of 22 January 1971, PREM 15/368, TNA
122 Message from Brandt to Heath of 27 January 1971, PREM 15/368, TNA
123 Bonn Embassy telegram to FCO of 27 January 1971, PREM 15/368, TNA
124 Minute from Nield to Heath of 29 January 1971, PREM 15/368, TNA
125 Record of meeting of 31 January 1971, PREM 15/368, TNA
126 FCO Planning Paper of 8 March 1971, PREM 15/369, TNA
127 Cabinet of 4 February 1971, CM (71) 8th Conclusions CAB 128/49, TNA
128 Record of meeting between Heath and Scheel on 5 February 1971, PREM 15/368, TNA
129 Minute from Robinson to O'Neill (FCO) of 21 February 1971, PREM 15/368, TNA
130 Record of meeting between Heath and Soames of 1 March 1971, PREM 15/368, TNA
131 Minute from Armstrong to Heath of 5 March 1971, PREM 15/368
132 Letter from Soames to Greenhill (FCO) of 10 March 1971. The letter was seen by Heath PREM 15/368, TNA
133 Minute from Barrington to Douglas-Home of 10 March 1971, PREM 15/369, TNA
134 Record of meeting of 15 March 1971, PREM 15/369, TNA
135 Cabinet of 18 March 1971 CM (71) 15th Conclusions, CAB 128/49, TNA
136 Minute from Tickell to O'Neill (FCO) of 16 March 1971, PREM 15/369, TNA
137 Minute from Rippon to Heath of 17 March 1971, PREM 15/369, TNA
138 Valedictory Despatch from Sir James Marjoribanks to Douglas-Home of 20 March 1971, PREM 15/347, TNA
139 Minute from Barber to Heath of 24 March 1971, PREM 15/369, TNA
140 Record of meeting between Rippon and Courcel of 26 March 1971, PREM 15/369, TNA
141 Minute from Rippon to Heath of 26 March 1971, PREM 15/369, TNA
142 Record of meeting between Heath and the Board of Shell on 31 March 1971, PREM 15/370, TNA
143 Minute from Rippon to Heath of 26 March 1971, PREM 15/369, TNA
144 Paris telegram to FCO of 27 March 1971, PREM 15/370, TNA
145 Record of meeting of 29 March 1971, PREM 15/370, TNA
146 Letter from Moon (No. 10) to the FCO of 31 March 1971, PREM 15/370, TNA
147 Account by Hargrove of meeting with President Pompidou on 3 April 1971, PREM 15/348, TNA
148 Belgian record of meeting between the Belgian Ambassador in Paris and Pompidou of 5 April 1971, PREM 15/348, TNA
149 Minute from Rippon to Heath of 1 April 1971, PREM 15/370, TNA

150 Heath: op.cit. pp. 605–606
151 Record of meeting between Heath and Brandt of 5 April 1971, PREM 15/397, TNA
152 Bonn Embassy Despatch to FCO of 16 April 1971, PREM 15/397, TNA
153 Letter from Soames to Greenhill of 21 April 1971, PREM 15/371, TNA
154 FCO telegram to Paris Embassy of 26 April 1971, PREM 15/371, TNA
155 Paris Embassy telegrams to FCO of 27 April 1971, PREM 15/371, TNA
156 Record of meeting between the French Ambassador and Rippon of 27 April 1971, PREM 15/371, TNA
157 Letter from Tickell (Paris Embassy) to Moon (No. 10) of 4 May 1971, PREM 15/371, TNA
158 Paris Embassy telegram to FCO of 4 May 1971, PREM 15/371, TNA
159 Record of meeting of 5 May 1971, PREM 15/371, TNA
160 Heath: *The Course of My Life*, p. 365
161 Paris telegram to FCO of 6 May 1971, PREM 15/371, TNA
162 Letter from Soames to Greenhill (FCO) of 7 May 1971, PREM 15/371, TNA
163 Record of meeting between Heath and Brandt of 6 May 1971, PREM 15/371, TNA
164 Treasury note of 18 May 1971, PREM 15/385, TNA
165 Heath: op.cit. p. 371
166 Despatch from Soames to Douglas-Home of 9 June 1971, PREM 15/372, TNA
167 Ibid.
168 Cabinet of 18 May 1971, CM (71) 26th Conclusions, CAB 128/49, TNA
169 Note by Armstrong of 21 May 1971 and Anglo-French agreed Record of Conclusions of the same date, PREM 15/372, TNA
170 Heath: op.cit. p. 372
171 *Hansard* of 24 May 1971
172 Despatch from Soames to Douglas-Home of 9 June 1971, PREM 15/372, TNA

8 Good thing, bad thing? The terms of entry and a country divided: 1971–1973

1 Cabinet of 24 May 1971, CM (71) 27th Conclusions, CAB 128/49, TNA
2 Letter from Gregson (No.10) to the Home Office of 24 May 1971 and minute from Simcock (No. 10) to Heath of 24 June 1971, PREM 15/543, TNA
3 Letter from Barrington to Moon of 27 May 1971, PREM 15/373, TNA
4 Paris Embassy telegram to FCO of 27 May 1971, PREM 15/373, TNA
5 Paris Embassy telegram to FCO of 25 June 1971, PREM 15/376, TNA
6 Communiqué after CSA consultations in London on 3 June 1971, PREM 15/366,TNA and *Hansard* of 21 July 1971
7 Letter from Armstrong to Ryrie of 24 May 1971, PREM 15/372, TNA
8 Letter from Armstrong to Ryrie of 3 June 1971, PREM 15/372, TNA
9 FCO telegram to EEC Embassies of 5 June 1971, PREM 15/373, TNA
10 Telegram from Rippon in Brussels to FCO of 7 June 1971, PREM 15/374, TNA
11 FCO telegram to EEC Embassies of 11 June 1971, PREM 15/374, TNA
12 Douglas Hurd: *An End to Promises* (Collins, 1979)
13 Paris Embassy telegram to FCO of 10 June 1971, PREM 15/366, TNA
14 Minutes from Thornton (Cabinet Office) to Armstrong of 11 and 14 June, PREM 15/367, TNA
15 FCO telegram to Paris Embassy of 11 June 1971, PREM 15/367, TNA
16 Paris Embassy telegram to FCO of 14 June 1971, PREM 15/374, TNA
17 Paris Embassy telegram to FCO of 16 June 1971, PREM 15/375, TNA
18 Paris Embassy telegram to FCO of 18 June 1971, PREM 15/367, TNA
19 Letter of 18 June from Soames to Armstrong, PREM 15/367, TNA
20 Minute from Armstrong to Heath of 22 June 1971, PREM 13/375, TNA

21 FCO telegram to Luxembourg Embassy of 23 June 1971, PREM 15/375, TNA
22 Cabinet of 24 June 1971, CM (71) 33rd Conclusions, CAB 128/49, TNA
23 *Hansard* of 24 June 1971
24 Ibid
25 Letter of 24 June 1971 from Marshall to Rippon, PREM 15/367, TNA
26 Statement of 1 July 1971 by the Australian PM, PREM 15/367, TNA
27 Letter from Heath to MacMahon of 2 July 1971, PREM 15/367, TNA
28 Despatch from Sir Morrice James to Douglas-Home of 7 July 1971, PREM 15/883, TNA
29 Letter from Trudeau to Heath of 12 July 1971, PREM 15/883, TNA
30 Hugh Noyes in *The Times* of 23 June 1971
31 Uwe Kitzinger: *Diplomacy and Persuasion* (Thames & Hudson: 1973) p. 297
32 Robert Jenkins: *Benn*, p. 381
33 Anthony Howard in *The Observer*, May 1971, quoted in Kitzinger op.cit, p. 299
34 David Owen: *Time to Declare*, Michael Joseph 1991, pp. 176–177
35 Roy Jenkins: *A Life at the Centre* (Macmillan: 1991) p. 320
36 Jenkins: op. cit. p. 320
37 Letter from Lord Drogheda to Heath of 29 July, and reply from Armstrong of 30 July, 1971, PREM 15/601, TNA
38 Record of conversation of 27 August 1971, PREM 15/380, TNA
39 Memo by Heath of 27 August 1971, PREM 15/511, TNA
40 Labour Party 'White Paper' of 31 August 1971, PREM 15/352, TNA
41 Cabinet Office minute of 6 September 1971, PREM 15/352
42 *The Economist* of 11 September 1971, PREM 15/352, TNA
43 Minute from Pym to Heath of 5 October 1971, PREM 15/574, TNA
44 Philip Ziegler: *Wilson: The Authorised Life* (Weidenfeld and Nicolson: 1993) p. 384
45 Jenkins, op.cit. p. 331
46 Owen, op. cit, pp. 185–187
47 PREM 15/380, TNA
48 *New York Times* of 22 October 1971, PREM 15/880, TNA
49 Letter from Heath to Brandt of 5 October 1971, PREM 15/880, TNA
50 Paris Embassy telegram to FCO of 22 October 1971, PREM 15/880, TNA
51 Minute from Heath of 21 November 1971, PREM 15/326, TNA
52 Minute to No. 10 of 15 December 1971, PREM 15/351, TNA
53 GEN 63(71) of 17 November 1971, CAB 130/538, TNA
54 Cabinet of 23 November 1971, CM (71) 58th Conclusions, CAB 128/49, TNA
55 Record of discussion on 28 October 1971, PREM 15/356, TNA
56 Letter from Armstrong to Soames of 24 November 1971, PREM 15/326, TNA
57 Minute from Heath to Prior of 25 November 1971, PREM 15/356, TNA
58 Minute from Tickell of 2 December 1971, PREM 15/889, TNA
59 Letter from Armstrong to Tickell of 2 December 1971, PREM 15/889, TNA
60 Record of meeting of 8 December 1971, PREM 15/889, TNA
61 Cabinet of 9 December 1971, CM (71) 62nd Conclusions, CAB 128/49, TNA
62 *Hansard* of 13 December 1971
63 Cabinet of 14 December 1971, CM (71) 63rd Conclusions, CAB 128/49, TNA
64 Sir Con O'Neill: *Report on the Negotiations of 1970–1972*, p. 347
65 Ibid, pxii
66 Author conversation with Sir Michael Butler
67 Record of meeting at Chequers on 2 January 1972, PREM 15/901, TNA
68 Letter from Wilson to Heath of 17 January 1972, PREM 15/880, TNA
69 Letter from Macmillan to Heath of 17 January 1972, PREM 15/880, TNA
70 FCO translation of *Paris Match* article of 8 January 1972, PREM 15/903, TNA
71 Despatch from Palliser to Douglas-Home of 20 January 1972, PREM 15/903, TNA
72 Draft (undated) by Robert Armstrong of mid-February 1972, PREM 15/879, TNA

73 Heath: op.cit. p. 394
74 Minute from Douglas-Home to Heath of 19 January 1972 and minute from Armstrong to Graham (FCO) of 28 January 1972, PREM 15/2077
75 Minute from Heath to Sir William Armstrong, et seq. of 31 January and 2 February 1972, PREM 15/876, TNA
76 Minute from Armstrong to the Cabinet Secretary of 4 February 1972, PREM 15/1512, TNA
77 Heath: op.cit. p. 384
78 Cabinet of 17 February 1972, CM (72) 7th Conclusions, CAB 128/50, TNA
79 Letter from Armstrong to Alexander (FCO) of 9 February 1972, PREM 15/906, TNA
80 Cabinet of 10 February 1972, CM (72) 6th Conclusions, CAB 128/50, TNA
81 Letter from Soames to Heath of 16 February 1972, PREM 15/903, TNA
82 Paris Embassy telegram of 16 March 1972, PREM 15/904, TNA
83 FCO brief of 17 March 1972, PREM 15/898, TNA
84 Records of discussions between Heath and Pompidou on 18/19 March 1972, PREM 15/904, TNA
85 Paris Embassy telegram to FCO of 24 April 1972, PREM 15/898, TNA
86 Paris Embassy Despatch of 5 May 1972, PREM 15/898, TNA
87 Record of meeting between Heath and Brandt on 21 April 1972, PREM 15/890, TNA
88 Record of 24 April 1972, PREM 15/890, TNA
89 Minute of 1 May from Armstrong to Hunt, PREM 15/890, TNA
90 Minute from Hunt to Armstrong of 10 May 1972, PREM 15/890, TNA
91 Letter to Heath from Sir John Partridge of 12 May 1972, PREM 15/1531, TNA
92 Letter from Armstrong to Graham (FCO) of 15 May 1972, PREM 15/890, TNA
93 Paris Embassy telegram to FCO of 3 June 1972, PREM 15/891, TNA
94 Letter from Alexander to Bridges of 7 June 1972, PREM 15/795, TNA
95 Paris Embassy telegram of 7 June 1972, PREM 15/795, TNA
96 Bonn Embassy telegram to FCO of 7 June 1972, PREM 15/891, TNA
97 Record of meeting between Heath and Krag on 9 June 1972, PREM 15/795, TNA
98 Letter of 13 June 1972 from Armstrong to Soames, PREM 15/875, TNA
99 Exchange of messages between Heath and Pompidou of 23 June and 7 July 1972, PREM 15/813, TNA
100 Cabinet of 27 June 1972, CM (72) 32nd Conclusions, CAB 128/50, TNA
101 Letter from Hunt to Robinson (FCO) of 19 June 1972, PREM 15/891, TNA
102 Cmnd. 3301: *Legal and Constitutional Implications of United Kingdom Membership of the European Communities*, 1967
103 Geoffrey Howe: *Conflict of Loyalty*, Macmillan 1994, p. 67
104 Letter from Sir Alan Neale (HMT) to No. 10 of 6 July 1972, PREM 15/1518, TNA
105 Record of meeting between Heath and the German Ambassador in London of 11 July 1972, and letter from Heath to Brandt of 17 July 1972, PREM 15/892, TNA
106 Record by Armstrong of meeting at the Elysée on 12 July 1972, PREM 15/813, TNA
107 Letter from Soames to Sir Alan Neale of 1 August 1972, PREM 15/813, TNA
108 Later Ambassador in Dublin, where he was assassinated by the Provisional IRA on 21 July 1976
109 Paris Embassy telegram to FCO of 18 August 1972, PREM 15/905, TNA
110 Record of meeting at Chequers on 24 August 1972, PREM 15/893, TNA
111 Minute from Douglas-Home to Heath of 25 August 1972, PREM 15/893, TNA
112 Minute from Hunt to Heath of 1 September 1972, PREM 15/893, TNA
113 Paris Embassy telegram of 2 September 1972, PREM 15/893, TNA
114 Record of meeting of 5 September 1972, PREM 15/893, TNA
115 Transcript of telephone conversation of 9 September 1972, PREM 15/893, TNA
116 Telegram from Home to Heath of 11 September 1972, PREM 15/893, TNA

117 Paris Embassy telegram of 21 September 1972, PREM 15/894, TNA
118 Oslo Embassy telegram of 26 September 1972, PREM 15/868, TNA
119 Conversation with author, the day after the referendum.
120 Oslo Embassy Despatch to FCO of 4 October 1972, PREM 15/868, TNA
121 Message from Heath to Brateli of 28 September 1972, PREM 15/868, TNA
122 Heath: op.cit. p. 394
123 Minute of 26 July 1972 from Armstrong to Heath, PREM 15/2077, TNA
124 *The Times* of 12 April 1972, PREM 15/2077, TNA
125 Exchange of minutes between Armstrong and Heath between 22 and 25 September 1972, PREM 15/2077, TNA
126 Letter to Armstrong of 19 October 1972, PREM 15/2077, TNA
127 Minute from Wright to Kenneth Stowe (PPS in No. 10) of 4 December 1975, PREM 16/859, TNA
128 *Sunday Times* of 8 October 1972, PREM 15/2077, TNA
129 *Daily Telegraph* of 9 October 1972, PREM 15/2077, TNA
130 Record of meeting with Heath of 8 October 1972, PREM 15/886, TNA
131 Minute from Hunt to Armstrong of 6 October 1972, PREM 15/894, TNA
132 Record of meeting of 8 October 1972, PREM 15/886
133 Paris Embassy telegram of 15 October 1972, PREM 15/895, TNA
134 MAFF briefing note of 17 October 1972, PREM 15/895, TNA
135 Record of meeting between Pompidou and Heath in Paris on 18 October 1972, PREM 15/896, TNA
136 Statement by Heath of 21 October 1972, PREM 15/895, TNA
137 Message from Armstrong to Sir Martin Charteris of 22 October 1972, PREM 15/895, TNA
138 Cabinet of 25 October 1972, CM (72) 46th Conclusions, CAB 128/59, TNA
139 *Hansard* of 23 October 1974
140 Ibid
141 Foreign Office record of the Summit (*The European Summit Conference, Paris – October 1972*), PREM 15/895, TNA
142 Ibid
143 The Werner Report, 1970
144 Margaret Thatcher: *The Downing Street Years* (Harper Collins: 1993) p. 741
145 Cabinet of 13 July 1972, CM (72) 36th Conclusions, CAB 128/50, TNA
146 Cabinet of 12 December 1972, CM (72) 57th Conclusions, CAB 128/50, TNA
147 Benn: *Office Without Power*, p. 428
148 Denis Healey quoted in Pimlott, op. cit. p. 597
149 Wilson papers quoted in Ziegler: op.cit. p. 387
150 Wilson: *Final Term*, p. 51
151 Ibid, p. 54
152 Pimlott: op.cit. p. 598
153 Letter from the Treasury et. seq. of 25 July 1973, PREM 15/1487, TNA
154 PREM 15/1490, TNA
155 GEN 119 (72) of 4 August 1972, CAB 130/605, TNA
156 GEN 119 minute of 29 September 1972, CAB 130/605, TNA
157 Minute from Royle to Heath of 17 October and reply from Heath of 26 October 1972, PREM 15/895, TNA
158 GEN 119 (72) (73) Vols. I and II, K119, CAB 130/606, TNA
159 Minute from Heath to all Cabinet Ministers of 9 November 1972, PREM 15/884, TNA
160 Cabinet of 14 December 1972, CM (72) 58th Conclusions, CAB 128/50, TNA
161 Heath: op.cit. p. 394
162 Minute from Barber to Heath of 1 December 1972, PREM 15/1518, TNA

9 The year of living dangerously: Britain's first year of European community membership: 1973–1974

1 Washington Embassy telegram to FCO of 16 January 1973, PREM 15/1976, TNA
2 FCO paper and Despatch from Washington Embassy of February 1973, PREM 15/1977, TNA
3 Record of discussion between Heath, Monnet and Palliser of 20 January 1973, PREM 15/1527, TNA
4 Record of meeting of 29 January 1973, PREM 15/1498, TNA
5 Cabinet of 30 January 1973, CM (73) 4th Conclusions CAB 128/51, TNA
6 Cabinet of 15 February 1973, CM (73) 7th Conclusions, CAB 128/51, TNA
7 Letter from Pym to Heath of 22 February 1973, PREM 15/1776, TNA
8 Minute of 5 March 1973, PREM 15/1776, TNA
9 Cabinet of 1 March 1973, CM (73) 12th Conclusions, CAB 128/51, TNA
10 *Times* Editorial of 27 February 1973 (*A Man for all Europe*), PREM 15/1576, TNA
11 Records of meetings in Bonn and Bonn Embassy telegram of 2 March 1973, PREM 15/1576, TNA
12 Ibid
13 Statement by Anthony Barber in the House of Commons on 6 March 1973, *Hansard*
14 Letter from Monnet to Heath of 7 March 1973, PREM 15/1494, TNA
15 Letter from Heath to Monnet of 19 March 1973, PREM 15/1494, TNA
16 Minute from Hunt to Heath of 14 March 1973, PREM 15/1494, TNA
17 Paris Embassy telegram to FCO of 21 March 1973, PREM 15/1554, TNA
18 Minute from Armstrong to Heath of 21 March 1973, PREM 15/1554, TNA
19 Record of meeting of 25 March 1973, PREM 15/1498, TNA
20 Paris Embassy telegram to FCO of 9 February 1973, PREM 15/2040, TNA
21 Minute from Hunt to Armstrong of 12 April 1973, PREM 15/1529, TNA
22 Minute of 14 April 1973, PREM 15/1529, TNA
23 Minute from Armstrong to Heath of 17 April 1973, PREM 15/1507
24 Paris Embassy telegram to FCO of 2 May 1973, PREM 15/1554, TNA
25 Paris Embassy Despatch of 4 May 1973, PREM 15/1554, TNA
26 Minute from Armstrong to Heath of 10 April 1973, PREM 15/1519, TNA
27 Letter from Palliser to Hunt of 8 May 1973 (also shown to the Chancellor of the Exchequer at Heath's request), PREM 15/1554, TNA
28 Minute of 14 May 1973, PREM 15/1519, TNA
29 Paris Embassy paper of 11 May 1973, PREM 15/1554, TNA
30 Paris Embassy telegram of 17 May 1973, PREM 15/1554, TNA
31 Message from Heath to Lord Cromer of 11 May 1973, PREM 15/1992, TNA
32 Letter from Greenhill to Bridges of 14 May 1973, PREM 15/1992, TNA
33 Minute from Trend to Heath of 2 May 1973, PREM 15/1541, TNA
34 Record of meeting of 10 May 1973, PREM 15/1984, TNA
35 Paris Embassy telegram to FCO of 17 May 1973, PREM 15/1554, TNA
36 Minute from Ewart-Biggs to Bridges of 17 May 1973, PREM 15/1554, TNA
37 Record of meeting of 21 May 1973, PREM 15/2075, TNA
38 Record of meeting of 21 May 1973, PREM 15/1519, TNA
39 Record of meetings on 21 May 1973, PREM 15/1526, TNA
40 Paris Embassy Despatch of 1 June 1973, PREM 15/1554, TNA
41 Cabinet of 24 May 1973, CM (73) 30th Conclusions, CAB 128/52, TNA
42 Paris Embassy telegram to FCO of 25 May 1973 reporting French Foreign Ministry Community briefing on the Heath/Pompidou talks, PREM 15/1554, TNA
43 Minute from Douglas-Home to Heath of 24 May 1973, PREM 15/1577, TNA
44 FCO and Bonn Embassy brief of 29 May 1973, PREM 15/1577, TNA
45 Letter from Henderson to Brimelow of 1 June 1973, PREM 15/1577, TNA
46 Record of meeting of 29 May 1973, PREM 15/1577, TNA

47 Minute from Armstrong to Bailey (HMT) of 5 June 1973, PREM 15/1519, TNA
48 Minute from Heath to Barber of 14 June 1973 and reply from Barber of 19 June 1973, PREM 15/1519, TNA
49 Minute from Armstrong to Heath of 21 June 1973, PREM 15/1519, TNA
50 Letter of 7 June 1973 from Cromer to Greenhill, PREM 15/1543, TNA
51 Minute from Heath to Bridges of 10 June 1973, PREM 15/1542, TNA
52 Letter from Armstrong to Acland (FCO) of 19 June 1973, PREM 15/1542, TNA
53 Minute from Armstrong to Heath of 29 June 1973, PREM 15/1542, TNA
54 PREM 15/1543, TNA
55 Treasury paper of 12 June 1973, GEN 138 (73) 9, CAB 130/625, TNA
56 Cabinet of 14 June 1973, CM (73) 31st Conclusions, CAB 128/52, TNA
57 Minute from Godber to Heath of 19 June 1973, PREM 15/2075, TNA
58 Twenty-five years later, in Brussels, President Chirac, speaking to the author, recalled Godber fondly.
59 Record of meeting of 5 July 1973, PREM 15/1561, TNA
60 Minute by Ewart-Biggs of 22 June 1973, PREM 15/2243, TNA
61 Paris Embassy telegram of 27 June 1973, PREM 15/2243, TNA
62 Record of meeting in 10 Downing Street on 27 June 1973, PREM 15/1519, TNA
63 Minute from Armstrong to Heath of 29 June 1973, PREM 15/2243, TNA
64 Minute from Hunt to Armstrong (and seen by Heath) of 6 July 1973, PREM 15/1512, TNA
65 'Waiting for Godot' (*Sunday Telegraph* of 2 September 1973), PREM 15/1498, TNA
66 Cabinet of 26 July 1973, CM (73) 39th Conclusions, CAB 128/52, TNA
67 Minute from Armstrong to Heath of 29 July 1973, PREM 15/1894, TNA
68 Paris Embassy Despatch of 31 July 1973, PREM 15/2073, TNA
69 Letter from Tomkins to Wright (FCO) of 31 July 1973, PREM 15/2076, TNA
70 Bonn Embassy telegram to FCO of 18 July 1973, PREM 15/1520, TNA
71 Minutes from Armstrong to Heath of 30 July and 7 August 1973, PREM 15/1520, TNA
72 Letter from Heath to Brandt of 12 September 1973, PREM 15/1520, TNA
73 PREM 15/1544, TNA
74 *Documents on British Policy Overseas*, Series III, Volume IV: *The Year of Europe: America, Europe and the Energy Crisis, 1972–1974*, Routledge 2006 [DBPO]
75 Ibid, p. 14
76 Letter from Sykes to Brimelow of 13 August 1973, PREM 15/1545, TNA
77 Letter from Heath to Armstrong of 3 September 1973, PREM 15/2243, TNA
78 Heath minute of 26 August 1973, PREM 15/2243, TNA
79 Heath record of 26 August 1973, PREM 15/1546, TNA
80 Heath record of 26 August 1973, PREM 15/2076, TNA
81 Minute from Armstrong to Heath of 17 September 1973, PREM 15/1507 and 2243, TNA
82 Records of conversations, PREM 15/1523, TNA
83 Paris Embassy telegram of 27 September 1973 and Armstrong letter to FCO, PREM 15/1523, TNA
84 PREM 15/1777, TNA
85 Minute from Davies to Heath of 2 October 1973, PREM 15/1523, TNA
86 Minute from Howe of 16 October 1973, PREM 15/1523, TNA
87 Minute from Pym to the Home Secretary (Robert Carr) of 16 November 1973, PREM 15/1523, TNA
88 Heath: *The Course of My Life*, p. 542
89 Letter from Nairne (CO) to Hurd of 8 October 1973, PREM 15/2075, TNA
90 Cabinet Office note of 10 October 1973, PREM 15/2076, TNA
91 Paris Embassy telegrams to FCO of 10 October 1973, PREM 15/1523 and PREM 15/1556, TNA

92 Record of meeting of 25 October 1973, PREM 15/1562, TNA
93 Minute of 5 October 1973, PREM 15/1523, TNA
94 Letter from Brandt to Heath of 25 October 1973, PREM 15/2075, TNA
95 Minute from Armstrong to Nairne of 23 October 1973 and minute from Hunt to Armstrong of 30 October 1973, PREM 15/1523, TNA
96 DBPO, op.cit. p. 28
97 Ibid, p. 29
98 Ibid pp. 33/34
99 Record of meeting of 16 November 1973, PREM 15/2093, TNA
100 Ibid, PREM 15/2093, TNA
101 German Chancellor and Foreign Minister who, with Aristide Briand, received the Nobel Peace Prize in 1926 for Franco-German reconciliation.
102 Record of meeting of 16 November 1973, PREM 15/2089, TNA
103 Record of discussion of 16 November 1973, PREM 15/2093, TNA
104 Record of discussion of 17 November 1973, PREM 15/2093, TNA
105 Minute from Douglas-Home to Heath of 20 November 1973, PREM 15/2080
106 Minute from Barber to Heath of 21 November 1973, PREM 15/2080, TNA
107 Record of conversation between Nairne and Thomson on 27 November 1973, PREM 15/2080, TNA
108 Minute from Heath of 7 December 1973, PREM 15/2080, TNA
109 Washington Embassy telegram to FCO of 24 November 1973, PREM 15/2089, TNA
110 Message of 28 November 1973 from Douglas-Home to Kissinger, PREM15/2089, TNA
111 PREM 14/1989, TNA
112 Washington Embassy telegram to FCO of 30 November 1973, PREM 15/1989, TNA
113 FCO telegram to Washington Embassy of 1 December 1973, PREM 15/1989, TNA
114 Article by Bernard Nossiter in the *Washington Post* of 30 November 1973, PREM 15/1989, TNA
115 Henry Kissinger: *Years of Renewal* (London, 1999) and Nigel Lawson, *The View from no 11*, quoted in Philip Ziegler (op.cit.) p. 374
116 Information given to the Author by Lord Armstrong
117 Ibid
118 Minute from Hunt to Heath of 10 December 1973, PREM 15/1496, TNA
119 FCO Guidance telegram of 10 December 1973, PREM 15/2041,TNA
120 UKRep Brussels telegram to FCO of 5 December 1973, quoted in DBPO op.cit, p. 37
121 Heath: op.cit. p. 393
122 Record of telephone conversation of 16 December 1973, PREM 15/2080, TNA
123 FCO telegram to UKRep Brussels of 16 December 1973, PREM 15/2080, TNA
124 Message from Heath to Douglas-Home of 17 December 1973, PREM 15/2080, TNA
125 Record of telephone conversation of 17 December 1973, PREM 15/2080, TNA
126 Minute from Armstrong to Nairne of 19 December 1973, PREM 15/2080, TNA
127 Cabinet of 20 December 1973, CC (73) 63rd Conclusions CAB 128/53, TNA
128 Bonn Embassy telegram to FCO of 22 December 1973, PREM 15/2080, TNA
129 Letter from Derek Mitchell (HMT) to Whitehall recipients, including No. 10, of 28 December 1973, PREM 15/2080, TNA
130 Cabinet of 17 January 1974 CM (74) 3rd Conclusions CAB 128/53, TNA
131 Minute from Douglas-Home to Heath of 17 January 1974, PREM 15/2080, TNA
132 Bonn Embassy telegram of 11 January 1974, PREM 15/2080, TNA
133 Minute from Hunt to Nairne of 21 January 1974, PREM 15/2076, TNA
134 Minute from Nairne to Hunt of 25 January 1974, PREM 15/2076, TNA
135 UKRep Brussels Despatch of 25 January 1973, PREM 15/2076, TNA
136 DBPO. op.cit. p. 43

10 Renegotiation and Referendum: 1974 – 1975

1 Record of meeting of British Ambassadors from EEC countries of 20 March 1974, PREM 16/72, TNA
2 *Let Us Work Together – Labour's Way Out of the Crisis*, February 1974
3 Record of meeting between Wilson and John Marshall of 29 April 1974, PREM 16/223, TNA
4 Author conversation with Sir Michael Butler and internal Foreign Office account of Renegotiation (Reneg).
5 Record of meeting of 20 March 1974, PREM 16/72, TNA
6 Record of meeting in Bonn on 21 March 1974, PREM 16/92, TNA
7 Bonn Embassy telegram of 23 March 1974, PREM 16/92, TNA
8 Ibid
9 Minute from Nairne to Hunt of 25 March 1974, PREM 16/92, TNA
10 Minute from Shore to Wilson of 7 March 1974, PREM 16/72, TNA
11 Minute from Shore to Wilson of 15 March 1974, PREM 16/72, TNA
12 Minute from Callaghan to Shore of 15 March 1972, PREM 16/72, TNA
13 Minute from Wilson to Shore of 25 March 1974, PREM 16/72, TNA
14 Reneg.
15 Cabinet of 14 March 1974, CC (74) 3rd Conclusions, CAB 128/54, TNA
16 Cabinet of 21 March 1974, CC (74) 5th Conclusions, CAB 128/54, TNA
17 Reneg.
18 Minute from Callaghan to Wilson of 26 March 1974, PREM 16/92, TNA
19 Cabinet of 25 March 1974, CC (74) 6th Conclusions, CAB 128/54, TNA
20 Record of meeting between Wilson and Kissinger in London on 28 March 1974, PREM 16/290, TNA
21 Paris Embassy telegram of 18 March 1974, PREM 16/72, TNA
22 Cabinet of 28 March 1974, CC (74) 7th Conclusions, CAB 128/54, TNA
23 Minute from Wilson of 1 April 1974, PREM 16/72, TNA
24 Roy Hattersley: *Who Goes Home? Scenes from a Political Life*, Abacus 1995, p. 152
25 *Financial Times* of 2 April 1974
26 Roy Hattersley: op.cit. p. 157
27 Conversation with author
28 Records of 1 April 1972, PREM 16/72, TNA
29 Cabinet of 4 April 1974, CC (74) 8th Conclusions, CAB 128/54, TNA
30 Tony Benn: *Against the Tide: Diaries 1973–76* (Hutchinson: 1989) p. 131
31 Paris Embassy Despatch of 17 April 1974, PREM 16/95, TNA
32 *Hansard* of 3 April 1974
33 Letter from Thorpe to Wilson of 8 April 1974, PREM 16/95, TNA
34 The author was in the street and heard him say it. It was, of course, picked up by the media as well.
35 Record by Wilson of conversation with Nixon in Paris on 6 April 1974, PREM 16/95, TNA
36 Bernard Donoughue: *Downing Street Diary: With Harold Wilson in No. 10* (Jonathan Cape: 2005) p. 93
37 PREM 16/73, TNA
38 S. African poet Roy Campbell who wrote an epigrammatic comment on some S. African novelists: '*You praise the firm restraint with which they write. I'm with you there of course. They use the snaffle and the curb all right. But where's the bloody horse?*'
39 Account of discussion given by Callaghan to Oliver Wright and minuted by Wright on 24 April 1974, PREM 16/73, TNA
40 Donoughue: op.cit. pp. 106–107
41 Reneg.
42 Cabinet of 2 May 1974, CC (74) 14th Conclusions, CAB 128/54, TNA

43 Cabinet of 9 May 1974, CC (74) 15th Conclusions, CAB 128/54, TNA
44 Reneg.
45 Press conference of 23 October 1975 quoted in: *The 1975 Referendum* by David Butler and Uwe Kitzinger (Macmillan: 1976) p. 31
46 Ibid.
47 Record of meeting between Wilson and Ortoli of 13 May 1974, PREM 16/73, TNA
48 Reneg.
49 Record of meeting of 13 May 1974, PREM 16/73, TNA
50 Cabinet of 16 May 1974, CC (74) 16th Conclusions CAB 128/54, TNA
51 Cabinet of 23 May 1974, CC (74) 17th Conclusions CAB 128/54, TNA
52 Minute from Ewart-Biggs to Tomkins of 10 June 1974, PREM 16/97, TNA
53 Letter from Henderson to Wright of 27 May 1974, PREM 16/73, TNA
54 Letter from Palliser to Wright of 4 June 1974, PREM 16/73, TNA
55 Reneg.
56 Letter of 14 June 1974 from Michael Jenkins (British diplomat seconded to the Thomson Cabinet) to Butler (FCO) of 14 June 1974, PREM 16/73, TNA
57 All correspondence in PREM 16/74, TNA
58 Foreign Office brief of 19 June 1974, PREM 16/11, TNA
59 Probably an RAF Andover. Wilson preferred this propeller-driven form of transport since, being slower than a jet aircraft, it gave him a lengthier period of peace and quiet.
60 Record of meeting between Wilson and Schmidt of 19 June 1974, PREM 16/73, TNA
61 Record of meeting between Wilson and Soames in 10 Downing Street on 24 June 1974, PREM 16/74, TNA
62 Record of meeting between Wilson and Tindemans in Brussels on 25 June 1974, PREM 16/11, TNA
63 Record of meeting between Wilson and Hartling in Brussels on 25 June 1974, PREM 16/11, TNA
64 Record of meeting of 25 June 1974 in Brussels, PREM 16/11, TNA
65 Record of meeting in Brussels on 26 June 1974, PREM 16/11, TNA
66 Cabinet of 27 June 1974, CC (74) 21st Conclusions, CAB 128/54, TNA
67 Cabinet of 2 and 4 July 1974 CC (74) 22nd Conclusions and 23rd Conclusions, CAB 128/54, TNA
68 Note for the record by Armstrong of 18 July 1974, PREM 16/74, TNA
69 Record of meeting in Paris on 19 July 1974, PREM 16/74, TNA
70 Minute by Harold Wilson on Paris talks of 19 July 1974, PREM 16/74, TNA
71 Undated manuscript exchange between Hunt and Wilson, PREM 16/97, TNA
72 Reneg.
73 Letter from Tomkins to Brimelow of 24 July 1974, PREM 16/97, TNA
74 Author translation of letter from Giscard d'Estaing to Wilson of 2 August 1974, PREM 16/97, TNA
75 Reneg.
76 Minute from Wilson to Armstrong of 4 August 1974, PREM 16/86, TNA
77 Minute by Nairne of 24 July 1974, PREM 16/86, TNA
78 Minute from Bridges to Armstrong of 2 September 1974, PREM 16/86, TNA
79 Message from Wilson to Shore of 7 August 1974, PREM 16/210, TNA
80 Minute from Shore to Wilson and other Ministers of 15 August 1974, PREM 16/210, TNA
81 TV interview with Robin Day on 1 August 1974, PREM 16/87, TNA
82 Minute of 13 August 1974, PREM 16/74, TNA
83 Cabinet of 5 September 1974, CC (74) 33rd Conclusions; and Cabinet of 10 September 1974, CC (74) 34th Conclusions, CAB 128/55, TNA
84 Record dictated by Wilson on 16 September 1974, PREM 16/78, TNA
85 Record by Wilson of discussion in Paris on 14 September 1974, PREM 16/78, TNA
86 Brussels Embassy telegram of 17 September 1974, PREM 16/75, TNA

87 October 1974 Labour Party Manifesto: *Britain will win with Labour*
88 No. 10 record of telephone conversation between Peart and Wilson of 19 September 1974, PREM 16/81, TNA
89 Transcript of BBC *Nationwide* TV interview of 27 September 1974, PREM 16/887, TNA
90 Minute from Callaghan to Wilson of 14 October 1974, PREM 16/85, TNA
91 Minute from Callaghan to Wilson of 23 October 1974, PREM 16/85, TNA
92 Letter from Bridges to Acland of 24 October 1974, PREM 16/75, TNA
93 Letter from Bridges to Acland of 25 October 1974, PREM 16/85, TNA
94 Record of meeting between Hattersley (accompanied by Butler) and Gundelach of 28 October 1974, PREM 16/75, TNA
95 Record of discussion between Wilson and Soames of 28 October 1974, PREM 16/85, TNA
96 Minute from Nairne to Wilson of 6 November 1974, PREM 16/76, TNA
97 Reneg.
98 Minute from Shore to Wilson and other Ministers of 1 November 1974, PREM 16/76, TNA
99 Minute from Callaghan to Wilson of 6 November 1974, PREM 16/76, TNA
100 Minute from Healey to Wilson of 8 November 1974, PREM 16/76, TNA
101 Minute from Peart to Wilson of 13 November 1974, PREM 16/76, TNA
102 Donoughue: op.cit. p. 251
103 Minute from Shore to Wilson of 25 November 1974, PREM 16/77, TNA
104 Personal minute from Callaghan to Wilson of 29 November 1974, PREM 16/77, TNA
105 Minute from Williams to Wilson of 29 November 1974, PREM 16/77, TNA
106 Minute from Armstrong to Wilson of 29 November 1974, PREM 16/77, TNA
107 Record of telephone conversation between Wilson and Callaghan of 1 December 1974, PREM 16/77, TNA
108 Donoughue: op.cit. p. 252
109 Ibid, p. 252
110 Reneg.
111 *Report of the Seventy-Third Annual Conference of the Labour Party, London 1974*, pp. 249–260.
112 Reneg.
113 James Callaghan: *Time and Chance.* p. 312
114 Record of meeting at Chequers on 30 November 1974, PREM 16/77, TNA
115 Letter from Henderson to Wright of 4 December 1974, PREM 16/101, TNA
116 Minute from Bridges to Armstrong of 4 December 1974, PREM 16/101, TNA
117 Donoughue: op.cit. p. 252
118 Record of telephone conversation between Wilson and Callaghan of 1 December 1974, PREM 16/77, TNA
119 Record of meeting between Callaghan and Giscard d'Estaing in Paris on 19 November 1974, PREM 16/76, TNA
120 Minute from Nairne to Armstrong of 3 December 1974, PREM 16/396, TNA
121 Reneg.
122 Record of meeting in Paris on 3 December 1974, PREM 16/84, TNA
123 Cabinet of 5 December 1974, CC(74) CAB 128/55, TNA
124 Donoughue: op.cit. p. 257
125 Speech to London Labour Mayors of 7 December 1974, quoted in Reneg.
126 Callaghan: op.cit. p. 315
127 Donoughue: op.cit. pp. 259–262
128 Donoughue: op.cit. pp. 260–263
129 Callaghan: op.cit. p. 315; Donoughue: op.cit. p. 261, and Communiqué of the Paris Summit
130 Communiqué of the Paris Summit

131 Cabinet of 12 December 1974, CC (74) 51st Conclusions, CAB 138/55, TNA
132 *Hansard* of 16 December 1974
133 Letter from Foot, Shore and Benn to Wilson 0f 27 November 1974, PREM 16/558, TNA
134 Cabinet of 12 December 1974, CC (74) 51st Conclusions, Minute 3 (Confidential Annex), CAB 128/55, TNA
135 Letter from Wilson to Heffer of 23 December 1974, PREM 16/558, TNA
136 Letter from Wilson to Foot of 24 December 1974, PREM 16/558, TNA
137 Correspondence between Benn and Wilson, PREM 16/558, TNA
138 Letter from Foot to Wilson of 3 January 1975, PREM 16/558, TNA
139 Minute from Hunt to Armstrong of 15 January 1975, PREM 16/403, TNA
140 Cabinet of 21 January 1975, CC(75) 4th Conclusions CAB 128/56, TNA
141 *Hansard* of 23 January 1975
142 *Hansard* of 11 March 1975
143 Minute from Wilson to all Ministers of 27 January 1975, PREM 16/404
144 Note by Wilson of 3 February 1975, PREM 16/395, TNA
145 UKRep Brussels telegram to FCO of 18 February 1975, PREM 16/395, TNA
146 Reneg.
147 Paris Embassy telegram of 22 February 1975, PREM 16/395, TNA
148 Reneg; and letter from Nairne to Acland of 21 February 1975, PREM 16/395, TNA
149 Letter from Healey to Schmidt of 3 February 1975, PREM 16/397, TNA
150 Minute from Healey to Wilson of 6 March 1975, PREM 16/306, TNA
151 Letter from Schmidt to Healey of 19 February 1975, PREM 16/397, TNA
152 Minute from Callaghan to Wilson of 24 February 1975, PREM 16/409, TNA
153 Paris Embassy telegram of' 27 February 1975, PREM 16/409, TNA
154 Paris Embassy telegram of 3 March 1975, PREM 16/409, TNA
155 Paris Embassy telegram of 6 March 1975, PREM 16/409, TNA
156 UKRep Brussels telegram of 3 March 1975, PREM 16/409, TNA
157 Donoughue: op.cit. p. 326
158 Message from Wilson to Schmidt of 6 March 1975, PREM 16/397, TNA
159 FCO telegram to Bonn Embassy of 9 March 1975, PREM 16/397, TNA
160 Cabinet of 6 March 1975, CC (75) 11th Conclusions, CAB 128/56, TNA
161 Donoughue: op.cit. pp. 329–330
162 Conclusions of Dublin European Council
163 Wellington High Commission telegram to FCO of 14 March 1975, PREM 16/396, TNA
164 Dublin telegram to FCO of 11 March 1975 and Conclusions of the Dublin European Council, PREM 16/397, TNA
165 Sir Michael Butler: *Europe: More than a Continent* (Heinemann: 1986)
166 Information given to the author by Sir Michael Butler
167 Record of meeting between Wilson and Soames of 6 March 1975, PREM 16/409, TNA
168 Statement on steel made by Wilson at Dublin on 11 March 1975, PREM 16/409, TNA
169 *Hansard* of 12 March 1975
170 Canard Enchaine cartoon of 12 March 1975, cited in *The 1975 Referendum* (Butler and Kitzinger) p. 44
171 Bonn Embassy telegram to FCO of 13 March 1975, PREM 16/383, TNA
172 Cabinet of 17 and 18 March 1975 CC (75) 14th Conclusions, CAB 128/56, TNA
173 *Hansard* of 18 March 1975
174 *Evening News* of 18 March 1975
175 Cabinet of 23 January 1975, CC (75) 5th Conclusions, CAB 128/56, TNA
176 *Hansard* of 23 January 1975

177 Report of the Referendum Unit (hereafter RRU) by J R Jameson of 17 June 1975, PREM 16/844, TNA
178 Cabinet of 6 February 1975, CC (75) 7th Conclusions, CAB 128/56, TNA
179 Harold Wilson: *Final Term*, p. 105
180 Minute from Armstrong to Wilson of 7 February 1975, PREM 16/404, TNA
181 Cabinet of 20 February 1975, CC (75) 9th Conclusions, CAB 128/56, TNA
182 Cabinet of 8 April 1975, CC (75) 18th Conclusions, CAB 128/56, TNA
183 RRU
184 RRU
185 Cabinet of 17 April 1975, CC (75) 21st Conclusions, CAB 128/56, TNA
186 *Hansard* of 22 April 1975
187 Cabinet of 24 April 1975, CC (75) 23rd Conclusions, CAB 128/56, TNA
188 *Hansard* of 7 May 1975
189 RRU
190 Minute from Callaghan to Wilson of 10 April 1975, PREM 16/411, TNA
191 *Britain's New Deal for Europe*, PREM 16/407, TNA
192 Britain's New Europe Deal, PREM 16/407, TNA
193 "*Why You Should Vote No*" (Statement by the National Referendum Campaign), PREM 16/407, TNA
194 Wilson: op.cit p. 106
195 Joe Haines: *Glimmers of Twilight* (Politico's: 2003) p. 49
196 Ibid p. 107
197 Guidance Note of 3 April 1975, PREM 16/406, TNA
198 Cabinet of 15 May 1975, CC (75) 24th Conclusions, CAB 128/56, TNA
199 Wilson: op.cit p. 105
200 Exchange of minutes between Wilson and Jenkins of 28 and 29 May 1975, PREM 16/407, TNA
201 Minute from Callaghan to Wilson of 3 April 1975, PREM 16/406, TNA
202 Letter from Armstrong to Barrett (Private Secretary, FCO) of 11 April 1975, PREM 16/406, TNA
203 Minute from Callaghan to Wilson of 13 May 1975, PREM 16/407, TNA
204 Minute from Wilson to Cabinet members of 14 May 1975, PREM 16/556, TNA
205 Donoughue: op.cit. p. 387
206 Wilson: op.cit. p. 106
207 Butler and Kitzinger: op.cit. p. 194
208 Minute from Nairne to Hunt of 8 May 1975, PREM 16/407, TNA
209 Minutes of 14 and 22 May 1975, PREM 16/407, TNA
210 *Gallup Poll* quoted in Butler and Kitzinger (op.cit) p. 250
211 Ibid p. 253
212 *Eurostat*, November 1975, quoted in op.cit p. 3
213 *Harris Poll* of 1–6 April 1975, op.cit. p. 256
214 *Hansard* of 9 June 1975
215 *Daily Telegraph* of 7 June 1975
216 *Financial Times* of 7 June 1975 (author italics)
217 Minute from Wilson to Callaghan of 10 June 1975, PREM 16/407, TNA
218 Cabinet of 26 June 1975, CC (75) 30th Conclusions, CAB 126/56, TNA
219 Callaghan: op.cit. 326
220 Bernard Donoughue: *The Heat of the Kitchen* p. 156/157
221 Letter from Sir Kenneth Stowe to the author of 13 October 2011
222 L P Hartley: *The Go-Between*

Bibliography

Benn, Tony: *Office Without Power, Diaries 1968–1972* (Arrow Books 1989)

Benn, Tony: *Against the Tide, Diaries 1973–1976* (Hutchinson 1989)

Brown, George: *In My Way, Memoirs* (Victor Gollancz Ltd 1971)

Butler, David and Kitzinger, Uve: *The 1975 Referendum* (The Macmillan Press 1976)

Butler, Sir Michael: *Europe More than a Continent* (Heinemann 1986)

Callaghan, James: *Time and Chance* (Collins 1987)

Campbell, Alan: *Anglo-French Relations a Decade Ago: A New Assessment, I and II*, International Affairs Vol. 58. Nos. 2 and 3 (Blackwell Publishing 1982)

Couve de Murville, Maurice: *Une Politique Etrangere 1958–1969* (Plon 1971)

De Gaulle, Charles: *Mémoires* (Editions Gallimard 2000)

Donoughue, Bernard: *The Heat of the Kitchen* (Politico's 2003)

Donoughue, Bernard: *Downing Street Diary: With Harold Wilson in No .10* (Jonathan Cape 2005)

Fenby, Jonathan: *The General: Charles de Gaulle and the France He Saved* (Simon & Schuster 2010)

Foreign & Commonwealth Office: *The Year of Europe and the Energy Crisis 1973–1974: FCO Documents on British Policy Overseas, Series III, Volume IV* (Whitehall History Publishing, Routledge 2006)

Haines, Joe: *Glimmers of Twilight* (Politico's Publishing 2003)

Hattersley, Roy: *Who Goes Home? Scenes from a Political Life* (Abacus 2003)

Healey, Denis: *The Time of My Life* (Michael Joseph 1989)

Heath, Edward: *The Course of My Life: My Autobiography* (Hodder & Stoughton 1988)

Horne, Alistair: *Macmillan: The Official Biography* (Macmillan 1988 and 1989)

Howe, Geoffrey: *Conflict of Loyalty* (Macmillan 1994)

Hurd, Douglas: *An End to Promises* (Collins 1979)

Jenkins, Roy: *A Life at the Centre* (Politico's 2006)

Kitzinger, Uve: *The Second Try: Labour and the EEC* (Pergamon Press 1968)

Kitzinger, Uve: *Diplomacy and Persuasion: How Britain Joined the Common Market* (Thames & Hudson 1973)

Ledwidge, Bernard: *De Gaulle* (Weidenfeld & Nicolson 1982)

Macmillan, Harold: *At the End of the Day: 1961–1963* (Macmillan 1973)

Macmillan, Harold: *The Macmillan Diaries: Prime Minister and After 1957–1966*, Edited by Peter Catterall (Macmillan 2011)

Milward, Alan S: *The Rise and Fall of a National Strategy 1945–1963* (Frank Cass 2002)

Morgan, Kenneth O: *Callaghan: A Life* (OUP 1987)

Newhouse, John: *De Gaulle and the Anglo-Saxons* (Andre Deutsch 1970)

O'Neill, Con: *Britain's Entry into the European Community: Report on the Negotiations of 1970–1972* (Frank Cass Publishers 2000)

Owen, David: *Time to Declare* (Michael Joseph 1991)

Parr, Helen: *British Policy towards the European Community: Harold Wilson and Britain's World Role 1964–1967* (Routledge 2005)

Pimlott, Ben: *Harold Wilson* (Harper Collins 1992)

Pine, Melissa: *Harold Wilson and Europe* (Tauris Academic Studies 2007)

Prittie, Terence: Adenauer: *A Study in Fortitude* (Tom Stacey 1972)

Stewart, Michael: *Life and Labour: An Autobiography* (Sidgwick & Jackson 1980)

Thorne, D R: *Alec Douglas-Home* (Politico's 2007)

Thorne D R: *Supermac: The Life of Harold Macmillan* (Chatto & Windus 2010)

Toomey, Jane: *Harold Wilson's EEC Application: Inside the Foreign Office 1964–1967* (University College Dublin Press 2007)

Williams, Charles: *The Last Great Frenchman: A Life of Charles de Gaulle* (John Wiley & Sons 1993)

Williams, Shirley: *Climbing the Bookshelves: The Autobiography* (Virago 2009)

Wilson, Harold: *The Labour Government 1964–1970: A Personal Record* (Weidenfeld & Nicolson and Michael Joseph 1971)

Wilson, Harold: *Final Term: The Labour Government 1974–1976* (Weidenfeld & Nicolson 1979)

Ziegler, Philip: *Wilson: The Authorised Life* (Weidenfeld and Nicolson 1993)

Ziegler, Philip: *Edward Heath: The Authorised Biography* (Harper Press 2010)

Index

'Abstention' or 'going it alone' 139, 176, 177, 180, 181
Acheson, Dean 14
Action Committee for United States of Europe 98, 313, 372
Adenauer, Konrad 30–1, 57, 59–60, 239; Blankenhorn and Dixon assess intentions of de Gaulle and 26, 30–1; correspondence with Kennedy 25, 32; dislike of British 11–12, 26; Fanfani advising Heath on 12; letter from Macmillan 10; meetings at funeral of 183–7; relationship with Macmillan 12
Agence France Presse 164, 438
"agreement to differ"' 566–8, 579
agricultural finance crisis 102–6, 107, 112–13
agriculture: British 120; a component of Franco-German Declaration 279; possibility of an agreement with EEC but excluding 127, 128, 198; wheat prices in UK 20, 92; *see also* Common Agricultural Policy
Aldington, Lord Toby 489
Alexander, Andrew 458
Algeria 23, 220
Allen, Sir Douglas 329
Alphand, Hervé 205, 326
alternatives to EEC, consideration of: 'Abstention' 139, 176, 177, 180, 181; Atlantic Free Trade Area (AFTA) 176–7, 180, 182, 192, 213–15; Belgian plan 254–6; Benelux proposals 277–8, 280, 281, 284, 288, 297, 301, 310, 311; at Chequers Cabinet October 1966 142–3, 144; Commission report on 285; de Gaulle makes references to 163, 164, 203,

206, 257; Franco-German Declaration 278–82, 284, 307, 309, 314; Germans searching for a compromise 258–60, 272–3, 282–3; Hancock's views on 329; North Atlantic Association 144; North Atlantic Free Trade Area 147, 180, 233; report 1967 to Cabinet on 176–8; Wilson resolutely opposed to 251, 278; *see also* Association
Ambassadors: class change in ranks of 14–15; communications with 11
Ambassadors meeting March 1974 511, 512–15
Amery, Julian 66
Arab-Israeli War 495
Are You Ready? 454, 455
Armstrong, Robert 407, 411–12, 423, 432, 437, 439, 442, 481, 544, 563; advises Heath to meet Pompidou 463; advises Heath to tell Wilson of Commissioner appointments 446–7; on Chequers meeting with Schmidt 559; and consideration of rejoining snake 465, 478, 479; Jobert meetings 439, 442–3, 465–6, 490–1; New Zealand and renegotiation meeting in Paris 573–4; note to Heath on Francophobia in FO 484–5; Paris Summit 1972 note 449–50; secret note on bilateral talks between Heath and Pompidou 402–3; tariff changes minute to Wilson 554–5; writes to Ryrie on role of sterling 407
Armstrong, Sir William 430–1
Association 44–5, 81, 206, 254, 257; Brown on 192; French prepare Convention of 23; Heath does not wish to pursue 28; Reilly advises

British application 1967 202; de Gaulle on history of Anglo-French relations 320; deeply suspicious of Soviet Union 494; defence collaboration with British 58–9, 131, 212, 297, 429; devaluation of franc 190, 345; differences with Germany on agriculture in Kennedy Round 76; dislike of 'l'offensive anglaise' 236–7; dislike of non-aggression pact with Soviet Union 63–4, 67–8, 69, 70, 71–2; Douglas-Home visit July 1970 363; EEC takes special measures to help 291; elections March 1963 463–4; elections March 1967 173; elections following May 1968 crisis 292–3; Ersboell's assessment of Germany and 531–2; floatation of franc 508; Foreign Office paper on Anglo-French relations 364–5; freeze in relations between Six 250, 251, 260, 264; gap between German inclinations on political cooperation and those of 484; German integration into Europe desirable to 489–90; Germans view relations with Britain as less important than relations with 26–7, 159–60, 179, 301, 311–12, 313, 315, 530–1; Germany a concern for 4–5, 58–9; hostility to dollar 278, 304, 373, 400, 441, 487; Kissinger complains of domination of Europe by 499–501; linking New Zealand and budget correcting mechanism in British negotiations 410–11, 571–2, 573; Luxembourg Compromise, view of 113, 396, 440; majority voting concerns 107, 112; monetary union policy 433, 441–3, 448; Nield reports to Heath on problem with 368; nuclear cooperation offer from US 38–9; nuclear policy under de Gaulle 39, 55, 59, 62, 65, 67–9, 72, 84; opposes British application opening statement in EEC Council 217–18; Palliser advises on how to deal with 237; Paris visit by Wilson and Brown May 1968 167–8; plans to meet without 27–8, 35, 309, 314; position in negotiations for British entry 381, 382–3, 387, 388–9, 394, 396; possibility of leaving EEC 82; proposals to trade budget correcting mechanism for reduced settlement on

New Zealand 570, 573; public opinion on EEC in 104, 124, 150, 173, 208, 242–3, 388; reaction to bilateral talks between Heath and Pompidou 405–6; referendum on enlargement 433; referendum on constitutional change 331; referendum to ratify Treaty of Accession 433, 435–6; relations with Britain and Germany in summer of 1973 487–8; relations with Britain at cross-purposes under Giscard 529–30; relationship more important than relationship with British to Germans 26–7, 159–60, 530–1; relationship of importance to Germany 56, 224–5, 234, 238, 512; secures payment of agricultural levies to EEC 349; significant differences with Germany on enlargement issue 285–6; Soames Affair and all time low in 319–31; speculation on actions at Council Meeting in December 1967 260–1; subtle change in policy on enlargement 299–300; waiting for General Election in Britain before making progress on renegotiation 535; wanting agreement on agricultural finance ahead of enlargement negotiations 343, 344, 346, 348; withdrawal from NATO 82, 85, 114–15, 122, 303

Franco-German Declaration 1968 278–82, 284, 286, 287, 288, 293, 305, 307, 309, 314

Franco-German Summit 1968 278, 279–82

Franco-German Summit 1972 442

Franco-German Treaty of Cooperation 1963 12–13, 27, 28, 33, 59, 77; Adenauer's presentation of 59–60; de Gaulle criticises Germans 146; Debré contradicts 305; fifth anniversary of 275–6; Kennedy on 31; lack of progress after signing of 72–3; signing of 30

Frank, Dr Paul 347

Frankfurter Allgemeine Zeitung 259–60

Freeman, John 295, 352

French language 393, 394, 415

Gaitskell, Hugh 50, 51, 97

Gallup Poll survey 36, 51, 146, 588

Gardiner, Lord 178, 195